Major Problems in American Sport History

MAJOR PROBLEMS IN AMERICAN SPORT HISTORY

GENERAL EDITOR
THOMAS G. PATERSON

Major Problems in American Sport History

Documents and Essays

SECOND EDITION

EDITED BY

STEVEN A. RIESS

Northeastern Illinois University

Bernard Bromell Research Professor Emeritus

Australia • Brazil • Japan • Korea • Mexico • Singapore • Spain • United Kingdom • United States

Major Problems in American Sport History: Documents and Essays, Second Edition
Edited by Steven A. Riess

Product Director: Suzanne Jeans

Product Manager: Ann West

Content Developer: Larry Goldberg

Content Coordinator: Megan Chrisman

Product Assistant: Liz Frazer

Media Developer: Kate MacLean

Rights Acquisitions Specialist: Jennifer Meyer Dare

Manufacturing Planner: Sandra Milewski

Art and Design Direction, Production Management, and Composition: PreMediaGlobal

Cover Image: Dempsey v. Firpo in New York City, 1 923, 1 924 (oil on canvas) by George Wesley Bellows (1 882–1 925) © Whitney Museum of American Art/Bridgeman

Library of Congress Control Number: 201 3951 260

ISBN-13: 978-1-133-31108-9

ISBN-10: 1-133-31108-3

Cengage Learning
200 First Stamford Place, 4th Floor
Stamford, CT 06902
USA

Cengage Learning is a leading provider of customized learning solutions with office locations around the globe, including Singapore, the United Kingdom, Australia, Mexico, Brazil, and Japan. Locate your local office at **www.cengage.com/global**

Cengage Learning products are represented in Canada by Nelson Education, Ltd.

To learn more about Cengage Learning, visit **www.cengage.com**

Purchase any of our products at your local college store or at our preferred online store **www.cengagebrain.com**

Instructors: Please visit **login.cengage.com** and log in to access instructor-specific resources.

Printed in the United States of America
2 3 4 5 6 25 24 23 22 21

For Josh, the next generation

Contents

Preface

Few nations over the past 200 years have been as sports crazy as the United States, and it is the American involvement with sport that is the subject of this anthology. The title of this volume, *Major Problems in Sport History*, indicates that the book's center of attention is on *sport*, a term that refers to the all encompassing set of institutions and cultural practices of the athletic world. Sociologists like Judith McDonnell, Heather Gibson, Janet Park, and others make an important distinction between *sport* and the related term, *sports*, which they use to refer to particular competitive contests like football, baseball, or golf.[1]

In Colonial America, when people spoke of sport, they meant any form of entertainment or diversion, but in the past two hundred years, the term has become more narrowly defined to refer to competitive contests governed by customs or rules that require physical activity and skills. Thus jockeys, baseball players, runners, and dart throwers engaging in contests are athletes, but chess and bridge players are not. The game may be against an individual, a team, or a record (even one's own best). Competitors across the globe may be amateurs, who play purely for enjoyment, *sport for sport's sake*, or professionals who are compensated for their efforts and exhibit their skills before a paying audience. An important exception is that the National Collegiate Athletic Association (NCAA) Division I and II college athletes can be compensated with a scholarship and living expenses.

Sport was considered, until recently, a male sphere, inappropriate for women, who were thought too frail for most sports other than such "feminine" activities as ice skating, horseback riding, swimming, tennis, and golf. The general public saw sports as a means for participants to display their manliness, and a vehicle to instruct boys how to become men, teaching values like courage and

---

1. See, e.g., Paul M. Pederson, Janet Park, Jerome Quarterman, and Lucie Thibault, *Contemporary Sport Management*, 4th ed. (Champaign, IL, 2011), 8.

competitiveness that were inappropriate for females. The main sports in the colonial era and in the Early American Republic included hunting, horse racing, boat racing, and boxing, and sports that abused animals, like cockfighting and baiting. The middle-class vigorously opposed such pastimes as an immoral waste of time that promoted gambling and led to the gathering of dangerous crowds. An important turning point came in the 1830s and 1840s when prominent middle-class writers created a positive sports creed that justified clean sports. Activities such as the German-imported sport of gymnastics and the newly evolved game of baseball were seen as positive social forces that promoted traditional values, built character, assimilated newcomers, taught sound morals, and promoted physical fitness. This ideology and the emergence of new sports led to a sporting boom after the American Civil War, heavily influenced by the processes of urbanization, industrialization, immigration, and bureaucratization. Amateur team sports like rowing, baseball, football, and track and field rapidly developed at colleges and high schools, and individual amateur sports like golf and tennis became very popular by the end of the century at elite country clubs. There was also a big boom in professional sports, primarily baseball, thoroughbred racing, and boxing in which highly skilled professional athletes were hired by entrepreneurs to entertain spectators. Sport became a means to promote ethnic identity, hometown pride in local teams, and to advance nationalism, first in competition against the British, and in 1896 at the Olympic Games. Sport also became a means to promote American business and culture around the world. However, sport was not yet a democratic institution, with participation limited by social class, race, and gender. The world of sport did become more democratic by the 1920s as the standard of living in the United States rose substantially, but it would not be until after World War II that professional sports like baseball, football, and basketball would be open to men of all races. Women made modest inroads into sport by the late nineteenth century, but they would not play a major role in American sports until the 1970s, following the rise of feminism and the enactment of Title IX of the Education Amendments of 1972.

Interest in American sport in the early twenty-first century is at an all-time high. Sports are enjoyed by men and women, children, adults, and senior citizens from all social, racial, and class backgrounds. We look to sports icons for our heroes, such as Muhammad Ali, Michael Jordan, and Billie Jean King, rather than our politicians, scientists, soldiers, or businessmen. Furthermore, sport is big business. In 2011, spectator and participatory sports reportedly generated over $200 billion, making it the 14th largest grossing sector of the economy. Americans spend billions of dollars on such participatory sports as fishing, hunting, and golf. Millions of fans attend sporting events, and even more watch on TV, helping to make professional sports franchises extremely valuable. The average Major League Baseball team in 2013 was worth $733 million, surpassed by the National Football League average of over a billion dollars. College sports are also big business. For example, the National Collegiate Athletic Association's revenue for 2011–2012 was nearly $871.6 million, mainly from TV, and six colleges own stadiums that seat over 100,000 fans.

The importance of sport in its own right, and the ways that the institution of sport reflects and mirrors the history of the broader society, was not really recognized until the 1970s. Before then academic snobbery looked down upon historians studying sport because it was not considered a serious subject, and writing about sport seemed a dangerous career move. Academic interest in sport history emerged in the early 1970s as a result of such factors as the rise of the New Social History; student demands for a more relevant curriculum; the growing importance of interdisciplinary history, especially as influenced by cultural anthropology; the democratization of the historical profession; and the establishment of the North American Society for Sport History (1972), an association that created a supportive intellectual community for historians interested in sport and founded the *Journal of Sport History* in 1974. However, the fundamental factor that encouraged sport scholarship was that historians began to realize that the analysis of the internal history of sport and the history of sport's interaction with the broader society elucidated certain central themes of American history, particularly class, ethnicity, race, and gender issues. One product of this growing awareness was Ken Burns's 18-hour documentary *Baseball*, first broadcast on national television in 1995, with an additional 4 hours added in 2010. Burns saw that analyzing baseball's myths, realities, symbols, and rituals provided an excellent vehicle for examining and understanding American mores, values, and beliefs.

The materials in this book should help students identify the major developments that took place over time in sport history, and explain how and why these trends occurred in the context of the broader American history. Readers will evaluate the role of such processes as urbanization, industrialization, bureaucratization, and immigration, along with such factors as capitalism, class, gender, race, ethnicity, technological innovation, urban politics, and diplomacy. Sport history includes in part the study of the internal history of individual sports like baseball, boxing, and football with their own rules and institutions. It also entails analyzing the changing interrelationships over time between sport and social institutions, political and economic structures, geography, group and individual behavior, and national values. Just as sport was influenced by the broader society and culture, society itself has been influenced by developments in sport, such as the integration of Major League Baseball in 1947 by Jackie Robinson.

This book, a volume in the Major Problems in American History series, seeks to provide educators and their students with essential, readable, and provocative documents and essays that illuminate the American sporting experience from a variety of viewpoints. The documents are primary sources, selected for how they illustrate major developments in the rise of sport and, often, how they illuminate the accompanying essays. Some documents are well known, and others relatively obscure, but all are important. They include government reports, court cases, contemporary newspaper articles, and memoirs. The essays in this volume were chosen to cover broadly the field of sport history, because of the particular significance of each essay to our understanding of sport history, and the quality of the writing, research, and analysis. Instructors will find many of these essays very familiar to them, but I hope a few recently published essays might be new to them as well.

The organization of this edition is typical of all volumes in the Major Problems series. The book begins with four essays that introduce different approaches to thinking about the history of American sport, followed by 14 chapters, organized chronologically and topically, that cover major issues about the subject. Each chapter begins with a brief introduction that defines the central issues covered and provides the historical context. The documents and essays are introduced by head notes that should help readers comprehend the meaning and significance of the following passages. All chapters conclude with a list of articles and books for further reading. In addition, students seeking a more detailed source for monographs in sport history are urged to consult two invaluable data bases, the more general *America: History and Life*, and the sport specific data base, *SPORTDiscus*.

The second edition is organized very similar to the first, but there are important major differences. While the chapter titles are largely the same as in the first edition, this new version gives greater attention to events beyond the eastern seaboard, to be more inclusive of American subcommunities, and to remedy the significant omission in the prior edition of a chapter on American sport and the global community. There has been a major changeover in the materials included. Nearly half of the 75 documents in the book (43 percent) are new. The turnover among the essays is even greater. Twenty-five of the 35 essays are new (71 percent). The large proportion of new essays reflects the enormous boom in sport history since the publication of the first edition. Monographs are now regularly published in all the leading historical journals along with the *Journal of Sport History*, the leading periodical among sport historians, plus excellent books have been written by historians on sport, particularly with university presses like the University of Illinois Press, the University of North Carolina Press, Syracuse University Press, and the University of Nebraska Press.

Following the exploratory and suggestive introductory chapter is a section on early American sport. The chapter on the colonial era examines the period when sporting practices were heavily influenced by the culture colonists brought over from England, the environment they encountered, and prevailing religious ideas, which is reflected in the documents. The essays include a classic analysis of horse racing among the elite, the most important sport in colonial America, and a second essay that analyzes the sporting practices at taverns, the main locus of male sociability in early America. The next two chapters examine sport in the young republic, beginning with one that investigates the relationship between sport and manliness, highlighted by essays and documents on gouging, boxing, and duels, the kinds of sports that respectable people abhorred. This is followed by a chapter titled "The Making of a Modern Sporting Culture, 1840–1870," which explains how the low-life culture of the sporting fraternity was supplanted by a more respectable, positive sporting culture that promoted clean sports that promised to build character, morality, and health. The section includes contemporary sources that speak to the making of an uplifting sports creed, and a classic essay by John R. Betts on the intellectual origins of middle class sport. This is complemented by an essay on baseball and its growing popularity at mid-century.

The next section of the book is the largest, which centers on the period from the late nineteenth century, when American sport boomed, up to the end of the Great Depression. It includes chapters on higher education, urbanization, space, social class, professionalization, gender, ethnicity and race, and athletic heroes. Chapter 5 examines the development of sport (mainly football and baseball) in institutions of higher education from the late nineteenth century through the 1930s, when intercollegiate sport was ostensibly amateur, played for fun by skilled athletes. Yet, as the documents and one of the essays point out, top football and baseball performers were compensated for their skills, with scholarships, and by circumventing the amateur codes, other assistance.

Chapter 6 deals with the relationship of sport to urbanization, the process of city building. Historians today believe that urbanization was a dominant factor in the evolution of American sports. This is connected to such variables as spatial relationships, the rise of mass transit, boosterism, and the commercialization of sport. One essay in this section examines the relationship between urban machine politics and the rise of professional sport, and the other analyzes the development of parks as a venue for middle and working class sport. This is followed by a related chapter on sport and social class. Class was a major factor in determining the sporting opportunities of Americans because of the importance of leisure time, accessibility, and expenses, not to mention the different values and attitudes of people from the upper, middle, and lower class to sport. The documents and essays in this section investigate the middle and upper classes that had the greatest sporting options in the late nineteenth and early twentieth centuries. Closely related to these chapters is one on the development of professional sport in the late nineteenth century and early 1900s. The Big Three were baseball, boxing, and horse racing, of which only baseball was legal throughout this era. Baseball, for years considered the national pastime, and the sport most extensively studied by scholars, gets the greatest attention in this chapter, especially among the documents, some of which are well known among baseball historians.

The next three chapters in this section deal with gender, race and ethnicity, and heroes. Gender is a major topic of this volume, with three chapters, plus a photo review on women's sport clothing. The documents in Chapter 9 scrutinize the in-roads made by upper middle and upper class women, particularly at renowned eastern women's colleges. The primary sources point out some startling achievements by women athletes, notably the story of the first woman to bicycle around the world and a woman who was a preeminent automobile racer in the early 1900s. One of the accompanying essays examines African American women's basketball at a historically black college, while the second, Elliott Gorn's analysis of prize fighting, the penultimate manly sport, returns to the connection between sport and manliness.

Chapter 10 examines the great significance of race and ethnicity in American sport. The documents mainly look at the African American experience, but also discuss Jim Thorpe, the great Native American sportsman, and the role of sport in interethnic relations, which did not always promote friendship and cooperation. One of the essays examines the issue of racism and manliness in the renowned Jack Johnson–Jim Jeffries heavyweight championship fight of 1920. The second essay analyzes the Italian American experience in sport as a means to promote acculturation, but not at the cost of ethnic identity.

Chapter 11 deals with a classic issue in sport, the creation of American heroes, who until the rise of sport had been soldiers, politicians, and entrepreneurs. There were a handful of sports heroes in the late nineteenth century, notably heavyweight champion John L. Sullivan, the "toughest man in the world," and Chicago White Stockings star Michael J. "King" Kelly. However, sports heroes mainly emerged in the twentieth century, abetted by the extensive sports coverage in the media, especially in the 1920s, the "Golden Age of Sports." Nearly every major sport had its hero, such as Babe Ruth (baseball), Jack Dempsey (boxing), Red Grange (football), Bobby Jones (golf), Helen Wills (tennis), and Charles Lindbergh (aviation). They were lauded because their tangible accomplishments represented American values (unlike celebrities who were famous just because they were well known). The essays in this section examine Red Grange, Olympian Babe Didrikson, and heavyweight world champion Joe Louis.

The four final chapters primarily deal with how sport since World War II became a truly democratic and meritocratic institution, how professional sport became a fully national enterprise that generated huge profits, and how twentieth century American involvement in sport expanded beyond our borders to sell sporting goods, promote our values, and advance our diplomatic goals. Chapter 12 examines the boom in women's sports since the 1970s, tied to feminism and the impact of Title IX. The documents include autobiographical accounts of two pre-Title IX stars, Wilma Rudolph and Billie Jean King, and also primary sources on Title IX and its implementation. One essay examines one of the earliest major sports ventures for women, All American Girls Baseball League, a professional league of female ballplayers active from 1943 to 1954. The second essay is a critical analysis of the implementation of Title IX at American colleges.

The next chapter examines the changing role of race in sport since World War II, spotlighting the integration of major league baseball and the impact of Muhammad Ali on prize fighting and the equal rights movement in sport. The essay on Jackie Robinson is drawn from Jules Tygiel's classic baseball's *Great Experiment: Jackie Robinson and His Legacy* (1983), and the one on Ali is drawn from David Zang's *Sports Wars* (2001), an iconoclastic take on recent American sport.

The business of American spectator sport is the subject of Chapter 14. It centers on Major League Baseball (MLB), the National Football League (NFL), and the NCAA's control of big-time college football. The documents mainly deal with the trials and tribulations of MLB that exemplify the conditions of pro team sports, such as national expansion, municipal support of professional franchises, labor-management relations (notably free agency), and the use of performance enhancing drugs. There are two essays by Michael Oriard, the leading student of football history, one on the ramifications of the NCAA's monopoly over college football, and another on how the NFL became a big business, marketing itself as the new national pastime. The third essay by Steven A. Riess studies the shift in ballpark ownership since the 1950s from private control to municipal possession. This business model was copied by the NFL, the National Basketball Association, and the National Hockey League.

The final chapter is completely new, placing American sport in a world context, covering a long time period, examining the diffusion of American baseball overseas and also the role of sport in American relations with foreign countries. The American sporting culture was largely formed from the experience of English colonists and other European immigrants who brought their favorite pastimes and their sporting culture to the new nation. However, beginning in the 1840s, Americans developed new sports, including baseball, football, basketball, and volleyball, which they took overseas. Baseball was exported by Americans to Japan and Hawai'i, but Cuban historian Louis Pérez's essay demonstrates how it was Cubans living in the United States who took the game back with them to Cuba, where it became a popular sport that represented freedom and democracy to the colonials, and eventually became their national sport. The connection between foreign relations and sport centered, in the twentieth century, on the Olympic Games. The United States used the quadrennial event to demonstrate its progressive character by being able to produce many champions, and by successfully hosting Olympic competitions. The Olympics also became a peaceful venue through which the American government tried to promote its foreign policies. International sport was a particular venue for the playing out of the Cold War after World War II. The second essay examines the historic significance of the U.S. victory over Russia in the semifinals of the 1980 ice hockey championships at Lake Placid, shortly before the American boycott of the Summer Games in Moscow because of the Russian invasion of Afghanistan.

I encourage students of sport history to become members of the North American Society of Sport History (http://www.nassh.org/NASSH_CMS/index.php). The organization welcomes student members with inexpensive rates that include a subscription to the *Journal of Sport History*.

A lot of people have helped me with the second edition of *Major Problems in American Sport History*. I thank Raymond Arsenault of the University of South Florida for prodding me to work on a second edition, and George Kirsch of Manhattan College and Linda Borish of Kalamazoo College for suggestions on revisions. Five reviewers conducted detailed evaluations of the first edition, offered extensive suggestions about reorganizing the book, dropping certain documents and essays, and topics for adding new entries, and I thank them for their extremely valuable critiques: Thomas Ashwell, University of New Hampshire; Karen Guenther, Mansfield University; Paul Keiper, Texas A&M University; Rita Liberti, California State University, East Bay; and Stephen Norwood, University of Oklahoma. Deborah Siegel, senior library specialist who does the interlibrary work at Northeastern Illinois University, helped enormously in accessing materials. At Cengage, Thomas G. Paterson, editor of the series, championed a second edition, along with Jeff Greene, who recently retired as editor of the Major Problems Series for Cengage/Wadsworth, who shepherded the first efforts of the new edition. A huge part of the essential work in helping me produce the volume was done by Larry Goldberg, my developmental editor. Sunetra Mukundan, Project Manager–Text Permissions, worked with me to secure permissions and keep down costs. Pradhiba Kannaiyan, Senior Project Manager, got me through the process of actual production, and Jennifer Meyer Dare, Senior Rights Acquisition Specialist, was extremely helpful in numerous ways. My daughter Jennifer Riess, my computer guru, helped me produce a graph depicting the relative value of major sports franchises in the United States. And finally, I thank my wonderful wife Tobi for editorial assistance, and her love and understanding.

S. A. R.

CHAPTER 1

What Is Sport History?

The analysis of American sport history is a relatively new area of scholarly inquiry. Intellectuals in general, including historians, all but ignored sport as a suitable field of inquiry. Articles and books were written on sporting subjects, but most were written by journalists for a general audience. The academic lack of interest in sport was particularly remarkable because the United States had a rich sporting heritage, which dated back to pre-Columbian American Indians. The earliest English colonists participated in athletic competitions, especially Southerners who became renowned for their horse racing. The United States, following the example of Great Britain, became a major sporting nation in the mid-nineteenth century that supported important amateur and professional traditions. Sport in the United States was at first primarily a participatory recreation, but by the late nineteenth century, it became increasingly professionalized and popular as a spectatorial entertainment.

Nonetheless, prior to 1960, only three scholarly books had been written on American sport history. Historians avoided the topic for several reasons. The primary reason was they believed there were more important subjects to examine such as political or diplomatic history, and that studying sport would not provide any broader understanding of American history. In addition, they disdained studying popular culture. They remained either indifferent to or defensive about the great importance of sport both as a major force on their college campuses and as a growing commercial enterprise. Lastly, professors were afraid their careers would be adversely affected by writing on sport.

Academic interest in sport history emerged in the early 1970s among younger scholars reacting to the democratization of the historical profession, to the rise of the New Social History, to student demands for a more relevant curriculum, and to the growing recognition by historians that sport and its interplay with society could inform us about the American experience. Scholars began by studying the history of individual sports, but they also examined sport in terms of society's political, economic, cultural, and social history. Sport history helped them analyze the behavior, values, and culture of social classes, ethnic groups, and races, and it is becoming an important vehicle for understanding gender issues.

ESSAYS

The four essays in this section examine different approaches historians take to writing the history of sport. The scholarly study of American sport history goes back to Frederick L. Paxson's "The Rise of Sport," published in 1917 in the *Mississippi Valley Historical Review (MVHR)*. He argued that the rise of sport in the late nineteenth century was a response to the rise of cities where Americans were deprived of a rigorous rural and frontier life. A student of the renowned Western historian Frederick Jackson Turner, Paxson asserted that with the loss of the frontier, Americans needed the new safety valve that sport represented to help residents of congested heterogeneous cities to cope with their problems and tensions and to sustain harmony. It would be thirty-six years before another essay on sport appeared in the prestigious *Journal of American History* (the former *MVHR*). Paxson's influential deprivation thesis was slightly modified by Arthur M. Schlesinger, Sr.'s *The Rise of the City, 1878–1898* (1938), which attributed the athletic boom to a reaction against restricting urban life. Urbanites were deprived of traditional fresh air recreations, and they turned to spectator sports to experience rural life vicariously. The deprivation model was reinforced by Foster Rhea Dulles, *America Learns to Play: A History of Popular Recreation* (1940), who noted that crowded urban conditions and the pace of industrial work made traditional village pleasures impractical; therefore, urbanites turned to escapist spectatorial entertainments as outlets for their "surplus energy and suppressed emotions." Dulles' mentor at Columbia University, John Allen Krout, had written the first academic survey, *Annals of American Sport* in 1929, a highly illustrated volume in the *Pageant of America* series published by Yale University Press. Two years later, Jennie Holliman published *American Sports, 1885–1931.*

The first American historian to specialize in sport was John R. Betts of Boston College, who in "The Rise of Organized Sport in America" (Ph.D. diss., Columbia University, 1951) argued that sport was not a reaction against the negative features of industrial labor or a romantic return to a lost pristine age. Instead, Betts asserted that sport arose mainly as a product of industrialization in cities rather than as a remedy to it. The industrial revolution created and expanded fortunes of elite sportsmen, while it helped the middle class raise their standard of living. The industrial revolution encouraged the commercialization of sport, and created new technologies that led to cheap, mass produced sporting equipment, and improved transportation and communication networks.

Contemporary interpretations for the rise of American sport emphasize the importance of American modernization or else the related process of urbanization. This perspective is central to the principal textbooks in American sport history, which include Benjamin G. Rader's *American Sports: From the Age of Folk Games to the Age of Televised Sports*, 6th ed. (2008), Elliott Gorn and Warren Goldstein's, *A Brief History of American Sport* (2004), Richard O. Davies' *Sports in American Life: A History*, 2nd ed. (2011), and Gerald Gems, Linda Borish, and Gertrud Pfister's *Sports in American History: From Colonization to Globalization* (2008).

In the first essay, Melvin Adelman, of Ohio State University, author of *A Sporting Time: New York City and the Rise of Modern Athletics, 1820-70* (1986), uses the concept of modernization to analyze the nature and reasons for the significant changes in American sport in the period 1820–1870 by focusing on New York City, the cultural, social, economic, and sporting capital of the United States. He argues that modernization is an excellent framework for understanding changes in the structures of sport, attitudes toward sport, and the functions of sport in the nineteenth century. The United States until the mid-nineteenth century was a traditional society in which status was determined by birth, the social structure was relatively rigid, behavior was controlled by long-established customs, people identified with primary groups, technology and education was limited, and the economy was largely agrarian. Then the United States began to transform itself into a modern nation, characterized by a dynamic and cosmopolitan society, and heavily influenced by technological innovations, with an open social structure.

Heavily influenced by Allen Guttmann's seminal *Ritual and Record: The Nature of Modern Sport* (1975), Adelman argues that it was at this point that American sport developed modern attributes, exemplified first by harness racing. American sport evolved from a traditional or folk stage of little organization, simple unwritten rules, local competition, no role differentiation, records or publicity, into a new phase of sophistication, characterized by organization, national competition, specialized roles, uniform rules, widespread dissemination of results, and extensive record keeping.

In the 1980s, a number of historians put the process of urbanization at the center for explaining the rise of American sport, particularly Stephen Hardy, Department of Sports Studies at the University of New Hampshire. He has written extensively on American sport from both the perspective of urban history, notably *How Boston Played: Sport, Recreation, and Community, 1865–1915 (1982)*, and as a leading scholar of sport management. In his contribution here, Hardy discusses the "urban paradigm" as it evolved from the ideas of Paxson to more current analyses that puts the city as the site of the emergence of sport and as an independent variable in shaping the direction of sport's evolution. Hardy sees the city as more than merely the site for the development of sport, but as a dynamic force composed of physical structures, social organizations, and value systems whose interaction over the course of time helped mold American sporting institutions, values, and behavior. He particularly focuses on the role of sport in community building.

The third essay is by Daniel A. Nathan, Department of American Studies, Skidmore College, who is the author of the prizewinning *Saying It's So: A Cultural History of the Black Sox Scandal* (2003). The selection from that book employed here focuses on the issue of collective memory, which he describes as "a way of expressing sets of ideas, images and feelings about the past that resonate among people who share a common orientation or allegiance." Not uncommonly, people, and societies create versions of the past that reflect their present day beliefs. It is "a cultural construction, an elaborate network of narratives and texts … that represents or explains the past." It is typically selective, incomplete, socially constructed, and based in the present. In the past, historians assume that memory was simply a recreation of the past "as it really was."

Nathan examines the producers of memories about two of the Black Sox players, outfielder Joe Jackson, the team's star player who took a bribe, yet batted .375 in the World Series, and third baseman Buck Weaver, a local Chicago boy, who knew about the fix, but did not take a bribe or play to lose, which diverted from the accepted historical version. These counter-memories neatly fit into certain public's perceptions of the truth.

The final essay in this section is by Jaime Schultz, an assistant professor of Kinesiology at Penn State University, author of the forthcoming *From Sex Testing to Sports Bras: Gender, Technology, & U.S. Women's Sport* (University of Illinois Press) and *Moments of Impact: Racial Politics, College Football, and The New Cultural History* (University of Nebraska Press). Her contribution promotes what she sees as a turn from social to cultural history of sport that emphasizes interpretation and quest for meaning. She examines such concerns as a) historical accuracy; b) subjectivity; c) experimenting with history; d) an emphasis on interpretation; e) greater attention to fictivity (relating to imaginative invention or fiction), narrativity (the process of telling or interpreting a story), and cultural memory; and f) new concerns for discourse (communication) and power.

Modernization and the Rise of American Sport

MELVIN L. ADELMAN

... Traditional society is marked by stability, localism, an ascriptive paternalistic hierarchy both in the family and society, an absence of specialized roles, and a dependence on muscle power. The past, present, and future are the same, and time moves in endless cycles. Traditional society is further characterized by the weaving together of family and community in labor, leisure, and religion. Ritual flows through the entire experience of traditional society, and no precise boundaries exist between the secular and religious life, or between work and leisure. The prevailing outlook is one of acceptance or of resignation toward life as it is; the repetition of past ways rather than innovative action is encouraged.

By contrast, modern society is dynamic, cosmopolitan, technological, and marked by a functional social structure that conforms to shifting political and economic structures; most of all, it is rational. The desire for change and the belief that it can be achieved through the application of rational analysis is central to modern society. From this set of assumptions flows many of the distinctive elements of modern society, especially the belief that the rational mode can be used to manipulate objects, the environment, people, and ideas. The modern personality type thus exhibits a significant drive for individual autonomy, initiative, and achievement....

The efforts of Guttmann and Dunning to differentiate the characteristics of modern sport and folk games (or premodern sport)—application of the concept of modernization to the study of athletics: While I have been influenced by their discussions and classifications, I differentiate premodern and modern sport in terms of six polar characteristics (see Table 1). The modernization of sport, like the modernization of society, entails movement from the premodern to the modern pattern.

As an analytic framework, modernization facilitates an examination of sport on two distinct, but interrelated and interacting, levels: the relationship between sport and the modernization of society and/or its component parts; and the evolution of modern sports structures and ideology. What both levels share, and what in fact unifies them, is the dominant role of rationalism in modern society. The increasing emphasis on rationalism and its logical extension, the desire to establish rational order, provides an important missing link in the analysis of modern sport. David Voigt correctly notes that "the appearance of a formal sport reflects man's rational attempt at channeling fun, and the rise of many formal sports in industrial society testifies to this faith in rationalism—a faith which values the formalization of most patterns of behavior." While scholars point to the emergence of the institutional character of athletics, in the past their studies have merely traced the growing presence of the structural components of rationality, the organization of sport, and the codification of its rules. The result is

TABLE 1 The Characteristics of Premodern and Modern Ideal Sporting Types

Premodern Sport	Modern Sport
1. Organization—either nonexistent or at best informal and sporadic; contests are arranged by individuals directly or indirectly (e.g., tavern owners, bettors) involved.	1. Organization—formal; institutionally differentiated at the local, regional and national levels.
2. Rules—simple, unwritten, and based on local customs and traditions; variations worked exist from one local to another.	2. Rules—formal, standardized, and written; rationally and pragmatically out and legitimated by organizational means
3. Competition—locally meaningful only; international no chance for national reputation.	3. Competition—national and superimposed on local contests; chance to establish national and international reputations.
4. Role differentiation—low among participants; loose distinction between playing and spectating.	4. Role differentiation—high; emergence of specialists (professionals) and strict distinctions between playing and spectating.
5. Public Information—limited, local, and oral.	5. Public information—reported on a regular basis in local newspapers, as well as national sports journals; appearance of specialized magazines, guide-books, etc.
6. Statistics and records—nonexistent.	6. Statistics and records—kept and published on a regular basis; considered important measures of achievement; records sanctioned by national associations.

more a description of what occurred than a coherent explanation of how and why it occurred or what it means.

The now classic articles of Oscar Handlin ["The Modern City as a Field of Historical Study," in Handlin, and John Burchard, eds., The Historian and the City (Boston, 1963), 1–9] and Louis Wirth ["Urbanism as a Way of Life," American Journal of Sociology 44 (1938): 1–24] on the nature and evolution of the modern city provide an excellent starting point for analyzing the relationship between sport and the city. Handlin noted that the generative impulse of the modern city emerged from three dramatic and interrelated societal changes that were external to it: the centralized national state, the new productive system, and the vastly improved communication system. These combined to increase the city's population, to endow it with a novel economic function, and to impose on it a fresh conception of order. While demographic increments had important ramifications for city life, the significant changes that took place in the modern city flowed from its role as the economic and communication center of the new productive system. These new tasks required the establishment of a rational order within the boundaries of the city. Both the desire and ability of the modern city "to impose a rational order upon the relations created by the new productive system" provided the city with its modern identity and resulted in "a thoroughgoing transformation in the urban way of life." This need to establish a rational order is the critical connection between the changing nature of the city and the changing structure of sport and can be examined in terms of Wirth's three components of urban society: physical space, organizational structures, and collective behavior.

The modern productive system required a new division of urban space based solely on the criteria of economic utility and value. This alteration resulted in the removal of traditional recreational areas and required that users of new and specifically designated sports areas compete economically for the land. The shift in land allocation thereby stimulated the creation of voluntary associations, private entrepreneurs, and even municipal government, all with greater amounts of capital, to become increasingly involved with sport. The emergence of these agencies dramatically illustrates that the complexities of urban life made it increasingly difficult for sport to exist on its previous informal and spontaneous basis.

The establishment of numerous voluntary sporting associations was at the heart and soul of the organized sports movement, but it was more than just a response to shifts in the physical contours of the city. Demographic increments, changes in the nature of social relations, shifts in urban social structure, the creation of new concepts of class, and the erosion of the former basis of status also stimulated the emergence of modern sports structures.

The increasing size and heterogeneous nature of the nineteenth-century urban population produced significant alterations in the form and function of social relations. Scholars have long recognized that the tremendous rise of urban voluntary associations during this period resulted from the emergence of the impersonal and fragmented city. Such associations performed important integrative functions by helping to stitch together diverse communal factions. With the various changes within the structure and meaning of the urban community, sporting clubs, similar to other organizations, acted at one level to promote an activity among individuals who shared a common interest but did not know each other on a personal basis.

Class structure also strongly influenced the formation of sports clubs. The initial thrust of organized sport came largely from the upper and upper-middle classes. While elite sports clubs were tied to the efforts of their members to institutionalize their status and disassociate themselves from the masses, the social backgrounds of individual members reflected the changing composition of New York's upper class during the half-century between 1820 and 1870. The middle class provided the organizational leadership for the two major spectator sports—harness racing and baseball—as well as several other sports. Ethnic groups promoted certain sports as a means of unifying their respective immigrant communities and preserving national identity in a foreign land. Artisans were not responsible for initially organizing any sport, but they engaged in a variety of organized sports and established their own clubs. Their participation in athletics was an expression of the tension created in the worker community by the onset of the modern productive system. On the one hand, involvement in sport was an extension of their desire to preserve traditional values and their ongoing veneration of physical prowess. On the other hand, artisan participation in certain sports, most notably baseball, was a reflection of their efforts to demonstrate their middleclass status. The lower class was conspicuous by its absence from organized sport. While the city's bottom strata engaged in boxing and no doubt participated in a variety of physical recreations, they neither sought nor had the financial wherewithal to formalize and institutionalize these behavioral patterns.

The most significant influence of the new rational order emerged via the role the city played in the construction of the ideology of modern sport. The growing fear that urban residents were physically degenerating and that the urban social order was decaying sparked the emergence of a new and more positive view of athletics. Spokesmen for the newer attitudes asserted that sport helped combat the problems created by the modern city in three specific, interrelated ways: by promoting good health, by encouraging morality, and by instilling positive character values.

While shifting attitudes toward athletics were a response to the rising concern about the changes in urban society, the desire to channel sport into socially productive outlets was at the heart of the new sports ideology. The claims that athletics promoted positive social benefits provided sport with greater dignity and importance but also illustrated that the fundamental justification of sport remained its utilitarian benefits. At a time when work and play emerged as distinct entities in urban life, proponents increasingly viewed the two as interrelated. The new relationship, however, was hardly one of equality. By training and adjusting urban men to the new social system, sport as a promoter of rational order became a servant of its creator, the modern productive system.

While the modern city was both a setting and a stimulant for the transformation of athletics, the creation of modern sports structures was not solely a by-product of societal change. The institutional needs of the various sports to establish their own order were equally responsible for the modernization of athletics. Since the modernization of each sport was in part a response to its particular requirements, the rate varied from sport to sport. Internal growth, competition, and commercialization combined to directly affect the degree to which modern sports structures evolved.

The increasing number of units within each particular sport and their emergence at more and different geographical locations made the older, local rules, norms, and sanctions inoperative. To facilitate the athletic experience within a growing sports universe required the development of uniform rules and the creation of governing agencies to administer the sport and provide a mechanism for rational change. The expansion of sport, moreover, produced an increased desire and need for more information, the result being burgeoning local coverage, the emergence of national sports journals, the creation of guidebooks and other sports manuals, and the developing importance of statistics.

The growing emphasis on competitive sport acted as a further stimulant for the transformation of athletics. A desire to demonstrate superiority—which is the essence of competition, particularly among individuals who do not know each other on a personal basis—required the formalization of behavioral patterns and contributed to the professionalization of sport, with a concomitant emphasis on training and specialized roles. The emergence of sports information and statistics and records was largely associated with the growth of competitive-professional athletics.

The commercialization of sport contributed to the modernization of sport in two ways: by facilitating the growth of competitive athletics beyond local boundaries and by aiding the rise of professional sports. In neither case was commercialization the cause of these developments, since both flowed from the search for superiority; in fact, the presence of competitive and professional elements within a particular sport always preceded commercialization. Rather, commercialization served as a catalyst for the expansion of competition and professionalism by providing a more rational and productive method of financing these developments. In addition, the increase in the number of commercial units nationally required that the various sports entrepreneurs coordinate and rationalize their business practices to maximize their profits. Critical to this process was equality of competition, uniform rules, systematic scheduling, and increased organization.

Urbanization and the Rise of Sport

STEPHEN HARDY

The "Urban Paradigm"

Historians agree that the engine for the evolution and rise of contemporary sport was an urbanizing, capitalist system that slowly transformed the landscapes of Europe and North America. As entrepreneurs rationalized production of agricultural and material goods, they disrupted traditional patterns of work, leisure, and

From Stephen Hardy, "Sport in Urbanizing America: A Historical Review," *Journal of Urban History*, Vol. 23, No. 6, September 1997, pp. 675–708, land use; they also fueled the growth of towns and cities. Holding the promise of a better life, places like London and New York attracted migrants of wildly diverse backgrounds who carried sports as part of their cultural baggage. Cities held the populations, the communication and transportation networks, the discretionary incomes, and the clearer segments of time that ... promoters ... needed to turn brawling into a manly art and science. At the same time, cities were the focus of widespread concerns for health, morality, and community, which continually served as rationales for new and reformed sports products.

This may be called the urban paradigm. It has dominated sport historiography since at least 1917, when Frederick Paxson argued in the *Mississippi Valley Historical Review* that burgeoning businesses like baseball, tennis, boxing, and golf had recently emerged as a new safety valve for a congested America that no longer had a frontier. Deprived of the outdoor life, urbanites suffered both stress and boredom; before succumbing to what John Higham later called "the frustrations, the routine, and the sheer dullness of an urban-industrial culture," Americans rediscovered and developed games and pastimes that could both excite and sooth.

If urban-industrial life—especially between the Civil War and World War I created a demand for sports, it provided the means. John Betts first argued the urban-product thesis in 1953; it has echoed in all subsequent works on sport and recreation. The most recent is David Nasaw's *Going Out: The Rise and Fall of Public Amusements*, which places the baseball boom (from 1880-1920) in a larger context of "the rise of public amusement ... a by-product of the enormous expansion of the cities. Commercial entertainments were an urban phenomenon. Their rise and fall were inevitably and inextricably linked to the fortunes of the cities that sustained them." [This] was especially true for the rising number of clerical and sales workers—a key sports market who comprised 11 percent of the workforce by 1920. When these urbanites stepped out for their evening hour, they entered a transformed world of electric power that lighted the streets, powered the trolleys hauling them to their destinations, and bathed the private boxing clubs and public dance halls in bold colors and images. Cities, then, were not just problems for which sports were an answer. Only cities had the technology, the densely packed markets of time and income, and the spirit of innovation to sustain the rapid growth of sports.

Nasaw's book reflects a turn taken in sport history during the last two decades. Moving beyond the "sweeping forces" approach of earlier studies—technological revolutions, frontier erosion, urban malaise—scholars began to examine how games like baseball, cricket, tennis, golf, and boxing related to the process of city building in specific cities. Using models suggested by Louis Worth, Eric Lampard, Roy Lubove, and Oscar Handlin, for example, Melvin Adelman and I considered sport as both cause and effect in the development of physical structures, social organizations, and ideologies in Boston and New York between 1820 and 1915. Other case studies ... placed similar emphasis on the nuances of context, the role of chance, and the effects of individual decision making or group conflict.

By the mid-1980s, the literature was extensive enough that Steven Riess won an NEH fellowship to write a synthesis, which was published in 1989 as

City Games: The Evolution of Urban Society and the Rise of Sport. Riess's monumental, exhaustive effort began with confidence in the urban paradigm: "Nearly all contemporary major Sports evolved, or were invented, in the city." Employing the city building model, Riess considered a parade of individuals and groups vying for control of space, social organization, and value systems in the walking city, the industrialized radial city, and the suburban era. He clearly captured the battles over playgrounds, clubhouses, and ballparks, as elites, workers, reformers, and basses sought to build their communities through sport. If Jacob Riis saw the team spirit in football or baseball as a means of overcoming ethnic and class divisions, the same sports fostered class exclusion at Andover or Harvard. If Frederick Law Olmsted offered his parks as serene and contemplative havens for all, urban workers and their ward politicians had other ideas. While Riess neatly sorted the ideology, he especially emphasized the spatial dimensions of sport and city building. The struggles for precious space, the sorting of space by class, ethnicity, and race, and the pursuit of available suburban space all dominate Riess's densely packed survey.

For Riess, the city games that shaped American sport arose in the swirling, madcap environment of nineteenth-century urban space. The following review focuses first on the recent literature that explores themes discussed by Riess and his predecessors; in particular, sport as a means of either escaping urban problems or building urban communities. The second half will consider newer themes—media, body culture, gender, and race—that move beyond the confines of specific cities into the larger realm of an urbanizing society....

Community Building

Sport was as much an embrace as an escape from modern urban industrial life. The literature is filled with examples of sport as a tool for building urban communities. Learning the language of baseball, developing a smooth golf swing, rallying for the provision of fresh-air play space have all linked somehow to community-building efforts. Historians have focused especially on the period from roughly 1840 to 1920, when so many towns grew into cities as immigrants from increasingly distant cultures swelled the burgeoning neighborhoods that were segmented by ethnicity, class, and race; as public officials documented with statistics the poverty, crime, squalor, and disease that journalists turned into popular copy. As all of this developed, many city people embraced sport as a weapon to help manage the jostling, sorting, blending, and contending that compacted their complex world.

The oldest topic of community building is the private world of clubs and voluntary associations. If the nineteenth-century city provided the fertile ground for the expansion of boxing, baseball, horse racing, rowing, and pedestrianism, the club—or voluntary association—was the basic unit of growth. For German Turners and their gymnastics, Scottish Caledonians and their field games, "native" shipwrights and baseball, Brahmin clerks and golf, or black porters and bicycling, clubs were the source of necessary financial and emotional support. As a recent *Brief History of American Sports* puts it, "in sport, as in religion, politics, or business, voluntary associations were the glue holding diverse Americans together." Most clubs were not heterogeneous communities; rather, they served to *sort* identities.... As Roger Lane points out, during the 1860s, the Pythian baseball club promoted the early game of baseball in Philadelphia's African American community; it was, however. limited to men from the most established families ... to provide collective capital for equipment and fields; to ensure a regular supply of players; and, equally important, to provide emotional support to adults playing kids games. For the black Pythians, numbers also provided some security against racial assaults.

Ethnic sports clubs reveal the paradoxes of community building in American cities. If the Turners, the Caledonian Societies, the Czech Sokols, and the Gaelic Athletic Associations embraced old or invented traditions as an obvious means of maintaining separate identity, what can one make of Woonsocket's Franco-American baseball clubs or South Philadelphia's Hebrew All-Stars basketball club? Baseball and basketball were utterly American. Historians claim, however, that American sports did not mean a betrayal of ethnicity. As Peter Levine concludes in his recent monograph *Ellis Island to Ebbets Field: Sport and the American Jewish Experience*, boxing, basketball, and baseball were all "transformed in the hands of Jewish athletes and spectators" into experiences that fused assimilation and ethnic pride. When Jewish fans cheered their local or national heroes, regardless of the sport "they turned such moments into community social celebrations of ethnic life."

Benny Leonard and other sports heroes take Levine out of the private space of the ethnic association and into the vibrant, contentious world of public space and public culture—street parades, museum exhibitions, ball games in the park, a day at the racetrack. These leisure activities, held on what Riess calls public or semipublic space, were by no means disconnected from issues of labor, class, or ethnicity. For over two decades historians have documented the close connections between labor and leisure ... This trend has upset some traditionalist, including Zane Miller, who recently complained of "a new genre of labor and urban history ... that [led] away from the question of the public interest."

Miller may have overlooked much of this literature. Baseball history is a case in point, particularly the work of Steven Riess. In his study of Progressive Era baseball, Riess revealed the intimate connections between the national pastime and urban political machines, trolley companies, and real estate speculators. Local bosses in Boston, New York, Philadelphia, and Cincinnati were often either club owners or close associates. They offered the team preferential treatment in municipal services or taxation; they gave inside information on plans for real estate and public transit. In return, the politicos used the ball clubs "as a source of honest graft and patronage, as an inducement to encourage people to travel on the traction routes they operated, and to improve their public image."

The placement of baseball parks was always an issue tying private profit to civic identity.... The same may be said for public parks and playgrounds. An earlier generation of progressive historians (e.g., Arthur Schlesinger Sr. and Blake McKelvey) viewed parks and playgrounds as the work of ... expert professionals ... to provide a piece of America's bounty to all citizens. In the last two decades, however, parks and playgrounds have been recast as cultural battlegrounds that echoed with skirmishes between workers, reformers, ethnic groups and their political representatives. Influenced by the work of E. P. Thompson and Herbert Gutman, labor and social historians in the late 1970s and 1980s began to look [to see] [w]ho actually decided where parks and playgrounds would be developed. Who determined and controlled the activities that occurred on these eminently public spaces? A whole range of groups contended over the issues. In Boston, Brahmins and arrivistes who supported [Frederick L.] Olmsted's vision of contemplative parklands lost battles to powerful ward bosses like Martin Lomasney, the "Mahatma" of Ward Eight, who defended the rights of his constituents to enjoy baseball, refreshment stands, and even mechanical flying horses on nature's greenswards. As a recent book on Central Park explains, while Olmsted believed the public could be "trained" to the proper use of a park, in fact, the public simply changed the meaning of a park.

In the Progressive Era, a host of new organizations and institutions linked sports to urban reform and community building. Leaders of YMCAs, settlement houses, playground associations, and public high schools all articulated vision in which games and sports—especially the team sports of baseball, football, and basketball—would foster a unity of purpose and sacrifice to overcome ethnic and class divisions....

This powerful melting-pot ideology still drives much of the public support for school and community sports. Historians, however, are less clear on how well it worked. For instance, Paula Fass analyzed the yearbooks of seven New York high schools from 1931 to 1947 and found that "members of different ethnic groups made definable distinctions among the sports offered at school. Natives, Italians, Germans, and to a lesser degree Irish, took to football. While the Italians rarely took up basketball, Jewish athletes embraced it as their own...."

Fass found one other distinct cluster in the yearbooks: "In every school with a meaningful population of black men, they were overrepresented on the track team.... [A]llmost, one third ... were on the team." Black students seemed to avoid most team sports, with the exception of basketball. Fass suggests that the individual and noncontact nature of track opened a niche for blacks "against whom discrimination would preclude "group involvement." African Americans had never figured into the Progressive blueprint for cultural integration in the schools or on the playgrounds.... In response, black neighbors had to help themselves, developing their own institutions—YMCAs, neighborhood unions, the National Urban League—to create their own space. They succeeded in developing numerous sports facilities and program in the early twentieth century, such as the Wharton Centre gymnasium in Philadelphia and church basketball teams in Chicago.

African American communities were not unified in their beliefs about the values of sports. Internal division over community building is a central feature, in James Coates's recent work on recreation and sport in Baltimore's African American community from 1890-1920. As Coates clearly reveals, Black professionals and "mental workers ... sought to dictate what was appropriate for the "people." The emerging black press was in the middle of this debate about leisure. The *Afro-American Ledger* ... and the NAACP's *Crisis* (1910) might join in a protest over segregation in the parks. But they were not united in their treatment of competitive sports. For instance, the *Afro-American* expanded its coverage of sports only after Jack Johnson's rise to the heavyweight boxing championship. And Johnson was a troubled champion who was as often attacked as defended in the pages of the black press.

On the other hand, sports could unify a community. Rob Ruck maintains that in the first half of the twentieth century, sandlot baseball and football helped Black Pittsburghers to overcome the differences that typically separated established from newly arrived groups. The two most prominent black baseball entrepreneurs represented the divide. Cum Posey, the son of Homestead's most distinguished black family, led the Homestead Grays; Gus Greenlee, a recent immigrant from Carolina who ran the numbers racket organized and bankrolled the Pittsburgh Crawfords.... [B]oth men, their teams, and their players represented "black Pittsburgh's potential for self-organization, creativity, and expression in these years."

The Limits of Urban Industrial Community

Despite the potential Ruck describes, sports seldom stood as permanent bridges between the social classes in any racial or ethnic community.... In her *Making a New Deal*, Lizabeth Cohen [claims] welfare capitalists ... wanted to overcome ethnic differences and union agitation to foster a sense of company community. Sports were central to this strategy. Western Electric's Hawthorne plant sponsored fourteen sports in the 1920s and provided extensive facilities, including a gymnasium, a track, and an elegant stadium. In Cohen's words, sports teams and leagues, from baseball to bowling, "aimed at developing an esprit do corps that transcended differences in ethnicity, age, and rank," but not with the intended outcomes: "Once workers had their own interests in common, employer-sponsored recreation could function to intensify employees' collective identity as easily as to diffuse it." Teamwork meant class-consciousness and union agitation. The young Congress of Industrial Organizations understood this well and began organizing its own leagues. As one packinghouse worker put it, "We work together on the job. Now we are playing together at night. It's making us all better friends so that we'll stick together in the organization whatever comes."

Cohen's study of Chicago workers underscores the view that class and ethnicity did not recede in the face of progressive urban sports programs. In fact, at least well into the 1930s, sports may have accentuated ethnic and class differences. There is one exception to this literature—baseball history....

According to [Gunther] Barth, ... [in *City People*] the experience of baseball—for fan and player alike—provided a common history of team records and statistics; people who were otherwise alienated could communicate through the language of box scores and batting averages. Baseball taught everyone an American morality that encouraged knowing and using the game's rules to get ahead.... Finally, claimed Barth, baseball taught appreciation of skill that framed the individual within the group.

David Nasaw borrows Barth's thesis in his book on public amusements ... [with] an important corrective. Where Barth echoed the old myth that Russian street peddlers, Irish ward heelers, and WASP bankers actually rubbed elbows as they formed a community around the home team Nasaw recognizes that baseball's magnates carefully manipulated ticket prices, specialized seating, and game times to control and segregate the crowds. As Steven Riess and Dean Sullivan have emphasized, baseball parks reflected the class and ethnic segregation of the city itself....

If the ballpark was segregated, how could baseball fuse classes and ethnic groups into an urban American culture? In truth, when baseball or any other sport promoted community, the vehicle was less the ballpark itself than the mythology promoted by reformers, politicians, and journalists....

Counter Memories and the Black Sox Scandal

DANIEL NATHAN

Most remembrances and renditions of the Black Sox scandal ... simplified the affair. The characters were largely stereotypical: they included avaricious, manipulative fixers and ballplayers, rubes duped into complicity, a few innocent victims, and a lone, wrathful avenger who restored order.

The setting was recognizable: the World Series. The preferred morals were plain: the wages of sin are (professional) death, so keep to the straight and narrow. In these ways one could argue that the Black Sox narrative did not evolve significantly in mainstream American collective memories and that the dominant discourse surrounding the scandal remained unchallenged.

Usually, however, when collective memories are (seemingly) stable and have been incorporated into popular consciousness—when they are institutionalized and enshrined in officially sanctioned traditions and narratives-counter-memories are not far afield. "Counter-memory," argues George Lipsitz in *Time Passages: Collective Memory and American Popular Culture* (1990), "is a way of remembering and forgetting that starts with the local, the immediate, and the personal." Unlike historical narratives that begin with the totality of human existence and then locate specific actions and events within that totality, counter-memory starts with the particular and the specific and then builds outward toward a total story. Counter-memory looks to the past for the hidden histories excluded from dominant narratives. For our purposes, counter-memory refers to evocations of the Black Sox scandal that deviate from or subvert the conventional or dominant ways it was commonly conceived. This is not to suggest a simple model of dominant narratives and memories versus resistant, countercultural narratives and memories; that is obviously too reductive and inaccurate, in part because dominant and competing narratives shift over time and in part because they sometimes exist simultaneously. Yet since collective memory is always linked to specific cultural contexts and places, we should examine some of the communities where unorthodox memories of the Black Sox held sway. In particular, how some local people remembered and made sense of Joe Jackson and Buck Weaver

---

provide us with vivid examples of counter-memory—perhaps collective counter-memories—at work.

In the decades immediately after the Big Fix, Joe Jackson represented numerous, sometimes conflicting, things for most people. Clearly he was still widely recognized as a ballplayer endowed with superior natural ability. The pitching great Walter Johnson of the Washington Senators put it succinctly in 1929: "The greatest natural hitter that I ever saw was Joe Jackson." To his family and friends, Jackson was shy, unassuming, and considerate. To many others, Jackson was a naive busher, a fool, a dupe, a pathetic simpleton. For still others, Jackson represented the worst sort of treachery, deceit, and betrayal; he was baseball's Judas, its Benedict Arnold. One critic suggests that Jackson was a pariah, an arch villain universally "anathema to every fan." Yet this was far from the case in much of Jackson's native South, where a resilient counter-memory of Jackson existed. For more than ten years after his expulsion from the Majors, Jackson played under his own name in the semiprofessional South Georgia League and in numerous promotional contests, where he was advertised in posters and treated warmly by fans. In August 1932, a year before he stopped playing organized baseball, Jackson was the subject of a where-are-they-now article by Ward Morehouse in the *New York Sun*. Morehouse described Jackson as "clear-eyed, ruddy-faced, big-bellied, slow-moving, soft spoken," and he noted that in Greenville, South Carolina, Jackson's home town, "this ballplaying country boy remains something of a hero. That 1919 business is forgotten. Whatever Joe's cronies may have thought then, they now regard him as a baseball genius who got a tough break." Morehouse's article was corroborated five years later by Richard McCann's "Baseball Remains Joe Jackson's First Love Seventeen Years after Ban." According to McCann, Jackson "is a respected citizen and a beloved neighbor here [in Greenville]. They just can't believe that Joe did anything wrong. Not their Shoeless Joe." To express their civic pride in Jackson, the people of Brandon Mills, South Carolina, twice held "Joe Jackson Night" in the forties to celebrate their native son's birthday.

Not long after one of those celebrations, in September 1942, the *Sporting News* published (much to Landis's consternation) a sensitive, sympathetic article by Carter "Scoop" Latimer entitled "Joe Jackson, Contented Carolinian at Fifty-Four, Forgets Bitter Dose in His Cup and Glories in His Twelve Hits in '19 Series." Latimer, who described Jackson as an old friend, noted that the "gift-bearing delegation of well-wishers at the surprise birthday party was typical of the boys who make almost daily pilgrimages to Joe's home or gang around him in the streets and on sandlots." It is, of course, an observation that undercuts the notion that Jackson betrayed and forever disillusioned the youth of America, or at least the boys in Greenville.

To drive that point home and to redeem one of their own, the South Carolina State Senate and House of Representatives passed a resolution in February 1951 to reinstate Jackson as a member in "'good standing' in professional baseball." Later that year, Jackson was inducted as a charter member of the Cleveland Indians Baseball Hall of Fame, which suggests that the counter-memory delineated here was not exclusive to the South. The prominent sports columnist Dan Daniel wrote that by "voting Joe Jackson, one of the notorious

Black Sox of 1919, into their diamond shrine, the electors in Cleveland have made a daring move which will bring prolonged and heated discussion wherever fans may gather." Jackson's election, Daniel argued, "honored a man of impugned baseball integrity." However, those who elected Jackson pointed out that his "integrity never was questioned in his six years of service with the Indians, from 1910, when he was acquired from the Athletics, until his 1916 transfer to the White Sox." As for his role in the 1919 World Series, many in Cleveland believed that Jackson "was the victim of a bum rap." That sentiment was amplified in Greenville, among other places—perhaps especially those below the Mason-Dixon line. After Jackson died in December 1951, Shirley Povich of the *Washington Post* remarked that Jackson "was the idol of the townsfolk who ascribed the whole talk of a fixed World Series as just another dirty Yankee trick."

For those who saw him as a convenient scapegoat, as a sacrificial lamb. as an icon of victimization—exploited by Comiskey, ensnared by (Jewish) city slickers, punished extralegally by Landis Jackson evoked powerful and resilient counter-memories of the Black Sox scandal. These counter-memories resisted the hegemonic version of the Big Fix the baseball establishment and much of the media promulgated; that is, that the fix resulted solely from the dishonesty and venality of the ballplayers and gamblers. "To the local folk," writes Eliot Asinof in *Eight Men Out*, Jackson was always "a hero. well liked and highly respected. He was never without their support, and the dignity of his talent never seemed to dwindle." In fact, it seems likely that Jackson was popular with and respected by some people partly due to his expatriate, outlaw status. The day before he died, Jackson apparently told an old Greenville friend: "I don't deserve this thing that's happened to me." Those who embraced counter-memories of the Big Fix no doubt agreed.

Buck Weaver likewise embodied and engendered counter-memories of the Black Sox scandal, especially on Chicago's South Side, where he lived until his death in 1956. Weaver—who by all accounts did not take the offered money to participate in the conspiracy, who played extremely well in the 1919 World Series, and who made several unsuccessful attempts to return to Major League Baseball—was generally treated with respect, warmth, and sympathy by those in his community. During the years immediately after his expulsion, it was not uncommon for him to "go out to the baseball diamonds at Washington Park … and hit fly balls to the kids," reveals Irving M. Stein in *The Ginger Kid: The Buck Weaver Story* (1992). "They loved Buck and he returned their affection." In 1927, recognizing that Weaver was still a talented ballplayer and a popular local celebrity, representatives of the Mid-West League, a semipro circuit in and around Chicago, voted unanimously to welcome Weaver as a player. During the course of his first season, Weaver was cheered by thousands of Chicagoans and honored with floral tributes and gifts. Stein observes that over the years the local media "sporadically focused on Weaver's situation expressing both sympathy and sorrow. Baseball fans in Chicago, in poll after poll, vouchsafed their confidence in Buck by naming him their choice as the best third baseman in either White Sox or Chicago history. While Buck was still playing semipro ball, south siders set up booths on busy street corners asking passersby to sign petitions asking for his reinstatement." At one point, those petitions numbered 30,000 signatures. In Chicago at least, it is reasonable to conclude, Buck Weaver was not a pariah; indeed, he was (and is) more often viewed as a victim of circumstance. Like Jackson, Weaver was widely understood as a convenient scapegoat for the affair. For those who remembered Weaver as a victim of association, as an innocent entangled in a conspiracy he did not participate in, as a man who refused to be an informer, as someone who was treated unfairly by a baseball commissioner who would not recognize different degrees of culpability, the Black Sox scandal was something other than a simple morality play.

Some Observations

All these Black Sox memories and stories supply us with an inkling of what personal understandings of the Big Fix may have been during the immediately succeeding decades. They do not, however, provide us with unproblematic evidence about how the Black Sox scandal was understood before it was reconstructed in more concrete cultural forms. The Black Sox scandal memories delimited here vividly demonstrate that collective memories—and meditations on those memories-are provisional and nebulous. It is difficult to reach anything but tentative conclusions about a collection of fragmentary remembrances. That may be the best conclusion to draw: where memory is concerned, conclusions are elusive. Nonetheless, it is possible to offer some observations about how Black Sox scandal memories were used and maintained during the thirty years after the scandal and about the process of collective remembering in general.

It may seem obvious, but it is worth saying: the Big Fix was remembered differently by individuals and communities in different places at different times. Always fragmentary and provisional, dynamic and ongoing, always an act or a process as opposed to an objective, static record to be recalled, memory is never monolithic. Still, since one of the most common ways both people and societies remember the recent past is through individuals, and because Landis ruled the professional game with iron-fisted panache until his death in 1944, the version of the Black Sox narrative he sought to convey remained alive (quite literally) for many Americans for most of this era. But because he occupied a prominent position, was widely respected, and had an intuitive flair for public relations (and self-aggrandizement), he exerted more influence than any other individual or institution in maintaining a particular remembrance of the affair. It seems that many Americans remembered the Black Sox scandal in the manner Landis preferred: an aberrant moral crisis (instigated by avaricious, immoral men) and a national tragedy, one that his tireless vigilance (and ruthlessness) would not permit again. Just as Landis brought order and stability to professional baseball, he did much to order and stabilize individual and collective memories of the event that brought him to power. This is not to suggest that Landis's hegemony over the deployment (and suppression) of Black Sox scandal memories was complete. For many people, especially those in places like Greenville, South Carolina, and Chicago these heroes were not easily transformed into scapegoats. Memory is not disinterested; it usually serves the interests of those doing the remembering.

Memories, collective no less than private, are not recalled in sociohistorical vacuums. As always, context matters. For many Americans, the time period examined here was tremendously unsettling. "In these years," maintains the historian Michael E. Parrish, "Americans had to cope both with unprecedented economic prosperity and the worst depression in their history. Which condition produced the greater collective anxiety remains an open question." Fighting World War II and living with the atomic bomb were no less anxiety-producing experiences for the next generation. The time was marked by the "uneasy coexistence of tradition and change and the relentless modifications of social institutions, habits and life-styles, linked in a complex, long-term relationship with economic change," argues the historian Ian Purchase. Amidst this type of dramatic transition, tradition is usually highly valued. So perhaps it is not coincidental that these years are also considered to be professional baseball's second Golden Age, a time of larger-than-life heroes and heroics, the era that Ruth built and that Gehrig, DiMaggio, Williams, Feller, Musial, and others maintained. Unwittingly, these men induced Black Sox amnesia, for their exploits confirmed the national pastime's good health and the vigor and integrity of those who played the game. Nevertheless, the scandal was consistently (though not exclusively) reactivated to reinforce dominant memories of the affair. One of the ways preferred narratives maintain their dominance and cultural currency is through repetition.

Finally, this chapter confirms that the historian James Wilkinson is correct: there is "a powerful tension between the desire to know and the availability of materials from which to derive that knowledge." A paucity of evidence is always a formidable obstacle for a historian, but adding to our burden is that few forms of knowledge are as evanescent and difficult to document as memory. While evidence is scarce and sketchy, counter-memories of the Black Sox scandal no doubt existed in numerous communities besides Greenville and Chicago. Banished ballplayers like Eddie Cicotte and Oscar "Happy" Felsch, both of whom confessed and who lived until the sixties, surely activated disparate memories of the episode. People in bars, pool halls, and barber shops all over the United States more than likely shared competing memories of the Big Fix. Only with great difficulty, effort, and luck will we ever know for sure.

The New Cultural Sport History

JAIME SCHULTZ

> It has often been suggested that sport should be studied as part of social history … While "cultural history" (in the sense of *Kulturgeschichte*) was once looked upon with suspicion, in recent years some historians have become interested in studying culture … When culture is conceived of as the set of shared conventions by which human beings orient themselves to the world and to each other, give *meaning* to their existence, and engage in a whole range of symbolic interactions, the importance of studying games and sports in historical contexts becomes apparent.

From Jaime Schultz, "Leaning into the Turn: Towards a New Cultural Sport History," *Sporting Traditions* 27:2 (2010): 53–59. Courtesy of the Australian Society for Sports History, www.sporthistory.org.

> An increasing body of literature suggests that important cultural values are reflected, interpreted, even critiqued by means of play, games, and sports.

Over a quarter of a century has passed since Roberta Park wrote the preceding passage that recommends a cultural approach to the study of sport. Her references to interpretation, meaning, and the symbolic presage a paradigmatic shift, though there are considerable differences between cultural history (the "classic" period of which can be traced from about 1800 to 1950) from "new cultural history," a designation that came into fashion in the late 1980s and has since become, according to Peter Burke, "the dominant form of cultural history—some would even say the dominant form of history—practiced today."

History "has always been a hybrid form of knowledge." Whereas social historians tended to draw insight from social theory and sociology, in the 1970s and 1980s, knowledge generated in anthropology, literary criticism, and cultural studies became evermore influential. What emerged was not a disavowal of work done under the "social" rubric, but a recognition and response to particular ontological and epistemological assumptions, including critiques of materialist notions of "the social" and a de-centering of class, dissatisfaction with prevailing social scientific paradigms, and refutation that language reflected a pre-existing reality. In overly simplistic terms, then, I characterize the shift from the social to the cultural model as one from that of explanation and an excavation for causes, to that of interpretation and an interrogation for meaning.

There are at least six points of convergence between new cultural history and the historiography of sport that warrant discussion here: 1) the impossibility of setting the record straight; 2) a surrender to subjectivity; 3) experimenting with history; 4) adopting an interpretive approach to sporting culture; 5) greater attention to fictivity, narrativity, and cultural memory and; 6) new concerns for discourse and power. The degree to which these themes manifest in the extant sport history literature varies. Consistent through each, though, are questions—perhaps even crises—associated with representation: its analysis, composition, articulation, fidelity to the past, determining power, and the historian's bearing on each of these processes.

The Impossibility of Getting It "Straight"

Wray Vamplew once declared that, "Setting the record straight, and thus preventing myths from becoming conventional wisdom, is the prime duty of all historians." His insistence on the responsibility of the researcher is important, but rather than trying to figure out what "really happened," those approaching "the record" from a new cultural history perspective recognize the impossibility of such a task. These historians might instead ask why those myths took hold, what political purpose they served, whether those principles have changed over time, and how we might reconcile their persistence in the present. Rather than getting the story "straight," Hans Kellner argues that historians should work to "get the story crooked"—to scrutinize the production of knowledge by analyzing historical narratives. "Crooked readings," writes Kellner, "unfocus texts in order to put into the foreground the constructed, rhetorical nature of our own knowledge of the past, and to bring out the purposes often hidden and unrecognized of our own retrospective creations."

This does not mean that concern for what "really happened" should be dismissed because of postmodernist denials of authenticity On the contrary, historians must have the "deepest respect for reality" while concomitantly granting that the past is unknowable and that history is a representation of that past, one of many versions pieced together from the historian's selection of the vestiges that remain. That evidence is "at once always already an interpretation and something that needs to be interpreted" and, in turn, emplotted and contextualized in ways that further impose meaning. Far from suggesting an anti-referentialist position, or that one cannot or should not study the past, this position highlights the limits of empiricism and affirms the idea that any attempt to represent the past inescapably creates meaning.

A Surrender to Subjectivity

In the first issue of the *Journal of Sport History*, Marvin Eyler addressed the topics of objectivity and subjectivity, writing: ".... The past can never be precisely replicated. It must be reconstructed. It is reconstructed on the basis of evidence which has been selected from pre-suppositions and for the historian's purpose. It is finally interpreted so that the historian arrives at as much truth of past actuality as is possible with his [*sic*] incomplete knowledge and fallible judgment."

Eyler's emphasis on reconstruction appears at odds with Douglas Booth's taxonomy, in which reconstructionists operate "under the assumption that they can discover the past as it really was" and "promote history as a realist epistemology in which knowledge derives from empirical evidence and forensic research into primary sources." I believe one would be hard pressed to find a sport historian with unwavering faith in the possibility of objectivity, as defined in the natural sciences. Instead, it seems to me that much of the debate swirling around subjectivity really has to do with issues of transparency—about the expression of critical reflexivity and its place in academic work.

To this end, Booth pushes scholars to be more skeptical about the "cult of the archives" and archival research. Martin Johnes counters with the claim that most historians analytically engage with their sources but that "the practice of writing and publishing in academic history means that this caution might not be obvious in the published work." So while academics might do more to demonstrate reflexivity, "preferably in the text but at least in the footnotes," it frequently contradicts the traditional standards of historical writing. With this in mind, one characteristic of the cultural paradigm is a surrender to subjectivity, that is, an open acknowledgement of the impossibility of objectivity, an evident expression of relativism, and a perceptible affirmation that any knowledge about this past is, and can only be, partial—in all its meanings. This is emphatically not the same as (though it does not exclude) authors self-consciously identifying their various subject positions within their scholarship; neither should it cater to self-indulgence. What it does require is a critical awareness of and appreciation for the researcher's role throughout different facets of the research process.

An Interpretive Approach to Culture

In the "story of the evolving, revolving 'cultural turn'" many scholars identify Clifford Geertz's *Interpretation of Cultures* as perhaps the "most influential text." In contrast to anthropologists and social scientists who approached the understanding of human experience from a positivist perspective, Geertz (citing Weber) explained that he understood culture as "webs of significance [humankind] has spun ... and the analysis of it to be therefore not an experimental science in search of law but an interpretive one in terms of meaning." Among Geertz's collection of essays, "Deep Play: Notes on the Balinese Cockfight" articulates a semiotic approach to discerning (sporting) culture, reading the event and those in attendance as social per "text"—as a story the Balinese tell themselves about themselves.

Geertz constructed this emphasis on signification around the notion of "thick description"—not a method *per se*, but an alternative to method that "has probably found its most ardent users, its most committed followers among historians; partly because it seems ... like a gentle exercise in common sense, written with elegance, and always embedded in a broad historical context—sounding very much like good history." The elision of historical and anthropological sensibilities is an important attribute of the cultural paradigm. As Robert Darnton argues, cultural history is the "anthropological mode of history," the aims of which are to read "for meaning—the meaning inscribed by contemporaries...."

[An important example in] ... the 1990s [of] ... Geertzian-inspired approaches ... in sport history [was] ... Michael Oriard's *Reading Football*, in which he proposed that, "football is indeed a cultural text." Rather than reading the actual game, Oriard reads it through the popular press—the "secondary texts" of the primary contest that "at least bring us close to the varied and changing readings of actual audiences." A wonderful manuscript in many respects, Stephen Hardy points out that Oriard "maybe too quick to assume that yesterday's readers would agree with his interpretation." Elsewhere, Peter Burke has made similar comments about what he sees as a "fundamental problem with the metaphor of reading", that is, "that it seems to license intuition."

Fictivity, Narrativity and Cultural Memory

Like Geertz, Hayden White holds iconic status in the turn towards culture; the two also share important convictions about the nature of scholarship. Geertz ... asserts that, "Anthropological writings are themselves interpretations.... They are 'something fashioned' ... not that they are false, unfactual, or merely 'as if' thought experiments". White similarly refers to histories as "verbal fictions, the contents of which are more invented than found and the forms of which have more in common with their counterparts in literature than they have with those in the sciences." The haziness between history and fiction understandably raises the hackles of many historians, but here the definition of the term fictive must be emphasized—it is not that anthropological or historical writings are made up, but rather that they are made.

Based on Northrop Frye's *Anatomy of Criticism*, White analyzed the works by "masters of nineteenth-century historical thinking" (e.g., Marx, Tocqueville,

Burckhardt) to argue that historians "prefigure" events into one of four main literary tropes (metaphor, metonymy, synecdoche, irony) that correspond to four literary modes of "emplotment" (romance, comedy, tragedy, satire). While historians might narrativise the past along multiple storylines, they tend to be wedded to these four "mythoi" which, in turn, affects the meanings of the histories they construct. It has been primarily within the new millennium that sports historians have explicitly referenced White's work, and narrativity holds exciting possibilities for the analysis of historical texts and in the 'writing up" of history.

White's tropic model has been less influential on sport history than has his appreciation of history as a narrative discourse. He encouraged "the realization that narrative is not merely a neutral discursive form that may or may not be used to represent real events ... but rather entails ontological and epistemic choices with distinct ideological and even specifically political implications." In turn, narrative is more than a delivery system for arguments and evidence but also (and more specifically) as a dedicated field of analysis for those increasingly sensitive to the complexities of language, perception, and memory." While Murray Phillips wrote that, with few exceptions, the "silence" about narratives in sport history "has been deafening," the topic has sidled into the field in a number of different ways. In particular, sport historians have begun to heed the concept of cultural memory, showing less interest in determining what "really" happened than with the ways what happened resonates in the present.... Analyzing these narratives gets to the heart of culturality—the importance of meaning for groups and individuals.

Discourse and Power

Peter Burke writes that "concern for theory is one of the distinctive features" of new cultural history, citing the works of Mikhail Bakhtin, Norbert Elias, Pierre Bourdieu, and Michel Foucault as appreciably influential. Foucault's genealogical methodology, his observations on the microphysics of power and their relationship to knowledge, epistemes of truth, and discursive regimes have been especially cogent. Post-structuralism deserves special mention here, for it has helped historians problematize the status of the social and discern culture as representational and linguistic.

Related to the understanding that language does not merely communicate reality but rather creates it, are issues of identity. When reviewing the field, sport historians operating within the social paradigm have suggested that certain "thematic topics" like class, "ethnicity and race, or different demographic groups," warrant greater assiduity. Again, these are fair assessments; people of color, the working class, and women have been (and, to some extent, continue to be) noticeably absent from the historical record. What a new cultural history perspective brings to light is that these categories are not descriptive, but determining. Nowhere is this more evident than in the works of feminist historians, primarily those influenced by Joan Wallach Scott, whose definition of gender "rests on an integral connection between two propositions: gender is a constitutive element of social relationships based on perceived differences between the sexes, and gender is a primary way of signifying relationships of power."

Early works on women and sport tended to operate from the standpoint of either victimization or valorization, examining, as examples, the ways in which females were excluded from the male preserve of sport, or those triumphant anomalies who thwarted convention and dared to compete. Yet, moving past compensatory or contribution measures that focused on "women worthies" and the "add women and stir" phases of history (or "herstory"), there was a "discernible shift during the 1980s" as scholars began to refocus their efforts from sex roles to the study of gender, especially those informed by post structuralism and deconstructionism. These latter, critical works, more than any others emanating from within the field, are most responsible for nudging sport history toward the cultural paradigm. In this regard, one cannot underestimate the works of Susan Cahn, Roberta Park, Catriona Parratt, Nancy Struna, and Patricia Vertinsky. Their inquiries into methodology, periodization, agency, the definition of sport, intersectionality and questions of difference, and their experimentations with representation have encouraged a radical reformulation of the ways in which many sport historians practice their craft.

To perceive gender as a culturally constructed relationship of power, as opposed to the essential, social aspect of the sexual dichotomy, helps move us away from the traditional binary conceptualization of man/woman, active/passive, culture/nature, public/private that affects and limits much of what we think about sport and society. Let me offer an example of what this insight can bring: when discussing sex testing in women's sports, Allen Guttmann suggests that two women who "disappeared from international competition" at the onset of these procedures were not "really women" and that the autopsy of another female athlete revealed that she "was a man". The result of these statements is to suggest that human beings must belong to one of two sex categories—that if these women refused to take or "failed" the examinations then they must therefore be men. Sex is an either/or proposition.

Conversely, a new cultural historical take on the same topic might be to engage a "critical attack on sex" or use sex testing as an opportunity for the "historicization and deconstruction of the terms of sexual difference." One might engage, to quote Lauren Berland and Michael Warner, in the "labor of ambiguating categories of identity...." [A]s Andrew Sparkes contends, "How we as researchers choose to write about others has profound implications, not just for how readable the text is, but also for how the people the text portrays are 'read' and understood." Accordingly, we should take into account the ways in which identities and subjectivities have been historically constituted, how they change over times, how they have been regulated and enforced, those instances that contest their construction, and our own complicity in these processes.

Doing Sport History Differently, Anew

Sport history's location within the cultural paradigm has been influenced by tensions and developments in other fields: anthropology, literary studies and criticism, postcolonial studies, cultural studies, and sociology, to name a few. Perhaps one of the most compelling shifts to occur in recent sport historiography involves reflexive engagement with meaning through the interpretation of symbolic and linguistic representations of physical culture. There is also an implication of social justice. Hayden White maintains that "the significance of the cultural turn in history and the social sciences inhere in its suggestion that in 'culture' we can apprehend a niche within social reality from which any given society can be deconstructed and shown to be less an inevitability than only one possibility among a host of others." This suggests the possibility of change, not just from past to present, but from present to future.

Conceptualizing history as a narrative-linguistic act and an empirical-analytic enterprise "does not mean that we cannot do history," writes Alun Munslow. "It means we do it differently, anew ... History understood for what it is—a representation—is not a 'problem' to be 'overcome' or a 'useful reminder' that historians trade in words and style." Certainly, there are factual statements that we do not dispute. But the processes of locating and understanding the facts, of making them consequential, of emphasizing some and omitting others, of situating them in context, and translating them into narrative form means that we must accept the idea that history is not the past, but one of its many possible depictions. If historians hope to comprehend the past on its own terms or grasp how inhabitants of the past interpreted an event, if they endeavor to stabilize knowledge about that past, then they obscure the politics of practicing history. Instead, by destabilizing that knowledge through critical, contextual, reflexive, empirically based work, historians can get on with the business of doing history differently, anew.

FURTHER READING

Booth, Douglas. *The Field: Truth and Fiction in Sport History* (2005).

Cahn, Susan K. "Sports Talks: Oral History and its Uses, Problems, and Possibilities for Sport History," *Journal of American History* 82:2 (1994), 594–609.

Davies, Richard O. *Sport in American Life*, 2nd ed. (2011).

Dyreson, Mark. "Sport History and the History of Sport in North America," *Journal of Sport History* 35 (2008), 405–14.

Gerlach, Larry. "Not Quite Ready for Prime Time: Baseball History, 1983–1993," *Journal of Sport History* 21 (Summer 1994), 103–37.

Gorn, Elliott and Warren Goldstein, *A Brief History of American Sports* (1993).

Guttmann, Allen. *From Ritual to Record: The Nature of Modern Sports* (1978).

Guttmann, Allen. *Sports Spectators* (1986).

Guttmann, Allen. *A Whole New Ball Game: An Interpretation of American Sports* (1988).

Hardy, Stephen. "The City and the Rise of American Sport, 1820–1920," *Exercise and Sports Sciences Reviews* 9 (1981), 183–229.

Johnes, Martin. "Texts, Audiences, and Post-Modernism: The Novel as a Source in Sport History," *Journal of Sport History* 34 (2007), 121–33.

Lewis, Robert M. "American Sport History: A Bibliographical Guide," *American Studies International* 29 (April 1991), 35–60.

Osmond, Gary and Murray G. Philips, "Reading Salute: Filmic Representations of Sports History," *International Journal of the History of Sport* 28:10 (July 2011), 1463–1477.

Park, Roberta J. "A Decade of the Body: Researching and Writing About the History of Health, Fitness, Exercise and Sport, 1983–1993," *Journal of Sport History* 21 (Spring 1994), 59–82.

Philips, Murray G. ed. *Deconstructing Sport History: A Postmodern Analysis* (2006).

Philips, Murray G., Mark E. O'Neill, and Gary Osmond, "Broadening Horizons in Sport History: Films, Photographs and Monuments," *Journal of Sport History* 34:2 (2007), 271–93.

Rader, Benjamin G. *American Sports: From the Age of Folk Games to the Age of Televised Sports*, 6th ed. (2008).

Riess, Steven A. *City Games: The Evolution of American Urban Society and the Rise of Sports* (1989).

Riess, Steven A. "From Pitch to Putt: Sport and Class in Anglo-American Sport," *Journal of Sport History* 21 (Summer 1994), 138–84.

Sammons, Jeffrey. "'Race' and Sport: A Critical, Historical Examination," *Journal of Sport History* 21 (Fall 1994), 203–78.

Vertinsky, Patricia. "Gender Relations, Women's History, and Sport History: A Decade of Changing Enquiry, 1983–1993," *Journal of Sport History* 21 (Spring 1994), 1–24.

CHAPTER 2

Sport in Colonial America

Sporting activities in what became the United States were first played by American Indians for religious, medicinal, and commercial purposes (gambling). However, in contrast to what occurred in Canada, native sports had little impact on the pastimes of overseas immigrants. How then did sport develop in colonial America? What was the impact of the settlers' culture (athletic traditions, morality, and religious customs) and the problems of living in a new and often dangerous environment? How did the character of their communities (Puritan Boston vs. Anglican Jamestown) shape their experience as it relates to sport? The colonists' favorite sports were drawn mainly from the frontier and rural character of their surroundings, although colonial villages, towns, and cities provided the primary sites for major sporting contests, for the first athletic clubs, and for the rudimentary commercialization of sport.

Seventeenth-century Puritans permitted lawful sports that were enjoyed in moderation and were recreational (i.e., improved participants' capabilities to perform their worldly duties). They barred blood sports, gambling activities, Sunday amusements, and any pleasures identified with Catholic or pagan rituals. However, as New England's population became more mixed in the eighteenth century and as its social structure widened, it became harder to limit sport. In the Anglican South, on the other hand, a livelier English sporting culture was maintained. Gambling sports like cockfighting and especially horse racing were extremely popular and reflected the manliness of the participants and spectators. Horse racing in the late seventeenth century, which consisted of impromptu short contests, reflected the elevated status of the great tobacco planters who dominated the land. By the middle of the eighteenth century, the gentry began importing thoroughbreds that could race for miles. Scheduled races supervised by elite jockey clubs were held at enclosed tracks in cities like Charlestown, Annapolis, and Williamsburg.

DOCUMENTS

The documents illuminate several perspectives on colonial sports and record evidence of the premodern sport enjoyed by early Americans. Document 1, generally known as King James I's *Book of Sports* (1618), was issued by the Crown as a political ploy. James sought to increase his popularity with the masses by sustaining traditional pastimes in the face of opposition by Puritan magistrates, while in the meantime, he wanted to undermine their growing power. Document 2 is a law passed by the Massachusetts General Court in 1653, and frequently amended to regulate Sunday behavior in the colony. The first laws limiting public activities on the Sabbath were enacted in the 1620s in Virginia and shortly thereafter in Massachusetts Bay. Devout Puritans tried to regulate proper behavior of all local residents, especially on Sundays, a day they believed should be devoted entirely to religious activity, barring all work and recreation on the Sabbath. The terms of the law indicate that most violators of the strict Sabbath were youths and non-Puritans. In Document 3, William Byrd II (1674–1744), an eminent Virginia planter, attorney, author, and fellow of the Royal Society of Great Britain, recounts a ring hunt in which the participants encircle an area rich in game and move into the center of the site, forcing the game into a constricted location where they have little chance of escaping the carnage. Document 4 is a review of Virginia racing in 1772 by a British traveler. By this time the elite of America had been racing thoroughbreds for over a generation at formal racetracks. Document 5 is the report of a cockfight attended by Elkanah Watson in 1787 shortly after he had purchased a 640-acre plantation in Virginia. Document 6 is an account by George Catlin, the noted painter and ethnographer of American Indians, of a lacrosse match he witnessed being played among the Choctaws during the 1830s. Such matches had been played well before the coming of Europeans, making American Indians the first people in what is now the United States to play team ball sports.

1. King James I Identifies Lawful Sports in England, 1618

Whereas upon our return the last year out of Scotland, we did publish our Pleasure touching the recreations of Our people in those parts under Our hand. For some causes Us thereunto moving, Wee have thought good to command these Our Directions then given in Lancashire with a few words thereunto added, and most appliable to these parts of Our Realms, to bee published to all Our Subjects.

Whereas wee did justly in Our Progress through Lancashire, rebuke some Puritans and precise people, and took order that the like unlawful carriage should not bee used by any of them hereafter, in the prohibiting and unlawful punishing of Our good people for using their lawful recreations, and honest exercises, after the afternoon Sermon or Service: Wee now find that two sorts of people, wherewith that country is much infected (Wee mean Papists and Puritans), have maliciously traduced and calumniated those Our just and honorable proceedings. And, therefore, lest Our reputation might, upon the one side (though innocently), have some aspersion laid upon it, and that, upon the other part, Our good people in that Country be misled by the mistaking and misinterpretation

From Kings James I, "'The Kinges' Majesties Declaration Concerning Lawful Sports," in *The King's Book of Sports*, ed. L. A. Govett (London: Elliott Stock, 1890).

of Our meaning: We have, therefore, thought good hereby to clear and make Our pleasure to be manifested to all Our good People in those parts.

It is true that at Our first entry to this Crown, and Kingdom, We were informed, and that too truly, that Our County of Lancashire abounded more in Popish Recusants [people who refused to attend Church of England services] than any County of England, and thus hath still continued since, to Our great regret, with little amendment, save that now of late, in Our last riding through Our said County, Wee find both by the report of the Judges, that there is some amendment now daily beginning, which is no small contentment to Us.

The report of this growing amendment amongst them, made Us the more sorry, when with Our own ears We heard the general complaint of Our people, that they were debarred from all lawful Recreation, and exercise upon the Sundays afternoon, after the ending of all Divine Service, which cannot but produce two evils: The one, the hindering of the conversion of many, whom their Priests will take occasion hereby to vex, persuading that no honest mirth or recreation is lawful or tolerable in Our Religion, which cannot but breed a great discontentment in Our people's hearts, especially of such as are, peradventure, upon the point of turning; The other inconvenience is, that this prohibition bars the common and meaner sort of people from using such exercises as may make their bodies more able for warre, when Wee, or Our Successors, shall have occasion to use them. And, in place thereof, sets up filthy tiplings [shop that sells liquor] and drunkennesse, and breeds a number of idle and discontented speeches in their Ale houses, For when shall the common people have leave to exercise, if not upon the Sundays and holy daies, seeing they must apply their labour, and win their living in all working daies?

Our expresse pleasure therefore is, that the lawes of Our Kingdom, and Canons of Our Church be as well observed in that County, as in all other places of this Our Kingdome. And on the other part, that no lawful Recreation shall bee barred to Our good People, which shall not tend to the breach of our aforesaid Laws, and Canons of our Church: which, to express more particularly, Our pleasure is, That the Bishop, and all other inferior Churchmen, and Churchwardens, shall, for their part, be careful and diligent, both to instruct the ignorant, and convince and reform them that are misled in Religion, presenting them that will not conform themselves, but obstinately stand out, to our Judges and Justices, Whom We likewise command to put the Law in due execution against them.

Our pleasure therefore is, That the Bishop of that Diocese take the like straight order with all the Puritans and Precisions within the same, either constraining them to conform themselves, or to leave the County according to the Laws of Our Kingdome, and Canons of our Church, and so to strike equally on both hands, against the cotemners of our Authority, and adversaries of Our Church. And as for Our good people's lawful Recreation, Our pleasure likewise is, Our good people be not disturbed, ... or discouraged from any lawful recreation, Such as dancing, ... Archery, ... leaping, vaulting, or any other such harmless Recreation, nor from having of May Games, Whitson Ales, and Morris-dances, and the setting up of Maypoles, and other sports therewith used, so as the same be had in due and convenient time, without impediment or neglect of Divine Service: ... But withal we doe here account still as prohibited all unlawful games to bee used upon Sundays only, as Bare and Bullbaitings, Interludes, and at all times, in the meaner sort of people, by Law prohibited, Bowling: And likewise we bar from this benefit and liberty, all such known Recusants, either men or women, as will abstain from coming to Church or Divine Service, that will not first come to the Church and serve God: Prohibiting, in like sort, the said Recreations to any that, though conform in Religion, are not present in the Church at the Service of God, before their going to the said Recreations.

Our pleasure likewise is That they to whom it belongs in Office, shall present and sharply punish all such as in abuse of this Our liberty, will use these exercises before the ends of all Divine Services for that day. And we likewise straightly command, that every person shall resort to his own Parish Church to hear Divine Service, and each Parish by itself to use the said Recreation after Divine Service.

Prohibiting likewise any offensive weapons to bee carried or used in the said times of Recreations, And Our pleasure is That this, Our Declaration, shall bee published by order from the Bishop of the Diocese, through all the Parish Churches, and that both Our Judges of Our Circuit, and Our Judges of Our Peace be informed thereof.

2. Restrictive Sabbath Statutes Enacted in Boston General Court, 1653

Upon information of sundry abuses and misdemeanors committed by several persons on the Lord's day, not only by children playing in the streets and other places, but by youths, maids and other persons, both strangers and others, uncivilly walking the streets and fields, traveling from town to town, going on shipboard, frequenting common houses and other places to drink, sport, and otherwise to misspend that precious time, which things tend much to the dishonor of God, the reproach of religion, and the profanation of his holy Sabbath, the sanctification whereof is sometimes put for all duties immediately respecting the service of God, contained in the first table: It is therefore ordered by this court and the authority, that no children, youths, maids, or other persons, shall transgress in the like kind, on penalty of being reputed great provokers of the high displeasure of Almighty God. and further incurring the penalties hereafter expressed, namely, that the parents and governors of all children above seven years old, (not that we approve of younger children in evil) for the first offense in that kind, upon due proof before any magistrate, own commissioner, or selectman of the town where such offense shall be committed, shall be admonished; for a second offense, upon due proof, as aforesaid, ten shillings; and if they shall again offend in this kind, they shall be presented to the county courts, who shall augment punishment, according to the merit of the fact. And for all youths

From "The Massachusetts Bay Colony," *Records of Massachusetts Bay* 3: 316–17 in *The Sabbath Recorder* 64:12 (March 23, 1908): 361.

and maids, above fourteen years of age, and all elder persons whatsoever that shall offend and be convicted as aforesaid, either for playing, uncivilly walking, drinking, traveling from town to town, going on shipboard, sporting or any way misspending that precious time, shall, for the first offense, be admonished, upon due proof, as aforesaid; for a second offense, shall pay as a fine, five shillings; and for a third offense, ten shillings; and if any shall farther offend that way, they shall be presented to the next county court, who shall augment punishment according to the nature of the offense; and if any be unable or unwilling to pay the aforesaid fines, they shall be whipped by the constable not exceeding five stripes for ten shillings fine; and this to be understood of such offenses as shall be committed during the daylight of the Lord's day.

3. William Byrd Observes a Fire Hunt, 1728

Considering how far we had walked, and consequently how hungry we were, we found but short commons when we came to our quarters. One brace of turkeys was all the game we could meet with, which almost needed a miracle to enable them to suffice so many voracious appetites. However, they just made a shift to keep famine, and consequently mutiny, out of the camp. At night we lodged upon the banks of Buffalo creek, where none of us could complain of loss of rest, for having eaten too heavy and luxurious a supper.

... In a dearth of provisions our chaplain pronounced it lawful to make bold with the Sabbath, and send a party out a-hunting. They fired the dry leaves in a ring of five miles' circumference, which, burning inwards, drove all the game to the center, where they were easily killed. It is really a pitiful sight to see the extreme distress the poor deer are in, when they find themselves surrounded with this circle of fire; they weep and groan like a human creature, yet cannot move the compassion of those hardhearted people, who are about to murder them. This unmerciful sport is called fire hunting, and is much practiced by the Indians and frontier inhabitants, who sometimes, in the eagerness of their diversion, are punished for their cruelty, and are hurt by one another when they shoot across at the deer which are in the middle. What the Indians do now by a circle of fire, the ancient Persians performed formerly by a circle of men: and the same is practiced at this day in Germany upon extraordinary occasions, when any of the princes of the empire have a mind to make a general hunt, as they call it. At such times they order a vast number of people to surround a whole territory. Then marching inwards in close order, they at last force all the wild beasts into a narrow compass, that the prince and his company may have the diversion of slaughtering as many as they please with their own hands. Our hunters massacred two brace of deer after this unfair way, of which they brought us one brace whole, and only the priming's of the rest.

From William Byrd, *A Journey to the Land of Eden and Other Papers* (New York: Vanguard Press, 1928), 214–15.

4. An Englishman's Positive Impressions of Virginia Racing, 1772

There are races at Williamsburg twice a year; that is, every spring and fall, or autumn. Adjoining to the town is a very excellent course, for either two, three, or four mile heats. Their purses are generally raised by subscription, and are gained by the horse that wins two four-mile heats out of three; they amount to an hundred pounds each for the first days runing, and fifty pounds each every day after; the races commonly continueing for a week. There are also matches and sweepstakes very often, for considerable sums. Besides these at Williamsburg, there are races established annually, almost at every town and considerable place in Virginia; and frequent matches, on which large sums of money depend; the inhabitants, almost to a man, being quite devoted to the division of horse-racing.

Very capital horses are started here, such as would make no despicable figure at Newmarket; nor is their speed, bottom, or blood inferior to there appearance; the gentlemen of Virginia sparring no pains, trouble or expence in importing the best stock, and improving the excellence of the breed by proper and judicious crossing.

Indeed, nothing can be more elegant and beautiful than the horses had here, either for the turf, the field, the road, or the coach; and they have always fine, long, full, flowing tails; but their carriage horses seldom are possessed of that weight and power, which distinguish those of the same kind in England.

Their stock is from old Cade, old Crab, old Partner, Regulus, Babraham, Bosphorus, Devonshire Childers, the Cullen Arabian, &c., in England; and a horse from Arabia, which was imported into America, and is now in existance.

In the southern part of the colony, and in North Carolina, they are much attached to *quarter-racing,* which is always a match between two horses, to run one quarter of a mile straight out, being merely an exertion of speed; and they have a breed that perform it with astonishing velocity, beating every other for that distance, with great ease; but they have no bottom. However, I am confident that there is not a horse in England, nor perhaps the whole world, that can excel them in rapid speed: and these likewise make excellent saddle-horses for the road. The Virginians, of all ranks and denominations, are excessively fond of horses, and especially those of the race breed. The gentlemen of fortune expend great sums on their race studs, generally keeping handsome carriages, and several elegant sets of horses, as well as others for the race and road; even the most indigent person has his saddlehorse, which he rides to every place, and on every occasion; for in this country nobody walks on foot the smallest distance, except when hunting; indeed a man will frequently go five miles to catch a horse to ride only one mile upon afterwards. In short, their horses are their pleasure and their pride.

From John Ferdinand Dalziel Smyth, *A Tour in the United States of America* (London: G. Robinson, 1784), II: 20–23.

5. Elkanah Watson's Misgivings on Cockfighting, 1787

In one of these excursions, I accompanied a prominent planter at his urgent solicitation, to attend a cock-fight in Hampton County, Virginia, a distance of twenty miles. We reached the ground about ten o'clock the next morning. The roads, as we approached the scene, were alive with carriages, horses, and pedestrians, black and white, hastening to the point of attraction. Several houses formed a spacious square, in the centre of which was arranged a large cock-pit; surrounded by many genteel people, promiscuously mingled with the vulgar and debased. Exceedingly beautiful cocks were produced, armed with long, sharp, steel-pointed gaffs, which were firmly attached to their natural spurs.

The moment the birds were dropped, bets ran high. The little heroes appeared trained to the business, and not the least disconcerted by the crowd or shouting. They stepped about with great apparent pride and dignity; advancing nearer and nearer, they flew upon each other at the same instant with a rude shock, the cruel and fatal gafts [iron hooks] being driven into their bodies, and at times, directly through their heads. Frequently one, or both, were struck dead at the first blow, but they often fought after being repeatedly pierced, as long as they were able to crawl, and in the agonies of death would often make abortive efforts to raise their heads and strike their antagonists. I soon sickened at this barbarous sport, and retired under the shade of a wide-spread willow, where I was much better entertained in witnessing a voluntary fight between a wasp and spider.

In viewing the crowd, I was deeply astonished to find men of character and intelligence giving their countenance to an amusement so frivolous and scandalous, so abhorrent to every feeling of humanity, and so injurious in its moral influence, by the inculcation of habits of gambling and drinking, in the waste of time, and often in the issues of fighting and duelling.

6. George Catlin Describes a Choctaw 1834 Lacrosse Match

Monday afternoon at three, o'clock, I rode out with Lieutenants S. and M., to a very pretty prairie, about six miles distant, to the ball-play-ground of the Choctaws, where we found several thousand Indians encamped. There were two points of timber about half a mile apart, in which the two parties for the play, with their respective families and friends, were encamped; and lying between them, the prairie on which the game was to be played.... Each party had their goal made with two upright posts, about 25 feet high and six feet apart,

From Elkanah Watson, *Men and Times of the Revolution, or Memoirs of Elkanah Watson.*, ed. Winslow C. Watson (New York: Dana and Co., 1856), 261–62.

From George C. Catlin, *Letters and Notes on the Manners, Customs, and Conditions of the North American Indians*, vol. 2 (London: David Bogue, 1844), 124–26.

Choctaw lacrosse. This ball-and-stick game had some forty variations. Note the multitude of participants. (Stock Montage, Inc.)

set firm in the ground, with a pole across at the top. These goals were about forty or fifty rods apart; and at a point just half way between, was another small stake, driven down, where the ball was to be thrown up at the firing of a gun, to be struggled for by the players. All this preparation was made by some old men, who were, it seems, selected to be the judges of the play, who drew a line from one bye to the other; to which directly came from the woods, on both sides, a great concourse of women and old men, boys and girls, and dogs and horses, where bets were to be made on the play. The betting was all done across this line, and seemed to be chiefly left to the women, who seemed to have martialled out a little of everything that their houses and fields possessed. Goods and chattels—knives—dresses—blankets—pots and kettles—dogs and horses, and guns; and all were placed in the possession of *stake-holders,* who sat by them, and watched them on the ground all night, preparatory to the play.

The sticks with which this tribe play, are bent into an oblong hoop at the end, with a sort of slight web of small thongs tied across, to prevent the ball from passing through. The players hold one of these in each hand, and by leaping into the air, they catch the ball between the two nettings and throw it, without being allowed to strike it, or catch it in their hands....

... In every ballplay of these people, it is a rule of the play, that no man shall wear moccasins on his feet, or any other dress than his breech-cloth around his waist, with a beautiful bead belt, and a "tail," made of white horsehair or quills, and a "*mane*" on the neck, of horsehair dyed of various colours.

This game had been arranged and "made up," three or four months before the parties met to play it, and in the following manner:—The two champions who led the two parties, and had the alternate choosing of the players through the whole tribe, sent runners, with the ball-sticks most fantastically ornamented with ribbons and red paint, to be touched by each one of the chosen players; who thereby agreed to be on the spot at the appointed time and ready for the play. The ground having been all prepared and preliminaries of the game all settled, and the bettings all made, and goods all "staked," night came on without the appearance of any players on the ground. But soon after dark, a procession of lighted flambeaux was seen coming from each encampment, to the ground where the players assembled around their respective byes; and at the beat of the drums and chaunts of the women, each party of players commenced the "ball-play dance." Each party danced for a quarter of an hour around their respective byes, in their ball-play dress; rattling their ball-sticks together in the most violent manner, and all singing as loud as they could raise their voices; whilst the women of each party, who had their goods at stake, formed into two rows on the line between the two parties of players, and danced also, in an uniform step, and all their voices joined in chants to the Great Spirit; in which they were soliciting his favour in deciding the game to their advantage; and also encouraging the players to exert every power they possessed, in the struggle that was to ensue. In the mean time, four old *medicine-men,* who were to have the starting of the ball, and who were to be judges of the play, were seated at the point where the ball was to be started; and busily smoking to the Great Spirit for their success in judging rightly, and impartially, between the parties in so important an affair.

This dance was one of the most picturesque scenes imaginable, and was repeated at intervals of every half hour during the night, and exactly in the same manner; so that the players were certainly !awake all the night, and arranged in their appropriate dress, prepared for the play which was to commence at nine o'clock the next morning. In the morning, at the hour, the two parties and all their friends, were drawn out and over the ground; when at length the game commenced, by the judges throwing up the ball at the firing of a gun; when an instant struggle ensued between the players, who were some six or seven hundred in numbers, and were mutually endeavoring to catch the ball in their sticks, and throw it home and between their respective stakes; which, whenever successfully done, counts one for game. In this game every player was dressed alike, that is, *divested* of all dress, except the girdle and the tail, which I have before described; and in these desperate struggles for the ball, when it is *up* (where hundreds are running together and leaping, actually over each other's heads, and darting between their adversaries' legs, tripping and throwing, and foiling each other in every possible manner, and every voice raised to the highest key, in shrill yelps and barks)! ... In these struggles, every mode is used that can be devised, to oppose the progress of the foremost, who is likely to get the ball; and these obstructions often meet desperate individual resistance, which terminates in a violent scuffle, and sometimes in fisticuffs; when their sticks are dropped, and the parties are unmolested, whilst they are settling it between themselves; unless it be by a general *stampedo,* to which they are subject who are down, if the ball happens to pass in their direction. Every weapon, by a rule of all ball-plays, is laid by in their respective encampments, and no man allowed to go for one; so that the sudden broils that take place on the ground, are presumed to be as suddenly settled without any probability of much personal injury; and no one is allowed to interfere in any way with the contentious individuals.

There are times, when the ball gets to the ground, and such a confused mass rushing together around it, and knocking their sticks together, without the possibility of any one getting or seeing it, for the dust that they raise, that the spectator loses his strength, and everything else but his senses; when the condensed mass of ball-sticks, and shins, and bloody noses, is carried around the different parts of the ground, for a quarter of an hour at a time, without any one of the mass being able to see the ball; and which they are often thus scuffling for, several minutes after it has been thrown off, and played over another part of the ground.

For each time that the ball was passed between the stakes of either party, one was counted for their game, and a halt of about one minute; when it was again started by the judges of the play, ... and so on until the successful party arrived to 100, which was the limit of the game, and accomplished at an hour's sun, when they took the stakes; and then, by a previous agreement, produced a number of jugs of whiskey, which gave all a wholesome drink, and sent them all off merry and in good humour, but not drunk.

ESSAYS

The following essays compare the sporting experience of two distinctly different colonial communities—the plantation society of the Anglican Chesapeake region, and the less stratified society of bourgeois Puritan Boston. In the first monograph, Timothy Breen, a renowned colonial historian at Northwestern University, employs the methods of cultural anthropology to analyze late seventeenth-century Virginia horse racing and to explain the significance of gambling among leading tobacco planters. He describes a society that was highly individualistic, materialistic, and honor-bound. Elite plantation owners utilized horse racing to certify social status, to express dominant values like risk taking, and to deflect potential social conflicts through their agreements and conventions that facilitated the horse races. In the second essay, Nancy Struna of the University of Maryland and author of *People of Progress: Sport, Leisure and Labor in Early Anglo-America* discusses the role of taverns in the sporting life of American colonists in Virginia and Maryland. Tavernkeepers were the first sports promoters, organizing sporting competitions like shooting matches, animal baiting sports, and table games to draw crowds of drinking men. There was always a lot of public concern about the social conduct in taverns (including drunkenness, gambling, idleness, and rowdyism), and local governments licensed and regulated their operation. Particular attention is given to the social significance of cockfighting and the role of class in colonial taverns.

The Cultural Significance of Gambling Among the Gentry of Virginia

TIMOTHY H. BREEN

... The great planters' passion for gambling, especially on quarter-horse racing, coincided with a period of far-reaching social change in Virginia. Before the mid-1680s constant political unrest, servant risings both real and threatened, plant- cutting riots, and even a full-scale civil war had plagued the colony. But by the end of the century Virginia had achieved internal peace. Several elements contributed to the growth of social tranquility. First, by 1700 the ruling gentry were united as they had never been before.... A sizable percentage of the Virginia gentry, perhaps a majority, had been born in the colony. The members of this native-born elite—one historian calls them a "creole elite"—cooperated more frequently in political affairs than had their immigrant fathers. They found it necessary to unite in resistance against a series of interfering royal governors [and] ... successfully consolidated their control over Virginia's civil, military and ecclesiastical institutions. They monopolized the most important offices; they patented the best lands.

A second and even more far-reaching element in the creation of this remarkable solidarity among the gentry was the shifting racial composition of the plantation labor force. Before the 1680s the planters had relied on large numbers of white indentured servants to cultivate Virginia's sole export crop, tobacco. These impoverished, often desperate servants disputed their masters' authority and on several occasions resisted colonial rulers with force of arms. In part because of their dissatisfaction with the indenture system, and in part because changes in the international slave trade made it easier and cheaper for Virginians to purchase black laborers, the major planters increasingly turned to Africans. The blacks' cultural disorientation made them less difficult to control than the white servants.... By the beginning of the eighteenth century Virginia had been transformed into a relatively peaceful, biracial society in which a few planters exercised almost unchallenged hegemony over both their slaves and their poorer white neighbors.

The growth of gambling among the great planters during a period of significant social change raises important questions not only about gentry values but also about the social structure of late seventeenth-century Virginia. Why did gambling, involving high stakes, become so popular among the gentlemen at precisely this time? Did it reflect gentry values or have symbolic connotations for the people living in this society? Did this activity serve a social function, contributing in some manner to the maintenance of group cohesion? Why did quarter-horse racing, in particular, become a gentry sport? And finally, did public displays such as this somehow reinforce the great planters' social and political dominance?

From Timothy H. Breen, "Horses and Gentlemen: The Cultural Significance of Gambling Among the Gentry of Virginia," William & Mary Quarterly 34 (April 1977): 239–57. Reprinted by permission.

In part, of course, gentlemen laid wagers on women and horses simply because they enjoyed the excitement of competition.... Another equally acceptable explanation for the gentry's fondness for gambling might be the transplanting of English social mores.... While both views possess merit, ... the widespread popularity of gambling among the gentry indicates that this type of behavior may have had deeper, more complex cultural roots than either of these explanations would suggest.

In many societies competitive gaming is a device by which the participants transform abstract cultural values into observable social behavior. In his now-classic analysis of the Balinese cockfight Clifford Geertz describes contests for extremely high stakes as intense social dramas. These battles not only involve the honor of important villagers and their kin groups, but also reflect in symbolic form the entire Balinese social structure. Far from being a simple pastime, betting on cocks turns out to be an expression of the way the Balinese perceive social reality. The rules of the fight, the patterns of wagering, the reactions of winners and losers—all these elements help us to understand more profoundly the totality of Balinese culture.

The Virginia case is analogous to the Balinese. When the great planter staked his money and tobacco on a favorite horse or spurred a sprinter to victory, he displayed some of the central elements of gentry culture—its competitiveness, individualism, and materialism. In fact, competitive gaming was for many gentlemen a means of translating a particular set of values into action, a mechanism for expressing a loose but deeply felt bundle of ideas and assumptions about the nature of society. The quarter-horse races of Virginia were intense contests involving personal honor, elaborate rules, heavy betting, and wide community interest; and just as the cockfight opens up hidden dimensions of Balinese culture, gentry gambling offers an opportunity to improve our understanding of the complex interplay between cultural values and social behavior in Virginia.

Gambling reflected core elements of late seventeenth- and early eighteenth-century gentry values.... Virginia gentlemen placed extreme emphasis upon personal independence. This concern may in part have been the [product] of the colony's peculiar settlement patterns. The great planters required immense tracts of fresh land for their tobacco. Often thousands of acres in size, their plantations were scattered over a broad area from the Potomac River to the James. The dispersed planters lived in their "Great Houses" with their families and slaves, and though they saw friends from time to time, they led for the most part isolated, routine lives.... Some planters were uncomfortably aware of the problems created by physical isolation....

Yet despite such apparent cultural privation, [planters] refused to alter their life styles in any way that might compromise their freedom of action.... Some of these planters even saw themselves as lawgivers out of the Old Testament.... Whatever the origins of this independent spirit, it bred excessive individualism in a wide range of social activities. While these powerful gentlemen sometimes worked together to achieve specific political and economic ends, they bristled at the least hint of constraint....

The gentry expressed this uncompromising individualism in aggressive competitiveness, engaging in a constant struggle against real and imagined rivals to obtain more lands, additional patronage, and high tobacco prices. Indeed, competition was a major factor shaping the character of face-to-face relationships among the colony's gentlemen, and when the stakes were high the planters were not particular about the methods they employed to gain victory. In large part, the goal of the competition within the gentry group was to improve social position by increasing wealth.

Some gentlemen believed that personal honor was at stake as well. Robert "King" Carter, by all accounts the most successful planter of his generation, expressed his anxiety about losing out to another Virginian in a competitive market situation. "In discourse with Colonel Byrd, Mr. Armistead, and a great many others," he explained, "I understand you [an English merchant] had sold their tobaccos in round parcels and at good rates. I cannot allow myself to come behind any of these gentlemen in the planter's trade." Carter's pain arose not so much from the lower price he had received as from the public knowledge that he had been bested by respected peers. He believed he had lost face. This kind of intense competition was sparked, especially among the less affluent members of the gentry, by a dread of slipping into the ranks of … the "common Planters."… The efforts of "these mighty dons" to outdo one another were almost certainly motivated by a desire to disguise their "originals" to demonstrate anew through competitive encounters that they could legitimately claim gentility.

Another facet of Virginia gentry culture was materialism. This certainly does not mean that the great planters lacked spiritual concerns. Religion played a vital role in the lives of men like Robert Carter and William Byrd II. Nevertheless, piety was largely a private matter. In public these men determined social standing not by a man's religiosity or philosophic knowledge but by his visible estate—his lands, slaves, buildings, even by the quality of his garments.…

The gentry were acutely sensitive to the element of chance in human affairs, and this sensitivity influenced their attitudes toward other men and society. Virginians knew from bitter experience that despite the best-laid plans, nothing in their lives was certain. Slaves suddenly sickened and died. English patrons forgot to help their American friends. Tobacco prices fell without warning. Cargo ships sank. Storms and droughts ruined the crops. The list was endless. [William] Fitzhugh warned an English correspondent to think twice before allowing a son to become a Virginia planter, for even "if the best husbandry and the greatest forecast and skill were used, yet ill luck at Sea, a fall of a Market, or twenty other accidents may ruin and overthrow the best Industry." Other planters, even those who had risen to the top of colonial society, longed for greater security.… However desirable such certainty may have appeared, the planters always put their labor and money into tobacco, hoping for a run of luck. One simply learned to live with chance.…

Gaming relationships reflected these strands of gentry culture. In fact, gambling in Virginia was a ritual activity. It was a form of repetitive, patterned behavior that not only corresponded closely to the gentry's values and assumptions but also symbolized the realities of everyday planter life. This congruence between actions and belief, between form and experience, helps to account for the popularity of betting contests. The wager, whether over cards or horses, brought together in a single, focused act the great planters' competitiveness, independence, and materialism, as well as the element of chance. It represented a social agreement in which each individual was free to determine how he would play, and the gentleman who accepted a challenge risked losing his material possessions as well as his personal honor.

The favorite household or tavern contests during this period included cards, backgammon, billiards, nine-pins, and dice. The great planters preferred card games that demanded skill as well as luck. Put, piquet, and whist provided the necessary challenge, and Virginia gentlemen ... regularly played these games for small sums of money and tobacco. These activities brought men together, stimulated conversation, and furnished a harmless outlet for aggressive drives. They did not, however, become for the gentry a form of intense, symbolic play such as the cockfight in Bali....

Horse racing generated far greater interest among the gentry than did the household games. Indeed, for the great planters and the many others who came to watch, these contests were preeminently a social drama. To appreciate the importance of racing in seventeenth-century Virginia, we must understand the cultural significance of horses. By the turn of the century possession of one of these animals had become a social necessity. Without a horse, a planter felt despised, an object of ridicule. Owning even a slowfooted saddle horse made the common planter more of a man in his own eyes as well as in those of his neighbors; he was reluctant to venture forth on foot for fear of making an adverse impression.... Such behavior seems a waste of time and energy only to one who does not comprehend the symbolic importance which the Virginians attached to their horses. A horse was an extension of its owner; indeed, a man was only as good as his horse. Because of the horse's cultural significance, the gentry attempted to set its horsemanship apart from that of the common planters. Gentlemen took better care of their animals, and, according to John Clayton, who visited Virginia in 1688, they developed a distinctive riding style. "They ride pretty sharply," Clayton reported, "a Planter's Pace is a Proverb, which is a good sharp hand-Gallop." A fast-rising cloud of dust far down a Virginia road probably alerted the common planter that he was about to encounter a social superior.

The contest that generated the greatest interest among the gentry was the quarterhorse race, an all-out sprint by two horses over a quarter-mile dirt track. The great planters dominated these events.... Members of the House of Burgesses, including its powerful speaker, William Randolph, were frequently mentioned in the contests that [came] before the courts. On at least one occasion the Rev. James Blair, Virginia's most eminent clergyman and a founder of the College of William and Mary, gave testimony in a suit arising from a race run between Capt. William Soane and Robert Napier. The tenacity with which the gentry pursued these cases, almost continuations of the race itself, suggests the victory was no less sweet when it was gained in court.

Many elements contributed to the exclusion of lower social groups from these contests. Because of the sheer size of wagers, poor freemen and common planters could not have participated regularly....

The gentry actively enforced its exclusive control over quarter-horse racing. When James Bullocke, a York County tailor, challenged Mr. Mathew Slader to a race in 1674, the county court informed Bullocke that it was "contrary to Law for a Labourer to make a race being a Sport for Gentlemen" and fined the presumptuous tailor two hundred pounds of tobacco and cask....

In most match races the planter rode his own horse, and the exclusiveness of these were two ways to set up a challenge. The first was a regularly scheduled affair usually held on Saturday afternoon. By 1700 there were at least a dozen tracks, important enough to be known by name, scattered through the counties of the Northern Neck and the James River valley. The records are filled with references to contests held at such places as Smith's Field, Coan Race Course, Devil's Field, Yeocomico, and Varina. No doubt, many races also occurred on nameless country roads or convenient pastures. On the appointed day the planter simply appeared at the race track and waited for a likely challenge.... A second type of contest was a more spontaneous challenge. When gentlemen congregated over a jug of hard cider or peach brandy, the talk frequently turned to horses. The owners presumably bragged about the superior speed of their animals, and if one planter called another's bluff, the men cried out "done, and done," marched to the nearest field, and there discovered whose horse was in fact the swifter.

Regardless of the outcome, quarter-horse races in Virginia were exciting spectacles. The crowds of onlookers seem often to have been fairly large, as common planters, even servants, flocked to the tracks to watch the gentry challenge one another for what must have seemed immense amounts of money and tobacco.... Attendance at race days was sizable enough to support a brisk trade in cider and brandy....

The magnitude of gentry betting indicates that racing must have deeply involved the planter's self-esteem. Wagering took place on two levels. The contestants themselves made a wager on the outcome, a main bet usually described in a written statement. In addition, side wagers were sometimes negotiated between spectators or between a contestant and spectator. Of the two, the main bet was far the more significant. From accounts of disputed races reaching the county courts we know that gentlemen frequently risked very large sums. The most extravagant contest of the period was a race run between John Baker and John Haynie in Northumberland County in 1693, in which the two men wagered 4000 pounds of tobacco and 40 shillings sterling on the speed of their sprinters, Prince and Smoaker. Some races involved only twenty or thirty shillings, but a substantial number were run for several pounds sterling and hundreds of pounds of tobacco. While few, if any, of the seventeenth-century gentlemen were what we would call gambling addicts, their betting habits seem irrational even by the more prudential standards of their own day: in conducting normal business transactions, for example, they would never have placed so much money in such jeopardy.

To appreciate the large size of these bets we must interpret them within the context of Virginia's economy. Between 1660 and 1720 a planter could anticipate receiving about ten shillings per hundred-weight of tobacco. Since the average grower seldom harvested more than 1500 pounds of tobacco a year per man, he probably never enjoyed an annual income from tobacco in excess of eight pounds sterling. For most Virginians the conversion of tobacco into sterling occurred only in the neat columns of account books. They themselves seldom had coins in their pockets. Specie was extremely scarce, and planters ordinarily paid their taxes and conducted business transactions with tobacco notes—written promises to deliver to the bearer a designated amount of tobacco. The great preponderance of seventeenth-century planters were quite poor, and even the great planters estimated their income in hundreds, not thousands, of pounds sterling.... The Baker-Haynie bet—to take a notable example—amounted to approximately £22 sterling, more than 7 percent of Fitzhugh's annual cash return. It is therefore not surprising that the common planters seldom took part in quarter-horse racing: this wager alone amounted to approximately three times the income they could expect to receive in a good year. Even a modest wager of a pound or two sterling represented a substantial risk.

Gentlemen sealed these gaming relationships with a formal agreement, either a written statement laying out the terms of the contest or a declaration before a disinterested third party of the nature of the wager. In either case the participants carefully stipulated what rules would be in effect. Sometimes the written agreements were quite elaborate....

Virginia's county courts treated race covenants as binding legal contracts. If a gentleman failed to fulfill the agreement, the other party had legitimate grounds to sue; and the county justices' first consideration during a trial was whether the planters had properly recorded their agreement. The Henrico court summarily dismissed one gambling suit because "noe Money was stacked down nor Contract in writing made[,] one of which in such cases is by the law required." Because any race might generate legal proceedings, it was necessary to have a number of people present at the track not only to assist in the running of the contest but also to act as witnesses if anything went wrong. The two riders normally appointed an official starter, several judges, and someone to hold the stakes.

Almost all of the agreements included a promise to ride a fair race. Thus two men in 1698 insisted upon "fair Rideing"; another pair pledged "they would run fair horseman's play." By such agreements the planters waived their customary right to jostle, whip, or knee an opponent, or to attempt to unseat him. During the last decades of the seventeenth century the gentry apparently attempted to substitute riding skill and strategy for physical violence. The demand for "fair Rideing" also suggests that the earliest races in Virginia were wild, no-holds-barred affairs that afforded contestants ample opportunity to vent their aggressions.

The intense desire to win sometimes undermined a gentleman's written promise to run a fair race. When the stakes were large, emotions ran high. One man complained in a York County court that an opponent had interfered with his horse in the middle of the race, "by meanes whereof the s[ai]d Plaintiff lost the said Race." Joseph Humphrey told a Northumberland County court that he would surely have come in first in a challenge for 1500 pounds of tobacco had not Capt. Rodham Kenner (a future member of the House of Burgesses) "held the defend[an]t horses bridle in running his race." Other riders testified that they had been "Josselled" while the race was in progress....

Planters who lost large wagers because an opponent jostled or "hollowed" them off the track were understandably angry. Yet instead of challenging the other party to a duel or allowing gaming relationships to degenerate into blood feuds, the disappointed horsemen invariably took their complaints to the courts. Such behavior indicates not only that the gentlemen trusted the colony's formal legal system—after all, members of their group controlled it—but also that they were willing to place institutional limitations on their own competitiveness. Gentlemen who felt they had been cheated or abused at the track immediately collected witnesses and brought suit before the nearest county court. The legal machinery available to the aggrieved gambler was complex; and no matter how unhappy he may have been with the final verdict, he could rarely claim that the system had denied due process.

The plaintiff brought charges before a group of justices of the peace sitting as a county court; if these men found sufficient grounds for a suit, the parties—in the language of seventeenth-century Virginia—could "put themselves upon the country." In other words, they could ask that a jury of twelve substantial freeholders hear the evidence and decide whether the race had in fact been fairly run. If the sums involved were high enough, either party could appeal a local decision to the colony's general court, a body consisting of the governor and his council.... For example, Joseph Humphrey, loser in a race for 1500 pounds of tobacco, stamped out of a Northumberland County court, demanding a stop to "farther proceedings in the Common Law till a hearing in Chancery."... All the men involved in these race controversies took their responsibilities seriously.... It seems unlikely that the colony's courts would have adopted such an indulgent attitude towards racing had these contests not in some way served a significant social function for the gentry.

Competitive activities such as quarter-horse racing served social as well as symbolic functions. As we have seen, gambling reflected core elements of the culture of late seventeenth-century Virginia. Indeed, if it had not done so, horse racing would not have become so popular among the colony's gentlemen. These contests also helped the gentry to maintain group cohesion during a period of rapid social change. After 1680 the great planters do not appear to have become significantly less competitive, less individualistic, or less materialistic than their predecessors had been. But while the values persisted, the forms in which they were expressed changed. During the last decades of the century unprecedented external pressures, both political and economic, coupled with a major shift in the composition of the colony's labor force, caused the Virginia gentry to communicate these values in ways that would not lead to deadly physical violence or spark an eruption of blood feuding. The members of the native-born elite, anxious to preserve their autonomy over local affairs, sought to avoid the kinds of divisions within their ranks that had contributed to the outbreak of Bacon's Rebellion. They found it increasingly necessary to cooperate against meddling royal governors. Moreover, such earlier unrest among the colony's plantation workers as Bacon's Rebellion and the plant-cutting riots had impressed upon the great planters the need to present a common face to their dependent laborers, especially to the growing number of black slaves who seemed more and more menacing as the years passed.

Gaming relationships were one of several ways by which the planters, no doubt unconsciously, preserved class cohesion. By wagering on cards and horses they openly expressed their extreme competitiveness, winning temporary emblematic victories over their rivals without thereby threatening the social tranquility of Virginia. These non-lethal competitive devices, similar in form to what social anthropologists have termed "joking relationships," were a kind of functional alliance developed by the participants themselves to reduce dangerous, but often inevitable, social tensions.

Without rigid social stratification racing would have lost much of its significance for the gentry. Participation in these contests publicly identified a person as a member of an elite group. Great planters raced against their social peers. They certainly had no interest in competing with social inferiors, for in this kind of relationship victory carried no positive meaning: the winner gained neither honor nor respect. By the same token, defeat by someone like James Bullocke, the tailor from York, was painful, and to avoid such incidents gentlemen rarely allowed poorer whites to enter their gaming relationships—particularly the heavy betting on quarter horses. The common planters certainly gambled among themselves. Even the slaves may have laid wagers. But when the gentry competed for high stakes, they kept their inferiors at a distance, as spectators but never players.

The exclusiveness of horse racing strengthened the gentry's cultural dominance. By promoting these public displays the great planters legitimized the cultural values which racing symbolized—materialism, individualism, and competitiveness. These colorful, exclusive contests helped persuade subordinate white groups that gentry culture was desirable, something worth emulating; and it is not surprising that people who conceded the superiority of this culture readily accepted the gentry's right to rule. The wild sprint down a dirt track served the interests of Virginia's gentlemen better than they imagined.

Sporting Life in the Taverns

NANCY STRUNA

Taverns were hubs of activity from daybreak, and sometimes before, to late evening and sometimes beyond.... In the evening the pace quickened: supper at seven o'clock, more drinks, a shooting contest and card play, a rendezvous in a back room, a round of dancing, a fight between inebriated adversaries, a

---

From *People of Prowess: Sport, Leisure, and Labor in Early Anglo-America*.

political or philosophical discussion. All and more were framed within the collage of tavern life.

Sports and other physical recreations were core activities in eighteenth century taverns. Card and dice games required only tables and chairs and were easily played, or perhaps better played, as people sat, conversed, and drank. Shooting contests in which the targets were things normally found indoors, such as candle flames that a marksman tried to "snuff," also occurred, as did dancing and more than a few fistfights.

Outside the tavern were space and, occasionally, equipment and facilities for other practices. Many keepers provided places for ninepins, if not formal alleys. Urban proprietors permitted this traditional bowling game in the lot or lane behind or next to the tavern, whereas rural taverns usually had enough land in front. The physical requirements were minimal and unstandardized; a narrow strip of ground, minimally twenty or thirty feet long, was sufficient to allow contestants to take turns at trying to knock down the pins, arrayed in three rows of three, with a wooden or stone "ball." Quoits was similar, in terms of both space and format. Originally a game played by agricultural laborers who took breaks in their work to toss stones at a target in a field, mid-eighteenth-century quoits required only a straightaway, a meg or stake, and a doughnut-shaped stone or piece of iron with a hole in the center. The object of the thrower was to "ring" the meg with the quoit [metal ring], or at least to toss the object closer to the stake than the opponents did. Eventually horseshoes would serve the same purpose.

Tavern grounds were also the sites for more physical matches between humans or animals. Cricket games between teams of gentlemen took place at taverns, as did the bull and bear baits that appealed to laborers. Horse races occasionally started or were arranged at the ordinary, and especially in the backcountry, tavernkeepers ... permitted and even promoted fistfights and wrestling bouts. Perhaps the most common sport on the grounds of the taverns, however, was cockfighting, which, outside New England at least, drew people of all ranks and races. Tavernkeepers were well aware of the popular interest in the event. Some of them built formal pits, which ranged from simple holes in the ground covered by boards when not in use to elaborate stagelike facilities. Others provided open spaces for matches, or single contests between fighting birds, as well as "mains," which were a series of fights.

Cockfighting flourished in the eighteenth century, especially from New York southward.... By the turn of the century cockfights were relatively common in the environs of New York City, owing in part to the region's trade goods and people with the West Indies and especially Barbados. In 1724 Hugh Jones, an Anglican minister posted in Virginia, noted that the sport was already popular there among common planters. Tavernkeepers in the Carolinas were building pits by 1732, and before midcentury the sport had spread to the towns surrounding Boston. By the 1740s it was a staple of tavern life, although the fights certainly occurred in other venues, and it was popular among servants and slaves, as well as free colonists.

Cockfighting was like other eighteenth-century sporting practices in that it was both simple and complex.... Owners loosed their fighting fowl in a ring, preferably an enclosed "pit" that provided protection for spectators. Spectators standing around ... watched the birds strike one another with beaks, claws, and metal spurs or gaffs, attached to each leg. The fight, which could be over in seconds or a few minutes, ended once one of the birds was either dead or too maimed to continue.

More complex were the preparations, ... pursued with a seriousness usually reserved for life-and-death struggles—or for horse races. Planters and tavern-keepers, as well as farmers and merchants, either raised or imported fowl that were specifically bred for limb speed and ferocity. They also clipped the birds' wings and feathers, fed them special diets, and trained them via mock fights to enhance their aggressiveness. Finally, some owners either assigned a servant or slave or hired a neighbor to care for the birds and oversee their training.

Why would colonists go to such lengths when there was little certainty that one's bird would survive to fight another day?.... Clifford Geertz, who observed the sport on the Indonesian island of Bali, provided the classic psychological explanation. The fighting cocks, Geertz wrote, were surrogates for their owners' personalities. Their battle required and displayed immense physical prowess, and it was often a fight for status, which was crucial to life itself and to individuals' conceptions of themselves in the hierarchical society on Bali. Owners thus saw the stakes as enormous, perhaps higher than they could ever realize or rationalize, and the practice of gambling and the multiple layers of wagers reinforced the stakes. Cockfights were, in short, instances of what Jeremy Bentham meant by the phrase "deep play." Everything and anything of significance was on the line in this contest.... Moreover, the owner of a winning fighting cock was not likely to recoup all that he—the owners were men—had invested, psychically or materially.

More recently Rhys Isaac applied Geertz's and Bentham's reasoning to cockfighting in mid-eighteenth-century Virginia.... In Virginia and elsewhere in the South, some Anglo-American men disavowed hard, physical work and valued particular physical recreations, as had their ancestors in Britain. Cockfighting thus linked them to prior generations for whom play, rather than work, was meaningful. It was, in short, a contemporary manifestation of the traditional leisure preference.

The contemporary social power of cockfighting rested on more than the ways of a still meaningful past, however.... [T]he sport had a particular appeal in light of the stratified social structure and prevailing rank, gender, and—in Virginia—race relations. According to Isaac, cockfights and other public sporting events enabled the human participants to suspend ordinary social conventions and boundaries. Indeed, cockfights were the produce of social rules suspended; they were practices negotiated by a variety of people in an extraordinary setting where what was ordinary did not hold sway. Owners of the cocks incorporated any training maneuver or match strategy deemed advantageous, regardless of the social position of its developer—a position that usually mattered in other contexts. Then, too, free men, women, and slaves attended the mains, not as passive spectators, but as wagerers, people whose gender and race differences did not deter the gambling contests among themselves. On occasion as well, members of both ranks, who otherwise would have competed in separate events, actually cooperated in constructing the central battle. They pitted their fighting chickens against one another's, literally on the same plain. For both, the fight—on which they might also wager substantial sums—was no laughing matter, and for the moment the divisions between them eroded. One who won, won big: some thing, perhaps money or tobacco of material value, and almost certainly respect or acclaim.

The social leveling effect of tavern sports such as cockfighting thus was real, but it was also fleeting, at least in the South....The sums won did not equal the investment of time and money, nor were they sufficient to propel the common planter into the upper rank, the great planter downward, or women and slaves anywhere. Moreover, except for cockfights, opportunities for interrank and interracial contests were infrequent. Separate contests for gentlemen, for common planters and small farmers, for laborers, and for slaves were more common, although gentry often supported the events of the others. Indeed, the practice of genteel patronage, which had itself become a custom, reinforced socially constructed and persisting rank and racial lines. As was the case with horse racing, gentlemen who permitted or actively supported cockfighting among their neighbors and laborers probably gained much, at least in terms of local goodwill and work force harmony, at relatively little cost. Beyond the shadow of the cock pit, the gentleman's extensive material holdings held sway.

Neither taverns nor tavern games and matches were inherently capable of overcoming persistent social constructions of difference, particularly but probably not only in the South. Some historians have claimed that taverns, regardless of location, were great democratic melting pots and that customers tended to put aside their differences and either to "belly up to the bar" or to congregate at the gaming tables and cock pits as if they were one people. This broad effect seems unlikely, especially given persisting rank, gender, and race divisions throughout the colonies. Occasionally, of course, in the context of popular public rituals such as horse races and cockfights, the physical environment of taverns, the fanatic interest in the sports, and the effect of liquor did encourage colonists to cross social boundaries.... Once a race or match had ended and the bottle was empty, social differences and divisions reemerged.

Particular differences actually deepened within the taverns and in the course of tavern sports as the eighteenth century advanced. One obvious pattern, as noted earlier, was the specialization of taverns by rank, occupation, and race. Taverners in turn provided for physical recreations of interest to their customers. Urban keepers whose clients were large landowners and merchants, for example, had billiard and card tables, and they were likely to have multiple rooms, one of which could be turned over to dancing for men and women, at least until assembly rooms appeared after mid-century. Taverns whose customers were hunters and trappers, small planters, laborers, seamen, and African Americans, both slaves and freed people, tended to sponsor or permit practices popular among their clients. In such places bull baits, shooting matches, ninepins, and country dances, among other practices, were common. Some taverns even became locally renowned as centers for particular vernacular sports.

For ordinary people, taverns appear to have been especially important recreational centers in the eighteenth century. This is not particularly surprising given the marginal infrastructure of facilities and institutions supporting popular sports. Moreover, taverns had long been social centers for ordinary people, and eighteenth-century colonists continued to see them as such.... Tavernkeepers ... actively catered to ordinary people; they came from their ranks and were neighbors, relatives, or friends. They thus permitted practices such as drinking and gambling that civil authorities had legislated against but that remained popular. They also kept their doors open for hours to accommodate the often irregular rhythms of ordinary peoples' lives, and they were not immune to the commercial possibilities of particular physical skills and performances. In the taverns many sporting entrepreneurs-exhibitors of equine skills, tumblers, acrobats, fighters, and eventually, people who claimed card playing and other gambling games as their means of making a living-found homes and audiences.

Taverns also had historically been places for respites, even refuges from the outside world, and their appeal as such persisted among ordinary people in the eighteenth century. In the taverns ordinary colonists could do what was either more difficult or impossible to do elsewhere. They could engage in shooting matches that stretched for hours and concluded only after an inebriated human assumed the role of target and ended up dead. They could go to a tavern after a disputed election, drink heartily, and then resume the unresolved contest with cudgeling.... They could even vent their rage at the ... privileged.... A fistfight with a gentleman or beating him senseless with a billiard cue was no small matter of besting one's superior in a society where opportunities for more permanent gains were limited.

Running through many of the accounts and records of tavern life is ... violence. Colonists rarely used the word; they spoke of assaults, beatings, and even battery instead. And there was probably a fine line between, and much ideological mediation of, actions understood or intended as violent ones on the one hand and the displays of strength, stamina, power, speed, and agility observed in physical recreations on the other. Moreover, the two sets of actions were not entirely separable, for instances of excessive force and other forms of abuse occurred in the course of some sports.... Occasionally fistfights and shooting matches between ordinary colonists culminated in violent ends, sometimes including the death of one of the contestants....

Criticisms of Taverns and Tavern Activities

The decade of the 1730s was pivotal in the history of tavern criticism. Prior to that time most concerns appeared in preambles to laws and in ministerial sermons. Thereafter membership in the chorus of criticism expanded, and the tone and content of the litany grew more harsh and pointed. Individuals and groups of colonists voiced their concerns through petitions, instructions to prospective tavernkeepers, letters in newspapers, and orally. Their messages originated in diverse movements—the Great Awakening, the Enlightenment, changes in the political cultures in some colonies, and the nascent economic diversification and restructuring—but they converged on a common theme. Taverns were no longer simply necessary establishments, or even necessary evils, the critics maintained. Especially but not only in urbanizing areas, they had become dens of iniquity that threatened the peace, stability, and moral rightness of colonial society, a society in which many of the critics had a stake. Whether as governors, officers in the churches, or private citizens, many of the objectors to contemporary tavern affairs were men who belonged to the upper and emergent middling ranks.

The attack on taverns was two-pronged. On the one hand, some critics maintained that tavernkeepers bore some responsibility for what the Braintree, Massachusetts, selectmen termed in 1761 the "present prevailing Depravity of Manners." They tolerated many behaviors, including "Quarreling and fighting," sexual license and other "lewd lascivious behavior," illegal sports and recreations, gambling, rioting, and excessive drinking. But the source of the "problem" extended beyond keepers who maintained lax discipline. Ordinaries had become the "haunts" of "loose, idle, and disorderly" persons, other detractors charged....

At the core of this "debauchery" lay a trio of particularly problematic behaviors, according to unsympathetic observers of taverns. One was "tippling," or habitual drinking, which was quite different from the ordinary, necessary, and nearly universal consumption of alcoholic beverages.... Tippling ... exceeded ordinary consumption, in terms of both frequency and amount, and it could lead to drunkenness. Drunkenness not only injured one's health, the critics charged, but also led to fighting, property destruction, riot, runaways, indebtedness, and poverty.

Tavern critics also maintained that tippling and drunkenness went hand in hand with idleness, another of the problematic behaviors. Drunkards, they believed, tended to be idlers, a combination that worsened the situation....

Implicit in this argument was the tavern opponents' belief that idleness was "uneconomic." It was unproductive, even wasteful, and it was surely not work—nor..., was it "leisure." Methodist and Baptist ministers in the South, where evangelical Protestantism was particularly vibrant, also argued that idleness was immoral.... Whether tavern visits and rhythms encouraged or accommodated idleness, however, was an open question....

Just as tavern critics linked drunkenness and idleness, so they also coupled idleness and the final "problem" behavior: gambling and, in an extreme form, gaming. Gambling was the practice of staking something of value ..., on one's or one's animal's prowess. It involved risk taking in a contest or a display, recreative or not, and for many colonists, gambling appears to have been the *sine qua non* of sporting matches and contests—horse races, bull baits, cards, and more. The greater the risk, as when the skills of the players were relatively equal or when multiple factors beyond the control of the participants might influence the outcome, the higher the stakes and the more numerous the wagers or bets....

This distinction between gambling and gaming was not unlike that between drinking and drunkenness, and it drew from a similar rationale. Gaming and drunkenness were out-of-the-ordinary, immoderate forms of gambling and drinking, respectively. Gambling, of course, was like drinking in that it was a common practice ... even in New England.... Certainly gambling knew no human boundaries. Africans wagered on their skills and, if they were slaves, those of their owners. Native Americans were also fond of gambling, and

European-American travelers regularly remarked on American Indians' wagering in sporting events. Women of all ranks and races bet, and even older age was not a deterrent....

Several historians have tried to account for the prevalence of—indeed, the passion for gambling, especially in the South.... Markedly integral to and integrated in life, gambling was neither irrelevant nor compensatory. It was not a means of providing for something a challenge, a thrill, or whatever that was absent from life, as some modern Americans have claimed. Rather, formalized and conventional, gambling was an expression of life itself in the eighteenth century.

For their part, contemporary critics, who rarely attended to the legal distinction between the practices or distinguished between urban and rural patterns, had few illusions about the consequences of gambling and gaming. Some of them recognized that gambling produced no money or anything else of material worth for the society. Gamblers merely exchanged goods or money, although the exchanges were never even: one won and another lost. Thus gambling, like idleness, was "uneconomic." Worse, opponents claimed, the practice might leave the loser destitute. Critics cited the personal and societal consequences of gambling among poor and dependent colonists who risked insolvency with even a small loss. Moreover, when the poor lost, the refrain against gambling continued, other people stood to lose as well: owners and employers whose money or goods the gamblers sometimes wagered, tavernkeepers who extended credit and then could not recoup it, and families and dependents who lost the money for food and shelter.

* * *

... [J]ust before the War for Independence began the Continental Congress and local committees of safety broadened the attack. As a part of the effort to "encourage frugality economy and industry," the order of Congress intoned, "We ... will discountenance and discourage every species of extravagance and dissipation, especially all horse-racing and all kinds of gaming, cock-fighting, exhibitions of shews, plays, and other expensive diversions and entertainments." On the other hand, ... tavern visits drinking and sporting practices continued. Some gentlemen and gentlewomen did halt their balls and horse races, but others did not. Ordinary colonists, as well, did not stop patronizing taverns or participating in proscribed activities. Among them customary practices persisted, and taverns remained critical gathering places for many colonists, especially those on the economic margins who lacked access to other forms and facilities for meeting, eating, and playing.

FURTHER READING

Blanchard, Kendall. *The Mississippi Choctaws at Play* (1981).

Boulware, Hunt. "Unworthy of Modern Refinement: The Evolution of Sport and Recreation in the Early South Carolina and Georgia Lowcountry," *Journal of Sport History* 35 (Fall, 2008), 429–448.

Carson, Jane. *Colonial Virginians at Play* (1965).

Culin, Stewart. *Games of the North American Indians* (1907).

Daniels, Bruce. *Puritans at Play: Leisure and Recreation in Colonial New England* (1995).

Ewing, William C. *The Sports of Colonial Williamsburg* (1937).

Hervey, John. *Racing in America, 1665–1865*, vol. 1 (1944).

Isaac, Rhys. *The Transformation of Virginia: Community, Religion, and Authority, 740–1790* (1982).

Jable, J. Thomas. "Pennsylvania's Blue Laws: A Quaker Experiment in the Suppression of Sport and Amusements," *Journal of Sport History* 1 (1974), 107–21.

Johnson, Karl E. "Problematizing Puritan Play," *Leisure/Loisir: Journal of the Canadian Association for Leisure Studies* 33 (2009), 31–54.

Ledbetter, Bonnie S. "Sports and Games of the American Revolution," *Journal of Sport History* 6 (Winter 1979), 29–40.

Mook, H. Telfer. "Training Day in New England," *New England Quarterly* 2 (December 1938), 675–97.

Powell, R. E. "Sport, Social Relations and Animal Husbandry: Early Cock-Fighting in North America," *International Journal of Sport History* 5 (1993), 361–81.

Stanard, William C. "Racing in Colonial Virginia," *Virginia Magazine of History and Biography* 2 (1894–1895), 293–302.

Struna, Nancy. *People of Prowess: Sport, Leisure, and Labor in Early Anglo-America* (1996).

Wagner, Hans Peter. *Puritan Attitudes Towards Recreation in Early Seventeenth-Century New England* (1982).

CHAPTER 3

Traditional Sport and the Male Bachelor Subculture, 1800–1860

In the days of the Early Republic, about 95 percent of the population lived in rural or frontier areas, and as late as the Civil War, 80 percent of Americans still lived in rural areas. Farmers and frontiersmen enjoyed traditional pastimes that required strength and skill and reflected their manliness and honor. Sports in the early nineteenth century were all premodern and exhibited little in the way of organization, specialization, rationalization, information, rules, or records. Sportsmen formed a male bachelor subculture whose traditional sports dominated American athletics into the 1840s. Their favorite sports included boxing, gouging (no-holds-barred fighting), horse racing, hunting, and cockfighting. Some of these sports, notably gouging, died out. Boxing and cockfighting went largely underground, and horse racing virtually collapsed in the North after 1845, though it survived in the South.

What accounted for this? Had the United States become "civilized"? What was the impact of the Second Great Awakening and the reform impulse of the Jacksonian Era? How did the rise of cities hinder traditional sports? What was the impact of the new, moral sporting pastimes that competed successfully for public interest and the new sporting ideology that justified those new games? Harness racing was one sport that emerged in the early nineteenth century and successfully adapted to the requirements of an increasingly rational society. How was it able to adjust to an increasingly urban environment to become the first fully modern sport and the most popular spectator sport at the middle of the nineteenth century?

DOCUMENTS

This section begins with the challenge posed by Andrew Jackson, a prominent plantation owner, politician, and horseman against Charles Dickinson for having publicly insulted him over a horse race gambling wager, and the responses. In the early 1800s, gentlemen might resolve an affair of honor with a potentially mortal duel with pistols. Dickinson agreed to the challenge, and their seconds set up the ground rules with the participants. Document 2, drawn from a short novel by James Hall, is a description of a vile billiard parlor in the 1820s. Document 3 is the report in the *American Turf Register and Sporting Magazine* of the first great footrace in American history, a match sponsored in 1835 by sportsman John Cox Stevens at Long Island's Union Course. Stevens had bet that a man could run ten miles in under sixty minutes, and he sponsored the race to prove it. Document 4 examines the brutality of prize fighting. In 1842 the renowned pugilist Yankee Sullivan arranged a fight between Christopher Lilly and Thomas McCoy, which was attended by 1,500 spectators in Hastings, New York. The fight lasted for two hours and forty-three minutes, when McCoy died in the ring. Sullivan and two other men who had arranged the match were convicted of fourth-degree manslaughter. The document consists of a report of the fight and an editorial from Horace Greeley's *New York Tribune*. Document 5 is a Boston policeman's report about a rat-baiting match he attended, which was one of the vilest sports of the subterranean male bachelor subculture. Document 6, drawn from the *New York Herald*'s front page coverage, reports the Fashion–Peytona horse race of 1845, attended by well over 50,000 spectators. It was the fifth and last Great Intersectional race that dated from the Sir Henry–Eclipse match of 1823. The reporter examines the ambiance of this major contest as well as the behavior of the huge crowd.

1. Andrew Jackson Challenges Charles Dickinson to a Duel, and the Response, 1806

To Charles Henry Dickinson

May 23rd. 1806.

Sir,

Your conduct and expressions relative to me of late have been of such a nature and so insulting that requires, and shall have, my notice—Insults may be given by men, of such a kind, that they must be noticed, and the author treated with the respects due a gentleman, altho (as in the present instance) he does not merit it—You have, to disturb my quiet, industriously excited Thomas Swann to quarrel with me, which involved the peace and harmony of society for a while—You on the tenth of January wrote me a very insulting letter, left this country and caused this letter to be delivered after you had been gone some days; and securing yourself in safety from the contempt I held you in, have a piece now in the press, more replete with blackguard abuse, than any of your other productions; and are pleased to state that you would have noticed me in a different way than through the press, but my cowardice would have found a pretext to evade that satisfaction, if it had been called for, ... I hope sir your courage will be an ample security to me, that I will obtain speedily that satisfaction due me for the insults offered—and in the way my friend,

From James Parton, *Life of Andrew Jackson* (New York: Mason Brothers, 1860), 292–94.

who hands you this, will point out—He waits upon you, for that purpose, and with your friend, will enter into immediate arrangements for this purpose....

Andrew Jackson

To Andrew Jackson

23d. May 1806.

Sir,

Your note of this morning is received, and your request shall be gratified— My friend who hands you this, will make the necessary arrangements....

Charles Dickinson

Arrangements of Thomas Overton and Hanson Catlet for Duel

Nashville May 24th 1806.

It is agreed that the distance shall be 24 feet, the parties to stand facing each other with their pistols down perpendicularly—When they are ready, the single word fire, to be given, at which they are to fire as soon as they please-Should either fire before the word given, we pledge ourselves to shoot him down instantly—The person to give the word, to be determined by lot, as also the choice of position.

We mutually agree that the above regulations shall be observed, in the affair of honor depending between Genl. Andrew Jackson and Charles Dickinson esqr.

Tho. Overton
Hanson Catlet

2. The Negative Image of Billiards in Early America, c. 1826

It was a large apartment, indifferently lighted, and meanly furnished. In the centre stood the billiard table, whose allurements had enticed so many on this evening to forsake the quiet and virtuous comforts of social life, and to brave the biting blast, and the not less "pitiless peltings" of parental or conjugal admonition. Its polished mahogany frame, and neatly brushed cover of green cloth, its silken pockets, and party-colored ivory balls, presented a striking contrast to the rude negligence of the rest of the furniture; while a large canopy suspended over the table, and intended to collect and refract the rays of a number of well trimmed lamps, which hung within its circumference, shed an intense brilliancy over that little spot, and threw a corresponding gloom upon the surrounding scene. Indeed, if that gay alter of dissipation had been withdrawn, the temple of pleasure would have presented rather the desolate appearance of the house of mourning.

The stained and dirty floor was strewed with fragments of segars, playbills, and nut shells; the walls blackened with smoke seemed to have witnessed the

From James Hall, *The Soldier's Bride and Other Tales* (Philadelphia: Key and Biddle, 1833), 255–72.

orgies of many a midnight revel. A few candles, destined to illumine the distant recesses of the room, hung neglected against the walls—bowing their long wicks, and marking their stations by streams of tallow, which had been suffered to accumulate through many a long winter night. The ceiling was hung with cobwebs, curiously intermingled with dense clouds of tobacco smoke, and tinged by the straggling rays of light which occasionally shot from the sickly tapers. A set of benches attached to the walls, and raised sufficiently high to overlook the table, accommodated the loungers, who were not engaged at play, and who sat or reclined, solemnly puffing their segars, idly sipping their brandy and water, or industriously counting the chances of the game, but all observing a profound silence which would have done honor to a turbaned divan, and was well suited to the important subjects of their contemplation. Little coteries of gayer spirits laughed and chatted aside, or made their criticisms on the players in subdued accents—any remarks on that subject being forbidden to all but the parties engaged; while the marker announced the state of the game, trimmed the lamps, and supplied refreshments to the guests.

3. The Great Foot Race of 1835

The great trial of human capabilities, in going ten miles within the hour, for $1,000, to which $300 was added, took place on Friday, on the Union Course, Long Island; and we are pleased to state, that the feat was accomplished twelve seconds within the time, by a native born and bred American farmer, Henry Stannard, of Killingworth, Connecticut. Two others went the ten miles—one a Prussian, in a half a minute over; the other an Irishman, in one minute and three quarters over the time.

As early as nine o'clock, many hundreds had crossed the river to witness the race, and from that time until near two, the road between Brooklyn, and the course presented a continuous line; (and in many places a double line) of carriages of all descriptions, from the humble sand cart to the splendid barouche and four; and by two o'clock, it is computed that there were at least from sixteen to twenty persons on the course.... [N]ine candidates appeared in front of the stand, dressed in various colors, and started at the sound of a drum.

The following are the names, &c. of the competitors...:

Henry Stannard, a farmer, aged twenty-four, born in Killingworth, Connecticut. He is six feet one inch in height, and weighed one hundred and sixty-five pounds. He was dressed in black silk pantaloons, white shirt, no jacket, vest, or cap, black leather belt and flesh colored slippers.

Charles R. Wall, a brewer, aged eighteen years, born in Brooklyn....

Henry Sutton, a house painter, aged twenty-three years, born in Rahway, New Jersey....

George W. Glauer, rope-maker, aged twenty-seven, born in Elberfeldt, Prussia....

From *American Turf Register and Sporting Magazine* (June 1835): 528–20.

Isaac S. Downes, a basket-maker, aged twenty-seven, born at Brookhaven, Suffolk county....

John Mallard, a farmer, aged thirty-three, born at Exeter, Otsego Co. New York....

William Vermilyea, shoemaker, aged twenty-two years, born in New York....

Patrick Mahony, a porter, aged thirty-three, born in Kenmar county, Kerry, Ireland....

John M'Cargy, a butcher, aged twenty-six, born at Harlaem....

There was a tenth candidate, a black man, named Francis Smith, aged twenty-five, born in Manchester, Virginia. Mr. Stevens was willing that this man should run; but as he had not complied with the regulation requiring his name to be entered by a certain day, he was excluded from contesting the race.

The men all started well, and kept together for the first mile, except Mahony, who headed the others several yards, and Mallard, who fell behind after the first half mile. At the end of the second mile, one gave in; at the end of the fourth mile, two more gave up; in the fifth, a fourth man fell; at the end of the fifth mile, a fifth man gave in; during the eighth mile, Downes, one of the fastest, and decidedly the handsomest runner, hurt his foot, and gave in at the termination of that mile, leaving but three competitors, who all held out the distance.

Stannard, the winner, we understand, has been in good training for a month. He is a powerful stalwart young man, and did not seem at all fatigued at the termination of the race. He was greatly indebted to Mr. Stevens, for his success; Mr. S. rode round the course with him the whole distance, and kept cheering him on, and cautioning him against over-exertion in the early part of the race; at the end of the sixth mile, he made him stop and take a little brandy and water, after which his foot was on the mile mark just as the thirty-six minutes were expired; and as the trumpet sounded he jumped forward gracefully, and cheerfully exclaimed. "Here am I to time"; and he was within the time every mile. After the race was over, he mounted a horse and rode round the course in search of Mr. Richard Jackson, who held his overcoat. He was called up to the stand and his success (and the reward of $1,300) was announced to him, and he was invited to dine with the Club; to which he replied in a short speech thanking Mr. Stevens, and the gentlemen of the Club for the attention shewn to the runners generally throughout the task....

4. Horace Greeley Decries the Slaughter of Boxer Thomas McCoy, 1842

... Christopher Lilly, by whose hands McCoy met his death, is a young man of English parentage and 'sporting' habits, about 23 years old. He lately fought a pugilistic battle with one Murphy, and came off victor. He has since been engaged in sparring exhibitions in the Bowery, where he met Thomas McCoy,

From Horace Greeley, "The Slaughter of McCoy," *New York Tribune*, September 19 and 20, 1842.

a Whitehall boatman, only 20 years old, of Irish parentage, and it seems a young man of fine character, marred by a fondness for pugilistic display and for the company and the scenes to which this taste introduced him. These two young men had been old acquaintances, and there was an unsettled grudge between them. They met at one of the flash groggeries where pugilism is the staple of excitement, soon after Lilly's victory over Murphy, which was the theme of general applause, in which McCoy refused to join. Being challenged for his opinion, he gave it against Lilly's achievement. This nettled the champion, who asked him to put on the gloves and try a round with him; McCoy refused, and instantly Lilly struck him a blow which laid him on the floor. He rose and rushed at the assailant, but they were separated and a regular fight instantly agreed on by their respective friends; $200 being the original stakes, but thousands were afterwards bet upon the result. The day was fixed, and the parties went directly into training.

On Tuesday morning last, being the day agreed on, the pitted boxers, their seconds, doctors, friends, judges, &c., and some thousands eager to be spectators, left in two steamboats for the selected battleground, near the little village of Hastings, in Westchester Co., 20 miles from this City....

McCoy had been sick, and was evidently in an inferior condition for such an affray.... He was also too high on flesh, showing that he had not been carefully trained for such brutality....

Let none say that his death was accidental. He openly avowed, on starting to the battleground, that he went to *"win or die."* He tied a *black* handkerchief to his post in the ring as his colors, to evince the same determination. Not one of the fifteen hundred who quietly looked on could have been ignorant that his life was the fearful stake of the contest....

... Lilly was cool, cautious and husbanded his strength; McCoy rash, eager, probably smarting under a sense of wrong, exposing himself constantly, and wasting his energy in furious, ineffective lunges. His *seconds* and backers had not even sense enough to caution him against his errors until he was virtually beaten. They saw him sweat like rain, and their only expedient was to deluge him repeatedly in cold water! The judges twice decided that Lilly struck "foul," giving the battle to McCoy; but his principal backer waived the "advantage," as he called it, and suffered the fight to go on! And their beautiful *doctor!* who was there, if for any thing, to save the life of their champion in extremity, saw the murder perfected without a word, only interpolating to *lance the eyes* of the victim, as directed, when they had been entirely closed by the blows of his antagonist!

It is of course understood that McCoy was a willing victim. He probably sought—he certainly did not shun—the conflict. At the opening of the fight, he drew from his pocket two $100 bills, and bet them on the result with his opponent. He evidently fought throughout under the influence of personal feeling....

Where were his seconds? his doctor? and the fifteen hundred spectators? The first urging on the fight; the second doing nothing; of the last a few murmured and two or three remonstrated aloud, but not one stirred to rescue him from inevitable death! ...

How shall we speak of the getters up and encouragers of this fight?—the gamblers, the brothel masters, and keepers of flash groggeries, who were ever the chief patrons of "the ring," and who were the choice spirits of this festival of fiends? They were in raptures as the well-aimed, deadly blows descended heavily upon the face and neck of the doomed victim, transforming the image of God into a livid and loathsome ruin; *they* yelled with delight as the combatants went down—often on their heads—with a force that made the earth tremble around them—as the blood spirited in rills from the fated sacrifice, or as his conqueror came down heavily upon him and lay there to beat the breath out of him, until taken off by the seconds! They enlivened the shocking scene, as McCoy's eyes closed beneath the blows of his antagonist, with "Shutters up! There's a death in the family!", "Finish him, Chris!" "Knock out his eye!" &c....

But why linger on the dreadful scene? At the *one hundred and twentieth* round, McCoy stood up as erect as ever, but with his eyes closed in funeral black, his nose destroyed, his face gone, and clots of blood choking the throat which had no longer power to eject them. He could barely walk, but still sparred with some spirit, though unable to get in a blow at his still vigorous antagonist, though the latter was evidently suffering severely from blows in his body. The fight had now lasted *two hours and forty-three minutes,* McCoy had received not less than *one hundred* square blows, and had been thrown or been knocked down *eighty-one times,* his opponent falling heavily as possible upon him. For the last time was this repeated; and, when Lilly was lifted off, McCoy was found lifeless, and sank inanimate as lead in his second's arms. 'Time' was called, but for him Time was no more! Lilly was declared victor, and, appearing little hurt and less disfigured, jumped with a cry of exhultation [*sic*] and sprang out of the ring! McCoy still gasped for breath, sucking his remnants of lips far back into his mouth by the violence of the effort. A moment more, and his struggles ceased—the widow's darling child had been immolated on the altar of *"Sport!"*—he was dead! And even in that moment of freezing horror—when it would seem that the blood of the hardiest ruffian must have curdled with conscious guilt and remorse, and a shadow darkened the most indurated brow—even then, in reference to the fact that *another* fight had been arranged to come off on this occasion, one voice was raised in the crowd, exclaiming, "Come, *carry off your dead, and produce your next man!"*—thus closed the fight at Hastings and the life of Thomas McCoy!

The Slaughter of McCoy, Its Causes, &C.

... In the first place, we rejoice to know that the originators and fosterers of pugilism in this country are almost entirely foreigners by birth. This species of ruffianism is not native here, nor is our atmosphere congenial to it. To say nothing of the combatants; the seconds, trainers, &c. of this fight, as of former fights, are, with hardly an exception, from abroad.... This is encouraging. This horrid vice—alas that we must more correctly say, this *form* of a horrid vice—has but a sickly hold on our soil, and may be wholly extirpated if proper exertions are made at the proper time. That time, we need not state, is now.

But again: the principal patrons of the pugilistic *science!* among us are the keepers of drinking-houses of the very worst description, professional gamblers, and a few who unite with one or both of these highly reputable and useful callings the keeping or protecting of brothels! To this rule there is hardly an exception. The three seconds who have run away were all keepers or drunkards at least; we believe one or more of them added to this one or both of the other vocations. The principal promoters and backers of the fight were what are called "king gamblers"—keepers of faro banks, roulette tables, and the like. We believe the world might be safely challenged to produce a single patron of 'the ring' who lives by industry in any useful calling.

We have now a few questions to ask, which we trust will be answered to the public satisfactorily and speedily. They are these: Who licenses foreigners of at best suspicious character to keep houses of public entertainment in our city? If those pugilistic grog shops are kept without licenses, whose duty is it to close them? Why is it not done?...

5. A Policeman Visits the Dissipated Rat Pits of Boston, c. 1860

A rat pit is one of those under-ground novelties occasionally seen in Boston by gaslight. The whereabouts, however, is not always exactly known to the uninitiated, the proprietors generally not choosing to either advertise or hang out a shingle to indicate the locality, ... nor when found is the establishment such as would be likely to impress the mind with an idea of grandeur or sublimity....

For many years one of these subterranean establishments was kept at "North End," which I have sometimes been called on to visit in my official capacity. The establishment consisted of a bar-room on the first floor from the street, not wide but deep, the counter running the whole length on one side. Behind this counter stood females, with *vermilion* cheeks and low-necked dresses, ready to deal out New York gin and cabbage-leaf cigars to all who had the *dosh* [money]....

In passing through this room (which was generally filled with pickpockets, petty knucks, [a small metal weapon worn over the knuckles] fumes of tobacco, smoke and bad gin) at the further end you find a trap-door leading down a flight of stairs to the *rat pit* below.

The pit consists of a broad crib of octagon form in the centre of the cellar, about eight feet in diameter and three and one half feet high, tightly secured at the sides. On three sides of the cellar are rows of board seats, rising one above the other, for the accommodation of spectators. On the other side, stands the proprietor and his assistant and an empty flour barrel, only it is half full of live rats, which are kept in their prison-house by a wire netting over the top of the cask. The amphitheatre is lighted with oil lamps or candles.... Spectators are admitted at twenty-five cents a head, and take their seats, when preparations for the evening's entertainment commence. The proprietor carefully lifts the edge of the wire netting over the rat barrel,

---

From Edward H. Savage, *A Chronological History of the Boston Watch and Police, From 1631 to 1865; Together with the Recollections of a Boston Police Officer, or, Boston by Daylight and Gaslight, From the Diary of an Officer Fifteen Years in the Service* (Boston: J.P. Dale, 1873), 160–62.

and with an instrument looking much like a pair of curling tongs, he begins fishing out his game, rat by rat, depositing each carefully inside the pit until the requisite number are pitted. The assistant has brought in the dog, *Flora,* a favorite ratter, which he is obliged to hold fast by the nape of the neck, so eager is she for the fray. Then commences the betting, which runs high or low according to the amount of funds in the hands of the sports.

"A dollar. She kills twenty rats in twelve seconds!" "I take that!" "Half a dollar on the rats!" "Don't put in them small rats!" "Two dollars on Flora in fifteen seconds!" "Done, at fourteen!" "No, you don't!" "Don't put in all your big rats at once!" "Five dollars on the rats in ten seconds!" (no takers.) ...

The bets having been arranged, time is called, and Flora is dropped into the ring. Flora evidently understands that her credit is at stake; but the growling and champing, and squealing, and scratching is soon over, and the twenty rats lie lifeless at the feet of the bloodthirsty Flora, when time is again called, and the bets decided, and all hands go up and liquor. This exhibition is repeated several times, with different dogs and lasts as long as the live rats hold out....

6. The *New York Herald* Reports on "The Great Contest: Fashion v. Peytona," 1845

It was an exciting, but very beautiful morning, exciting because the contest between the North and the South for the dominion of the turf was to be settled, before the shades of evening closed on the well-trodden race ground. It is well understood that the ambiguity of the relative pretensions of the two great sections of the country to this honor, is the natural result of former well balanced successes.... In addition to the sectional feeling and the strong rivalry of sportsmen, and in one sense partizans—the vast sums of money pending on the race, attached a degree of absorbing interest to the result, quite proportionate to the great demonstration that took place.

More than three thousand persons crossed the South Ferry ... before 8 o'clock for the races. As the morning progressed, the crowd increased rapidly, and a sense of tumult, disorder and confusion ensued.... All seemed eager to reach the ground. Long trains of carriages, filled with all sorts of people, reaching to Broadway, lined Whitehall Street. Here was the magnificent barouche of the millionaire, full of gay, laughing, dark-eyed *demoiselles,* jammed in between a Bowery stage and a Broadway hack—here were loafers and dandies, on horseback and on foot ... Southerners ... with anxious faces, but hearts full of hope.... [A]ll business seemed laid aside.... Omnibuses of all dimensions, cabriolets, chariots, drays, wagons, and every description of vehicle were put in requisition....

By twelve o'clock about 30,000 persons had passed over the south and 20,000 over Fulton ferries.

We saw many distinguished sporting characters, politicians, editors, reporters, managers, actors, printers, devils, &c....

From *New York Herald,* May 5, 1845.

The first train started from the terminus of the railway, Brooklyn, at 7 o'clock, followed by others at 8, 9 1⁄4, 9 3⁄4, and 10 1⁄2 o'clock. With each of these trains one of our corps started, to not only note whatever might occur ..., and also because it is fitting that the *Herald* should be represented, if not identified with all marvelous progressive movements of our race. A terrific rush from the ferry boats to the cars was the work of a moment.... A large number of cars had been fitted up with temporary seats ..., however, happy was the wight [brave being] who got a seat ... for forty minutes or so, for the lawful consideration of twenty-five cents....

* * *

The enclosed area, whose circumference of a mile formed the Course, was the resort of the carriages and horsemen.... Immediately on the right of the Judge's stand, and opposite to the great stand for spectators, on the other side of the course, a dense mass of vehicles of all descriptions congregated. Among these the most striking were a number of the city omnibuses, which had been engaged for the day by a full complement of passengers, who from the roofs ... were enabled to have a capital view of the race. As may be expected, the occupants of them were of a more mixed class than those who lolled in private carriages, or those engaged *special* for the occasion....

* * *

On the stand there could be fewer than thirty thousand persons; every train added countless hosts, for the first race of everybody who obtained admission, was to the grand stand, and the solicitude to secure places increased in the direct ratio of the difficulty of finding them, so that the onset of the last was impetuous in the extreme. A harder day's labor no men performed that day, than those who had charge of the stairs. We saw several altercations with fellows who attempted to get on the stand without tickets, but they were invariably foiled.... The lower portion of the stand was occupied by refreshment tables on one side and faro and roulette, and all sorts of gaming tables on the other. Betting and gambling and guzzling went on at a rapid rate....

At about 2 o'clock the excitement ... was tremendous. In the vicinity of the judges' stand, and the enclosed space before the grand stand the multitude heaved and fell like the bellows of the ocean in a mighty storm, and from amidst this excited throng, looking up at the stands, the immense sea of faces, and the hoarse murmur of expectation that spread through the thronged buildings, was one of the most extraordinary scenes that can well be imagined. Here might be seen representatives from all parts of the Union.... In one corner might be heard the Bowery boy arranging his final bet with a Northern blood, for some cool hundreds on Peytona. In the general eagerness to obtain a favorable position to view the coming race, many, at the peril of life and limb, were climbing on the different parts of the buildings, and the efforts of those who, though "not shaped for sportive tricks," still persisted in climbing to the roof eaves.... Two tall trees that stand toward the head of the course were filled with those who, probably not relinquishing the idea of paying for grand stand or jockey club tickets, selected the commanding situation, and patiently waited in their perches for hours.... The track all round was lined inside by vehicle of every description and shape, from the rickety oyster cart ... to the aristocratic turn-out of the "upper ten thousand"....

On the Course itself there was the utmost difficulty in preserving the track clear from intruders, and to the efficiency of a few may be ascribed the comparative order which was at length established. A young gentleman, mounted on a black horse, was quite conspicuous in the part he took, riding up and down, and most fearlessly charging the intruding multitude with his whip. The indomitable Captain Isaiah Rynders, mounted on his famous white charger, rendered most valuable services, and never have we seen such perfect self-possession and invincible good humor as was displayed on this occasion by the leader of the Empires. He was loudly cheered by the members of the Jockey Club, and by his address to the crowd, appealing to their feelings of pride as northerners, to show the Southerners assembled that fair play could be given to their horse, succeeded in obtaining a clear course.... Yankee Sullivan, and others, including Bill Harrington, who with the rest ..., most ably seconded the efforts of the rest. Justice Matsell, by his appearance, was of most essential service, and where-ever a notorious character, or suspicious-looking individual, fell under the influence of his eye, their stay was short....

We observed Mr. Prescott Hall in the Judge's stand exerting his lung to the utmost preserve order, but beyond that we did not see any particular action on his part ... but the exertions requisite appeared to have been left entirely to the twenty or thirty constables who were expected to control the hundred thousand people on the Course.

The booths and temporary stands with refreshments that were erected outside were crowded during the whole day.... The gambling fraternity were by no means inactive on the occasion, and the extraordinary force of example that always tempts people to gamble at a race course was fully followed here. Roulette, sweat-cloth, thimble-rig [a dishonest game played with three thimbles and a pea] and all the usual games were in full operation during the whole day.... There was one feature we noticed with pleasure, which was the almost universal absence of all the gross scenes of intemperance that used formerly to disgrace our racecourses, and despite all the attraction for the various drinkables in the different booths, the crowd generally seemed to partake more of the eatables and the different temperance beverages of soda water, lemonade and the like....

★ ★ ★

The Race

About half past two o'clock, the bugle sounded to bring forth the horses.... Mr. J. Laird topped the pig-skin across Fashion, dressed in a purple jacket and red and gold cap. The "indomitable Barney" mounted Peytona. Two finer animals and abler jockies ... there is not in the States. Having gone to the scales, Laird made his weight to 125 lbs.; and Barney his to 118....

After some endeavors on the part of those in authority, the track was well cleared as could be expected under the circumstances.... At 33 minutes past two o'clock the horses were saddled and mounted, and at the first tap they went forth in gallant style, Peytona having the pole, but a most beautiful start—nose and nose. They kept thus together round the bottom, Peytona gently falling off, but yet keeping her nose close to the tail of her rival.... They kept thus to the first quarter, the same to the half. At the third quarter they were close together, Peytona ... at the drawgate [a gate controlling an artificial channel for conducting water] ... came in front, and led to the judges stand a length and a half in front. For the second mile they appeared to keep in this position round the bottom, but owing to the clouds of dust prevailing just then, only an occasional glimpse could be caught of them, but they seemed to maintain a similar position round the top to the drawgate, where Fashion appeared to come in front, but on reaching the judge's chair, Fashion's nose was close up with that of Peytona, on the inside. For the third mile they kept well thus together round, to the nearing of the half mile post, where the heavy patch before alluded to occur, Fashion appeared to gain somewhat, but shortly after Peytona reached her flank, nipping her hard, but Fashion appeared immediately afterwards to make the gap wider. At the drawgate, Fashion appeared two lengths in front, but on nearing the judge's stand, Peytona had her nose close on the flank of her opponent. It was not pretty evident that Barney had it all his own way, and could do just as he pleased with the affairs, and faces became elongated, while others could scarce keep their feet.... Round the bottom they kept well together, but owing to dust, &c., there was no seeing further, until they reached the drawgate towards home, where Fashion appeared to have the lead, but it was immediately taken from her, and Peytona came home two lengths in front, making the first heat in 7m. 39s., amid the most unbounded of cheers....

* * *

After the interval of twenty minutes the horses were again ready, and the crowd resumed their positions round the course; this time wound up to the pitch of frenzy....

* * *

At the first attempt they did not go forth, and were pulled up short, owing to what appeared a rather premature tap. They returned and commenced again, de novo. At the second attempt they went forth Peytona leading a neck, Laird well up round the bottom to the quarter; on approaching the half Fashion went in front, and led to the three-quarter. Here the crowd broke in at the lower drawgate, which caused some confusion for a few moments, but owing to the vigilance of those now engaged, was soon got under. Fashion led to the drawgate, where they came together to the Judge's chair, head and head, no telling who had the lead. For the second mile Fashion appeared to have the lead to the quarter, the other well up they kept so up the back stretch; at the three-quarter it was just so. Fashion still kept the lead, closely waited upon by Peytona; it was thus round the top, but at the drawgate they were again well together, Fashion having the track, but at the end of the second mile, notwithstanding Fashion's advantage Peytona led to the Judge's stand a head in front. For the third mile they kept so to the quarter; a table cloth might have covered the pair to the half-mile post. They kept just so to the three-quarters; at the drawgate Fashion led on the inside, but Peytona had got her and led her home a length in advance. "Now comes the tug of war." Peytona maintained her position, both well together, she gained a little on her round the bottom, but apparently with little effect; at the half they were well together, which was maintained to the three-quarters, but here the mob closed in so as to obscure sight from the club stand. Fashion appeared to have the lead, but on approaching the drawgate, notwithstanding the mob closing on the track, Peytona led a way clear length in advance in 7.45 1/4.

We have only time to say that it was quite a waiting race; "Barney" knew what he had to do, and did it nobly, and doubtless more he would have done if it had been required.

ESSAYS

In the first essay, Elliott J. Gorn, the Joseph A. Gagliano Professor of History at Loyola University, Chicago, one of the preeminent scholars of American sport history, employs his expertise in folklore, working-class culture, and gender relations to illuminate the meaning of gouging. This "rough-and-tumble" fighting in the early nineteenth-century frontier provided an important means to display one's courage, manliness, and honor. In the second essay, James Parton, the greatest biographer of mid-nineteenth century American political leaders, discusses the famous duel between lawyer, horse breeder, politician, and future president, Andrew Jackson, who arranged a race between his stallion Truxton and Ploughboy, owned by Charles Dickinson's partner and father-in-law, Joseph Erwin. The organizers and the owners agreed on an $800 forfeit appearance bond if a horse could not compete. Erwin's horse went lame and the forfeit was paid, but only after disagreement over the terms. Dickinson felt that Jackson had slurred Erwin and himself, and declared him "a worthless scoundrel, a poltroon and a coward." In response, Jackson, who had already fought duels, challenged Dickinson to a combat, although his twenty-five-year-old foe was considered the finest marksman in Tennessee. As Parton points out, Jackson planned to take Dickinson's shot, and if he survived, stand as a man of iron, and shoot back and kill his rival.

In the final essay, Sergio Lussana, a postdoctoral student at the Institute of Advanced Studies at the University of Warwick examines enslaved masculinity in the antebellum South, focusing on male interdependence through such pastimes as boxing, a part of an all-male subculture through which slaves created their own ideas about masculinity, friendship, solidarity, and resistance. Slave owners at times organized matches between their slaves or those of another plantation owner to entertain the master, and slaves also arranged their own boxing and wrestling matches for their own purposes. The narrative points out the role of these sports in enabling slaves to shape their own identity, develop their own perspectives on manliness, and promote male social solidarity.

The Social Significance of Gouging in the Southern Backcountry

ELLIOTT J. GORN

"I would advise you when You do fight, Not to act like Tygers and Bears as these Virginians do—Biting one anothers Lips and Noses off, and *gouging* one another—that is, thrusting out one anothers Eyes, and kicking one another on the Cods, to the Great damage of many a Poor Woman." Thus, Charles Woodmason, an itinerant Anglican minister born of English gentry stock, described the brutal form of combat he found in the Virginia backcountry shortly before the American Revolution. Although historians are more likely to study people thinking, government, worshiping, or working, how men fight—who participates, who observes, which rules are followed, what is at stake, what tactics are allowed—reveals much about past cultures and societies.

As early as 1735, boxing was "much in fashion" in parts of Chesapeake Bay, and forty years later a visitor from the North declared that, along with dancing, fiddling, small swords, and card playing, it was an essential skill for all young Virginia gentlemen. The term "boxing," however, did not necessarily refer to the comparatively tame style of bare-knuckle fighting familiar to eighteenth-century Englishmen. In 1746, four deaths prompted the governor of North Carolina to ask for legislation against "the barbarous and inhuman manner of boxing which so much prevails among the lower sort of people." The colonial assembly responded by making it a felony "to cut out the Tongue or pull out the eyes of the King's Liege People." Five years later the assembly added slitting, biting, and cutting off noses to the list of offenses. Virginia passed similar legislation in 1748 and revised these statutes in 1772 explicitly to discourage men from "gouging, plucking, or putting out an eye, biting or kicking or stomping upon" quiet peaceable citizens. By 1786 South Carolina had made premeditated mayhem a capital offense, defining the crime as severing another's bodily parts....

... Not [only] assaults on persons or property but slights, insults, and thoughtless gestures set young Southerners against each other. To call a man a "buckskin," for example, was to accuse of the poverty associated with leather clothing, while the epithet "Scotsman" tied him to the low-caste Scots-Irish who settled the southern highlands....

Descriptions of these "fist battles," as [Philip] Fithian called them, indicate that they generally began like English prize fights. Two men, surrounded by onlookers, parried blows until one was knocked or thrown down. But there the similarity ceased. Whereas "Broughton's Rules" of the English ring specified that a round ended when either antagonist fell, southern bruisers only began

From Elliott Gorn, " 'Gouge and Bite, Pull Hair and Scratch': The Social Significance of Gouging in the Southern Backcountry," *American Historical Review* 90 (February 1985): 18–22, 27–28, 31–35, 39–43.

fighting at this point. Enclosed not inside a formal ring—the "magic circle" defining a special place with its own norms of conduct—but within whatever space the spectators left vacant, fighters battled each other until one called enough or was unable to continue. Combatants boasted, howled, and cursed. As words gave way to action, they tripped and threw, gouged and butted, scratched and choked each other....

Around the beginning of the nineteenth century, men sought original labels for their brutal style of fighting. "Rough-and-tumble" or simply "gouging" gradually replaced "boxing" as the name for these contests. Before two bruisers attacked each other, spectators might demand whether they proposed to fight fair—according to Broughton's Rules—or rough-and-tumble. Honor dictated that all techniques be permitted. Except for a ban on weapons, most men chose to fight "no holts barred," doing what they wished to each other without interference, until one gave up or was incapacitated.

The emphasis on maximum disfigurement, on severing bodily parts, made this fighting style unique. Amid the general mayhem, however, gouging out an opponent's eye became the sine qua non of rough-and-tumble fighting, much like the knockout punch in modern boxing. The best gougers, of course, were adept at other fighting skills. Some allegedly filed their teeth to bite off an enemy's appendages more efficiently. Still, liberating an eyeball quickly became a fighter's surest route to victory and his most prestigious accomplishment. To this end, celebrated heroes fired their fingernails hard, honed them sharp, and oiled them slick. "'You have come off badly this time, I doubt?'" declared an alarmed passerby on seeing the piteous condition of a renowned fighter. "'Have I,' says he triumphantly, shewing from his pocket at the same time an eye, which he had extracted during the combat, and preserved for a trophy."

As the new style of fighting evolved, its geographical distribution changed. Leadership quickly passed from the southern seaboard to upcountry counties and the western frontier.... Rough-and-tumbling was best suited to the backwoods, where hunting, herding, and semisubsistence agriculture predominated over market-oriented, staple crop production....

The social base of rough-and-tumbling also shifted with the passage of time. Although brawling was always considered a vice of the "lower sort," eighteenth-century Tidewater gentlemen sometimes found themselves in brutal fights. These combats grew out of challenges to men's honor—to their status in patriarchal, kin-based, small-scale communities—and were woven into the very fabric of daily life.... Although they valued hierarchy, individual status was never permanently fixed, so men frantically sought to assert their prowess—by grand boasts over tavern gaming tables laden with money, by whipping and tripping each other's horses in violent quarter-races, by wagering one-half year's earnings on the flash of a fighting cock's gaff....

Piety, hard work, and steady habits had their adherents, but in this society aggressive self-assertion and manly pride were the real marks of status. Even the gentry's vaunted hospitality demonstrated a family's community standing, so conviviality itself became a vehicle for rivalry and emulation. Rich and poor might revel together during "public times," but gentry patronage of sports and festivities kept the focus of power clear. Above all, brutal recreations toughened men for a violent social life in which the exploitation of labor, the specter of poverty, and a fierce struggle for status were daily realities.

During the final decades of the eighteenth century, however, ... many in the planter class now wanted to distinguish themselves from social inferiors more by genteel manners, gracious living, and paternal prestige than by patriarchal prowess. They sought alternatives to brawling and found them by imitating the English aristocracy. A few gentlemen took boxing lessons from professors of pugilism or attended sparring exhibitions given by touring exponents of the manly art. More important, dueling gradually replaced hand-to-hand combat. The code of honor offered a genteel, though deadly, way to settle personal disputes while demonstrating one's elevated status....

★ ★ ★

By the early nineteenth century, rough-and-tumble fighting had generated its own folklore. Horror mingled with awe when residents of the Ohio Valley pointed out one-eyed individuals to visitors, when New Englanders referred to an empty eye socket as a "Virginia Brand," when North Carolinians related stories of mass rough-and-tumbles ending with eyeballs covering the ground, and when Kentuckians told of battle-royals so intense that severed eyes, ears, and noses filled bushel baskets. Place names like "Fighting Creek" and "Gouge Eye" perpetuated the memory of heroic encounters, and rustic bombast reached new extremes with estimates from some counties that every third man wanted an eye. As much as the style of combat, the rich oral folklore of the backcountry—the legends, tales, ritual boasts, and verbal duels, all of them in regional vernacular—made rough-and-tumble fighting unique.

It would be difficult to overemphasize the importance of the spoken word in southern life. Traditional tales, songs, and beliefs—transmitted orally by blacks as well as whites—formed the cornerstone of culture. Folklore socialized children, inculcated values, and helped forge a distinct regional sensibility.... Southern society was based more on personalistic, face-to-face, kin-and-community relationships than on legalistic or bureaucratic ones. Interactions between southerners were guided by elaborate rituals of hospitality, demonstrative conviviality, and kinship ties—all of which emphasized personal dependencies and reliance on the spoken word. Through the antebellum period and beyond, the South had an oral as much as a written culture.

Boundaries between talk and action, ideas and behavior, are less clear in spoken than in written contexts. Psychologically, print seems more distant and abstract than speech, which is inextricably bound to specific individuals, times, and places.... Literate peoples separate thought from action, pigeon-holing ideas and behavior. Nonliterate ones draw this distinction less sharply, viewing words and the events to which they refer as a single reality. In oral cultures generally, and the Old South in particular, the spoken word was a powerful force in daily life, because ideation and behavior remained closely linked.

The oral traditions of hunters, drifters, herdsmen, gamblers, roustabouts, and rural poor who rough-and-tumbled provided a strong social cement. Tall talk around a campfire, in a tavern, in front of a crossroads store, or at countless other meeting places on the southwestern frontier helped establish communal bonds between disparate persons.... But words could also divide.... Men were so touchy about their personal reputations that any slight required an apology. This failing, only retribution restored public stature and self-esteem. "Saving face" was not just a metaphor....

The oral narratives of the southern backcountry drew strength from these national traditions yet possessed unique characteristics. Above all, fight legends portrayed backwoodsmen reveling in blood. Violence existed for its own sake, unencumbered by romantic conventions and claiming no redeeming social or psychic value. Gouging narratives may have masked grimness with black humor, but they offered little pretense that violence was a creative or civilizing force....

The danger and violence of daily life in the backwoods contributed mightily to sanguinary oral traditions that exalted the strong and deprecated the weak. Early in the nineteenth century, the Southwest contained more than its share of terrifying wild animals, powerful and well-organized Indian tribes, and marauding white outlaws. Equally important were high infant mortality rates and short life expectancies, agricultural blights, class inequities, and the centuries-old belief that betrayal and cruelty were man's fate....

Rather than be overwhelmed by violence, acquiesce in an oppressive environment, or submit to death as an escape from tragedy, why not make a virtue of necessity and flaunt one's unconcern? To revel in the lore of deformity, mutilation, and death was to beat the wilderness at its own game. The storyteller's art dramatized life and converted nameless anxieties into high adventure; bravado helped men face down a threatening world and transform terror into power. To claim that one was sired by wild animals, kin to natural disasters, and tougher than steam engines—which were displacing rivermen in the antebellum era—was to gain a momentary respite from fear, a cathartic, if temporary, sense of being in control. Symbolically, wild boasts overwhelmed the very forces that threatened the backwoodsmen....

★ ★ ★

More than realism or fantasy alone, fight legends stretched the imagination by blending both. As metaphoric statements, they reconciled contradictory impulses, at once glorifying and parodying barbarity. In this sense, gouging narratives were commentaries on backwoods life. The legends were texts that allowed plain folk to dramatize the tensions and ambiguities of their lives: they hauled society's goods yet lived on its fringe; they destroyed forests and game while clearing the land for settlement; they killed Indians to make way for the white man's culture; they struggled for self-sufficiency only to become ensnared in economic dependency. Fight narratives articulated the fundamental contradiction of frontier life—the abandonment of "civilized" ways that led to the ultimate expansion of civilized society....

... Although rough-and-tumble fighting appears primitive and anarchic to modern eyes, there can be little doubt that its origins, rituals, techniques, and goals were emphatically conditioned by environment; gouging was learned behavior. Humanistic social science more than sociobiology holds the keys to understanding this phenomenon.

What can we conclude about the culture and society that nourished rough-and-tumble fighting? The best place to begin is with the material base of life and the nature of daily work. Gamblers, hunters, herders, roustabouts, rivermen, and yeomen farmers were the sorts of persons usually associated with gouging. Such hallmarks of modernity as large-scale production, complex division of labor, and regular work rhythms were alien to their lives....

Boatmen, hunters, and herdsmen were often separate from wives and children for long periods. More important, backcountry couples lacked the emotionally intense experience of the bourgeois family. They spent much of their time apart and found companionship with members of their own sex. The frontier town or crossroads tavern brought males together in surrogate brotherhoods, where rough men paid little deference to the civilizing role of women and the moral uplift of the domestic family. On the margins of a booming, modernizing society, they shared an intensely communal yet fiercely competitive way of life. Thus, where work was least rationalized and specialized, domesticity weakest, legal institutions primitive, and the market economy feeble, rough-and-tumble fighting found fertile soil.

Just as the economy of the southern backcountry remained locally oriented, the rough-and-tumblers were local heroes, renowned in their communities.... Legendary champions were real individuals, tested gang leaders who attained their status by being the meanest, toughest, and most ruthless fighters, who faced disfigurement and never backed down....

Given the lives these men led, a world view that embraced fearlessness made sense. Hunters, trappers, Indian fighters, and herdsmen who knew the smell of warm blood on their hands refused to sentimentalize an environment filled with threatening forces. It was not that backwoodsmen lived in constant danger but that violence was unpredictable. Recreations like cockfighting deadened men to cruelty, and the gratuitous savagery of gouging matches reinforced the daily truth that life was brutal, guided only by the logic of superior nerve, power, and cunning. With families emotionally or physically distant and civil institutions weak, a man's role in the all-male society was defined less by his ability as a breadwinner than by his ferocity. The touchstone of masculinity was unflinching toughness, not chivalry, duty, or piety. Violent sports, heavy drinking, and impulsive pleasure seeking were appropriate for men whose lives were hard, whose futures were unpredictable, and whose opportunities were limited. Gouging champions were group leaders because they embodied the basic values of their peers. The successful rough-and-tumbler proved his manhood by asserting his dominance and rendering his opponent "impotent."... And the loser, though literally or symbolically castrated, demonstrated his mettle and maintained his honor....

Above all, the ancient concept of honor helps explain this shared proclivity for violence. According to the sociologist Peter Berger, modern men have difficulty taking seriously the idea of honor. American jurisprudence, for example, offers legal recourse for slander and libel because they involve material damages.

But insult—publicly smearing a man's good name and besmirching his honor—implies no palpable injury and so does not exist in the eyes of the law. Honor is an intensely social concept, resting on reputation, community standing, and the esteem of kin and compatriots. To possess honor requires acknowledgment from others; it cannot exist in solitary conscience. Modern man, Berger has argued, is more responsive to dignity—the belief that personal worth inheres equally in each individual, regardless of his status in society. Dignity frees the evangelical to confront God alone, the capitalist to make contracts without customary encumbrances, and the reformer to uplift the lowly. Naked and alone man has dignity; extolled by peers and covered with ribbons, he has honor.

Anthropologists have also discovered the centrality of honor in several cultures. According to J. G. Peristiany, honor and shame often preoccupy individuals in small-scale settings, where face-to-face relationships predominate over anonymous or bureaucratic ones. Social standing in such communities is never completely secure, because it must be validated by public opinion whose fickleness compels men constantly to assert and prove their worth. Julian Pitt-Rivers has added that, if society rejects a man's evaluation of himself and treats his claim to honor with ridicule or contempt, his very identity suffers because it is based on the judgment of peers. Shaming refers to that process by which an insult or any public humiliation impugns an individual's honor and thereby threatens his sense of self. By risking injury in a violent encounter, an affronted man—whether victorious or not—restores his sense of status and thus validates anew his claim to honor. Only valorous action, not words, can redeem his place in the ranks of his peer group.

Bertram Wyatt-Brown has argued that this Old World ideal is the key to understanding southern history. Across boundaries of time, geography, and social class, the South was knit together by a primal concept of male valor, part of the ancient heritage of Indo-European folk cultures. Honor demanded clan loyalty, hospitality, protection of women, and defense of patriarchal prerogatives. Honorable men guarded their reputations, bristled at insults, and, where necessary, sought personal vindication through bloodshed. The culture of honor thrived in hierarchical rural communities like the American South and grew out of a fatalistic world view, which assumed that pain and suffering were man's fate. It accounts for the pervasive violence that marked relationships between Southerners and explains their insistence on vengeance and their rejection of legal redress in settling quarrels. Honor tied personal identity to public fulfillment of social roles. Neither bourgeois self-control nor internalized conscience determined status; judgment by one's fellows was the wellspring of community standing.

In this light, the seemingly trivial causes for brawls … —name calling, subtle ridicule, breaches of decorum, displays of poor manners—make sense. If a man's good name was his most important possession, then any slight cut him deeply. "Having words" precipitated fights because words brought shame and undermined a man's sense of self. Symbolic acts, such as buying a round of drinks, conferred honor on all, while refusing to share a bottle implied some inequality in social status. Honor inhered not only in individuals but also in kin and peers; when members of two cliques had words, their tested leaders or several men from each side fought to uphold group prestige. Inheritors of primal honor, the southern plain folk were quick to take offense, and any perceived affront forced a man either to devalue himself or to strike back violently and avenge the wrong.

The concept of male honor takes us a long way toward understanding the meaning of eye-gouging matches. But backwoods people did not simply acquire some primordial notion without modifying it. Definitions of honorable behavior have always varied enormously across cultures. The southern upcountry fostered a particular style of honor, which grew out of the contradiction between equality and hierarchy. Honorific societies tend to be sharply stratified. Honor is apportioned according to rank, and men fight to maintain personal standing within their social categories. Because black chattel slavery was the basis for the southern hierarchy, slave owners had the most wealth and honor, while other whites scrambled for a bit of each, and bondsmen were permanently impoverished and dishonored. Here was a source of tension for the plain folk. Men of honor shared freedom and equality; those denied honor were implicitly less than equal—perilously close to a slave-like condition. But in the eyes of the gentry, poor whites as well as blacks were outside the circle of honor, so both groups were subordinate. Thus, a herdsman's insult failed to shame a planter since the two men were not on the same social level. Without a threat to the gentleman's honor, there was no need for a duel; horsewhipping the insolent fellow sufficed.

Southern plain folk, then, were caught in a social contradiction. Society taught all white men to consider themselves equal, encouraged them to compete for power and status, yet threatened them from below with the specter of servitude and from above with insistence on obedience to rank and authority. Cut off from upper-class tests of honor, backcountry people adopted their own. A rough-and-tumble was more than a poor man's duel, a botched version of genteel combat. Plain folk chose not to ape the dispassionate, antiseptic, gentry style but to invert it. While the gentleman's code of honor insisted on cool restraint, eye gougers gloried in unvarnished brutality. In contrast to duelists' aloof silence, backwoods fighters screamed defiance to the world. As their own unique rites of honor, rough-and-tumble matches allowed backcountry men to shout their equality at each other. And eye-gouging fights also dispelled any stigma of servility. Ritual boasts, soaring oaths, outrageous ferocity, unflinching bloodiness—all proved a man's freedom. Where the slave acted obsequiously, the backwoodsman resisted the slightest affront; where human chattels accepted blows and never raised a hand, plain folk celebrated violence; where blacks could not jeopardize their value as property, poor whites proved their autonomy by risking bodily parts. Symbolically reaffirming their claims to honor, gouging matches helped resolve painful uncertainties arising out of the ambiguous place of plain folk in the southern social structure.

Backwoods fighting reminds us of man's capacity for cruelty and is an excellent corrective to romanticizing premodern life. But a close look also keeps us from drawing facile conclusions about innate human aggressiveness. Eye gouging represented neither the "real" human animal emerging on the frontier, nor nature acting through man in a Darwinian struggle for survival, nor anarchic disorder and communal breakdown. Rather, rough-and-tumble fighting was ritualized behavior—a product of specific cultural assumptions. Men drink together, tongues loosen, a simmering old rivalry begins to boil; insult is given, offense taken, ritual boasts commence; the fight begins, mettle is tested, blood redeems honor, and equilibrium is restored. Eye gouging was the poor and middling white's own version of a historical southern tendency to consider personal violence socially useful—indeed, ethically essential.

★ ★ ★

Rough-and-tumble fighting emerged from the confluence of economic conditions, social relationships, and culture in the southern backcountry. Primitive markets and the semisubsistence basis of life threw men back on close ties to kin and community. Violence and poverty were part of daily existence, so endurance, even callousness, became functional values. Loyal to their localities, their occupations, and each other, men came together and found release from life's hardships in strong drink, tall talk, rude practical jokes, and cruel sports. They craved one another's recognition but rejected genteel, pious, or bourgeois values, awarding esteem on the basis of their own traditional standards. The glue that held men together was an intensely competitive status system in which the most prodigious drinker or strongest arm wrestler, the best tale teller, fiddle player, or log roller, the most daring gambler, original liar, skilled hunter, outrageous swearer, or accurate marksman was accorded respect by the others. Reputation was everything, and scars were badges of honor. Rough-and-tumble fighting demonstrated unflinching willingness to inflict pain while risking mutilation—all to defend one's standing among peers—and became a central expression of the all-male subculture.

Eye gouging continued long after the antebellum period. As the market economy absorbed new parts of the backcountry, however, the way of life that supported rough-and-tumbling waned. Certainly by mid-century the number of incidents declined, precisely when expanding international demand brought ever more upcountry acres into staple production. Towns, schools, churches, revivals, and families gradually overtook the backwoods. In a slow and uneven process, keelboats gave way to steamers, then railroads; squatters, to cash crop farmers; hunters and trappers, to preachers. The plain folk code of honor was far from dead, but emergent social institutions engendered a moral ethos that warred against the old ways. For many individuals, the justifications for personal violence grew stricter, and mayhem became unacceptable.

Ironically, progress also had a darker side. New technologies and modes of production could enhance men's fighting abilities. "Birmingham and Pittsburgh are obliged to complete ... the equipment of the 'chivalric Kentuckian,' "Charles Agustus Murray observed in the 1840s, as bowie knives ended more and more rough-and-tumbles. Equally important, in 1835 the first modern revolver appeared, and manufacturers marketed cheap, accurate editions in the coming decade. Dueling weapons had been costly, and Kentucky rifles or horse pistols took a full minute to load and prime. The revolver, however, which fitted neatly into a man's pocket, settled more and more personal disputes. Raw and brutal as rough-and-tumbling was, it could not survive the use of arms. Yet precisely because eye gouging was so violent—because combatants cherished maimings, blindings, even castrations—it unleashed death wishes that invited new technologies of destruction.

With improved weaponry, dueling entered its golden age during the antebellum era. Armed combat remained both an expression of gentry sensibility and a mark of social rank. But in a society where status was always shifting and unclear, dueling did not stay confined to the upper class. The habitual carrying of weapons, once considered a sign of unmanly fear, now lost some of its stigma. As the backcountry changed, tests of honor continued, but gunplay rather than fighting tooth-and-nail appealed to new men with social aspirations. Thus, progress and technology slowly circumscribed rough-and-tumble fighting, only to substitute a deadlier option. Violence grew neater and more lethal as men checked their savagery to murder each other.

The Jackson-Dickinson Duel of 1806

JAMES PARTON

The place appointed for the meeting was a long day's ride from Nashville. Thursday morning, before the dawn of day Dickinson stole from the side of his young and beautiful wife, and began silently to prepare for the journey. She awoke, and asked him why he was up so early. He replied, he had business in Kentucky across the Red river, but it would not detain him long. Before leaving the room, he went up to his wife, kissed her with peculiar tenderness, and said

"Good bye, darling. I shall be sure to be at home tomorrow night."

He mounted his horse and repaired to the rendezvous, where his second and half a dozen of the gay blades of Nashville were waiting to escort him on his journey. Away they rode, in the highest spirits, as though they were upon a party of pleasure. Indeed, they made a party of pleasure of it. When they stopped for rest or refreshment, Dickinson is said to have amused the company by displaying his wonderful skill with the pistol. Once, at a distance of twenty-four feet, he fired four balls, each at the word of command, into a space that could be covered by a silver dollar. Several times he cut a string with his bullet from the same distance. It is said that he left a severed string hanging near a tavern, and said to the landlord as he rode away,

"If General Jackson comes along this road, show him *that*!"

It is also said, that he laid a wager of five hundred dollars that he would hit his antagonist within half an inch of a certain button on his coat. I neither believe nor deny one of these stories; but so many of the same kind are still told in the neighborhood, that it is safe to conclude that, on this fatal ride, Dickinson *did* affect much of that reckless manner which was once supposed to be an evidence of high courage. The party went frisking, and galloping lonely forest

From James Parton, *Life of Andrew Jackson* (New York: Mason Brothers, 1860), 271, 295–301.

roads, making short cuts that cautious never attempted, dashing across creeks and rivers, making the woods ring and echo with their shouts and laughter.

Very different was the demeanor of General Jackson and the party that accompanied him. General Thomas an old revolutionary soldier, versed in the science, and familiar with the practice of dueling had reflected deeply upon the conditions of the coming combat, with the view to conclude upon the tactics most likely to save his friend from son's unerring bullet. For this duel was not to be the amusing mockery that some modern duels have been. This was to be *real*. It was to be an affair in which each man was to strive with his utmost skill to effect the purpose of the occasion—disable his antagonist and save his own life. As the principal and the second rode apart from the rest, they discussed all the chances and probabilities with the aim to decide upon a course which should result in the disabling of Dickinson and the saving of Jackson. The mode of fighting which had been agreed upon was somewhat peculiar. The pistols were to be held downward until the word given to fire; then each man was to fire *as soon as he pleased*. With such an arrangement, it was scarcely possible that both the pistols should be discharged at the same moment. There was a chance, even, that by extreme quickness of movement, one man could bring down his antagonist without himself receiving a shot. The question anxiously discussed between Jackson and Overton was this: Shall we try to get the shot, or shall we permit Dickinson to have it? They agreed, at length, that it would be decidedly better to let Dickinson fire first. In the first place, Dickinson, like all miraculous shots, required no time to take aim, and would have a far better chance than Jackson in a quick shot, even if both fired at once. And in spite of anything Jackson could do, Dickinson would be almost sure to get the first fire. Moreover, Jackson was *certain* he would be hit; and he was unwilling to subject his own aim to the chance of its being totally destroyed by the shock of the blow. For Jackson was resolved on hitting Dickinson. His feelings toward his adversary were embittered by what he had heard of his public practicings and boastful wagers. "I should have hit him, if he had shot me through the brain," said Jackson once. In pleasant discourse of this kind, the two men wiled away the hours of the long journey.

A tavern kept by one David Miller, somewhat noted in the neighborhood, stood on the banks of the Red river, near the ground appointed for the duel. Late in the afternoon of Thursday, the 29th of May, the inmates of this tavern were surprised by the arrival of a party of seven or eight horsemen. Jacob Smith, then employed by Miller as an overseer, but now himself a planter in the vicinity, was standing before the house when this unexpected company rode up. One of these horsemen asked him if they could be accommodated with lodgings for the night. They could. The party dismounted, gave their horses to the attendant negroes and entered the tavern. No sooner had they done so, than honest Jacob was perplexed by the arrival of a second cavalcade—Dickinson and his friends, who also asked for lodgings. The manager told them the house was full; but that he never turned travelers away, and if they chose to remain, he would do the best he could for them. Dickinson then asked where was the next house of entertainment. He was directed to a house two miles lower down the river, kept by William Harrison. The house is still standing. The room in which Dickinson slept the night, and *slept* the night following, is the one now used by the occupants as a dining-room.

Jackson ate heartily at supper that night, conversing in a lively, pleasant manner, and smoked his evening pipe as usual. Jacob Smith remembers being exceedingly pleased with his guest, and, on learning the cause of his visit, heartily wishing him a safe deliverance.

Before breakfast on the next morning the whole party mounted and rode down the road that wound close along the picturesque banks of the stream.

About the same hour, the overseer and his gang of negroes went to the fields to begin their daily toil; he longing to venture within sight of what he knew was about to take place.

The horsemen rode about a mile along the river; then turned down toward the river to a point on the bank where they had expected to find a ferryman. No ferryman appearing, Jackson spurred his horse into the stream and dashed across, followed by all his party. They rode into the poplar forest, two hundred yards or less, to a spot near the center of a level platform or river bottom, then covered with forest, now smiling with cultivated fields. The horsemen halted and dismounted just before reaching the appointed place. Jackson, Overton, and a surgeon who had come with them from home, walked on together, and the rest led their horses a short distance in an opposite direction.

"How do you feel about it now, General?" asked one of the party, as Jackson turned to go.

"Oh, all right," replied Jackson, gayly; "I shall wing him, never fear."

Dickinson's second won the choice of position, and Jackson's the office of giving the word. The astute Overton, considered this giving of the word a matter of great importance and he had already determined *how* he would give it, if the lot fell to him. The eight paces were measured off, and the men placed. Both were perfectly collected. All the politeness of such occasions were very strictly and elegantly performed. Jackson was dressed in a loose frock-coat, buttoned carelessly over his chest, and concealing in some degree the extreme slenderness of his figure. Dickinson was the younger and handsomer man of the two. But Jackson's tall, erect figure, and the still intensity of his demeanor, it is said, gave him a most superior and commanding air, as he stood under the tall poplars on this bright May morning, silently awaiting the moment of doom. "Are you ready?" said Overton.

"I am ready," replied Dickinson.

"I am ready," said Jackson.

The words were no sooner pronounced than Overton, with a sudden shout, cried, using his old-country pronunciation,

"FERE!"

Dickinson raised his pistol quickly and fired. Overton, who was looking with anxiety and dread at Jackson, saw a puff of dust fly from the breast of his coat, and saw him raise his left arm and place it tightly across his chest. He is hit, thought Overton, and in a bad place, too; but no; he does not fall. Erect and grim as Fate he stood, his teeth clenched, raising his pistol. Overton glanced at

Dickinson. Amazed at the unwonted failure of his aim; and apparently appalled at the awful figure and face before him, Dickinson had unconsciously recoiled a pace or two.

"Great God!" he faltered, "have I missed him?

"Back to the MARK, sir!" shrieked Overton, with his hand upon his pistol.

Dickinson recovered his composure, stepped forward to the peg and stood with his eyes averted from his antagonist. All this was the work of a moment, though it requires many a tell it.

General Jackson took deliberate aim, and pulled the trigger. The pistol neither snapped nor went off. He looked at the trigger, and discovered that it had stopped at half cock. He drew it back to its place, and took aim a second time. He fired. Dickinson's face blanched; he reeled; his friends rushed toward him, caught him in their arms, and gently seated him on the ground, leaning against a bush. His trowsers (*sic*) reddened. They stripped off his clothes. The blood was gushing from his side in a torrent. And, alas! here is the ball, not near the wound, but above the opposite hip, just the skin. The ball had passed through the body, below the ribs. Such a wound could not but be fatal.

Overton went forward and learned the condition of the wounded man. Rejoining his principal, he said, "He won't want anything more of you, General," and conducted him from the ground. They had gone a hundred yards, Overton walking on one side of Jackson, the surgeon on the other, and neither speaking a word, when the surgeon observed that one of Jackson's shoes was full of blood.

"My God! General Jackson, are you hit?" he exclaimed, pointing to the blood.

"Oh? I believe," replied Jackson, "that he has pinked me a little. Let's look at it. But say nothing *there*," pointing to the house.

He opened his coat. Dickinson's aim had been perfect. He had sent the ball precisely where he supposed Jackson's heart was beating. But the thinness of his body and the looseness of his coat combining to deceive Dickinson, had only broken a rib or two, and raked the breast-bone. It was a somewhat painful, bad-looking wound, but neither severe nor dangerous, and he was able to ride, to without much inconvenience. Upon approaching the house, he went up to one of the negro women who was churning and asked her if the butter had come. She said it was just coming. He asked for some buttermilk. While she was getting it for him, she observed him furtively open his coat and look within it. She saw that his shirt was soaked with blood, and she stood gazing in blank horror at the sight, dipper in hand. He caught her eye, and hastily buttoned his coat again. She dipped out a quart measure full of buttermilk, and gave it to him. He drank it off at a draught; then went in, took off his coat, and had his wound carefully examined and dressed. That done, he dispatched one of his retinue to Dr. Catlett, to inquire respecting the condition of Dickinson, and to say that the surgeon attending himself would be glad to contribute his aid toward Mr. Dickinson's relief. Polite reply was returned that Mr. Dickinson was past surgery. In the course of the day, General Jackson sent a bottle of wine to Dr. Catlett for the use of the patient.

But there was one gratification which Jackson could not, even in such circumstances, grant him. A very old friend of General Jackson writes to me thus: "Although the General had been wounded, he did not desire it should be known until he had left the neighborhood, and had therefore concealed it at first from his own friends. His reason for this, as he once stated to me, was that as Dickinson considered himself the best shot in the world, and was certain of killing him at the first fire, *he did not want him to have the gratification even of knowing he had touched him.*"

Poor Dickinson bled to death. The flowing of blood was stanched, but could not be stopped. He was conveyed to the house in which he had passed the night, and placed upon a mattress which was soon drenched with blood. He suffered extreme agony, and uttered horrible cries all that long day.

At nine o'clock in the evening he suddenly asked why they had put out the lights. The doctor knew then that the end was at hand; that the wife, who had been sent for in the morning would not arrive in time to close her husband's eyes. He died five minutes after, cursing, it is said, with his last breath, the ball that had entered his body. The poor wife was hurried away on hearing that her husband was "dangerously wounded," and met, as she rode toward the duel; a procession of silent horsemen escorting a rough migrant wagon that contained her husband's remains.

Slave Boxers on the Antebellum Plantation

SERGIO LUSSANA

Formerly enslaved with about seventy-five others on a cotton plantation in Jackson County, Alabama, John Finnely recalled one of the few amusements he and his fellow slaves shared in their days of bondage. For "'joyments," remembered Finnely, "'weuns have de co'n huskin' an' de nigger fights." Finnely delighted in his recollection of the slave fights he witnessed growing up in antebellum Alabama, noting that although the fights were "mo' fo' de w'ite fo'k's 'joyment," die slaves were also "lowed to see it." According to Finnely, the masters of different plantations matched their slaves by size and then bet on them. Finnely's master had one slave who weighed 150 pounds and who was an "awful good fightah"; he was "quick lak a cat an' powe'ful fo' his size an' he lak to fight." The fighter, named Tom, would always "win de battle quick"…. Such was Finnely's love of the fights that he disclosed that the contests had made him reconsider his plans for running away to freedom: "I's think an' think 'bout gittin' freedom… Den I's think ob some ob de 'joyment on de Marster's place dat I's lak, sich as de co'n huskin', nigger fights, an' de singin' an' den I's don't know w'at to do."

Finnely's account illuminates a part of antebellum slave life that has generally been overlooked by historians, that of organized fighting practices and their role in the lives of enslaved men…. [T]here is evidence that enslaved men engaged in various pursuits, such as wrestling, as a way to demonstrate their physical

---

From Sergio Lussana, "To See Who Was Best on the Plantation: Enslaved Fighting Contests and Masculinity in the Antebellum Plantation South," *Journal of Southern History* 76 (November 2010): 901, 904–11, 914–17, 919–922.

prowess.... [H]istorian T. J. Desch Obi has traced the rich martial arts tradition of West and West Central Africa across the Atlantic to the slave communities of North and South America and the Caribbean.... This article will build on Desch Obi's work by analyzing slave testimony to recreate the world of organized slave fights and to explore the implications of these activities for the identities of men enslaved in the antebellum American South.

At present, the historiography on enslaved men is particularly undeveloped because historians have tended to view the normative slave experience as male and hence have neglected to analyze enslaved men from a gendered perspective. The lack of focus on enslaved men and masculinity markedly contrasts with the plethora of work in recent years on masculinity in the white antebellum South [notably] Bertram Wyatt-Brown's *Southern Honor: Ethics and Behavior in the Old South* (1982).... By exploring the lives of men and using masculinity as a category of analysis, these works have considerably deepened our knowledge of the unique social and cultural worlds of the antebellum American South. The historiographical direction of this article owes much ...historians researching gender and the lives of enslaved women. Deborah Gray White's *Ar'n't I a Woman? Female Slaves in the Plantation* South (1985) pioneered this approach in slave studies.... These studies continue to teach historians of slavery that gender was central to defining the experiences of enslaved men and women... and served as "a primary way of signifying relationships of power."

... [I]ssues of black masculinity ... in scholarly accounts of slavery ... have usually been studied through the provider/protector roles performed by enslaved men within the context of slave courtship and marriage. This article intends to move beyond the now familiar terrain of the roles of enslaved men and women in courtship, marriage, and the family. It will do so by focusing on organized fighting activities such as wrestling and boxing that were engaged in by enslaved men in the antebellum South. Drawing on the insight of various anthropologists and sociologists, the article argues that these organized fighting activities provided enslaved men with a vital and meaningful context in which to assert and display autonomous masculine identities distinct from both enslaved women and slaveholders on the plantations of the antebellum South. It suggests that through these activities, enslaved men took part in African-derived community forming rituals that underscored rank, status, and leadership roles in the slave community and fostered male solidarity. Moreover, building on the work undertaken by Stephanie M. H. Camp on the female slave body, the article contends that these fighting activities were potentially important avenues of male bodily resistance to the symbolic and economic imperatives of slavery.

The primary source material used in this article includes published narratives written by former slaves and previously unused accounts of enslaved wrestling that appear in the extensive oral interviews conducted with former slaves between 1936 and 1938 by the Federal Writers' Project of the Works Progress Administration (WPA). The article utilizes historical evidence from the late antebellum period....

Although formerly enslaved men typically reported engaging in mostly noncombative games as small boys, such as ring games, wolf-over-the-river, and hide-and-seek, some also participated in wrestling. Too young to enter the field and commence serious labor, slave boys typically ran errands and performed light chores; thus, they had more time for recreation than enslaved adults did. It was not unusual for slave children, while at play, to be joined by the master's children; as Gabriel Gilbert reported, "de li'l white folks and nigger chillen uster jis' play 'roun' like brudder and sister." On these occasions, Gilbert added, the slave boys "hab fights and us fight de white boys and niggers jis' de same."

Nonetheless, serious wrestling and other fighting activities tended to be reserved for the older boys and men of the plantation. Furthermore, as slave boys came of age, they soon learned that fighting with the progeny of their white masters was unacceptable.... The free time of ... older men was shaped by the "particular combinations" of local work, environment, and the Christian calendar." The task system in the Low country afforded slaves a relative degree of autonomy after their tasks were completed. Under the task system, the owner or overseer allocated each slave a particular job every morning, and on finishing their tasks, the enslaved persons typically spent the rest of the day working their own gardens, fishing, or hunting. Formerly enslaved in South Carolina, Sam Polite recalled, "You haf for wuk 'til tas' t'ru W'en you knock off wuk, you kin wuk on your land." In the upcountry, work was organized through a gang labor system, whereby the enslaved typically labored from sunrise to sundown, affording them time only at night to tend garden patches and complete chores for their families.... As Mark M. Smith has noted, "All time on the plantation, whether work or leisure, was ultimately the master's to bestow, manipulate, and define."

The enslaved were nonetheless able to claim time for recreational pursuits. Most slaves in the upcountry and Lowcountry were granted Saturday nights and Sundays off, and some had Saturday afternoons off as well. Matthew Hume recalled that his fellow slaves in Kentucky were "free from Saturday noon until Monday morning," during which time the majority would "drink, gamble and fight." Holidays such as Christmas and the Fourth of July were special days when no work was undertaken. Depending on the owner, the Christmas holidays could last from a few days to two weeks. Events such as corn shuckings (harvest festivals) ... were intense periods of work that culminated in organized parties, barbecues, games, dancing, and wrestling for the enslaved.... In addition ... many slaves defied the temporal restrictions imposed by the owners and engaged in their own pursuits at night away from the eyes of the slaveholder.

Often, fighting activities for enslaved men were controlled and monitored by the slaveholder. Isaac Wilson relayed that whereas the master provided a "playground fer de slave chillum ter play in," the master had the older ones "run foot races, wrestle an' box." Wilson commented that some said these exercises were designed "to make de slaves develop an' long winded," but he nevertheless reported that he "had many a gran' time in deir." Another man reported that the masters had slaves "wrestling and knocking each other about" every Saturday night. Henry Bibb gave perhaps the most descriptive account of such fights:

> Those who make no profession of religion, resort to the woods in large numbers on that day to gamble, fight, get drunk, and break the Sabbath.

> This is often encouraged by slaveholders.... The[y] get them to wrestling, fighting, jumping, running foot races, and butting each other like sheep. This is urged on by giving them whiskey; making bets on them; laying chips on one slave's head, and daring another to tip it off with his hand; and if he tipped it off, it would be called an insult, and cause a fight. Before fighting, the parties choose their seconds to stand by them while fighting; a ring or a circle is formed to fight in, and no one is allowed to enter the ring while they are fighting, but their seconds, and the white gentlemen. They are not allowed to fight a duel, nor to use weapons of any kind.... After fighting, they make friends, shake hands, and take a dram together, and there is no more of it.

... Kenneth S. Greenberg points out ... that the fighting replicated the form of the duel "without its substance." One could hence argue that the impotence of enslaved men in this context served to validate the mastery of their owners. However, Bibb's narrative also makes clear that this was not a fight to the death and that after the contest the two fighters shook hands and shared a drink....

... Desch Obi notes of intraplantation matches that "while serious," such fights were not "life-threatening" contests and thus were "not necessarily damaging to the contestants or in conflict with the bondsmen's honor code."

The most common accounts of organized slave fights record those held at corn shuckings.... Carter J. Jackson recalled how they had some "good fights" between men on the plantation at corn shuckings, but "no one was killed."... "[T]hey matched fights between the Niggers from the different plantations. The Masters of the two men fighting managed the fight to see it was fair." As Jackson's testimony demonstrates, organized crossplantation wrestling and boxing bouts were staged by the slaveholders, who supervised the events....

Sometimes, masters raised some of their enslaved men as prizefighters and arranged fights with other slaves from different plantations for money throughout the year....

An extraordinary account survives from an enslaved spectator who described in detail one of these interplantation prizefights organized by the slaveholding class for money. John Finnely, ... recalled an occasion when a challenger to his master's prizefighter, Tom, came to the neighborhood. Finnely witnessed the "vicious fight" that ensued:....

> De fight am held at night by de pine torch light. A ring am made by de fo'ks standin' 'roun' in de circle an' de niggers git in dat circle. Deys fight widout a rest 'til one give up or can't git up.... Nothin' barred 'cept de knife an' clubs.
>
> Well sar, dem two niggers gits into de ring. Tom, dat am de Marster's nigger, him stahts quick lak him always do but de udder nigger stahts jus' as quick an' dat 'sprise Tom. It am de fust time a niggers jus' as quick as him.... Den it am hit, kick, bite, an' butt anywhar, anyplace, anyway fo' to best de udder. Fust one down an' de udder on top apoundin', den 'tis de udder one on top. De one on de bottom, bites knees or anything dat him can do. Dat's de way it goes fo' ha'f an houah....

> Finally dat udder nigger gits Tom in de stomach wid his knee an' a lick 'side de jaw at de same time. Down goes Tom an' de udder nigger jumps on him wid both feet, den straddles him an' hits wid right, left, right, left, right, side Tom's head. Dere Tom layed makin" no 'sistence.... Both am bleedin' an' am awful sight. Well, dat nigger relaxes to git his wind or something an' den Tom, quick lak a flash, flips him off an' jumps to his feet. Befo' dat nigger could git to his feet, Tom kicks him in de stomach, 'gain an' 'gain. Dat nigger's body stahts to quiver an' his Marster says, '"nough." Dat am de dostest dat Tom ever came to gittin' whupped dat I's know ob.

Finnely portrays an intensely brutal prizefighting match, ... [as] both contestants bled and subsequently produced an "awful sight." Indeed, as opposed to intraplantation matches for amusement purposes, "professional" slave prizefighting matches could be especially violent when big money was at stake, with the emphasis on employing any technique ... [to] win the contest.

However, it must be noted that Finnely ... enjoyed watching the fights, ... and that Tom, the fighter, did "lak to fight" in these contests. Additionally, as in the Bibb fight, the contest was not literally a fight to the death, and the master of Tom's opponent stepped in and ended the fight when his protégé's body started to "quiver."... [S]laves fighting on behalf of their master could expect certain privileges, such as reduced workloads, ... better diet, ... promotion to positions of authority on the plantation, respect from the slave community, and in rare instances manumission....

Fighting activities organized by slaveholders were hence not solely exploitative of enslaved men.... Fighting activities can ... act as a form of empowerment. In the context of slavery, the implications of this self-empowerment could be significant. To understand this idea, it is helpful to think of the "three bodies" theory utilized by Stephanie Camp in her research on enslaved women. For Camp, "Enslaved people ... possessed at least three bodies. The first served as a site of domination" .... on which the owner "inscribed" his authority. "The second body was ... the 'colonized body,' where "sexual and nonsexual violence, disease, and exploitative" labor were experienced. The third body was the "reclaimed body." In the struggle for mastery over bodies, enslaved women could reclaim this body from ... the master by seeking pleasure in activities such as dancing, drinking, and attending illicit parties. [T]third body potentially acted as a vital political site and source of resistance in opposition to the economic and symbolic imperatives of slavery. One can draw on this idea to analyze enslaved men as well: organized fighting activity under slavery served as a sphere in which male contestants were able to exercise mastery over their bodies....

Closely analyzing Finnely's narrative corroborates these observations. Finnely's choice of language is telling because of the references to stamina, speed and surprise, and strength. Their prominence suggests that they were specific qualities that were looked for in a match.... Finnely notes that the match was ultimately determined by endurance and stamina.... The elements of speed and surprise were also celebrated.... Certainly, speed and surprise ultimately clinched victory for Tom. He was pinned down and was dealt a series of blows to his head from the other fighter, but as the other man relaxed for an instant, … Tom then kicked the opponent repeatedly in the stomach until his body "quiver[ed]" and his master stepped in and called an end to the fight. Additionally, Tom's sheer strength and endurance are emphasized by his ability to come back from what seems to be the final barrage of blows.… The reference to the opponent's quivering body portrays Tom as the stronger and ultimately superior fighter. Tom had controlled his body, through stamina, speed and surprise, and strength, whereas his opponent had failed the test, allowing his body to shake, thus signaling the end of the match.

Moreover, the crucial point is that Tom proved he was master of his body and these qualities in the public sphere. Finnely underscores the importance of such public performance.… Tom's reputation as a fighter was … earned in the public eye of his fellow slaves and, indeed, of the whites who organized the fight.… Tom's fighting skills were challenged and tested.… Tom … answered the call to "best de udder" publicly, consequently proving himself to his peers. This idea of public display and "testing" is integral to David D. Gilmore's cross-cultural study of contemporary constructions of masculinity, which concludes that "manhood" for most males is a "critical threshold" that boys must pass through "testing."… For Gilmore, masculinity is something that has to be proved in the company of one's peers.… E. Anthony Rotundo has argued that a man's identity in early-nineteenth-century America "was inseparable from the duties he owed to his community." Rotundo terms this "communal manhood." Likewise, Bertram Wyatt-Brown has argued that in the antebellum white South a man's identity was decided among … "the larger 'family' of peers and superiors called community."

For enslaved men, possessing the skills and attributes of a fighter proved a vital source of self-respect and personal empowerment and a way to validate masculinity. Josiah Henson boasted in his fugitive slave narrative that he grew to be "a robust and vigorous lad" who, upon reaching fifteen years of age, could "run faster and farther, wrestle longer, and jump higher" than anybody else. Having a "robust and vigorous" body like Henson's not only endowed its possessor with pride and self-respect but also secured respect and admiration from others in the slave community. William Smith described his father as "a double-jointed man and very strong" and recounted how others would comment on his father's physique. "Man, was he strong!" said Smith; "de folks told me all about him … [H]e was all muscle. Even de mawster had told de others dat dey had better not fight him, 'cause he was so strong dat he could break dere necks." These "reclaimed" strong, muscular bodies could be celebrated as ideal masculine features for enslaved men, earning respect from other men and potentially attracting the attentions of enslaved women. Additionally, exhibitions of stamina, speed and surprise, and strength in the ring afforded enslaved men the opportunity to prove they possessed qualities useful for evading the patrol gangs that roamed the South.

Indeed, a fighter's "reclaimed" masculine body could also serve as a site of direct resistance to white oppression. Respondents in the WPA narratives recalled that fighters, owing to their huge build, could often resist whipping from whites and cause their owners problems. The Reverend Perry Sid Jamison, a former slave, remembered "one colored boy" who "wuz a fighter." "He wuz six foot tall and over 200 pounds" and "would not stand to be whipped by de white man."... The journal of former slave Wallace Tumage underscores how being "an expert wrestler" gave him the courage to stand and fight his overseer. Tumage describes how he "spoke very saucy" to the overseer when asked to account for his recent absence from the plantation.... These examples provide intriguing evidence to support Camp's suggestion that "the body, so personal, was also a political entity, a site of both domination and resistance." For enslaved men, the fighter's body was not necessarily exploited. Rather, the fighter's "reclaimed" body could serve as an important political site of resistance, a "symbolic and material resource" that was fiercely contested between the slave and the owner.

Most important, bouts of fighting were not organized and supervised solely by the slaveholders. Enslaved men at times coordinated their own fights, against the wishes of owners and in spite of the threat of punishment. Glascow Norwood stated that fights took place at dances, where the participants would "tie up and fight lack mad dogs." He continued, "dey had to keep de fights a secrete, fo' de owners ob de slaves sho' didn't like no fighting 'round you all see, hit wuz like dis, dey would get crippled up and wouldn't be worth nothing to wuk." Mark Oliver recalled that the slaveholders did not care how late the enslaved stayed up and danced; however, "the strictest rule they had was about fighting".... Indeed, not only did organized fighting potentially endanger the productivity of the slaveholder's labor force by rendering contestants "worth nothing to wuk," but it could also significantly devalue the slaves as property.... By engaging in organized fighting activities against the wishes of the owner, enslaved men could exercise mastery over their own bodies and thereby contest the owner's power. Determining the fate of each other's body, away from the view and control of the master, amounted to a form of resistance for enslaved men. Damaged bodies equated to reduced efficiency at work and ultimately devalued the slaves as property. In more extreme cases, death caused by organized fighting resulted in a significant loss of property for the slave owner." In the words of Stephanie Camp, these acts "had real and subversive effects on slaveholding mastery and on plantation productivity—both of which rested on elite white spatial and temporal control of enslaved bodies."

One former slave's testimony recorded by a WPA interviewer gives considerable detail concerning the recreational activities of the enslaved on a Saturday afternoon. One of the "sports" that the enslaved were "very fond of" was the "free for all":

> Here a ring was drawn on the ground which ranged from about 15 ft. to 30 ft. in diameter depending on the number of contestants who engaged in the combat. Each participant was given a kind of bag that was stuffed with cotton and rags into a very compact mass...[that] would weigh on an average of 10 pounds, and was used by the

> contestants in striking their antagonist. Each combatant picked whichever opponent he desired and attempted to subdue him by pounding him over the head with the bag.... The contest was continued in this manner till every combatant was counted out, and a hero of the contest proclaimed. Some times two contestants were adjudged heroes, and it was necessary to run a contest between the two combatants before a final hero could be proclaimed. Then the two antagonists would stage a battle royal and would continue ... till one was proclaimed victorious.
>
> Sometimes these Free-For-All battles were carried on with a kind of improvised boxing gloves ... Very often, as many as 30 darkies of the most husky type were engaged in these battles, and the contests were generally attended by large audiences ... mostly on Saturday afternoon; these physical exhibitions were the scenes of much controversial conflict, gambling, excessive inebriation and hilarity.

Although the narrative fails to explicitly state who organized these fighting contests, it does offer clues that these were likely slave-organized bouts.... Unlike some of the master-controlled contests in which owners matched the contestants, the enslaved in this instance were afforded a significant degree of agency. Furthermore, the large participation of the enslaved ... and ... references to ... the stuffed bags and padded "boxing gloves" suggest that this was not a bloody prizefight staged between two enslaved men chosen by the master, but rather a communal recreational activity organized by the enslaved community.

Viewed through David Gilmore's anthropological lens, the passage reveals how for enslaved men, the testing and proving of their fighting qualities could provide a significant validation of a masculine identity. The contest functioned on an elimination basis. After a man picked the opponent he desired, battle ensued, and "[t]he contest was continued in this manner till every combatant was counted out, and a hero of the contest proclaimed." In the words of one former slave, the object of such a match was "to see who was bes' on de plantation." The last man standing was crowned a "hero," and when two men were adjudged heroes, it was "necessary" to run a contest between the two before a "final hero" could be proclaimed. This "battle royal" would decide who was ultimately "victorious." These matches could function as a vital avenue for enslaved men to establish leadership roles, status, and rank among themselves and in the community in general. Those who made it toward the final stages of the contests would have gained the highest respect and reverence among their male peers.... Fighting contests held among the male population of the slave community were thus important arenas in which enslaved men could assert and display distinctly gendered identities, which were judged, recognized, and validated by their peers. In addition, qualities such as bravery, fairness, and expert knowledge of rules could also be displayed in public. As former slave Carter J. Jackson stated, "the best man whipped and other one took it."

Drawing on the insights of anthropologists who have studied West African wrestling practices, one can understand how wrestling matches and other similar fighting activities among the enslaved of the antebellum South functioned not only as a means of establishing male rank order and leadership roles but also as a "community-forming" ritual. Sigrid Paul's study of the wrestling tradition in Africa highlights that games and sports activities cannot be considered in isolation from their "sociocultural contexts."... In the majority of cases, wrestling functioned as a rite of passage for boys reaching puberty.... Wrestling served as a prerequisite of initiation into [age] groups. Wrestling ... contests were an important means of establishing male rank order, leadership roles, and friendship bonds, as well as fostering social solidarity within the village. Intervillage matches were also commonplace and proved crucial in establishing contact with other isolated villages and forming alliances. Collective competition against other villages bred solidarity and served to reify ethnic identifies. As Paul states, "whereas intervillage wrestling on the one hand functioned to establish and stress internal, local solidarity, on the other it both emphasized rivalry between contending groups and their mutual interdependence and potential solidarity at a wider regional level."

Paul's study ... provides insights into the functional importance of combat activities organized among the enslaved in the antebellum American South. Certainly, Desch Obi's recent analysis of African martial arts traditions in the Atlantic world notes that as in Africa, the enslaved in America "united and defined themselves as a new community via performance rituals." "[F]ar from being mere 'leisure,'" Desch Obi concludes, enslaved fighting activities were "nothing short of African-based community-forming and individual-empowering rituals." Furthermore, as in Africa, organized fights among the enslaved male plantation population could serve as an important sphere for male bonding and fostering group solidarity.... By organizing their own fighting bouts together on the plantations of the antebellum South, enslaved men could reaffirm the boundaries of a homosocial world that excluded enslaved women and the interference of the master. Plantation fights could thus dramatize sex roles and serve as a social act that underscored specific gendered demarcations cultivating male group solidarity.

Additionally, collective competition against neighboring plantations had the potential to promote stronger interplantation relations among men. By promoting interplantation contact and interaction, wrestling matches could emphasize, in the words of Sigrid Paul, "mutual interdependence" and "potential solidarity at a wider level." Conversely, fighting could serve in some cases to reify neighborhood differences and accentuate interplantation rivalry.... Harry Smith's slave narrative recounted an interplantation wrestling match that escalated out of control and degenerated into chaos. He recalled that during corn shuckings the slaves from the Plum Creek plantation formed a team called the Plum Creek Tigers and those from Salt River named themselves the Salt River Tigers. On one occasion, after they had been dancing and wrestling with each other, Smith picked a fight with one of the opposite boys.... Each team "urged the boys on," and fighting subsequently broke out among men from both plantations in "dead earnest." Smith described how some "hammered each other with the pickets until the white men came out with guns and threatened to shoot them if they did not stop." Smith's narrative demonstrates how fighting contests not only had the potential to bring men from other plantations together and thus cultivate cross-plantation alliances and friendships, but also could conversely accentuate interplantation rivalry and, in the process, further intraplantation solidarity and identity.

Smith's narrative raises an interesting issue, that of conflict. As indicated above, Sigrid Paul, in her research on traditional African wrestling, has found that wrestling contests functioned as a means of settling quarrels. Similarly, Desch Obi has noted that in Biafran society, wrestling could be used as a form of "conflict resolution." This was also the case among the slave communities of North America. For example, fighting matches could be staged between two men to settle a courting dispute. One former female slave recalled how two men fought over her; "dey bof' wanted me, an' couldn' decide no other way!" The ring was thus a place where disputes could be resolved and interpersonal tensions could be discharged. In this respect, organized fights could function as a form of social control. The ring could also be a place where a man's reputation was defended. Lula Jackson reported how an insult could trigger a contest: "[O]ne man would walk up to another and say 'You ain't no good.' And the other one would say, 'All right, le's see.' And they would rassle." However, it should be noted that fighting practices also had the potential to exacerbate antagonisms between two individuals as well as to foster solidarity between men....

The various accounts of fighting contests between the enslaved in the antebellum South offer an important window into the lives of those enslaved men who participated. In addition to the provider/protector roles that some enslaved men managed to perform under the dehumanizing system of slavery, organized fighting contests further offered enslaved men a significant avenue through which to recognize, affirm, and validate masculine qualities that were publicly displayed, tested, and judged among their peers.... [O]rganized fighting practices such as wrestling played an important role in the lives of some enslaved men. Whether the bouts were staged by the owner or by the enslaved themselves, male fighters could publicly display prized fighting attributes such as stamina, speed, surprise, and strength, consequently exercising mastery of their bodies—an important empowering feat when considered in the context of slavery. These fighting attributes had the potential to transform perceptions of the enslaved male body; physical virility learned and developed in the ring could also function as a political site of resistance to the slave owner's domination. Resisting whippings from overseers and disrupting the day-to-day productivity of plantation operations as a result of exercising bodily self-mastery and inflicting injury or even death on other slaves were everyday gendered forms of resistance by enslaved men. Moreover, slave-organized fights among men were both "individual-empowering" and "community-forming" rituals. Through these matches, enslaved men could rank and order themselves, consequently establishing status among one another and leadership roles in the male and wider communities. Not only was the ring a crucible in which masculinity could be tested and proved in front of peers, but it could also function as a sphere for fostering male bonding and solidarity, and a means of conflict resolution.

FURTHER READING

Adelman, Melvin L. *A Sporting Time: New York City and the Rise of Modern Athletics, 1820–1870* (1986).

Bennett, Bruce. "The Making of Round Hill School," *Quest* 4 (April 1965), 53–64.

Betts, John R. "Sporting Journalism in Nineteenth Century America," *American Quarterly* 5 (1953), 39–56.

Betts, John R. "The Technological Revolution and the Rise of Sport, 1850–1900," *Mississippi Valley Historical Review* 40 (1953), 231–56.

Betts, John R. "Mind and Body in Early American Thought," *Journal of American History* 54 (1968), 787–805.

Borish, Linda J. "Farm Females, Fitness and the Ideology of Physical Health in Antebellum New England," *Agricultural History* 64 (Summer 1990), 17–30.

Borish, Linda J. " 'Do Not Neglect Exercise nor Recreation': Rural New Englanders, Sport and Health Concerns," *Colby Quarterly* 32 (March 1996), 25–35.

Cogan, Frances B. *All-American Girl: The Idea of Real Womanhood in Mid-Nineteenth Century America* (1989).

Chisholm, Ann. "Nineteenth-Century Gymnastics for U.S. Women and Incorporations of Buoyancy: Contouring Femininity, Shaping Sex, and Regulating Middle Class Consumption," *Journal of Women's History*, 20 (Fall 2008), 84–112.

Dawson, Kevin. "Enslaved Swimmers and Divers in the Atlantic World," *Journal of American History* 92 (March 2006), 1327–1355.

Dyreson, J. K. "Sporting Activities in the American-Mexican Colonies of Texas, 1821–1835," *Journal of Sport History* 24 (Fall 1997), 269–84.

Fielding, Lawrence W. "War and Trifles: Sport in the Shadows of Civil War Army Life," *Journal of Sport History* 4 (Summer 1977), 151–68.

Freedman, Stephen. "The Baseball Fad in Chicago, 1865–1870: An Exploration of the Role of Sport in the Nineteenth Century City," *Journal of Sport History* 5 (Summer 1978), 42–64.

Geldbach, Erich. "The Beginning of German Gymnastics in America," *Journal of Sport History* 3 (Winter 1976), 236–72.

Goldstein, Warren. *Playing for Keeps: A History of Early Baseball* (1989).

Green, Harvey. *Fit for America: Health, Fitness, Sport, and American Society* (1986).

Kirsch, George B. *The Creation of American Team Sports: Baseball and Cricket, 1838–1872* (1989).

Levine, Peter. "The Promise of Sport in Antebellum America," *Journal of American Culture* 2 (1980), 623–34.

Lewis, Robert. "American Croquet in the 1860s: Playing the Game and Winning," *Journal of Sport History* 18 (1991), 365–86.

Park, Roberta J. "The Attitude of Leading New England Transcendentalists Toward Healthful Exercise, Active Recreation, and Proper Care of the Body: 1830–1860," *Journal of Sport History* 4 (Spring 1977), 34–50.

Park, Roberta J. "'Embodied Selves': The Rise and Development of Concern for Physical Education, Active Games and Recreation for American Women, 1776–1865," *Journal of Sport History* 5 (Summer 1978), 5–41.

Story, Ronald. "The Country of the Young: The Meaning of Baseball in Early American Culture," in Alvin Hall, ed., *Cooperstown Symposium on Baseball* (1991), 324–42.

Todd, Jan. *Physical Culture and the Body Beautiful: Purposive Exercise in the Lives of American Women, 1800–1870* (1998).

Vertinsky, Patricia. "Sexual Equality and the Legacy of Catharine Beecher," *Journal of Sport History* 6 (Spring 1979), 39–49.

Whorton, James C. *Crusaders for Fitness: The History of American Health Reformers* (1982).

CHAPTER 4

The Making of a Modern Sporting Culture, 1840–1870

American sport began a dramatic transformation in the mid-nineteenth century, a period when sport was premodern and primarily participatory. Sport at that time defined manly behavior as aggressive, vigorous, courageous, and unchildlike. However, during this era, sport began to modernize, and the stage was set for the sporting boom of the post–Civil War period.

How was this achieved? How important was it to transform sport from a morally suspect amusement into a respectable and progressive recreation? What was the role of the new positive sporting creed and the development of modern sports?

The United States in the 1830s and 1840s was in the midst of the Second Great Awakening, a religious revival that anticipated the Second Coming of Christ. The movement raised the religious consciousness of middle-class evangelical Protestants who strongly opposed the pastimes of the male bachelor subculture on moral grounds. Secular reformers who felt that such uncivilized behavior was inappropriate for citizens of a Great Republic also opposed traditional amusements. They chastised gambling and blood sports for attracting the worst elements in society, teaching idleness and debauchery, and for not recreating participants and spectators.

Religious and secular reformers joined forces during the Jacksonian Era to create the first great period of American social reform when they sought to raise moral standards, fight slavery, promote democracy, and cope with problems of urban growth such as slums, drunkenness, rising crime rates, and epidemics. Many of these reformers, like Thomas Wentworth Higginson and Catharine Beecher, envisioned physical culture and clean outdoor sports as a potential answer to many social problems.

A positive sports creed emerged that recognized the possibility that clean sports could provide an alternative to vile games and promote public health, improve morality, and develop character. Good role models were provided by immigrant sports organizations like the German Turnverein, which emphasized gymnastics. Several sports became popular, including cricket, croquet, and cycling, but the most important was the new team game of baseball, which soon became the national pastime. Baseball and cricket particularly seemed to fit in well with the requirements of the new positive sports creed. These two games, as baseball became more difficult and dangerous to play, were perceived as manly sports that promoted health, built character, and promoted morality. The sports creed not only promoted sports but also influenced the growing park movement, which in turn encouraged municipalities to set aside public space to facilitate healthful, uplifting recreations. The first such space was Central Park in New York, which was completed in 1858 and designed to include special places for games like baseball and cricket. However, park planner Frederick Law Olmsted, who supervised the construction of Central Park, personally preferred receptive (inactive) recreation that protected the park's grounds over active (sporting) recreation, and his vision had a great impact on the park's early use.

DOCUMENTS

Document 1 is drawn from the classic essay "Saints and Their Bodies," written in 1858 by the Rev. Thomas Wentworth Higginson, a Boston Brahmin and a leading social reformer. He, like many other reformers, was a champion of physical fitness. Higginson was a "muscular Christian" who advocated the union of a sound mind, body, and spirit. Document 2 is by Catharine Beecher, a member of a famous New England family, an early feminist, and one of the leading advocates of athletic activity for women. Beginning in 1832 with *Course of Calisthenics for Young Ladies*, Beecher had long encouraged physical fitness by recommending walking, swimming, horseback riding, and exercises to alleviate women's frailty. In *Letters to the People on Health and Happiness* (1855), she evaluated American women and offered suggestions for alleviating their ill health. Document 3 is a compilation of rules for the New York Knickerbockers for baseball on September 24, 1845 formulated collectively by leading club members, including Alexander Cartwright, William Rufus, Daniel Lucius Adams, William R. Wheaton, William H. Tucker, and Louis F. Wadsworth, most of whom had played a version of baseball with other clubs. These rules defined the New York version of baseball, which became the national pastime. Document 4 describes the newly popular co-ed sport of ice skating at Central Park, which opened in New York City in 1858 and became a model for municipal park construction after the Civil War. Document 5 is an 1859 editorial from the *New York Herald* that compares baseball and cricket. The editor lauded both sports but explains why baseball had more popular appeal. Document 6 is an essay from the *Spirit of the Times*, a highly influential middle-class sports weekly, that praised the formation of the first major nonethnic athletic society in America, the New York Athletic Club, which became the model for future high-status athletic clubs in the United States.

1. Thomas W. Higginson Analyzes the American Clergy and Their Need for Physical Fitness, 1858

... There is in the community an impression that physical vigor and spiritual sanctity are incompatible.... But, happily times change.... Our moral conceptions are expanding to take in that "athletic virtue" of the Greeks.... The modern English "Broad Church" aims at breadth of shoulders, as well as of doctrines.... [Kingsley's]

From Thomas W. Higginson, "Saints and Their Bodies," *Atlantic Monthly* 1 (March, 1858), 82–95.

critics charge him with laying down a new definition of the saint, as a man who fears God and can walk a thousand miles in a thousand hours....

... One of the most potent causes of the ill-concealed alienation between the clergy and the people, in our community, is the supposed deficiency, on the part of the former, of a vigorous, manly life.... What satirists upon religion are those parents who say of their pallid, puny, sedentary ... offspring, "He is born for a minister," while the ruddy, the brave and the strong are as promptly assigned to a secular career!...

Physical health is a necessary condition of all permanent success. To the American people it has a stupendous importance, because it is the only attribute of power in which they are losing ground. Guarantee us against physical degeneracy, and we can risk all other perils,—financial crisis, Slavery, Romanism, Mormonism, Border Ruffians, and New York assassins.... Guarantee us health, and Mrs. Stowe cannot frighten us with all the prophesies of Dred; but when her sister Catharine informs us that in all the vast female acquaintance of the Beecher family there are not a dozen healthy women, we confess ourselves a little tempted to despair of the republic.

The only drawback to satisfaction in our Public-School System is the physical weakness which it reveals and helps to perpetuate.... The teacher of a large school in Canada went so far as to declare to us, that she could recognize the children born this side of the line by their invariable appearance of ill-health....

There are statistics to show that the average length of human life is increasing; but it is probable that this results from the diminution of epidemic disease, rather than from any general improvement in *physique*.... Indeed, it is generally supposed that any physical deterioration is ... peculiar to the United States....

No one can visit Canada without being struck with the spectacle of a more athletic race of people than our own. On every side one sees rosy female faces and noble manly figures....

* * *

Who, in this community, really takes exercise? Even the mechanic commonly confines himself to one set of muscles.... But the professional or business man, what muscles has he at all? ... Even to ride sixty miles in a day, to walk thirty, to run five, or to swim one, would cost most men among us a fit of illness, and many their lives. Let any man test his physical condition, we will not say by sawing his own cord of wood, but by an hour in the gymnasium or at cricket, and his enfeebled muscular apparatus will groan with rheumatism for a week. Or let him test the strength of his arms and chest by raising and lowering himself a few times upon a horizontal bar, or by hanging by the arms to a rope, and he will probably agree with Galen in pronouncing it *robustum validumque laborem*. Yet so manifestly are these things within the reach of common constitutions, that a few weeks or months of judicious practice will renovate his whole system, and the most vigorous exercise will refresh him like a cold bath.

To a well-regulated frame, mere physical exertion ... is a great enjoyment, which is, of course, enhanced by the excitement of games and sports. To almost every man there is joy in the memory of these things; they are the happiest associations of his boyhood....

* * *

But, as far as there is a deficiency in these respects among us, this generation must not shrink from the responsibility. It is unfair to charge it on the Puritans. They are not even answerable for Massachusetts; for there is no doubt that athletic exercises, of some sort, were far more generally practiced in this community before the Revolution than at present. A state of almost constant Indian warfare then created an obvious demand for muscle and agility. At present there is no such immediate necessity. And it has been supposed that a race of shopkeepers, brokers, and lawyers could live without bodies. Now that the terrible records of dyspepsia and paralysis are disproving this, we may hope for a reaction in favor of bodily exercises.

... In one way or another, American schoolboys obtain active exercise. The same is true, in a very limited degree, even of girls. They are occasionally, in our larger cities, sent to gymnasiums,—the more the better.... A fashionable young lady is estimated to traverse her three hundred miles a season on foot; and this needs training. But outdoor exercise for girls is terribly restricted, first by their costume, and secondly by the remarks of Mrs. Grundy.... Still, there is a change going on, which is tantamount to an admission that there is an evil to be remedied. Twenty years ago, if we mistake not, it was by no means considered "proper" for little girls to play with their hoops and balls on Boston Common; and swimming and skating have hardly been recognized as "lady-like" for half that period of time.

* * *

... American men, how few carry athletic habits into manhood! The great hindrance, no doubt, is absorption in business; and we observe that this winter's hard times and consequent leisure have given a great stimulus to outdoor sports. But in most places there is the further obstacle, that a certain stigma of boyishness goes with them. So early does this begin, that we remember, in our teens, to have been slightly reproached with juvenility, because, though a Senior Sophister, we still clung to football. Juvenility! We only wish we had the opportunity now.

2. Catharine Beecher Criticizes Women's Frailty and Recommends What Should Be Done About It, 1855

You have read often of the Greeks. Some twenty centuries ago ... they were remarkable, not only for their wisdom and strength, but for their great beauty, so that the statues they made to resemble their own men and women have, ever since, been regarded as the most perfect forms of human beauty.

The chief reason why they excelled ... was the great care they took in educating their children. They had two kinds of schools—the one to train the minds, and the other to train the bodies of their children. And though they

From Catharine Beecher, *Letters to the Healthy on Health and Happiness* (New York: Harper & Bros., 1855), 9, 107–8, 120–33, 172.

estimated very highly the education of the mind, they still more valued that part of school training which tended to develop and perfect the body....

But the American people have pursued a very different course. It is true that a large portion of them have provided schools for educating the minds of their children; but instead of providing teachers to train the bodies of their offspring, most of them have not only entirely neglected it, but have done almost every thing they could do to train their children to become feeble, sickly, and ugly. And those, who have not pursued so foolish a course, have taken very little pains to secure the proper education of the body for their offspring during the period of their school life.

In consequence of this dreadful neglect and mismanagement, the children of this country are every year becoming less and less healthful and good-looking. There is a great change in reference to this matter within my memory. When young, I noticed in my travels the children in school-houses, or on Sunday in the churches almost all of them had rosy cheeks, and looked full of health and spirits. But now, when I notice the children in churches and schools, both in city and country, a great portion of them either have sallow or pale complexions, or look delicate or partially misformed....

★ ★ ★

Every year I hear more and more complaints of the poor health that is so very common among grown people, especially among women. And physicians say that this is an evil that is constantly increasing, so that they fear ere long, there will be no healthy women in the country.

... A change is possible.... Nothing is needed but a *full knowledge* of the cause, and then the *application of that practical common-sense and efficiency to this object....*

I have been led to this effort by many powerful influences. More than half of the mature years of my own life have been those of restless debility and infirmities, that all would have been saved by the knowledge contained in this work.

... The more I traveled, and the more I resided in health establishments, the more the conviction was pressed on my attention that there was a terrible decay of female health all over the land, and that this evil was bringing with it an incredible extent of individual, domestic, and social suffering, that was increasing in a most alarming ratio....

In my own family connection, I have nine married sisters and sisters-in-law, all of them either delicate or invalids, except two. I have fourteen married female cousins, and no one of them but is either delicate, often ailing, or an invalid. In my wide circle of friends and acquaintance all over the land out of my family circle, the same impression is made. In Boston I can not remember but one married female friend who is perfectly healthy.

... The thing which has pained and surprised me the most is the result of inquiries among the country-towns and industrial classes in our country. I had supposed that there would be a great contrast between the statements gained from persons from such places, and those furnished from the wealthy circles, and especially from cities. But such has not been the case....

★ ★ ★

Next to pure air, *healthful exercise and amusements* are the most important remedies for the evils set forth.

3. The New York Knickerbocker Rules of Baseball, 1845

1st.—Members must strictly observe the time agreed upon for exercise, and be punctual in their attendance.

2nd.—When assembled for exercise, the President, of in his absence, the Vice-President, shall appoint an Umpire, who shall keep the game in a book provided for that purpose, and note all violations of the By-Laws and Rules during the time of exercise.

3rd.—The presiding officer shall designate two members as Captains, who shall retire and make the match to be played, observing at the same time that the player's opposite to each other should be as nearly equal as possible, the choice of sides to be then tossed for, and the first in hand to be decided in like manner.

4th.—The bases shall be from "home" to second base, forty-two paces; from first to third base, forty-two paces, equidistant.

5th.—No stump match shall be played on a regular day of exercise.

6th.—If there should not be a sufficient number of members of the Club present at the time agreed upon to commence exercise, gentlemen not members may be chosen in to make up the match, which shall not be broken up to take in members that may afterwards appear; but in all cases, members shall have the preference, when present, at the making of the match.

7th.—If members appear after the game is commenced, they may be chosen in if mutually agreed upon.

8th.—The game to consist of twenty-one counts, or aces; but at the conclusion an equal number of hands must be played.

9th.—The ball must be pitched, not thrown, for the bat.

10th.—A ball knocked out of the field, or outside the range of the first and third base, is foul.

11th.—Three balls being struck at and missed and the last one caught, is a hand-out; if not caught is considered fair, and the striker bound to run.

12th.—If a ball be struck, or tipped, and caught, either flying or on the first bound, it is a hand out.

13th.—A player running the bases shall be out, if the ball is in the hands of an adversary on the base, or the runner is touched with it before he makes his base; it being understood, however, that in no instance is a ball to be thrown at him.

14th.—A player running who shall prevent an adversary from catching or getting the ball before making his base, is a hand out.

15th.—Three hands out, all out.

16th.—Players must take their strike in regular turn.

From *Rules and Regulations of the Knickerbocker BaseBall Club*, Adopted September 15, 1845.

17th.—All disputes and differences relative to the game, to be decided by the Umpire, from which there is no appeal.

18th.—No ace or base can be made on a foul strike.

19th.—A runner cannot be put out in making one base, when a balk is made on the pitcher.

20th.—But one base allowed when a ball bounds out of the field when struck.

4. The *New York Times* Recommends Skating at Central Park, 1859

Such a throng of skaters and spectators as collected yesterday at the Central Park has never before been equaled. The City cars were absolutely insufficient to accommodate the crowds that flocked to the skating carnival. From daylight until after dark the stream of visitors was continuous, including all ages, sexes and conditions in life, from the ragged urchin with one broken skate, to the *millionaire* in his richly-robed carriage. The Park presented a scene of brilliancy and animation more enlivening than on any day of the popular Saturday afternoon concerts, while the healthful glow on every cheek was a flattering testimonial to the efficacy of this noble breathing-spot of the City. Although the early comers had no very good skating to boast of, they certainly had a decided advantage over those who deferred the visit until late in the afternoon, for long before mid-day the ice was in a most deplorable condition.

The Caledonia Club, and their rivals in the manly sport of curling, were among the first on the pond, and were for a time busily engaged in practicing for their contemplated match. But, as the crowd increased, it was found impossible to keep a place sufficiently clear for them, while the cracking, cutting-up, sinking and melting ice finally compelled an abandonment of the match for the day. But the skaters, to the number of several thousands, in the face of obstacles that would have deterred any but New Yorkers, and perhaps even them on any other day, persisted in their evolutions, rejoiced in their gyrations, and exhibited their skill by tortuous meanderings through the crowd,—presenting an exhilarating scene equal to the liveliness of a thousand ball-rooms. The collisions, the tumblings down, the wetting of clothing, the uncertain foothold of the beginners, as well as the skill of amateurs, afforded ample recreation to all and especially to the thousands who lined the banks. The drives commanding a view of the pond were crowded throughout the day, while at one time as many as a hundred carriages were drawn up near the shore to afford the occupants an extended view.

The number of ladies in vehicles and on foot was quite remarkable, and it was a common sight to see a gentleman with two pairs of skates on one arm, and a bundle of crinoline on the other. But few ladies, however, participated in the skating, partly owing to the bad condition of the ice on the pond appropriated to

---

From "The Skating Carnival: Great Rush to the Central Park" [editorial], *New York Times*, December 27, 1859.

their use, and partly from the fact that they prefer to enjoy the sport by moonlight, when they are not so conspicuous. Had the ice permitted yesterday, a class of ladies would have been instructed in the art; but as it was, they had to postpone their lesson. Their diminutive ponds were flooded in the afternoon, so that the first cold snap will atone for yesterdays disappointment.

The condition of the ice in the afternoon was a source of general regret, but did not prevent the majority from attempting the fun in spite of the lowering of the signals that the pond was in good condition. So great was the crowd on the narrower and southern position of the pond, that about 1 P.M., the Police had orders to clear it. This was no easy task, for the skaters had rather the advantage of their pursuers, and darted hither and thither with a celerity that baffled the authority of the meagre force of the Central Park Police. At length a string of laborers was stretched across the pond, and, advancing, cleared nearly all before them—those who sifted through being captured by the officers, and the unruly ones taken to the station-house. In this way that portion of the pond was cleared in three quarters of an hour, most of the people leaving quietly upon request. But the effort to pursue the same plan on the larger portion of the pond, above the new iron bridge, signally failed. The agile skaters dodged the Police line easily, for the sweeping-machine could not be made to extend the width of the pond. If the sweepers went in the middle, the skaters nimbly slid by at the ends. If the sweepers undertook to spread out, the skaters sailed fleetly under their hands.

In vain did the officers of the law become indignant and exasperated and irate. The plan wouldn't work; and they finally gave up in sheer despair, contenting themselves with the reflection that if the people would run the risk of getting soaked, or even drowned, it wasn't their fault. So the skating went on unmolested, and the little boys took especial pains to collect in crowds near the signs of "danger." Yet no serious accident occurred, as there doubtless would have been had the facilities for getting on the pond been greater. Fortunately the sinking of the ice at the edges left a circuit of water about two inches deep and three feet wide, which made all without skates run the risk of wet feet before joining the crowd of skaters. It is to be hoped that either the Croton Board or the thaw will allow the pond to be speedily flooded so that ice may be formed which will not be as rough as a mill-stone.

One thing the skaters ought to understand and appreciate, and that is, that the police regulations are for their own comfort and safety, and should be obeyed with that alacrity which has characterized the orderly conduct of the great majority of visitors to the Central Park.

5. The *New York Herald* Compares Cricket and Baseball, 1859

Cricket … has not extended much … for two reasons: first, because base ball—an American national game—was in possession, and was too like cricket to be superceded by it, and secondly, in the points on which it differs from cricket it

From "Comparing Cricket and Baseball" [editorial], *New York Herald*, October 16, 1859.

is more suited to the genius of the people. It is rapid and simple. Even if there were no base ball in existence cricket could never become a national sport in America—it is too slow, intricate and plodding a game for our go ahead people.

Base ball has been from time immemorial a favorite and popular recreation in this country; but it is only within the last fifteen years that the game has been systematized and clubs formed for the purpose of playing at stated periods and under a code of written laws. The Knickerbocker Club, for New York, organized in 1845, was the first and since then numerous clubs have sprung up in this city and Brooklyn, and throughout the country. But the great increase has been within the last three or four years....

The good effect produced on the health and strength and morals of the young men engaged in this outdoor exercise is the theme of all who are conversant with them. It has taken them from the unhealthy haunts of dissipation indoors, and given them a taste for manly sport which cannot fail to have a beneficial effect, not only in the physical development of our citizens, but on the national character. No 'refreshments' are allowed on the occasion of matches, which are visited by thousands of spectators, including a large number of ladies.

★ ★ ★

... There is great art in pitching and the pitcher's position in base ball corresponds with the bowler's in cricket, though not quite so important. The ball must be pitched, not jerked, nor thrown, that is, the hand is held down to the hip or below it, and it must be aimed for the centre of the home base, or at the batman. It must not touch the ground before it reaches the batman, but the art of pitching consists in throwing it with such force that the batman has not time to wind his bat to hit it hard or so close to his person that he can only hit a feeble blow.... The batman strikes overhand at the ball. In cricket, he strikes underhand, because the ball is thrown low, and must strike the ground before it reaches the batman.

... In cricket the batman is never compelled to run till he thinks proper, so that he has rarely any risk in making at least one run of sixty feet between the two wickets.... If he has time he runs back again, and counts another, and so on.... Hence the English game is so slow and tame, and the American so full of life. In the latter the player is compelled to go. If the ball is caught, either flying or on the first bound from the earth, after being struck with the bat, the batman is put out without counting; or if it is held by the adversary on the first base before the striker touches it, or if at any time he is touched by the ball in the hands of an adversary without some part of his person being on the base. Formerly it was sufficient to strike the adversary with the ball by throwing it at him. This practice is now abolished as it was dangerous and unnecessary to the game....

The base ball bat must be round.... The cricket bat is flat.... In cricket the batman has his legs cased in leather for protection, and so has the wicket keeper who stands behind him to catch the ball after it glides off his bat or hand. The wicket keeper has also strong gloves. Behind the batman in base ball stands a catcher, who, if he catches the ball flying or on the first hop puts out the batman. Thus the batman in both games correspond, also the pitcher corresponds with the bowler, and the catcher with the wicketkeeper, and these three are the men who, in both games, do the principal part of the work. In both games each man on each side must take the bat, in turn; in both games a bowler and a pitcher, a wicket keeper and a catcher are selected for their peculiar skill, and they play those parts throughout....

In base ball the game centres around the bases; in cricket it centres around the wickets. In base ball the batman, when he runs, is put out by being touched with the ball when he is off his base. In cricket the batman is put out if he is caught outside of an enclosure in front of the wicket by his adversary, who does not touch him with the ball, but knocks down his wicket either by throwing the ball at it or by throwing it to the wicket keeper or any other player, who, with ball in hand, knocks it down. Thus running and throwing and catching are equally important in both games.

In the game of cricket the wicket consists of three round stakes, called stumps, placed upright in a row, twenty-seven inches out of the ground, and on the top is placed a small piece of wood called a bail ..., which ... with the least touch given to it or the stumps, it comes off, and puts the batman out. There are two of these wickets, pitched opposite to each other, at a distance of twenty-two yards ...; at each of these stands a batsman to defend them with the bat against being knocked down by the ball ... Cricket is played by eleven on each side. The eleven who go in—that is, get first possession of the wickets and bats ..., send two of their number to take those positions, and the remaining nine continue out of play till they are called in succession ... until the whole eleven are thus put out.... Each side has two innings.... The object of the batman is to score by runs between the wickets; the object of his adversaries is to prevent him, by knocking down his wicket with the ball. The attack is made on the wicket which he has both to defend and make the runs as best he can. If his wicket is fairly down he is put out, and another ... takes his place. The bowler from beside one of the wickets bowls at the opposite one to knock it down. The batman stops the ball with his bat or strikes it away. In this consists the greatest art of the game. The ball must be bowled, and ... the hand must not be above the shoulder when delivering the ball ... Sometimes the bowler bowls it with great force and very low, direct for the wicket.... Sometimes the artful bowler throws the ball ... at an angle, in order to deceive, and gives it a twist when leaving his hand, which makes it come right to the wicket.... If the batman drives the ball out of the bounds, it is called a "lost ball," and counts six for him without running.... If a ball is caught in the air without touching the ground no run is reckoned, but the striker is not put out....

★ ★ ★

... There is only one bowler on the ground ... but after every fourth ball the bowler changes over and bowls at the other wicket. The batman who guards that wicket which is not bowled has the privilege of making his run to the other wicket, when the ball is struck, just the same as the striker, and they generally run together, crossing each other.

★ ★ ★

The only points in which the base ball men would have any advantage over the cricketers, in a game of ball, are two—first, in the batting, which is overhand, and done with a narrower bat, and secondly in the fact of the ball being more lively, hopping higher, and requiring a different mode of catching. But the superior activity and practice of the Eleven in fielding would amply make up for this, even if they have not already practiced base ball....

In cricket a very smooth ground is wanted on account of the bowling as the ball must strike the ground before it reaches the batman or strikes the wicket, and every obstruction on the surface would spoil the bowling. In base ball very smooth ground is not required, but a rather larger space than is necessary for cricket....

... It occupies on an average about two hours to play a game of base ball—two days to play a game of cricket.

From the foregoing description and comparison for the two games, the reader will see that base ball is better adapted for popular use than cricket. It is more lively and animated, gives more exercise, and is more rapidly concluded. Cricket seems very tame and dull after looking at a game of base ball. It is suited to the aristocracy, who have leisure and love ease; base ball is suited to the people. Cricket is the better game for warm weather, base ball when it is cold. In cricket, those actually engaged except three—the bowler, the batman and the wicket keeper—do little or nothing three-fourths of the time; and for half the day, sometimes longer, nine out of one side are not on the field at all. In the American game the ins and outs alternate by quick rotation, like our officials, and no man can be out of play longer than a few minutes. Still, the game of cricket is one of great merit and skill, and we should be glad to see it cultivated by all who have sufficient time for the purpose. Both games seem suited to the national temperament and character of the people among whom they respectively prevail.

6. The *Spirit of the Times* Examines the Founding of the New York Athletic Club, 1868

We have very great satisfaction in announcing that the first semi-annual games of the New York Athletic Club will take place upon November 11th. It is a gratifying fact that healthy and strengthening pastimes are daily growing into greater favor with the community, which the vitality and the increasing prosperity of the athletic organizations in this city amply testify. We believe that the benefit of such institutions as that to whose exhibition we have alluded can not be too highly appreciated by any class of the people; but we would more especially urge their value on the youth of our cities and colleges, whose business pursuits and recreations are unexceptionally of a sedentary character. To those young men who are for many hours of the day excluded from air and exercise, the cultivation of their physical power becomes a necessity if they would escape the doom of early

From *Spirit of the Times* 19 (October 10, 1868): 121.

senility; and it must necessarily be through their exertion and combined support if these organizations are to become permanent and flourishing....

The New York Athletic Club, although but in its infancy, shows remarkable promise of becoming the leading institution of its kind in this country, and will, doubtlessly, in course of time, fill the same position in this country occupied by the London Athletic Club in England. The club was founded some few months ago by a number of gentlemen who were fully aware of the benefits to be derived from such an organization, and foresaw the probable advantage to be subsequently gained from it by the young men of New York. The prospects are undoubtedly encouraging, and give considerable assurances of success; but we would suggest that, in order to complete the organization and render it perfect, those designing to become members (who hesitate, thinking the club insufficiently formed) should at once join and put their shoulder to the wheel, and in a very short time every obstacle will be no more. It cannot be expected that a club like the present can become an accomplished fact without some little difficulties have been wrestled with and successfully overcome. It is the intention of the members of the club to extend its patronage to all species of gymnastics, rowing, swimming, and skating; but at present the funds of the organization being unequal to the fulfillment of these designs, it has been determined to institute a series of semi-annual games, in which pedestrianism is to take the prominent position.... In the spring of 1869 the ... grounds for the club ... on which a running track will be constructed and the necessary buildings erected. In its efforts to acquire stability and strength, the New York Athletic Club has our hearty support and cordial approval, believing as we do, that in such recreations becoming dear to the young men of the nation, we have an additional safeguard against the truth of the dismal doctrine of the degeneration of the human species.

In the approaching games the various Caledonian clubs of this city have been invited to contest, so that a very interesting exhibition may be looked for with confidence. The exercises comprise jumping, leaping, racing, putting the shot, and throwing the hammer. Naturally enough, the Caledonian Club, which has for so long occupied the most prominent position as an athletic club in this city, will strain every nerve to keep ahead of its friendly but vigorous rival.... For its approaching exhibition the club has secured the Empire City Skating Rink, an enormous structure with a ground-floor and raised seats, having a capacity to accommodate an audience of at least ten thousand persons. As the display will take place by gaslight, a very large attendance may be anticipated.

ESSAYS

The first essay by John R. Betts, a pioneer in the scholarly study of sport, is a seminal study in American sport history that was published in the prestigious *Journal of American History* in 1968. Betts argues that the interest in mind and body goes back to the Enlightenment, European educational innovators, and romanticism. Their ideas were picked up by American educators, physicians, and journalists in the 1840s who sought to counter the problems of urbanization and industrialization by improving men and women's health, character, and morality by getting them involved in clean, uplifting sports. Their ideas, and the emergence of elevating sports like gymnastics and baseball, led to the popularization of sport among the middle class.

The second essay, by George B. Kirsch of Manhattan College, the author of several important books on American sport, examines the growth of baseball as a spectator sport as it evolved from an amateur to a professional game, with particular attention to the behavior and social composition of baseball crowds. The term "baseball" dates back to the eighteenth century, but the first game of what we would recognize as modern baseball was played in 1845 in Brooklyn between the New York Nine and the Brooklyn Club, prior to the first game played by the Knickerbockers, which was against the New York Nine one year. A decade later, there were over 125 teams in metropolitan New York.

The Making of a Positive Sports Ideology in Antebellum America

JOHN R. BETTS

The [*American Journal of Education* in 1826-27] pointed out the need for city playgrounds and gymnasiums, as well as the benefits of hunting, cricket, handball, and golf. Boston's *North American Review* cited James G. Carter's *Essays upon Popular Education*, while the Boston Medical Intelligencer described the decline of gymnastics during the Middle Ages and its revival by Guts Muths, [Friedrich] Jahn, and company. Robert Dale Owen had been a student at Fellenberg's Hofwyl, where he joined in the public games, annual walking tours, and daily gymnasium exercises, which he considered so conducive to vigor, health, good temper, morality, and intellectual vitality. Francis Neefe, the Pestalozzian, was attracted to New Harmony, Indiana, whose *Gazette* discussed the values of gymnastics....

Gymnastics were introduced in Massachusetts, New York, and Virginia almost simultaneously. Jefferson and the organizing trustees provided for gymnastic exercises at the University of Virginia in 1824; William Bentley Fowle of the Boston Monitorial School declared, "I hope the day is not far distant when gymnasiums for women will be as common as churches in Boston"; John Griscom, who had visited the schools of [Swiss educators Johann] Pestalozzi and [Philipp von] Fellenberg, introduced gymnastics into his New York high school; and George Bancroft, acquainted with the influence of Pestalozzi and [Johann] Fichte in Berlin's schools, joined with Joseph Cogswell in organizing the Round Hill School in Northampton, Massachusetts. Round Hill played an historic role. Though they would provide a liberal education, Cogswell and Bancroft announced, "We would also encourage activity of body, as the means of promoting firmness of constitution and vigor of mind, and shall appropriate a regular portion of each day to healthy sports and gymnastic exercises." In the *Prospectus* of 1823, claimed

---

From John R. Betts, "Mind and Body in Early American Thought," *Journal of American History* 54 (September 1968): 793–805, by permission of Oxford University Press.

they were "the first in the new continent to connect gymnastics with a purely literary establishment." Calisthenics, the mile run on the school's own track, archery, tumbling, games, and long walking trips were part of the daily schedule. To Round Hill came a disciple of Jahn, Charles Beck, who constructed a gymnasium and translated his master's *Treatise on Gymnasticks*, saying that play and enthusiasm could counteract pecuniary ambitions absorbed early in life.

Emigré scholars followed Beck in extending the movement. Charles Follen, newly appointed at Harvard, opened a school gymnasium and then founded the Boston (Tremont) Gymnasium in 1826. When he resigned his position, he expressed the hope that the gymnasium would "spread over all this free and happy land." In his *Lectures on Moral Philosophy*, the young German scholar claimed that "this methodical exercise of every part of the human frame, is the only way to make the body a sure and well- trained servant of the mind, always ready to obey its master's call." German idealism had influenced a number of intellectuals, including Ralph Waldo Emerson, Theodore Parker, and Margaret Fuller; and Follen was one of the links to idealist literature.

Francis Lieber, who was familiar with the idea of the gymnasium and the Turner movement, accepted an invitation extended by a group in Boston to come ... from London in 1827. The German scholar wrote, "... I only want benevolent and sincere intention from those citizens, who declared to patronize the Gymnastics, this important branch of education." In a visit with Lieber at Boston, the sixty-one-year-old President John Quincy Adams plunged into Lieber's swimming pool from a six-foot springboard. Adams remarked that he hoped there would be many similar establishments to improve public health. The President thought that swimming was superior to gymnastic exercise, after hard intellectual exertion.

New Englanders were adopting gymnastics. Henry and Sereno Dwight opened a New Haven gymnasium. Apparatus was secured by the Mount Pleasant Classical Institute in Amherst, the Berkshire Gymnasium at Pittsfield, and the Woodbridge School at South Hadley. Amherst, Brown, Williams, Bowdoin, and Andover Seminary students participated in the sport. School journals deplored the endless hours of rigid posture in tiny, over-heated classrooms. Philip Lindsley from Princeton, the new president of the University of Nashville, advised: "Attach to each school house a lot of ten acres of land, for the purpose of healthful exercise, gardening, farming, and the mechanical arts." The true university would teach a broad spectrum of literary and scientific subjects and would include fencing, riding, swimming, and gymnastics. Frontiersmen had their rail splitting, ploughing, turkey shoots, and brawls on county-court day; but physical education was moving into the West and South on the coattail of the educator.

College enthusiasm waned as manual-labor experiments were introduced, and apparatus on some school and academy greens rusted with age. Even so, Richard Henry Dana found Harvard students exercising at cricket, football, boxing, fencing, and swimming. Academies, well-established by 1820, entered their golden age in the next two decades, years marked by a rising middle class as well as more education-oriented rural communities. Typical of the most progressive academies, in terms of physical education, were the Dummer School,

Phillips Andover, Exeter, Chauncy Hall, and Salem Latin in New England; in New Jersey there was the Lawrenceville School; and more than two thousand academies, many military in nature, appeared in the South. Football (soccer style) was popular at Exeter by 1800, and after-school games proved a diversion to boarding students everywhere. Both Emma Willard at Middlebury, Vermont, and Zilpah Grant at Derry, New Hampshire, sprained ligaments during calisthenics.

Educators and physicians were increasingly cognizant of the dependence of mental health upon physical well-being. Even the decline in the mortality rate was ascribed, in part, to physical education. Dr. William P. Dewees of the University of Pennsylvania Medical School urged imitating European educators in promoting exercise: "The play of a child is a sort of intellectual occupation. The mind at this age prompts to perpetual exercise and noisy motion." Gymnastic exercise, he concluded, gives "tone and vigour to all parts of the body," and improves morality as well. Though public concern for health had been limited in the past, reformers were now aroused by George Combe's *Constitution of Man* (1828) and by Dr. Andrew Combe's *Principles of Physiology* (1834). The latter recalled Sinclair's *Code of Health* and declared that social play and sports were more meaningful than aimless walking. One scholar has observed, "American health reformers cited the Combes [book] as theologians cited the Bible."

The *Journal of Health*, published by an association of Philadelphia physicians, proposed following the example of Sheffield, England, and providing public gymnasiums and baths open to the laboring classes at a minimal fee. An advocate of *mens sana in corpore sano*, the *Journal* printed articles on calisthenics, riding, and sports, paid court to the goddess of health, cited Strutt's *The Sports and Pastimes of the People of England*, and apparently approved John Frost's lecture to Middlebury students on the benefits of sparring. Mind and body were indissolubly linked in human development. The young woman was urged to dance in moderation and to ride horseback without corset and buckles (which prevented "the free expansion of her chest") as a cure for nervousness, tremors, palpitation, paleness, headache, indigestion, and poor appetite. Such riding often did "more good than all the art medicinal." The *Journal* saw a variety of benefits of exercise: gymnastics were an antidote for hypochondria, and golfers in Scotland had frequently lived an extra decade. It also ranked the lack of exercise with such "poisons of modern invention" as rum, tobacco, and tea as a cause of the physical decline of modern man.

Physical strength of Americans in an urban society was inferior to that of their ancestors ... according to many reformers. The *New York Mirror* became concerned over health and physical degeneration, claimed "a healthy man in New York would be a curiosity," regretted the early fading of women's beauty, deplored the routine of schools, colleges, and seminaries, noted the total neglect of exercise in all social classes, and appealed for more writing on the subject of health. Businessmen foolishly excused their inactivity as the result of lacking time, and thousands were going to unnecessarily early graves.

Health faddists were on the march. Sylvester Graham, a temperance lecturer, concerned himself with vegetarianism, overindulgence, adequate sun-light, bathing, dress reform, sex hygiene, and exercise. The Graham journal of *Health and*

Longevity appeared in 1837 and related physical fitness to great achievement. Plato, Aristotle, Cicero, and Caesar had appreciated the dependence of a sound mind on a healthy body, it was argued, and so had Shakespeare, Gibbon, Byron, Scott, and Davy. The *Boston Health Journal and Advocate of Physiological Reform* carried Graham's appeal. He found exercise a tonic, thought horseback riding a preventive of pulmonary consumption, and warned, "Aged people, after they have retired from the active employments of life, must keep up their regular exercise, or they will soon become feeble and infirm."

Medical men rivaled health cultists in discussing physical fitness. Dr. William A. Alcott edited the *Moral Reformer and Teacher on the Human Constitution.* His *Library of Health* encouraged swimming and gymnastics and praised exercise as a means of avoiding consumption. The profession was especially concerned with the war on cholera, yellow fever, influenza, and other epidemics, but the well-being of individuals was thought to hinge in good part on exercise. Dr. John Collins Warren spoke to the American Institute of Instruction on the importance of physical education and lectured annually thereafter on the value of exercise in the development of the organic structure of the body. A study of muscular action was presented in *Human Physiology* by Dr. Robley Dunglison of the University of Virginia, while Dr. John Jeffries discussed "Physical Culture The Result of Moral Obligations" in the *American Quarterly Observer.*

The plight of the American woman's physical development and health was emphasized in the medical and physiological writings of such physicians as William Alcott, E. W. Duffin, J. M. Keagy, Charles Caldwell, John Bell, Caleb Ticknor, and Abel L. Peirson. Alcott cited the English girl's vigor in his *Young Woman's Guide to Excellence* as a curative for deformity of the spine and noted Pestalozzi's influence. Caldwell, a student of [American Dr.] Benjamin Rush, had toured Europe and held the chair of medical and clinical practice at Transylvania University when he published *Lectures on Physical Education* in 1834 and *Thoughts on Physical Education* in 1836. The doctor noted the increase of insanity and dyspepsia, which he blamed on political and religious agitation and the pursuit of wealth. Observing Dr. William Beaumont's discovery of the role of gastric juices in digestion, Caldwell recommended abandonment of excessive mental exertion, regulation of passion, and the practice of muscular exercise. Physical education, he contended, was vital to the destiny of the republic: "Its aim should be loftier and more in accordance with the destiny and character of its subject to raise man to the summit of his nature. And such will be its scope in future and more enlightened ages." John Bell related exercise to femininity and grace in *Health and Beauty: An Explanation of the Laws of Growth and Exercise.* Caleb Ticknor discussed walking and riding in his *Philosophy of Life.*

Abel Peirson, who had studied in Paris, edited the *Medical Magazine.* The prejudice against girls exercising in the open air, he declared, was aggravated by the passing of the spinning wheel with its muscular demands and by the imposition of a social code which permitted only sledding and battledore as feminine sport. Poor girls! "There is no amusement which could be contrived, better suited to improve the shape of females, by calling into action all the muscles of the back, than the game of billiards. But this game has unfortunately come into bad repute, from being the game resorted to by profligate men of pleasure, to destroy each other's health, and pick each other's pockets." According to the learned doctor, French women surpassed other Europeans in lightness of step, symmetry of form, and retention of agility and vivacity into old age. From duchess and leader of *ton* to chambermaid and peasant girl, this vitality was due to the French love of dancing. Feminist leaders also championed physical education for women. Catherine Beecher pioneered with *Suggestions respecting Improvements in Education* (1829) and *Course of Calisthenics for Young Ladies* (1831); Mary Lyon at Mount Holyoke inaugurated a callisthenic quadrille; and Margaret Coxe featured exercise in her *Young Lady's Companion* as an antidote to the ravages inflicted by a half century of increasing luxury.

The wakening spirit caught hold of the educational movement. Professor Edward Hitchcock of Amherst cited the case of President Timothy Dwight of Yale as an example of the restorative powers of walking. He claimed that three or four hours daily were not too much to devote to moderate outdoor activity. Statistically, he found that 186 great men of ancient, medieval, and modern times had lived to the average age of seventy-eight, possibly due to physical culture as well as constitutional endowments. Andover seminarians heard Dr. Edward Reynolds of Boston deplore "the measured ministerial walk." "Look at Germany," he advised, and imitate the ancients: "The same necessity which sent Plato and Aristotle to the gymnasium after severe mental labor, still exists with the hard students of our day." Princeton's *Biblical Repertory* lauded the intellectual benefits of rational gymnastics:

> They not only minister present health, but look forward prospectively to firmness of constitution in subsequent life. Most of the Gymnastic games, also, are of a social kind, and awaken an intense interest in the competitors; absorbing the attention, sharpening the perception, and communicating alertness to the motions of the mind as well as the body. Thus they become invaluable auxiliaries to the more direct methods of promoting intellectual culture.

Theodore Weld's Society for Promoting Manual Labor in Literary Institutions encouraged active sports: "Their effects upon the economy are universal—are felt everywhere. A glow of pleasure, as indescribable as it is exquisite, diffuses itself over all the organs.... The vigor of the intellect is revived, and study once more becomes easy and successful." Publisher Mathew Carey acknowledged the importance of Weld's work.

Other testimonials to exercise were given by numerous professors, ministers, and leading citizens. Thomas Grimke of Charleston declared the habit of exercise "creates a greater capacity for mental labor, a more enduring energy, a loftier enthusiasm, a more perfect harmony in the whole system of intellectual powers." Francis Wayland, president of Brown University, recommended three hours of exercise per day: "No man can have either high intellectual action, or definite control over his mental faculties, without regular physical exercise. The want of it produces also a feebleness of will, which is as fatal to moral attainment as it is to intellectual progress." In his inaugural address, Mark Hopkins of

Williams claimed many students spent too much time in drinking, smoking, and eating rather than in exercises such as sawing wood, walking, or gardening. "It is now agreed," he observed, that the health of the body is to be one great object of attention, not only for its own sake, but from its connection with a sound state and vigorous action of the mind. The editor of the *American Annals of Education and Instruction*, William Channing Woodbridge, duly recorded the views of the *Boston Medical and Surgical Journal* and discussed the sports of children. Samuel R. Hall recognized play as the only source of pleasure for some school children, because "brilliancy and force of thought are the natural fruits of activity." And Orestes Brownson commented on the "Necessity and Means of Physical Education" at the American Institute of Instruction.

Thought on exercise in the age of Jackson focused upon the common schools. The *New York Mirror* in 1833 warned: "The seeds of many diseases, which sweep hundreds and thousands ..., are planted at school by the injudicious ambition of teachers, who entirely overlook the body in their efforts to over-cultivate the mind. Parents forget, in their zeal to clothe the brows of their children with the early laurel for the triumphs of learning that learning itself is valueless without health...." Pedagogues became aware of the refreshment of the mind provided by exercise. Victor Cousin's widely discussed *Report on the State of Public Instruction in Prussia* revealed that all Prussian primary schools supported gymnastic exercises, for graceful carriage strengthened "the good qualities of the soul." Jacob Abbott's *The Teacher* recommended battledore and softball at recess. The Essex County Teachers' Association in Massachusetts called for a quarter-acre area for play and exercise at each schoolhouse. Alexander Dallas Bache asserted, "A system of education, to be complete, must combine moral, intellectual, and physical education." Commissioned by Nicholas Biddle and the trustees of Girard College to study European schools, Bache noted the presence of commons or playgrounds for every school on the Rugby model. Central High School in Philadelphia and Houston Public School in New York featured the playground. Entering upon his historic superintendency of Massachusetts schools and aware of the new conditions of urban life, Horace Mann read the *Constitution of Man* in 1837. Thus he commenced a long friendship and correspondence with George Combe, whom he considered the greatest living man. The first issue of Mann's *Common School Journal* appeared in 1838, asserting the involvement of mind and body and expressing dismay over the deterioration of the health of people: "Mental power is so dependent for its manifestations on physical power, that we deem it not extravagant to say, that if, amongst those who lead sedentary lives, physical power could be doubled, their mental powers would be doubled also.... Gradually and imperceptibly a race may physically deteriorate, until their bodies shall degenerate into places, ... wholly unfit to keep a soul in."

During the 1830s sports gained a foothold in the press because of the rising interest in horse racing, prize fights, and walking matches. Popular publications were the *American Turf Register*, the *Spirit of the Times*, Horatio Smith's Festivals, *Games and Amusements*, Robin Carver's *Book of Sports*, and a few manuals on archery and games, treasured by lucky youngsters.

The rise of sports coincided with the social changes of the times—for example with the growth of an affluent middle class in the North and a leisured aristocracy in the South. It coincided with the emergence of a spirit of reform: interest in Utopian experiments, women's rights, penal legislation, capital punishment, a peace crusade, care of the insane, temperance, public education, and the abolition of slavery. Greater attention to outdoor recreation may also have been related to unemployment and the depression of the late thirties and early forties. At any rate, labor editors concerned themselves with health and with the shorter work day. Men puzzled over the flaws in an urbanizing society. Albert Brisbane, a popularizer of Fourierism, charged American schools with hostility to both Nature and health; corporal dexterity and health, he thought, "were sources of Internal riches." Only a few reformers, however, seriously advocated increased attention to public health and better conditions for the working classes and the poor, ... recommended by William Ellery Channing in 1840, by Dr. Lemuel Shattuck in his study of the overcrowding and the tenement life of Boston, and by the first report of the *New York Association for the Improvement of the Condition of the Poor* (1845).

Sporting and athletic interest increased in the early forties as reports of English activities became more common. Pierce Egan's *Book of Sports* and Donald Walker's *British Manly Exercises* capitalized on the acquaintance of many with *Bell's Life in London*, the *Sporting Magazine*, and James Gordon Bennett's *Herald,* which pioneered in sports news. The transcendentalist *Dial* even published Henry David Thoreau's translation of Pindar's *Olympic Odes*. Walt Whitman used the columns of the *Brooklyn Daily Eagle* in the mid-forties as a forum for discussing school playgrounds. In a pre-Freudian speculation on a young boy's drive for power, Emerson observed: "In playing with bat-balls, perhaps he is charmed with some recognition of the movement of the heavenly bodies, and a game of base or cricket is a course of experimental astronomy, and my young master tingles with a faint sense of being a tyrannical Jupiter driving spheres madly from their orbit." In the early forties, too, Caldwell's *Thoughts on Physical Education* (1836) and Dr. J. Lee Comstock's *Outlines of Physiology* (1837) were reissued and remained popular. Shortly before his historic surgical experiment with Dr. William Morton's ether at Massachusetts General Hospital, Dr. Warren published his lecture in expanded book form and urged open-air exercise for factory workers.

Though specialization had begun to crowd discussion of personal hygiene and exercise out of professional medical journals, popular interest seemed to persist and grow. The water-cure system of Vincent Priessnitz of Silesia, who came to the United States in 1831, stressed walking, skipping, jumping, and running, "but what lady dare do these things in these days of refinement?" The perils of urban comfort brought a revival of the gymnasium. Sheridan's gymnasium in New York catered to clergymen, lawyers, physicians, merchants, artists, artisans, and schoolboys. Harvard scholars in 1842 worked out under T. Belcher Kay, instructor in "the art of self-defense" to Francis Parkman, who prided himself on "a rapid development of frame and sinews." In New Haven, however, activity lagged badly. A student commented on the contrast with Cambridge in England: "There is one great point in which the English have the advantage over us: they understand how to take care of their health ... every Cantab takes his two hours' exercise per diem, by walking, riding, rowing, fencing, gymnastics, &c. How many Yalensians take one hour's regular exercise?..." Taking note, men of Yale and Harvard formed sculling crews in 1843 and 1844.

Despite obstacles and even some religious objections, progress in physical culture continued. Playgrounds were adopted in Cincinnati.... New York state schools recognized the need of muscular exercise, and teachers "in almost every school district" were said to have access to Andrew Combe's *Principles of Physiology*. Illustrative of professional activity were the work of the American Physiological Society by 1837 and the publication of *Human Physiology for the use of Elementary Schools* by Dr. Charles A. Lee. Charles Dickens, though noting the American deficiency in exercise and being shocked by the emaciated prisoners of New York's Tombs, visited the Perkins Institute in Boston and found blind boys engaged in active sports, games, and gymnastics. George B. Emerson lent the prestige of his name to the encouragement of walking, riding, gardening, sleighing, and general. exercise in the open air and sunlight. In the *Sixth Annual Report of the Board of Education* Mann expounded on the oxygenizing of the blood through "the athletic exertions of manual labor or of gymnastic sports," far superior to passive activities like sailing. Lack of space in cities led to physical degeneration, Mann thought, but he was pleased with recreational improvements in the schools during the decade up to 1845. Dr. David Thayer's gymnasium, he observed, was a boon to Boston clerks, students, lawyers, and clergymen; and he similarly praised Mrs. Hawley's gymnastic school for young misses. The Michigan superintendent of education, O. C. Comstock, declared exercise was "essential to physical health, mental vigor and delightful study."

Urban people, grappling with the need for schools and sound pedagogy, also faced mounting sanitation, housing, and health problems in a society marked by its high mortality rate. The labor of immigrant workers on canals and railroads and in factories and the vigorous life of farmers and frontiersmen more than met their requirements of physical activity. But there were impediments for others, such as old myths about night air and fashionable prejudices against athletic women. Early Victorian society in England, having reached a more advanced stage of industrialism, might hunt the fox, attend Ascot, encourage schoolboy games, introduce athletics and rifle shooting into the army and the military academies, and become disciples of Isaak Walton; but their contemporaries in America required an extra generation or two before the leisure provided by a maturing industrial system would become general enough to extend the health and sporting interests of the privileged classes to the populace at large. Religious hostility to amusement and recreation proved to be a continuing deterrent, and social acceptance of the machine raised doubts about the value of bodily strength and muscle. Still, the development of a nationwide system of education, the encouragement of child-centered educational programs, the immigrant's fondness for his active games, and the fear of physical degeneration made a breakthrough in attitudes toward recreation and sport by the late thirties and early forties. Rowing clubs in Boston, New York, Philadelphia, Savannah, and Detroit; throngs attending thoroughbred racing and trotting; matches between runners, pedestrians, and prize fighters; formation of numerous hunting and fishing clubs; sailing and yachting clubs in Atlantic coastal communities and on the Great Lakes; adoption of mass football, gymnastics, cricket, or crew at eastern colleges—all bore witness to the sporting fever.

Mind and body were more intimately related to one another by the development of a native literature of pedagogues and physicians, by an awareness of English concern for exercise and German educational reforms, and by a mounting public recognition that the Puritan gospel of work lost some of its validity in a highly commercial, urban environment. Outdoor life took on greater appeal in the romantic call back to the solitude or to the primitive challenge of Nature; the woodland haunts of "Frank Forester" (Henry William Herbert) lured the angler and the hunter. Emulation of the frontiersman's vigor contributed to the mounting concern over the debility of college students, the fair sex, office workers, and children in the crowded tenement. Soon the voices of Edward Everett, Thoreau, Oliver Wendell Holmes, and others would aid the cause.

Events of the mid-forties were prophetic of things to come. As the nation looked to the threat of war with Mexico, the New York Yacht Club organized, and the Knickerbocker Club established the rules of baseball. In the near future German forty-eighters would establish Turner societies, Scottish Caledonians would introduce their native games, and Irish crewmen would race in city regattas. Only in the generation after the Civil War would expectations be realized; but in the quarter century between 1820 and 1845 educators, physicians, and reformers had begun to develop a philosophical rationale concerning the relationship of physical to mental and spiritual benefits derived from exercise, games, and sports. From the diffusion of ideas developed by the medical profession under the influence of the Enlightenment and by educators and reformers affected by the romantic spirit, Americans were alerted to the threat against their physical and mental powers that came with the confinements of the home and school and the more sedentary habits of the city.

Baseball Spectators, 1855–1870

GEORGE B. KIRSCH

... On August 23, 1860 about 15,000 people packed around ... [the Putnam Base Ball Club's grounds in Brooklyn] to witness the deciding game of the championship series between the Atlantics and the Excelsiors. These two crack teams had split the opening contests—the Excelsiors won the first easily, but lost the second by a single run. The excitement among the baseball fraternity was intense, as rumors circulated that the Excelsiors would not be allowed to win a close contest. During the early play one of the Atlantics agitated part of the

---

From *The Creation of American Team Sports: Baseball and Cricket, 1838–72*.

crowd by refusing to yield immediately to an umpire's call. Then, in the top of the sixth, with the Excelsiors ahead, 8–6, a group of rowdies renewed their "insulting epithets and loud comments on the decision of the umpire." Joseph Leggett, the Excelsiors captain, warned the spectators that his team would withdraw if the hooting continued. Members of the Atlantics then appealed to their supporters to let the game go on, as one hundred policemen tried to restrain the unruly crowd. But the troublemakers only increased their yelling and abuse of the umpire and the Excelsiors, promoting Leggett to order his players off the field. A large crowd pursued them, and pelted their omnibus with stones as they drove off. Most newspapers blamed the disorders and interference on gambling, and condemned the behavior of those spectators who had disrupted the contest. It was unfortunate that "sports which are healthful and respectable in themselves should be rendered disreputable by their surroundings, commented the *Brooklyn Daily Eagle*, which then added that "a little further decadence will reduce the attendance at ball matches to the level of the prize ring and the race course."

[This episode] provide[s] dramatic proof of the importance of spectators during the formative years of baseball.... Interclub and special all-star matches were more than just competitions among the players. They were also public entertainments and major events in the recreational life of thousands of city dwellers. To fully understand the cultural aspects of modern sport in the United States during the formative years, it is thus important to know who attended these contests, why they came, how they experienced them, and how they influenced the games and the sports themselves....

During the early years of team sports in America, amateur clubs generally did not restrict attendance at their matches. An early cricket manual defined the policy that baseball officials also observed: "It is always a proper courtesy, and tends to the popularity of this noble exercise, to allow any respectable and quiet strangers to come on the ground to witness either play or practice; but it is always good policy, likewise to have it understood by the visitors that it is a privilege, not a right." Before the 1860s promoters charged admission fees only for the all-star baseball games and international cricket contests. Since spectators also had to pay for their transportation, these special matches tended to attract those from the middle- and upper-income groups. When leading teams played interclub games on neighborhood ball grounds, however, especially in Brooklyn, Newark, and Jersey City, the crowds included many people who were not financially comfortable. For example, when the Knickerbockers played the Excelsiors before about 6,000 people in August 1859, it was noted that "a means of rational enjoyment was offered freely to all who chose to avail themselves of it, the only passport requisite being, orderly conduct while on the ground, thus giving to those of the community whose circumstances prohibit their participation in any sport attended with expense, an opportunity to relieve themselves temporarily at least of the cares and anxieties of daily life." On Boston Common, at Camac's Wood in Philadelphia, at Hoboken's Elysian Fields, and at virtually all of the early ball fields, both blue- and white-collar workers and their families watched amateur antebellum team sports.

After the Civil War promoters and clubs charged an admission fee for many of the top matches, in part because they wished to exclude spectators from the poorer classes. Yet there is considerable evidence that baseball games continued to draw fans from a wide variety of social groups during the 1860s. In describing the huge throng that attended an 1865 contest between New York's Mutuals and Brooklyn's Atlantics, the *Clipper* noted that it was composed of all classes, with minority representation of "roughs," the "blackleg fraternity," and pick-pockets. An 1867 upstate New York championship game brought out a mixed collection of "judges, lawyers, bankers, doctors, clergymen, merchants, clerks, mechanics, students, railroad men, laborers, farmers, officials, editors, printers' devils, boot-blacks, and so on, all anxious to see a good game." …

The events that generated the most excitement and attracted the largest crowds before the Civil War were … the 1858 New York City versus Brooklyn all-star series at the Fashion Race Course … and the 1860 Atlantic versus Excelsior matches in Brooklyn. Most of these drew crowds of at least 5,000, with a few going well over 10,000. Many who came to the first of the Fashion Course baseball games were prosperous, arriving in fancy wagons and coaches. But apparently not all who watched the third and deciding game were as well heeled, for "a large deputation of overgrown boys from Brooklyn occupied a prominent position in the Grand Stand, and they materially interfered with the pleasure of the game by their noisy and very partial comments on the decisions of the Umpire, when unfavorable to the Brooklyn Nine…."

The popularity of early American baseball … cannot be judged solely by the numbers who witnessed these special matches, because they were exceptional public amusements that received a great deal of newspaper publicity. A better indicator of the relative appeal … is the attendance at the regular contests among the leading and lesser clubs. In New York, Brooklyn, Philadelphia, Boston, and a few other large cities the premier baseball games regularly attracted a few thousand people, despite inconvenient travel and hot weather. The *Clipper* estimated the throng at the 1865 Mutuals–Atlantics match to be between 18,000 and 20,000….

People attended these early sporting events for widely different reasons, and experienced them in as many different ways. Players frequently appeared at important matches to observe the skills of their fellow athletes and future opponents. Sportswriters such as Henry Chadwick stressed the aesthetic appeal of baseball—they commonly referred to "the beautiful game of baseball"—and often presented a detailed critique of the quality of the play, and complimented clever … pitching, fine fielding, and strong batting. Charles King Newcomb, a Philadelphia man of letters, thought that baseball provided object lessons in art and science….

Many spectators enjoyed hard hitting, while others appreciated the fine points of scientific batting and acrobatting fielding…. But the *Clipper* complained that "the majority of spectators of a ball match are ignorant of what constitutes scientific batting, and consequently they applauded only the long, heavy hits for home runs. It criticized both the lively balls then in use and the tendency of batters to try to satisfy the fans' desire to see the long ball…. Other writers considered fielding to be the "essence of the game" and lobbied for the elimination of the rule permitting an out when a ball was caught on the first bound, arguing that taking it "on the fly" was more difficult and more exciting for spectators.

The advent of unofficial championships and open professionalism after the Civil War drew thousands to ballparks, but also raised suspicion about the legitimacy of some of the contests, which sometimes dampened enthusiasm among the fans. The rivalries among the Athletics, Atlantics, Mutuals, Red Stockings, and other great teams certainly stimulated interest. But as admission fees became more common during the late 1860s, journalists began to demand that the patrons of baseball get their money's worth. Several newspapers complained about clubs that charged a price for practice or exhibition games. In 1866 Philadelphia's *Sunday Dispatch* scolded the Athletics for displaying a "miserly spirit" in collecting ten cents for an intrasquad session "wherein the players are only anxious to 'keep their hands in,' and not to show their skill." The *Clipper* took the Atlantics and the Athletics to task for not informing the public in advance about whether several contests were exhibitions or regular matches.

According to several of the sporting weeklies, rumors of fixed games did reduce the size of the crowds.... The *Clipper* asserted that games that called out 10,000–15,000 spectators in 1867 and 1868 did attract 5,000 fans in 1869. The following year the *Spirit* explained that only 1,000 people witnessed a Chicago White Stockings victory over the Atlantics because the Brooklyn club was "getting into such bad repute, from the constantly flying rumors of 'sells' and 'thrown' games, that few people care to expend their time and money in going to witness what may turn out to be merely a 'hippodroming' exhibition."

... After the Civil War the baseball boom fed a gambling fever, especially at championship matches. In 1867 a reporter for the *Newark Daily Advertiser* described the scene at an Athletic–Atlantic game: "a few men, with their hands full of greenbacks, were walking around the skirts of the crowd calling for takers of bets at a hundred dollars to twenty that the Athletics will beat two to one." He estimated that "over one hundred thousand dollars changed hands." The next year, pools of bets were sold at a game between the Atlantics and the Haymakers of Troy, New York. According to the *Troy Budget*, it was "lamentable to see what an extent the betting mania reaches." The paper declared that betting "pervades all classes. At the game played with the Mutuals on Tuesday women brought their money and bet on their favorite Haymakers to the last cent in their possession. We hear of Lansingburg sewing girls who sent down their five, ten, and twenty dollars each by male friends to bet on the Haymakers."

While the artistry of players, the excitement of the competition, and the chance to profit were all major attractions of early American team sports, many also enjoyed the spectacles that the leading events provided. As Warren Goldstein has pointed out, there were important similarities between the cultures of baseball and the theater during this era. The sportsmen played out the drama of a match on their special stage, dressed in costumes that symbolized their club affiliation. Like the world of the theater, baseball had associations with both respectable society and the less reputable life of Victorian popular amusements.

People flocked to games for many of the same reasons that they came to see plays that were produced for the masses; their tastes were both high-brow and low-brow. Some simply wanted to watch an exciting contest on a beautiful day, while others anticipated a good time spiced with some liquor and wagering....

The special events that drew thousands produced a carnival atmosphere, as the great crowds attracted con men, tradesmen, vendors, and thieves. At the Fashion Course series spectators arriving at the entrance encountered "thimble-riggers and card sweaters" who were trying to swindle a few dollars out of the "greenies." At the second game between the Atlantics and Excelsiors in August 1860, on the outskirts of a huge throng of onlookers were "various itinerant tradesmen and vendors of eatables and drinkables." Fans crowded into fancy colored tents to quench their thirst with beer or stronger spirits, such as "Jersey lightning," which increased the business of the police force. Pickpockets plagued these contests and others, prompting newspapers to report their activities and warned people to be on the alert. After the war pickpockets flocked to feature events, "such a favorable opportunity seldom occurring for picking up stray pocket-books, watches, etc." At an 1867 game between the Mutuals and the Irvingtons several "Newark rowdies" staged a fight in order to give some thieves an opportunity to work the crowd.

Most sports clubs made a special effort to encourage ladies to attend their matches by providing them with tents, seats, refreshments, and other accommodations. Sportsmen believed that female spectators would enhance the respectability of their pastimes while restraining the behavior of males in the crowds. The sporting weeklies and daily press cooperated by urging women to patronize both cricket and baseball. The *Brooklyn Daily Eagle*, for example, recommended baseball as "a rational and manly pastime, which our wives, sisters, and sweethearts can witness, and enliven us with their presence, without the fear of a word or deed that would call the blush to the cheek of the most fastidious." Frank Queen, editor of the *Clipper*, solicited the approval of the ladies for the new sports. Although he suspected that women came to sporting events primarily for social reasons, he wanted the ladies to exert their positive influence on troublemakers: "Let our American ladies visit the cricket grounds, the regattas, the baseball matches, and the most rough or rude among the spectators would acknowledge their magic sway.... When ladies are present ... no class of our population can be found so debased as not to change their external behavior immediately, and that change is always for the better...."

... Females did appear in sizeable numbers at ballgrounds, especially for the premier interclub and all-star contests. On several occasions they showed their approbation of the new sport as moral, wholesome recreation by presenting the participants with American flags or bouquets of flowers.... [D]elegations of women frequently participated in postgame awards rituals. Newspaper descriptions of their attire suggest that most of the women who attended these matches, albeit primarily for social reasons, were form the "respectable" classes. Others came out of curiosity or because of the beauty and excitement of the play. More than a few were well-posted on the fine points of the sport and were vociferous fans.... Some women apparently joined in the gambling, as well—for example at the second game of the 1858 Fashion Course series, "in many instances ladies were found exchanging little wagers among themselves." Whatever their motives, their appearance at ballgames proved that team sports had become respectable recreations for the American middle class....

The presence of female spectators at baseball and cricket matches proved that the two sports had achieved respectability, but it is doubtful that the women really inspired the players or restrained the hecklers, gamblers, and rowdies.... Heated rivalries generated much emotion, which led to physical and verbal interference and fighting by club followers and assorted troublemakers. Baseball players and club managers were sensitive to the problem of crowd control, and attempted to cope with it by appeals to the spectators, which usually worked. Some of the Brooklyn baseball clubs owned their own grounds, and hired police to maintain order and to remove objectionable persons. Brooklyn's Excelsiors enjoyed a reputation for preserving peace at their field in South Brooklyn, while the Atlantics at Bedford did not control their grounds and therefore had more trouble with spectators. On a few occasions, such as the deciding game of the Atlantic–Excelsior series of 1860, even the police were unable to restrain the crowd.

During the amateur era most of the baseball matches were played on open grounds. When thousands appeared to witness a contest, clearing the field of spectators was no easy task, and keeping them away from the players during the game could also be difficult. Generally the crowd cooperated by staying behind lines marked as bounds, but sometimes club followers got too close to the action—for example, outfielders might have to retrieve balls from amongst a forest of legs.

Fights and other disturbances among boys and men in the crowds also created problems for baseball clubs. In July 1860 a Jersey City resident reported that "spectators are seriously annoyed on the Hamilton's grounds by the misconduct and noise of rude and rowdyish boys." He urged officials "to see that good order is preserved, and that the nuisance caused by groups of yelling, hooting and wrestling boys mixing themselves with the quiet spectators, and sometimes insulting the visiting club, should be prevented." ... An old-timer remembered that in the 1860s the conduct of the players was excellent, but he recalled "many nasty melees among spectators after the games." He ... followed "an adherent of the Atlantics ... several blocks to a drugstore where his wounds from [a] gunshot were treated. Near-riots were frequently the results of clashes between hucksters and drivers who on top of their vehicles in Columbia av. hurled remarks at each other until these ended in fistic encounters. But this was all off the field of honor." There were also a few fights between white and black spectators, including one at Charleston, South Carolina in 1869.

The intense partisanship that frequently marked baseball matches reflected a contentiousness that plagued most antebellum American cities. Urban violence and mob activity were commonplace in the divided and tumultuous world of these fast-growing centers. The riot which ended the Atlantic–Excelsior series was only a symptom of the nationalism and social class antagonism that troubled many communities—the Irish, working-class Atlantics versus the Excelsior gentlemen, for example. A *Clipper* editorial identified the true cause of all urban disorder as "the *spirit of faction* ... in which the foreign element of our immense metropolitan population, and their native offspring, especially, delights to indulge." While noting that gambling contributed to the trouble, that periodical stated that the real evil lay in "the bitterness of party spirit and sectional strife," in fire department fights, in lower-class gangs, and in sectarian religious jealousies. "In short," it continued, "whether it is 'our country,' 'our party,' 'our company,' 'our club,' or 'our church,' the same evil spirit rules the actions and paralyzes the virtuous tendencies of all who succumb to its baneful influence, replacing kindly feelings with bitter hatred, and manly emulation and generous rivalry with revengeful retaliation." According to the *Clipper*, the remedy lay "in the self control of contending clubs and parties, and in a strict adherence to the rules that guide the actions of a man of honor and a gentleman." Of course, proper conduct in the world among the contestants did not guarantee peace and quiet among the spectators. When issues of social class or nationality appeared, as they apparently did in the Atlantic–Excelsior matches of 1860, there was always the potential for problems in the crowd.

The commercialization of baseball after the Civil War did not bring any drastic changes in the behavior of audiences. Some promoters and enthusiasts thought that the coming of more enclosed grounds and admission fees ranging from ten to fifty cents for most games would restrict spectators to a more select and well-mannered crowd. But this was not usually the case, in part because many from the lower classes were willing to pay to see the feature events. Also, thousands of fans congregated outside the fences and often found ways to view the sport over or through the barriers. One reporter marveled at the numbers waiting at the entrance to deposit their quarters to see a Mutuals–Athletics contest in 1867: "One would imagine that in these times of high rents and low wages that the patronage of the base ball arena would be somewhat limited at such a high tariff as a quarter of a dollar; but the fact is a quarter is nothing for such an hour or two's exciting sport as a well contested ball match yields."

Those who were unable or unwilling to pay often could still see the action (and create a disturbance). When the Athletics routed the Atlantics in 1868 at the Union Grounds at Williamsburg, Brooklyn, "several thousands managed to witness the game without disbursing the required admittance fee." The *Clipper* reported: "Owners of trucks and other vehicles drove a brisk trade by stationing their establishments close to the high fence surrounding the ground, and letting out 'standing room only' to those who preferred this method of looking on. Others secured the prominent 'peek-holes' in the fence, while others still, after the game was under way and the attention of officers was centered in the exciting contest, boldly took up their position on the fence and held them to the close."

Charging admission to enclosed fields did lead to better accommodations for ladies, the press, and the general paying public, but it did not eliminate fan interference, fights, or crowd disorders. An 1866 contest between the Athletics and the Atlantics ended in the bottom of the first inning after a fight between police and spectators and a rush of people onto the field disrupted play. Fisticuffs in the stands were commonplace.... People who paid twenty-five or fifty cents for admission also fought over good seats, and were enraged when others blocked their view or that of their lady friends....

[Baseball achieved popularity] by providing chances for betting, excitement, excellent play, and gambling at a colorful and respectable public amusement.... Thousands of people attended the special contests that excited the sporting fraternity, while smaller but equally enthusiastic crowds witnessed lesser matches. Early amateur ... baseball gave the players a chance to exercise and have fun, while creating a new form of public recreation that all could enjoy. As fans flocked to these ball games for their own particular reasons, they also experienced them in their own special ways. Baseball provided its great popularity and showed its potential for commercialism which promoters would exploit after 1865....

FURTHER READING

Adelman, Melvin L. *A Sporting Time: New York City and the Rise of Modern Athletics, 1820–1870* (1986).

Akers, Dwight. *Drivers Up! The Story of American Harness Racing* (1938).

Berryman, Jack W. "Sport, Health, and the Rural-Urban Conflict: Baltimore and John Stuart Skinner's American Farmer, 1819–1820," *Conspectus of History* 1(1982), 43–61.

Betts, John R. "Sporting Journalism in Nineteenth Century America," *American Quarterly* 5 (1953), 39–56.

Betts, John R. "The Technological Revolution and the Rise of Sport, 1850–1900," *Mississippi Valley Historical Review* 40 (1953), 231–56.

Betts, John R. "Mind and Body in Early American Thought," *Journal of American History* 54 (1968), 787–805.

Block, David. *Baseball Before We Knew It: A Search for the Roots of the Game* (2005).

Borish, Linda J. "The Robust Woman and the Muscular Christian: Catharine Beecher, Thomas Higginson, and Their Vision of American Society, Health and Physical Activities," *International Journal of the History of Sport* 4 (September 1987): 139–51.

Cohen, Kenneth. "Well Calculated for the Farmer," *Virginia Magazine of History & Biography* 115:3 (2007): 371–411.

Dizikes, John. *Sportsmen and Gamesmen* (1981).

Gammie, Peter. "Pugilists and Politicians in Antebellum New York: The Life and Times of Tom Hyer," *New York History* 75 (July 1994), 265–96.

Gorn, Elliott. *The Manly Art: Bare-Knuckle Prize Fighting in America* (1986).

Holliman, Jennie. *American Sport, 1785–1835* (1931).

Kirsch, George B. *The Creation of American Team Sports: Baseball and Cricket, 1838–72* (1989).

Kirsch, George B. *Baseball in Blue and Gray: The National Pastime During the Civil War* (2003).

Levine, Peter. "The Promise of Sport in Antebellum America," *Journal of American Culture* 2 (1980), 623–34.

Malcolm, Dominic. "The Diffusion of Cricket to America: A Figurational Sociological Examination," *Journal of Historical Sociology* 19 (June 2006), 151–173.

Miles, Edwin A. "President Adams' Billiard Table," *New England Quarterly* 45 (1972), 31–43.

Moss, George. "The Long Distance Runners of Ante Bellum America," *Journal of Popular Culture* 8 (1974), 370–82.

Robertson, W. H. P. *The History of Thoroughbred Racing in America* (1964).

Sparks, Randy J. "Gentleman's Sport: Horse Racing in Antebellum Charleston," *South Carolina Historical Magazine* 93 (January 1992), 15–30.

Struna, Nancy. "The North-South Races: American Thoroughbred Racing in Transition, 1823–1850," *Journal of Sport History* 8 (Summer 1981), 28–57.

Thorn, John. *Baseball in the Garden of Eden: The Secret History of the Early Game* (New York: Simon & Schuster, 2011)

Wiggins, David K. "Sport and Popular Pastimes: Shadow of the Slavequarter," *Canadian Journal of the History of Sport and Physical Education* 11 (May 1980), 61–88.

Yates, Norman W. *William T. Porter and the Spirit of the Times* (1957).

CHAPTER 5

Higher Education and the Growth of American Amateur Sport, 1890–1940

Intercollegiate athletics provided one of the most important breeding grounds for organized sport in America. This started with interclass competitions in the early 1800s due to the example of Oxford and Cambridge in staging intercollegiate contests that existed virtually nowhere else.

The first interschool competition in the United States occurred in 1852 between Harvard and Yale crews, with Harvard winning. Six years later, the College Union Regatta was organized as the first intercollegiate sports league. Crew was followed as an intercollegiate sport by baseball in 1859, football in 1869, and track and field in 1873. Baseball was the principal college sport until the late 1880s, when the "big game" became the annual Thanksgiving Day football match between traditional rivals.

Why did football supplant baseball? Was it profits? By the early 1890s the Yale eleven was earning over $50,000 a year. The test of manliness? The rituals of the "big game"? Spectators saw games marked by brute strength and power—mass momentum with little deception or guile. Did the sport fulfill its promise? Faculties usually supported intercollegiate competition, which supposedly taught proper social skills, promoted manliness, advanced civilization, boosted school spirit, and advertised the institution's name. However, historians generally agree that the ideals of football and the realities of the game were far apart. How and why were the goals of amateur college sport undermined? Were they realistic goals? What was the role of the professional coach? In what ways were they role models? How did college presidents, alumni, and students contribute to subverting the ideals of amateurism?

Recruiting violations were commonplace, and it was easy to keep players eligible despite poor academic performances. By the 1890s the fervor for intercollegiate sport had spread westward, especially to growing state universities that were seeking both publicity and larger enrollments. Shortly thereafter historically black colleges also established intercollegiate sports programs in emulation of the mainstream colleges.

Around the turn of the century, football underwent a lot of external appraisals and self-criticism due to violence and the deaths of several players. This scrutiny led to the Intercollegiate Athletic Association in 1906 (renamed the National Collegiate Athletic Conference in 1910), which established nationwide playing rules and eligibility requirements. What was the relationship between developing a more wide-open game that employed the forward pass and the commercial aspects of the sport? The exciting play on the field, the development of gridiron heroes ("All-Americans"), the entertaining rituals that accompanied the game, and the ability of schools to get graduates and others to identify with the team helped make college football extremely popular. In the 1920s some of the greatest sports heroes were football players like Red Grange, who played in stadiums (increasingly publicly financed) that seated 80,000 or more spectators.

College sports were not an exclusively male sphere. In the late nineteenth century, elite women's colleges supported physical education as part of their curriculum, but the students preferred team sports. Matches between classes led to a brief era of intercollegiate competition at the turn of the century; however, female physical educators believed such activities promoted inappropriate values, and succeeded in curtailing intercollegiate contests with the substitution of the more social play days.

DOCUMENTS

Document 1 reports on the Harvard–Oxford boat race of 1869, the first international intercollegiate competition. Document 2 comprises Walter Camp's recommendations to college athletes that they play with high standards of sportsmanship. Camp was a star football player at Yale from 1875 to 1882, when it fielded the dominant team in America. He subsequently coached Yale to their greatest seasons, authored twenty books on sports, was largely responsible for drawing up the game's rules, and selected the All-American teams from 1889 to 1924. Document 3 is a report by Richard Harding Davis, one of the foremost journalists of his day, describing the social festivities surrounding the 1893 championship Thanksgiving Day football match between Yale and Princeton. In Document 4, muckraker Henry B. Needham examines how college athletic associations subsidized star athletes who were actually professionals rather than simon-pure amateurs. Next, Alice Katherine Fallows (1862–1932), a prominent author and journalist who wrote about many topics, including college women, discusses the sporting options for women at elite eastern women's colleges, and the social functions of participating in sport. Finally, Hildrus A. Poindexter (1901–1987), a noted black bacteriologist who studied tropical diseases, recounts in his autobiography, *My World of Reality*, his football exploits in the 1920s at Lincoln University, a historically black college. African American colleges tried to emulate other colleges academically, socially (with fraternities and sororities), and in extracurricular activities, including sports. The latter promoted school spirit among undergraduates, faculty, and alumni.

1. The *New York Times* Reports on an International Match: The Harvard–Oxford Boat Race, 1869

The two greatest commercial nations of the world were engaged yesterday, not in the usual pursuit of gain, but in watching an extraordinary trial of strength between eight young men. There is no race but the Anglo-Saxon with whom such a competition would have been possible. We may, without boasting, add that only Americans would have traveled three thousand miles from home in order to challenge the strongest crew ever seen upon foreign waters, under circumstances unavoidably adverse to themselves. It was impossible from the first that the conditions could be made quite equal on both sides. The Oxonians are at home on the Thames, and every man in their boat had already taken part in one or more successful struggles with a crew only second to their own. They were animated with all the confidence and buoyancy which a recent victory naturally inspires. They had nothing to learn about the river, and no changes to make in regard to the construction of their boat. Moreover, they had the sympathy of nine-tenths of the spectators with them, and in a trial which imposes the severest strain on all the powers this is an advantage difficult to overestimate.... The American crew had little more than three weeks active training, ... they have been obliged to change their boat twice or thrice, and to recast the crew more than once....

... It has been superiority of physical strength quite as much as any moral qualities which has given the Anglo-Saxon race a noble supremacy in the world. A people which looks upon an athlete as a useless incumbrance upon the face of the earth, or as a paradox in nature, is not likely to hold its own for centuries together. It is often alleged that in this country we are too apt to neglect a purely physical training—the systematic and careful development of strength and muscle—in the education of our youth. If that charge were well-founded, nothing could so quickly remove all occasion for repeating it as a contest like that of yesterday. We undertake to say that boat-racing will henceforth be more popular than ever among us. Young men now beginning their college studies will be stimulated to earn the distinction which the Harvard crew so brilliantly won for themselves yesterday in the old and the new world. Emulation of this kind is of the greatest value to a people in an age when the young are thrust into the battle of life before there has been time for a full expansion of their powers. A weak, sickly, flabby race may be a pleasing spectacle to theorists who live chiefly in the clouds, but for the destiny yet lying before us we cannot have too many of the attributes which are popularly included in the word "manliness." There are situations in which "mind" can do nothing, and we are forced to base our hopes upon "matter." An international boat race between nations like the American and the English cannot, therefore, be regarded as a trivial incident. We are unable, indeed, to regard a single trial of the kind as a decisive test of the superiority either of a race and breed, or of a system of rowing. But it

From "The Boat-Race," [editorial] *New York Times*, August 28, 1869.

challenges the world to admire physical pluck, endurance, hardiness, a sound constitution, and other gifts which we were intended to cultivate and rejoice in no less than in the pretentious intellectual forces. How many men are there on either side of the Atlantic whose nerves would have enabled them even to begin the task which these young men from Harvard nearly carried to a successful issue yesterday?

... We honor the Harvard men for persevering against all difficulties in one of the most gallant contests ever recorded, and we hope that we shall some day have the opportunity of congratulating the Oxonians on a similar exhibition of mettle....

2. Coach Walter Camp on Sportsmanship, 1893

"Be each, pray God, a gentleman!" ... Do you live up to it? Or are you letting it come down a little here and there; so little, perhaps, that you hardly notice it until you make comparison? A gentleman against a gentleman always plays to win. There is a tacit agreement between them that each shall do his best, and the best man shall win. A gentleman does not make his living, however, from his athletic prowess. He does not earn anything by his victories except glory and satisfaction.... There is still no harm where the mug or trophy hangs in the room of the winner is indicative of his skill; but if the silver mug becomes a silver dollar, either at the hands of the winner or the donor, let us have the laurel back again.

A gentleman never competes for money, directly or indirectly. Make no mistake about this. No matter how winding the road may be that eventually brings the sovereign into the pocket, it is the price of what should be dearer to you than anything else,—your honor....

If you are enough of a man to be a good athlete, and some one asks you to use that athletic ability upon their behalf, don't take money for it, or anything that amounts to pay. If you are on the school team or nine and go into training, don't break faith with your captain, yourself, and your fellows by surreptitious indulgences.... If you are the captain and you find a man breaking training in spite of your orders, and you consider it advisable to put him off, don't be afraid to do it. Gentlemen are not cowards, mentally or physically.

If a man comes to you and endeavors to affect your choice of a college by offers of a pecuniary nature, he does not take you for a gentleman or a gentleman's son, you may be sure. Gentlemen neither offer nor take bribes.

Now, my young college friend, it is your turn. Remember it is upon you that the eyes of the preparatory school-boy are fixed, it is toward you that the younger brother looks for example, and whatever you do in your four years' course, you will see magnified by the boys who come after you. Support your class and your college in every way compatible with your position. Gentlemen are not stingy, nor are they selfish. Play it if you can and your class or college needs you. Pay if you can afford it, but do not allow a false pride to lead you

---

From Walter Camp, "Walter Camp on Sportsmanship," in *Walter Camp's Book of College Sports* (New York: Century, 1893), 1–9.

into subscriptions beyond your means. Don't be ashamed of enthusiasm. A man without it is a man without a purpose.

I remember a little incident of my own college course. I was a freshman, and knew almost no one in college except a certain junior. I had entered in two events in the fall athletic games, one a quarter mile, the other a hurdle race. I had run the quarter and been beaten, although I finished second. My opponents had all been upper classmen, and I received no little encouragement from their friends. I felt very lonely and disgusted with myself and life in general when I got on the mark for the hurdle. I had but two competitors, and both had been cheered when they came to the scratch. Suddenly as we were getting on our marks I heard a voice half-way down the course call out, "You can do 'em," and I saw my junior friend waving his hat to me. It was not a classical remark, but it made me feel better. I was clumsy in getting off, and when we came to the sixth hurdle was nearly five yards behind the other two, but from that time on I could hear my friend roaring out, "Go in!" "You've got 'em yet!" "Now you're over," as I went up each flight. I *did* finish first, and I had hardly touched the tape before he was patting me on the back. I don't suppose it cost him much to yell for a poor freshman, but I know that I always thought of him as one of the best fellows I ever knew, and in after years I have remembered enough of the feeling that was in my heart toward him, to go out and try to make some others feel that even a freshman has friends.

Apropos of this, a word to non-contestants.... A gentleman is courteous. It is not courtesy upon a ball-field to cheer an error of the opponents. If it is upon your grounds, it is the worst kind of boorishness. Moreover, if there are remarkable plays made by your rivals you yourselves should cheer, conceal any chagrin you may feel at the loss it may be to your side, but be courteous to appreciate and applaud an exceptional play by the opponents....

Finally, to non-contestants, I want to say a word regarding "celebrating." Primarily, do not, I beg of you, do anything because it looks smart. Enjoy yourselves, but do not try to "show off." ... A little unusual hilarity, a tendency to believe that everything is expressly for the collegian, can be upon these occasions overlooked and forgiven, but be ready to appreciate the point beyond which it is carried too far; be ready to apologize quickly and instantly where offense is taken. Show that behind the jolly fun there is the instinct and cultivation of a gentleman's son....

Now for the contestants. I wish I could impress indelibly upon your minds the fact that with you rests the most enduring standard for amateur sports. With no disrespect to any class or condition—with the best regard for all strong legislation in outside athletic bodies—I say that the collegian's standard of purity in his sports should be the highest. The very fact of having the leisure to devote four years to a higher education, should be taken to involve the duty of acquiring a keener perception of right and wrong in matters where right and wrong depend upon a delicacy of honor. Gentlemen do not cheat, nor do they deceive themselves as to what cheating is. If you are elected the captain of a nine, team, or crew, read over your rules, and note exactly who are allowed as contestants by those rules, not by the custom of some predecessor, nor by what you think some rival will do, but by the rules themselves. Having done that, never let a thought enter your head of making use of any man not clearly and cleanly eligible....

What if, at the time, your side may be the weaker? Don't be a coward on that account. Face it like a man, and say with your whole heart that you are on the side of the men who want no chance of retreat or escape, only a fair contest and certain victory or defeat at the end of it....

Be each, pray God, a gentleman!

3. Richard Harding Davis Scrutinizes the Rituals of the Thanksgiving Day Football Game, 1893

There is nothing more curious or more interesting in the history of New York city within the last decade than the development of the Thanksgiving-day Game. Ten years ago the game was a sporting event, and nothing more.... Today the sporting character of the event has been overwhelmed by the social interest it has aroused in itself, and which has enveloped it and made it more of a spectacle than an athletic contest. But it is still the greatest sporting event and spectacle combined that this country has to show.... No one who does not live in New York can understand how completely it colors and lays its hold upon that city, how it upsets and overturns its thoroughfares, and disturbs its rapid routine of existence....

Ten years ago Thanksgiving day in New York was an event of moment and meaning; there still clung to it the semi-religious significance that gave it its place.... But the game up at the polo grounds caused many desertions and annual mutinies.... It was not that they cared so much for football, but there was nothing better offered, and, in short became "the thing to do." ...

Now ... the city surrenders herself to the students and their game as she never welcomes any other event, except a Presidential election.... She begins to prepare for them early in November ... with the colors of two rivals, and from Ninety-fourth Street in Harlem to lower Broadway, ... and from the east side to the North River, the same colors in every form and texture hang on the outer walls, and the cry is that "they come." But long before they come, every other young woman you meet, and every little boy, and elderly men even, begin to parade Broadway with bows of blue stuck on their persons, or long strips of orange and black ribbon ... which proclaim their allegiance and their hopes.... Service in many of the churches ... were held one hour earlier than usual last Thanksgiving day, because the rectors found they could not get a full congregation unless the service was over in time to allow the worshipers to make an early start for Manhattan Field....

Everything on four wheels and that will hold twenty men on its top ... goes up Fifth Avenue on Thursday morning. It is like a circus procession many miles long. It begins at ten in the morning, four hours before the game, when the coaches meet in front of the Fifth Avenue and the Brunswick hotels, where a crowd has gathered to cheer them as they start. The streets are empty, for it is

From Richard Harding Davis, "The Thanksgiving Day Game," *Harper's Weekly* 37 (December 1893): 1170–71.

a holiday, and the sounds of the bugle calls and coach horns and the riflelike cheer of Yale and the hissing sky-rocket yell of Princeton break in on the Sabbath-like quiet of the streets like the advance of an army going forth triumphantly to war. There is everything, from the newest English brake to omnibuses, draped from their tops to the level of the street with cloths of yellow and blue, hung in festoons or dropped in four straight curtains from each corner and dragging in the mud and with wheels covered up entirely or decorated with ribbons around their spokes, and suggesting monster revolving pin-wheels.... All blanketed in the true colors, ... every coach carries twenty shouting men and exciting young women smothered in furs; and the flags, as they jerk them about, fill the air with color; and the coaches themselves toss like shops in a heavy sea, rocking from side to side, and sinking and rebounding on their springs as the men on top jump up and down in time to the rhythm of the rival cheers.

Every coach load yells for all the pretty girls on the next coach if they wear the proper colors and race scornfully past those who do not; and from the Washington Arch to the layers of flats in Harlem there are holiday-makers out along the route to see the procession pass, standing in some places three and four deep along the sidewalk. And from houses all along the course there are bits of bunting and big flags; sometimes it is only a strip of paper muslin fluttering from the eighth story window of a cheap apartment-house, and again it is a big silken banner swinging from the housefront of some important friend of one or the other of the two colleges.... And as the decorated horses and bedecked hansoms and brakes and coaches and omnibuses go galloping up the Avenue there are special cheers of the orange flag and the big black P in front of the Sloanes and the Alexanders and the Scribners, and for the blue banners and white Y before the homes of the Whitneys and the Vanderbilts.

Manhattan Field, where the game has been held of late years, and where it took place last week [attended by] thirty thousand.... When every other one ... stood up and yelled and waved a blue or an orange and black flag, the effect was worth crossing an ocean to see. There are certain traditions of these games which are interesting, and which were observed last weekend with much enthusiasm. One of these is the singing of words expressive of the sentiments of the rival colleges to the tunes of hymns and popular songs in which the names of the "star" players are handed down to immortality....

It is also interesting to the stranger to note how systematically the cheering is given, how it is timed to destroy the effect of the rival cheering, and that certain men are selected to lead and give the time for these yells, who hold a position similar to that of a leader of an orchestra. This year there was a new and an unintentionally pretty effect in the introduction of blankets by the substitutes, in the place of "sweaters." They found that it took too long to pull a jersey on and off a player while he was waiting for a comrade to revive, or for the two captains to discuss a disputed point with the referee, and that throwing a blanket around him kept him warmer. So this year the substitutes lay around the lines stretched at full length on blankets of double length, and whenever time was called, as it was at almost every fifth minute of each half, they would swarm over the field, ... and smother the eleven men of their college....

There is no change so noticeable in the Thanksgiving day game as the difference in the manner in which it is reported for the daily papers. It is no longer considered enough to cover it with two men—one to write the introduction, and [the] other to describe the play. Now each paper sends its star men, its artists, and photographers, and engages many ex-players of reputation to describe the game from the points of view of adherents of each college, and to make diagrams which show where the ball was at every minute.... At the last Thanksgiving day game that I helped to report for the *Evening Sun*, there were seventeen men assisting one another....

4. Henry Beach Needham Decries the Professionalization of College Athletes, 1905

For the good of sport, a distinction is made between an amateur and a professional. This distinction does not in itself involve a moral question. It is a classification in the interest of fair play. The professional, having made something of a business of athletics, presumptively outclasses the amateur who plays only for enjoyment and recreation. Therefore, contests in which professionals of any degree are pitted against amateurs are ... "unequal, if the facts are known, unfair, if the facts are concealed."

[In 1898] the Conference on Intercollegiate Athletics ... simply stated, a student becomes ineligible who accepts compensation, "direct or indirect" for his athletic services....

Winning at Any Cost

The *paid* coach has to win. If he develops a winning team, his services will be retained; if his team meets with defeat, there is something radically wrong with his methods. He has not "delivered the goods." ...

In 1899 Columbia determined to go in for football. There had been no eleven for eight years, during which time the athletic energies of the university had been devoted mainly to rowing—the cleanest of all sports. Columbia saw greater advertising possibilities in football.... Played in New York, the games would attract large crowds, and sufficient revenue ... to support athletics in general. A coach was engaged at a salary which the average college professor accepts gladly. A Yale athlete, George Foster Sanford ... knew the secrets of Yale's success, and was willing to teach them to a rival college for a proper consideration.... He had to have apt pupils. The game as developed required men of weight and muscle. Such men ... he could not find matriculated at Columbia.... So this enterprising coach got several "stars" outside—or rather had the manager of the team hire them. He put them in Columbia uniforms, and they beat Yale.... His salary was raised to $5,000 per year.

... Thanks to the influence of the colleges, there is growing up a class of students tainted with commercialism.... They are resolved that their athletic ability shall put them through college, and they propose to go to the institution offering the best "opportunities." ... Said Professor Hollis, for seven years

---

From Henry B. Needham, "The College Athlete: How Commercialism is Making Him a Professional," *McClure's Magazine* 25 (June 1905): 115–28.

chairman of the Harvard Athletic Committee: "The evils of college athletics are the evils of every-day life. Commercialism is a characteristic of American life."

"Opportunities" at Prep School and College Contrasted

James J. Hogan, captain and right-tackle of the Yale eleven ... entered Exeter, a poor boy, at the age of twenty-three. That was over eight years ago. He had been earning his own living when he set about to complete his education....

Harvard joined Yale and Princeton in competition for this great prep athlete. Hogan went to Yale, which is not far from his home....

The career of this athlete at the university has been one of marked success. Hogan with his room-mate ... occupies a suite in Vanderbilt Hall—the most luxurious of the Yale dormitories.... He takes his meals at the University Club ... an expensive undergraduate organization.... After the football season of 1903, ... the Yale trainer ... with Hogan, then captain elect of the Yale eleven, as a traveling companion made a ten-day trip to Cuba. The athletic association paid for the excursion, which cost ... $25 per day for Hogan.

... Hogan receives $100 a year, the income of the John Bennetto Scholarship. In addition, ... his entire tuition is abated. The baseball association gives to Hogan (and two teammates) the score-card privilege. From the sale of the cards at the intercollegiate games and from the advertising, these athletes take the entire proceeds.... At Yale the football and baseball score-card privileges are regarded as "sort of scholarship for athletes."

Bartering a Reputation

Hogan's income is further augmented by commissions paid him by The American Tobacco Company, whose agent he is. It is well known about the campus that, through the influence of the Yale captain, the "Egyptian Deities" and the "Turkish Mogul" cigarettes were placed on sale at "Mory's." These brands are spoken of at Yale as "Hogan's cigarettes." ...

It is not to be argued that this employment affects Hogan's amateur standing. The "business arrangement" is important only as showing the growth of commercialism in collegiate sport. Hogan entered Yale a skillful player. College coaching made of him a "star." He was selected as captain of the varsity football team, which added greatly to his popularity, practically insuring him election to a senior society. The success of the eleven gave him a wide reputation. This reputation and popularity—largely a gift of the university—have been bartered, doubtless unconsciously on Hogan's part, for dollars and cents—money sent by sympathetic fellow students in acquiring a taste for certain brands of cigarettes.

The Tramp Athlete

[Andrew L.] Smith is the man who goes to college with the *one* idea of engaging in athletics.... As full-back of the eleven of Pennsylvania State College, he played a "magnificent game" against the University of Pennsylvania, October 4, 1902.

The following Monday he was practising [*sic*] with the University of Pennsylvania second eleven.... He immediately began to attend classes.... The following fall he played for his new college.... Then it became known that, between October 4th and November 7th, 1902, when practicing with the "scrub" and attending classes at the University of Pennsylvania, he played three games ... for *Penn State*.... Smith was thereupon ... declared ineligible.

... Yet this man was permitted to represent Pennsylvania on the gridiron last fall (1904), and to the victory of Harvard he contributed greatly. Afterwards, in the middle of his senior year, he was dropped from college. His football days [were] over, and he was no longer a useful member of the college community....

The only justification of Pennsylvania's unsportsmanlike behavior is found in Harvard's attitude toward this sister institution.... It was noised about that Harvard would "drop Penn" if a decisive victory was won in 1904. Pennsylvania, therefore, in order to continue in the competition of the "Big Four" *had* to produce a winning team.

An Example and a Moral

... William Clarence Matthews, the young colored student, who is best known to the public as short-shop on the varsity nine for three years, and as an end-rush in the last football game against Yale ... has worked his way through the university, practically completing his four years' course in three years....

Matthews is a product of Tuskegee, where he fitted himself for Phillips Andover.... At Harvard he had a Price Greenleaf Aid, paying $200 his freshman year, but since then has had no scholarship.... As at Andover he has worked his way, doing what he could during the college year ..., and working steadily during the summers in hotels, or on Pullman sleeping cars. This year he has taught in one of the North Cambridge night-schools.

Here is a man who, to maintain his standing as an amateur, has repeatedly refused offers of forty dollars per week and board to play semi-professional baseball in summer....

"The trouble with accepting favors ... to help one through college is that in the end you find they have *made you dependent*."

Here is the answer to those who advocate the indirect subsidizing of athletes.

"Mr. Washington taught us at Tuskegee ... that the best help a man can get is an opportunity to help himself."

5. Alice Katherine Fallows on Sports at Vassar and Wellesley Colleges, 1903

In the larger significance of athletics for girls each college has developed its own picturesque climax and test of physical ability. At Vassar, field-day in the spring is the focus of many athletic hopes and ambitions. Interclass basket-ball matches set

From Alice Katherine Fallows, "Athletics for College Girls," *Century* 66 (May 1903): 58–65.

the whole college on tiptoe with excitement, … but field-day … seems … even more the characteristic expression of Vassar's athletic spirit. It falls on a certain Saturday in late spring. One-hundred-yard dash, 220-yard dash, relay race, running high jump, running broad jump, standing broad jump, fence vault, basket-ball throw, base-ball throw, putting the eight-pound shot—all these things are on the Vassar field-day program.

The records are surprising as an illustration of what girls can accomplish; but the physical achievement of the day is not all. In the scheme of college development that interclass struggle for the championship has another significance. A pink V on a Vassar girl's sweater means that she has broken a record. Symbol of ability, key to many of the good things of life, the athletic freshman longs for this letter with all her soul. But … her first exultant thought is not, "I've won my V," but, "I've helped my class." An ambition wider than one's ego—that is what a college contest helps to teach its girl participants.… If athletics, then, can teach a girl to work for her class first and herself afterward, it is not a small achievement.…

At Wellesley, field-day in the fall is a fillip for the enthusiasm of the girls whose interest is in field-sports.… [S]even "organized" sports, which collectively claim a membership of three hundred and fifty students. Tennis, golf, field-hockey, low hurdling, relay-racing, and basket-ball, six of the magic seven, all have their enthusiastic supporters. But rowing is preeminently the Wellesley specialty. "Float" is its climax and reward, the picturesque water contest which has been the pride of students and the joy of beholders from the earliest days of the college.

The preparation for float is arduous. It means winter exercise in the gymnasium, tiresome preliminary practice at the rowing machine before the candidate is permitted to touch an oar to water, and, lastly, practice on the lake. But practice plus ability wins a girl the right to row with the other seven for the glory of her class. On a June afternoon comes the beautiful sequel of all these toiling hours—that rhythmic procession of boats that sweeps up and down while thousands of friendly eyes watch from the bank. The winning crew is judged by its skill and form rather than by its speed. Afterward the best of the individual oarsmen in all the crews are chosen to row in the varsity crew, and proud indeed is the class that has the most representatives.…

Wellesley requires gymnastic drill of its students, as other colleges do, for the first year; but of late it has been laying special stress on the recreative side of athletics.… "Girls who don't know how to play must be taught to play," is the motto. The athletic director, believing heartily in the benefit of self-forgetful exercise, has been making a determined effort to infuse enjoyment into this particular performance of Wellesley duty, and to wake up those in her charge to the pleasure of sport for sport's sake. The trustees have begun to see the matter from the same point of view, and have provided not only a gymnasium and an athletic field with a fine cinder track, a boat-house, and tennis-courts, but playgrounds and a bath-house as well. They also provide instruction in the various sports, as they do in gymnastics, and examiners to look out for the health of the participants in the games, just as they do for the members of the gymnastic classes.

This is an interesting development of girls' athletics, and a phase in which Wellesley is the pioneer; for while other colleges have recognized the benefit of enjoyment in exercise, they have not made an organized effort to secure it.

However colleges may differ in athletic creeds and doctrines, the aim of all is the same—to make girls stronger and healthier. Unless carefully gathered statistics are to be utterly discredited, all colleges are at least partly accomplishing this aim; for the average of health throughout the women's college world is vastly better than it ever was in the days of nondescript, take-it-as you-please exercise. The increase of interest in voluntary exercise and athletics among girl students should be most encouraging to those who desire their symmetrical development. No college now feels itself complete without a student athletic association, usually a strong, robust organization, and a center of encouragement for all forms of physical activity.

6. Football at Lincoln University, a Historically Black College in the Early 1920s

HILDRUS A. POINDEXTER

Football was the major athletic event at Lincoln in the 1920s. To be a member of the varsity … put the student in a preferred category … I was fresh from the steel industry of Detroit where I had worked as a laborer and molder. I had never played football, but I reported to the coach for the purpose of joining the freshman squad.…

... The rules of limiting the varsity to only the three upper classmen were not rigidly adhered to in the Colored Intercollegiate Athletic Association (CIAA). A good player on the freshman team might … play with the … varsity.… I was tried as a fullback, but fumbled too much.… Finally, … as a guard, I … was the left guard of choice.…

[D]uring the sophomore year … Paul Robeson … would come … one day a week from [his] graduate studies in Law… to coach.… I worshiped Robeson and absorbed his every principle and tactic for playing on the line. I learned to charge fast, low, and hard. I learned to punish an opponent and to accept punishment without complaint … It was the custom … after some weeks of practice and coaching, for the selection of a first string team.…

This varsity squad would eat together at a … "training table," … train as a unit, travel first class … and would even get some consideration from the teachers for absenteeism.…

[T]he grapevine [told] me that a conspiracy was … formed … to eliminate me by concentrated attacks designed to cripple me.… I was overcharged with rage. [O]ne opponent [ended] in the hospital, … another … turned in his uniform, and I was … established as the left guard.…

There was adequate local and national recognition. I was named to the second CIAA All American Team in 1922 and was the first CIAA All American left guard in 1923. [P]ress coverage was small.…

From Hildrus A. Poindexter, *My World of Reality: An Autobiography* (Detroit, Balamp Publishing, 1973), 33–36.

In the early 1920s Lincoln University was in its heyday in football, playing teams as Howard, Hampton, Morgan, West Virginia State, Union, Tuskegee, Wilberforce, St. Paul's Polytechnic Institute....

I played in 20 CIAA football games. The two schools that gave me the hardest time were Hampton and West Virginia State. In two of the games against Hampton, Lincoln used the Dartmouth shift as a result of Coach Shelbourne ... [an All-American] at Dartmouth. I had less than 50% successes against All American [linebacker] "Red" Dabney [who] used knees, fist, thumbs, cleats, and his 230 lbs Shelbourne to maim me, but in true Paul Robeson fashion, no complaint was registered....

ESSAYS

The two essays in this section examine both the commercialization and the integrity of sport at the college level in the United States. In the first essay, Robin Lester, who studied with Daniel Boorstin at the University of Chicago, and was for two decades a headmaster at prestigious independent secondary schools, analyzes three of the essential aspects of big-time, highly commercialized sport at the University of Chicago—the roles of spectators, athletes, and the football coach. The University of Chicago was established in 1892 as a major research university. Its president, William Rainey Harper, recruited top scholars to the university with Rockefeller money. However, Harper knew it would take some time to gain recognition through scholarship, so he also invested heavily in sports to quickly gain national attention. He brought in former Yale star athlete Amos Alonzo Stagg to coach by offering the promise of a high salary and faculty status. Stagg built the football program, as well as other sports, into a national powerhouse that brought fame and profit to his institution. In the second essay, Scott A. McQuilkin, who received his Ph.D. at Penn State University, and is currently Vice President for Institutional Advancement at Whitworth College, examines in depth one of the major problems colleges encountered in preserving amateurism, which was the widespread practice of their athletes playing baseball for compensation during their summer vacations. A clear violation of the amateur code, players regularly tried to circumvent the rules and, if caught, were rarely punished by pliant administrations.

The Rise of the Spectator, the Coach, and the Player at the University of Chicago, 1895–1905

ROBIN D. LESTER

Harper's University fostered the growth of football so successfully at the turn of the century that Chicago gained the leadership of intercollegiate football in the West in 1905. Maroon football had two extraordinary assets. First, located in the nation's second most populous [city], the university could count on many players and spectators.... Second, Amos Alonzo Stagg was the perfect athletic entrepreneur to match William Rainey.

The Rise of the Spectator

The most significant development during the period was the rise of the spectator—the widespread acceptance and use of the Chicago football enterprise by the students, faculty, and alumni of the university community and by the larger civic community.... The university became very successful in selling its athletic product and even of applying monopolistic principles, as a kind of "athletic Darwinism." Although some of its academics grew chary of the strong community interest and nascent control by 1900, most judged that the activity was useful to the university's larger purpose.

... The "windy city" newspaper boosters maintained their civic reputation with unsupportable claims for the Stagg men. The journalists themselves were a prime market for the game, even as they became the chief salesmen; they soon believed and printed virtually everything that Stagg told them.

Boosterism came full circle in 1902 when the first "Gridiron Fest" was sponsored by the Chicago Press Club. Coaches, athletic managers, football officials, and players joined the propagandists in the formal unification of the press and the new intercollegiate football industry.

The university strategy in taking the game to the Chicago community was divulged by Horace Butterworth, manager of Maroon athletics.... He reasoned that early season victories promoted attendance and enthusiasm for the later contests; this approach accounts for the scheduling from 1896 to 1905 of teams which managed only twenty-seven points in thirty-six early season games, while Chicago scored 1,116 points. Butterworth described the Chicago marketplace as possessing two elements—the "society element" and the public. Athletic Director Stagg added a third constituency, "the college people" (he estimated 50,000), by which he meant the citizens who had attended other institutions whose loyalty might be partially transferred to the Chicago Maroons....

... Chicago was a limited football marketplace in the early 1890s because few Chicagoans knew the game either as players or spectators. The public's interest in football picked up when the sport was introduced into the secondary schools during the 1890s, but the greatest single influence on public perception was the football enterprise that Harper and Stagg built. There was a steady supply of university contests played on the Midway from 1896–1905 (almost 90 percent of all Chicago games were played at home) and a persistent publicity which argued that the honor of the collegiate and civic community was at stake on the Maroon gridiron.

Chicago students showed a ready acceptance of the idea that the intercollegiate team was "theirs" and that the game had some validity for institutional comparisons.... The games became a weekly meeting place for the new and old members of the university community.... The campus community suffered and rejoiced communally over their team's performances: "Rockefeller gifts were celebrated like football victories and football victories like the second coming...."

The development of consistent support by alumni occurred later than the development of student and faculty support and was contemporaneous with the support of the larger civic community. Chicago was in a unique position during the 1890s, for, although it opened and functioned as a fully staffed university with a comparatively large student body, it took about a decade of graduations to produce a sufficiently large and interested alumni.... The Chicago alumni were joined around 1900 by other universities' alumni to provide enthusiastic backing for Stagg's teams and a collateral desire to demand victory regardless of means.

During the first decade, alumni interest in the athletic fortunes of the university teams was informal, and little organization beyond the seating of alumni in the Chicago section of the stands was accomplished.... The first successful concerted effort by the alumni to influence athletic policy occurred at the annual [pre-Thanksgiving Day] dinner in 1902 where some critical remarks were directed to Stagg's alleged ineptitude at recruiting top high school athletes. This alumni influence combined with the increasing sense of team ownership felt by the civic and journalistic communities was so strong that Stagg and his staff were stirred to more active recruiting and periodic reports to the alumni; in return, the alumni-civic coalition provided long-running protection for his winning program and rendered coach Stagg a campus untouchable. Harper and Stagg were more than willing to go along with the demands for victory even when the result was the bending and warping of the original stated values of their intercollegiate athletic program.

The selling of the Maroon football team went well at Harper's University.... From 1903 through 1905 Stagg scheduled twenty-eight games in Chicago, five away. Football revenue had so outgrown football expenses that the surplus was devoted to maintaining the other activities in the Department of Physical Culture; and increasingly, this dependence on football was becoming a major argument for maintaining the large commercial football enterprise at Chicago and elsewhere.

The Rise of the Coach

Amos Alonzo Stagg rose to a position of considerable power in Harper's University.... Stagg's rise was due to his special relationship to Harper, his dominant personality, the precedentless department which he headed, the innovative "profession" of coaching of which he was a pioneer and the enlargement of his national reputation based upon his unparalleled entrepreneurial and football genius.

President Harper and Coach Stagg grew increasingly close and mutually dependent.... Harper was constantly vigilant about the best way to present the Maroon football show to the paying customers....

The relationship of Harper with Stagg also had its trials. Harper showed unhappiness over his coach's management in 1895 when a university summer baseball team (one of Stagg's delights was to play in these more informal games), composed partially of non-university students, played teams the president deemed inappropriate: "We have had a series of games with negroes [*sic*] etc. which has brought disgrace upon us." ... Few African-Americans played for Stagg, but for that matter, few were enrolled at Chicago. Perhaps the most celebrated black athlete was Henry Dismond, one of Stagg's sprinters who held a world record.

The Harper-Stagg colleagueship was severely strained at times because the coach was frequently at the heart of a campus imbroglio and often was himself the focus of antagonism. People sometimes viewed his insistence upon what he considered points of "principle" frequently was seen by others as overly forceful or even tactless behavior. Stagg was a man of imperious character who frequently saw issues more simply than his faculty colleagues...: "I understand that I am not to be hampered in any way in my work.... [Comptroller] Rust is not to request *reasons why* this or that expenditure; that I am not compelled to *explain* to him for what ever purpose certain money is to be used ... and am not to be called to account by *him* for the same." Harper backed Stagg and it was not until the University Council and the Board of Trustees many years later investigated the special autonomy Stagg enjoyed that his department was brought into line with others....

Stagg's impatience with those who might challenge his point of view was not confined to his relations with university officials.... The Intercollegiate Conference of Faculty Representatives, the Midwest's pioneer athletic governance organization ..., formed in 1895–96 ... provided the context for such protests. President C. K. Adams of the University of Wisconsin leveled extensive charges against Stagg in 1898 to the effect that it was the duplicity of Stagg that had ruined athletic relations between Wisconsin and Chicago....

Coach Stagg's successful athletic career with early physical education training at Springfield had prepared him to serve as the pioneer of a new profession, the college coach.... The same societal forces behind the "cult of efficiency" ... was a part of the culture which produced the nation's football coaches. The vulnerability of the coaches to "the great strength of the business community and the business philosophy in an age of efficiency" was considerable and these influences molded their work—few were allowed to remain simply as coach-educators. The professionalization of the college coach can be seen in Stagg's career: he moved from the player-coach of the first generation of coaches into the "scientific" coach-manager and the celebrity-entrepreneur-coach stages of successive generations.... Many other coaches followed his model, e.g., football coaches assumed control over all other intercollegiate activities as "athletic directors" because of the dominant economic position of football on the campuses about twenty to thirty years after Stagg. Stagg even led the chosen few toward the final coaching stage—the celebrity-entrepreneurs of the twentieth-century American university who often occupied a cultural and financial niche well above their college president or state governor....

Stagg was lauded by a leading Chicago newspaper in 1902 as "better known than anyone connected with the University of Chicago, Dr. W.R. Harper and John D. Rockefeller alone excepted." ... A mystique surrounded his activities on the gridiron and extended well beyond its perimeter.... It is not improbable that Amos Alonzo Stagg personified, for many Americans, a purer, less materialistic, lost Christian America.

Stagg's preeminence lay in the acquaintances and contacts he maintained in the East, as well in his position as a leading coach and athletic director.

His co-authorship of the first avowedly "scientific" football book *A Scientific and Practical Treatise on American Football for Schools and Colleges* in 1893 had also brought considerable attention.... In 1904, Stagg became the first non-eastern representative on the Football Rules Committee which legislated the rules of the sport for the entire nation....

University of Chicago football teams became nationally known because of their precedent-setting inter-regional trips and games.... The 1898 game with Pennsylvania at Philadelphia's venerable Franklin Field was not only an important institutional milestone, it was the match "that put western football on the map." Penn was considered the best team in the country that year based on a twenty-four game winning streak.... Chicago, featuring the play of back Clarence Herschberger, led at the half and surprised the East with a new style of play that featured deception and quickness.... Veteran observer Caspar Whitney ranked Chicago equal to the best of the East that year. At the end of the season, Herschberger became the first non-eastern ... player selected by Walter Camp on his All-American team....

... Stagg's football teams consistently played more difficult schedules than their opponents. Perhaps the profit instinct was operating here, for well known, successful opponents insured greater revenues, but Chicago regularly played two or three times the number of major opponents as the other members of its conference. For example, Chicago's 1904 schedule included seven major university teams out of eleven opponents; Michigan played two major opponents in nine games, Wisconsin two of seven ... and Minnesota two of ten....

The Rise of the Player

The most concise statement of the change in the place of football in the player's life at Harper's University came from a Maroon veteran in 1897: "I have no more fun in practice games.... It is nothing less than hard work." ... The status of the player changed as well as the spectator and coach, and the period 1895 to 1905 was marked by the displacement of the student-player by the player-student....

The role of the football player was becoming an identifiable one; it can be described as the two-fold development of the player as a "campus commodity" and as a "campus physical elite." The young student-player who complained of the business-like manner with which he was expected to approach the sport of football in 1897 became an anachronism by 1905, for by then he was required to continue his football training year-round.

The basis for Stagg's new cult of player efficiency can be seen in his explanation of the award of the coveted "C" monograms to Chicago athletes—the Order of the C was "the first athletic-letter club ever formed," according to him. Stagg controlled these awards and he noted that they were based upon the athlete's "merit, amount of work done, and usefulness to the team and the university." ...

... [A]n excellent supply of college level players for the university's use was ... available locally. Chicago was in the median enrollment position among Intercollegiate Conference schools and from 1902, Stagg ... he had excellent players for years after that.... The player commodities were supplied by the high schools and by the Chicago Football League which sponsored a "prairie" (sandlot) game for youths....

The Recruitment of the Campus Commodities

Stagg and Harper developed a number of recruiting methods which enabled them to improve markedly the quality of Chicago's football teams. Shortly after the turn of the century they sought to create a special relationship with interscholastic players and officials. [In 1902] Harper himself presented an ingenious plan (hatched by Stagg) to the Board of Physical Culture and Athletics [regarding] the widespread recruitment of schoolboy athletes....

... [The proposal] ... established a bold experiment of using the nine "affiliated" prep schools in Illinois and Indiana as places of employment for Maroon athletes and as athletic "feeder" schools ... [and] for using the public schools in much the same way....

Finally, the sixth recommendation ... legitimated an event which had already been planned and scheduled by Stagg: ... "That interscholastic meets be held of the Academies and high schools in relationship to the University." Within eight days the "First Annual Interscholastic Track Meet" was history, as about 200 athletes from forty schools who had won state meets in Illinois, Michigan, Wisconsin, and Iowa competed at Marshall Field.... The visiting athletes, termed "young prospectives," were housed in university fraternity houses and were entertained in "great style" by the athletic management and by enthusiastic student groups.

The coaching staff's decision to engage in a recruitment drive and capture beefy and/or speedy campus commodities constituted a change from their public position on the matter. Stagg had often railed against "scouting" by other universities and their alumni; in 1900 he had argued that recruiting was contrary to the "spirit of amateurism." Two unsuccessful football campaigns later, Stagg and the Board "discovered that something had to be done if Chicago expected to compete with other western universities." ...

The Chicago coaches, the football captain, and interested faculty members met periodically to assess their recruitment progress.... The recruitment success of 1902 was enlarged in 1903 with the prophetic, "Maroons Sound Doom of Yost's Great Eleven," due to the snaring of "one of the greatest collections of giants ever collected in the West." ... The Chicago newspapers greeted each Midway acquisition as a civic resource and with bold headline: ... "Hogenson Captured for the Maroon Team," ... "Stagg gains Another Star Prep Athlete," and "Stagg Secures Star."

President Harper worked with the coaching staff to initiate the recruiting system. He led the organization of the university alumni early in 1904 ... at his annual football dinner.... "We have 6000 alumni in and about Chicago. Why do not these alumni see that the university gets its fair share of the athletic material?" Harper then urged that a committee be appointed to organize the alumni into "a recruiting organization." ...

The interscholastic track meet grew rapidly in its importance for the Chicago football enterprise.... "Stagg's Interscholastic" was the premier meet in the West by 1905....

A battle over the recruitment of prominent Chicago high school players erupted in 1903 between Chicago and Michigan. The scalps were difficult to count, for some of Stagg's new wards had not completed high school and it was not always easy to pry them into Chicago. Fielding Yost of Michigan also recruited his share of Chicago public high school juniors in 1903....

This undignified recruiting scramble by two major universities drew some criticism, but not from the eminent academics within those institutions. The criticism came from the public press and from high school administrators and officials. ... [which] one respected columnist had described late in 1902 ... [as] "most unworthy of the dignity and purposes of a great institution of learning." ...

The most telling indictment of the player recruitment chaos came from Chicago Superintendent of Schools Edwin G. Cooley. Cooley was an alumnus of the university (Ph.B., 1896) and an acquaintance of President Harper. The Superintendent described the Chicago-Michigan approaches to Chicago school boys in 1903 as "practically stealing boys out of high school for athletic purposes before their high-school courses are completed." ...

Vagabond players peddled their football playing abilities to the highest-bidding school at the turn of the century, and in the absence of standardized eligibility regulations, the bidders were many. Illustratively, two candidates for the 1902 Chicago team practiced one week, disappeared, and emerged at the Michigan practice field. One of the tourists returned to Chicago's team followed by the other; Wisconsin was then rumored to have captured their fancy. Finally, one went to Ann Arbor to play, the other remained at Chicago.

The most difficult recruitment for Chicago's football enterprise occurred in 1905 with the acquisition of Walter Steffen, future All-American, from a Chicago high school. His attendance at the Midway did not end the battle for his services, however, for ... the universities of the Middle West ... did not scruple to recruit athletes enrolled at other institutions. According to his father, Steffen had "matriculated, paid his tuition, bought his books and attended classes for a week" at Chicago when he left for Madison, Wisconsin.... [H]e attended football practice to ascertain the football future that Wisconsin, and perhaps he, could expect. Steffen returned to Chicago after a three day absence...." When the valuable young man returned to the Maroon practice field, President Harper quietly forgot his threats to require an explanation for Steffen's absence from President Van Hise of Wisconsin; Coach Stagg stated that the athletic department would take "no official notice" of Steffen's confused behavior.

The Retention of the Campus Physical Elite

Retaining players proved as difficult as recruiting them, and the elevation of players to a special status in order to retain their services produced the physical elite on the Midway....

The specter of ineligibility was constant for the Chicago players. At least five of the best players on the 1900 team were found academically deficient in July.... [T]he Chicago faculty generally showed a benign interest in the football team.... [A] player who complained of the anti-football professor was given a special make-up examination by Professor O.J. Thatcher of the History Department, who was in constant attendance at team practices. The errant player was soon back on the field.... [In fall 1903, the team's GPA was 2.01 even though just 3 of 23 players took the normal course load of three major classes.]

Coach Stagg himself kept a watch on his players and was not above using an informal conversation with an instructor as an appeal for a player's eligibility. When his captain flunked a course after Stagg claimed he was told by the instructor the player would pass, Stagg wrote a protest to Harper....

The physical elite were given other special considerations as well. Early in the century a set of chimes was installed in newly constructed Mitchell Tower, and Stagg had the idea of a special playing of the carillon for the Maroon athletes, especially for those who tended to miss curfew, and gave a sizeable gift toward that end. His gift was to provide "a nightly curfew to the men in training." ...

The special nightly ringing of the carillon for the benefit of the athletes was consistent with the new elitist status of the group. The concern for the football players' welfare led to a special diet for them at a "training table." The original training plan was to ask all football candidates to live on or near the campus to enable them to eat together.... The university ... [put] a portion of Snell Hall at the disposal of Stagg's men and by 1902 the newest and most luxurious residence hall was reserved for the intercollegiate athletic teams. Hitchcock Hall, termed the "millionaires' den," became the site for the training table and quarters for about thirty players....

The separation of the football team from the rest of the student body was accomplished with no discussion of its effect upon student life and values. The idea of separate and unequal training facilities for the players was viewed simply as an efficient use of the physical elite. But students petitioned ... to move the athletes and their training table to the midst of the commons so that mutual acquaintance and "school spirit" could develop properly.... The plea was to no avail.

If the physical man was furnished at the training table and at the training quarters, the mental and emotional man was also served. Academic advice came from the faculty members most interested in the success of the team and from Coach Stagg who watched his men's study habits carefully. President Harper inaugurated a special tutorial program for football players by requesting instructors to coach them in troublesome areas. The emotional balance of the football team was sometimes strained during the season as the pressures for winning mounted. When the Maroons suffered "Nervous Fits" in 1905, Stagg suspended practice sessions and took the team ... to exclusive Onwentsia Golf Club in Lake Forest for a weekend of relaxation at university expense.

The administration and many faculty were lavish in their praise of the function which the new physical elite performed on campus. The football captain was elected at President Harper's annual dinner; he became the most revered undergraduate figure....

... The players were given post-game theater parties, dinners, and trips to other campuses to view football games, accompanied by proud professors and paid for by the game receipts.... Thanksgiving dinner after the traditional Michigan game had an important place on the players' calendar, especially when select female students were included as guests of the young gladiators and themselves became an auxiliary elite....

The rise of the intercollegiate football player as a campus commodity and as campus physical elite can be illustrated in the career of Walter Eckersall, the most acclaimed intercollegiate athlete in University of Chicago history and a consensus all-time All-American quarterback....

The future star was born and grew up in the Woodlawn area of Chicago, adjacent to the university.... At Hyde Park High School Eckersall set a ten second flat Illinois 100 yard dash record in 1903 that stood until ... 1928.... One year Hyde Park played Brooklyn [Poly Prep], the best eastern school team, for the "high school national championship" and won 105–0....

Walter Eckersall brought more publicity to the University of Chicago than any other student in the institution's history, with the possible exception of the kidnap-murderers, Nathan Leopold and Richard Loeb.... The Michigan enemy composed an Eckersall chant, hopefully fatal, but implicitly laudatory: "... Eckie, Eckie, break your neckie...."

... Eckersall ... compiled an atrocious academic record, but he was permitted to pursue that path until his football eligibility ended.... From his first quarter at Chicago as a sub-freshman (since he had not completed college preparatory work), the quarterback led his teammates off—as well as on—the field, in failing grades and in total absences from his classroom work.... [H]e and six other first-year students who were flunking participated in intercollegiate track meets for freshmen. Their participation and the press coverage prompted an embarrassed University Council to reconsider the basis of eligibility for freshmen, but the inquiry petered out when Harper assumed responsibility with Stagg for the involvement of the errant students.

The reconstruction of Eckersall's eligibility began during the spring quarter of 1904 to ensure his football play that autumn. He was enrolled in two history courses for Senior College (upper division) students. His enrollment in "The Renaissance Age" would appear peculiar as the course was described as appropriate for those wishing to do graduate work in history.... Eckersall's registration would appear peculiar, that is, if the teacher were other than the Chicago athlete's friend, Oliver J. Thatcher. Appropriately, Eckersall was given a "C" ... by Thatcher who did not flunk a single student in the class of sixty-seven....

... He maintained his eligibility to participate in intercollegiate athletics, but he found that after three and two-thirds years of higher education, he was still classified in the Junior Colleges (lower division). His lack of the full secondary school preparation for his college work was partly responsible—at least eight of his courses were applied toward making up his admissions deficiencies.... [He left the university after the 1906 autumn quarter after finishing his football eligibility.]

⋆ ⋆ ⋆

The patronage of President William Rainey Harper, the spectator and player supply offered by the dynamic Midwestern metropolis, and the single-minded "saintly" coach had combined to ensure that the Chicago football enterprise was hugely successful by 1905. President Harper had adopted university founder John D. Rockefeller's Darwinian *modus operandi* closely enough to recruit professors and players alike and to use them successfully in promoting the new academic creation. It was, moreover, Harper's and Stagg's keen sense of the basics of the institution and their artful collaboration in the athletics of Darwinism which promoted football within and without the university. Their institution and football were now synonymous, stable, and famous.

Summer Baseball and the College Amateur Tradition

SCOTT A. McQUILKIN

> A boy may be given a "position" for the summer in the town where many ball games are to be played. His position may consist of [briefly] tending a soda fountain, ... with an emolument of about $50 a week and expenses.... Or ... after the game the manager ... may bet him $50 he cannot jump over a bat held one foot from the ground—but he doesn't play for money.
>
> E. H. Nichols, Harvard Baseball Coach (1913)

National Collegiate Athletic Association (NCAA) secretary Frank Nicolson recounted in 1912 how, of all the major issues before the association at its inaugural meeting, only in summer baseball had the membership failed to achieve satisfactory results. The ... issue that needed to be resolved ... to justify the NCAA's existence, centered on college players who had for years turned to baseball as a means of summer employment. The question before college officials ... was whether college students who accepted pay for playing baseball during the summer, ... had thereby become professionals and should suffer the loss of their intercollegiate eligibility. The debate over summer baseball would be fought, however, on a broader basis than just college baseball. Many athletic authorities reasoned that the amateur concept was at stake. Any compromise on professionalism in baseball, they believed, would lead to rapid growth in professionalism in other sports.... More significantly, college baseball stood alone in the latitude its players were granted with regard to adherence to amateur law....

... [S]ummer baseball ... rank[ed] in importance behind only brutality in football during the NCAA's first decade.... Initiated by intercollegiate athletics' Big Three of Harvard, Yale, and Princeton, summer baseball practices were then copied by athletes of their lesser but still elite brethren of the northeast and eventually modeled ... by virtually all baseball-playing colleges and universities. Under scrutiny was the custom whereby undergraduates engaged in "sordid" professionalism or were employed under the guise of menial hotel jobs to finance their baseball activities. Although [most] faculty and administrators ... desired

---

From Scott A. McQuilkin, "Summer Baseball and the NCAA: The Second 'Vexation,'" *Journal of Sport History* 25:1 (1998), 18–42. Reprinted with permission.

reform, tolerance for this notable exception eventually won out. For even though the consensus ... was that institutions were obligated to follow the rules, that summer baseball was based in deception, and that amateur principles possessed inherent values, after an initially strong surge of opposition to summer baseball a tolerance more pragmatic than philosophical emerged. The eventual outcome of the summer baseball conflict would include a lesson in the NCAA's part hypocritical, part pragmatic means of "solving" this contentious issue as well as a student victory over amateur constraints in pursuit of self-interest.

Summer Baseball Before the NCAA

... Summer baseball first gained popularity during the 1880s and 1890s.... A purse was collected from among the hotel's patrons at season's end and divided among the players. Players were not discouraged from taking the money, nor was any consideration given to the forfeiture of one's college athletic eligibility.... The openness with which undergraduate men played on summer nines changed, however, in the latter years of the nineteenth century.

Opposition to summer baseball arose among college officials as word spread of how hotels employed college baseball players during the summer months. Men who competed intercollegiately, and who were bound to their institution's eligibility guidelines, were accused of skirting the amateur code.... College players therefore determined to render themselves unimpeachable. Those who wanted to play baseball for money during the summer would no longer earn income as a shortstop or as a pitcher. They were obliged, rather, to acquire employment at a hotel in service as a waiter, bellboy, or clerk....

... The object of every organizer of a summer resort team was to procure a roster of men of marked social traits.... amateurs [who] came from the most prestigious and highly esteemed colleges and universities; for if baseball skill were the sole criterion for selection, then teams would not have been made up largely of college players.... If the boys were paid openly, they would be published as professionals, lose their right to represent their respective schools, and consequently lose their standing in summer baseball. To be known as baseball hirelings, Caspar Whitney later assessed, would have destroyed their "peculiar value to the hotel. Their social prestige would be gone; their amateur cachet lost." Thus, gifted college baseball players, housed as nonpaying guests ... deceived their schools and maintained their amateur standing.... For Harvard baseball coach Edward H. Nichols, speaking in 1913 to NCAA delegates and providing historical perspective on thirty years of summer baseball practices, it had seemed curious that boys so poor that they needed scholarships to attend college ... finance[d] a stay in an expensive hotel for an entire summer. Perhaps it was because ... they could "find $50 in their jeans every Saturday night, and wonder as much as they please where it comes from."

With veiled financial arrangements such as this at summer resorts, amateur violations related to summer baseball became, not surprisingly, difficult to enforce. Students could ... lie about being paid, or ... insist that income was gained from work done apart from the playing field. Many players ... remained beyond detection with the assistance of college authorities who cared less for athletic morals than for won-loss records. The only way to convict a student for playing summer baseball was if he or the man who paid him told of the arrangement....

This lack of accountability occurred because the affairs of summer baseball players were protected by hotel owners, and oftentimes supported by students on their home campuses. At Brown University, for instance, where the school's baseball roster had traditionally been dotted with players of questionable amateur status, what students did in the summer to earn money was cited as an individual's own business....

The public perception was ... that leading universities—Harvard, Yale, Princeton, Penn, Amherst, Dartmouth, Brown, Williams, and Columbia—had committed themselves to playing strictly amateurs in college baseball. Violations of the amateur code were more likely attributed to smaller, less prestigious, institutions that sought to gain ... notoriety through winning athletic teams.... [W]hen it came to the dodging of eligibility rules, none were better than the athletes of America's oldest colleges and universities. Coaches, athletic committee members, and even faculty athletic representatives, the men consigned to uphold and direct amateur standards, were oftentimes complicit in the exemption of summer baseball players from amateur law.

Brown University, ... was castigated in 1894 as "the culmination of evil" because the majority of its baseball squad had played summer baseball.... Princeton quarterback Phil King ... [drew] a salary during the summer as a member of the Cape May Baseball Club, with no adverse effect to his gridiron status. Penn ... was forced to remove seven players from its baseball roster in 1896 for having played summer ball. What separated Brown from the other schools was its pioneer ruling approving ... summer baseball [in] 1903....

At relatively the same time ... Harvard was confronted with a conflict of its own. Walter Clarkson, the Crimson's star pitcher and loser of only four pitching decisions in almost four seasons, admitted to having signed a contract with the New York Highlanders of the American League.... Clarkson had been suspected of having been a salaried summer baseball player for several years, [yet] no case could ever be mounted against him, and therefore his participation on the Harvard nine continued....

... Henry B. Needham, a muckraking journalist whose accusing pen influenced American reform more broadly than just intercollegiate athletics, believed it was "easier to convict a legislator of bribe taking ..." than to convict a college man of evading the rules.... Needham believed this was true because for every Caspar Whitney who abhorred any hint of professionalism, there was an influential college educator who thought baseball played for love or for money could enhance character. Any bad-mouthing of sports professionalism, some believed, therefore ran counter to the principles of the market economy, for in all areas of life, when a man could do something well enough that it could be assigned a monetary value, he was encouraged to do more of it. That professional baseball players were among the highest paid Americans verified the sport's value as a business venture.

... Amateur Athletic Union (AAU) president James E. Sullivan was distressed when [Yale and Harvard] ... voted to liberalize their rules of amateurism [in 1905]. No longer would men who had accepted pay for play be ruled terminally ineligible. Rather, the newly adopted rule stated that any athlete who arrived … by the age of nineteen, having previously received money for athletic services, would be placed in good standing at the discretion of the college after a lapse of two years. Sullivan immediately denounced the two schools.… The argument about summer baseball was turned over in 1906 to … the National Collegiate Athletic Association.

The NCAA and Summer Baseball

… [C]ollege authorities were willing to hazard a course of collective intercession into college athletics … because of their … belief that harmony and justice were dependent on purposeful social planning. Progressives formed voluntary associations, of which the NCAA was one, to collect data [to] … establish reforms.… Intercollegiate athletic leaders attempted this … reform through oration and debate at annual NCAA conventions. Behind brutality in football, … summer baseball … was at the forefront of these discussions.

At the time of the NCAA's genesis, the ways in which college baseball players were associated with summer nines had expanded. Some players still played for seaside or mountain resorts under the cover of employment. Others … were paid at the end of the season when a collection was taken up from the guests. With the advent of semiprofessional town teams, skilled players could also work regular jobs for a living and then float from place to place on weekends filling roster spots for … cash.… How players maintained their anonymity remained unchanged, as many opted to compete under an alias.… [A] journalist wrote in 1907 of what the public could soon expect to hear from college campuses at the close of the summer baseball season: Newspapers could be expected to publish incriminating evidence against college athletes; faculty would then be prompted to debate whether to uphold amateur principles in baseball; idealists would worry about the state of intercollegiate baseball and the moral depravity of the young men involved; students and athletic committees would remain discretely silent; while the general public laughed at the clever player earning an honest dollar.…

The first NCAA district report [1906] … noted the problem of summer baseball and how it related to amateurism. A committee on summer baseball was subsequently created to investigate the issue. No doubt, though, the NCAA's Executive Committee, … had already established an anti-summer baseball agenda. Article 7 of the inaugural by-laws stated: "No student shall represent a college or university in any intercollegiate game or contest who has at any time received, either directly or indirectly, money, or any other consideration, to play on any team or for his athletic services as a college trainer, athletic or gymnasium instructor, or who has competed for a money prize or portion of gate money in any contest, or … competed for any prize against a professional."

… To be eligible for intercollegiate competition, however, a student was expected to … sign an eligibility card according to his "honor as a gentleman.… Of the four questions posed, only the last one was devoted to a specific sport: "Have you ever played baseball on a summer team?" …

The response ... was frequently a lie because student sentiment towards summer baseball had not wavered. Adequate financial offers from summer teams were welcomed.... Students knew ... that star football players had for years been given scorecard privileges worth hundreds of dollars. To be denied an income during summer vacation seemed irrational to many students. Violations of amateur law to play on a resort or town team, therefore, fit well within "the ordinary undergraduate scheme of morality...." Alexander Meiklejohn from Brown ... claimed that students skilled in deception, and even the most honorable athletes corrupted by peer pressure, operated on the principle that any faculty rule could be broken and the punishment evaded under two conditions: If the rule lacked adequate enforcement, permitting all to break it, and if the rule seemed unfair and unjust. Summer baseball was certainly notable for its random sanctioning, students found summer baseball codes unreasonable as well.

Amateur law was thus viewed by many students as an unnecessary hindrance. In his district report to the NCAA assembly in 1913, University of the South professor Walter Hullihen announced ... students envied the athlete skillful enough to obtain a salary, no matter how small, for his ability. "Very rarely," Hullihen continued, "does the American undergraduate hear any argument against professionalism stronger than that it is a violation of 'amateur law' ... to be classed ... with the law against chapel cuts, class absences, and other abominations of the oppressors which should be evaded as far as possible."

The NCAA ... [worried that] if the question was not resolved, ... professionalism would spread throughout ... intercollegiate sport. Amos Alonzo Stagg articulated this ethical "thin edge of the wedge" argument before delegates of the 1908 NCAA Convention.... Many like Stagg were alarmed that any measure of professionalism permitted in college baseball would necessarily expand to ... other sports. Anarchy would be the order of the day.... Coaches and players ... of [other] sports could be expected to clamor for equal consideration.... Certainly it would be difficult to convince track athletes, wrestlers, swimmers, or football players, ... in need of summer earnings to defray education expenses, of the justification for one branch of athletics to have its own, less restrictive standards....

[If] summer baseball were allowed, Stagg prophesied ... professional football would appear and ultimately thrive. The nation's largest industrial cities, where the summer baseball problem was the most extreme, could be expected to field teams of ex-college players void of the amateur spirit. What would prevent such an occurrence, Stagg naively believed, was a genuine amateur spirit held among college football players that opposed commercialism.

NCAA leaders thus believed themselves ... charged with protecting the impressionable moral character of students from professional influences. The adoption of an indulgent summer baseball rule, reformers feared, would lead to an abundance of "pollution to the college community." For Stagg, ... a rule permitting summer baseball "would be an unceasing catastrophe which would wreck one of the finest institutions in the whole social structure of our country," as well as undermine the moral forces at work in college and high school athletics." Moral conduct of games would recede to take on the characteristics of a former era of foul language, unfair tactics, and brutality....

The underlying theme of this spirited opposition to professionalism was a stern judgment on the professional's morality. Professionalized men were thought by many to be a little less ready to admit that a game well lost was better than a game badly won. The infiltration of this mentality into college sport was viewed as a hindrance to college authorities seeking adherence to the letter, as well as the spirit, of amateur law....

Acceptance on college campuses of the men who had been compensated for their baseball abilities by resort and town teams could foreseeably lead to the solicitation of skilled players whose main objective was baseball rather than education. While surely better baseball would result, and some professionals assuredly were men of high ethical and moral standards, the issue was one of fairness. Unfair competition would result if men who played for fun and recreation were forced to compete with men who played for compensation. Collegiate players, ... would be forced to devote more time to baseball in order to win a spot on a professionally dominated collegiate roster, adversely affecting their educational interests.... Even more objectionable for Harvard coach Edward H. Nichols was the potentiality that colleges would be represented by "eminent professionals like Mr. Cobb, without giving a chance to the bona fide student." Although a career in professional baseball was "right in its way," according to Nichols, more could be expected in the way of usefulness and productiveness from a man with a college education.

Not all NCAA leaders, however, were as quick to embrace the oft-spoken hyperbole of Stagg.... Many in favor of a rule permitting summer baseball contested amateur law on the basis of its parallel application to intercollegiate football. How was it possible, they questioned, that a baseball player, earning pay for his athletic abilities for the direct purpose of paying his college tuition, could be ruled ineligible while football players were subsidized by the colleges? Both benefitted equally from their athletic abilities, the summer resort player at a rate of perhaps $150 per month compared to the football player who received free board at a training table. At least the baseball player was employed outside the college. The rules of amateurism seemingly differentiated between the professional and the amateur in a narrow and arbitrary manner. No doubt a case could be made that both classes of athletes were professionals, if indeed either was. Other students on college campuses were not restricted from earning money in the same way that athletes were. Rarely, for instance, were students who earned money for singing or playing an instrument considered professional musicians....

It ... was generally accepted among college faculty that students utilized their specific talents to bankroll tuition expenses.... Doing so did not necessarily make these men professionals in their chosen occupation. To be fair to the summer baseball players, then, J. P. Welsh of Penn State recommended athletes be judged solely on their status as bona fide students.... Welsh favored removing barriers that precluded professional athletes from representing colleges on the baseball diamond. Professionals would thereby be encouraged to seek college degrees while fulfilling their athletic ambitions as well.... Summer baseball men should be left alone in the "full, free, untrammeled exercise of his American citizenship," which entitled him "to 'life, liberty, and the pursuit of happiness,' which sometimes means money." More attention should have been paid, instead, to the true "canker sore in college athletics," the salaried tramp athlete with no interest in school.

Yale's Walter Camp, ... was not in favor of paying college athletes, and he opposed the practice of permitting college men to compete in athletics who demonstrated little interest in academics. Camp was not, however, a foe of summer baseball [although] he believed it best that players not be permitted to receive money for playing in the summer.... Camp believed revisions were in order when eligibility rules were constructed so as to prevent a college athlete from participating in a sport during the summer when it was particularly appropriate.... The only players inhibited by the restrictions of amateurism, Camp asserted, were the star players ..., the only athletes skilled enough to be sought after....

Baseball and crisis-laden football were considered worth saving because of their social value. Intercollegiate athletic programs were treasured or tolerated in direct proportion to the social welfare they generated. In this context, the permissiveness of summer baseball threatened the civic righteousness that many believed had developed during the first decade of the twentieth century. Threats to progressive human advancement, however, did not stop NCAA member institutions from conceding to the realities of summer baseball.

The Liberalization of Amateur Principles

The most acute stage of the summer baseball question passed sometime ... following the 1908 NCAA Convention debate. Although criticism ... continued to ebb and flow throughout the first decade of the NCAA's existence and was highlighted by occasional punctuating events, such as when Jim Thorpe was forced to relinquish his Olympic medals in 1913 for having received a small sum of money for playing summer baseball in North Carolina, institutions by this time had generally given up their efforts to prohibit ... summer baseball. Many NCAA delegates had come to view the breaking of summer baseball rules as trivial. They opted instead for guidelines that permitted students to play summer baseball rather than for rules that forced them to "deceive and falsify" their eligibility record. Even NCAA president Palmer Pierce noted that it had become no longer practicable to enforce the amateur rule in college baseball.... Better, to permit students to play for money with certain restrictions....

... [T]he amount of attention paid to summer baseball at NCAA conventions ran parallel to public and university spectator interest in the sport. As early as 1911, college baseball was being described in contemporary literature as a sport that failed to incite the interest of men and women in the bleachers.... The game was said to be "needlessly slow and drawn out" and reflected a tediousness not seen in the professional game. [P]rofessional baseball drew most of the country's best talent, thus causing college exhibitions to suffer in comparison....

With the decline in college baseball's popularity, and without any sense of a national summer baseball accord, institutions enacted guidelines covering a range of amateur tenets. Numerous faculty … found it increasingly troubling that they were compelled to monitor the summer activities of athletes….

Members schools of the Missouri Valley Conference were especially divided. … [In 1911] three conference schools abolished baseball as an intercollegiate sport rather than be parties to the "fraud and deception." … On the West Coast, some schools permitted summer baseball….

In the southern United States, summer baseball regulations were loosely enforced…. [S]ome schools reportedly permitted playing ball for money, some … to play on hometown teams, other schools threw up their hands in surrender …; while still others permitted the activity so long as the student was not receiving pay from his own institution…. [N]umerous southern schools adopted the position that small towns, many of which fielded a team, were dependent on their college players' return home for the summer. When amateur rules kept college players from their only summer opportunity, it was determined to be unfeasible to enforce amateur law. It was therefore not the evasive ethics of collegiate players that needed adjustment, but rather amateur codes….

… [I]nstitutions of the Rocky Mountain and Southwest regions made summer baseball an exception to their otherwise rigid eligibility rules….

Although eastern schools typically adhered to the party line … against summer baseball … as early as 1909, 10 of the 16 northeastern district colleges permitted summer baseball. Those who allowed their players to maintain collegiate eligibility typically fell back on the argument that students could be educated "into sympathy with amateurism."

Their intent was to make official … the common and reasonable practice of allowing the players of their institutions to play for their town teams…. Summer baseball was thus permissible except on teams governed by the national agreement between the professional National and American Leagues….

… [R]epresentatives from some prestigious northeastern schools continued to publicly malign summer baseball as inimical to amateur standards…. Fred Marvel of Brown, although expressing his district's collective distaste for summer baseball, noted the apprehension of athletic representatives about recommending rules that would apply to every NCAA institution…. Pessimists about reform …, agreed with the notion that colleges would always formulate their policies to fit local conditions and that a sweeping rule against the practice of summer baseball would be ineffective. In a number of America's most prestigious schools, however, the anti-summer baseball posture had been noticeably altered. Even intercollegiate athletics' Big Three had conceded to the realities of summer baseball, well beyond the scope of their two-year moratorium on intercollegiate baseball participation for 19-year-olds devised in 1905…. Five Yale men … were ruled ineligible by the Yale Athletic Committee in the fall of 1915 for having accepted free board the previous summer while playing in Quogue, Long Island. Princeton men were blamed for having blown the whistle on the Yale players, who, … had received permission from a Yale coach to play…. It is therefore ironic that a defense … would be headed by athletic officials from rivals Princeton and

Harvard ... who both requested the Yale men be permitted to play based on similar circumstances occurring with players of their own schools. Because both Harvard and Princeton had reinstated several of their own men under parallel circumstances, their athletic committees, from an attitude of sportsmanship, supported the reinstatement of the Yale players.... Provisional rules were ultimately formed at the conference that would allow college athletes to play summer ball, provided the players gained prior permission from college authorities. ... [T]he five Yale men had their eligibility reinstated.

At Penn and Columbia, a liberalized climate for summer baseball had likewise emerged. Dr. Arthur W. Goodspeed, chairman of the Faculty Committee on Athletics at Penn, advocated early in 1914 that college men be able to play summer baseball without the threat of losing their athletic eligibility.... President Butler of Columbia, the same man who squashed football on the Columbia campus in 1905, ... saw no objection to a student playing baseball for money during his vacation rather than waiting tables....

This newfound tolerance also affected the fervor for amateurism shared by the NCAA, the AAU, and the IC4A [and] a defined amateur code was agreed upon. One objection by the NCAA caused Chairman Gustavus Kirby of the AAU to drop the wording "associating with professionals" from the code.... because the NCAA had rejected this phrase for the adverse effects it would have on collegians playing or having played summer baseball.... They were only recognizing what was well known ... that summer baseball rules were not enforceable, that amateur principles were embraced in blind faith by neither students nor faculty, and that association with professional athletes did not necessarily correlate into the corruption of a student's ... character.

By 1916, ... 105 out of 137 surveyed colleges permitted summer baseball for compensation.... College baseball players were ... granted a peculiar exemption from amateur law. While other collegiate athletes were bound to uphold standards that precluded the procurement of an income from their athletic talents, summer baseball players recreated for profit.

FURTHER READING

Bernstein, Mark F. *Football: The Ivy League Origins of an American Obsession* (2001).

De Martini, Joseph R. "Student Culture as a Change Agent in American Higher Education: An Illustration from the Nineteenth Century," *Journal of Social History* 9 (1976), 526–41.

Doyle, Andrew. "'Causes Won, Not Lost': College Football and the Modernization of the American South," *International Journal of the History of Sport* 11 (February 1994), 231–51.

Durick, William G. "The Gentlemen's Race: An Examination of the 1868 Harvard–Oxford Boat Race," *Journal of Sport History* 15 (1988), 41–63.

Ingrassia, Brian M. *The Rise of Gridiron University: Higher Education's Uneasy Alliance with Big-Time Football* (2012).

Lester, Robin Dale. *Stagg's University: The Rise, Decline, and Fall of Football at Chicago* (1995).

Lewis, Guy M. "The Beginning of Organized Collegiate Sport," *American Quarterly* 22 (1970), 222–29.

Miller, John J. *The Big Scrum: How Teddy Roosevelt Saved Football* (2011).

Moore, J. Hammond "Football's Ugly Decades, 1893–1913," *Smithsonian Journal of History* 2 (1967), 49–68.

Oriard, Michael. *Reading Football: How the Popular Press Created an American Sporting Spectacle* (1993).

Pont, Sally. *Fields of Honor: The Golden Age of College Football and the Men Who Created It* (2001).

Riesman, David and Reuel Denney, "Football in America: A Study of Cultural Diffusion," *American Quarterly* 3 (1951), 309–25.

Savage, Harold J. et al., *American College Athletics* (1929).

Schmidt, Raymond. *Shaping College football: The Transformation of an American Sport, 1919–1930* (2007).

Smith, Ronald A. *Sports and Freedom: The Rise of Big-Time College Athletics* (1988).

Smith, Ronald A., ed., *Big-Time Football at Harvard, 1905: The Diary of Coach Bill Reid* (1994).

Sperber, Murray. *Shake Down the Thunder: The Creation of Notre Dame Football* (1993).

Waterson, John Sayle. *College Football: History, Spectacle, Controversy* (2002).

CHAPTER 6

Sport and the Rise of the Industrial Radial City, 1870–1930

The coming of the modern city dramatically influenced the development and character of American sport. Antebellum American cities were "walking cities," which were small, commercialized towns characterized by unspecialized land uses. In contrast, the new industrial radial city of the 1870s had a much larger population, and it encompassed far more space, which was usually gained through annexation. It had highly specialized land uses, a central business district, distinctive class-based residential areas, and it was economically grounded in industrial production. These cities covered large areas and required innovative forms of mass transit, which culminated in the electric-powered streetcars and subways in the 1890s and early 1900s.

How did the growth of cities shape our sporting heritage? The sporting options of urbanites were directly affected by such diverse issues as changing land use patterns, local politics, ethnicity, race, wealth, and the social values of a city's dominant and subordinate groups. As cities grew, older forms of sport that required a lot of space were displaced. The loss of traditional recreational spaces encouraged a boom in the park movement that advocated construction of large suburban parks on the model of New York's Central Park.

What was the impact on sport of overcrowded urban neighborhoods? What kinds of sports could be played in urban slums? It was difficult to play a regular game of baseball in the more densely populated neighborhoods, and youths would have to initiate special ground rules if they played in narrow alleys. How successful was the playground movement's quest for small play spaces in crowded inner-city neighborhoods?

Another consequence of urbanization was the great increase in potential markets for commercialized sports. Entrepreneurs established professional sports leagues and built ballparks, race tracks, and indoor arenas and gymnasiums to cater to the growing demand for spectator sports. Innovative businessmen also established a vast sporting goods industry that took advantage of a host of new products and innovations in industrial production to manufacture cheap mass-produced goods to satisfy growing consumer demands for athletic equipment.

DOCUMENTS

The documents in this section describe certain sporting facilities available to urbanites, the importance of those sites for the benefit of the community, and the sporting options available to city people. Document 1 is composed of two *New York Times* editorials evaluating the status of New York's Central Park. The editorials laud the park as an important site for receptive (nonactive) public recreation, but they also criticize the inadequate access of the park both for people other than the well-to-do and for its strict policy of keeping patrons off its grass. Document 2, an 1888 *New York Times* editorial, explains how a professional baseball team boosted a city's pride, even though the players were all out-of-towners. Document 3 focuses on boosterism in a *New York Times* editorial at the turn of the century that urged the municipality to take over the new Madison Square Garden, which was built in 1890. Designed by renowned architect Stanford White, it was the most famous sports arena in the United States and the second tallest structure in New York City. The original Garden, operated by William Vanderbilt from 1879 to 1886, had already hosted many great sporting events, including the Horse Show, boxing matches starring John L. Sullivan, and long-distance running races. Document 4 deals with Josiah Quincy III, the progressive mayor of Boston from 1896 to 1899, following in the footsteps of his father and grandfather, who was a big supporter of public works, especially aimed at helping the poorer residents enjoy an improved quality of life. He was heavily involved in increasing Boston's investment in parks, playgrounds, and public baths to enhance public health. The document included here is his report to the City Council in 1898, supporting the financing of public swimming pools. Finally Document 5 in this section is taken from the autobiography of Barney Ross (1909–1967), an all-time great fighter who was the first to simultaneously hold three world championships (lightweight, light welterweight, and welterweight) during 1933–1934. He had a lifetime record of 74-4-3, and the remarkable distinction of never having been knocked down. He recounts growing up in the impoverished Jewish West Side of Chicago where after his father was shot to death by robbers in his grocery store, and his mother had a nervous breakdown, young Beryl Rosofsky turned to the streets and became a thug. This lifestyle prepared him well to become a prizefighter.

1. The *New York Times* Evaluates the Accessibility and Utility of Central Park, 1873, 1875

… How great a boon these grounds have been to the public may be judged from the fact that during last year nearly 11,000,000 persons visited them, the average daily number being about 30,000, or about twenty-three per cent larger than on any former year. On one fine Sunday, in September, the visits ran up to 109,000. Thus far, however, these beautiful grounds are more for the recreation

From *New York Times*, March 6, 1873, and November 15, 1875.

of the rich than the poor, as the average number of visits made daily in carriages and on horseback was 14,000, while the average number of pedestrians was about 9,000. This proportion will undoubtedly constantly change. Means will be contrived for carrying the masses of the people from the crowded tenement-house quarters, cheaply to these charming scenes. We hope in the future for what may be called "workmen's cars," going at low rates from the poorer wards, directly to the park, on Saturday afternoons. The children, too, of the laboring people, will more and more spend their holidays there. It must be remembered that the great and valuable use of the Central Park, in the future, will be its affording a bit of quiet, rural scenery, and a breath of fresh country air to the people of the poorer and middle classes. The rich can get their pleasures anywhere, but hundreds of thousands of persons of small means are forced to find their only out-door enjoyment in this, almost our only park. In this view, it is of the utmost importance that nothing should be done for the future which should destroy its quiet, rural character. Enough space already has been given up to drives and stately promenades; enough is already occupied by, or devoted to, public buildings. What the laborers and the children of the poor and the tired business men most need are simple, pleasant country scenes, with solitary rambles and quiet walks.

... [T]he rules about not walking on the grass are now enforced so rigidly that sending children to the Park is rather a punishment for them than a treat. Policemen hunt them about as if they were little criminals who were "wanted" at head-quarters. The children are obliged to keep on the hard, narrow paths, like prisoners in a yard. In every park in the country but our own, children are allowed to play on the grass—and certainly Central Park grass has cost enough to be good for something. Prospect Park, Brooklyn, is the delight of young and old, because of the absence of those vexatious restrictions with which the Central Park Commissioners do their best to drive the public out of their own property. Indeed, Prospect Park is now in every way a much more beautiful park than ours. Between the malaria of the lakes, and cast-iron rules, and the way in which policemen threaten and bully every little child who wanders for a minute on the grass, the Commissioners are likely soon to have the Central Park all to themselves....

2. The *New York Times* Lauds Baseball and Community Pride, 1888

A considerable number of intelligent and respectable citizens of New-York are daily disgusted at the evidence of the interest taken by a still more considerable number of persons whom they assume to be less intelligent and respectable in the game of baseball. They regard it as monstrous and absurd that the papers should devote so much space to chronicling the procedures of nine persons of no eminence except for their capabilities of throwing, catching, and hitting

---

From *New York Times*, September 23, 1888.

balls and of running short distances with rapidity. They deplore the effect of these chronicles upon the young, and they resent the absence from the public prints of matter more interesting to themselves which they assume is displaced to make room for the accounts of baseball matches. Those of them whose disgust has not prevented them from learning anything at all of its subject point out that it is not even a local pride that is properly involved, since the players are mercenaries who may appear this season in the green shirts and scarlet stockings and blue caps of one community, and next year in equally kaleidoscopic raiment betokening a new allegiance.

This is all true, and yet the zealots of baseball, at least in this city, have some reason on their side, though they may not be able to produce it. However illogical it may be that local pride should be aroused by the victories of one team of professional baseball players over another or touched by its defeats, yet, as a matter of fact, that feeling is enlisted on the part of a considerable fraction of the population in the varying fortunes of the so-called "New-Yorks," and we hold that anything whatsoever that can excite the local pride of New-York is so far a good thing. For local pride is much the same thing as public spirit, which at least cannot exist without it, and there is no city in the world that is more deficient in public spirit than New-York, or that ought to welcome more anything that tends to stimulate that quality.

It is in some respects a misfortune for a town to be the biggest in its country, though doubtless it is a misfortune that other towns would gladly assume. Its inhabitants are too apt to assume that its bigness puts it out of competition and that it is superfluous for it to be anything else but big. The New-Yorker who goes to Boston or to Philadelphia or to Chicago is sure to have the excellences and advantages of those towns respectively pointed out to him by the inhabitants thereof, and he is equally sure to regard the indication as "provincial," assuming that the establishment by the census that there are more "head" of New-Yorkers than of Bostonians or Philadelphians renders any other indication of its superiority unnecessary. He is only internationally sensitive. When he goes to London or Paris, or when a Londoner or Parisian is under his charge in his own city, he is apt to wish that he had something else to point out than the bigness in which their cities exceed his own. He would like them to admire New-York, though he is above soliciting the admiration of his countrymen....

If New-York were not so big as to be out of competition in that respect it would doubtless be a better place to live in, and anything that brings it into direct competition with other cities, even in so trivial a matter as playing baseball, has wholesome elements. It is not at all municipally important that the New-Yorks should win the championship, but it is important that New-Yorkers should be anxious that their city should excel in anything. When *Iroquois* won the Derby it was plausibly said that the victory raised the United States higher in the estimation of the general mass of Englishmen than any other they had ever achieved. A cynical philosopher, replying to a person uninterested in aquatic sports, who betrayed the same impatience with the inordinate attention paid by the press and the public to the international yacht races that we are now remarking upon with reference to baseball, defended the public interest upon the ground that the *America's* Cup was really the only trophy the country had to show. Possibly a similar remark about the possession of the champion baseball pennant by New-York would be equally exaggerated, but at all events the competition proves that it does not quite suffice for all New-Yorkers that New-York is big. If this sentiment were extended in more rational directions there might actually come an irresistible public demand that New-York should become the best paved, cleaned, and policed city and the most attractive place of residence in the United States. Meanwhile, any stir of local pride is to be welcomed that makes a beginning in the direction of that distant and Utopian end.

3. The *New York Times* Considers Madison Square Garden as a Civic Institution, 1900

... The representatives of the owners of Madison Square Garden cannot be blamed for trying to sell their property to the Government for a Post Office. Such a sale would enable them to unload a burden some of them have been carrying for many years for the benefit of all the rest of us, and which they may well desire that somebody else shall now take up. Neither can the representatives of the government be blamed for dealing to acquire a site for the Post Office which is at least far more eligible than the site now occupied for that purpose....

They ignore the importance of the civic and municipal functions which the amphitheater of the Madison Square Garden now fulfills, and has fulfilled since its erection. There are certain shows and celebrations which cannot be given anywhere else, and which add immensely to the attractiveness of the city, and also to the profits of the men who do business in it, that simply could not be given in the absence of a Madison Square Garden to give them in. The Horse Show is the most conspicuous of these entertainments. It cannot be rivaled or approached in any other American city, mainly for want of so good a place in which to hold it. It is safe to say that it is the municipal possession which is most envied of New York by citizens of the other great cities.

Why should it not be made, in name as well as in fact, a municipal possession, as other things have been, through private munificence? The proposition is by no means so startling or so anomalous as it may at the first glance seem. The city is empowered, under its charter, to acquire real estate "for any public use or purpose." Surely there is not difference in principle between acquiring land for the purpose of public entertainment and instruction and devoting to such a purpose land of which the title is already in the city. And this latter has repeatedly been done, with the general approbation. For the New York Public Library the city has given both ground and building. For the Metropolitan Museum of Art, for the Museum of Natural History, for the Zoological Garden, or the Botanical Garden, it has given the land. In all these cases it has gone into partnership with private munificence and public spirit. None of these enterprises, perhaps, could

---

From *New York Times*, February 28, 1900.

sustain itself but for the perfectly legitimate assistance it has derived from being made free of rent and taxes. Here is another public enterprise not less important, which has been demonstrated not to be self-sustaining purely as a commercial enterprise. Why should the city not lend its countenance to this also?

It is to be noted that in every one of the other cases private citizens have given earnest of public spirit and munificence before the city has been called in to aid. That condition should not be relaxed in this instance. If there is in the community enough of interest in the purposes which the Madison Square Garden subserves to induce subscribers to make a free gift to the city of the building of the Madison Square Garden, they would have made an excellent case for the city to treat them as it has treated other admirable and public-spirited enterprises, by aiding them to carry on their public work. This it could do by taking title to the land on which the building stands. As a continuous corporation the city could not lose by such an investment. In fact, it would be a good investment, since it would be provided that after a certain or an uncertain term of years, when the place should have outlived its usefulness as a unique place of public entertainment, the whole property should revert to the city, to be put to the more profitable uses of which it would have become ready.... The sole question is, or ought to be, whether there is public spirit enough among the rich men of New York to retain for public uses the place which has so admirably served those uses ever since it was built.

4. Mayor Quincy of Boston Supports Municipal Swimming Pools, 1898

I have recently been considering with the Bath Commission the propriety of deepening the Frog Pond upon the Common, and converting it during the summer season into a swimming pool. It appears from the estimates which have been prepared that this pond could be deepened to a uniform depth of four feet, which would be suitable for the purpose proposed, at an expense of about $3500 and the necessary bath-house accommodation could be provided, by the temporary use of two polling booths, for about $1000. The plan contemplates a bathhouse projecting over the pond, so that bathers would enter and leave the water only under its shelter; it is not proposed to allow them to enter or leave the water from any other point. The pool is intended to be used only by boys of school age during the daytime, though possibly by adults as well during the evening, and of course suitable bathing dresses would be required.

If it were thought necessary or advisable, a fence or screen could be provided extending entirely around the pond. According to estimates which have been prepared, a suitable canvas screen 12 feet in height, supported on ornamental iron posts, could be provided for $1800, and the cost of an ornamental, portable shingled fence, built in sections, of the same height would be about the same. If there seemed to be a demand for it, as I think would be the case,

---

From Boston City Council, *Report of the Proceedings of the City Council of Boston for the Year Commencing January 3, 1898, and ending December 21, 1898* (Boston: Municipal Printing Office, 1899), 942.

instruction in swimming might be provided at this point during the summer season. As everything could be movable, the pond would be restored to its present condition early in the autumn.

The Bath Commission has by vote given its indorsement to this proposal to try the experiment of putting the Frog Pond to this new use, and after giving the matter considerable thought, I am fully prepared to recommend to the City Council that the requisite authority for trying this experiment be given. If such use of this pond proved in any way to be undesirable, it need not be continued; and in order to place the project strictly upon an experimental basis, it might be as well to confine the authority to the coming season.

The area of the Frog Pond is about 38,500 square feet, or about six-sevenths of an acre, and an opportunity for bathing and swimming for a large number of persons would therefore be afforded. The location is of course a very central one, and a very large population resides within an easy distance of it. The City Engineer estimates that it would cost over $15,600 to build a new swimming pool of this area, and the cost of purchasing such an amount of land in any central location would doubtless be considered prohibitory. It is admitted that a large number of boys, and perhaps of adults, would gladly avail themselves of the privilege of bathing in this pond if it were afforded to them, as I believe would prove to be the case, it seems to me that the only question is whether the greatest good of the greatest number would be promoted by making this new use of property already owned by the city. Of course the success of the experiment would depend upon the manner in which the bathing was regulated and upon the maintenance of proper order, but I believe myself that this would be satisfactorily managed.

It may be suggested that the portion of the Common now used for a playground would be a more suitable location for such a swimming pool, but aside from the very much greater expense of construction, I find that a pool of the same size could not be constructed there without occupying altogether too large a portion of the available space and unduly restricting the important use of this area for playground purposes. I therefore recommend the passage of the accompanying order. Respectfully submitted,

Josiah Quincy, Mayor.

Ordered that the Superintendent of the Public Grounds be authorized to deepen Frog Pond upon the Common for the purpose of making the same available for a swimming pool; and that the Department of Baths lie authorized to allow bathing in such swimming pool between June 20th and September 20th of the current year, under such rules and regulations as they shall prescribe with the approval of the Mayor, such rules to provide among other things, that only boys shall be allowed to bathe in the Pond during the daytime, that bathers shall enter and leave the water only under the shelter of a bathhouse projecting over the Pond, and that proper bathing dresses be worn; and for such purposes said Department is hereby authorized to erect any temporary structures, to be approved by the Mayor, adjacent to said Pond, the same to be entirely removed by October 1st next, such structures to include a screen at least 12 feet high enclosing the pond. Assigned to the next meeting.

5. The Mean Streets of Chicago in the 1920s and the Making of a Prize Fighter

BARNEY ROSS

I went down to the Four Deuces[an Al Capone owned speakeasy and brothel].... I hung around for a few days till I met Arnie Falzo, one of my opponents in our street-gang fights. [He] ... was doing odd jobs for the gang. He brought me ... to Al [who] ... knew all the details of Pa's murder:.... "You got no business getting mixed up in rackets, you couldn't be a hood if you wanted to...."

... Finally he said maybe I could run errands for him and he'd keep me in pocket money.... I also ran errands for Al [Capone]'s brother, and for other gang members like the Fischetti brothers ... and Jack McGurn.

... Many of the gang members who used to send me on errands soon wound up as corpses in the gang wars. The St. Valentine's Day Massacre of 1929 meant more to me ... because I knew ... the seven men ... killed.

My career as messenger-boy for gang leaders ended abruptly one morning when Capone told me it was time for me to stop hanging around his place and time to "get off the streets."... "Here's a twenty ..." "Buy your family something and go back to school or get a job...."

... I met up again with Arnie Falzo. I hadn't seen him for a while and he told me he'd joined a gang called the "42's"[a Chicago teenage street gang] ... young toughs who'd graduated from the street fights, gotten themselves guns, and were now pulling off armed hold-ups, and hi-jackings....

... Arnie ... told me the gang was going to pull a stick-up [and asked if I wanted in]....

I nodded, as if to say yes, and walked off. But ... memories of Pa kept crowding my mind.... Once I seemed to see Pa standing right in front of me, ... shouting at me, "*Nayn*! Beryl, *nayn!*" ... I kept remembering how Pa's customers had always looked up to him and how he talked about Reb Rasofsky as a man of learning and honor.... I just couldn't do that to Pa and to the things Pa stood for.

The 42's became a real terror gang, one of the worst in Chicago. For a while, they really rode high. But two years later, Arnie Falzo was killed by the cops trying to escape the scene of a hi-jacking job. Eventually, three other fellows ... were killed in gang fights, two who lived just a block away from me went to the electric chair, and seven others were sent up for prison terms ranging from ten to thirty years. Pa's memory and Pa's teachings had saved me from a terrible fate.

From Barney Ross with Martin Abramson, *No Man Stands Alone: The True Story of Barney Ross* (Philadelphia: J. B. Lippincott, 1957), 65–68, 84.

ESSAYS

The two essays in this section reflect the great interest urban historians have in how urbanization has influenced the direction of sport history and how, in turn, the rise of sport has affected urban life. They look at the city not only as the site of sport but also as a part of the process of city building—the interplay of its physical structures, organizations, and values.

Drawn from his broader study of sport in Boston, *How Boston Played*, Stephen Hardy examines in detail how and why municipal parks were built in Boston in the late nineteenth century despite the varied interests of important local political blocs. He emphasizes the agency of Irish working-class people in securing the kinds of parks they wanted with space to play ball rather than the staid suburban parks advocated by the middle class.

Steven A. Riess, professor emeritus at Northeastern Illinois University, examines the integral role of machine politicians in the development of prize fighting, horse racing, and baseball (the three major professional sports at the turn of the century) in New York City, the national capital of professional sport. New York politics was heavily influenced by its powerful Tammany Hall machine, but in cities all across the country, local politicians were prominent sports entrepreneurs, who relied upon their clout to facilitate their sporting interests.

Parks for the People: The Rise of Public Parks in Boston, 1869–1900

STEPHEN HARDY

... The development of a public park system marks a significant chapter in Boston's sport history. For one, the parks represented the first major civic response to the amusement question. Indeed, parks provided much of the open space upon which Bostonians pursued their favorite sports. But the parks issue also embodied many of the philosophies and arguments aired in a city rudely awakened to the fact that urban growth was not all positive. Commercial and industrial success rested on top of a much denser population that included hordes of immigrants; the by-products of "progress" included an inexorable sprawl of housing, a choking pollution of the air, and the erosion of cultural homogeneity. In large part, public parks were first presented as a reform to many of these problems. But the record of park development reveals that simple solutions were not easily implemented. Urban growth was accompanied by widening divisions between social classes and interest groups within the city's boundaries. Residents in new and old neighborhoods sought to control the use of local space. New political machinery had developed to represent their divergent interests. The working of this changing social and political

From Stephen Hardy, *How Boston Played: Sport, Recreation and Community, 1865–1915* (Boston: Northeastern University Press, 1982), 65–84.

order complicated, challenged, and transformed the park system in Boston. Their complexity argues against simple notions about the nature and process of this important urban reform.

Most historians have viewed parks and their close relation, playgrounds, as the creation of middle- and upper-class reformers who desired to provide order for both the urban landscape and its inhabitants. As a recent article on Frederick Law Olmsted, consultant and chief architect for the Boston park system from 1875 to 1895, maintains, "Olmsted's parks seemed to offer an attractive remedy for the dangerous problem of discontent among the urban masses." ... Olmsted and other early park advocates quickly and continually discovered that factional strife and class resentment could erupt and envenom debates on the placement, benefits, and beneficiaries of nature's blessings. In Boston, as in Worcester, the larger urban constituency—laborers and clerks, artisans and bookkeepers, natives and immigrants, men and women—expressed their interests, either directly or through their political representatives. Their pressure forced adjustments in the initial visions of genteel reformers like Olmsted and his supporters.

The park movement in Boston was part of an active, conscious search for order amid the environmental, political, social, and cultural dislocations.... Much of the initiative clearly lay with established middle- and upper-class groups who designed their programs for all Bostonians. But it would be wrong to think that the remainder of Boston's population sat passively as major public policy filtered down from above. On the contrary, both the form and essence of public parks developed in ways determined by interest groups representing a wide range of citizens, as one discovers by comparing the early rhetoric with the later reality.

The main story begins in 1869, when the pressures of increased growth and a heightened awareness of the Common's inadequacies resulted in a series of proposals for public park systems. Unfortunately, the fear of higher taxes, coupled with the conviction that the nearby suburbs provided ample scenery, prevented the approval of such early legislation as the Park Act of 1870. The debate over parks continued unchecked, however, and within five years Boston's citizens had swayed enough to approve the Park Act of 1875. Accordingly, the mayor appointed three commissioners (approved by the city aldermen) who were charged to entertain citizens' proposals and examine possible acquisitions "with regard to many different points such as convenience of access, original cost and betterments, probable cost of improvements, sanitary conditions and natural beauty." The commissioners retained Frederick Law Olmsted as a consultant until 1878, when he was appointed chief landscape architect for the park system.

Early park advocates claimed (convincingly enough) that the entire city benefited from and supported the movement. As one popular newspaper urged:

> A public park is now a great necessity and not an expensive luxury. It is the property of the people, rich and poor together, and the only place where all classes can daily meet one another face to face in a spirit of fraternal recreation.

Another claimed on the eve of the park referendum:

> The moment anything is done under the act it will open a new field for laborers, and at the same time enlarge the possessions in which their wives and children will have an equal inheritance with the most favored. Indeed, the great benefit of public parks is gathered by those who are not rich.

Park boosters, often among Boston's most prominent and established residents, felt their arguments represented those of all citizens, rich and poor. Their formula for reform was simple. Parks would offer both escape from and control of the traumas caused by the rapid spread of houses, factories, and people, with their congestion, noise, and pollution. Parks would provide something the much-revered small town always had offered; open space and rural scenery. Thus, while park proponents tended to revel in the prospect of a booming Boston, they also desired to brake its unchecked growth by imposing at least three qualities that the small-town community seemed to offer: fresh air and open space, healthy citizens, and pervasive morality.

It was not so much that park proponents wanted to make Boston a small town. They desired, rather, to balance urbanization with a form of ruralization. With parks the city would always retain part of what it had had in the past. Few denied the inexorable nature of the population's advance.... Unfortunately, the congestion of humanity threatened the existence of open space and pure air, and so endangered the lives of individual inhabitants as to threaten the life of the city itself.

During the heated debates of 1881, the critical year of parkland acquisition, one alderman emphasized the changes that had occurred in his thirty-seven years as a Bostonian. The city had been smaller, but at the same time, "the boys could go anywhere, the lands of all seemed to be public.... Now you will find a sign up, 'No trespassing'; 'Keep off the grass.'" He warned his colleagues that they voted not for their generation, but for "those that follow us...."

Shaping the city environment by means of well-planned open space was matched in urgency by the concern for health. It was a well-circulated belief that parks were the "lungs of the city."... Parks would be part of a triad of services which, along with pure water and efficient sewage systems, would "make the cities in all ways healthful and beautiful. The weight of the medical profession aided the momentum for parks. Physicians cited numerous statistics and studies to show that urban areas suffered higher death and disease rates, which could in large part be traced to foul air and insufficient sunlight. Particularly alarming were the facts disclosing high rates of cholera infantum and stillbirths in cities like Boston. The haunting conclusion remained that "unless open spaces of sufficient extent are provided and properly located, we shall create and shut up in this city the conditions, of which disease, pestilence and death will be the natural offspring."

Others saw a different therapeutic value in parks. One alderman wove the sights and sounds of parks into a logical argument about the requisites of labor and wealth. Since wealth rested on labor, and labor involved expenditures of force, "it follows that without recuperation and recreation of force, the ability of each individual to labor is diminished and his power to add to the wealth of the community is lost."...

Physical health, or the lack of it, was delicately entwined with the issue of public morality. To those concerned with a degenerating social order, the benefit of public parks in this area was unrivaled.... It was, said Dr. [Edward] Crane, the "close atmosphere" of his house and street that drove the tired workman to the saloon to seek relief. If only he had a park accessible to him, the poor laborer would seek it with his family "as instinctively as a plant stretched toward the light." The park would "educate him and his family into the enjoyment of innocent amusements and open-air pleasures." Somehow, by an association with nature, the workingman and his family would experience a florescence of morality previously stifled by the choking air of city streets. Thus the parks would help resolve the nagging problem of urban amusements....

... By 1876, as the speakers at a public park rally made clear, it was necessary for the city to provide asylums for ... wholesome activities. The cost of parks would be far less than the cost of the jails, prisons, and police used in repressing wasteful indulgences like liquor and gambling. Parks would provide the blue sky, the gurgling brook, and the green trees that acted as immeasurable moral agents in the village. The country would elevate the minds and manners of the urban poor. If the masses could not get to the country, let the city "bring the country to them, and give them a chance, at least, to experience its humanizing and blessed influence." Since parks belonged to all the people, rich or poor, all could mingle freely in a neutral cultural asylum. Fresh air would naturally improve the temperament of working-class men and women, for they would be induced "by public orders and public favor to elevate themselves and their condition in society" by associating with their betters through the medium of nature.

Boston needed parks to preserve her environment, her health, and her morality. But she also needed parks to prove her legitimacy as a first-class American city.... The best public schools, art museums, conservatories of music, and schools of design could not ensure Boston's reputation as the Athens of America if she lacked the spirit by which public parks were developed. A City Council committee concluded that "if Boston cannot afford such an expenditure to secure the priceless benefit of parks, it must be because she has entered the ranks of cities like Newburyport and Salem, which have ceased to grow." Civic boosterism clearly accelerated the growing demand for public parks. Boston's top business firms favored parks as a grand advertisement of the city's commercial health, and claimed that their beauty would attract wealthy merchants from around the globe. Moreover, these plush pleasure grounds would convince the prosperous classes to retain their homes within the city's limits and eschew the flight to rural suburbs. As Oliver Wendell Holmes maintained, parks would help provide the city "with the complete equipment, ... of a true metropolis."

The argument supporting public parks was clear. They would improve the physical environment of the city and, more important, elevate the living conditions of her inhabitants. Rich and poor alike would enjoy the benefits of nature, placed in perpetuum within the city limits. Families in the impoverished North End or in the elegant Back Bay could rest assured that fresh air would be forever available to their children and to their children's children. Finally, Boston, by displaying the spirit necessary for such a project, would reestablish her reputation as America's premier city.

There can be no doubt that a broad consensus supported the position of park advocates. By 1900, the park system surrounding Boston was, in large part, complete.... By means of parkways, expanses of greenery were effectively linked throughout the city....

But while Bostonians agreed upon the general benefits that parks could produce, they differed over answers to several specific questions that arose during the implementation of the plan proposed by Olmsted and the commissioners. These questions and their resultant friction revolved around three interrelated concerns. First, where in the city should parks properly be located? Second, for whose benefit were the parks ultimately intended? Finally, how exactly were parks to improve the leisure, and through it the life, of all citizens? ...

The task of locating a park or parks was not an easy one. While advocates stressed the benefits to be enjoyed by the entire city, politicians and citizens' lobbies were more concerned about the advantages or disadvantages of placing parks within their particular neighborhoods.... Each section of the city concluded that all would be best served by locating a park within its boundaries.

By 1881, the year in which the City Council considered the bulk of park bonds, this parochialism had become so acute as to threaten the very purpose of a park system.... A City Council committee pleaded that "an end be put to sectional contentions respecting park lands." Yet as the votes in the Common Council indicate, local interests rivaled general concerns. Every area of the city, from East Boston to West Roxbury, was represented by a politician who steadfastly maintained both the urgent need for a park in his district and the general benefits to be derived from placing one there.

The voting patterns on two key proposals ... display the type of parochialism that worried Olmsted. For instance, in 1877 the first proposal to purchase land for a Back Bay park failed because of negative votes from members of the Common Council representing the congested inner wards and the outlying suburban wards. The proposal succeeded only when it was reevaluated as a necessary instrument for the improvement of the city's sewage system. Second, and more clearly, one can view the local interest pattern in the December 1881 vote on the purchase of land for the West Roxbury (Franklin) Park, the linchpin of Olmsted's system.... Opposition to the suburban park came from congested wards in the inner city. At the same time, councilors from wards adjacent to the park were almost unanimous in their approval of the costly ($600,000) acquisition.... Many citizens viewed park benefits in local, not general terms. The debates and votes on the placement of public parks thus exhibited the polarity in urban politics so well described in historical literature: centralized reform groups at odds with localized political machinery. In this case one sees Olmsted's grand vision matched against legitimate neighborhood and ward interests. The parks commissioners were forced to deal with an ever-increasing parochialism that reared its head early and often, as when many Ward 3 voters qualified their rejection of the 1875 Park Act by voting "No, unless Copps Hill is taken."

These attitudes continued even after the parks were completed. Some neighborhoods objected when "outsiders" availed themselves of local greenery. For instance, in 1892 a group of South Boston residents complained to the commissioners that Marine Park "had been an injury to South Boston on account of the rabble it had attracted there." Sunday arrests had involved far too many "Cambridge people"; they worried that the park had attracted "undesirable visitors to the neighborhood."...

But despite Olmsted's fears, parochial interests never seriously threatened the success of the park system. On the contrary, they may have *ensured* success, by forcing central planners to accommodate local interests. Olmsted and the parks commissioners might have had more than topographical considerations in mind when they designed a *series* of parks spread about Boston's various districts. Perhaps they realized the growing importance of neighborhood communities within the larger city boundaries. The overall park plan succeeded politically in 1881 because it offered a chain or package, with a little something for everyone....

There was another side to the problem of locating parks. Most of the acreage, as originally conceived and as expanded by local pressure, was situated in less-congested wards. While land was more available and cheaper here, the anomaly raised serious questions. For whom were parks really intended? The rich or the poor? ...

With elitist sentiment lurking under the surface of public proclamations, it was no wonder that the *Boston Daily Advertiser* worried about approval of the Park Act of 1875, noting that "in some of the northerly wards there will be formidable opposition, the laborers and others having been made to believe that in some way the act will be against their interests." Many had doubts. The councilors from inner-city wards realized that "the people" could not enjoy distant parks as easily as some believed. As one representative from Ward 7 reminded his colleagues, the poor workingman was not likely to march his family across town on a hot summer night just "to enjoy the benefits of the park which Boston, in its wisdom and philanthropy, has furnished for the laboring classes."...

One clearly deduces from the public record a sense of working-class frustration with the outlying parks.... Many continued to regard much of the system as essentially "rich man's parks," to enjoy which required either a carriage, or, later, an automobile.

But the changing political structure provided workingmen with more clout than they had previously enjoyed. Working through their local representatives in the City Council, the people of Charlestown effectively lobbied for a park in their area. During the mid-nineties, John F. Fitzgerald, the ward boss of the North End, continually pressured the commissioners for a park in his district. His unfailing energy and political savvy ensured the project's success despite the city's financial troubles. The North End park was thereafter his personal "monument." In like manner, the West End could count on strong political support to increase the capacity and facilities of its Charlesbank gymnasium. The inhabitants of the inner city did not reap the promised fruits of the outlying "emerald necklace," but they traded off support for rural parks in return for open space in their local neighborhoods. Much of this open space would take the form of small parks and playgrounds. These breathing spaces did not fit the classic model of an Olmsted park. They offered only limited foliage or serenity. But they did offer working people something tangible, and their development represented an important accommodation in the original vision of the park system.

The final area of contention was closely related and involved the question of appropriate activities for park patrons. Park advocates claimed that properly placed enclaves of "rus in urbe" would elevate the life of all citizens. Parks would provide true recreation for Boston's collective body and soul. The practical question, however, became whether or not the masses could be educated into the "proper" use of parks....

The central figure in this issue was, of course, Frederick Law Olmsted, who guided the Boston Park System until 1895.... Because of his national influence and, of course, his position as chief architect, his views were indelibly stamped on the policies of the Boston parks commissioners....

Olmsted believed that the city was the source of civilization's great advances, but he also saw that its population density could induce a reactive alienation, a "quickness of apprehension, a peculiarly hard sort of selfishness." As an antidote to this pejorative side of urban life, Olmsted, along with other urban reformers, looked to recreative amusements. Expanding the concept of recreation, he wrote:

> All forms of recreation may, in the first place, be conveniently arranged under two general heads. One will include all of which the predominating influence is to stimulate exertion of any part or parts needing it; the other, all which cause us to receive pleasure without conscious exertion. Games chiefly of mental skill as chess, or athletic sports, as baseball, are examples of means of recreation of the first class, which may be termed that of *exertive* recreation; music and the fine arts generally of the second or *receptive* division.

Olmsted obviously fashioned his views of parks around the notion of receptive recreation.... To Olmsted, ... action had little or no place in a public park. Boston's parks commissioners took Olmsted's views to heart and banned almost all active pursuits in the park system. There would be no "orations, harangues or loud outcries," no parades, drills, or processions, no individual music making. The rules allowed little legitimate activity beyond quiet picnics, meditations, and tours.

This tranquility would not last; the patrons had their own ideas about the activities that ought to occur in a park. They continually pressured for accommodation in the regulations, and, in Olmsted's view, constantly threatened the integrity of his receptive-recreation grounds....

The growth of interest in athletic sports proved to be a major problem for the parks commissioners. While the wealthy could join suburban country clubs for playing space, the majority of the population looked to the new parklands for sports. The commissioners tried to suppress this appetite, particularly that of baseballers, and finally declared in 1884: "No entertainment, exercises, or athletic game or sport shall be held or performed within public parks except with the prior consent of the Park Commission." Olmsted was in full agreement, citing similar rules in Hartford, Baltimore, Chicago, Buffalo, New York, and Philadelphia. Only a corner of Franklin Park was allotted to active sports, and that for children only.

Yet by the turn of the century, the City Council and public pressure had forced the commissioners to permit virtually every popular sport within the confines of the parks. Cricket clubs battled baseball interests for exclusive privileges. By the mid-1890s, several parks were the scene of scheduled football matches; tennis courts and a golf course were laid out in Franklin Park; the parkways whirled with wheels, many in procession and in parade! At the turn of the century, "horseless carriages" began to intrude; by 1902 they had received full privileges. Although certain sports were restricted to particular places and times, and much of the sporting activity was funneled to the related playground system, the evidence in the Parks Department minutes clearly indicates that the concept of public parks in Boston was altered, by special-interest groups, to include provisions for active sports....

Athletic sports were probably eventually accepted as legitimate park recreations because they represented a less severe encroachment than commercial amusements. As soon as the parks neared completion, the commissioners were inundated with license petitions from operators of hurdy-gurdy machines, merry-go-rounds, photo tents, refreshment stands, and amusement theaters, to name but a few. The operator of one theater argued that "the purpose of amusing the public is a public benefit entirely consistent with the use of the public parks." Further, the operators claimed that they desired only to satisfy an overwhelming demand for their services.

Alderman Martin Lomasney, the powerful boss of Ward 8, accurately voiced one attitude of the inner city when he opposed a rule outlawing mechanical "flying horses" or similar commercial amusements on the Sabbath:

> I don't believe we should be activated by the same spirit that prevailed in the days of the old Blue Laws, when on Sunday you would have to walk down Washington Street carrying a Bible in your hand and not speak to anybody on the street.... Certain people in the North End and in South Boston can reach these parks Sundays who cannot reach them any other day, and I don't believe they should be deprived of going on the flying horses if they wish to do so.

The laborer who found his relief in a nickel beer and free lunch at the saloon, or in a 25-cent seat at the Columbia Theatre, might well expect similar offerings at the parks. Olmsted's vision had to accommodate Lomasney's. Working through their connections on the City Council and even on the Parks Commission, commercial amusements operators succeeded in placing merry-go-rounds, photo tents, refreshment stands, and vending machines among the elm trees, brooks, and beaches....

The development of a park system involved an active and conscious attempt by Bostonians to shape and control the physical aspects of their community. In this respect, the Parks Department can arguably be described as the city's first municipal planning board. Olmsted and his successors successfully blended the available topography to reconcile beauty and space for recreation with basic needs like adequate drainage and traffic flow. Beyond all else, the park system was a farsighted response to a prevailing belief that the city was fast gobbling up both open spaces and a way of life; it was what Olmsted called a "self-preserving instinct of civilization." The islandlike quality of these parks today is testimony to the accuracy of that instinct.

If the Boston case is at all representative, however, it cautions the historian to take special care in categorizing urban park systems as a vehicle of genteel reform or social control whereby an elite class, whatever its members' motives, could readily manipulate the behavior of inferiors. Considerable evidence suggests this as the intent of many park advocates, but its basis lies largely in the arguments of early proposals.... An equally compelling body of evidence, the public record, displays the active role which the "popular mass" took in altering this vision. Special interest groups—neighborhood citizens' lobbies, athletic clubs, amusement operators—all representing a wide range of social classes, continually worked directly and through their political representatives to influence major decisions in park placement and policy. These groups succeeded in getting parks where they wished them; they pursued their own choice of recreation on the park grounds. Thus, the park movement in Boston was a reform that issued from the "bottom up" as well as from the top down. Because of this, the ultimate product of reform differed from the intended product....

Professional Sports and New York's Tammany Machine, 1890–1920

STEVEN A. RIESS

The close connection between commercialized sport and urban politics was probably first evident in prizefighting. As early as the 1830s and 1840s, gangs of New York youths worked actively with Tammany Hall in seeking the immigrant vote for the Democratic Party.... The most famous was Irish-born John Morrissey, the American boxing champion from 1853 to 1858.... Morrissey utilized his fame to get elected to the Congress.... Ward leaders and public officials in this era often became boxing patrons, arranging bouts for side bets at hangouts like Harry Hill's Dance Hall, a favorite meeting place for the sporting crowd [and] rewarded favored fighters with jobs as emigrant runners, bouncers, tavern keepers, and policemen.

... After the Civil War, Tammanyites remained interested in boxing, but formal matches were difficult to pull off because the violent and bloody sport was illegal. Contests had to be fought in out-of-the-way sites such as barns,

From Steven A. Riess, "Professional Sports and New York's Tammany Machine," Raymond A. Mohl, ed., *The Making of Urban America* (Wilmington, DE: Scholarly Press, 1988), 102–18.

barges, or saloon backrooms. Some of the important exhibitions in the early 1880s were held at Madison Square Garden, ... until 1885, when the promoters gave up after repeated police interference....

Prizefighting staged a revival in the New York metropolitan area in the early 1890s, and New York regained its preeminence in the sport. The main site of bouts was Coney Island, a wide-open resort that was becoming a major sporting center.... The principal boxing club there was the Coney Island Athletic Club (CIAC), organized in May 1892 by Boss John McKane, the political kingpin of the town of Gravesend, and various other machine politicians. McKane owned the arena, provided political protection, and prevented any big bouts at Coney Island unless he had a share of the action....

The CIAC was only one of several boxing clubs in the metropolitan area sponsored and protected by local politicians. These clubs operated even though professional boxing was illegal. For example, in 1895 the New Puritan Boxing Club of Long Island City held its matches at a site owned by the town's former mayor, James Gleason. His partners included Big Tim Sullivan and former Justice Dick Newton, recently released from a jail sentence for corrupt electioneering. In 1898 when Brookyn merged with New York, Long Island City became an integral part of Greater New York. Furthermore, by 1898 he also monopolized boxing in New York State, except in Brooklyn, where the new CIAC was protected by Democratic Boss Hugh McLaughlin.

Tim Sullivan was first elected to the state assembly in 1886 at the age of twenty-three and moved to the Senate in 1893. He served in the U.S. Congress from 1902 to 1906, but in 1908 he returned to his power base in the state senate.... Sullivan was associated early in his career with such gangsters as Monk Eastman, Kid Twist, and Paul Kelly, who provided him with intimidators and repeaters at election time. In return, organized crime was allowed to flourish. Big Tim was idolized by his constituents as a friend of the poor. He provided them with patronage, relief, outings, and any other assistance. Sullivan was a great sportsman ... [who] raced horses, gambled heavily, and, after 1895, dominated the New York poolroom business.

In 1896, under Sullivan's guidance, a bill passed the legislature and was approved by the governor legalizing "sparring" matches of up to ten rounds at licensed athletic clubs. New York became the only state with legalized boxing.... Within two years, he would monopolize boxing in New York State, except in Brooklyn, where the new CIAC was protected by Democratic Boss Hugh McLaughlin.

Tammany control of the police department further obviated fears of harassment at ... politically connected athletic clubs. Police Chief Bill Devery rarely interfered with boxing bouts, even well-advertised matches like the heavyweight championship match in 1899 between titleholder Bob Fitzsimmons and challenger James J. Jeffries at the new CIAC, ... Devery ..., [who] owed his rise to the sponsorship of Boss Croker and Tim Sullivan, [had a] career was marked by several episodes of incompetence and corruption....

Legalized boxing lasted only until 1900, when the state legislature repealed the Horton Act because of the sport's brutality, the gambling menace, and the

Tammany influence in boxing. Approximately 3,500 contests had been staged over five years, mainly in New York City....

The repeal of the Horton Act did not completely stop boxing, since it survived surreptitiously in saloon backrooms and at club smokers. Private clubs circumvented the law by holding three-round exhibitions for the entertainment of "members," who paid a one-dollar "fee" to join the club. The most prestigious of the membership clubs was Tim Sullivan's National Athletic Club, which reputedly had 3,000 members. By 1908 fifteen clubs in New York held weekly bouts....

Tammany politicians tried in vain for several years to legalize boxing again. Prospects brightened in 1911 when the Democrats took over control of both the state legislature and the governor's mansion for the first time in years. This enabled Senator James J. Frawley, a former president of the Knickerbocker Athletic Club, to pass a bill legalizing ten-round, no-decision boxing contests. The sport was placed under the supervision of an unpaid three-man State Athletic Commission responsible for licensing athletic clubs and fighters. A 5 percent tax was levied on the box office take, which came to nearly $50,000 in 1912. The Frawley Act resulted in a renewed interest in boxing, and by the end of 1912 there were eighty-nine licensed boxing clubs in the state, forty-nine in New York City. The bouts were held in small neighborhood boxing clubs and large downtown arenas like Madison Square Garden.

Prizefighting operated under the Frawley Act until 1917, when the law was repealed by a Republican administration led by Governor Charles S. Whitman. The prestige of the sport remained low. Its brutality, the low-life types associated with it, and incessant gambling and rumors of fixes did little to improve the standing of boxing as a sport. The Athletic Commission ... became overtly politicized by the Republicans, who regained control of the state legislature and the governorship in 1915.... Whitman called for repeal late in the session as a party measure, getting his bill approved on a strict party vote. Not one Democratic senator voted to abolish boxing. Whitman's battle against boxing was a politically astute move signifying to upstate voters that the Republican party stood for tradition and high moral values, unlike the Democrats who had supported an immoral blood sport with dubious connections to urban political machines and gangsters.

The repeal of the Frawley Act was a major blow to American prizefighting. The sport was legal in twenty-three states in 1917, but was severely restricted, if not completely outlawed, in the major markets of New York and Chicago. Even in San Francisco, which had temporarily supplanted New York as the boxing capital after the repeal of the Horton Act, the sport was greatly curtailed by a 1914 state law limiting matches to four rounds. The outlook for boxing improved markedly during World War I, however, because the sport was used to help train soldiers for combat. Consequently, boxing's image became much better. Even the reform-minded *New York Times* became an advocate of pugilism.... In 1920, under the direction of Senate Minority Leader Jimmy Walker, a loyal son of Tammany, the legislature enacted a law permitting twelve-round matches, with the support of Democratic Governor Al Smith.

Judges were empowered to choose a victor if the contest went the distance. An unpaid athletic commission was established to supervise the sport and license boxing clubs, trainers, and fighters.

The passage of the Walker Act enabled New York City to regain its position as the national center of boxing. In the 1920s local fight clubs became important sources of top-flight fighters. Most major American bouts were held at Madison Square Garden. The promoter there was Tex Rickard, probably best known for his successful work in pulling off the Jeffries–Johnson championship fight of 1910 in Reno, Nevada.... An out-of-towner, Rickard generated a lot of jealousy among local promoters and politicians, compelling him to provide passes, favors, and bribes to bring off ... match[es]. By 1920, Rickard had learned his lesson and developed important connections with Tammany Hall, including Al Smith. The governor interceded on Rickard's behalf with the owners of Madison Square Garden, helping the promoter get a ten-year lease for $400,000....

Politics dominated not only the "sport of pugs" but also the "sport of kings." Despite the aristocratic image of the sport, horse racing often came under severe moral scrutiny from church leaders and moral reformers because of the gambling, crooked races, and animal abuses associated with the turf. More than any other sport, racing depended upon betting for its appeal and survival. Consequently, thoroughbred racing at the turn of the century was widely forbidden. Where the sport did operate, as in New York, it was heavily influenced by machine politicians and politically active elites, such as William C. Whitney, Thomas Fortune Ryan, and August Belmont II. These men used sport to facilitate cross-class coalitions in the Democratic Party to help protect their transit franchises. Streetcar executives out of necessity became intimately involved in urban politics; they needed inside information, long-term leases, and rights of way. Elite sportsmen like Ryan and Belmont owned and operated racetracks. Along with machine politicos like Croker and Tim Sullivan, they owned, bred, and raced thoroughbreds, and wagered heavily at the track. Sullivan and other professional politicians were also prominent in the business of gambling, usually as organizers and promoters of bookmaking and off-track poolroom, or betting parlor, syndicates. The elite and plebeian members of the sporting fraternity worked together on issues of mutual concern, such as the facilitation of racetrack operations and the legalization of on track betting. They were bitter enemies, however, when it came to off-track betting, which, while totally banned, was seldom halted.

Thoroughbred racing ... enjoyed a boom in the 1820s and 1830s but faltered in the North after the depression of 1837.... The turf did not revive in the North until 1863, when John Morrissey staged races at the resort town of Saratoga Springs to attract elite vacationers. He was supported by wealthy sportsmen Leonard Jerome, William R. Travers, and John Hunter, who apparently were not adverse to working with a former Tammany shoulder hitter.

The Saratoga experiment was such a resounding success that Jerome, Chairman August Belmont of the national Democratic Party, and other elite sportsmen organized the American Jockey Club (AJC) in 1866 to sponsor races in the vicinity of

New York City. Jerome played a leading role in securing 230 acres in Westchester, where a racetrack was built and named Jerome Park in his honor....

Not all of the 862 original members of the AJC ... were socially elite.... The membership included such politicians as the notorious Tammany Boss William M. Tweed....

New York horsemen needed considerable political savvy to circumvent the legal barriers to gambling, the backbone of the sport. An antipool law was passed by the state legislature in 1877 in response to the widespread wagering on the Tilden–Hayes election. Despite fears that this law would hurt track attendance, the turf continued to flourish, largely because the auction pool system of betting was replaced by bookmaking. The locus of racing moved to the Coney Island area, a forty-cent, one-hour train ride from mid-town Manhattan. Local politicians were expected to protect the tracks from rigorous enforcement of the penal codes. In June 1879, William A. Engeman, builder of the Brighton Beach Hotel and politically well connected, established a proprietary racetrack at Brighton Beach. The track was quite successful, and, by 1882, Engeman was netting $200,000 per year. Late in 1879, Jerome organized the prestigious Coney Island Jockey Club (CIJC), which included Belmont, William K. Vanderbilt, and Pierre Lorillard, Jr.... Finally, in 1885, the politically astute Dwyer brothers, plungers who had made their fortune as butchers, opened Gravesend as a proprietary track. These three tracks were tolerated and protected by local politicians under the direction of Boss McKane, who permitted pool-selling to flourish....

In 1887 representatives of the racing interests passed the Ives Pool Law forbidding off-betting but permitting betting at the tracks during the May to October racing season. The state also levied a tax on the race courses to raise money.... The new law resulted in a boom in racing and gambling. It led directly to the formation of the Metropolitan Turf Alliance (MTA) in 1888, an association of over sixty well-connected bookmakers who sought to monopolize the bookmaking privilege at the tracks.... Another result was that, in 1889, John A. Morris constructed Morris Park Racetrack in Westchester to replace Jerome Park, which the city had purchased for a reservoir. Morris ... had made his fortune operating the infamous Louisiana Lottery. He was politically influential, ... and his Tammanyite son was the district's assemblyman. Managed by the New York Jockey Club, Morris Park had the largest grandstand and the longest track in the United States. The facility cost several hundred thousand dollars and was regarded as palatial by contemporaries. It immediately became an important resort for the social set that traveled to the track in expensive carriages....

Poolroom operators learned to adapt and stay in business despite the Ives Act. Poolrooms were mainly located in midtown or the Tenderloin.... Occasional raids were instigated by reformers like Anthony Comstock of the Society for the Suppression of Vice, but the poolrooms usually operated with impunity. The poolroom operators were well protected by Mayor Hugh Grant and other Tammany friends, ... by payoffs to police and local political powers. Machine-appointed jurists were also supportive....

... Early in the spring of 1893, the police instigated a major attack against local poolrooms, possibly at the instigation of Boss Richard Croker. The

Tammany boss had recently purchased the famous Belle Meade stud and wanted New York tracks to prosper so he could race his horses there. In addition, Croker was a good friend of the Dwyers, who had often given him betting tips, and he hoped to protect their interests. With Croker's support, and despite the opposition of Tim Sullivan, the state legislature enacted the Saxton Anti-Poolroom Law making the keeping of a poolroom a felony.

The status of horse racing was seriously threatened one year later by a coalition of social reformers, clergymen, and other Tammany opponents. This group used the September 1894 state constitutional convention as a forum to ban all horse-race gambling. There was widespread sentiment against betting, particularly at illegal poolrooms.... Opponents were bolstered by the closing in December 1893 of New Jersey's tracks, which had been totally controlled by corrupt machine politicians. The New York State constitutional convention adopted a proposal banning horse-race betting completely. When the proposal was approved by voters in fall elections, the end of racing appeared imminent.

Racing interests waged an all-out campaign to save the sport. Calmer minds recognized that the convention might have gone too far. Even the reform-minded *New York Times* sought to save racing, which it believed helped improve the breed. The turf had powerful friends in Albany. Racing advocates flexed their muscle in the passage of the Percy-Gray Act, establishing a state racing commission to supervise the sport....

Off-track betting was also back in business, even though a new law had been passed accompanying Percy-Gray that banned such betting. The enterprise now came under the protection of Big Tim Sullivan, and, under his patronage, off-track betting soon reached its apogee. Sullivan's operation had Croker's approval. As many as 400 poolrooms belonged to the syndicate, each paying from $60 to $300 per month for the privilege of staying in business.... The poolroom operations were extraordinarily successful, and in 1902 the syndicate earned $3.6 million....

Thoroughbred racing's greatest crisis came in 1908, when Governor Charles Evans Hughes in his annual address to the state legislature called for the end of racetrack gambling.... The progressive governor believed that gambling on races was both a moral outrage and a flagrant violation of the state constitution.... He used his influence to get Republicans behind a bill to abolish on-site betting.... Hughes ... convened a special session of the legislature, which passed the Agnew-Hart bill by a margin of one vote in the Senate. This victory was described by a Hughes biographer as his "most dramatic venture in the area of moral reform."

The new law severely hampered the racing industry, a $75 million business nationwide. The major tracks tried to remain open by allowing oral betting, which the courts ruled was legal, but attendance declined by two-thirds. In 1910 the legislature passed the Agnew-Perkins Act, making racetrack owners liable for any gambling violations at their facilities. The result was that tracks still operating immediately went out of business. In 1911 and 1912 there was no thoroughbred racing in New York. However, in 1913, Judge Townsend Scudder ruled in the *Shane* case that track managers were liable only if they had wittingly permitted bookmakers to operate. As a consequence, Belmont Park and two minor tracks, Jamaica and Aqueduct, reopened. But such historic racetracks as Gravesend and Sheepshead Bay, each worth about $2.5 million, never reopened.

... Baseball owners were regarded as selfless, civic-minded men who sponsored teams out of a concern for the public welfare. But in reality, owners were not drawn from the "best people." New York baseball magnates included a heavy representation of machine politicians. They used their clout to benefit their teams, which provided patronage, financial and psychic rewards, and good public relations.

Baseball in New York from its earliest days was closely tied to local politics. Tammany was an early sponsor of amateur baseball teams, the most important being the Mutuals, established in 1857. By the 1860s, when Tweed had become involved with the club, it was already one of the leading amateur nines. Players were subsidized with patronage jobs in the sanitation department and the coroner's office. In 1871, when the Mutuals joined the first professional league, the National Association of Professional Baseball Players (NA), its board of directors included the sheriff, several aldermen, two judges, and six state legislators. One of only three teams that played in all five NA campaigns, the Mutuals in 1876 joined the new National League (NL). But late in the 1876 season, after refusing to make a costly western trip, the Mutuals were expelled by the NL.

New York City was without major league baseball until 1883, when Tammanyites John B. Day and Joseph Gordon and former minor leaguer John Mutrie were awarded franchises in both the NL and the year-old American Association (AA) that played at different ends of the first Polo Grounds at 110th Street. The Metropolitans won the 1884 AA pennant, but floundered afterwards, and the franchise was sold to the Brooklyn Bridegrooms after the 1887 season. The owners devoted most of their attention to the ir Gothams of the NL (renamed the Giants in 1885), who won the World Series in 1887 and 1888, but in 1889, political pressure forced them to move to Jersey City, then to Staten Island, and then to a new Polo Grounds at 155th Street. A competitor was established across the street in 1890 by the new Players' League, a cooperative venture of capitalists and players revolting against the reserve clause. The financial backers were prominent Republicans, who bought out the Giants in 1891 after the collapse of the Players' League, and moved the NL club into their site, thereafter known as the Polo Grounds. Tammany regained the Giants at the end of 1894, when Andrew Freedman, an intimate friend and business partner of Boss Croker, purchased the club for $48,000. Freedman held no elective office but wielded great influence through Croker and in his own right as a member of Tammany's powerful Finance Committee. In 1897, Freedman became treasurer of the national Democratic Party....

Freedman of the Giants used his clout to cower other owners, and sportswriters claimed that he then ran his team as a Tammany appendage. The object of considerable abuse from fans, the press, and fellow owners for mismanagement and encouraging rowdy baseball, and disappointed with his profits, Freedman decided to sell out after the 1902 season. Besides, he had more important matters to attend to, principally the construction of the New York subway system, in which he invested $1.7 million. Freedman sold most of his Giants stock for $125,000 to John T. Brush, an Indianapolis clothier. Brush had himself just sold his Cincinnati Reds baseball team to a local syndicate consisting of Mayor Julius Fleischmann, Republican Boss George B. Cox, and Water Commissioner August Herrmann, Cox's right-hand man. According to one journalist, Brush had been forced to sell out to the machine, which threatened to cut a street through the ballpark.

Despite the sale, the Giants remained the Tammany team. Still a minority stockholder, Freedman was more than willing to use his clout for the club. Brush died in 1912, and his heirs sold the team in 1919 for $1 million to Tammanyite Charles Stoneham, a curb-market broker of limited integrity....

The Giants were enormously successful on the diamond in the early 1900s under [John] McGraw's management. They won six pennants from 1904 to 1917 and became the most profitable team in organized baseball. From 1906 to 1910 the club annually earned over $100,000, and by 1913 earnings surpassed $150,000. After World War I, baseball experienced an enormous boom in the city, largely because of the legalization of Sunday baseball. In 1920 the Giants established a league record $296,803 in profits....

The Giants had Manhattan to themselves until 1903, when the rival American League (AL) secured a New York franchise. The junior circuit had failed to organize a New York team earlier because Freedman controlled virtually all the potential playing sites through his political power and real estate interests. Even after Croker was exiled to England on the heels of Seth Low's election as mayor in 1901, Freedman and his Tammany friends still had enough power to stymie any interlopers....

... In March 1903 the AL granted a franchise to a syndicate headed by Joseph Gordon, a figurehead for the real owners—poolroom king Frank Farrell and former Police Chief William Devery. They soon constructed a field on a rock pile at 165th Street that Freedman apparently had ruled out as unsuitable for baseball. Devery and Farrell paid the local district leader $200,000 for excavation and another $75,000 to build a grandstand....

The Highlanders (known as the Yankees since 1913) failed to prosper, either on or off the field.... Devery and Farrell sold out in 1915 for $460,000 to brewer Jacob Ruppert, Jr., and C. Tillinghast Huston, a rich civil engineer. Ruppert was a prominent member of the sporting fraternity who bred and raced dogs and horses. A great fan of the Giants, he was a notable member of Tammany Hall, served on its Finance Committee, and had been selected personally by Croker in 1897 to run for president of the city council.... One year later he was chosen to run for Congress from a Republican district, was elected in an upset, and went on to serve four undistinguished terms....

New York owners took advantage of their political connections to enhance their baseball operations in valuable ways. Clout was used to deter interlopers from invading the metropolitan area. Influence at city hall provided access to the best possible information about property values, land uses, and mass transit, all essential matters when teams built new ballparks. This was especially crucial once teams began constructing permanent, fire-resistant ballparks that cost in excess of $500,000. In 1911 the Giants built their new Polo Grounds in Washington Heights on the site of the old field that had burned down.... A decade later the Yankees moved into their own ballpark in the Bronx....

Political connections facilitated various mundane but necessary business operations. Teams without such protection could find themselves vulnerable to political pressure and high license fees. Cities also provided teams with a variety of municipal services, including preseason inspections to check for structural defects in the ballparks.... The most important ongoing service was police protection. Officers were needed to maintain order among those waiting to get into the park, keep traffic moving, and prevent ticket scalping. Inside the grounds, police prevented gambling and kept order among unruly spectators who fought with other fans, umpires, and even players.... New York teams got free police protection inside the grounds until 1907 when the reform police commissioner Thomas A. Bingham stopped it....

The prominence of professional politicians, particularly urban bosses, as promoters and facilitators of professional sports was not limited to New York. It was a nationwide pattern common to urban areas with a citywide machine and cities where the local ward machine model prevailed....

As befitted their venal reputations, the machine politicians were especially prominent in prizefighting and horse racing, sports that operated under severe moral disapproval and widespread legal restrictions. In New Orleans, ... John Fitzgerald, [the] referee of the seventy-five-round bare-knuckle championship fight in 1889 between John L. Sullivan and Jake Kilrain ... was elected mayor in 1892, though he was later impeached. After the sport was banned in New York in 1900, San Francisco became the major site of pugilism. Its leading promoters all were affiliated with Boss Abe Ruef, who received payoffs to guarantee licenses for staging bouts.

In horse racing, it was commonplace for proprietary tracks to be affiliated with political machines. Off-track betting operations were always closely allied to urban bosses for the necessary protection. In New Jersey, for instance, racing in the early 1890s at the state's six major tracks was controlled by machine politicians. Although horse-race gambling was nearly always illegal, notorious outlaw tracks like Guttenberg and Gloucester operated with impunity, servicing the sporting fraternity from New York and Philadelphia. Gloucester was owned by Bill Thompson, the local political boss, while Guttenberg received its protection from the notorious Hudson County machine that enabled it to operate year-round. In Chicago, the racing center of the Midwest, certain track officials were so closely allied to the local machines that the sporting press claimed its horsemen were outdoing Tammany. The most flagrant example in the early 1890s was Garfield Park, a proprietary track owned by West Side bookmakers. Their political clout emanated from Mike McDonald, reputed head of syndicate crime; Bathhouse John Coughlin, boss of the infamous Levee District; and Johnny Powers, "Prince of Boodlers" in the city council and boss of the Nineteenth Ward. These political connections were also important in Chicago's bookmaking circles, since nearly all the handbook operators were tied to local ward machines.

The national pastime was not as tightly controlled by machine politicians as either prizefighting or horse racing, but nonetheless, professional baseball was dominated by notable politicos. Historian Ted Vincent has found that politicians made up nearly half of the 1,262 officials and stockholders of the nineteenth-century ball clubs he studied.... The pattern established in the nineteenth century continued until the 1920s. Between 1900 and 1920 every American and National League team's ownership included professional politicians, traction magnates, or friends or relatives of prominent power brokers. A similar situation existed in the minor leagues.... All the teams welcomed political connections as a means to protect the franchise against interlopers, to secure vital inside information from city hall, and to obtain preferential treatment from the municipal government.

Baseball best exemplified the pastoral world that white Anglo-Saxon Americans sought to maintain and protect in the face of industrialization, immigration, and urbanization. The sport helped to certify the continuing relevance of traditional values. But, paradoxically, baseball was in large measure controlled by men who typified all that mainstream America detested in the immigrant-dominated cities.

FURTHER READING

Boyer, Paul. *Urban Masses and Moral Order in America, 1820–1920* (1978).

Cavallo, Dominick. *Muscles and Morals: Organized Playgrounds and Urban Reform, 1880–1930* (1981).

Churchill, David S. "Making Broad Shoulders: Body-Building and Physical Culture in Chicago 1890–1920," *History of Education Quarterly* 48 (Fall 2008), 341–70.

Domke, Martin. "Into the Vertical: Basketball, Urbanization, and African American Culture in Early-Twentieth-Century America," *Aspeers* (April 2011), 131–50.

Gems, Gerald R. *Sport and Culture Formation in Chicago, 1890–1940* (1997).

Gems, Gerald R. "Welfare Capitalism and Blue-Collar Sport: The Legacy of Labour Unrest," *Rethinking History* 5-1 (March 2001), 43–58.

Hardy, Stephen. *How Boston Played: Sport, Recreation, and Community, 1865–1915* (1982).

Hardy, Stephen, and A. G. Ingham. "Games, Structures, and Agency: Historians on the American Play Movement," *Journal of Social History* 17 (1983), 285–301.

Kuklick, Bruce. *To Every Thing a Season: Shibe Park and Urban Philadelphia, 1909–1976* (1991).

Lucas, John A. "Pedestrianism and the Struggle for the Sir John Astley Belt, 1878–1879," *Research Quarterly* 39 (1968), 587–95.

Marsden, Gerald. "Philanthropy and the Boston Playground Movement, 1885–1907," *Social Science Review* 35 (1961), 48–58.

McCarthy, Michael P. "Politics and the Parks; Chicago Businessmen and the Recreation Movement," *Journal of the Illinois Historical Society* 65 (1972), 158–72.

Riess, Steven A. *City Games: The Evolution of American Urban Society and the Rise of Sports* (1989).

Riess, Steven A. *The Sport of Kings and the Kings of Crime: Horse Racing, Politics, and Organized Crime in New York, 1865–1913* (2011).

Rosenzweig, Roy. *Eight Hours for What We Will: Workers and Leisure in an Industrial City, 1870–1910* (1983).

Rosenzweig, Roy, and Elizabeth Blackmar. *The Park and the People: A History of Central Park* (1992).

Somers, Dale A. *The Rise of Sports in New Orleans, 1850–1900* (1972).

Vincent, Ted. *The Rise and Fall of American Sport: Mudville's Revenge* (1994).

CHAPTER 7

Sport and Class, 1870–1930

Although historians do not consider the issue of class as an essential factor in the shaping of American history compared to the European experience, they do recognize its importance as a variable. Most people in this era were manual laborers, followed by a large middle class of white-collar workers and farm owners. The upper class comprised the richest five percent of Americans who owned about a third of the total national wealth. Their standards of taste and refinement were established by a small elite of well-born white Anglo-Saxon Protestants who came from old money, married into the most distinguished families and had access to power. What was the impact of this social structure upon American sporting practices? In particular, how did income and discretionary free time determine sporting options? How did social status influence sporting choices?

The upper class, whose members had the broadest options in selecting their favorite recreations, preferred very expensive sports that were inaccessible to people of lower social rank. They used their sporting participation to certify their high social status and separate themselves from the upper middle class. Contemporary social critic Thorstein Veblen disparagingly characterized their behavior with the term "conspicuous consumption."

The middle classes had opposed the antebellum sport of the male bachelor subculture because in their opinion it was immoral, debilitating, and not recreational. However, middle-class interest in sports grew with the development of modern sports and the articulation of a sports creed that rationalized sports as a positive social force. The middle classes had sufficient discretionary income, leisure time, and access to sporting facilities to become very active in physical culture.

Lower-class Americans also participated in sports, particularly artisans in the preindustrial era, who had considerable control over their pace of work and free time. However, working-class opportunities came but under significant limitations during the post–Civil War era as the industrial revolution escalated. What was the impact of the rise of the factory system on wages, working conditions, and leisure time? Industrialization at first had a negative impact on working-class participation as certain jobs like shoe-making were de-skilled and as all workers lost control over the workplace and the pace of work. By the late nineteenth century, 85 percent of industrial workers were semiskilled or unskilled. They earned low wages and worked extremely long hours, usually six days a week and they lived in inner-city slums. How did these conditions affect their sporting opportunities? On the other hand, craftsmen (who worked shorter hours for higher pay) and blue-collar city employees, like policemen, encountered relatively few hindrances in their leisure activities. After the turn of the century, hours of work declined in most industries, but it was not until the 1920s, when most workers enjoyed significantly higher standards of living, that blue-collar Americans could enjoy a full range of sporting pleasures.

DOCUMENTS

Document 1 reports in detail various aspects of the March 1879 Astley Belt race at the old Madison Square Garden. This was a series of six-day "go-as-you-please" races that began in London in 1878. The winning prize for each event was up to $20,000; in addition, the winner of the series received a gold and silver belt donated by Lord Astley. The events were enormously popular and drew capacity crowds to see men struggling to run 500 miles and more in six days. England's defending champion, Charles Rowell, successfully defended his title by covering 530 miles in six days, and for the first time in history, two other competitors also bettered the 500-mile mark. Document 2 by Caspar Whitney, a noted late nineteenth-century journalist who specialized in high-status sports, explores the nature of the exclusive country club. The clubs were located in suburban locales with facilities that enabled men and women to enjoy a variety of expensive outdoor sports. In addition, the clubs provided a place where the rich could separate themselves from lesser groups in a convivial atmosphere. Document 3 examines the reasons for the cycling fad in the early 1890s, when bicycle riding became an enormously popular middle-class pastime. Cycling had previously been a very difficult sport to master until the invention of the English safety bicycle, which had two equal-sized pneumatic tires and a chain drive rear wheel, a vast improvement over the hard to ride high wheelers they supplanted.

Document 4 on the Chicago Women's Athletic Club was written by Bertha Damaris Knobe, editor of the women's department of the *Chicago Tribune.* The organization, created in 1898 "by ladies for ladies," provided a "retreat where health, grace, and vigor can be restored." The WAC claims to be the first athletic club for American women. Its building, located along the city's "Magnificent Mile" in the Near North Side, was proclaimed a Chicago landmark in 1891.

Document 5 examines what one journalist feels is the growing commercialization of amateur track and field because certain athletic clubs were recruiting top athletes with such attractive inducements like jobs that require no real work, and also because of the far-reaching control that A. G. Spalding & Brothers, the preeminent American sporting goods company, had over the Amateur Athletic Union that regulated amateurism in the United States. The criticism of commercialization is particularly aimed at working-class ethnic clubs that were achieving considerable prominence at the turn of the century when several American Olympic gold medal winners were policemen.

1. The Apex of Professional Track: The Astley Belt Race of 1879

As we write the contestants in the fifth race for the belt presented by Sir John Astley are hard at work in Madison Square Garden, this city, having started at 1 A.M. on Monday, Sept. 22. Notwithstanding that the price of admission was placed at a dollar, the crowd present at the start was fully as great as upon the occasion of the previous contest for the same trophy at this place, the throng fully testing the capacity of the Garden. By dint of hard work, day and night, from Saturday morning, a pretty good track composed of sifted loan and tanbark, with a light top dressing of sawdust, had been prepared. It was not as wide by three feet as before, but still it afforded plenty of room for the thirteen competitors, each one of whom had a tent to himself, furnished with everything necessary.... The most intense excitement prevailed among the spectators, and it was with great difficulty that they could be prevented from encroaching upon the track; but there was a strong force of police present, and, considering the immense crowd, comparatively good order was maintained. The pedestrians were started promptly at one o'clock A.M. Monday, Sep. 22, and nearly all commenced the long journey at a walk, notable exceptions being Hazael and Rowell, the former going off with an easy lope and the latter again setting to work with the dog-trot so familiar to New-Yorkers. Rowell was the favorite with the betting fraternity, the bookmakers offering 1½ to 1 against him, 2½ to 1 against Weston, 3 to 1 against Hazael, 10 to 1 against Guyon, 30 to 1 against Panehot or Ennis, 20 to 1 against Krohne or Hart, 35 to 1 against Merritt, and as much as 50 to 1 against the others. The bookmakers had their stands erected in the centre of the main floor, and drove quite a thriving business.... The only man who kept to a walk for any length of time after starting was Fedemeyer, whose long hair and beard and odd attire caused him to present a strange appearance. He walked steadily for several hours, and then, finding that he was getting further and further behind, he changed his gait to a jog, which did not carry him along much faster, and he retained the last place. A great deal of interest was manifested in the colored boy Hart, who walks much better than he runs, and whose style is very much like that made familiar to New Yorkers by O'Leary. He is a tough-looking lad, and seems likely to make an excellent record during the week....

While we are writing, those of the competitors who by their performance have proved themselves worthy of participating in the fifth contest for the trophy offered by Sir John Astley, and emblematic of the championship of the world in long-distance, go-as-you-please pedestrianism, are still contending for the supremacy, and nearing the end of a race which, from a sporting point of view as well as financial, has been decidedly more successful than any other similar six-day tournament ever held here or in England. In no other contest of like duration have the chances appeared so even as in this, nor the public interest been excited and sustained from first to last by the spectacle of the four or five leading men separated from one another by so short a distance, and all doing so well that

From *New York Clipper* (September 27, 1879): 210.

the foremost man is forced to continually crowd the fastest previous record, and occasionally exceed it. It had been expected by nearly everybody except Manager Hess that the placing of the price of admission at one dollar to all parts of the house was a mistake which would have the effect of limiting the attendance during the middle of the week. Had the competition proved a one-sided affair, no doubt these anticipations would have been realized; but the character of the contest increased to such an extent the interest already felt in the result that the public extended a more than liberal patronage throughout the six days. Taken as a whole, the class of people who have visited the Garden during the week have been superior to the general character of the supporters of like events, and, while we hold that the privilege of gratifying their desires should not be placed beyond the reach of the masses of the people, there can be no doubt that to this fact is attributable the excellent order which has been maintained. The arrangements for keeping the people informed of the state of the contest were about on a par with previous tournaments, the positions of the six leading competitors being indicated on a huge blackboard placed at the east end of the building, upon which the miles made by each man were placed opposite his name. The lap-scoring was done by means of dials painted on a long board fence erected at the outer edge of the inner circle and facing the north, opposite to which was the scorers' and press-stand, built up against the wall in front of the ladies gallery. The fence alluded to might have been made a little lower, as it was just high enough to prevent the spectators on the main floor and on the south side of the house from obtaining a view of the finish. The scoring was attended to by members of different athletic clubs, some of whom were experienced in the business and attentive, while others were inexperienced and seemingly careless as well, which was no recommendation to persons appointed to discharge duties of so important a nature. The track is not so wide by about three feet as before, and being made in a hurry, was rather soft at first, but has been well looked after, and the pedestrians have had little reason to complain of it since the first day. As we had from previous experience been led to anticipate, the attempt to prevent smoking even on the floor of the house (except along the edge of the track) was a pronounced failure, as it always must be on such occasions, and where the lessees are anxious to sell all the poor cigars they can at high prices....

2. Caspar W. Whitney Probes the Evolution of the Country Club, 1894

... The history of the country club, as much as anything else, bears witness to our tendency to superlative development. From having not a single country club in the entire United States of America twenty-five years ago, we have ... in half that period, evolved the handsomest in the world.... The country club has done appreciable missionary work in bringing us in contact with our fellows, where

---

From Caspar Whitney, "Evolution of the Country Club," *Harper's New Monthly Magazine* 90 (December 1894): 16–33.

another than the hard business atmosphere envelops us, and in enticing us for the time being to put aside the daily task.

... Country-club benefits remain so abundant as not to be easily computed.... It has at the same time cultivated a love of out-doors for itself, and stood as the rallying point for every sport in America in which the horse is a factor.... With the creation of country clubs long drives became a possible and delightful feature of the year....

Only a careful study of our country's history and its social traditions will give us a full appreciation of what the country club has done for us. It has ... , corrected to a large extent the American defect of not being able or at least not willing to stop work and enjoy ourselves: it has brought together groups of congenial, cultivated people....

It is impossible to overestimate the blessings of the country club in adding comforts to country living that before were utterly unattainable, and in making it possible to enjoy a degree of that rural life which is one of England's greatest attractions....

... The need of a rendezvous was ... realized in the establishment, in 1882, of the Brookline Country Club, the first of the genus in America, albeit some of the hunting clubs had been and are to this day filling a similar sphere.

Probably the country club has rendered its greatest service in tempting us out of doors, and cultivating a taste for riding and driving that has so largely benefited both sexes. With the evolution of the country club we have been developing into a nation of sportsmen and sportswomen. Indeed, sport of one kind or another and the origin of the country club are so closely connected, it is exceedingly difficult to decide which owes its existence to the other. It may be asserted that country clubs, generally speaking, have been created by the common desire of their incorporators to make a home for amateur sport of one kind or another. Some grew directly out of sport, as, for instance, the Country Club of Westchester County, which was originally planned for a tennis club, the Rockaway, Meadow Brook, and the Buffalo clubs, that were called into existence by the polo and hunting men. Others owe their existence to a desire to establish an objective point for drives and rides, and a rendezvous within easy access of town like the Brookline and Philadelphia Country clubs. Others have been called into being as the centralizing force of a residential colony, as Tuxedo....

If sport has not been the *raison d'être* of every club's establishment, it is at all events, with extremely few exceptions, the chief means of their subsistence. Practically every country club is the centre of several kinds of sport, pursued more or less vigorously as the seasons come and go....

The one distinguishing feature of the country club ... is its recognition of the gentle sex, and I know of none where they are not admitted either on individual membership or on that of *paterfamilias*....

It is the sporting side of the country club, however, that gives it life and provides entertainment for its members: the club and our sporting history are so closely interwoven as to be inseparable. Polo, hunting, and pony-racing owe to it their lives, and to the members we are largely indebted for the marked improvement in carriage horseflesh during the past five years. They founded the horse show, made coaching an accepted institution, and have so filled the year with games that it is hard to say whether the country-club sporting season begins with the hunting in the autumn or with tennis in the spring, for there is hardly any cessation from the opening to the closing of the calendar year.

Once upon a time the country was considered endurable only in summer, but the clubs have changed even that notion: all of them keep open house in winter, some retain a fairly large percentage of members in residence, and one or two make a feature of winter sports. Tuxedo holds a veritable carnival, with tobogganing, snow-shoeing, and skating on the pond, which in season provides the club table with trout....

Spring opens with preparations for polo, lawn-tennis, and yachting. Not all country clubs have polo and yachting, but every one has courts, and several hold annual tournaments that are features of the tennis season, and where the leading players are brought together....

All the clubs dabble in live-pigeon trap-shooting, which is regrettable, for it is unsportsmanlike, to say nothing of the cash prizes, professionalizing the participants. It is a miserable form of amusement and unworthy the name of sport.... Hunting and polo in the early days constituted the sole sport of the country club members, but the introduction of other games in the last five years has divided the interest that was once given to them entirely....

Probably the most characteristic country-club scene, however, is created by the pony-race meetings given on the tracks with which several of the clubs are provided. Here there is ample opportunity for the hysterical enthusiasm so dear to the feminine soul, and plenty of time between events for them to chatter away to their hearts' content. Here, too, there is the certainty of seeing one's friends not only in the carts and on top of the coaches that line the course, and on the temporary little grand stand, erected for the near-by residents of the club colony, but frequently riding the ponies....

... On such an occasion the social and sporting sides of the club are revealed at their best. Turn your back to the race-course and you well might fancy yourself at a huge garden party....

As the eldest and one of the most picturesquely located, the Country Club of Brookline deserves precedence. It had its origin in J. Murray Forbes's idea of an objective point for rides and drives, and was organized in 1882. No other club possesses a hundred acres of such beautiful land within such easy access, for it is only five and a half miles from the State House ... and, better still, in its immediate neighborhood none of the rural effects have been marred.

The club-house, originally a rambling old building, is very picturesque, and has been enlarged from time to time to meet requirements. Its piazza overlooks the race-course, in the centre of which is one of the best of polo fields.... There is a shooting-box, where clay pigeons are used, a toboggan-slide, golf-course, and good tennis-courts, both grass and gravel....

Who shall deny the country club to have been a veritable blessing, what with its sport and pleasure and health-giving properties that have brushed the cobwebs from weary brains, and given us blue sky, green grass, and restful shade in exchange for smoke-laden atmosphere, parboiled pavements, and the never-ceasing glare and racket of the city? And womankind too has partaken of country-club as she should of all blessings, in relaxation from the petty trials of house-keeping, and the parade and deceits of "society," while the hue of health has deepened in her cheeks.... Beginning life as somewhat of a novelty, the country club has become so familiar an institution that we wonder, ... how we ever managed to get on without it.

3. Philip G. Hubert, Jr., Reflects on the Bicycle: The Marvel of Its Day, 1895

... [T]he bicycle is one of the great inventions of the century.... A bicycle is better than a horse to ninety-nine men and women out of a hundred, because it costs almost nothing to keep, and it is never tired. It will take one three times as far as a horse.... In touring with a bicycle I can make fifty miles a day as comfortably as twenty miles on foot, and I can carry all the clothing I need, besides a camera and other traps. The exercise is as invigorating as walking, or more so, with the great advantage that you can get over uninteresting tracts of country twice as fast as on foot. In fact, as any bicyclist knows, walking seems intolerably slow after the wheel; even easy-going tourists, with women in the party, can make forty miles a day and find it play. Perhaps even greater and more important than its use as a touring machine is the bicycle as an every-day help to mechanics, factory hands, clerks, and all people who live in or near small towns. Thanks to this modern wonder, they can live several miles away from their work, thus getting cheaper rents and better surroundings for their children; they can save car-fares and get healthful exercise. For the unfortunate dwellers in cities it offers recreation after working-hours and induces thousands who would never walk to get out into the air and find out for themselves that life without out-door exercise is not living.

How tremendous has been the change in the fortunes of the nickel-plated steed within the last five or six years.... The bicycle was still a toy five or six years ago. Half a dozen manufacturers exhibited their wares, and the pneumatic tire, then a curiosity imported from England, was viewed with interest, but much doubt as to its practical usefulness. The wheel was still something of a curiosity as a machine for grown men, while women who braved public opinion far enough to ride one in public were looked upon with suspicion.

The high 52-inch wheel, upon which the rider perched himself at the risk of his neck, was still the only one in common use, and had the "Safety" pattern not appeared, it is pretty certain that we should see but little more of the bicycle now than we did then. When I look at the high wheel to-day I rather wonder that any one was ever reckless enough or skilful enough to ride it. It was a matter of weeks to learn to get on it at all, and of months to ride it well.... At best the big wheels ... were fit only for athletic young men.... When a wheel was offered

From Philip G. Hubert, Jr., "The Bicycle: The Wheel of To-day," *Scribner's* 17 (June 1895): 692–697.

that anyone—man, woman, or child—could learn to ride well inside of a fortnight; that exposed the rider to no dangerous falls while learning, and that possessed all the speed of the high wheel with none of its dangers, then, seemingly, every one began to talk bicycles. Now no one is too old or too young to ride a "Safety," and the woman who objects to bicycling is soon likely to be looked upon as more eccentric than her sister who skims along the road in bloomers.

While the "Safety" pattern made the bicycle possible to everyone, of course the pneumatic tire is a great invention.... Upon a perfectly smooth board floor less power was required to propel a steel-rimmed wheel than one with a pneumatic tire. But let a few fine pebbles be sprinkled upon the track and then the power required for the steel tire had to be doubled and even tripled, while that for the pneumatic tire required only a slight increase.... With the pneumatic tire the pebble simply makes a dent in the soft tire, which passes over it without rising. A country road, or almost any road except a smooth floor, offers to the wheel a succession of minute obstacles....

Various estimates have been made of the output of bicycles for 1895, the figures running as high as four hundred thousand. The sales of wheels last year are said to have been two hundred and fifty thousand....

In one respect the bicycle show was peculiar; all classes seemed to be represented. At the horse show, for instance, or the dog show, the mechanic is never seen; at the bicycle show I noticed hundreds of men, evidently prosperous mechanics, who had come to see more of a machine that offered them at once economy and recreation, a healthful exercise and a saving of car-fares in getting to and from their daily work....

I was glad to find a manufacturer who would admit that we should some day get good machines for less than $50. Personally I am satisfied that a poor bicycle is a most costly affair. At the same time, the price asked for the best machines, ... dropped this year from $125 to $100 for standards, still seems out of proportion to the actual cost. It is ... hard to see why a good bicycle cannot be sold at a fair profit for $50 or less.... This year's cut in prices is a promise of better things to come.

4. An Elite Chicago's Women's Sports Organization: The Chicago Women's Athletic Club

BERTHA DAMARIS KNOBE

When the fashionable Chicago Women's Athletic Club opened its doors to society dames several years ago it ranked as the only athletic club for women in the world, and the most expensive woman's club in the country. It offered an elegant $100,000 equipment for beautifying through physical culture and, in return, it asked the unprecedented initiation fee of $100, with proportionate dues for privileges. Though a unique and costly experiment, inviting the pessimistic prophecy of short life, it stands to-day stamped with the successful membership

---

From Bertha Damaris Knobe, "Chicago Women's Athletic Club," *Harper's Bazaar* 39 (June 1905): 537–46.

of seven hundred and the promise from its promoter of new $600,000 quarters replete with every luxury and beauty-preserving appliance. The fact that it serves as a prototype for a similar organization, recently launched under the leadership of Mrs. John Jacob Astor, by the society women of New York, deprives it of the proud prestige of being the "only athletic club exclusively for the fair sex" though the sincerest flattery of imitation has its compensations....

Commensurate with the high price of membership, this club has sumptuous quarters unmatched outside of London. The building, to begin with, occupies a most desirable downtown site on Michigan Avenue, opposite the classic Art Institute solitarily adorning the lake-front park, and thus overlooking this attractive space and the opalescent water of Lake Michigan. Every morning the handsomest carriages rolling down this thoroughfare stop before the imposing edifice ... the members ushered in by an obsequious man in uniform, finds many athletic pleasures amid luxurious surroundings. The initiation fee of $100 is supplemented by annual dues of $40, and payment for every service after one officially arrives, but the appointments, from the white marble swimming-pool of Oriental splendor to the perfect cuisine in the great green dining-room, afford the creature comforts so common in the American man's club, and so exceptional in that of the American woman. The fair fortunate with purses sufficiently inflated to meet these assessments are naturally women of social position; indeed, from the beginning the two promoters—the president, Mrs. Philip D. Amour, widow of the multimillionaire, and the secretary and manager, Mrs. Paulina Harriette Lyon—have made personal standing the prerequisite. The honorable membership includes notables such as Mrs. William B. McKinley, and the regular roll such names as Mrs. Cyrus McCormick, ... thus bespeaking strict preservation of this standard.

Though in that experimental beginning masculine paragraphers, believing the club a passing fad, declared the women would plant pond lilies in the pool and pose in the gymnasium as hostesses for pink teas, those society dames have taken to athletics most seriously. Not unexpectedly this delightful trysting-place has developed into a fashionable centre for social affairs, but, at the same time, the number increases of enthusiasts who espouse either the gentle methods of beauty-making known as to Greek maidens of old, or the more ardent muscle-making exercise of to-day.... [T]he member may surrender to the soothing manipulations of the masseuse, ... or, perhaps, an occasional lesson in aesthetic calisthenics, when she goes through grace committed by several persons on the Lord's day, not only by children playing in the streets and other places, but by youths, maids and other persons, both strangers and others, full movements to the rhythm of music.... The swimming-pool, gymnasium, and bowling-alley, on the other hand, offer allurement for more strenuous physical development, and members are by no means exceptional who do a backward turn from the springboard into the pool, swing by their toes on the trapeze, or scientifically stroke the punching-bag.

... [I]n common with the English woman's club which usually approximates that of the American man, this Chicago Women's Athletic Club roundly repudiates intellectual attainment, speaking officially, for the luxurious life of relaxation. After a social turn in the upper reception room ..., the member usually proceeds to her private dressing room. Having exchanged her street gown for the club costume, a dark-blue blouse with big scarlet collar and short divided skirt, she enters the great circular gymnasium on the first floor, entirely finished in hard wood and provided with rope ladders, performing bars, running-track, and other athletic paraphernalia.

During the morning the gymnasium serves as a popular meeting-place. Under skilled instructors there are regular classes, from fancy dancing ... to most intricate bouts in the fine art of fencing. The already-mentioned training in aesthetic calisthenics has been supplemented lately by menti-physical culture under a man teacher, who directs these society women in evolution of arms to expand the chest or rotary motion of body to reduce the waist, and, as soft music keeps rhythmic time to movements, explains in "new-thought" parlance; "Beauty is not a matter of muscle and bone, however symmetrical they may be, but mind-spirit, will, ego, whatever you please to call it-must be in harmony with the voluntary muscle." Between classes basket-ball or bowling, perhaps, claims one coterie, and at all times, more daring individuals keep up perpetual motion in mid-air so to speak, the sudden ascent of a maiden on a pole or unexpected descent of a matron on a rope being offset by the more difficult aerial feats.

Following these exhilarating hours in the gymnasium, many seek the swimming pool, the expert not unusually going head first from the springboard or doing a few fancy turns on the performing-rings along one side before the final plunge. That the scene of their aquatic sport is probably unequaled in splendor ... , every inch of the tank and corridor with its massive pillars is of white marble.... Occasionally a game of water polo invites to spirited contests, though members prefer to practice their special accomplishments, the modern mermaid who swims the length of the pool underwater being outdone only by the one who apparently sits down on the surface before turning a series of back somersaults. At one end of the pool is the visitors' gallery of white marble....

These morning amusements over, the fair athletes separate for more individual diversion. If one seeks repose she hastens to the resting-rooms on the second floor. Twenty-one rooms open out of a leisure-inviting quadrangle....

Though the sterner sex are not associated with the club ... an encouraging number are becoming habitués at the luncheon hour, each being sponsored by a member....

5. Charles J. Lucas Criticizes the Commercialization of Amateur Athletics, 1906

The Amateur Athletic Union is a national organization intended to maintain and to regulate non-professional athletics throughout the country.... The national Amateur Athletic Union is in the hands of a board of governors representing ... various associations.... The controlling interest resides in New York and, to be more particular, in the hands of the Metropolitan Union. This body in turn is

From Charles J. Lucas, "Commercializing Amateur Athletics," *World Today* 10 (March 1906): 281–85.

largely under the control of Mr. James E. Sullivan, secretary-treasurer of the Amateur Athletic Union.

... The Amateur Athletic Union has done large service to the cause of amateur sport. This was particularly true when territorially athletics were limited to the cities lying east of the Alleghenies. The new prominence of western universities and athletic clubs has, however, given rise to a number of rather distressing situations. Furthermore there have been at work certain very marked tendencies making for the commercializing of the athletic club and its athletes. As a result the A.A.U. to-day is in serious need of reformation.... It is provincial rather than national; it can not control the action of athletic clubs belonging to the Metropolitan district; and it is becoming increasingly a creature of a business house....

Fred Lorz, a member of the Mohawk Athletic Club, New York City, who tried to steal the Marathon race at the Olympic Games in St. Louis in 1904, was suspended for life by the Amateur Athletic Union. Eight months later he was reinstated through the efforts of eastern men on the ground that he was temporarily insane. This reinstatement was in the face of affidavits by George Hench, St. Louis correspondent of the Associated Press ... and Mrs. J.T. Beals, official photographer of the Fair, and myself. We all saw Lorz riding in an automobile and talked with him as he ran in the race after riding eleven miles....

For a number of years the New York Athletic Club had dominated eastern amateur sport. Year after year the Mercury foot representatives had captured A.A.U. championships until the fall of 1903, when John Flanagan and other crack men were dropped by the New York Athletic Club. Then it was that the Greater New York Irish Athletic Club was organized with James E. Sullivan as its first president, and the now notorious Celtic Park, Long Island was selected as the home of the club. It was not long before Mr. Sullivan became tired of the position and believing in pure amateur sport resigned his position. The club went after the best men in the districts, securing Myer Prinstein, who forsook the honest Twenty-second Regiment Engineers' team for the Irish team; Martin Sheridan of the Pastime Athletic Club, one of the oldest and most honored A.A.U. Clubs, and a number of other athletes.

It was not long before the New York Athletic Club saw its boasted supremacy threatened. In 1904 the Irishmen won both the junior and senior A.A.U. championships at St. Louis. With the backing of Tammany, the Irish-men began a war on Mr. Sullivan in the hope that he would permit them to carry on match races at Celtic Park, which, from an amateur standpoint were impossible....

And now will come the worst attack upon amateur sport ever witnessed. The Greater New York Irish Athletic Club has a number of sinecures in the way of government jobs at its disposal for college men, together with huge gate receipts at Celtic Park. The New York Athletic Club has a sumptuous clubhouse and beautiful Travers Island, not to mention various sinecures put at its disposal through the kindness of members who want victory at any cost. Who will win? The Irish club has already secured Hymen, formerly of Pennsylvania, who has a government job on Long Island. Amateur sport has got to such condition in and around New York that resort is made to the courts when A.A.U. officials legislate so as to displease the Tammany crowd....

A decided detriment to amateur sport throughout the United States is the control of A.G. Spalding & Brothers over the Amateur Athletic Union.... The Spalding discus is the official discus; the Spalding basketball is the official ball ... ; the Spalding football is the official ball for intercollegiate contests.

Last spring Garrells, of Michigan, made a world's record with a discus not of the Spalding manufacture. Mr. Sullivan promptly stated that the record would not be allowed....

Mr. J.E. Sullivan is secretary-treasurer of the national Amateur Athletic Union. He is also president of the American Sports Publishing Company, by whom is published the Spalding Athletic Library, one of the most effective mediums for advertising the Spalding products.... He is commonly considered as being the general manager for advertising of A.G. Spalding.... And finally, it was Sullivan who prevented the exhibition in the Physical Building at St. Louis of any athletic and gymnastic equipment except that manufactured by A.G. Spalding & Brothers.

ESSAYS

The two essays in this section examine the role of social class in the sporting experience of Americans. The first, by Donald Mrozek of the Department of History, Kansas State University, discusses how ultra-rich Americans utilized their wealth to promote their particular sporting interests. They were not interested in sport to regenerate themselves, but to display their wealth and status. The second essay by Steven A. Riess, which was recognized as the best article of the year in the *International Journal of Sport History* for 1991, focuses on middle-class sport. Riess examines the process by which middle-class men began relying upon sports as a means for defining their manliness. During the nineteenth century when the middle classes shunned sport because it represented anti-Victorian values, respectable men gained their sense of manliness from hard work, marriage, and fatherhood. However, in the late nineteenth century, as they became less independent in their careers, and as sport became a positive social force, these men turned to sport to demonstrate their masculinity.

Sporting Life as Consumption, Fashion, and Display—The Pastimes of the Rich at the Turn of the Century

DONALD MROZEK

It has been argued that the newly emerging class of extravagantly rich Americans whose wealth was rooted in industrial capitalism came to challenge the role of social leadership and political power of the traditional American gentility. Later historians have questioned the degree of antipathy between old and new wealth. But in sport, quantities of money meant the ability to govern the games that

From Donald Mrozek, *Sport and American Mentality, 1880–1910* (Knoxville: University of Tennessee Press, 1983), 103–135.

could be played. Although ultra-rich Americans did not dictate institutionalized sport among other classes, they made possible the emergence of certain sports that required large outlays of money for facilities and their maintenance. Most important in the interplay of varying attitudes about sport in the early twentieth century, the ultra-rich—the Vanderbilts, the Harrimans, and others—embodied an alternative sensibility about sport. They conducted it as a mode of consumption and as a fashion, and what regeneration they were likely to experience through sport flowed from its social outlets. That the remnant of the gentility, such as Roosevelt and Lodge, might have harbored such sentiments at an unconscious level is possible; but that they could have pursued them deliberately is nearly inconceivable. In this difference lay the curious contribution of the ultra-rich toward attitudes about sport....

... Democracy of nearly any description had no place in the world of the very rich. Using their sports as badges of social status, the ultra-rich generally confined themselves to pursuits whose cost put them out of reach of ordinary Americans. Yachting, polo, fox-hunting, tennis, and golf—these were the characteristic sports of the American rich. Indeed, their penchant to use sport as a means of establishing social exclusiveness and prestige showed itself not only in the activities that they favored but in their departure from various sports that they could not control....

In this passion for exclusiveness, the very rich, who sought means of certifying their worth, often made the criticisms of Thorstein Veblen seem a miracle of understatement. In the words of Price Collier, they were "a widely advertised, though fortunately small, class, diligent in making themselves conspicuous, who, having been recently poor, are trying to appear anciently rich." In a 1911 volume predicting their passing, Frederick Townsend Martin called them the "idle rich."... It was a criterion that differed fundamentally from the standards of duty and dedication to the public interest which held such deep appeal for middle- and upper-middle-class Americans. Yet the new ultra-rich were accorded a peculiar publicity; and, while excluding those of an inferior economic class from the scenes of their sport, they nonetheless assumed a certain paradoxical visibility, through which they became the embodiment of the quest for pleasure and self-gratification.

Simultaneously a source of personal amusement and a component of an exclusionary social system, the sports of the very rich industrial magnates and financiers were thus special in kind, special in place, and special in function. The characteristic sportive activities of the rich took place in distinctive environments shaped for their pursuit—whether a country club or even a whole compound such as at Newport, Rhode Island. Sport further served as a device for governing their etiquette and signifying their status. Ironically, the rich found their own way of giving meaning to Grantland Rice's maxim that what mattered was "how you played the game"; and social manners frequently predominated over athletic prowess in determining who really won or lost. Yet, for this reason, sport itself seemed all the more real, as it was tied to the very core of one's social goals and aspirations. Sport thus gained an added constituency that perceived it to have value, fastening on it as a nonproductive amusement and an instrument of display.

The Exclusionary Sports of the Rich

By the very sporting ventures they chose, the American rich set patterns of behavior that distinguished them from the masses and even from much of the respectable middle class. Infected with a desire to set fashion ... the wealthy elite often opted for the customs of the British upper classes—a phenomenon that showed itself in the sudden vogue of tennis and golf and invited satire in the rise of fox-hunting. A key means of distinguishing fashionable sport from common amusement was the price tag. Those requiring expensive and well-maintained facilities had a special appeal for the rich, who affected a lack of interest in the cost of their undertakings while glorying in the ability to pay it. It was the attitude of J. Pierpont Morgan who, when asked how much it cost to maintain his yacht, replied that anyone who had to ask could not afford one....

Although many advocates of pure amateurism from varying economic backgrounds were concerned to avoid excessive attention from journalists and sports fans lest it lead to commercialism and subversion of gentlemanly values, the desire for privacy harbored among the rich was another matter entirely. The seclusion of the country club, for example, halted not the corruption of American life but the dilution of upper-class society. Yet, while seeking privacy at one level, the rich invited public attention at another, partly because their exclusionary measures provoked idle curiosity and also because the magnificence of their display could hardly have escaped notice under nearly any circumstances. The first American country club, Brookline, opened in 1882 as a center for Boston's elite in polo, racing, and the hunt. Soon it added golf links, making available to its aristocratic membership yet another sport whose expense barred it from the common citizen. The Newport Country Club, spearheaded by sugar magnate Theodore A. Havemeyer, attracted founding members from the moneyed class such as Cornelius Vanderbilt, Perry Belmont, and John Jacob Astor. Similarly, men of wealth took the spotlight when they joined in 1908 to promote tournament play through the National Golf Links of America; and the roster of promoters included the fashionable names of William K. Vanderbilt, Harry Payne Whitney, and Henry Clay Frick....

Among wealthy women, the same bias against workers and the common middle class appeared as among men. Anne O'Hagan's "Athletic Girl," described in *Munsey's Magazine* for August 1901, had little truck with the common working woman. Even for O'Hagan, some gymnasiums seemed to set unreasonably steep and exclusionary fees.... [One gym] cost ... a hundred dollars a year. Other clubs whose appointments were "less Sybaritic" charged membership dues on the order of forty dollars per year. O'Hagan rather blithely noted that, "if one has the distinction of being a working woman," ten dollars would suffice to obtain gymnastic instruction. Although O'Hagan found ten dollars an inconsiderable amount of money, the working girl for whom this represented a week's pay may have thought differently. Among many Americans, bodily exercise was still essentially a private matter; and the inaccessibility of gymnasiums on economic grounds meant the exclusion of large numbers of Americans.... As a result, glib pronouncements about the availability of gymnasiums with pillowed couches and well-trained maids said "Let them eat cake" to people who struggled for bread....

Women of upper-class instincts and means thus tended to isolate themselves from the preponderance of Americans of their sex. Welcoming greater interest in sports and games, they nonetheless used it—perhaps unconsciously—in ways that only sharpened their distinctiveness from men and from working women....

... Suggestive of the importance of class distinction, the desirability of tennis for women evidently stemmed from its social effects as much as from its hygienic benefits. According to Elizabeth C. Barney, ... the enjoyment of tennis revolved around the "social intercourse" at the club house. The game strengthened and unified the community by drawing together the young people who played and the matrons who watched.... This sporting scene served as a common ground upon which women could develop social values, much as the sporting options open to men enabled them to realize their own ideals; but the codes for women differed from those of the men. For Elizabeth Barney ... tennis served to organize polite society and to put a healthy flush in its cheeks.

The flow of fashion which illuminated the wealthy woman's sporting habits extended into the physical trappings that surrounded them, such as clothing styles and accessories. In a society that prized conspicuous consumption and wasteful dress, the realm of sport had the advantage of adding a whole new set of activities for which special costumes could be devised and socially mandated.... Commentators promoted the wasteful and unproductive behavior that Thorstein Veblen termed conspicuous consumption, emphasizing the value of certain sports—often marginal sports ... such as croquet and fencing—in enhancing the worth of woman as an object of pecuniary display.

The conduct of sports themselves became an object of fashion, and social grace competed—successfully—against athletic ability in the design and management of tournaments. In woman's events as in men's, strict control was exerted over admission to play in ostensibly national events. Elizabeth Barney, for example, reported that upper-class women were able to contribute "beautiful form" to the mixed doubles matches in tennis ... at the country club; and they carried the same spirit over into tournament play. The *crème de la crème,* Barney noted, made their way, in 1894, to the Ladies' National Championship at the Philadelphia Country Club, which ranked with "the foremost in tone and social standing, and every thing that it does is in the best of style." The tournament operated on rules that ensured protection ... from contact with their social inferiors. Matches were determined by invitation only, in a way that openly violated the supposedly democratic quality of modern sport, and only those of "assured social position" would think to submit their names for screening....

The enthusiastic and influential physical educator Dudley A. Sargent observed, in an article published in 1901, that fashion actually accounted for the rise and fall of many sports themselves, rather than merely the costumes for their pursuit. Archery and fencing, for example, would be pursued as "fads and ... then become obsolete." Obedient to society's edicts, the *beau monde* took up even serious sports as "the proper thing" and dropped them with equal unintelligence when style changed....

Special Places for Special Sportsmen

Although there was a strong current in America toward sharing certain sports which were national in sweep and were usually conducted in public places, the new rich bucked the trend and created a more specialized environment for sports. The country club was their most repeated form, and lavish clubhouses designed by leading architectural firms served as centers of social interchange as well as focal points of golf and tennis.... Separated and distinct from work, sport had become an autonomous focal point in the life of the rich. Unlike middle-class Americans who claimed that sport ingrained in players those qualities that empowered them to do life's work, the rich favored sport for its inutility. Their country clubs, then, became symbols of a quite different, pleasure-oriented ethic, which was to make a major contribution to the American notion of leisure.

The physical segregation of sporting activities in a special place for their pursuit, which was an intrinsic feature of the country club, had equivocal implications. On the one hand, it suggested the isolation of play, as ritualized in the games at the club, from work. On the other hand, it made a comprehensive and interactive, if separated, system out of the activities which were conducted there.... In short, the sporting life of the rich thus assumed an institutional shape, one which affirmed the viability of sport as an autonomous enterprise and one whose very comprehensiveness helped to provide foundation for the belief that a man might even pursue sport as a calling and an independent source of meaning in one's life....

... Many of the business features that had appeared in the earlier resorts were absent at Newport. Gambling went private, and even the admission of spectators to competitions in sports such as tennis was restricted on social grounds. Although the aim was to create an isolated playground for the rich in which social distinction exceeded athletic ability in the pursuit of diversion, the effect was also to lay the groundwork for the concept of the "destination resort."...

... Eager for acceptance among the more reputable classes, [John] Morrissey evidently hoped to curry their favor by catering to their desire for amusement. He built lavish facilities at Saratoga which pampered his guests ... but he soon identified a restiveness among the patrons, who seemed to crave more elaborate, exciting, and active entertainments. He succeeded in enlisting the advice of the prominent New York stockbroker William R. Travers, whose ideas contributed much to the quality of the early racing seasons.

... Morrissey's interests in sport grew principally from his growing need to keep Saratoga a commercial success; and even his desire for social acceptance could not possibly be fulfilled unless he continued to attract the rich and well-born as guests....

The enclosure and definition of space, ... give it cultural and even ceremonial meaning. In the late nineteenth century, this process exemplified the passion for discipline and order in life that pervaded middle-class society, and it enhanced the sense of importance shown toward the activities pursued within it. With the establishment of the grand compound of the rich at Newport, there came upon the American scene such a defined and enclosed space that was devoted exclusively to leisure; and, although sport was not the only entertainment or amusement pursued within its confines, it occupied a major place and thus became integrated into the concept of leisure itself. Although this latter phenomenon prevailed only within a rarified community at the time, namely the very rich, it lent credence to an interpretation of the worth and respectability of sport that was quite different from what was encouraged by the middle class and the remnant of the gentility. …[S]port no longer needed to be a "healthful amusement" that readied one for work; it could become an end in itself, to be sought only as a means of diversion and pleasure.

… In a process that began in 1859, Newport emerged as the summer social center of the "great American families," who had previously been scattered about in resorts of their own choosing. The gravitation toward Newport suggested a certain nationalization, or centralization, of America's rich upper crust; and this, in turn, was to lend itself to a standardization of behavior and amusements among the wealthy.… Even then, it was a refuge from the world and its troubles, or … a world unto itself with its own cares and concerns. In a sense, even the absorption into the social rounds that became a staple of Newport's image and self-image furthered the sense of insulation from the practical affairs of business and politics, sharpening the sense of protective enclosure.…

Nonetheless, the annual renewal of social ties at Newport itself became a kind of competition, in which sporting events and social occasions became devices for the definition and measurement of status, as had not been the case before, except perhaps in the colonial Tidewater. The relationship applied within the social elite and also between wealthy society as a whole and the rest of America.… [T]he actual performance of athletic feats was less important than the grace and style with which people performed them; and instances in which competitive excellence was prized—notably in yachting—themselves hinged partly on the purchase of expensive, specially designed vessels and on the maintenance of a substantial crew and staff. Even in yachting, however, a social note obtained; and extravagant expenditures conspired with contempt for "new money" to govern participation in competition on the waters off Newport. The dedicated British yachtsman Sir Thomas Lipton was snubbed widely at Newport since he had made his money in trade, and much too recently at that.…

The tendency of the rich at Newport to use sport as part of a whole system of leisure showed itself in their disdain for games that needed no more than an open field and a ball. Instead, they lavished their attention on pastimes that demanded much time, special facilities, expensive equipment, and, sometimes, extensive travel. Although the enthusiasm for yachting, lawn tennis, fox-hunting, and the like was often genuine, so was their social role. As J.P. Morgan put it succinctly, "You can do business with anyone, but you can go sailing only with a gentleman." The devotion of resources to sport and other aspects of leisure thus became more than an emblem of wealth, although it was assuredly that; it also became a means of delineating leisure as an institution whose complexity invited members of the wealthiest classes to pursue it as if it were life's very purpose.

This kernel of difference helps to account for the interest of the American rich in the sporting life of the British upper class. It has been suggested that

American sport was largely an imitative extension of British sport.... Among the very rich the imitation ascended toward parody. The wealthy Americans aped what they thought to be the sporting traditions of the British upper class in an effort to stay in international fashion and to act convincingly as an American aristocracy by recreating the behavior of a confessedly leisured society.... Polo ponies were kept in lavish stables, sleeping on monogrammed linen sheets.... Pink-coated riders pursued the fox across the fields of disgruntled Rhode Island farmers.... The passion for things British, for example, encouraged the rich to show interest in lawn tennis, although the game's survival also depended on its suitability to the needs of the American rich. First brought to New York by Mary Outerbridge after a vacation in Bermuda, where she had observed the game played by British officers, tennis soon became a fixture of Newport's summer season. Partly because it brought the well-dressed spectators together at the Casino, Tennis Week—the informal name for the National Lawn Tennis Tournament—emerged as the most estimable sporting event of the season. The very choice of a grass surface gave it an air of greater style, since it required much more careful and costly maintenance than hard-packed clay. Players in the tournament, ... initiated in 1881, came from the ranks of social fashion.... Clad in knickers, blazers, and caps, they competed in a mild game, paced by "the genteel pat of the ball against languid strings." Richard D. "Dicky" Sears, who won the first championship match and held the title for eight consecutive years, came from a reputable Boston family.... [I]nvitations to compete [were not] allowed by the Casino's board of governors to players outside the Newport social set until the turn of the century. As with the rest of Newport's summer activities, tennis was as much a matter of style as one of athletics.

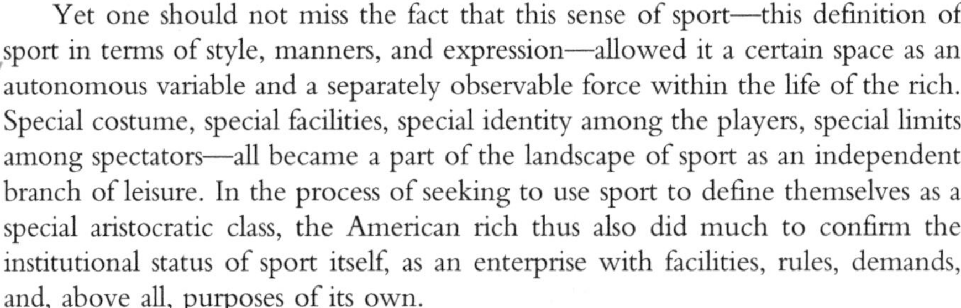

Yet one should not miss the fact that this sense of sport—this definition of sport in terms of style, manners, and expression—allowed it a certain space as an autonomous variable and a separately observable force within the life of the rich. Special costume, special facilities, special identity among the players, special limits among spectators—all became a part of the landscape of sport as an independent branch of leisure. In the process of seeking to use sport to define themselves as a special aristocratic class, the American rich thus also did much to confirm the institutional status of sport itself, as an enterprise with facilities, rules, demands, and, above all, purposes of its own.

The Special Role of Sport for the Ultra-Rich

Although the ultra-rich pursued sport as a fashion, it was still something that could be a calling. In this regard, they veered sharply from the gentility.... Traditionalists such as Roosevelt found little to approve in the antics of the ultra-rich. Roosevelt never condoned the use of sport for purely personal purposes, arguing that it was a means through which one prepared for societal tasks. Yet, among the very rich, ever more elaborate trappings were forged in service of selfish goals, seeking to use material splendor as proof of personal importance. At the same time, however, the likes of Roosevelt also objected to the implications of the physical separation of the very rich from the great majority of

Americans.... The very process of physical exclusion that showed itself in the growth of country clubs and in the development of the wealthy colony in Newport ran afoul of the gentility and the middle class, even as it made the undiluted pursuit of a sporting life a more credible and creditable option among the rich themselves.... For the very rich, however, the dignity of sport inhered in the lavishness of circumstance and in the impertinence of its pursuit. Truly, the ultra-rich were pioneers of sport as a leisure activity which required no justification. Precisely this, which so alienated and disgusted the traditional gentility because it seemed to debase sport by subordinating it to motives that were trivial because they were merely personal, constituted the major contribution of the turn-of-the-century rich to the development of twentieth century attitudes toward sport.

... The ultra-rich came to their sport partly from the vantage of excess "spare" time.... In an age that equated activity with life itself, it seemed senseless and unacceptable to fall into total indolence or passivity. It was in this context of the general need for the sensation of action and the specific need for the impression of economic inutility that the very rich helped to create the American sense of leisure. Contrary to Marx's sense that it was simply uncommitted spare time or rest, the wealthy American capitalist made leisure a rather exhausting round of organized amusements and consumer activities. Transcending or even just ignoring the traditionalists' focus on duty and service, the ultra-rich thus developed a sense of leisure and leisure time that was permeated by activities and suffused with an underlying conviction of the primacy of experience. It was insufficient to have free time, unless you showed it.

... Even as the common sense of what constituted the sports hero came to center on the primacy of deeds over virtues, so did the more general sense of a hero of culture center on action over character ... [T]he rich ... did much to create the concept of the "sportsman." The very rich could establish influence—other than their manifest economic power—only by accumulating objects and by establishing a record of elitist activities. The absence of usefulness in sport was more than charming, then; for it made sport a superb instrument for the creation of leisure. Ironically, the wealthy Americans' emphasis on the intertwined goals of self-gratification, identity, relief from the tedium of a stultifying structured life, and expressive display resembled the supposed preferences of the laboring class more closely than those of the economic and social middle. In this way, the very rich helped to advance notions about sport and its role in purposeless leisure which would simultaneously compete with the middle class's concentration on the work-ethic and service and encourage the working class to see sport as a part of the American Dream. Like the very rich, workers could prove their achievement of leisure only by expressing this fact through action, as deeds increasingly assumed greater eloquence than words in the formulation of American ideas. Sport had become a fixture among the idle rich; and Americans who cherished a belief in upward material mobility were prone to follow the reigning models of the culture....

The very clarity of the sporting system among the rich made it possible for them to avoid the ambivalence, ambiguity, and occasional sophistry that plagued the exponents of middle class and genteel virtues. Wealth—not virtue—was its own reward; and it was association with wealth that kept a sport worthy of further interest. At the same time, wealth served to guard and insulate a sport so that it remained not only limited in clientele but rarified in its social role.... Whatever social benefit the very rich saw in sport was "social" only in the small sense, serving to sharpen lines of status. But the effects of sport in individual gratification, in what Veblen called a renewed "clannishness," and in activity-oriented leisure were numerous and systemic. Untroubled by issues of moral purpose, the rich thus established the prototype of the sportsman as an unrestricted consumer.

What the defenders of the older tradition criticized as "monomania" in sport, whether among the rich or among the professionals, passed as a form of virtue among the ultra-rich. The wealthy Americans luxuriated in expensive yachts, "Sybaritic" clubs, and costly holidays. Yet the middle class and the gentility proved ineffective in stamping out their influence.... Theodore Roosevelt ['s belief] that the [wealthy hunts]man could afford both the trip and any attendant loss of income suggest the limits of democratic thought and opportunity among the middle class and the gentility. At least the very rich made the best of it, turning a rather vulgar instinct for display into a form of candor. Thus impervious to the internally flawed arguments of their critics, the rich stood as a significant point of gravitation within the realm of sport and so also as a constituency lending sport an aura of legitimacy.... [G]iven their privileged and powerful position, they had a largely radical effect, which finally touched the mass of Americans just as deeply as did the self-appointed protectors of American values.

Sport and the Redefinition of American Middle-Class Masculinity, 1840–1900

STEVEN A. RIESS

At the onset of the Victorian era, middle-class American men had little interest in sport or physical culture. They were shopkeepers, professionals, agents, clerks, and farmers—hard-working, devout, future-orientated individuals who had little precious free time to take away from the serious business of earning a living. With the exception of clerks, generally young men learning the business with the expectation of a future entrepreneurial career, middle-class men were competitive workers who were their own bosses. They frowned upon popular mass sports ... as a waste of time, immoral, illegal and debilitating.... Yet by mid-century a respectable middle-class sporting culture was beginning to evolve, and after the 1870s, it boomed. This article will explain how middle-class men's concerns with their masculinity contributed to make sport an integral part of their lives. Sport redefined for them their sense of manliness and provided mechanisms to achieve it.

From Steven A. Riess, "Sport and the Redefinition of American Middle-Class Masculinity," *International Journal of the History of Sport* 8 (May 1991): 5–22. Reprinted by permission of Taylor & Francis Group, www.tandfonline.com.

The Rise of a Respectable Middle-Class Sporting Culture, 1840–70

... Athletics and physical culture had historically always been an almost exclusively male activity, and prowess in sporting competitions ... regarded as a mark of manliness [with] such characteristics as courage, determination, strength and vigor. At the start of the Victorian era ... , the leading sportsmen were members of a traditionally oriented male bachelor sub-culture.... The sporting fraternity was composed of urban machine politicians, artisans, seasonal workers, Irish immigrants, and men from the dregs of society along with young elite rakes.... They participated in sports for fun, to develop camaraderie, and to display their honor and manliness. Their favorite contests were illegal blood and gambling sports.... The pre-modern life-style and values of the male bachelor sub-culture expressed a social ethic totally antithetical to the bourgeoisie.... An antebellum middle-class man ... gained his identity through work, not leisure, earned his money through hard work, ... and was a good and steady provider for his family. He was reliable, independent, and resisted temptation who ... did not shun domesticity for the saloon or poolroom, but rather made family and home the centerpiece of his life.

Middle-class opposition to sport and physical culture began to wane in the 1840s and 1850s ... when the country was starting to modernize. As the United States began to undergo the processes of urbanization, industrialization, immigration, and "civilization," the nature of sport underwent substantial changes and began to appeal to urban middle-class needs and sensibilities. This development was the product of the role models of immigrant and upper-class sportsmen, the evolution of new sports congruent with middle class values and behavior, and, most importantly, the influence of a new positive sports creed. This ideology was popularized by Jacksonian reformers who believed that non-violent, clean, gambling-free, outdoor physical exercise and sport would be socially functional activities that could counter the growing urban pathology and social anomie....

... The ideology posited that participation in clean sport would improve public health, raise moral standards and build character; and provide a substitute for the vile practices of the sporting fraternity.... Leaders in the physical-fitness movement included religious leaders (Unitarian Rev. William Ellery Channing), utopians (Robert Dale Owen), educators (Horace Mann), transcendentalists (Ralph Waldo Emerson), scientists (Lemuel Shattuck), physicians (Dr. Oliver Wendell Holmes), and health faddists (Sylvester Graham)....

... The severest critic of middle-class lassitude was Dr. Holmes, a noted oarsman in his own right, who ... in "The Autocrat of the Breakfast Table" denounced "the vegetative life of the American" who he compared unfavorably with the English gentry, a popular role model for the American elite since the colonial era. Holmes rated American college students poorly in comparison with the vigorous Oxbridge athletes, and recommended they learn from their English brothers who rowed and engaged in other sports.... Holmes foresaw a rapid decline of the race, certain that "such a set of black-coated, stiff-jointed, soft-muscled, paste-complexioned youth as we can boast in our American cities never before sprang from loins of Anglo-Saxon lineage."...

The advocacy of improved public health and the city's need for fresh air and space to play out-of-doors led to the development of a municipal park movement, based largely on British antecedents....

The municipal park movement, ... was led by journalists, ... physicians, and scientists.... Their primary purpose was to improve the urban public's physical and mental health by providing access to fresh air, beautiful vistas, and playing space. The movement's first major achievement was New York's Central Park, opened in 1858. The original design by Frederick Law Olmsted and Calvert Vaux set aside space for formal gardens and wooded areas for receptive recreation and areas for playgrounds and cricket fields for more active sports. Central Park was a huge success, and became a model for suburban parks across the country after the Civil War.... Since these facilities were situated far from the centers of population, costly to reach, and at first stressed receptive over active recreation, ... the new parks were ... primarily for the middle- and upper-class.

... Middle-class urbanites were confident they could transmit their high moral standards to their children but were concerned about the more exuberant behavior of lower-class urban youth in increasingly impersonal, large heterogeneous cities.... Rising crime rates, periodic riots and rampant hooliganism reflected growing anomie and the erosion of basic values.... Middle-class moral guardians promoted moral leisure activities to curtail the behavior of working-class youth who were independent of the traditional customs and social controls that regulated village life and found themselves with ample opportunities for immoral commercialized entertainments. Rational recreations like sports and physical training were expected to provide a healthy alternative to such dissipating pastimes as drinking, fornication and gambling....

... Historian Melvin L. Adelman argues that character building aspect of the sports creed developed in the 1850s as an adjunct to the morality thesis but became more prominent after the Civil War when sports participation was identified as a moral equivalent of war. The key to the character-building argument was the assumption that participation in sports promoted manliness. Sport was regarded as almost inherently a male sphere, inappropriate for Victorian women, and the contemporary press described nearly all sports as manly. Advocates of the sport creed not only believed that competitive sports engendered traits that were essential to middle-class success—self-discipline, self-denial, and even courage—but also that sedentary white-collar workers could utilize sports to demonstrate manliness at a time when manliness was widely identified with physical labor. Athletes were real men who had graduated from childhood and were prepared for the battles of life or death (i.e., war).

The character-building qualities of sport were widely promoted by the apostles of muscular Christianity, an English-based philosophy that sought to harmonize the mental, physical and spiritual dimensions of man....

The idea that a man who was moral and devout could and should also be physically fit tied in very well with prevailing middle-class values and the new sports creed. Holmes, Emerson, and Unitarian ministers Edward Everett Hale and Thomas Wentworth Higginson all became leading spokesmen for muscular Christianity ... , such a strong justification for sporting activities that it largely eliminated all but the most conservative pietistic opposition to athletics, especially when physical culture was sponsored by the evangelical Young Men's Christian Association (YMCA). The "Y" movement began in England in 1844 and was brought to America seven years later to assist farm youth to adjust to urban life in a moral environment. By 1860 it was supporting moral athletics and gymnastics as "a safeguard against the allurement of objectionable places of resort."… In the late nineteenth century the YMCA became one of the most important facilitators of sport and physical training for middle-class youth and young men.

Sexuality was an essential, if implicit, aspect of the character-building element of the sporting ideology. Muscular Christians and other mid-Victorians saw sport as both a sexual substitute and a check on effeminacy, concerns that became increasingly important over the course of the nineteenth century. Sports reformers wanted to create a manly Christian gentleman who "was the athlete of continence, not coitus, continuously testing his manliness in the fires of self-denial." The middle classes not only disdained the sexual liberties of … the male bachelor sub-culture but were also worried about a loss of sexual energy and sperm which were believed to have a finite, irreplaceable limit. Sport would provide an alternative expenditure of energy and help build manliness which would give young men the strength to resist the "secret vice" (masturbation). Moral men could earn their manhood on the playing field instead of the bedroom.

Clean sport was viewed by contemporaries as a means to counter effeminacy. In 1859 the *New York Herald* attributed the feminization of culture in part to the absence of sports in America…. Through sport men would retain such physical qualities as ruggedness and hardiness, instead of degenerating into foolish fops. It was manliness the nation needed, not flabby sick weaklings, if it was to fulfill its destiny.

At mid-century middle-class young men who were convinced by the new sports creed that physical culture was an excellent and useful activity had a number of options to choose for their recreation. They nearly always preferred sports, usually competitive sports, to boring calisthenics…. Virtually any sport that did not rely on gambling for its appeal or brutalize other men or beasts was regarded as appropriate for respectable, forward-looking, middle-class men or individuals with middle-class aspirations. But unless the activity was "manly," requiring a high level of dexterity, physical skill and courage, and not played by women, it would not be considered character-building…. Bicycle-riding was originally a manly sport because riding a velocipede, or "boneshaker," in the 1860s was difficult to master and uncomfortable to ride. Similarly, it took a "man" to master the ordinary, or high wheeler bicycle, an odd-shaped vehicle introduced in 1876 with a huge front wheel and tiny rear wheel that was often ridden on dangerous, poorly constructed roads. However, once technological innovations produced the light weight safety bicycle of the 1890s, with same size pneumatic tires that easy to maneuver, riding became a popular fad among millions of Americans including middle-class women. Cycling then was only manly among "scorchers" (speeders), or participants in strenuous 100-mile outings….

… Middle-class men at mid-century … preferred agonistic activities more in line with the competitive middle-class spirit … , particularly team ball games which commentators regarded as particularly effective in indoctrinating respectable young men with Victorian ideals of masculinity. This was ironic because team games were not really congruent with the independent nature of middle-class work then. But over the course of the century, as white-collar jobs became less independent with the rise of bureaucratization, team games would fit in more and more with the character of non-manual employment.

Cricket was the first major team sport.… Few contests were played in the United States until 1840 when English merchants, agents, and artisans in New York formed the St. George Cricket Club. A cricket fad soon developed and it was the most popular ball game until the late 1850s.…

Cricket eventually lost out to baseball for several reasons; it was an English game; its historic rules and regulations did not readily adapt to American needs; the game took too long for busy Americans; and it was hard to play. Americans had not yet developed a ball-playing tradition, in spite of the English example, and ball-playing was regarded at least until the 1840s as a boy's amusement. The English perception of cricket as a very manly game and appropriate recreation for young men and adults did not readily transfer to the United States. In the 1840s, journalists … who covered the rise of a respectable sporting culture were generally strong supporters of cricket because they identified it as a masculine amusement … because it required physical and mental exertion that was beyond a child's capabilities.… The *New York Clipper* lauded the sport for testing mental and physical ability and strength of character. Immigrant journalist Henry Chadwick, … applauded cricket for teaching such virtues as sobriety, self-denial, fortitude, discipline, fair play and obedience.… Cricket was a manly activity both because of the skill involved and the courage required to defend the wicket against a bowler's speedy throw.

The modern game of baseball was established in 1845 by members of early clubs including the Knickerbockers Base Ball Club, middle-class men who played for outdoor exercise and amusement.… In the early 1850s the game began to gain popularity, mostly among white-collar men influenced by the new sports creed and the example of cricket. Baseball soon got more press coverage, became organized with the formation of the National Association of Base Ball Players in 1858.

From 1857, journalists began describing baseball as a masculine game, and even the "national pastime." *Beadle's Dime Base-Ball Player* (1860), edited by Henry Chadwick, identified the manly attributes of the game: "Baseball to be played thoroughly, requires the possession of muscular strength, great agility, quickness of eye, readiness of hand, and many other faculties of mind and body that mark the man of nerve."

… Yet, there was still doubts about baseball's manliness because the level of skill required was noticeably less than cricket. Writers advocated a change in the fly rule which allowed catching a batted ball on the bounce, to make the sport more difficult and less of a children's game. Chadwick and others recommended that it had to be caught on the fly.… The NABBP did not adopt this rule change until 1864 for fear it would make baseball too much like cricket and because players were afraid of getting hurt! This innovation persuaded Chadwick to turn his allegiance from cricket to baseball, a manly exercise valuable for American youth and more suited to the American character....

The coming of the Civil War slowed the rise of middle-class sport, but the necessary conditions had been established which led to an enormous boom in middle-class athletic activity soon after the war's end. The new sports creed was accepted as the conventional wisdom and employers who had once criticized their workers for neglecting their duties to play baseball, changed their minds. In the late 1860s, Chicago department store moguls, John V. Farwell and Marshall Field, became so convinced that baseball taught such Victorian values as thrift, sobriety, virtue and hard work that they organized company teams and gave players time off for practice and games. A respectable, gambling-free sporting culture was evolving, based on behavior and attitudes consonant with Victorian values which stressed the functionalism of competitive athletics. Sport was now a useful recreational activity appropriate for respectable middle-class young men who would be transformed into manly specimens, sound of body and pure of heart.

The Martial Spirit, Teamwork and Middle-Class Sport, 1870–1900

Sport in the late nineteenth century continued to shape the middle-class sense of manliness. Middle-class masculinity was still mainly based on the role of breadwinner and head of household, but ... men were undergoing a serious identity crisis that sport could help resolve. The enormous changes under way with the rise of Big Business and the corporate state were causing a loss of individuality and self-esteem. The bureaucratization of the work-place created a great demand for managers, professionals, salesmen and clerks. These salaried workers were now subordinates, no longer independent workers or entrepreneurs, and they did not enjoy the same sense of creativity and accomplishment previously enjoyed by the old middle class. A second identity crisis was that young men questioned their own courage, having been too young to have fought in the Civil War and unsure if they could measure up to the bravery of their fathers, uncles, and brothers who had worn the blue or gray. Finally, a third crisis was the feminization of American culture which had led to the over-civilization of society. Protestantism was becoming feminized, with church pews dominated by women, stressing feminine values like humility and meekness, and unable to reach out to young men. The eastern elite establishment and other opinion-makers were becoming frightened that the Anglo-Saxon male had become effete, was losing his sexual identity, and was becoming impotent.... In the 1890s concerns for manliness were epitomized by such new words as "sissy," "stuffed shirt," and "molly-coddle." Manliness was less a stage of development out of childhood than the opposite of femininity.

One important response by middle-class men to this self-questioning was to turn to vigorous physical activity as a means of proving their manliness to themselves and others. They participated in a wide variety of strenuous, clean, outdoor sports to develop strength, courage and virility, and regain confidence in their masculinity. The preeminent exponent of using a "strenuous life" to achieve and certify one's masculinity was Theodore Roosevelt, the elite New York civic reformer and future president. Roosevelt had outgrown a sickly childhood by a regimen of daily vigorous exercise and participation in such sports as boxing, riding and hunting and promoted a cult of masculinity through widely read essays he wrote.... Roosevelt did not advocate manly activities merely for the physical joy it brought, or even its sense of accomplishment, but because the qualities that strenuous recreation endowed would make men into leaders who would contribute significantly to the common weal. In 1893 Roosevelt argued in "The Value of an Athletic Training" that "in a perfectly peaceful and commercial civilization such as ours there is always a danger of placing too little stress upon the more virile virtues—upon the virtues which go to make up a race of statesmen and soldiers, of pioneers and explorers." The young reformer recommended that men remedy the situation by participating in exercise and manly out-of-door sports....

Among the sports Roosevelt recommended were big-game hunting, boxing and football.... While hunting and boxing were individualistic sports that may have been excellent means of building manliness, middle-class men ... preferred team sports which were sociable, entertaining, sufficiently hazardous, ... and highly congruent with their future work options. The new game of football, which became the most prominent sport at eastern colleges, seemed particularly relevant to the needs of upper-middle-class and elite sons.... Football was quite appropriate for a nation ripe for a clean, violent, virile yet gentlemanly sport. Coming after the carnage of the Civil War in an era dominated by the social Darwinian concept of the survival of the fittest, football appeared the best sport to teach well-born young men the virtues of the martial life (subordination and co-operation, presence of mind, endurance, precision and courage) without the carnage of war....

... Students preferred intercollegiate athletics over traditional extracurricular activities like debating and literary clubs because sports was exciting, promoted a sense of community, and operated independently of adult supervision. Furthermore, they believed that participation in team sports would help prepare them for a modern, bureaucratized society.

The college game was extremely violent, dangerous and at times, brutal. The style of play in the 1890s emphasized mass and momentum rather than deception and wide-open offenses; passing was virtually non-existent.... Players wore little protection, and the number of injuries and deaths was staggering (twelve deaths in 1902 alone).... The bloodshed and such ungentlemanly behavior encouraged critics like Harvard President Charles Eliot and E.L. Godkin, editor of the *Nation,* to urge the banning of the sport.

Proponents of football turned several criticisms on their heads. Most sports journalists joined with coaches and the majority of athletic administrators in supporting the game, believing that its violence and danger made it a manly sport and a moral equivalent of war.... Professor Woodrow Wilson of Princeton, a former college coach, believed that football, like other sports, developed precision, presence of mind and endurance, but particularly promoted co-operation, self-subordination and discipline. Director Eugene L. Richards of the Yale Gymnasium described football as "the most manly and most scientific game in existence." Harvard coach Lorin Deland, designer of the devastating flying wedge, and Yale's renowned coach Walter Camp co-authored *Football* in 1896 in which they argued that the physical and moral courage learned on the gridiron was excellent training for life....

However, baseball, the most popular sport played and watched by middle-class men, was probably more influential in building manly characteristics among most middle-class young men.... Millions played baseball on a recreational basis, and thousands played in more organized settings; by the 1880s every city usually had an amateur white-collar workers' league. Furthermore, middle-class fans had the money and leisure time to observe and learn from the manly behavior of professional ballplayers.

Baseball was not only a manly game because of the courage needed to play (standing in the batter's box against a fast pitcher; sliding hard to break up the double play), but was even identified by certain commentators with a martial spirit.... More importantly, baseball was a team game highly congruent with the bureaucratic middle-class work-place, yet also offered an opportunity to exercise individuality that could not be done on the job. Baseball provided a milieu where traditional and contemporary values could be merged. Sedentary workers did their own job, while developing a sense of team spirit and co-operation essential in their jobs, learning to sacrifice for the good of the team (company). They gained pride and enhanced self-esteem through the team's success.

By the end of the Victorian era, the college athletic hero was an important role model for children and adolescents. Juvenile pulp-fiction portrayed young athletic heroes as manly individuals who achieved prowess in sports, yet maintained a proper balance between mind and body. The prime example was Frank Merriwell, a fictional character first introduced by Burt L. Standish (Gilbert Patten) in 1896. The series, which at its peak sold over 500,000 copies a week, followed the exploits of Frank and his brother through Fardale School and Yale. Merriwell excelled at all forms of athletics, and had the uncanny knack of making the winning score on the last play of the game. Frank was a model scholar-athlete, whose "look of manliness ... stamped him as a fellow of lofty thought and ambition." Readers were taught that if they were good sports, stellar athletes and manly Christians, they would develop all the best traits of manliness and their future success was assured.

The intercollegiate sports program provided a model for secondary school students to emulate. High school students in the late nineteenth century were middle class or above, and shared the same values as collegians. They copied many college extracurricular activities, like inter-school athletic competition under the control of student organizations. Students and educators shared the conventional wisdom that athletics built character and trained values that could be readily transferred to the business world. The manly ethic of sports was most prominent though at elite boarding schools, which, following the lead of Groton headmaster Endicott Peabody in 1884, adopted the muscular Christianity philosophy and made athletics compulsory. Competitive sports were employed, in emulation of student life at elite eastern colleges and the English public schools, to build up youths physically, morally and spiritually as they learned to play by the rules, control their emotions, and carry out their responsibilities as members of disciplined teams. Sociologist Christopher Armstrong argues that "as games became the most popular schoolboy activity, manliness tended to overshadow Godliness and good learning." Headmasters hoped to train future leaders who would first prove themselves on the playing field and go on to "become good Christian soldiers, as prepared for moral combat or war as properly trained football players were for the big game." Once-pampered boys would leave Groton, St. Paul's or Exeter ready for the manly playing fields of New Haven or San Juan Hill.... These sportsmen were gentlemen who could now control and channel their aggression, unlike lower-class athletes who were supposedly over-aggressive and out of control.... Presumably many of the same lessons were also taught at public schools like Boston Latin and Brooklyn Tech.

Conclusion

Sport in the Victorian era played an important role in redefining the criterion of middle-class masculinity, moving beyond the man's relationship to his work and family to include his character and physical self. Then, once sport defined the attributes of respectable manliness, it was employed to indoctrinate proper bourgeois virtues in succeeding generations. At the onset of the Victorian period sport had been totally antithetical to middle-class behavior. Sports were violent, dangerous, immoral, prone to gambling, and occurred in exclusively male settings of dubious character. Sport had originally promoted a manly ethic congruent with the nature of life in pre-modern societies where life was harsh, hazardous, often uncivilized, and unpredictable. These values fit in well with life on the frontier, southern plantations, the open range, mining camps, and rough urban neighborhoods, but did not fit in well at all with life in settled communities or at the workplace under industrial capitalism.

The respectable urban middle class began to participate in sport at mid-century as they learned from immigrants, social critics, health faddists and other social reformers that physical culture could be enjoyed free of nefarious influences, and that participation was fun and uplifting at the same time. A new sport ideology developed that promoted team sports and other athletic pastimes that were consonant with the social values of hard-working, religious, future-orientated Victorians and promised to improve health, morality and character (that is, manliness). Sedentary students and workers who were worried about their fitness and the unmanly nature of their work were drawn to sports to improve their health and gain respect for their manliness. Sport was no mere child's play, but would create muscular Christians: rugged, disciplined manly gentlemen would be produced out of effete childlike youths. These men would be responsible, physically fit, moral adults, who continued to live within traditional middle-class norms, abstaining from pre-marital sex, living within the virtues of domesticity, and serving as good providers.

Sport boomed as a middle-class recreation in the late nineteenth century and contributed significantly to the redefinition of middle-class manliness. The rise of bureaucratization, the threat posed by the new immigrants, an uncertainty of measuring up to brave ancestors, and the feminization of culture encouraged middle-class young men to test their manliness through vigorous physical activity, especially team sports. Participation in strenuous, if not dangerous, clean outdoor sports would develop strength, courage and virility, while restoring self-confidence. Sport tested one's mettle and prepared one for adulthood. Followers of the strenuous life would grow up to become self-controlled, disciplined men of action who were team players in the work-place, bearers of the white man's burden, who would protect the race against inferior immigrant strains and surmount the feminization of American culture.

FURTHER READING

Baltzell, Edward D. *Sporting Gentlemen: Men's Tennis from the Age of Honor to the Cult of the Superstar* (1995).

Betts, John R. *America's Sporting Heritage, 1850–1950* (1974).

Boddy, Kasia. *Boxing: A Cultural History* (2008).

Chisholm, Ann. "Nineteenth-Century Gymnastics for U.S. Women and Incorporations of Buoyancy: Contouring Femininity, Shaping Sex, and Regulating Middle-Class Consumption," *Journal of Women's History* 20 (Fall 2008), 84–112.

Cumming, John. *Runners and Walkers: A Nineteenth-Century Chronicle* (1981).

Gelber, Steven M. "Working at Playing: The Culture of the Workplace and the Rise of Baseball," *Journal of Social History* 16 (June 1983), 3–20.

Gems, Gerald R. "Welfare Capitalism and Blue-Collar Sport: The Legacy of Labour Unrest," *Rethinking History* 5 (March 2001), 43–58.

Harmond, Richard. "Progress and Flight: An Interpretation of the American Cycling Craze of the 1890s," *Journal of Social History* 5 (1971), 235–57.

Jable, J. T. "Cricket Clubs and Class in Philadelphia, 1850–80," *Journal of Sport History* 18 (1991), 205–223.

Lewis, Guy. "World War I and the Emergence of Sport for the Masses," *Maryland Historian* 4 (1973), 109–122.

Kirsch, George. *Golf in America* (2009).

Miner, Curt. "Hardhat Hunters: The Democratization of Recreational Hunting in Twentieth Century Pennsylvania," *Journal of Sport History* 28 (Spring 2001), 41–62.

Mrozek, Donald. *Sport and American Mentality, 1880–1910* (1983).

Pesavento, Wilma J. "Sport and Recreation in the Pullman Experiment, 1880–1900," *Journal of Sport History* 9 (Summer 1982), 38–62.

Pope, Steven W. *Patriotic Games: Sporting Traditions in the American Imagination, 1876–1926* (1997).

Rader, Benjamin G. "Quest for Subcommunities and the Rise of American Sport," *American Quarterly* 29 (1977), 355–69.

Riess, Steven A. *City Games: The Evolution of American Urban Society and the Rise of Sports* (1989).

Smalley, Andrea L. "'Our Lady Sportsmen': Gender, Class and Conservation in Sport Hunting Magazines, 1873–1920," *Journal of the Gilded Age & Progressive Era* 4 (October 2005), 355–80.

Tobin, Gary. "The Bicycle Boom of the 1890s: The Development of Private Transportation and the Birth of the Modern Tourist," *Journal of Popular Culture* 7 (Spring 1974), 838–49.

Uminowicz, Glenn. "Sport in a Middle-Class Utopia: Asbury Park, New Jersey, 1871–1895," *Journal of Sport History* 11 (1984), 51–73.

Vincent, Ted. *The Rise and Fall of American Sport: Mudville's Revenge* (1994).

Weir, Robert. "'Take Me Out to the Brawl Game': Sports and Workers in Gilded Age Massachusetts," *Historical Journal of Massachusetts* 37 (Spring, 2009), 28–47.

Willis, Joseph D., and Richard G. Wettan. "Social. Stratification in New York City Athletic Clubs, 1865–1915," *Journal of Sport History* 3 (Spring 1976), 45–63.

CHAPTER 8

The Commercialization and Professionalization of Sports, 1870–1930

There were limited opportunities to make money from sport in the United States prior to the late nineteenth century. The first sports entrepreneurs were innkeepers who sponsored animal-baiting contests and hunting matches. Athletes during the antebellum period competed for prizes in boxing, pedestrianism (long-distance running), and horse racing. However, these events were haphazardly organized and staged only on an irregular basis. Then a big sporting boom occurred in the late nineteenth century. How have historians explained this development? What were the roles of the modernization of sports, the rapid growth of urban populations, changing standards of living, and the emergence of ambitious entrepreneurs poised to exploit potential new markets? What was the relationship between these entrepreneurs and the professional athletes employed to draw in the crowds?

Unlike amateurs, who played at sport, professionals worked at playing excellently. Cycling, football, and basketball joined the list of minor professional sports like track and field and rowing; nonetheless, the major sports remained prize fighting, thoroughbred racing, and baseball. Pugilism was still shunned by respectable folk for reasons of violence and gambling, and major fights had to be held in secret because boxing was banned everywhere until the 1890s. Thereafter prize fighting was only briefly permitted in various towns until 1920, when it was permanently allowed in New York. Thoroughbred racing, the "sport of kings," was revived by elite horsemen during the 1860s, and elite and proprietary tracks were established in major cities. There were as many as 314 racetracks in the United States in the late nineteenth century. However, the turf was widely forbidden around the turn of the century because of gambling, crooked races, and animal abuse, and there were just 25 tracks in operation by the early 1910s. Then the sport had an enormous revival in the

1920s, supported by working-class urbanites who enjoyed gambling, state legislators seeking new sources of revenue, and machine politicians financed by organized crime who were seeking to rejuvenate gambling.

The preeminent professional sport was baseball, whose first professional league, the National Association of Professional Base Ball Players, was organized in 1871. It was supplanted five years later by the National League (NL). Major League Baseball became a profitable business by the 1880s, attracting competing major leagues, and encouraging the organization of minor leagues (forty-six in 1912). The American League was the sport's most successful interloper, gaining full recognition from the NL in 1903.

The commercialization of sports also resulted in the rise of a sporting goods industry. Technological innovations and extreme division of labor and separation of parts in factories made possible the mass production of cheap sporting goods like gloves, bats, and balls. Inventors developed new types of equipment like the safety bicycle. Sporting goods companies were established to efficiently manufacture and distribute sporting goods, and to become important suppliers for outlets such as department stores and mail-order catalogs.

DOCUMENTS

Several of the documents in this section examine various aspects of professional baseball, which was the unquestioned national pastime at the turn of the century. Document 1, taken from the *New York Sun* in 1884, describes the social composition of late nineteenth-century major league baseball crowds. It is followed by a critical analysis of employee–employer relations by John Montgomery Ward, the star shortstop of the New York Giants. Ward, a trained lawyer as well as a major leaguer, founded the Brotherhood of Professional Baseball Players in 1885, the first athletic labor union, which organized its own major league in 1890. Document 3, written by sociologist and author Josiah Flynt, who was an expert on the underworld, examines one of the biggest problems thoroughbred racing faced, which was the menace of illegal off-track gambling by bookmakers and poolroom operators.

Document 4 is by H. Addington Bruce, a journalist reared and educated in Canada, who authored a classical statement of the positive functions that baseball was said to play during the Progressive Era. Document 5 summarizes Supreme Court Justice Oliver Wendell Holmes, Jr.'s landmark 1922 decision that exempted Major League Baseball from federal antitrust laws. Baseball today is the only major sport that is exempt from antitrust legislation.

At the end of the section, there are reproductions of advertisements for sporting equipment that appeared in the semiannual Sears, Roebuck and Company catalog, first published in 1888. By 1895 it was a 532-page book that educated the company's mainly rural clients about the affordability of a wide range of consumer products, including sporting goods. Note the affordable prices of the bats, gloves, and balls.

1. The *New York Sun*'s Portrayal of a Typical Baseball Crowd, 1884

The first thing that impresses one on a visit to the Polo Grounds on any day of the week is the number of spectators. It makes no difference what day it is or which clubs are to compete, there are always crowds on hand to witness a match. On Fridays and Saturdays there are more persons than on other days. But a match between two of the more prominent nines of the League will call out 7,000 or 8,000 persons, no matter what the day may be. The wonder to a man who works for his living is how so many people can spare the time for the sport. They are obliged to leave their offices down town at 2 or 3 o'clock in order to get to the Polo Grounds in time, and very many of them are constant attendants on the field. The next thing that impresses the visitor is the absolute and perfect knowledge of base-ball which every visitor at the grounds possesses. Nearly every boy and man keeps his own score, registering base hits, runs and errors as the game goes along, and the slightest hint of unfairness on the part of the umpire will bring a yell from thousands of throats instantaneously. The third notable characteristic ... is the good nature, affability, and friendliness of the crowd. The slim schoolboy ten years of age, and the fat, lager-beer saloon proprietor of fifty talk gracefully about the game as it progresses as though they had known each other for years. Men exchange opinions freely about the game with persons they never saw before and everybody seems good-natured and happy.

The majority of the Men are intensely interested in the game. Most of them come well provided with their own cigars, and sedulously evade the eye of the man who peddles "sody-water, sarss-a-parilla lemonade, pea-nuts and seegars." There is little drinking of any sort and much smoking.... At times when the umpire renders a decision that does not meet with popular approval, there will be a terrific outbreak, and for the next ten minutes the offending one is guyed unmercifully. Every decision he renders is received with jeers, and sarcastic comments are made upon the play. The good sense of the crowd gets the better of this boyishness, however, and unless the umpire is decidedly biased, which rarely occurs, the crowd soon settles back into its accustomed condition of contentment.

Perhaps the most enthusiastic and expert spectators at the Polo Grounds are the stockily built young Irishmen. They may be bartenders, light porters, expressmen, clerks, loungers, policemen off duty, or merchants out on a holiday. One of them is a type of a thousand others. He is usually square shouldered and well built. Probably he has had a taste of athletics himself and plays....

It has often been remarked that there are at the Polo Grounds every day AN EXTRAORDINARY NUMBER OF FAT MEN. No one can tell why this is. It is said that men of extraordinary avoirdupois who find it impractical, inelegant, and more or less sensational to throw hand-springs, steal base, and run swiftly at

---

From *New York Sun*, June 16, 1884.

250 pounds weight, enjoy the spectacle of the cat-like and rapid movements of the athletes on the field....

A good many gray heads and gray beards are to be seen on the grand stand. They belong to men who have been base-ball enthusiasts from boyhood up. They enjoy the sport more than they would any play, horse or boat race, and they are full of reminiscences of the game. Scattered in among them are bright-face boys, who are well dressed, well mannered and intelligent. They are looked upon by the men as of enough importance to warrant sober treatment, and their opinions are as gravely accepted as those of men. Another pronounced type is the young businessman. Hundreds of spruce, well-dressed and wide-awake young men who are apparently clerks, brokers or business men from downtown are to be seen about the grounds. They talk balls and strike, but principally ball. They do not know as much about it as ... the solid young Irishmen, but they make up in enthusiasm what they lack in knowledge. Their interest in the game consists largely in the money they have on it. They always bet freely among themselves, and return home happy or crestfallen, according to their winnings.

There are among the ladies who attend ball matches a few, perhaps a dozen in all, who thoroughly understand the game and are actually and warmly interested in the sport. Most of them, however, have such a superficial knowledge of the game that they grow tired before the ninth inning is reached, and conceal their weariness when they leave early, by expressing a desire to avoid the crowd.

2. John Montgomery Ward Asks, "Is the Base-ball Player a Chattel?" 1887

... The first reserve agreement was entered into by the club members of the National League September 30, 1879. By that compact each club was conceded the privilege of reserving for the season of 1880 five of its players of the season of 1879.... The five men so chosen ... were ... forced either to sign with the club reserving them at its own terms or withdraw.... The club thus appropriated to itself an absolute control over the labor of five of its men, and this number has since been enlarged to eleven, so that now the club controls practically its entire team....

In order to justify this extraordinary measure and distract public attention from the real causes making it necessary, the clubs tried to shift the blame to the players. They declared that players were demanding extortionate salaries, and that the rule was needed as a protection against these. They attempted to conceal entirely that the real trouble lay in the extravagant and unbusiness-like methods of certain managers and in the lack of good faith between the clubs themselves.... And was it really against the players or against themselves that the clubs were obliged to combine for protection? The history of base-ball deals between different clubs is full of instances of broken faith, and in most such cases where a player was involved the favorite procedure has been to white-wash the clubs and black-list the player....

From John Montgomery Ward, "Is the Base-ball Player a Chattel?" *Lippincott's Magazine* 40 (May 1887): 310–19.

In the enactment of the reserve-rule the clubs were probably influenced by three considerations: they wished to make the business of base-ball more permanent, they meant to reduce salaries, and they sought to secure a monopoly of the game.

At the close of each season there was always a scramble for players for the following year.... There was no assurance to the stockholders of a continuing fixed value to their stock, for the defection of a few important players might render it almost worthless. But with the right of retaining the pick of its players the club was assured of a good team, and the stock held its value.

Again, in this annual competition for players, clubs often paid extravagant salaries to certain very desirable men, and the effect was to enlarge the average scale so that it was assuming undue proportions. But with the privilege of retaining its best men at its own figures, the average salary would be forced down....

The third consideration was the desire to create a monopoly. It was just beginning to be seen that base-ball properly managed might be made a lucrative business.... With all the picked players reserved to it and the prestige thus given, it was thought that the League might easily retain the control of the business....

The effect of this was that a player reserved was forced to sign with the club reserving him, or quit playing ball altogether.... As new leagues have sprung up, they have been either frozen out or forced into this agreement for their own protection, and the all-embracing nature of the reserve-rule has been maintained. There is now no escape for the player.... Like a fugitive-slave law, the reserve-rule denies him a harbor or a livelihood, and carries him back, bound and shackled, to the club from which he attempted to escape. We have, then, the curious result of a contract which on its face is for seven months being binding for life....

On the other hand, what reciprocal claim has the player? Absolutely none! ... The club reserves the right to release the player at any time, "at its option," by ten days' notice, and that its liabilities under the contract shall thereupon cease and determine. That is to say, the club may hold the player as long as it pleases, and may release him at any time, with or without cause, by a simple ten days' notice; while the player is bound for life, and, no matter what his interests or wishes may be, cannot terminate the contract, even by ten years' notice.

... The reserve-rule ... inaugurated a species of serfdom which gave one set of men a life-estate in the labor of another, and withheld from the latter any corresponding claim.... Its justification, if any, lay only in its expediency. It was a protective measure which gave stability to the game by preserving the playing strength of the teams, and it acted as a check on the increase of salaries....

... The rule itself was an inherent wrong, for by it one set of men seized absolute control over the labor of another, and in its development it has ... grown so intolerable as to threaten the present organization of the game. Clubs have seemed to think that players had no rights, and the black list was waiting for the man who dared assert the contrary. Players were cowed into submission....

... The reserve rule ... is ... being used not as a means of *retaining* the services of a player, but for increasing his value for the purpose of sale.... The clubs claimed that the right to retain the services of a valuable player was necessary for the conservation of the game, and with that understanding the players tacitly acquiesced in the seizure. They never received any consideration for the concession....

These are, in part, the relations which exist between base-ball players and the associations by which they are employed. Is there a base-ball official who will claim them to be governed by any semblance of equity? Is it surprising that players begin to protest, and think it necessary to combine for mutual protection?

Encouraged by the apparent inactivity of the players, the clubs have gone on from one usurpation to another until in the eye of the base-ball "magnate" the player has become a mere chattel. He goes where he is sent, takes what is given him, and thanks the Lord for life. The demand exceeding the supply, the growth and cultivation of young players has become an important branch of the business. They are signed in large numbers, and, if they turn out well, are disposed of as a valuable commodity to the highest bidder. If they fail, they are simply released....

... The whole thing is a conspiracy, pure and simple, on the part of the clubs, by which they are making money rightfully belonging to the players. Even were we to admit, for the sake of argument, that the reserve-rule does give a right to sell, we naturally ask, What consideration did the club ever advance to the player for this right? What did the Chicago Club ever give Kelly in return for the right to control his future services? Absolutely nothing; and yet that club sells that right, so cheaply acquired, for ten thousand dollars! ... Any such claim by one set of men of a right of property in another is as unnatural to-day as it was a quarter of a century ago....

... The interests of the national game are too great to be longer trifled with in such a manner, and if the clubs cannot find a way out of these difficulties the players will try to do it for them. The tangled web of legislation which now hampers the game must be cut away, and the business of base-ball made to rest on the ordinary business basis.... The players will catch the spirit of the new order; base-ball, to them, will be more of a business and less of a pastime; contract-breaking will be impossible, and dissipation will disappear; the profession of ball-playing will be looked upon as a perfectly honorable calling, and the national game be more than ever the greatest of outdoor sports....

3. Josiah Flynt Delineates the Evils of Off-Track Pool-Rooms, 1907

The pool-room as it exists in New York city is more or less of a distinct type. Before [District Attorney] Jerome seriously got after the pool-rooms I have been told that there were not less than two thousand ... in the metropolis....

I was talking with a friend at Forty-third Street and Broadway ... and I said, "I want to get down a bet. Where shall we go?"

"Come along with me," he replied.

We walked up Broadway two blocks ... and stopped at No. 146.... To all appearances it was vacant.... We went ... to the basement door, where my

From Josiah Flynt, "The Pool-Room Spider and the Gambling Fly," *Cosmopolitan* 42 (March 1907): 513–521 and "The Men Behind the Pool-Rooms," 42 (April 1907): 639–48.

friend knocked. His knock was answered without delay, and the door swung upon a few inches. A man about twenty-five years old, well-dressed, Jewish in type, looked through the opening. The look that he and my friend exchanged was sufficient to make good for our entrance into that particular spider's den....

We climbed some stairs leading to the parlor floor.... On reaching the first landing we met a second guard.... This fellow was heavy, red-faced, and brutal looking,... but he knew my friend by sight, and nodded....

There were about a hundred men in the room. Nearly all of them were smoking and the place was stiflingly close....

... Nothing less than five dollars was accepted as a bet. On that day I had invested fifty cents in a paper which declared that it gave all the selections of the best handicappers in New York....

I noticed that the original prices did not appear against the horses after the card had been hung up. I found out, also, that it was a common practice to "shave" the prices from the time they reached the pool-room.... Most of the shaving was done in the "place" and "show" prices....

As soon as the card on the first ... race had been hung up, the money began to be pushed through one of the small windows.... Each better wrote on a slip of paper the name of the horse he wished to play, that amount he wished to bet, and the position.... This slip with the money, was handed in at one of the windows.

In the total of two thousand pool-rooms in New York city, fifty were for women exclusively. In these rooms social caste was unknown. The betting fever has no favorites. The woman of wealth and social standing mingles with women of the half-world and with shop-girls.... Inside the pool-room there is an intimacy among these women, born of a common passion for gambling. These rooms were often conducted under a "stall," or a pretense of legitimate business. They were "button-factories," "millinery-shops" ... but in reality pool-rooms.

... In the West the word "pool-room" means many things. At Hot Springs [AR] it means a magnificently appointed hall resembling the office of a stock broker.... In other cities west of New York, the pool-room may be located in a store-building in the heart of the city. Usually it is in the rear of a saloon. In Chicago, however, there are no pool-rooms of the kind familiar to the New Yorker. Instead Chicago has the handbook....

"Handbook" is used to describe those books made without the apparatus necessary in the pool-room proper. A pencil, a pad of paper, and the memory of the Bookmaker are all that is required. The handbook, in the beginning, was a child of necessity. When the police raid the wide-open pool-room, betters and Bookies are driven into the street.... Suckers ... are willing to make their bets on the curb-stone, in saloons, in cigar-stores, or in any other makeshift place where there is a man with a book. In New York, where the handbook has not been such a necessity to the betting public as in Chicago, there has been so much "welching" as to bring it onto disrepute. In most cities the handbook is a distinct gambling institution; it is the walking pool-room.... The most popular pool-room and handbook man in Chicago is "Mont" Tennes.... In one year he made ninety thousand dollars in the handbook business. His place at 123 Clark Street has been raided oftener than any other betting place in America....

The determination with which Tennes has defied the police and the care he has taken to provide immediate release for customers arrested in his place have endeared him to the Suckers....

So rapid has been the growth of the pool-room evil in late years, in response to the horse-racing madness of the people that there are comparatively few pool-rooms or handbooks backed and controlled by one individual. No matter where you find them, pool-rooms or handbooks are controlled by a syndicate—a close combination with police attachment. In one city there may be one syndicate, or there may be several. In New York there are sub-syndicates operating in different parts of the city. They are all dependent for their existence, also for friendship, on one man—"Big Tim" Sullivan. Of course there are also the systems known as the Sullivan, the Peter DeLacey, and the "Jere" Mahoney syndicates.

Each one of these syndicates has a clearing house and information headquarters. The first is a place where the managers of the several books attached to that particular syndicate settle with the syndicate managers on the play of the day before. When police conditions are mixed it is found more convenient to send an agent of the syndicate around to the different books to make the settlement. The syndicate tries to back the books connected with it. Each book, however, has its individual manager ... a man familiar with the betting trade in a certain district....

The Chicago pool-room crowd is next in importance to the one in New York. Its political machinations and its police attachments are of the same character.... It came into existence ... as the result of more or less similar conditions. There was a growing sentiment against the wide-open gambling-house of Western style and the police raids on that class of institution.... There was the complacent public that tolerated one of the most pernicious systems for wrecking men that ever infested the country. There was the false cry of the track-owner that a healthy sport was being carried on and should not be interfered with because a few meanly inclined individuals were criminal enough to turn "the sport of kings" into a gambling device.

The meanest man, because he is the biggest, of the Chicago pool-room crowd is James O'Leary.... The genial Jim brought to his new business the reputation of being a "good fellow."... Nicholas Hunt ... , [who was] the inspector of the Hyde Park police district ... , and O'Leary were friends. Hunt directed the appointment of the police captain at the stock-yards.... The stock-yards police showed a wholesome respect for ... O'Leary. But with the passing of the old-fashioned forms of gambling and the growth of playing the ponies, O'Leary did away with faro, roulette, "stud" poker, and craps, and equipped his place as a pool-room. He became the biggest individual operator in Chicago.... He anticipated the coming of the day when public sentiment would suppress the pool-room.... So he built a shack outside of the city, and equipped it with telegraph and telephone wires ... He advertised his place far and wide.... At one time he went so far as to employ a press-agent....

Whether in New York, Chicago, or elsewhere, the type of the big pool-room man—the man higher up—is about the same. He is either a politician or the friend of politicians. To be precise, he is "in right."

4. H. Addington Bruce Analyzes Baseball and the National Life, 1913

... Veritably baseball is something more than the great American game—it is an American institution having a significant place in the life of the people, and consequently worthy of close and careful analysis.

Fully to grasp its significance, however, it is necessary to study it, in the first place, as merely a game, and seek to determine wherein lie its peculiar qualities of fascination. As a game, as something that is "playable," it of course must serve the ordinary ends of play. These, according to the best authorities on the physiology and psychology of play, are threefold: the expenditure of surplus nervous energy in a way that will not be harmful to the organism, but, on the contrary, will give needed exercise to growing muscles; the development of traits and abilities that will afterwards aid the player in the serious business of life; and the attainment of mental rest through pleasurable occupation....

... Success and progress depend chiefly on the presence of certain personal characteristics. Physical fitness, courage, honesty, patience, the spirit of initiative combined with due respect for lawful authority, soundness and quickness of judgment, self-confidence, self-control, cheeriness, fair-mindedness, and appreciation of the importance of social solidarity, of "team play"—these are traits requisite as never before for success in the life of an individual and of a nation.... But it is safe to say that no other game—not even excepting football—develops them as does baseball.

One need attend only a few games, whether played by untrained schoolboys or by the most expert professionals, to appreciate the great value of baseball as a developmental agent. Habits of sobriety and self-control are established in the players if only from the necessity of keeping in good condition in order to acquit one's self creditably and hold a place on the team. Patience, dogged persistence, the pluck that refuses to acknowledge either weariness or defeat, are essential to the mastery of the fine points of batting, fielding, or pitching—a mastery which in turn brings with it a feeling of self-confidence that eventually will go far in helping its possessor to achieve success off as well as on the "diamond."

So, too, courage, and plenty of it, is needed at the bat—courage not simply to face the swiftly moving ball, but to "crowd" the "plate" so as to handicap the pitcher in his efforts to perform successfully and expeditiously the work of elimination.... The courage of the batsman ... had no small share in winning for the "Giants" the National League honors in 1911 and again last year.

As an agent in the development of the "team spirit" baseball is no less notable. The term "sacrifice hit" eloquently expresses one phase of the game which must leave on all playing it an indelible impression of the importance in all affairs of life of unselfish co-operation....

... Baseball is also a splendid mind-builder. The ability to think, and to think quickly, is fostered by the duties of its every position as well as by the

---

From: H. Addington Bruce, "Baseball and the National Life," *Outlook* 104 (May 1913): 104–107.

complicated problems that are constantly arising in its swiftly changing course of events. Time and again games have been won, or the way has been cleared to victory, by the quickness of a player or a manager in appreciating the possibilities of a critical situation and planning a definite plan of campaign to meet the emergency....

So incessant and so varied are the demands made on the ball-player's intelligence that any one who really knows the game will be inclined to indorse unreservedly the published declaration of that most successful baseball-player and most successful businessman, Mr. Albert G. Spalding:

"I never struck anything in business that did not seem a simple matter when compared with complications I have faced on the baseball field. A young man playing baseball gets into the habit of quick thinking in most adverse circumstances and under the most merciless criticism in the world—the criticism from the 'bleachers.'..."

... With the passage of time the technique of the game has been improved to an extent that makes it more of a developmental agent than it was even ten years ago. Lacking the strength, skill, and experience of the professional player, the schoolboy whose efforts are confined to the "diamond" of the vacant lot or public park plays the game under precisely the same rules as the professional, and with no less zest and earnestness, and profits correspondingly. To be sure, in playing it he does not dream for an instant that he is thereby helping to prepare himself for the important struggles of maturity. He plays it merely because he finds it "good fun"—merely because, in its variety and rapidity of action, in the comparative ease with which its fundamental principles may be learned, and in its essentially co-operative yet competitive character, it affords an intensely pleasurable occupation. It is, in truth, a game which makes an irresistible appeal to the instincts of youth precisely because it so admirably meets the principal objects of play—mental rest through enjoyment, exercise for the muscles, the healthy expenditure of surplus nervous energy, and practice and preparation for life's work....

... An instinctive resort to sport [is] a method of gaining momentary relief from the strain of an intolerable burden, and at the same time finding a harmless outlet for pent-up emotions which, unless thus gaining expression, might discharge themselves in a dangerous way.... It is no mere coincidence that the great sport-loving peoples of the world—the Americans, the English, the Canadians, and the Australians—have been preeminent in the art of achieving progress by peaceful and orderly reform....

Baseball, then, from the spectator's standpoint, is to be regarded as a means of catharsis, or, perhaps better, as a safety valve. And it performs this service the more readily because of the appeal it makes to the basic instincts, with resultant removal of the inhibitions that ordinarily cause tenseness and restraint. For exactly the same reason it has a democratizing value no less important to the welfare of society than is its value as a developmental and tension-relieving agent. The spectator at a ball game is no longer a statesman, lawyer, broker, doctor, merchant, or artisan, but just a plain every-day man, with a heart full of fraternity and good will to all his fellow-men—except perhaps the umpire. The oftener he sits in grand stand or "bleachers," the broader, kindlier, better man and citizen he must tend to become.

Finally, it is to be observed that the mere watching of a game of baseball, as of football, lacrosse, hockey, or any other game of swift action, has a certain beneficial physical effect. It is a psychological commonplace that pleasurable emotions, especially if they find expression in laughter, shouts, cheers, and other muscle-expanding noises, have a tonic value to the whole bodily system. So that it is quite possible to get exercise vicariously, as it were; and the more stimulating the spectacle that excites feelings of happiness and enjoyment, the greater will be the resultant good. Most decidedly baseball is a game well designed to render this excellent service....

5. Supreme Court Justice Oliver Wendell Holmes, Jr., Explains Why Baseball Is Not Subject to Antitrust Laws, 1922

Mr. Justice Holmes delivered the opinion of the court.

... The plaintiff is a baseball club incorporated in Maryland, and with seven other corporations was a member of the Federal League of Professional Base Ball Clubs, ... that attempted to compete with the combined defendants. It alleges that the defendants destroyed the Federal League by buying up some of the constituent clubs and in one way or another inducing all those clubs except the plaintiff to leave their League, and that the three persons connected with the Federal League and named as defendants, one of them being the President of the League, took part in the conspiracy. Great damage to the plaintiff is alleged. The plaintiff obtained a verdict for $80,000 in the Supreme Court and a judgment for treble the amount was entered, but the Court of Appeals, after an elaborate discussion, held that the defendants were not within the Sherman Act....

The clubs composing the Leagues are in different cities and for the most part in different States. The end of the elaborate organizations and sub-organizations that are described in the pleadings and evidence is that these clubs shall play against one another in public exhibitions for money, one or the other club crossing a state line in order to make the meeting possible.... Of course the scheme requires constantly repeated travelling on the part of the clubs, which is provided for, controlled and disciplined by the organizations, and this it is said means commerce among the States....

The business is giving exhibitions of baseball, which are purely state affairs. It is true that, in order to attain for these exhibitions the great popularity that they have achieved, competitions must be arranged between clubs from different cities and States. But the fact that in order to give the exhibitions the Leagues must induce free persons to cross state lines and must arrange and pay for their doing so is not enough to change the character of the business.... The transport is a mere incident, not the essential thing. That to which it is incident, the exhibition, although made for money would not be called trade or commerce in the commonly accepted use of those words. As it is put by the defendants, personal

From *Federal Club v. National League*, 259 U.S. 200 (1922).

effort, not related to production, is not a subject of commerce.... To repeat the illustrations given by the Court below, a firm of lawyers sending out a member to argue a case, or the Chautauqua lecture bureau sending out lecturers, does not engage in such commerce because the lawyer or lecturer goes to another State.

If we are right the plaintiff's business is to be described in the same way and the restrictions by contract that prevented the plaintiff from getting players to break their bargains and the other conduct charged against the defendants were not an interference with commerce among the States.

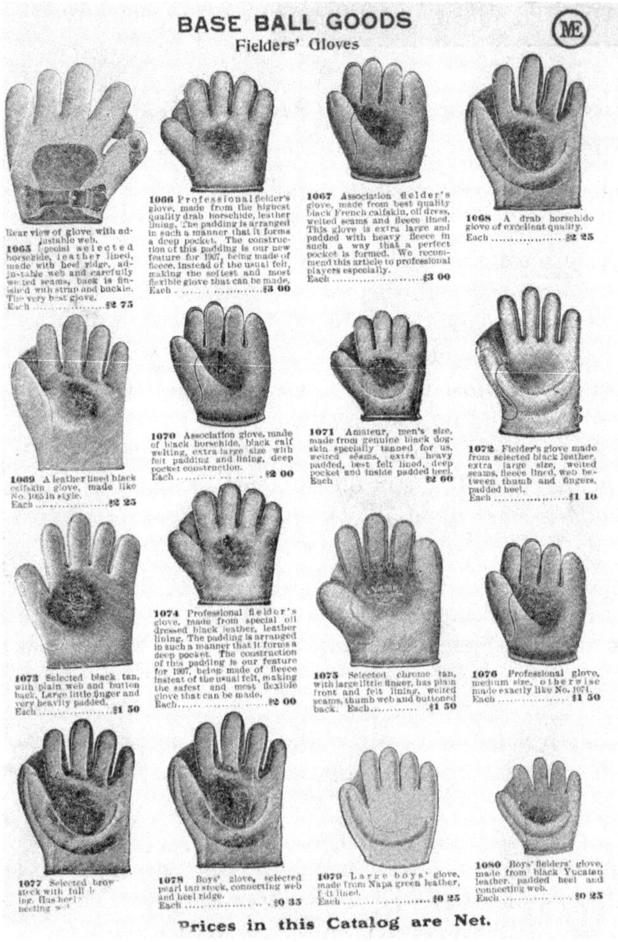

Turn of the Century Sporting Goods Catalogue. By the late nineteenth century, Americans could purchase cheap mass produced sporting goods equipment from department stores, small retailers, specialty shops and mail-order catalogues. This advertisement shows gloves manufactured by the Victor Sporting Goods Company, founded in 1898, in Chicopee Falls, MA. The company specialized in making gloves with a preformed and deep set pocket, especially for catchers whose position was very dangerous. Fielder's gloves were very small and rigid by today's standards. A boy's glove cost as little as $0.25 (equal to $7.05 today), while a high quality glove cost $2.25 in 1900 ($63.50 today). (Historical/Bettmann/CORBIS)

ESSAYS

The two essays in this section examine how two professional sports initially became organized. The first essay was written by Robert K. Barney, a distinguished scholar of Olympic history, who was the long-time director of the International Centre for Olympic Studies at the University of Western Ontario, as well as a devotee of the National Pastime, with his associate, Frank Dallier. In their essay, they examine the role of William Hulbert, a Chicago businessman, in creating the National League in 1876 as the successor to the first professional league, the National Association of Professional Base Ball Players (1871–1875). Hulbert, an ardent Chicago booster, and president of the White Stockings (the future Cubs ball club) sought to bolster his city's national reputation by creating a league on business principles that would flourish for years to come. In the second essay, Guy Reel, Associate Professor of Mass Communications at Winthrop University, and the author of *The National Police Gazette and the Making of the Modern American Man, 1879–1906*, focuses on the role of Irish immigrant Richard K. Fox (1846–1922) in making boxing a paying business. Fox arrived in the United States in 1874, became a journalist, and purchased the *National Police Gazette* two years later. He converted the weekly scandal sheet into a sporting periodical, and reinvented the boxing business by promoting championship fights fought for purses instead of side bets.

The Making of the National League

ROBERT K. BARNEY AND FRANK DALLIER

[William A.] Hulbert was born on October 23, 1832, in Burlington Flats, Otsego County, New York State ... some 20 miles from Cooperstown.... Hulbert moved with his parents to Chicago at two years of age, was educated in the city's public schools, and attended the Beloit (WI) Academy for one year, 1851–1852. Returning to Chicago, Hulbert made his way in business, most notably in coal wholesale groceries, and eventually gained membership on the Chicago Board of Trade.... He was ... an ardent baseball fan.... In 1870 Hulbert purchased three shares of stock in the White Stocking Ball Club, ... beginning ... a formal affiliation with baseball that would result in several significant contributions to the National Pastime, [most notably] as a pivotal figure in the establishment of the National League....

"Lamp Post in Chicago"

Besides being an ardent baseball fan and business opportunist, Hulbert was a dedicated booster of his home city. Baseball had become nationally recognizable by 1870, making his investment in a professional team the exciting prospect of combining a business venture with community service. Hulbert's civic pride in being

From "'I'd Rather Be a Lamp Post in Chicago Than a Millionaire in any Other City': William A. Hulbert, Civic Pride, and the Birth of the National League," by Robert K. Barney and Frank Dallier, is reproduced from *NINE: A Journal of Baseball History and Culture* with permission from the University of Nebraska Press. Copyright 1994.

a Chicagoan is illustrated by one of his more flamboyant statements: "I would rather be a lamp post in Chicago than a millionaire in any other city."

Upon becoming a White Stockings stockholder in 1870, Hulbert began to take an increasingly lively interest in the proceedings of the club's power structure. [In] 1875, not only was Hulbert named to the club's board of directors, he was also elected its president. "[H]is reputation as a community leader and shrewd businessman made him the obvious choice."

At the time … the club was a member of the National Association of Professional Base Ball Players, a player-controlled organization in its fourth year of operation. By 1875, the National Association's image and credibility were in serious jeopardy. Persistent rumors of player association with professional gamblers, as well as noted instances of alcohol abuse, were but two factors which contributed to rising public censure.

The first major incident involving Hulbert and the National Association occurred in July of 1875 when [he] startled the baseball world by securing the written contracts for the 1876 season of Albert Spalding, Ross Barnes, Cal McVey, and James "Deacon" White of Boston's Red Stockings, and Ezra Sutton and Adrian "Cap" Anson of Philadelphia's Athletics. In his first major act … Hulbert pried six of the Association's best players away from two of its best teams….

The National Association Executive, incensed by Hulbert's blatant player raid on Eastern club talent, convened an emergency meeting … to issue a threat to the Chicagoan that if he carried through with his piracy, Chicago would be banned permanently from the organization. This had little effect…. Hulbert's primary goal was to build the White Stockings into a formidable professional baseball team, and, to his way of thinking, [this] meant acquiring as many of baseball's best players as he possibly could…. As a result, … the relationship between the National Association and Hulbert was tumultuous from the start.

The confrontation … quickly led the White Stockings president to consider a plan to form a completely new baseball association, one which his own creativity and assertive control might reflect…. In the wake of Spalding becoming a White Stocking, Hulbert … lost little time in enlisting his confidence. "Spalding, I have a new scheme," said Hulbert, during one of their early personal talks, "lets us anticipate the Eastern cusses and organize a new association before the March meeting (1876)."

Hulbert's decision to confide in Spalding may seem unorthodox … as Spalding had but recently signed with the White Stockings and, further, was merely a player. Spalding, however, was not just any player; he was without question the sport's marquee performer, … baseball's best pitcher. By confiding in Spalding, Hulbert guaranteed that his proposed new association would have the support and presence of the game's best player.

Orrick C. Bishop of St. Louis appears to have been the second person that Hulbert approached with the idea of forming a new association. Bishop was a prominent St. Louis lawyer/judge, as well as a member of the St. Louis Browns Board of Directors…. On September 25, 1875, he wrote:

> I suggest to get the matter started the Four Western Clubs (Cincinnati, Louisville, St. Louis & Chicago) have a meeting…. At that meeting we

> can arrange and settle the Western program and come to conclusion as to our general policy with the Eastern Clubs. At the convention you and I can carry the day on anything we want. Then finally established, with four powerful clubs welded together, we can easily influence such of the remainder as we desire to join us—... Early in the field and united—cornering the whole paying territory—What shall prevent us from having things right—Don't say a word, think my plan out, and let me know your conclusion.

Late in 1875, Hulbert initiated correspondence with still other individuals he envisioned as being instrumental in his plans for launching a new league, well known baseball men such as St. Louis's Charles A. Fowle, Louisville's Charles E. Chase and W. N. Haldeman, and Cincinnati's John J. Joyce. A strong endorsement of Hulbert's plans emerged, along with personal commitment from each owner towards formalizing the grand scheme at a conference to be held in Louisville....

Louisville Conference

The historic Louisville Conference took place on December 16 and 17, 1875. From Hulbert's perspective, the conference was eminently successful. His plan was generally accepted (at least in the west); the birth of the National League of Professional Base Ball Clubs (National League) became official some three weeks later.

There remained much work to accomplish in readying the National League for its inaugural season. Two important issues had to be resolved. One concerned the proposed constitution: the document had to be framed in legal terms. As well, the Eastern clubs of the now dismembered National Association (Philadelphia, Boston, New York, New Haven, and Hartford) had to be approached on the viability of their joining Hulbert's new creation.

The legalization of the National League Constitution took place in St. Louis on January 9, 1876. In a letter to Louisville's Chase, who was unable to attend ... , Hulbert recounted the results of the St. Louis Conference, underscoring his own pivotal role:

I arrived at St. Louis Tuesday morning and spent the day with Messrs. Fowle and Bishop in conference at the Hotel—I verbally unfolded the plans that I thought would serve the needs of the Professional clubs in ways of organization, and Mr. Bishop taking notes in regular order. You and I think familiar with the general features of my plan—as to the mode of conducting offices by a board of five, submission of differences to arbitration etc.... Well when I had finished I found that both gentlemen were highly pleased with the plan and ready to adopt and support it and before adjournment.... [W]e met the next day with Mr. Hazard added. Bishop had left original spaces in his draft for the insertion of amendments and we took up the document what was of great length—section by section—giving each a thorough discussion.... The result is for every one of us highly satisfactory and we are of opinion that we have produced a document that will be very strong.

With the incorporation of its constitution, the National League took its first step towards legal foundation, indeed, its institutionalization....

Hulbert, of course, cannot be accorded sole credit for the entire contents of the National League Constitution. The National Association's playing rules, for instance, were transferred verbatim to the new constitution. As directed by Hulbert, copies of the rules document were provided to the committee by Spalding.... The National Association's playing rules were inserted into the National League Constitution because there was no evidence to suggest that the style of play under its rules framework had contributed to the league's negative image.

Hulbert's Philosophy

Playing rules were one thing; the philosophy undergirding the new league's operation was quite another issue. Hulbert felt that the narrow objectives and business approach *of* the old National Association were fundamental causes for many of its problems. Consequently, he conceived a new set of objectives and a fresh business plan for the National League. Those objectives were outlined in the League's original constitution:

1. To encourage, foster and elevate the game of base ball;
2. To enact and enforce proper rules for the exhibition and conduct of the game;
3. To make base ball playing respectable and honorable;
4. To protect and promote the mutual interests of professional base ball and professional base ball players;
5. To establish and regulate the base ball championship of the United States.

Hulbert's aim at disassociating the new National League from the ... negative image of its immediate predecessor ... was expressed in an agenda which committed the enterprise to honesty, fair play and, above all, integrity of the highest order.

In order to achieve the League's stated objectives, Hulbert developed a business plan that ... noted baseball historian ... Harold Seymour, has described as an embodiment of "the reducing theory of professional baseball." The so-called reducing theory was a plan that would transform professional baseball from being a loosely-structured, poorly-managed large business to a tightly structured, well-managed small business. At the centre of Hulbert's plan was his belief that the National League should "put the life of the player in the hands of the organization that employs him." To Hulbert, professional baseball was, in basic terms, simply a business, and, as such, its control should be lodged in the hands of its businessmen, rather than its players. Once under the control of businessmen, the National League would be directed towards developing "none but first class clubs." To Hulbert, "first class clubs" meant those legally incorporated and based in a city with a population of at least 75,000 people. There would be no more than eight clubs in the National League; Hulbert considered a number larger than this to be unmanageable. Each club would play each other ten times throughout the season, and no league member club could employ a player expelled from another league team. Game admission fees would be standardized at 50 cents per person; the gate receipts from each game to be divided between the participating teams in accordance with a pre-game arrangement. As Hulbert saw it, such a format would provide the structure necessary for transforming professional baseball into a tightly-organized, well-managed small business.

Almost equal in importance to the initial National League organizational meetings held in St. Louis in December 1875, were the attempts of Hulbert and his Western colleagues to garner membership in their enterprise by the most recognized Eastern baseball clubs. Hulbert's inclination ... was to offer an "olive branch" to the alienated Eastern adversaries, one focused on "convincing the Eastern Clubs that it's best for all that the quarrels and troubles of the past should be forgot ... and in order that like troubles may not disturb us in the future as we prepare a new partnership."

To this point, Eastern baseball clubs had been completely ignored ... Hulbert harbored distinct anxieties that this factor alone might compromise their efforts and result in the refusal of Eastern clubs to join the new league. An anxious Charles Fowle accompanied Hulbert as the two Western baseball "sharps" entrained for New York in late January in order to meet representatives of Boston, Philadelphia, New York, and Hartford on the issue of Eastern club membership.

The now storied New York Conference between representatives of Eastern and Western clubs of a prospective National League was held at the Grand Central Hotel on February 2, 1876. Hulbert and Fowle had prepared for organized resistance from Eastern club executives, but, ... "we had an easy time, for surprisingly none of our Eastern friends were in condition to make effective resistance." The conference concluded with the unanimous adoption of the National League Constitution and the election of Morgan Bulkeley, a respected Connecticut politician, to position of League President.

... Newspaper reaction to the newly formed National League was positive. The *Boston Herald* reported: "The leading professional clubs have by their representatives lately taken a step which seems calculated to work some needed improvements in the whole system or code of professional ball playing."

Likewise, the *Chicago Tribune* trumpeted: "The most important measure ever adopted by the professional baseball clubs of this country has been considered and approved by a council of representatives of the eight principal clubs of the country, in a session at the Grand Central Hotel." The *Tribune* also acknowledged Hulbert's role as visionary and architect of the National League: "It should go on record that the President of the Chicago Club is to be credited with having planned, engineered and carried out the most important reform since the history of the game."

There was at least one exception to an almost universal endorsement of the National League ... expressed by Henry Chadwick in New York's popular sporting journal, the *Clipper*. Baseball history's noted scribe and commentator offered a dire prediction for the new enterprise: "Judging from what took place in the metropolis this past week, it would seem that this important work was not entrusted to men of experience for in our opinion, a sad blunder has been committed—it cannot be called a convention—which, on Wednesday Feb. 2, terminated in the 'National League of Professional Clubs.'" Though previously associated with the operation of the National Association, Chadwick had not been invited to the Grand Central Hotel Conference. Hulbert's seemingly intentional slight offended Chadwick, who, in turn, promptly used his association with the *Clipper* to vent his negative feelings.

Hulbert's anxieties grew as the National League's inaugural season approached. There were several problems that could potentially hinder the new endeavor's success. He outlined three of the most vexing in a letter to Bill Cammeyer, manager of the New York Mutuals: (1) team compliance with the Constitution, (2) producing a consistent yet high level of competitive play, and (3) overcoming the public perception that professional baseball was corrupt. Hulbert was especially concerned with the problem of perceived corruption: "I am no saint but I utterly despise the miserable skunks and deadbeats who make a living out of betting on public sport. They are ruining every out door *pastime*. Let us do what we can to break up this band."

Despite Hulbert's apprehensions, the inaugural season of the National League generally exceeded most expectations. Hulbert's Chicago White Stockings won the pennant. More importantly, newspaper coverage demonstrated wide public support for the new league. On the down side, however, both the New York and Philadelphia clubs elected to end their respective seasons early, each ceasing operations prematurely toward the end of August. Each had experienced dismal campaigns. Poor play led to poor attendance which, in turn, resulted in financial deficits. To prevent incurring further financial loss, both teams decided against completing the remainder of their scheduled league games. The decision to end the season early directly violated the National League Constitution. In … the face of such action the constitution mandated the expulsion of both clubs: "The membership of any club belonging to this League shall be forfeited, if the League by two-thirds vote shall so determine, under the following circumstances, namely: 1st. By disbanding, or by failing or refusing to keep engagements in regard to games with other clubs."

Crisis

Crisis struck the National League. Should it enforce its constitution and risk surviving without teams in New York and Philadelphia? Or, should the National League ignore a direct violation of its constitution and risk losing its integrity as an organization?

Exerting his considerable influence during this crisis, Hulbert saw only one legitimate course of action, the substance of which he outlined to Boston Red Stockings owner N. T. Apollonio:

> I'll be dammed, before I will have fellowship with either of them any longer. We are of age and had plenty of experience when we not in NY last Febry (*sic*), and every man of us fully comprehended the situation and every man of us honestly strove to reduce our fair and equal agreement to writing, and the two things intended were, first, ever*y club*

> *shall play ten games with every other* and no club shall employ a man expelled from another club. These are two things that are the corner stone of the league. I know of no other possible use for a combination of clubs except to enforce these two things.

Hulbert concluded by stating: "I believe as a matter of fact that the Mutuals and the Athletics are already excluded. I believe the constitution fairly interpreted puts them out." League President Bulkeley was silent on the matter. However, Hulbert's stance was quite clear. No team or teams were bigger than the National League and firmly establishing this precedent was paramount to the National League's long term survival.

The proceedings, whereby the fate of New York and Philadelphia was determined, took place at the National League's first Annual League Conference held in December 1876. By then, Bulkeley had resigned. As might be expected, the outspoken Hulbert led the attack on ousting the Mutuals and Athletics from the league. As baseball historian David Q. Voigt has noted: "Hulbert was pitiless; after presenting the charges, he demanded and got a unanimous vote for dismissal." Out went New York and Philadelphia.

If there were any doubts as to which person wielded the real power in the new league, there were none following Hulbert's vitriolic reaction on the New York/Philadelphia matter. His leadership status could no longer be denied; indeed, it was confirmed by his unanimous election to the presidency of the National League shortly before the adjournment of the 1876 Annual League Conference.

The new circuit faced the 1877 campaign with more resolve than optimism. No new teams were added to replace expelled New York and Philadelphia, leaving Chicago, Cincinnati, Boston, Hartford, Louisville, and St. Louis to vie for the pennant. Shrunken membership aside, national interest in the League's affairs was not enhanced by the premature retirement of Albert Spalding as an active player. The League's most celebrated star, Spalding's departure had added misfortune for Hulbert; without Spalding's services, Chicago failed to contend for the 1877 pennant.

Hulbert and the Collapse of the Louisville Group

The favorites for the 1877 pennant race were the Boston Red Stockings and the Louisville Grays. Louisville appeared especially strong. They were led by the pitching of James "Terror" Devlin the strong fielding and hitting of outfielder "Gentleman" George Hall and shortstop "Butcher" Bill Craver. The Grays started the season in strong fashion, winning 15 of their first 20 games. They continued their strong play … into early August [when] Louisville went into a prolonged slump … [and a] seemingly insurmountable lead melted in the face of Boston's late season charge. Harry Wright's team won the pennant by seven games, clinching the championship on September 30th. The Grays, mathematically eliminated from winning the pennant, suddenly began to play inspired baseball, winning all but one of their remaining games to clinch second place by the season's end on October 10th. As the season ended in mid-October, the National League was embroiled in a major scandal. Louisville's collapse had devastated their fans.

Questions of impropriety circulated, the most alarming of which raised the suspicion of gambler/player collusion. Hulbert ordered an investigation into the accusations, the examination to be conducted by W. N. Haldeman and Charles E. Chase, the Grays' president and vice-president, respectively. Upon completion of the investigation, a chagrined and angry Chase announced that three of Louisville's best players: Devlin, Craver, and Hall, along with lesser rated infielder Al "Slippery Elm" Nichols, had deliberately thrown games. They were immediately expelled from the team.... Hulbert's greatest fear had become reality; the National League had been irrefutably linked to that most unsavory of all ills affecting early professional baseball's integrity—corruption in the form of player/gambler collusion.

Hulbert knew that drastic reaction against the four guilty players was the only response that might have a chance at restoring the public's confidence in the integrity of the National League, indeed, for professional baseball itself. Hulbert viewed the forthcoming League meetings as an appropriate forum where this fact might be drummed home. As Hulbert wrote to Bob Ferguson (Hartford's manager): "Now it strikes me the exposure and conviction upon their own confession of the four men named, makes our forthcoming League meeting an excellent time and place to strike an effective blow."

The 1877 National League Convention emerges as one of the most memorable occasions in professional baseball history. At those meetings Louisville's four guilty players were permanently banned for life from the National League. The baseball world was in shock. Few had expected President Hulbert to demand, let alone receive, support for such harsh punishment. The four banished players were outraged, arguing that as first-time offenders their punishment was much too severe. True to form, Hulbert refused to compromise, claiming that collusion with gamblers was not the type of mistake that warranted a second chance. The offending players had put their interests ahead of those of the National League. No indiscretion carried any graver consequence for the game; the punishment fit the crime. And so ended Hulbert's first year as League president. His leadership ability had been severely tested. He had responded quickly and forcefully to the challenges. The National League had survived.

The Reserve Clause

Matters associated with National League by-law legislation (known simply as the Reserve Clause), enacted at a secret meeting in Buffalo in September 1879, became the next serious challenge to Hulbert's leadership. Basically, the clause allowed each National League club the right to protect five players from being signed by other teams. The Providence Grays announced its five "sacrosanct" players for the 1880 season, one of whom was its celebrated infield/player-manager, George Wright. In early 1880, however, Wright was enticed by his notable older brother, Harry, manager of the Red Stockings, to join the Boston nine. George Wright appeared in the Red Stockings' opening game despite the fact that he remained on the Providence club's reserve list. A protest of Boston's action ensued immediately; so did an airing of the affair in the daily newspapers of a number of the nation's most baseball-conscious cities.

The validity of the owner-oriented (player restrictive) clause was challenged on several fronts, most vigorously, of course, by the Wright brothers themselves. Commensurately, fresh aspersions were cast on the integrity of the National League. Hulbert, though, was equal to the challenge. Writing to new Red Stockings president, Arthur H. Soden, Hulbert decreed that the game be eliminated from the Championship Series and Wright given a stiff warning and "should he ever violate the Reserve Clause again he shall be banned from the National League for life." Clearly, Hulbert believed capital punishment to be a worthy deterrent. The one game stint in a Red Stockings uniform was the first and last appearance for George Wright in National League play during the 1880 season. Relative calm descended on the National League after the Wright affair; the validity of the Reserve Clause had been upheld; the integrity of the National League remained intact.

Though problems continued to plague the League, the framework for its long-term survival was solidly entrenched. The National League had faced similar problems in its fledgling years encountered by most businesses launching operations for the first time, and, like young businesses achieving success in their endeavors, had gained the respect and confidence of the primary consumer, in this case, the baseball public.

But Hulbert himself, was beset by problems other than those associated with baseball. Following the 1881 season, his health deteriorated badly, ironically, at the same time that the National League's health began to improve.... Over the winter of 1881-1882, Hulbert's condition became grave. On April 10, 1882, the National League lost its founding architect and first true czar.

Hulbert's baseball career lasted only seven years. Nevertheless, he had left his mark.... There were many public tributes paid to him, but the newspaper which knew him the most intimately, the *Chicago Tribune*, characterized his baseball accomplishments best:

His great force of character, strong will, marked executive ability, unerring judgment of men and measures. and strict integrity and fairness were of incalculable value the League, and he was rightly considered to be the brains and backbone of the organization. In him the game of baseball had the most useful friend and protector it has ever had; and in his death the popular pastime suffers a loss the importance of which cannot easily be exaggerated.

Richard Fox and the Modernization of the Squared Circle in the Late Nineteenth Century

GUY REEL

During the 1880s, *National Police Gazette* publisher Richard Kyle Fox helped create modern boxing by conducting promotions, offering prize belts, and publicizing the exploits of boxing great John L. Sullivan. Fox used the *Gazette* not just to

---

From Guy Reel, "Richard Fox, John L. Sullivan, and the Rise of Modern American Prize Fighting," *Journalism History* 27:2 (Summer 2001), 73–85. Reprinted by permission of the author.

chronicle the adventures of buxom showgirls or to sensationalize the latest heinous crime; it also was a pulpit to denounce hypocrites who opposed the modern sport of boxing. Through his … [luck], and good fortune in having the deeds of a legend such as Sullivan to play up, Fox became one of the most influential sports figures of the nineteenth century; and it made him a millionaire. Sullivan was just as fortunate, becoming world famous. This article tells the story of Fox; Sullivan, and the *Police Gazette* during … Fox's lengthy tenure as editor and publisher. The *Gazette*, while it is perhaps best known for its emphasis on sex and crime as a precursor to today's tabloid journalism, also should be remembered for its unrelenting, early support of professional prize fighting.

One of the most oft-repeated stories in boxing circles in late nineteenth-century New York was that of the meeting between … Fox and … Sullivan. As the story goes, Fox, an Irish immigrant to New York City who had built his publishing empire from almost nothing, … in early April 1881 … went to Harry Hill's saloon … The bar and dance hall … was well known among the sporting crowd of gentlemen; it also was a popular place for prostitutes and gamblers.… Fox was accompanied by his well-known sports editor, William E. Harding, and the two were given the royal treatment by Hill.…

Sullivan had disposed of … Steve Taylor, several nights earlier on the stage of the same room where the men were eating. Before that bout, Sullivan had made his usual boast, saying he would pay fifty dollars to any man in the room who could last four rounds with him.…

Fox, in his brash manner, supposedly told Hill to ask Sullivan to come across the dance hall and meet him. Hill delivered the message, but Sullivan, a known binge drinker who was surrounded by admirers and several bottles of champagne, was in no mood to take orders from anyone. He told Hill to relay the message that if Fox wanted to meet him, then he had to come to his table.

Fox had spent the last five years making the *National Police Gazette* into one of the most important magazines in New York. Through the 1880s and most of the 1890s, its circulation was about 150,000, and it was able to garner most of its revenues through advertising, with agate rates of a dollar a line, the same as such contemporary publications as *Leslie's Popular Monthly* and the *Ladies Home Journal*. The *Gazette* was known as a journal of sports, celebrities, sensational crimes, and oddities of human behavior; and its weekly editions featuring woodcut illustrations and blaring headlines were eagerly anticipated in the nation's barbershops and barrooms. So Fox, a self-important, crusading man, was taken aback by what he perceived as a personal affront by the young, husky fighter. He determined that the Bostonian should be taken down a notch, and over the next several years he would campaign far and wide for a worthy opponent for Sullivan.

In this crusade, Fox would master the art of boxing promotion by becoming one of the first to sponsor ring matches with belts, cash, and other prizes awarded to the winners.… [H]e would use pulp as a pulpit to fight against laws banning prize fighting, and … turn the *Gazette* into what its banner proclaimed it was—the "leading illustrated sporting journal in America." But he did not stop at ordinary sports. He gave *Police Gazette* belts to dancers, rat catchers, drinkers, oyster openers, and even great steeple climbers.…

Fox and his weekly magazine helped create modern boxing.... During the period from 1881, when Sullivan and Fox met, through 1889, when Sullivan finally went into semi-retirement after one of the most remarkable boxing records in history, perhaps no other one-two combination did more to popularize boxing—and bring it into modern respectability—than Fox and Sullivan. One historian has compared the *Gazette*'s promotionalism to the staged competitions of the "battles of the network stars" seen in the late twentieth century.... Fox was a sort of P.T. Barnum of journalism—a man who knew how to create a spectacle and make money off it at the same time.

... Fox's efforts at promotion and publicity fit an age that saw rapid growth in press agentry, promotion, and advertising. Public relations developed during this period as a profession and as a sophisticated tool for attracting the public's attention to entertainment, products, or services. Using the same types of promotional efforts as public relations practitioners, he came to be an organizer and publicist of events—boxing matches as well as others—that, in turn, created publicity for his magazine and boosted his circulation. Thus, Fox was part of a tradition of promotion and press agentry whose patterns were ... "drawn, cut and stitched by the greatest showman and press agent of all time—... Phineas Taylor Barnum."

By the mid-1850s, circuses, which needed publicity to attract crowds because they traveled from city to city, had become regular sources of advertising revenue for newspapers and other publications. Other types of attractions, such as Wild West shows and vaudeville, also used advertising and promotion to boost attendance.... "Buffalo Bill" Cody ... Barnum, and other showmen employed press agents to make contacts with newspapers and seek publicity.... Advertising agencies were formed after the Civil War, and many of them sponsored staged, or "pseudo events" to promote wares....

This type of promotional activity was common among publishers. In 1895, the *Chicago Times Herald* staged a highly publicized race to promote the new automobile. Other newspapers sponsored rowing contests or essay contests....

Many of the promotional stunts by newspapers and magazines were journalistic in nature.... On November 13, 1871, an expedition led by New York [*Herald*] journalist Henry Morton Stanley found missing British explorer David Livingstone.... Twelve years later, Joseph Pulitzer's *World* sent ... Nellie Bly, around the world to determine if she could beat the time suggested by Jules Verne in his *Around the World in Eighty Days*. She completed the journey in seventy-two days.

During this era, newspapers and magazines also seized upon the growth of sports as a way to boost circulation and promote themselves.... Particularly when it came to boxing, Fox operated with all of the zeal of his competitors. It is not an exaggeration to call him one of the most influential sports figures of the nineteenth century.... [O]ne factor in the growing popularity of boxing was the enmity between Fox and Sullivan, but ... key ... was the development of publications as a vehicle for marketing and promotion. Fox's determination and salesmanship, along with his willingness to join court battles over illegal prizefighting and his eagerness to editorialize against boxing opponents, also helped position him as a key figure in the growth of pugilism.

George Wilkes and Enoch Camp founded the *Gazette* in 1845: … "We offer … a most interesting record of horrid murders, outrageous robberies, bold forgeries, astounding burglaries, hideous rapes, vulgar seductions, and recent exploits of pickpockets and hotel thieves in various parts of the country."… [M]en and boys proved to be the most faithful readers of the *Gazette*.… By 1857, Wilkes was driven into ruin by a financial panic. He was forced to sell the *Gazette* to George W. Matsell, [former] New York City chief of police. But he proved to be an uninspiring leader and unloaded the publication to two engravers to whom he owed money. By 1876, the *Gazette* appeared to be nearly dead. But then it passed into Fox's hands.

Fox was born in Belfast in 1846 and moved to America in 1874 with less than five dollars.… [T]rained as a printer …, he got a job with the *Gazette* and within two years had engineered a takeover. Using Wilkes' model, he intended to shock and titillate readers. Printed on pink-tinted paper to attract attention and selling for a nickel, the *Gazette* soon became one of the most lurid journals of its day, featuring buxom showgirls, sex, and various crimes, including murder. To the network of barbershops and saloons he added hotels … to attract traveling businessmen.… In 1880, astonished to see his circulation top 400,000 when he featured weekly coverage of the Joe Goss–Paddy Ryan fight, he vowed to make his journal the most important of the prize ring.…

Fox hired a crew of rewrite men, who used the reports from stringers nationwide to make his pages as readable as possible.… Eventually the *Gazette* would be distributed in twenty-six countries, and it made Fox a millionaire. At his death in 1922, … he had given away more than $250,000 in medals, prize money, stakes, and promotional payments.

That Fox would use his position to promote a sport such as boxing is not surprising. It was a behind-the-scenes sport with a huge potential for growth. But before Sullivan arrived on the scene, boxing was a thoroughly discredited activity. Bare-knuckle boxing, for which prizes were usually awarded, was illegal and barbaric. In this atmosphere, different groups emerged—those who supported the legal "amateur sparring," … and the more disreputable crowd who favored illegal prize fighting.… [D]espite prohibitions in New York and elsewhere, prize fighting, with its allure of spectacle, took place (sometimes with police knowledge).

One of those fights was on May 16, 1881, on a barge towed … to a dock on the Hudson River … On that evening, aboard the barge to avoid authorities because the fight was illegal under an 1859 New York ordinance, Sullivan fought John Flood, a barrel-chested longshoreman.… The first blow of the fight sent Flood reeling, and after eight rounds Sullivan collected the winner-take-all stakes of $1,000.… The *Gazette* did not sponsor the fight, but it capitalized by publishing a woodcut of the scene aboard the barge, in … apparently the first artistic representation of Sullivan in action.

Following the Flood fight, Fox wasted no time in coming up with a new challenger for Sullivan. Paddy Ryan, another Irish immigrant, was backed by Fox with a stake of $1,000. In those days, each fighter's camp posted a certain amount of money, and the winner took the entire purse. Rules varied and therefore were agreed upon before each fight.…

Boxing backers developed rules in order to silence some of the criticism, and the twenty-nine London Prize Ring Rules, generally adopted in 1838, were among the first efforts to corral the violence. However, those rules allowed for bare-knuckle brawling, a practice later forbidden under the rules authored by the Englishman Henry Sholto Douglas, the eighth marquis of Queensberry. The 1866 Queensberry rules outlawed wrestling and grappling holds, required boxing gloves, and established three-minute rounds, with a minute of rest in between. The rules, slow to be uniformly adopted, usually designated a specific number of rounds, but fighters often agreed to … "fight to the finish." By Sullivan's day, boxing was illegal in all thirty-eight states, including New York, but the enforcement varied widely. Some states permitted boxing "exhibitions" or amateur boxing; others had penalties so minor that any prohibition was virtually meaningless. There is no evidence that Fox lobbied for a change in laws, but he did lobby for a change in attitudes; the *Police Gazette* lauded the sport as a "manly art" that promoted fitness as well as sharpness of mind and feet. Thus, a new era of legality dawned when Sullivan was defeated by "Gentleman Jim" Corbett in 1892 using gloves under the Queensberry rules; … and gave new legitimacy to the sport.

For the Ryan–Sullivan fight, Fox … ultimately guarantee[d] half of the purse of $5,000, with Hill designated as the stakeholder. The attention given to the fight was unequaled; Fox trumped his competitors by offering weekly coverage of the training. The men met in Mississippi City, Mississippi, on February 7, 1882, even after the Mississippi Legislature heard of the planned fight and passed a bill banning prize fighting.… On January 28, a train left New York City carrying so many people that, according to the *Gazette*, "Gotham was depleted of her fancy element almost entirely." In defiance of the boxing ban, the men squared off in front of the Barnes Hotel in Mississippi City.

In order to fully cover the fight, the *Gazette* added eight pages to its normal run of sixteen. Even the fighting colors of the men were described in minute detail. Ryan's colors, the colors of the *Police Gazette* champion, "were said to represent America, Ireland and New York: … red, white and blue …"

In the supplement available a week after the fight, an artist titled it "The Battle of the Giants," but only one giant emerged. Sullivan dispatched Ryan with "sledgehammer smashes.…" Sullivan won by knockout in the ninth round.

Fox offered Ryan $5,000 for another fight with Sullivan, and a rematch was eventually held almost three years later, with Sullivan winning again.… [The *NPG*'s] special supplement on the fight had sold more than 300,000 copies, which was twice its normal run. Given the immense publicity that Sullivan afforded the sport of boxing, it was obvious that a win by Sullivan only served to set up the next big fight, which could be trumpeted in the *Gazette*. But Sullivan could not resist needling Fox, and called the *Gazette* championship belt a "dog collar." Even though he knew Sullivan was probably good for the sport and thus good for the *Gazette*, Fox took offense at such comments, and he next brought in British middleweight Tug Wilson to serve as an opponent. Sullivan at first said Wilson (a squat five foot, eight inches tall) was too small to fight, but he eventually became convinced when enough prize money was put up. More than 5,000 people paid as much as five dollars a seat, making it the biggest crowd yet to come see Sullivan. The fight was held in Madison Square Garden on July 17, 1882, and Sullivan performed poorly. He failed to knock out Wilson, who used evasive maneuvers to keep Sullivan off balance. Wilson backpedaled, fell down intentionally, or was knocked down nine times in the first round alone; but he avoided most of Sullivan's serious blows. It had been an obvious setup to beat the terms of the match—that a man could not "last" with Sullivan for four rounds. An angry Sullivan accused his manager, Billy Madden, of double-crossing him, and the two parted ways temporarily.

In many ways the heyday for Fox and the *Gazette* was 1882 [when] he opened a new building.... outfitted with a magnificent museum, another tourist attraction and promotional vehicle for Fox. The museum featured examples of the publication's awards, mostly presented by Fox himself, as well as large oil paintings of the leading figures of the day....

The publicity reached all levels, from ... newsboys ... to Theodore Roosevelt, who muttered that the *Gazette* could be found in the hands of every Western ruffian.... Fox often boasted of a barely legible note he received from Sempronius, Texas, dated December 20, 1879: "Please send me a copy of your paper (*The Police Gazette*), and greatly oblige—Jesse James."

.... In early 1883, followers of the *Gazette* were treated to yet another kind of journalism in Fox's public crusade to legitimize prize fighting, both legally and for the tastes of "polite society." In his attempt to find a challenger for Sullivan, Fox brought in a another foreigner, a New Zealander, Herbert A. Slade, who was known as the Maori ... to fight Englishman Jem Mace in a "sparring exhibition."... But the Mace–Slade match hit a snag when a warrant was sworn out for the arrest of Fox as the instigator of a prize fight. The main contention of Fox and his lawyers was that while prize fighting was prohibited under the 1859 ordinance, "exhibitions," in which contestants wore padded gloves, were legitimate. In the *Gazette*'s columns, opponents of fighting were portrayed with the utmost contempt. Activist Henry Bergh ... was said sarcastically in the *Gazette* to be against the Mace–Slade fight because he could not get the men to box for the benefit of the "Society for the Prevention of Cruelty to Bald-Headed Men."

Fox finally obtained a hearing, and in state court, his lawyers argued that boxing was a legitimate form of entertainment and exercise. Judge Donohue ... found that sparring was not necessarily an unlawful act. The *Gazette* could not resist a little crowing. The headline for February 17, 1883, said: "ANOTHER VICTORY!/The "*Police Gazette*" Triumphs Once More over Bigots and Sneaks...."

Mace and Slade did eventually spar in Manhattan, Baltimore, and other eastern cities, with Slade performing convincingly enough to win a battle against Sullivan on August 6, 1883, knocking him out in three rounds.

[T]he *Gazette* was not concerned solely with Sullivan. In its regular boxing column it featured many fights and a lot of fighters, including Daisy Daly, the women's champion from California, and Harry Woodson, the "Black Diamond." Throughout his life Sullivan refused to fight black fighters, but Fox had no qualms about promoting them in many bouts.... [O]n April 14, 1883, the front page of the *Gazette* carried its standard large woodcut illustration, showing a well-dressed woman standing over another, who was unconscious on the floor. The second woman was being fanned awake by a gentleman escort ... The women were wearing boxing gloves. The caption read, "KNOCKED OUT IN ONE ROUND."

The Sullivan fights remained the biggest draw for Fox, however. In April 1883, the Boston Strong Boy drew 25,000 to an exhibition in his hometown. Meanwhile, Madden had traveled to England with $5,000 of Fox's money to find a contender; Charley Mitchell emerged, and he was put up against Sullivan on May 14, 1883....

Sullivan won again, hammering Mitchell over the ropes at one point. According to Fox and those associated with him, the Mitchell fight netted him about $20,000, although some historians believe this figure is high.

Like all good sensational journalists before and after him, Fox attempted to give his readers information about the personal side of his subjects—and the more scandalous the better. During the post–Civil War era, the press was changing in response both to the shifts in society—immigration and industrialization—and to its own needs. Cultural changes demanded changes in coverage which, in turn, led to changes in the way journalism was practiced. The press evolved ... from simple, opinion broadsheets manned frequently by two-person print shops to newspapers containing complex reporting. Historian Hazel Dicken-Garcia noted the latter papers reprinted "items as received to physically pursuing news across communities, nation, and world, to 'dressing up' information to entice readers, to 'manufacturing' news to retain them." These changes led to charges of sensationalism, trivialization, or invasion of privacy (all ... criticisms of the *Gazette*), but they also led to standards and ethical practices ... even though the first ethical codes for journalists would not be adopted until the twentieth century. Fox was not particularly restricted by the rise of new standards, but the *Gazette* did highlight its ability to secure "private information from our correspondents" to underscore its credibility.

As Sullivan gained fame, stories circulated about him and his wife, Annie Bates Bailey Sullivan. When they married on May 1, 1883, there were rumors that Sullivan beat his wife and that the two drank and engaged in quarrels. Fox's pursuit of the story was another example of his intimate, celebrity-style journalism.... [I]t prompted one ... to refer to his magazine as *The National Enquirer* of the nineteenth century. During this period, the *Gazette* was so popular that its imitators multiplied....

In June 1883, one of the most sensational stories emerged when Annie alleged to police that her husband had beaten her and destroyed some of their furniture, but no warrant was issued for his arrest. Later that month, reports ... were that he had beaten not only his wife but her sister. But when Fox sent a reporter, ... [b]oth women denied the story....

Mitchell and Sullivan were scheduled for a rematch in the summer of 1884. Fox used all of his journalistic skill to promote the fight, and thus sales. The *Gazette* listed in fine print more than a column of names of those who were at ringside, including William K. Vanderbilt, reputed to be the richest man in the world; Rev. Henry Ward Beecher; Rev. De Witt Talmadge, and a host of New York aldermen, assemblymen and police.... After some preliminary bouts, there was a delay.... Sullivan finally walked slowly into the arena. He mounted the ring with difficulty and announced that he was sick and unable to fight.... Most agreed that Sullivan might have been sick, but he was also "drank as a Lord."

Later in 1884, Fox again brought in a foreign contender in an attempt to create another attention-getting matchup for Sullivan, and as an added publicity stunt, he unveiled the most impressive of his championship belts. The winner was to receive the *Police Gazette* Diamond Belt, which was fifty inches long, eight inches wide, and speckled with silver and gold. A ring in the center was encircled by diamonds with the top featuring a fox's head. With the belt valued at $2,500, Fox was not accused of lacking promotional zeal. In the early moments of the November 18 fight, Sullivan appeared to be handling the contender, Alf Greenfield of Birmingham, England, but the fight was most notable for what happened next. Superintendent George Washington Walling of the New York City Police Department ordered the men to stop fighting, saying the fight had gone beyond being a sparring match because the men were attempting to knock each other out.... Sullivan and Greenfield were tried on a charge of prize fighting.

As the trial unfolded, Fox's bankrolling of the defense began to pay off. Captain Williams ... , called for the prosecution, became a good witness for the defense. He testified that he had seen harder hitting, and more blood spilled, in bouts presented by the Police Athletic Association. Then, Sullivan took the stand, much to the delight of the crowd, and testified that he and Greenfield were merely attempting to put on a show....

Judge Barrett ... charged the jury "if it was a physical contention for supremacy, then the defendants are guilty under the statute." The jury filed out.... Thy came back after eight minutes.... "Not guilty." In 1930, a historian noted the evidence showed that the money spent by Fox ... was well spent....

Although the foreign recruiting was clearly beneficial for Fox, it was costly, so by 1885 he began to turn more often to American fighters in an attempt to find someone who could pose a legitimate challenge to Sullivan. In the following year, he became the backer of Kilrain (born John Joseph Killion). In preparation for his fight with Sullivan, Kilrain, trained by Mitchell, went to England to fight the English champion, Jem Smith. After 106 rounds of bare-knuckle fighting in two-and-a-half hours, the fight was declared a draw.... That was enough for Fox, who called Kilrain his new "*Police Gazette* Champion." The *Gazette* headline screamed, "NIGHT OF BUTCHER."

Sullivan unofficially lost his title when he failed to make a timely answer to Kilrain's challenge to fight. But that helped Sullivan, who became the "people's champion," and instead of boxing, a "war of printers' ink" occupied the sporting world for months. Sullivan finally issued a challenge to Kilrain to fight for a purse of $20,000, $10,000 to be put up by each side with the winner taking all. Fox immediately backed Kilrain with $10,000, and on July 8, 1889, the men battled for hours, also in Mississippi, in what is considered by boxing historians to be one of the greatest prize fights of the history of boxing.

The *Gazette*'s series of headlines printed on July 20, 1889, told the story:

John L. Wins!/A Terrific Battle of 75 Rounds, Lasting 2 Hours and 16 Minutes./ At Richburg, Miss./Thousands Gather at the Ring-side to Witness the Fight./Jake Ill at the Start./Notwithstanding this Fact, He Fights John L. to a Standstill./No Strength to Follow it Up./He Is Badly Used Up at the Finish, but Succumbs Gracefully./John L. Not Unscathed./He Has Two Black Eyes, a Split Ear and a Disfigured Face./ …

Sullivan had beaten Fox again, but the *Gazette* had the last laugh. It spent several column inches chronicling Sullivan's mildly unfortunate adventure on the way home from the fight. Mississippi authorities had authorized the arrest of the fighters, but they escaped the state without incident. Sullivan, however, was detained at a train stop in Nashville, Tennessee, but was released when the judge found that "under the law prize fighting was a misdemeanor in Mississippi and was not an extraditable offense."

Sullivan, who continued his heavy drinking ways, fell into the trap that has caught many aging champions—he did not know when to quit. After several years of retirement mixed with traveling exhibitions, he finally was defeated in 1892 by Corbett. But for many, the true end of Sullivan was the Kilrain fight. In 1938, historian Frank Luther Mott wrote, "Thus ended the feud of Mr. Fox and Mr. Sullivan; and what Mr. Fox's many champions could not do, John Barleycorn accomplished in short order."

… Though Fox had failed to ultimately find a challenger to beat Sullivan, he succeeded in every other category. He achieved his millionaire status by the 1890s, and the paper thrived until the Spanish–American war in 1898. The *Gazette* continued to be successful promoting boxing after Sullivan had left the arena, campaigning against other sports, such as college football, as "silly, pretentious and hypocritical." As the nineteenth century ended, the *Gazette* began to lose readers, although it survived, with Fox still at the helm promoting boxing. Some believe the *Gazette*'s death-knell [occurred in] the 1920s, when women began being allowed in barbershops for female hair-styling. The racy *Gazette*, the "barbershop Bible," was no longer considered proper fare in a province integrated by women.

It also would be incorrect to make too much, as many writers have, of the feud between Sullivan and Fox.… Fox was shrewd enough to realize that Sullivan was good for boxing, and … his magazine, and most accounts of Sullivan in the *Gazette* (with the exception of the asides about his drinking) appear to be reasonably objective.… Fox needed Sullivan, and Sullivan needed Fox.

It is not an exaggeration to call Fox one of the most influential sports promoters of the nineteenth century, and he is credited by historians with helping the sport grow at a crucial time.… Through his journalism, his showmanship, and his pioneering presentation of title belts, he probably did more to popularize boxing outside the ring than anyone else in the nineteenth century. His promotional skills, his sense of sensationalism, and his taste for what might not be considered proper in "polite society," as well as his willingness to bankroll court fights to expose hypocrisy and the uneven enforcement of boxing laws, positioned him to be a champion of prize fighting. That he had a champion of the caliber of Sullivan to celebrate and vilify served him only too well. He seized the moment and through a combination of journalistic aggressiveness, boastfulness, confidence, and luck, he helped to create modern prize fighting.

FURTHER READING

Alexander, Charles C. *John J. McGraw* (1988).

Alexander, Charles C. *Our Game: An American Baseball History* (1991).

Burk, Robert F. *Never Just a Game: Players, Owners, and American Baseball to 1920* (1994).

Chacar, Aya S., and William Hesterly. "Innovations and Value Creation in Major League Baseball, 1860–2000," *Business History* 46 (July 2004), 407–38.

Crepeau, Richard. *Baseball: America's Diamond Mind* (1980).

Fielding, Lawrence W., and Lori K. Miller. "The ABC Trust: A Chapter in the History of Capitalism in the Sporting Goods Industry," *Sport History Review* 29 (May 1998), 44–58.

Gershman, Michael. *Diamonds: The Evolution of the Ballpark* (1993).

Hardy, Stephen. "Entrepreneurs, Organization and the Sport Marketplace," *Journal of Sport History* 13 (1984), 14–33.

Hardy, Stephen. "'Adopted by All the Leading Clubs': Sporting Goods and the Shaping of Leisure," in Richard Butch, ed., *For Fun and Profit* (1990), 71–92.

Hardy, Stephen. "Entrepreneurs, Structures, and the Sportgeist: Old Tensions in Modern Industry," in Donald G. Kyle and Gary Stark, eds., *Essays on Sport History and Mythology* (1990), 83–117.

Hillenbrand, Lauren. *Seabiscuit: An American Legend* (2002).

Jable, J. Thomas. "The Birth of Professional Football: Pittsburgh Athletic Clubs Ring in Professionals in 1902," *Western Pennsylvania Historical Magazine* 62 (1979), 136–47.

Levine, Peter. *A. G. Spalding and the Rise of Baseball: The Promise of American Sport* (1985).

Lowenfish, Lee. *The Imperfect Diamond: A History of Baseball's Labor Wars*, rev. ed. (1992).

Macht, Norman L. *Connie Mack and the Early Years of Baseball* (2007).

Macht, Norman L. *Connie Mack: The Turbulent and Triumphant Years, 1915–1931* (2012).

Maltby, Marc. *The Origin and Early Development of Professional Football* (1997).

Murdock, Eugene C. *Ban Johnson: Czar of Baseball* (1982).

Peterson, Robert W. *Cage to Jump Shots: Pro Basketball's Early Years* (1990).

Pietrusza, David. *Judge and Jury: The Life and Times of Judge Kenesaw Mountain Landis* (1998).

Rader, Benjamin G. *Baseball: A History of America's National Game*, 3rd ed. (2008).

Reel, Guy. *The National Police Gazette and the Making of the Modern American Man, 1879–1906* (2006).

Riess, Steven A. "In the Ring and Out: Professional Boxing in New York, 1896–1920," in Donald Spivey, ed., *Sport in America* (1985), 95–128.

Riess, Steven A. *Touching Base: Professional Baseball and American Culture in the Progressive Era*, rev. ed. (1999).

Riess, Steven A. *The Sport of Kings and the Kings of Crime: Horse Racing, Politics, and Organized Crime in New York, 1865–1913* (2011).

Ritter, Lawrence. *The Glory of Their Times* (1966).

Robertson, W. H. P. *The History of Thoroughbred Racing in America* (1964).

Seymour, Harold. *Baseball: The Early Years* (1960).

Seymour, Harold. *Baseball: The Golden Years* (1971).

Smith, Leverett T. *The American Dream and the National Game* (1975).

Sullivan, Dean A., ed. *Early Innings: A Documentary History of Baseball, 1825–1908* (1995).

Voigt, David Q. *American Baseball: From Gentleman's Sport to the Commissioner System* (1966).

Voigt, David Q. *American Baseball: From the Commissioners to Continental Expansion* (1970).

Westcott, Rick. *The Mogul: Eddie Gottlieb, Philadelphia Sports Legend and Pro Basketball Pioneer* (2008).

PHOTOGRAPH ESSAY

Uniforming Sportswomen

One of the most remarkable recent developments in American sport has been the boom in women's athletics. The photographs in this section illustrate that this was a slow process. At the turn of the century, sport was barely considered an appropriate activity for women, and those who did participate were constrained by traditional clothing that made free, rapid movement uncomfortable and difficult. Upper- and middle-class young women had more opportunities than others to engage in high-status sports such as golf and tennis and more strenuous college contests such as baseball and rowing. Often idealized as the "Gibson girl"—attractive, slim, and physically fit—the woman athlete of this period wore a shirtwaist and long skirt that provided greater freedom than most contemporary apparel. However, female physical educators led a fight against competitive sport for women because they believed it was manly, immodest (as it involved wearing bloomers and playing in front of men), debilitating, and corrupting. From the 1920s until the early 1970s, women athletes had few outlets other than sports that were considered suitably feminine, such as figure skating, tennis, and golf.

As recently as 1972, when Title IX of the Education Act became law and made gender-based discrimination illegal at all institutions receiving federal aid, only about four percent of American girls participated in athletics, compared to 50 percent of American boys. In that year women composed only about one-seventh of the American Olympic team. Since then there has been a revolution in women's athletics. More women have become serious competitors, and they have successfully challenged barriers in such sports as the marathon. By 1996 about one-third of American girls participated in school sports, nearly half of college varsity players were women, and women made up nearly three-sevenths of the Olympic squad.

Chicago golfers, c. 1900. Golf was expensive, elitist, sociable, and nonstrenuous, and it did not require exposing one's body. (H. C. Rew/Chicago Historical Society)

Chicago tennis players, c. 1910. Tennis was less exclusive than golf. Most women tennis players wore restrictive clothing, but the better, more active players began wearing looser apparel. (John Becker/ Chicago Historical Society)

A 1920s basketball squad from the Jewish People's Institute, a settlement house on Chicago's West Side. This team was one of the best in the United States. The JPI provided a rare opportunity for young working-class women to participate in sports. (Chicago Historical Society)

Dorothy Herrick leaping over a hurdle, Boston College of Secretarial Science athletic meet, 1921. This athlete's uniform made hurdling difficult. In 1928, there were just five women's track events in the Olympics, and no hurdling races. (Underwood & Underwood/Chicago Historical Society)

Dorothy Griesheber and Wilma Bieber striking a fencing pose, Chicago, 1930. Fencing was one of the first sports advocated for women in the early 1900s, especially in Europe, because of the sport's aristocratic associations. Although it required aggressiveness, fencing was considered to be graceful and cerebral, and it became an Olympic event in 1924. (*Herald and Examiner*/ Chicago Historical Society)

Archery meet, Chicago, 1930. For centuries aristocratic women enjoyed archery. The sport required little physical exertion and no special clothing. At the 1904 Olympics, archery was the only sport for women. Participants then belonged to exclusive women's clubs. (*Chicago Daily News*/Chicago Historical Society)

Women Softball Players at Japanese Relocation Camp, May 1942. Maye Noma behind the plate and Tomi Nagao at bat in a practice game between members of the Chick-a-dee softball team at the internment camp of Manzanar, CA. Softball was a popular sport at relocation camps, providing an escape from the arduous conditions of daily life. The game was so popular that the Pinedale Assembly Center near Fresno had twenty-two women's clubs. These players wore pants, although women in the All American Girls Professional Baseball League (1943–1954) played in short skirts. (Historical/CORBIS)

Olympic National Team, 2012. By 1996, American Olympians ran with bare midriffs and tiny shorts made out of low-friction Lycra; uniforms are far skimpier than their male peers. For aerodynamics? To sell sex? Shown is the national team of Sanya Richards-Ross, Allyson Felix, Francena McCorory, and Deedee Trotter, who won the women's 4 × 400-meter relay at London's Olympic Stadium on Aug. 11, 2012. (AP Photo/Lee Jin-man)

CHAPTER 9

Gender and Sport in Modern America, 1870–1940

For most of American history, people assumed that sport was a manly activity. Why was sport a gendered activity? Sport was identified as exertive activities that required ruggedness, strength, courage, and vigor. The male bachelor subculture identified prowess in sport, as well as the ability to drink and seduce women, as excellent indicators of manliness. Muscular Christians, who came from an entirely different perspective—sport for them promoted sound morals—also regarded the playing fields as a first-rate site for young men to certify their manliness. Manliness in the mid-nineteenth century had meant the end of boyhood. In the late nineteenth century, people continued to consider athletic prowess as a manly activity through which men could demonstrate how far removed they were from any feminized influences such as religion, education, and culture. This was especially important for upper-class and middle-class men who had not served in the military, engaged in "manly" (physical) labor, or socialized at private men's clubs. Sport provided a venue for them to test their mettle and to prove they were not sissies or "mollycoddles," but rather robust, energetic, and vital.

If sport was considered manly, what place was there for women in athletics? Middle-class women participated in sociable coed sports like ice skating and croquet, but vigorous athletics were inappropriate for women. The conventional wisdom was that Victorian women had little need for physical fitness and that active sports were unfeminine. True believers in the cult of domesticity saw a woman's role as being in the home raising children and establishing a moral environment for her family. Women were warned against sport because they were too weak, could learn such bad (male) values as pride and aggressiveness, could have such good (female) qualities as self-control and modesty undermined, and would become masculine and unprepared for domesticity. What woman would dare participate in sports?

The first sportswomen were mainly from the upper and upper-middle classes whose social status protected them from ridicule. They participated in physical activities such as cycling and other sports that were sociable, feminine, and not too strenuous. They would play tennis and golf—often at their fathers' country clubs. For a number of years, well-to-do young women also engaged in competitive intercollegiate sports under modified rules. The participation by such "new women" in sport reflected their increasingly active roles in society. However, female physical educators successfully resisted intercollegiate competition because it promoted masculine values ("win at all costs"). They preferred sport for sport's sake in intramurals and play days that largely supplanted interschool contests. Sport remained inappropriate for most American women, especially young working-class women who had limited free time, had few opportunities to learn to play sports, and were pressured by parents and friends to conform to conventionally defined norms of femininity and respectability.

DOCUMENTS

Documents 1 and 2 are written by Theodore Roosevelt (TR), twenty-sixth president of the United States. In the first essay, originally published in *St. Nicholas Magazine* when TR was vice president, he discusses how American boys become men by playing sports. No American spoke as forcefully about the manly qualities of sport as Theodore Roosevelt, the leading advocate of the strenuous life theory. Young Ted was a sickly child who was encouraged by his father to exercise and box to improve his health. He boxed at Harvard with considerable success, and years later returned to boxing for recreation, sparring while he was president. In Document 2, he argues that amateur boxing promoted manly virtues. Roosevelt befriended prominent prizefighters, yet decried professional boxing, which he felt was debasing and demoralizing.

The rest of the documents in this section focus on American women, beginning with the remarkable story of Annie "Londonderry" Cohen Kopchovsky (1870–1947), a Jewish immigrant from Riga, Latvia, and mother of three, the first woman to bicycle around the world. Two Boston club members offered $10,000 to anyone who could ride a bicycle around the world in fifteen months. Annie took up the challenge, even though she had never ridden before. Kopchovsky advertised many products during her journey to pay expenses. She was paid $100 by the Londonderry Lithia Spring Water Company to ride with their blurb on her bicycle, and also to adopt the firm's name as her own. She began her journey on June 25, 1894, and returned home to Boston on September 24, 1895. Kopchovsky wrote the newspaper account included here, but note that she had a tendency to "embellish" her experiences. Document 4 by Anne O'Hagan, reporter, author, and editor, describes women's growing participation in sports and includes a detailed analysis of sport's positive features for women's health and clothing. Document 5 is an essay by Senda Berenson, director of Physical Education at Smith College at the turn of the century. She describes the positive values of women playing a form of basketball that she adapted from the men's game to fit women's particular skills and values. In Document 6, Dr. Dudley A. Sargent, perhaps the leading professor of physical education in America, with forty years' experience at Harvard, answers the widespread fears that sports were making girls masculine. Finally, Joan Newton Cuneo of New York City, wife of a well-known banker, discusses her career as the first competitive female automobile racer. In 1905, for instance, she was the only woman in the inaugural Glidden Tour; a 1,350-mile trek from St. Louis to New York, sponsored by the American Automobile Association (AAA) to promote safer roads and well-built, reliable automobiles. A skilled mechanic, Cuneo set a number of speed records, including in 1909 a mile in 5:05 during a five-mile timed race, breaking her own world record of 6:04. That year she came in second in a fifty-mile race in New Orleans, to Ralph De Palma, one of the preeminent racers of the day. However, the AAA soon banned women from competitive racing. Nonetheless, in 1911, she had the opportunity to drive a car at 112 miles per hour.

1. Theodore Roosevelt Explains How Sport Makes Boys into Men, 1900

... During the last few decades there certainly have been some notable changes for good in boy life. The great growth in the love of athletic sports, for instance, while fraught with danger if it becomes one-sided and unhealthy, has beyond all question had an excellent effect in increased manliness. Forty or fifty years ago the writer on American morals was sure to deplore the effeminacy and luxury of young Americans who were born of rich parents. The boy who was well off then, especially in the big Eastern cities, lived too luxuriously, took to billiards as his chief innocent recreation, and felt small shame in his inability to take part in rough pastimes and field-sports. Nowadays, whatever other faults the son of rich parents may tend to develop, he is at least forced by the opinion of all his associates of his own age to bear himself well in manly exercises and to develop his body—and therefore, to a certain extent, his character—in the rough sports which call for pluck, endurance, and physical address.

Of course boys who live under such fortunate conditions that they have to do either a good deal of outdoor work or a good deal of what might be called natural outdoor play do not need this athletic development. In the Civil War the soldiers who came from the prairie and the backwoods and the rugged farms where stumps still dotted the clearings, and who had learned to ride in their infancy, to shoot as soon as they could handle a rifle, and to camp out whenever they got the chance, were better fitted for military work than any set of mere school or college athletes could possibly be. Moreover, to misestimate athletics is equally bad whether their importance is magnified or minimized. The Greeks were famous athletes, and as long as their athletic training had a normal place in their lives, it was a good thing. But it was a very bad thing when they kept up their athletic games while letting the stern qualities of soldiership and statesmanship sink into disuse ... In short, in life, as in a football game, the principle to follow is: Hit the line hard; don't foul and don't shirk, but hit the line hard! ...

From Theodore Roosevelt, "The American Boy," in *The Strenuous Life: Essays and Addresses* (New York: Century, 1900), 155–67.

2. Theodore Roosevelt Advocates Amateur Boxing, 1913

Having been a sickly boy, with no natural bodily prowess, and having lived much at home, I was at first quite unable to hold my own when thrown into contact with other boys of rougher antecedents. I was nervous and timid. Yet from reading … and from hearing of the feats performed by my Southern forefathers and kinsfolk, and from knowing my father, I felt a great admiration for men who were fearless and who could hold their own in the world, and I had a great desire to be like them….

[W]ith my father's hearty approval, I started to learn to box. I was a painfully slow and awkward pupil, and certainly worked two or three years before I made any perceptible improvement whatever. My first boxing-master was John Long, an ex-prize-fighter….

On one occasion, to excite interest among his patrons, he held a series of "championship" matches for the different weights, the prizes being, at least in my own class, pewter mugs of a value, I should suppose, approximating fifty cents. Neither he nor I had any idea that I could do anything, but I was entered in the lightweight contest, in which it happened that I was pitted in succession against a couple of reedy striplings who were even worse than I was. Equally to their surprise and to my own, and to John Long's, I won….

This was, as far as I remember, the only one of my exceedingly rare athletic triumphs which would be worth relating. I did a good deal of boxing and wrestling in Harvard, but never attained to the first rank in either, even at my own weight. Once, in the big contests in the Gym, I got either into the finals or semi-finals….

When obliged to live in cities, I for a long time found that boxing and wrestling enabled me to get a good deal of exercise in condensed and attractive form. I was reluctantly obliged to abandon both as I grew older…. While President I used to box with some of the aides, as well as play single-stick with General Wood. After a few years I had to abandon boxing as well as wrestling, for in one bout a young captain of artillery cross-countered me on the eye, and the blow smashed the little blood-vessels….

When I was in the Legislature and was working very hard, with little chance of getting out of doors, all the exercise I got was boxing and wrestling…. Naturally, being fond of boxing, I grew to know a good many prize-fighters, and to most of those I knew I grew genuinely attached. I have never been able to sympathize with the outcry against prize-fighters. The only objection I have to the prize ring is the crookedness that has attended its commercial development. Outside of this I regard boxing, whether professional or amateur, as a first-class sport, and I do not regard it as brutalizing. Of course matches can be conducted under conditions that make them brutalizing. But this is true of football games and of most other rough and vigorous sports. Most certainly prize-fighting is not half as brutalizing or demoralizing as many forms of big business and of the legal work carried on in connection with big business. Powerful, vigorous men of strong animal development must

---

From Theodore Roosevelt, *Theodore Roosevelt: An Autobiography* (New York: MacMillan, 1913), ch. 2.

have some way in which their animal spirits can find vent. When I was Police Commissioner I found ... that the establishment of a boxing club in a tough neighborhood always tended to do away with knifing and gun-fighting among the young fellows who would otherwise have been in murderous gangs..... [T]hey had to have some outlet for their activities. In the same way I have always regarded boxing as a first-class sport to encourage in the Young Men's Christian Association. I do not like to see young Christians with shoulders that slope like a champagne bottle. Of course boxing should be encouraged in the army and navy....

When I was Police Commissioner, I heartily approved the effort to get boxing clubs started in New York on a clean basis. Later I was reluctantly obliged to come to the conclusion that the prize ring had become hopelessly debased and demoralized, and as Governor I aided in the passage of and signed the bill putting a stop to professional boxing for money. This was because some of the prize-fighters themselves were crooked, while the crowd of hangers-on who attended and made up and profited by the matches had placed the whole business on a basis of commercialism and brutality that was intolerable. I shall always maintain that boxing contests themselves make good, healthy sport.... There should always be the opportunity provided in a glove fight or bare-fist fight to stop it when one competitor is hopelessly outclassed or too badly hammered.... Of course the men who look on ought to be able to stand up with the gloves, or without them, themselves; I have scant use for the type of sportsmanship which consists merely in looking on at the feats of some one else.

3. Annie Londonderry Cycles Around the World in 1894–1895

I am a journalist and a "new woman"—if that term means that I believe I can do anything any man can do. Nellie Bly, the readers of the Sunday World all know, went around the world in seventy-two days and beat the record. But she had the comforts of steamships and parlor cars.

I have been around the world on a bicycle and I think that beats the record of any feminine undertaking to date.

The first idea of this trip came into my head when I heard in June a year ago of a wager that had been made that no woman could traverse the globe on a wheel. I accepted the burdensome end of the wager and determined to win it. The *Sunday World*, as usual, was interested in the project.

I knew nothing whatever about a bicycle. I had never ridden one, and there I had agreed to ride one around the world. Of course, the first thing to do was to get a bicycle and learn to ride. Two lessons sufficed for the learning and then I announced my readiness to start.

Conditions of the Trip

These are the conditions under which the trip was taken: I was to start from Boston, Mass., with nothing but one suit and my bicycle; was allowed five

---

From Annie Londonderry, "Feat of a Bloomer Girl," *San Francisco Call*, September 26, 1895, 2.

cents per diem for expenses; was permitted to earn money to defray my expenses in any honorable way other than by my profession as a journalist; was obliged to speak only the English language; was obliged to earn $5,000 over and above my expenses; was obliged to register at certain specified points, and secure the vouchers of the various American consuls that I had reached these various stages in my journey.

Well, of course, the only thing I could do as a starter in Boston was to transform myself into an advertising medium; received $100 from one firm and smaller sums from others, and in a few hours I was enabled to equip myself properly and present myself in front of the State House for the start. Lieut.-Gov. Wolcott made a little speech and wished me success and then I was off. This was June 26, 1894.

I found it altogether different riding on the uneven road than in the academy, and my progress was at first slow and painful. I reached Providence in due time, but it was not a record-breaking ride. After a good rest I made myself known and was engaged as a clerk in a drugstore for a day I received $5 for my work. From Providence I came to New York. I remained here three weeks. It was necessary for me to earn enough money here to defray my expenses across the ocean. Again I became an advertising medium, and received $600 for carrying four ribbons for as many firms.

Roughing It

... I had some very funny experiences en route. It was my first attempt at "roughing it," and I'm afraid I was a sorry specimen of a tramp. I had to sleep out of doors, under haycocks, in barns—anywhere, in fact, where I could find shelter. I could not beg, but the people en route were very kind, as a rule, and I did not suffer except from the unaccustomed strain of riding the wheel.

Nine weeks from the time I left Boston I rode into Chicago with three cents in my pocket. I had worn a short riding skirt thus far but in Chicago I swallowed my pride and donned bloomers. I quickly saw that this despised garment was the only practical thing to wear, and I will say right here that those bloomers won for me everywhere the respect and consideration which a woman has the right to expect. After the novelty had worn off I felt a certain degree of independence which I had never before experienced.

A Word for Bloomers

I firmly believe that if I had worn skirts I should not have been able to make the trip. It must not be thought that I lost the attention which is supposed to be associated with feminine apparel. I was everywhere treated with courtesy, and for the benefit of my sisters who hesitate about donning bloomers I will confess that I received no less than two hundred proposals of marriage.... I mention this to prove that bloomers are no handicap to matrimonial aspirations.

In Chicago I exchanged my forty-five pound wheel for one weighing only twenty pounds. Again I decorated myself with advertising ribbons in exchange for $185 in cash and started back to New York.... The bicycle clubs en route gave me an opportunity to earn money, and when I reached New York again, in eighteen days after leaving Chicago, I had enough money to pay my passage to Havre.

I sailed on *La Touraine.* I made myself known to the passengers and earned 150 francs lecturing. This was stolen from me the first day of my arrival in Havre.... The American Consul printed a large placard which explained in French the object of my visit and asking for an opportunity to earn some money.

Earning Money Rapidly

The French people were very quick to catch the spirit of the occasion and I was overwhelmed with offers of one kind and another. I distributed dodgers [small handbills], gave exhibitions of riding, sold my photograph and served as clerk in different stores. In this way I collected $1,500 in five days....

Attacked by Highwaymen

One night I had an encounter with highwaymen near Lacon [about 30 miles north of Marseilles]. I think they were waiting for me, for they knew I had been earning money in Paris. There were three men in the party, and all wore masks. They sprang at me from behind a clump of trees, and one of them grabbed my bicycle wheel, throwing me heavily. I carried a revolver in my pocket within easy reach, and when I stood up I had that revolver against the head of the man nearest me. He backed off but another seized me from behind and disarmed me. They rifled my pockets and found just three francs. They were magnanimous enough to return that money to me. My shoulder had been badly wrenched by my fall, and my ankle was sprained, but I was able to continue my journey....

Again in America

When I reached Yokohama I needed just 86 yen to secure my passage across the Pacific. The American Consul refused to interest himself in my trip. He said: "You've been receiving so much attention from the French that you'd better let them see you through." I took him at his word and appealed to the French Consul. He introduced me to friends, who gave me the chance to earn 250 yen.

I sailed for San Francisco on the steamer *Belgic,* arriving there March 23, ... forty-eight days ahead of schedule. I was glad enough to get away from the land of rats and rice and into a country where one could get a decent bed....

Well, when I reached San Francisco I felt as if my journey was ended. I never made a greater mistake in my life. The hardest part of the entire trip was through Southern California and the desert in Arizona. At Stockton I was nearly killed by a runaway, and was laid up five weeks. My experience in China had undermined my nervous system, and I collapsed under what would have been a trifle at another time. The enforced rest did me a lot of good, though.

Otherwise I would not have been able to have made my way through the desert. I succeeded in acquiring the trick of jumping my wheel from railroad tie to railroad tie, a really not difficult thing to learn, and I traveled along the railroad quite comfortably.

The Worst Part of the Trip

I had a journey of 165 miles through the sand.... At Yuma, Ari., a woman refused to give me a drink of water. It was the first act of inhospitality I had experienced and in my own country, too. Her excuse later, when questioned by the local newspaper men, was: "I didn't know her. I thought she was a tramp."

At another place I was given some stale bread and then forced to saw wood in payment. I explained that I had never before tackled a woodpile and told her of my journey. I had to chop wood, nevertheless.

In another place I could find no shelter and spent the night in a graveyard. I slept comfortably with a grave for my pillow and was awakened by a shrill voice exclaiming: "Hi, there! Get off my old man's grave!" Inasmuch as the command was backed by an uplifted broom, I obeyed in a hurry.

Well, I reached Chicago safely on Thursday, Sept. 12, fourteen days ahead of the time allowed by the agreement. This completed my journey, for I had already touched Chicago and I had thus completed the girdle around the world. The gentleman who had won the wager presented me with the stake—$10,000—and in addition I had the $5,318.75 which I had earned. My expenses for the entire time had been $1,200. I rode 9,604 miles on the wheel, and the ocean travel and walking in addition made a grand total of 26,000 miles trave[r]sed in the fourteen and one-half months.

4. Anne O'Hagan Describes the Athletic American Girl in 1901

To whomsoever the athletic woman owes her existence, to him or her the whole world of women owes a debt incomparably great. Absolutely no other social achievement in the behalf of women is so important and so far reaching in its results.... With the single exception of the improvement in the legal status of women, their entrance into the realm of sports is the most cheering thing that has happened to them in the century just past.

The Benefit to Body and Mind.

In the first place, there is the question of health. The general adoption of athletic sports by women meant the gradual disappearance of the swooning damsel of old romance, and of that very real creature, the lady who delighted, a decade or so ago, to describe herself as "high strung," which, being properly interpreted, meant uncontrolled and difficult to live with. Women who didn't like athletics were forced to take them up in self defense; and exercise meant firmer muscles,

---

From Anne O'Hagan, "The Athletic Girl," *Munsey's Magazine* 25 (August 1901): 729–38.

better circulation, a more equable temper, and the dethronement of the "nervous headache" from its high place in feminine regard.

The revolution meant as much psychologically as it did physically.... In dress, ... no boon has been granted to woman so great as the privilege of wearing shirt waists and short skirts. When the tennis players of ten or fifteen years ago first popularized that boneless, free chested, loose armed bodice they struck a blow for feminine freedom.... The woman who plays golf has made it possible for the woman who cannot distinguish between a cleek [number one golf iron] and a broom handle to go about her marketing in a short skirt; she has given the working girl, who never saw a golf course, freedom from the tyranny of braids and bindings....

To have improved half the race in health, disposition, and dress would seem almost enough for one movement to have accomplished. But athletics have done more than this. They have robbed old age of some of its terrors for women, and they promise to rob it of more....

When "Play" Was "Wisely Banished."

Twenty-five years ago a woman so fortunate as to live in the country probably rode on horseback—primarily as a means of locomotion, however. She could also play croquet. The city woman might walk, and she too might play croquet, if she had a large enough lawn; but that was about the sum of the sports permitted.

The change began with the gradual introduction of physical training into the schools. Today there is not a girls' school of any standing that does not include in its curriculum a course in gymnastics, and encourage or insist upon some sort of outdoor exercise.... Boards of education require that the newer school buildings shall be properly equipped with gymnasiums....

The Growth of College Sports.

From being the chief factor in the athletic life of the women's colleges, the gymnasiums have grown to be distinctly subsidiary. They supplement the outdoor exercises which the location of most of the institutions for higher education makes so natural and attractive. Each has its specialty in the line of sport, and the young woman, who wins a championship in rowing, swimming, track events, basket ball, bicycling, or whatever it may be, is a lionized creature who tastes for once the sweets of the cup of utter adulation.

At Wellesley, where the distinctive sport is rowing, Float Day is the banner festival of the year. No girl is allowed to row upon the crews who is not able to swim, but, ... the only contest permitted is in rowing form, not in speed. Bryn Mawr has by far the most complete and elaborate of the gymnasiums connected with the women's colleges, and its basket ball is famous wherever college women, past, present, or to be, are gathered together....

There are many reasons why college athletics for women are the most important of all. In the first place, a girl who, while struggling for a degree, develops a taste for outdoor sports, never loses it. The chances are ten to one that as a grandmother, she will be an active pedestrian or mountain climber.... Moreover, it is college athletics that have the greatest effect upon the physique of women. Once they have attained their full growth, exercise may keep them well, or make them stout or thin, but it will not have the marked effect upon their bodily development that it has upon that of a growing girl.

Physical Culture in the Cities.

Once upon a time the young woman who came out of college was somewhat at a loss how to expend her energy and to keep up her sports. Bicycles, golf, and the country clubs have altered that. Moreover, ... there are, in the large cities at any rate, excellent gymnasiums. In New York, for instance, apart from the gymnasiums in all the schools, in the working girls' clubs, and in the various branches of the Young Women's Christian Association, there are at least six well known private gymnasiums where women may pursue physical culture to their hearts' content and the good of their bodies....

Between three and four hundred women are enrolled as pupils of the Savage Gymnasium, which, both in attendance and equipment, is the largest in New York. There are classes and there is individual work. Fencing and boxing, both of which have many ardent disciples, are taught privately. Girls of five and women of fifty and sixty are among the patrons....

The cost of being a gymnast in New York varies. There is one gymnasium with pillowed couches about the room, soft, lovely lights, and walls that rest weary eyes; where a crisp capped maid brings the exerciser a cup of milk during her rest upon the divan, where her boots are laced or buttoned by deft fingers other than her own. For these privileges and the ordinary ones of gymnastic training the charge is a hundred dollars a year.

Forty dollars covers the cost in less Sybaritic circles, and if one has the distinction of being a working woman, ten dollars will pay for gymnastic instruction and privileges. The gymnasiums connected with the Christian Associations, the working girls' clubs, the settlements, and the like are even less expensive.

What New York offers women in gymnastic opportunities, all the other large cities duplicate. Chicago, indeed, is in advance of the metropolis, for it has a woman's athletic club, the only large and successful one now in operation in this country. It was started more than a year ago through the efforts of Mrs. Pauline H. Lyon, who interested Mrs. Philip Armour, Mrs. Potter Palmer, ... and other wealthy women in the project. A business building was remodeled to fit the needs of the club, the cost being about sixty thousand dollars. In addition to the gymnasium proper, a swimming tank ... has been constructed.... A Swedish teacher of swimming was engaged, and the gymnasium instructor is also a graduate in the Swedish methods. There are bowling alleys, rooms for fencing, a Turkish bath, parlors, library, a tea room, dining room, and everything that such a club could possibly require....

Women on the Golf Links.

With the gradual athletic development of women, the tendency of men to regard their gymnasiums and country clubs as close corporations from which women must be barred at any cost, is disappearing. Of all the twelve hundred golf clubs which dot the United States ... only one was instituted upon the monastic principle of excluding women....

There are, however, many courses where women are not allowed to play on Sundays and holidays. There is excellent and almost universal masculine testimony to the fact that on crowded days nothing so discourages a man as women playing before him on the golf links....

... The best drive of the champion women players is equal in distance to the average drive of the average man. Miss Beatrix Hoyt, ... three times the national woman's champion, has a drive of from a hundred and twenty to a hundred and sixty yards. A good average drive for a man is a hundred and fifty yards....

... In the rest of the game the well trained woman has an equal chance with a man.... At Shinnecock Hills there is a separate course for women known as the "red" course. It is of nine holes, but the distances are not short. Until a woman has played this course at least three times in a certain minimum number of strokes, she is not allowed to play upon the "white," or eighteen hole course....

In some places women have been more enterprising than men in the matter of forming clubs. The Morris Country Club, of Morristown, New Jersey, was started and managed by women alone. In the associations of golf clubs there are both women's and men's. There is a Women's Metropolitan Association, under whose direction the women's championship matches have been played. There is a women's association of the clubs around Boston, though there is not yet a men's....

... The aim of athletics among women has been the establishment and maintenance of a high general standard of health and vigor, rather than some single brilliant achievement.

So far, with a few notorious exceptions, ... women have made freedom and fun their objects in athletics; and there are certain indications that this temperate view of the subject is gaining ground even in the ranks of the record breaking sex itself.

5. Senda Berenson Asserts the Value of Adapted Women's Basketball, 1901

Within the last few years athletic games for women have made such wonderful strides in popularity that there are few directors of physical training who do not value them as an important part of their work. They have become popular, too, not as the outcome of a "fad" but because educators everywhere see the great value games may have in any scheme of education. Gymnastics and games for women are meeting less and less opposition, and gaining larger numbers of warm supporters because our younger generation of women are already showing the good results that may be obtained from them in better physiques and greater strength and endurance.

Now that the woman's sphere of usefulness is constantly widening, now that she is proving that her work in certain fields of labor is equal to man's work and

From Senda Berenson, "Significance of Basketball for Women," in Senda Berenson, ed., *Line Basketball for Women* (New York: A.G. Spalding, 1901), 20–27.

hence should have equal reward, now that all fields of labor and all professions are opening their doors to her, she needs more than ever the physical strength to meet these ever increasing demands. And not only does she need a strong physique, but physical and moral courage as well.

Games are invaluable for women in that they bring out as nothing else just these elements that women find necessary today in their enlarged field of activities. Basket ball is the game above all others that has proved of the greatest value to them....

It is said that one of woman's weaknesses is her inability to leave the personal element out of thought or action. If this is so—and there is some ground for such a supposition—a competitive game like basket ball does much to do away with it. Success in this game can be brought about only by good team-play. A team with a number of brilliant individual players lacking team-work will be beaten always by a team of conscientious players who play for each other. This develops traits of character which organization brings; fair play, impersonal interest, earnestness of purpose, the ability to give one's best not for one's own glorification but for the good of the team—the cause.

... Just as basket ball may be made an influence for good so may it be made a strong influence for evil. The gravest objection to the game is the rough element it contains. Since athletics for women are still in their infancy, it is well to bring up the large and significant question: shall women blindly imitate the athletics of men without reference to their different organizations and purpose in life; or shall their athletics be such as shall develop those physical and moral elements that are particularly necessary for them? We can profit by the experience of our brothers and therefore save ourselves from allowing those objectionable features to creep into our athletics that many men are seriously working to eliminate from theirs.... It is a well known fact that women abandon themselves more readily to an impulse than men.... This shows us that unless we guard our athletics carefully in the beginning many objectionable elements will quickly come in. It also shows us that unless a game as exciting as basket ball is carefully guided by such rules as will eliminate roughness, the great desire to win and the excitement of the game will make our women do sadly unwomanly things....

The modifications in the rules contained in this pamphlet were carefully considered and are entirely the fruit of experience. The two important changes are the division of the playing field and the prohibiting of snatching or batting the ball from the hands of another player.

The division of the gymnasium or field into three equal parts, and the prohibiting of the players of one division from running into the domain of another seems an advantage for many reasons. It does away almost entirely with "star" playing, hence equalizes the importance of the players, and so encourages team work. This also encourages combination plays, for when a girl knows she cannot go over the division line to follow the ball, she is more careful to play as well as possible with the girls near her when the ball comes to her territory. The larger the gymnasium the greater is the tax on individual players when the game is played without lines. It has been found that a number of girls who play without division lines have developed hypertrophy of the heart. The lines prevent the players from running all over the gymnasium, thus doing away with unnecessary running, and also giving the heart moments of rest. On the other hand, the lines do not keep the players almost stationary, as some believe. A player has the right to run anywhere she may please in her own third of the gymnasium.

The divisions, then, concentrate energy, encourage combination plays, equalize team work and do away with undue physical exertion.

Allowing snatching or batting the ball from another person's hand seems the greatest element toward encouraging rough play in the game. It is apt to encourage personal contact; it has an intrinsic quality that goes against one's better nature; it has an element of insult in it. When a player gets the ball it should be hers by the laws of victory, ownership, courtesy, fair play. To prevent this rule, however, from making the game slow and spiritless, a rule was made that a player should not be allowed to hold the ball longer than three seconds under penalty of a foul. Preventing snatching or batting the ball has also developed superb jumping; for a player knows that since she cannot snatch the ball away from her opponent, by jumping in the air as high as possible she may catch the ball before it gets to her opponent.

When the game was first started many saw the danger of "dribbling." The objectionable element was done away with by not allowing the players to bounce the ball more than three consecutive times or lower than the knee. Since then the Y.M.C.A. rules have done away with dribbling together. It seems a good rule to eliminate it when the game is played without division lines—where a player by dribbling can easily get from one basket to the other—but that necessity is overcome with division lines. To allow a player to bounce the ball three times gives an opportunity for having possession of the ball longer than three seconds when she wishes to use a signal or combination play. On the other hand, by demanding that the ball shall be bounced higher than the knee gives a quick opponent a fair opportunity to bat the ball away when it is between the floor and the player's hands....

The original rules allow only five on a team. We have changed the rules to allow any number from five to ten players on a team. My own conviction is that the smallest number of players should be six instead of five, for when the game is played with division lines the work in the centre is much too hard for one player. Some of the strongest and quickest work is done in the centre. The size of the gymnasium should decide the number of players on a team....

Should people imagine that these modifications take the fire and spirit out of the game, they can either try it with their own teams "without prejudice," or witness a game where such modifications are adopted to be convinced of their mistake. Perhaps it may not be out of place to quote some passages from an account which appeared in one of our leading newspapers with reference to a game played with modified rules at one of our colleges for women: "the playing was very rapid and extremely vigorous. From the time the ball went into play until a goal was tossed there was no respite. The playing could not properly be called rough. There was not an instance of slugging, but the ball was followed by the players with rushes, much the way it is on the gridiron. One who supposes it is a simple or weak game would be surprised to see the dash and vigor with which it is entered into. It is a whirl of excitement from start to finish, and yet, with all the desperate earnestness and determination with which the game is played, there is excellent control and much dexterity shown. There is splendid temper and true sportswomanlike spirit in the game. The services of a referee to end a dispute are seldom needed, and there are no delays on account of kicking. The amount of physical strength and endurance which is cultivated is readily apparent. One might suppose that it would be a namby pamby exhibition with much show, many hysterical shrieks and nothing of an athletic contest; but nothing could be more contrary to facts. True, there is no slugging or exhibition of roughness, but the play is extremely vigorous and spirited, and is characterized by a whirl and dash that is surprising to the uninitiated. The possession of self-control, both of temper and physical action, was clearly in evidence yesterday, even during the most exciting stages of the game."

6. Dr. Dudley A. Sargent Asks, "Are Athletics Making Girls Masculine?", 1912

... Heretofore women have been more creatures of the kitchen and fireside than of the great outdoors, and the present generation of young women who will become the mothers of the next generation have more muscle and more lung capacity than their own mothers. The growth of athletics for girls is largely responsible for this. Colleges for women have more or less grudgingly made room in their curricula for gymnastics and athletics, and the non-collegiate world has followed suit and made athletic sports accessible to women....

Many persons honestly believe that athletics are making girls bold, masculine and overassertive; that they are destroying the beautiful lines and curves of her figure, and are robbing her of that charm and elusiveness that has so long characterized the female sex....

Do Women Need as Much Exercise as Men?

From a physiological point of view woman needs physical exercise as much as man. She has the same kind of brain, heart, lungs, stomach and tissues, and these organs in her are just as responsive to exercise as in men. Fundamentally both sexes have the same bones and muscles. They are much larger, however, in the average male than in the average female.

The average male weighs about one hundred and thirty-five pounds without clothes and is about five feet seven inches in height, while the female weighs about one hundred and fifteen pounds and is about five feet two inches in height. The male has broad, square shoulders, the female narrow, sloping ones. The male has a large, muscular chest, broad waist, narrow hips and long and muscular legs, while the female has little muscle in the chest, a constricted waist, broad hips, short legs and thighs frequently weighted with adipose tissue.... In point of strength the female is only about one-half as strong as the male....

From Dudley A. Sargent, "Are Athletics Making Girls Masculine? A Practical Answer to a Question Every Girl Asks," *Ladies' Home Journal* 29 (March 1912): 11, 71–73.

No Athletic Sport Prohibitive to Women

I have no hesitation in saying that there is no athletic sport or game in which some women cannot enter, not only without fear of injury but also with great prospects of success. In nearly every instance, however, it will be found that the women who are able to excel in the rougher and more masculine sports have either inherited or acquired masculine characteristics. This must necessarily be so, since it is only by taking on masculine attributes that success in certain forms of athletics can be worn. For instance, … [s]he could not hope to succeed in rowing or in handling heavy weights without broadening the waist and shoulders and strengthening the muscles of the back and abdomen.…

… Nor do the limitations which I have mentioned apply to young girls from ten to fifteen years of age, who, if properly trained, will often surpass boys of the same age in any kind of game or athletic performance. But it is at these ages that girls have neat, trim and boyish figures. If girls received the same kind of physical training as boys throughout their growing and developing period they could make a much more creditable showing as athletes when they become adult women. The interesting question is, would such girls become more womanly women, and the boys more manly men?…

The Best Sports for Girls

There are no sports that tend to make women masculine in an objectionable sense except boxing, baseball, wrestling, basket-ball, ice hockey, water polo and Rugby football. These sports are thought better adapted to men than to women, because they are so rough and strenuous.…

These Make Women More Masculine

Physically all forms of athletic sports and most physical exercises tend to make women's figures more masculine, inasmuch as they tend to broaden the shoulders, deepen the chest, narrow the hips, and develop the muscles of the arms, back and legs, which are masculine characteristics. Some exercises, like bowling, tennis, fencing, hurdling and swimming, tend to broaden the hips, which is a feminine characteristic.…

Just how all-round athletics tend to modify woman's form may be judged by comparing the conventional with the athletic type of woman. The conventional woman has a narrow waist, broad and massive hips and large thighs. In the athletic type of woman sex characteristics are less accentuated, and there is a suggestion of reserve power in both trunk and limbs. Even the mental and moral qualities that accompany the development of such a figure are largely masculine,…

Sports Should Be Adapted to Women

… While there is some danger that women who try to excel in men's sports may take on more marked masculine characteristics … this danger is greatly lessened if the sports are modified so as to meet their peculiar qualifications.… All the apparatus used and the weights lifted, as well as the height and distance to be attained in running, jumping, etc., should be modified to meet her limitations.

Considering also the peculiar constitution of her nervous system and the great emotional disturbances to which she is subject, changes should be made in many of the rules and regulations governing the sports and games for men, to adapt them to the requirements of women.

Modify Men's Athletics for Women

... Women as a class cannot stand a prolonged mental or physical strain as well as men.... Give women frequent intervals of rest and relaxation and they will often accomplish as much in twenty-four hours as men accomplish.... I have arranged the schedule of work at both the winter and summer Normal Schools at Cambridge so that periods of mental and physical activity follow each other alternately, and both are interspersed with frequent intervals of rest.

The modifications that I would suggest in men's athletics so as to adapt them to women are as follows: Reduce the time of playing in all games and lengthen the periods of rest between the halves. Reduce the heights of high and low hurdles and lessen the distance between them. Lessen the weight of the shot and hammer and all other heavy-weight appliances. In heavy gymnastics have bars, horses, swings, ladders, etc., adjustable so that they may be easily adapted to the requirements of women. In basket-ball, a favorite game with women and girls, divide the field of play into three equal parts by lines, and insist upon the players confining themselves to the space prescribed for them. This insures that everyone shall be in the game, and prevents some players from exhausting themselves....

I am often asked; "Are girls overdoing athletics at school and college?" I have no hesitation in saying that in many of the schools where basket-ball is being played according to rules for boys many girls are injuring themselves in playing this game. The numerous reports of these girls breaking down with heart trouble or a nervous collapse are mostly too well founded.... These instances generally occur in schools or colleges where efforts are made to arouse interest in athletics by arranging matches between rival teams, clubs and institutions, and appealing to school pride.... The individual is not only forced to do her best, but to do even better than her best, though she breaks down in her efforts to surpass her previous records.

There will be little honor or glory in winning a race, playing a game, or doing a "stunt" which every other girl could do. It is in the attempt to win distinction by doing something that others cannot do that the girl who is over-zealous or too ambitious is likely to do herself an injury. For this reason girls who are ambitious to enter athletic contests should be carefully examined and selected by a physician or trained woman expert....

7. The Early Career of Car Racer Joan N. Cuneo

Many people have asked me how I happened to enter the automobile racing game, and what satisfaction could have resulted from risking my life in such a manner, just for the love of driving a car. My answer has always been that I felt that if anything seemed worth doing I always wanted to do it to the very

---

From J. N. Cuneo, "Woman's Automobile Racing Record," *Country Life* 19 (15 November 1910): 127.

best of my ability, and looking over my racing records it is with great satisfaction that I find that each event under the varying conditions was an improvement on the previous one, and each cup and each medal and trophy meant one step higher in the automobile racing world.

During the summer of 1905 I had entered and driven my car through the Glidden tour, and in September a challenge came to me through the newspapers to come to Atlantic City and show what I could do handling a car at speed on the beach.

My car was in the shop being painted and overhauled, but out she came and was shipped by express to Atlantic City, and competing with four men driving gasoline cars I came in second in the one-mile race, being timed 1 minute 18 2-5 seconds. I was proud of my first record, but not satisfied. I knew if I had a faster car I could do better, so order a 1906 model, and before the body was put on, being invited to give an exhibition at the Dutchess County Fair at Poughkeepsie, September 19th, 1905, I drove my new chassis up there and had my first experience at track racing.

It was a case of love at first sight, and my love for track driving increased each time I drove around one. There was trouble with the oiling system on the car, and my mile exhibition in 1 minutes 22 1-5 seconds was a keen disappointment to me. On our drive home the cause of the trouble was found and remedied and we were arrested for speeding.... A gold medal was presented to me for driving at Poughkeepsie.

November 1st, 1905, I drove my car in a three-mile race on Point Breeze track at Philadelphia, winning a silver cup from three other contestants; time 4 minutes 8 seconds—which was good time for an 18 horse power car in those days.

In April, 1906, I was invited to Atlantic City again, and drove a mile exhibition in 1 minute 15 seconds, and made a world's record for middleweight gasoline cars, in 1 minute 23 3-5 seconds for which I received a gold and diamond medal.

At the Rockland County Fair, Orangeburg, N.Y., in September 1906, I drove an exhibition mile on the half-mile track in 1 minute 31 seconds, which was a record for the track, and still stands, I believe....

In the spring of 1907 I drove in a hundred-mile race at the Bennings track in Washington, and came in third, being timed 2 hours 23 minutes.

Touring contests then kept me busy until the New Orleans Mardi Gras celebration when there were three days of automobile racing on the track there, February 21st, 22d, and 23d, 1909. Competing with Ralph De Palma, George Robertson, Louis Stang, Robert Burman, Jimmie Ryal and others, I beat the last three named in every event I drove in, and George Robertson in all but one. De Palma's specially built track racer was too fast for my car, but I had good cause to be very proud of my records down there. During the three-day meet a one-mile event in 1 minute 1-5 second went to my credit, a silver cup for five miles in 5 minutes 5 seconds ... a gold horn for ten miles in 10 minutes 8 seconds, and the much coveted gold trophy for the National Amateur Championship ... for five miles in 5 minutes 8 seconds.... In the fifty mile race ... I came in second to De Palma. My time was 52 minutes 40 seconds, which broke the world's record at that time....

I had made record time in practice on the Fort George, Fort Lee and Wilkes-Barre hill climbs, and for the Briarcliff and Long Island Derby road races, but was not allowed to compete because, unfortunately, I am a woman!

After driving from New York to Atlanta on the *Herald* tour without even a puncture to break the monotony of the trip, I drove my car around the new Atlanta Motordrome, two miles, in 1 minute 56 seconds, carrying full touring equipment and four passengers. The same day, the first time I had ever even sat in the car, I drove a big racer around the same two-mile tack in 1 minute 45 seconds....

After making these various racing records without accident to myself or others, after driving through the 1908 Glidden tour with a perfect score—which all in the motor world know is one of *the most* difficult, if not the most difficult, of automobile acquirements—I would very much like to challenge any man driver to-day to show a better record in all around driving from the easy few-day touring contests to the beach racing, motordrome contests, hill climbs, road racing, one mile, then half mile dirt track, and ending with the Glidden tour.

ESSAYS

The two essays in this section explore how sports defined appropriate parameters for gendered behavior and how, in turn, being male or female established stark parameters around an individual's sporting options. In the first essay, drawn from *The Manly Art: Bare-Knuckle Prize Fighting in America* (1986), one of the outstanding books in sport history, Elliott J. Gorn analyzes how the art of self-defense helped define for men the penultimate qualities of a manly individual. In the mid-nineteenth century, boxing demarcated several qualities of manliness for the male bachelor subculture, which included courage, self-discipline, and self-control. In the late nineteenth century, the potential to gain such traits through sparring made the sport popular with certain segments of the upper and middle classes who were worried about their own manliness and ability to measure up to their brave and virile ancestors.

The second essay is by Professor Rita Liberti of the Department of Kinesiology, California State University, East Bay. She specializes in women's sport history, and in particular the female African American experience. In this chapter she discusses the importance of sport and image during the late 1920s and 1930s among coeds at Bennett College, an all-women's institution in Greensboro, North Carolina.

Liberti examines the values aspiring middle-class women attributed to intercollegiate basketball competition at Bennett, where like in other historically black colleges, excellence in sports provided an opportunity to demonstrate racial pride and competence. Women were becoming more self-aware, assertive, and self-confident, taking upon themselves greater challenges, that were beyond the purview of traditional black southern womanhood. Women athletes strove to clothe their activity in respectability. The qualities that basketball had been designed to teach—discipline, teamwork, and determination—made it problematic to physical educators, parents, and males, who opposed competitive basketball for challenging traditional gender roles.

Manliness in the Squared Circle

ELLIOTT J. GORN

Within the magic circle of the ring, not only were concepts of wealth altered, but gender too became inverted. With the breakdown of the household-based artisan economy, sexual identity grew increasingly bifurcated. Moreover, men and women were encouraged to moderate their passions and keep them from interfering with the goal of economic success. In the bourgeois canon, masculinity meant, above all, taking responsibility, controlling one's impulses, and working hard in order to support a family. Being a good provider was the touchstone of being a man, so probity, dependability, and resistance to temptation defined a middle-class male ideal. The very word manly was usually conjoined with "independence" or "self-reliance," thus linking the bourgeois concept of masculinity with autonomy and self-possession, key elements of Victorian character which flowed from diligent labor. Not all Victorian men fulfilled the role; many slid back into less morally rigid ways. The sporting underworld could stir the envy of those who felt themselves deprived of the freedom and openness they perceived in working-class culture. Despite these deep feelings of ambivalence, however, the bourgeois male ideal remained compelling, and it was reinforced by a new female role. For middle-class women, the home became a separate sphere, not a place of production but a haven where their superior morality refined men, nurtured children, and inculcated tender emotions. This domestic ideal placed women at the center of moral life, freeing men to go out into the corrupting world, then return to a purifying sanctuary.

If the fundamental test of masculinity was, by Victorian lights, being a good breadwinner, if work was a man's primary source of self-definition, the measure of his worth, and proof of his manhood, then many working-class men in industrializing cities were doomed to failure. Of course, those who performed heavy or dangerous tasks could take pride in their strength and stamina. But fathers now had diminishing legacies of wealth or skill to pass on to sons, and for most men, earnings were small and opportunities limited. Put simply, daily labor undermined rather than buttressed masculinity. It made sense, then, that many workers turned to a more elemental concept of manhood, one they could demonstrate during leisure hours. Toughness, ferocity, prowess, honor, these became the touchstones of maleness, and boxing along with other sports upheld this alternative definition of manhood. The *manly* art defined masculinity not by how responsible or upright an individual was but by his sensitivity to insult, his coolness in the face of danger, and his ability to give and take punishment.

Reprinted from Elliott J. Gorn, *The Manly Art: Bare-Knuckle Prize Fighting in America*, 140–47, 198–202.

Sociologists have talked of a "bachelor subculture" to capture a phenomenon so common to nineteenth and early twentieth century cities: large numbers of unmarried males finding their primary human contact in one another's company. In some large cities unweddedness was so common that at mid-century, 40 percent of the men between twenty-five and thirty-five years of age were single. Irish immigrants contributed to this tendency, bringing a tradition of late marriage and high rates of bachelorhood to America, but even among the native-born, working men in the nineteenth century tended not to marry until their late twenties. The bachelor subculture, however, included betrothed men as well as unattached ones. Sullivan, Hyer, and Morrissey, for example, were all married, but their wives seemed almost tangential to their lives as the champions passed their nights drinking and carousing among friends. With the breakdown of the household economy, men and women spent diminishing amounts of their work time together, and many chose to take their leisure too in gender-segregated realms. In saloons, pool halls, and lodges as well as in gangs, firehouses, and political clubs, men gathered to seek companionship, garner one another's esteem, and compete for status.

Here, implicitly, was a rejection of the cult of domesticity so characteristic of bourgeois Victorian life. Members of the bachelor subculture expected women to be submissive; they also tended to view them as either pure and virginal or exciting and whorish. Women were both exploitable and less than central to men's affective lives. Rather than spend their nonworking hours within the confines of the family circle—where women's allegedly superior moral nature and "instinctive" sense of self-sacrifice tamed men and elevated children—members of the sporting fraternity chose to seek rough male companionship. It was not only men, however, who felt stifled by the domestic ideal. The Victorian home emotionally suffocated many middle-class women as well, and to compensate for the deprivations caused by their gender-based role, they sought one another's company. The homoerotic tone of letters women wrote to each other and the sensual descriptions of their meetings at spas where they went for physical and emotional therapy had less to do with simple homosexuality (though no doubt homosexual acts and relationships occurred) than with women reaching out for the warmth, love, and emotional contact that homelife denied.

There was a parallel in the bachelor subculture that supported the ring. Of course heterosexual prowess was an important element of masculinity; fathering a family, picking up unattached women, and frequenting prostitutes all demonstrated virility. But maleness seemed most emphatically confirmed in the company not of women, but of other men. The loving descriptions of boxers' bodies so common in antebellum fight reports grew less from narrowly defined homosexuality than from a common male aesthetic. Men perceived men as creatures of beauty because they focused so much emotional attention on one another. In the saloon, the firehouse, or the gang, many working-class males found their deepest sense of companionship and human connectedness. The boxer's physique was a palpable expression of such masculine values as strength, power, and stamina. With his body alone the prize fighter attained financial autonomy. Conversely, women were associated with those family responsibilities made so onerous by low pay and lack of economic opportunity. Rather than accept domesticity as the highest good—and domesticity, after all, was a bourgeois luxury; working-class women often toiled in factories or as laundresses or maids—many laboring men sought refuge from the family in all-male peer groups where heroic prize fighters symbolized independence through physical prowess.

Here the concept of male honor helps us understand the culture of the ring. Honor, as historians have recently applied the term, is distinct from the more modern ideals of conscience and dignity. The Victorian man of character possessed a particularly well-developed conscience (an internalized sense of morality stressing strict self-control) and a profound belief in human dignity (especially faith in the fundamental equality of all men). Thus each Christian faced God alone, businessmen were responsible for the fulfillment of their contracts, and good citizens acted on inviolable principles to perfect society. Although the approbation of others was gratifying for such men, good deeds brought their own internal satisfactions and immoral acts evoked a sense of guilt.

But honor more than conscience or dignity depended on external ratification. It was conferred when men acknowledged one another as peers, often in symbolic acts such as buying drinks, spending money lavishly, or toasting one another's accomplishments. Honor had no existence outside group life, for only reputation and the esteem of others conferred it. Honorific societies have tended to be tightly knit and nonbureaucratic, placing special emphasis not on inward virtues but on outward signs that must be approved or rejected by one's status equals. The objects of honor have varied across time and cultures. They have included the protection of the chastity of wives and daughters, grand displays of hospitality, and tests of male prowess. But regardless of the specifics, an individual had honor only when his kin or his fellows said he did. Honor was denied him when his peers refused to acknowledge his status as an equal, and no amount of arguing could restore it. Only acts of valor, especially violent retribution, expunged the sense of shame, proved one's mettle, and reasserted one's claim to honor.

The fights between boxers and the collectivities they belonged to—fire brigades, gangs, political factions, saloon cliques, militia companies, and so forth—were often animated by a sense of lost honor, of having had one's status impugned. Stake money for fighters, turf between gangs, and elected office for political parties, these were tangible objects to contend over, but the real battle was for peer recognition, for a sense of distinction that made a man first among equals in the small male cliques of working-class society. Saloons were so central to the culture of the ring in part because here, with alcohol lowering inhibitions, men affirmed their right to drink together or, alternatively, to cast aspersions that only blood could redeem. The ethic of honor had roots in the Old World, but it continued to thrive where individuals were concerned less with morality or piety, more with flaunting their status among peers through acts of masculine prowess. In mid-nineteenth-century America, then, character, conscience, and dignity were hallmarks of middle-class culture, while honor remained central to the lives of the poor and marginal, the acid test of personal worth in the male peer society.

The Rites of Violence

Perhaps most important, the bloodiness displayed in the ring was symptomatic of the violence endemic to urban working-class life. Unemployment and poverty were constant threats, and a cycle of alternating depression and inflation made the antebellum years particularly unstable. New York City's per capita wages fell by roughly 25 percent in the decade before mid-century. Moreover, the *New York Times* estimated in the middle of the 1850s that a family of four needed a minimum yearly income of six hundred dollars, double the salary of many laborers and well over what the majority of working-class men earned. In the impersonal market economy, lack of job security and inequalities of wealth and power were becoming intractable problems.... Staggering numbers of men were killed or maimed on the job. Indeed, by 1860 there were four Irishwomen for every three Irishmen in New York City, partly because of desertions, partly because of breadwinners' need to travel in search of work, but also as a result of brutally high job-related mortality rates. In addition, poor diet, overcrowding, and lack of modern sanitation contributed to waves of deadly epidemics. Between 1840 and 1855 the city's mortality rates rose from one in forty to one in twenty-seven, and nearly half of all New York children died before reaching age six.

The death sounds of livestock slaughtered in public markets, the smell of open sewers, the feverish cries of children during cholera season, the sight of countless men maimed on the job, all were part of day-to-day street life. The poor lived as their ancestors had, in a world that did little to shield them from pain. Men tolerated violence—created violence—because high death rates, horrible accidents, and senseless acts of brutality were a psychological burden that only stoicism or bravado helped lighten.

This context makes sense of the ring's violence. Boxing, as well as cockfighting, bullbaiting, and ratting, did not just reflect the bloodiness of life. Rather, these and similar sports shaped violence into art, pared away its maddening arbitrariness, and thereby gave it order and meaning. Here, ideally, was true equality of opportunity, a pure meritocracy free of favoritism and special influence. At their best, the ring and the pit rendered mayhem rule-bound instead of anarchic, voluntary rather than random. Boxers, like fighting cocks and trained bulldogs, made bloodshed comprehensible and thus offered models of honorable conduct. They taught men to face danger with courage, to be impervious to pain, and to return violence rather than passively accept it.

As members of male peer societies steeped in the conflicts of their day, prize fighters embodied community values, giving them concentrated symbolic expression. Often harsh and brutal, working-class life required a dramatic form to express its reality. Boxing acknowledged, rather than denied life's cruelty, even celebrated it. In the midst of nagging hatreds and festering rivalries, often unleashed by flowing alcohol and blustering attacks on masculine honor, the cool restraint needed to sign articles, train, organize excursions, and bring off matches made bloodletting comprehensible. A properly carried out fight was a performance, a pageant, a ritual, that momentarily imposed meaning on the savage irrationalities of life. Out of chaos the ring created an aesthetic of violence based on bodily development, fighting skills, and controlled brutality.

This is not to argue that boxing and similar sports supplanted real with vicarious brutality. On the contrary, as recent research reveals, symbolic displays of violence tend to promote further violence. Even as pugilism brought order to bloodiness, made it comprehensible by confining it to two men who represented larger collectivities and fought by rules, the ring also upheld, indeed gloried in the fact that brutishness was part of man's fate. Not the pious homilies of evangelicals, the sentimental humanitarianism of reformers, nor the optimistic progressivism of the middle class, prize fighting as a metaphor declared that there was limited good in this world, that every man's victory implied another's loss, that the way was harsh and bloody for all, and that hardship, even death, were the soul mates of life. The ring thus expressed an outlook in which pain and defeat were ineluctable parts of living, a notion almost heretical in this rationalistic age.

Despite the divisions among sporting men, then, all were united by disruptive change in their patterns of work, alienation from bourgeois or evangelical ways, and shared attitudes toward wealth, labor, leisure, masculinity, and honor. Working-class men adopted their own forms of expressive culture, and prize fighting symbolically affirmed their distinct ethos. If not a political threat to new alignments of social and economic power, the ring at least offered cultural opposition; if not a challenge to evangelical or bourgeois authority, here at least was a denial of the values that undergirded oppressive social relationships.

Above all, the manly art gave men a way to get a symbolic grip on the contradictions in their lives, to see these conflicts neatly arranged and played out. It offered an alternative to the Victorian vision of an ever-improving world, stressing instead a constant balance between victory and defeat. As drama, the prize fight depicted pain as the portion for both winner and loser, violence as a necessary means to human ends, and loyalty to one's communal group along with honor in defending one's good name as the very highest human ideals. The ring celebrated the high-stakes gamble, the outrageous boast, the love of strife. Prize fighting made Old World virtues such as prowess, courage, and virility the essence of manhood, while loving descriptions of muscles and sinews gave palpable expression to naked physical beauty as a source of masculine pride.

Of course the culture of the ring had an ugly, disturbing side. Bare-knuckle fighting attracted some social misfits who reveled in brutality. Boxing could become an outlet for bully boys who enjoyed inflicting pain, sociopaths who responded only to their own pleasure at others' suffering. The special order of the ring moreover, sometimes broke down under the tensions it symbolically reconciled, unleashing further violence. Prize fighting also defined masculinity in a narrow way that encouraged male exploitation of women and alienated men from a whole range of softer emotions within themselves. But at its best the ring dramatized a world of victory for the socially downtrodden, realistically counterpoised to defeat and bloodshed. It offered colorful, satisfying rituals that embodied the most profound human strivings but always presented them in mercilessly unsentimental terms. Boxers responded to a violent world by embracing violence, by accepting brutality and returning it with interest, by being as tough and savage as life itself.

In all of these ways bare-knuckle prize fighting was woven into the texture of working-class culture during the antebellum era. A plethora of urban street institutions supported the ring, as boxing helped crystallize the ethos of laboring men. Pugilism gave controlled expression to the schisms of working-class life, not in order to drain away violent passions but to make those divisions comprehensible and thereby transform chaos into meaning. Divided by neighborhood, ethnic, and workplace tensions, large segments of the lower classes were nonetheless united in opposition to key Victorian values, values on which an onerous new social system was built. Every bout inverted bourgeois and evangelical assumptions about such fundamental social phenomena as money, gender, and violence. More, the prize ring conveyed its own alternative outlook. Pugilism was an autonomous expressive form that symbolically opposed the drift of modern society. In crucial ways, then, boxing during the age of heroes captured the values, the ethos, the distinct culture of countless working men who felt dispossessed amidst the Victorian era's heady optimism.

... By late in the century countless American men of good families were personally familiar with boxing. The small numbers who had attended sparring classes given by the old professors of pugilism before the Civil War now became a multitude. Young men from the wealthiest backgrounds, such as Theodore Roosevelt at Harvard and William C. Whitney at Yale, fought with gloves in college during the 1870s. By the 1880s cabinet secretaries such as James G. Blaine and Zackary Chandler, former governor Flower and ex-senator Conklin of New York, all took sparring lessons. Exclusive athletic clubs hired boxing coaches, YMCAs offered instruction, and self-defense manuals proliferated. The New York Athletic Club even sponsored the first national amateur boxing championship, in 1878. *Frank Leslie's Magazine* acknowledged pugilism's recent popularity when it bewailed the worship of brute force which filled New York City sparring rooms and urged that "prize-fighters be once more regarded as outlaws and not as public entertainers."

Quite the opposite occurred, for amateur sparring's newfound popularity helped redeem professional ring fighting. The New York Athletic Club, for example, retained middleweight champion Mike Donovan to teach "gentlemen eminent in science, literature, art, social and commercial life." Unlike his professional ancestor, William Fuller, Donovan did not hesitate to assist at and arrange regular prize battles, apparently offending none of his elite clientele. Other cities followed New York's lead. The gentlemen of San Francisco's Olympic Club were so pleased with their sparring master, prize fighter James J. Corbett, that they paid him $2,500 per year. Boston elites also learned the fistic arts in their own private institutions. The Cribb Club, for example, where ring fighter Jake Kilrain gave lessons, had over one hundred enrollees by the mid-eighties, among them businessmen, lawyers, physicians, and journalists. Nomination by two members and the approval of an election committee were required for admission. Similarly, the Commercial Athletic Club charged an initiation fee and monthly dues to discourage all "unruly and turbulent spirits."

Even an occasional Christian voice now spoke up for the prize ring. Reverend Brobst of Chicago's Westminster Presbyterian Church believed the Sullivan Kilrain fight in 1889 contained important lessons for the faithful. Before going into training, the principals were "drinkers, sensual, beastly" men. But once articles had been signed, Brobst noted, the opponents resisted all temptation: "Talk about taking up your cross, Christians! You ought to be ashamed of yourselves. Take a lesson in hardship and denial from these pugilists!" The ends of prize fighting might be corrupt, but the means were divine, for hard training brought boxers to physical and mental perfection. Here was an important change from earlier decades. Although a few writers had praised the abstemiousness of boxers in training, no minister in the era of Heenan, Hyer, and Morrissey would have dared refer to prize fighters as paragons of Christian virtue. But Brobst argued that men in the ring offered models of will power, fortitude, and endurance to the faithful. Boxing was a metaphor for a grim world of stern competition, where toughness was both a religious and a secular duty. "Take a lesson," Brobst admonished his congregation, and no doubt many did, seeking spiritual enlightenment at the next convenient bout.

In one form or another, then, boxing became familiar to men of solid social standing. Courage and confidence, self-command and graceful bearing, vigor and decisiveness, pugilism fostered all of these traits. The animal world, psychologist G. Stanley Hall declared, was filled with the struggle for survival. Man's aggressive "instinct" sometimes embroiled him in senseless combat, yet anger was a valuable trait and real men rejoiced in noble strife. Hall—who championed the concept of a distinct adolescent stage of life, with its own psychology—believed that boys must learn to fight, lest they grow up to be unmanly and craven milksops. Boxing lessons were the perfect means to channel aggression, tempering adolescent violence yet engendering courage, force of will, and self-assertion.

Soon respectable journals advocated pugilism. Daniel L. Dawson, writing in *Lippincott's Monthly,* argued that sparring was among the very best forms of exercise, encouraging not only muscular development but also courage, temperance, and quickness of thought. *Outing,* which claimed to be *the* gentleman's magazine of sport, travel, and outdoor life, became a repository of information for genteel boxers. Essays not only discussed leverage, mechanics, and physiology; they upheld the moral worth of pugilism. Amateur bouts, A. Austin declared in "The Theory and Practice of Boxing," were tests of character, forcing men to confront their moral strengths and weaknesses.

Some writers now called for the reform of prize fighting. Charles E. Clay, who wrote about yachting and exotic travel for *Outing,* did a series of articles based on his personal boxing experiences. The gentlemanly fighter, like Eakins's men in the ring, was beautiful: "His shoulders are broad, but graceful and sloping, and from them the arms, with full and rounded biceps, fall so easily and naturally to their proper position at the sides! ... The chest expansive, and well filled out, shows plenty of room for the lungs to work. The deltoid and shoulder muscles are all thoroughly developed, and go to form a strong and shapely back." But the benefits were more than merely physical, for boxing taught pluck and endurance. Those who entered the ring developed the resourcefulness, the confidence, and the command to overcome life's daily obstacles and become leaders among men. However, Clay added, only the rules of glove fighting made boxing so excellent for moral and physical training; the old bare-knuckle ways must go.

Duffield Osborn concurred. His "Defense of Pugilism," published in the *North American Review* in 1888, argued that as civilization grew over refined, it degenerated into "mere womanishness." The rigorous self-denial of boxers in training, their unflinching courage in the face of pain and fatigue, helped counter these pernicious tendencies. Those who valued "high manly qualities" ought therefore to array themselves against the "mawkish sentimentality" that threatened to transform Americans into "a race of eminently respectable female saints." Boxing, Osborn concluded, must be reformed and supported.

John Boyle O'Reilly, poet, editor of the *Boston Pilot,* and an acknowledged leader of the Irish-American middle class, became the ring's most articulate champion. Prize fighting was too valuable to be sullied by gangsters and criminals. "Let it stand alone," O'Reilly argued, "an athletic practice, on the same footing as boating or football." Sparring was the perfect recreation for businessmen whose nerves were frayed by competition and energies depleted by the frenetic pace of life. No other sport exercised the trunk, limbs, eyes, and mind so well. The intensity of sparring made it ideal training for the young: "The boxer in action has not a loose muscle or a sleepy brain cell. His mind is quicker and more watchful than a chess player's. He has to gather his impulses and hurl them, straight and purposeful, with every moment and motion." Watching honest professionals fight with gloves also taught valuable lessons in manly fortitude and confidence. "Where else in one compressed hour," O'Reilly asked, "can be witnessed the supreme test and tension of such precious living qualities as courage, temper, endurance, bodily strength, clear-mindedness in excited action, and above all, that heroic spirit that puts aside the cloak of defeat though it fall anew a hundred and a thousand times, and in the end, reaches out and grasps the silver mantle of success?" Ideal training for all citizens, boxing must be rescued from gamblers and thugs and restored to gentlemanly luster.

Pugilism, then, was filled with meaning for turn-of-the-century America. Bloodletting, merciless competition, and stern self-testing in the ring addressed the newly perceived need of middle- and upper-class men for more active life. Alive in every nerve, the boxer was in complete control of his body, negating by example the pervasive fears of over civilization, nervous breakdowns, and neurasthenia. The ring countered effeminizing tendencies, preparing men for the life of strife.

The physical and mental acuteness of two fighters in combat offered an intriguing symbol for a society extolling "manly competition" in the market place and a culture beginning to substitute a cult of personal experience for tight self-control. Pugilists were models of poise and courage for an old upper-class that felt threatened from above by new industrial wealth and below by immigrant hordes and labor radicals. Prize fighting upheld fantasies of untrammeled masculinity for a new white-collar class locked into distinctly unvirile, corporate jobs. As a spectator sport, boxing symbolically reconciled contradictory cultural imperatives. Pugilists were models of aggressiveness but also of self-discipline and self-control. Moreover, the fans, by passively imbibing images of ultramasculine action, by sitting back and watching others bleed, could have it both ways, extolling prowess while filling the role of consumer.

And here was the problem. Upper- and middle-class men were enthralled by the drama, the violence, the pageantry of the ring, but few were willing to accept prize fighting because of its associations with gangs, criminality, and the urban underworld. Change was needed, to purge the sport of its rowdy, even criminal elements yet retain the old vibrancy. For such men as Roosevelt and O'Reilly, the solution was to assimilate professional boxing to amateur rules....

Sport and Image Among African American College Women in the 1920s and 1930s

RITA LIBERTI

Recently, the efforts of a handful of sport history scholars have added significantly to our knowledge and understanding of the collegiate athletic experiences of African American women....These studies suggest that among elite black colleges and universities, the tendency throughout the 1920s and 1930s was to abandon their earlier commitment to women's intercollegiate basketball. School leaders at Howard, Fisk, Morgan, and Hampton believed that women's participation in competitive intercollegiate basketball ran counter to a middle-class feminine ideal grounded in refinement and respectability. Thus, support once given to intercollegiate basketball was channeled to less competitive structures, such as intramurals and play-days, emphasizing activities deemed more suitable for female involvement including badminton, archery and table tennis.

While some African American schools actively sought to dismantle their female basketball programs through the late 1920s and early 1930s, others were just beginning to invest institutional resources. Reflecting on this increased involvement, in 1927, the *Chicago Defender* concluded that "women [*sic*] athletics are booming among dixie institutions." Many public and private black colleges and universities across the South participated in women's basketball competition in some fashion.... In North Carolina, several private black institutions initiated women's intercollegiate basketball teams in the 1920s including Shaw University, Livingstone College, Barber-Scotia College, Immanuel Lutheran College, and Bennett College in Greensboro. The wide range of institutional support of women's basketball by black colleges and universities reflects the broad spectrum of responses and attitudes concerning female participation in sport during the 1920s–1940s.

Bennett is a fascinating exception to the pattern of elite black colleges discontinuing basketball for women during the 1930s and, as a result, provides a unique opportunity to examine African American women's sport history.

From Rita Liberti, ""We Were Ladies, We Just Played Basketball Like Boys": African American Womanhood and Competitive Basketball at Bennett College, 1928–1942," *Journal of Sport History* 26:3 (Fall 1999): 567–84. Reprinted with permission.

I intend to explore the tension between a middle-class ideology, which partially supported traditional conceptualizations of gender relations, and the support Bennett gave competitive female athletic participation in basketball. Although disagreement existed within the black community concerning the propriety of female involvement in competitive basketball, Bennett College enthusiastically supported a team, becoming one of the most successful basketball programs in the nation by the mid 1930s. However, by the early years of the 1940s Bennett discontinued intercollegiate basketball, and instead focused energy and resources on intramural and play-day events.... [T]his transition not only reflected a middle-class ideology which precluded women's participation in rigorous athletic activity, but also illustrated the multiple—and often contradictory and shifting—roles of black middle-class women during this period.

Black women who enrolled as students and athletes in colleges and universities during this period both challenged and yielded to the boundaries of class, race, and gender arrangements in their community. This on-going process of negotiation exposes a history shaped by multiple and intersecting identities. The juxtaposition of black women's collegiate athletic experiences with those of black men and white women, for example, provides further evidence of the varied historical experiences which emerge among particular groups.... As [Patrick] Miller notes, black male collegiate athletic achievement during the interwar years was promoted as another avenue for blacks to demonstrate their worthiness of inclusion into the dominant culture. Although women's collegiate athletic experiences were generally viewed as acceptable by the black community, their activities in sport were not put forth with the same intensity and enthusiasm. Occasional ambivalent reactions to female athleticism by members of the black community reflected adherence by some to more restrictive notions of gender and the unease surrounding women's involvement in rigorous sport. However, opposition to female participation in athletics was not universal in the black community, in part because the life experiences of women necessitated and exposed a wider range of attitudes.

The view of female physicality in the black community, which did not necessarily preclude being a woman and a participant in athletic competition, translated into different participation patterns for black and white women enrolled in colleges in the South. Although dissimilar in the level of involvement in competitive intercollegiate athletic activities that their respective communities deemed suitable, white and black women who enrolled as students in colleges shared a common bond in their efforts to, at times, challenge existing gender ideologies. Pamela Dean's study of the athletic activities of white women at Sophia Newcomb College and North Carolina Normal and Industrial College illustrates the diversity of women's experiences generated from competing ideals of womanhood.

As Dean argues, whether at Newcomb College or at the Normal College, white women constructed athletic activities within the confines and parameters of wider cultural misgivings concerning female participation in physical games. In much the same way, the basketball history at Bennett College reflects the same negotiation of prescriptive class and gender ideologies.

The Methodist Episcopal Church founded Bennett College in 1873 as a coeducational institution for African Americans. The College's initial mission was to train men for the ministry and women as teachers to help meet the enormous need to educate newly freed blacks. In 1926 the Woman's Home Missionary Society of the Methodist Episcopal Church decided to refocus the direction of the school from a coeducational to a women's college, with the emphasis on teacher training remaining in the forefront.... From its inception, Bennett College served as an important venue allowing black women to be active participants in the struggle for racial equality and justice.

Under the leadership of college president Dr. David Jones, the enrollment of the newly re-organized Bennett quickly rose from just 10 women in 1926 to 138 by 1930. The growth of basketball at Bennett seemed to parallel the general development of the college, with intercollegiate athletic contests beginning during the 1928–29 academic year. In addition to giving early support to intercollegiate basketball, Bennett also was committed to the general health and physical well-being of all of its students, requiring them to take two years of physical education....

The support that college officials at Bennett provided to its basketball program and other extra-curricular activities reflected the broader goals of the college—to "provide its students with opportunities for the development of self-expression, leadership, and skill along individual lines of interest." Bennett students from the 1930s recall the encouragement President Jones and other college faculty gave to the basketball program. Ruth Glover, star Bennett forward from 1934 to 1937, remembers that Jones was in attendance at all home games and "was right there on the sidelines rooting!" Teammate Almaleta Moore adds that for away contests Jones offered his vehicle and driver to transport the basketball squad.... Bennett student Frances Jones, daughter of President Jones, explains that basketball served as the centerpiece for campus activity, in part because African Americans had such limited access to other forms of recreation and leisure activities in the segregated South. In addition, ... "we all loved our basketball" and ... "we beat everybody...."

[P]resident David Jones was well aware of the obstacles that black women encountered, and he worked to create an environment at the college to prepare students to enter the world and be full participants in it. According to Jones, the "role of Negro women in the past has been a heroic one as mother, teacher, and civic leader. The responsibilities of the educated Negro woman of the future will be no less burdensome or challenging." Understanding the significance of sexism and the implications that structure had upon higher education for women, Jones stated:

> The struggle of women to achieve status in the American economy has been a long and sometimes discouraging and baffling effort. The idea that the woman's place is in the home is so deep-rooted, and the resistance of men to female competition so keen that the achievements of women in politics, in economics, in science have been won oft-times only because of superior qualifications and because of compensatory effort on the part of the so-called weaker sex.

Under Jones's leadership, the educational mission of Bennett was to train women on a number of different levels and in a wide range of settings to bring about the most effective positive change for the entire race.... Emphasis on academic rigor, civil responsibility, and homemaking were the elements of a Bennett College education.... The components of this strategy were not meant as competing ideals, but ... as the best means to effect social change.

Bennett sought to uphold middle-class standards of refinement and respectability among its students in part to counter lingering stereotypes of African Americans as immoral and uncivilized. Although efforts to "uplift" the entire race rested upon middle and upper class African Americans, as "keepers of social standards ... and guardians of spiritual values" black college women in particular were considered conveyers of character and culture. Historian Stephanie Shaw notes many educated blacks believed that upstanding behavior by black college women reflected positively not only on the individual woman but also on the entire black community. College personnel carefully molded and monitored students' behavior, deeming actions seen as unbecoming for a "lady" inappropriate and discouraging them. [B]eing a lady meant, for one thing, dressing the part, with a clear understanding that the dress code had much more serious implications than fashion. [Ruth] Glover explains: "Oh, you didn't go shoppin' or uptown ... without your hat and gloves...." Moreover, white assaults on the black community were often centered on the notion that African American women contributed to the moral degradation with unkempt and uncivilized homes. As a result, homemaking became a core element in the educational process at many black colleges and universities, including Bennett College.... Bennett required each student to satisfactorily complete a course entitled "The Art of Right Living" which, among other goals, aimed to "help students find and solve their own problems in relation to personal hygiene, food and nutrition, clothing, family and community relationships...."

Not only did their academic preparation equip Bennett women with the skills to enhance the lives of others in the black community, but basketball also presented another way in which these women could give something back ... After graduating ... all of the basketball players of the 1930s that I interviewed entered careers as teachers and as basketball coaches....

With an educational philosophy similar to that of many black colleges and universities...., Bennett College consistently emphasized the notion of the relationship between college educated blacks and the community.... [A]dministrators and faculty strove to ensure that the school was "far from being an ivory tower, ..." but rather supported student initiative to take academic learning beyond the classroom to assist in the development of racial pride and justice. Historian Glenda Gilmore argues that black women ... graduates ... took with them "more than just a finite body of knowledge or set of skills"; rather they were "armed with a full quiver of intellectual weapons to aim at ... discrimination."

The 1937–38 protest and boycott of the downtown movie theatres in Greensboro, led by Bennett first year student Frances Jones, reflected an educational structure and philosophy which instilled civic duty and responsibility. When students learned that white theatre owners in North and South Carolina refused to show films in which "Negro and white actors appear[ed] on an equal social basis" as opposed to stereotyped depictions of blacks, they organized a campaign by members of the black community to stop their support of the movie establishments. After months of picketing their efforts were successful, leading the *Carolina Times* to conclude that "the step taken by the students in the two Negro schools in Greensboro shows more courage on the part of Negro youth than we have any record of anywhere else in the south."... Frances Jones recalls that the success of the boycott was significant because it symbolized ... that segregation was no longer considered an impenetrable, indestructible "solid wall...." She remembers that the continued support that President Jones gave his students throughout the protest exemplified that he demanded excellence in all of his students and encouraged their participation in various activities that fostered pride and self-respect.

Interestingly, while Bennett officials created an environment that supported acts of civil disobedience in protest of racial injustice, they continually demanded that students exhibit behavior that maintained a level of dignity. In an effort to instill ideals such as good manners, proper conduct, and self-control, college officials at Bennett and other black schools enforced strict rules and rigid codes of behavior for all students, especially women.... Bennett women were rarely given the opportunity to leave campus unless on officially sanctioned business and, in such a case, a chaperone accompanied them. Participation in basketball provided student-athletes with a degree of autonomy greater than their peers. Travel to away basketball contests presented such a rare and special occasion ... it led some of the Bennett players to resist and ultimately bend the rules [such as] "sneaking the team mascot out of the dormitory" so that, she too, could travel with the team. Practice sessions were also considered an opportunity to escape the regulations the general student body had to follow. Basketball practice for Bennett ... lasted from 9 to 11 PM. As the other students returned to the dormitory from the library, athletes made their way to the gym....

Bennett faculty and administrative staff members may have extended the higher level of personal freedom to basketball players because they were committed to the notion that physical development on the basketball court or in a physical education class reinforced their efforts to impart conduct becoming a "lady." [C]ollege literature promoted the physical education program by asserting that the activities "involve total body control as they take place under conditions requiring physical exertion, intellectual accuracy and emotional control simultaneously." Having the chance to travel ... was sometimes used by players as a way to mock a segregated South, turning racism on its head if only for a brief moment. Moore remembers that "we would be riding along the highway and you'd meet some white fellas thumbing ... and we'd hang our heads out the window and say, Jim Crow car!"

The moral standards Bennett women were trained to practice and possess off the basketball court occasionally contrasted with opponents' ideas concerning respectable actions and appropriate behavior. Such was the case when Bennett, after a very successful 1934 season, competed in a three-game series against the *Philadelphia Tribune* women's team. The contests even attracted the white press, which ordinarily gave little attention to events in the black community.

[O]ver one thousand spectators attended the initial game ... , reflecting the enormous interest in women's basketball in the community. The *Greensboro Daily News* prefaced the upcoming series: "After having met and defeated in rapid succession all of the college teams that would accept to play, the undefeated Bennett College team, seeking larger worlds to conquer, will risk its reputation against Otto Briggs' *Tribune* female team ... led by the indomitable, internally famed and stellar performer, Ora Washington, national women's singles champ in tennis, comes with an enviable reputation."

The *Tribune* team was housed on the Bennett College campus ... Lucile Townsend remembers their arrival, particularly her first impression of Ora Washington: "She looked like the worst ruffian you ever wanted to see. She looked like she'd been out pickin' cotton all day, shavin' hogs, and everything else." Washington's rugged appearance stood in opposition to the feminine ideals that ... black college educated women were trained to regard as "earmarks of a lady" which included "always being well-groomed, appropriately dressed, scrupulously clean in body and attire with hair carefully arranged."

Townsend recalls that the first game of the series was played in downtown Greensboro at the Sports arena, and "ordinarily colored didn't play there ... it was the largest place we had ever played and I was scared."... The game itself was also a departure for the Bennett team from encounters with high school and college opponents. Although Townsend had played in a number of ... physical contests, none compared to the match-up.... She recalls, "I told the referee she's [Ora] hittin' me in the stomach every time I jump ... he caught her when she hit me one time ... I doubled over and went down."

The series between Bennett College and the *Philadelphia Tribune* team not only illustrates the popularity of women's basketball but also highlights the tensions, ambiguities, and divisions present in the black community along class and gender lines during this period. Like other black college women, Bennett students were taught to always present themselves in a refined and dignified manner. Reflecting on the actions by Ora Washington and the *Tribune* team, both on and off the basketball court, Lucille Townsend drew a clear line of distinction between herself and the members of the Philadelphia squad...." [T]hey were a different class of people."

Although Bennett lost the three games against the *Philadelphia Tribune* team, the 1934 and 1935 seasons were extremely successful for the Bennett cagers, with twenty-four victories and no defeats versus college, high school, and community teams. Ruth Glover explains Bennett College's basketball dominance through the mid-1930s: "We used to practice against a group of high school boys ... They would come down and teach us the tricks of the trade ..."

[I]nteraction between the sexes was viewed by some within the black community as unladylike and thus discouraged. In this instance, however, whatever conflict, if any, was present in the minds of Bennett personnel was surpassed by the desire to elevate the level of play of the women's basketball program by practicing against local high school boys.

By the 1934 *Tribune* series, basketball was an extremely popular activity at Bennett, despite the continuing and growing ambivalence within the black community concerning the suitability of the competitive game for girls and women. The National Association of College Women (NACW) ... spoke out strongly against intercollegiate competition for black women.... Under the auspices of the NACW, a conference composed of Deans and Advisors to women in black colleges and universities was held at Howard University in 1929.... The position of intercollegiate athletics for women was the central focus of one of four issues ... it tackled.... The *NACW Journal* summarized the position of the women in attendance: Inter-collegiate athletics should not be encouraged with all their undesirable physiological and sociological features. Interclass and intraclass games serve every good purpose of the inter-collegiate games, and avoid all the harmful effects.

Similarly, Maryrose Reeves Allen, Director of the Physical Education program for women at Howard University ... , deemed activities such as dance, light games, archery, and badminton appropriate physical activities.... In 1938 she wrote that, "the heavier sports ... have no place in a woman's life: they rob her of her feminine charms and often of her good health."

The tension between femininity and athleticism is best illustrated in the writings of Ivora (Ike) King, sport columnist for the *Baltimore Afro-American,* who argued that "the girl who is too athletic is on the wrong track to becoming a wife. Men want feminine women, not creatures who are half like themselves and the other half resembling something else.... Men want women all women.... Heterosexual appeal rested firmly on a woman's ability to remain within the confines of particular gender roles." For King, in denying her femininity the athletic woman threatened to corrupt her gendered and sexual identities and in doing so forfeited her existence as a real woman.

To Bennett women, however, a feminine ideal of black womanhood and participation in competitive athletics remained negotiable.... [According to] Glover, this did not mean that the Bennett women felt they compromised their respectability or womanliness by playing basketball: "We were ladies too, we just played basketball like boys." [B]eing athletic *and* female was not a contradiction for Bennett women..... For these women, ... the notion that being female and athletic was dichotomous, remained a falsehood....

Thus, while some within the black community opposed all basketball competition for girls and women, others encouraged the sport but sought to place limitations on the style of play, preferring girls' rules. Throughout the 1920s and 1930s the debate ... over the suitability of five- or six-player basketball competition for girls and women was played out on several occasions in the black press. Proponents of games played under girls' rules argued that five-player basketball was too rough for women and that "girls always look inadequate and butter-fingered under boy's [*sic*] rules." J.H.N. Waring, Jr., principal and girls' basketball coach at Downington Industrial and Agricultural School in Pennsylvania, ... argued that the five-player game was too strenuous and did not bring out "the finer qualities in girls." Furthermore, ... five-player rules did not draw spectators because the limited physical capabilities of girls and women resulted in slow and unexciting play. He insisted too, that games were "disgusting to athletic fans who do not enjoy seeing young school girls pulling and tugging and roughing each other like so many alley cats." Waring … feared for the physical well-being of the athletes who competed, but also because such participation disturbed his own sensibilities concerning appropriate behavior for girls and women.

[On the other hand], a former basketball player and current coach argued in … the *Baltimore Afro-American* in 1930 that, "Girls of today are red-blooded, virile young creatures, and are no longer content to conform to the masculine ideal of feminine inferiority and frailty. The clinging vine has given way to the freely moving, sensibly clad young Amazon of today. Such fineness of physique cannot be maintained or secured through the inadequacies of girls' rules in basketball." These oppositional views reflected the tensions and negotiations of the boundaries of black womanhood that were ongoing during the 1920s and 1930s.

Despite the wide range of opinions …, girls' rules began to influence college play in North Carolina.… [and by] 1936 … [they] began to compete using six player rules. The move … "hampered the style of quite a number of the old varsity members" on Bennett's team, but they still claimed a share of the state title with Shaw University, making it their fourth championship of the decade. Following an undefeated 1937 season, … the *Chicago Defender* dubbed Bennett "the nation's best female cage team"; but this would be the last state championship that Bennett won.

Not only were basketball rules in a state of transition at Bennett College, … but direction and control of the sport was also in flux. Throughout the 1920s and 1930s black physical educators and others interested in female participation in sport debated whether men should coach women's athletics, and some supported the notion that women should organize and direct female involvement in sport and physical activity. Although female physical educators were on staff from the inception of Bennett, … male coaches directed the basketball team for many … years.… By the late 1930s this pattern of male coaching dominance began to change somewhat. In 1938 female physical education instructor Mildred Ann Burris became only the second female coach at Bennett.…

Though Bennett continued to support intercollegiate basketball through the 1941 season, by the late 1930s its athletic interests also appeared headed in another direction. In 1939 the college became the first of four black North Carolina schools to join the Women's Sports Day Association (WSDA) … founded in 1938 by several female physical educators.… The goals … clearly promoted the personal philosophy of Allen, endorsing a structure that was non-competitive and activities that "develop in women the qualities of beauty of movement, poise, femininity by affording each individual who participates an opportunity to play in an atmosphere of dignity, courtesy, and refinement." The WSDA promoted a class-bound ideal of womanhood grounded in female frailty, and its influence was reflected in the activities pursued on the Bennett campus. In November of 1940 Bennett served as "hostess" to the … other colleges in the Association, … at the first of two Sports Days. Each school sent twenty-five women who were then divided among the other participants into teams so that "group sportsmanship among the colleges [was] emphasized." This was a significant shift for Bennett from intercollegiate basketball, which emphasized competition, travel, and winning.… By 1942 the shift was complete and Bennett withdrew its support of women's intercollegiate basketball.

... [G]iven the promotion of play-days by the WSDA and the continued anti-competition rhetoric put forth by the NACW, it is highly likely that intercollegiate basketball for women at black colleges in North Carolina ... came under increasingly heavy scrutiny.... On the state level, Bennett was not alone in its increased focus on play-days versus intercollegiate basketball competition for women ... through the 1940s.

This transition to less-competitive activities during the early 1940s [at] Bennett College signaled the end to a brief, yet illuminating, period in the history of African American women's sport. The tensions surrounding female athleticism on the Bennett campus and in the black community at large reflected diverse responses and attitudes concerning women's involvement in sports ... and provides scholars with insights into the ways in which class informs race and gender identity.

From the late 1920s through the 1930s, Bennett's administration, faculty, and student-athletes balanced and negotiated various understandings of class, race, and gender arrangements as they supported competitive women's basketball.

... Bennett personnel articulated a position which illustrated the societal tensions that worked to forge their identity as a black women's college. In a presentation to the NACW in 1937, Bennett faculty member Merze Tate argued that "The presidents of women's colleges are not endeavoring to turn out an army of masculine counterparts...." Tate's interest in sculpting public perception of Bennett as an institution for women that did not "masculinize" women may have been in response to fears among some in the wider African American community that college educated black women disrupted gender norms and might make unsuitable marriage companions to men. Aware of societal gender restrictions, Bennett College officials balanced those tensions while challenging assumptions in educating black women....

The particular conceptualization of womanhood that some middle-class blacks constructed, including those at Bennett, simultaneously endorsed and rejected aspects of middle-class femininity. The complexity of that continual process of cultural construction is symbolized in women's basketball, which evolved and changed over the course of a decade and a half, much like the fluid notion of what it meant to be black, female, and middle-class ... These multiple identities at times merged and blended, and in other instances were contradictory forces, exposing a history which cannot be categorized as static or fixed, but rather dynamic and shifting. Bennett College basketball from the late 1920s to the early 1940s illustrates the tensions between individual agents creating their own histories amid societal expectations and constraints.

FURTHER READING

Bederman, Gail. *Manliness & Civilization: A Cultural History of Gender and Race in the United States, 1880–1917* (1995).

Chapman, David L. *Sandow the Magnificent: Eugene Sandow and the Beginnings of Bodybuilding* (1994).

Ernst, Joseph. *Weakness Is a Crime: The Life of Bernarr McFadden* (1991).

Gorn, Elliott. *The Manly Art: Bare-Knuckle Prize Fighting in America* (1986).

Green, Harvey. *Fit for America; Health, Sport, Fitness and American Society* (1986).

Isenberg, Michael. *John L. Sullivan and His America* (1988).

Mangan, J. A., and Roberta Park, eds. *From "Fair Sex" to Feminism: Sport and the Socialization of Women in the Industrial and Post-Industrial Eras* (1987).

Marks, Patricia. *Bicycles, Bangs, and Bloomers: The New Woman in the Popular Press* (1990).

Melnick, Ralph. *Senda Berenson: The Unlikely Founder of Women's Basketball* (2007).

Mrozek, Donald. *Sport and American Mentality, 1880–1910* (1983).

Reiger, John F. *American Sportsmen and the Origins of Conservation* (1975).

Roberts, Gerald F. "The Strenuous Life: The Cult of Manliness in the Era of Theodore Roosevelt," Ph.D. diss., Michigan State University (1970).

Shattuck, Debra S. "Bats, Balls and Books: Baseball and Higher Education for Women at Three Eastern Women's Colleges, 1866–1900," *Journal of Sport History* 19 (Summer 1992), 91–109.

Shattuck, Debra S. "Women's Baseball in the 1860s: Reestablishing a Historical Memory," *NINE: A Journal of Baseball History and Culture* 19 (Spring 2011), 1–26.

Smith, Ronald A. "The Rise of Basketball for Women in Colleges," *Canadian Journal of History of Sport and Physical Education* 1 (1970), 1–21.

Verbrugge, Martha. *Able Bodied Womanhood: Personal Health and Social Change in Nineteenth-Century Boston* (1988).

Verbrugge, Martha. *Active Bodies: A History of Women's Physical Education in Twentieth-Century America* (2012).

Vertinsky, Patricia. *The Eternally Wounded Woman: Women, Doctors, and Exercise in the Late Nineteenth Century* (1990).

Warner, Patricia Campbell. *When the Girls Came Out to Play: The Birth of American Sportswear* (2006).

Whorton, James. *Crusaders for Fitness: The History of American Health Reformers* (1982).

Zheutlin, Peter. *Annie Londonderry's Extraordinary Ride: Around the World on Two Wheels* (2007).

CHAPTER 10

Race and Ethnicity in American Sport, 1900–1940

Ethnic and racial factors played an enormous role in the development of sport. The original immigrants who came from Western Europe between 1840 and 1880 brought a vital athletic tradition that they sought to maintain in the United States. How did their experience compare to that of the millions of new immigrants from Eastern and Southern Europe who arrived in the period 1882–1914 from premodern cultures where sport was largely unknown?

Though these newcomers found American sports to be a waste of time, their American-bred children became very interested in sports. Were the athletic experiences of second-generation Jews, Italians, and Poles similar to those of second-generation Germans and Irish? Second-generation Americans idolized leading athletic heroes, followed their favorite teams in the penny newspapers, and played sports themselves. However, their options were limited by poverty and by parental disapproval. These young men looked to sport as a means to gain respect, prove they were not greenhorns, and even make money. They were most successful in those sports that fit in with their environment, like boxing and basketball. How did their sporting experiences compare to those of American-born people of color? Native Americans produced several prominent major-league ballplayers, and the Carlisle Indian School fielded powerful football teams that competed with distinction against the top collegiate elevens. African Americans also participated in high level sports, but they encountered more discrimination than any other group. In the late nineteenth century, many leading jockeys were African Americans, and there were excellent professional African American baseball players and prize-fighters. However, prejudice forced them out of organized baseball and most other sports by the turn of the century. African Americans were only allowed to remain in the low-status sport of boxing, and following Jack Johnson's tenure (1908–1915) as heavyweight champion, none received an opportunity to fight for that prestigious title until Joe Louis in 1937.

DOCUMENTS

The documents in this section emphasize how the host society was prejudiced against ethnic and racial groups, and they also point out the importance of sports in promoting community pride. Documents 1 and 2 examine the Native American athletic experience. In one, Captain Richard Henry Pratt, founder of Carlisle, directed his players to be good sportsmen because of the positive impact it would have upon prevailing racial prejudice of white Americans toward the Native American. Then in the next document, *Outing* magazine analyzes the significance of track and field star Jim Thorpe's confession to having been a professional athlete. Thorpe had played in organized baseball prior to the 1912 Olympics, where he won both the decathlon and the pentathlon, gaining recognition as the world's greatest athlete. Thorpe first gained national renown as an All-American football player at Carlisle in 1911 and 1912. He later played both major league baseball and professional football. The third item is a *St. Louis Post-Dispatch* article (reprinted in the black *New York Age*) that tried to rationalize in very derogatory terms of the apparent superiority of African American ballplayers. In Document 4, African American catcher Frazier "Slow" Robinson recounts his experience working with pitcher Satchel Paige, the greatest star of the Negro Leagues. New York Yankees center fielder Joe DiMaggio rated Paige as the best pitcher he ever faced, and Cleveland Indians pitching star Bob Feller considered the best pitcher he ever saw. Paige started playing in 1926 and for two decades dominated black baseball as well as confounding major leaguers he challenged in barnstorming tours. Satchel joined the Cleveland Indians of the American League in 1948, at the age of forty-two, one year after Jackie Robinson integrated Major League Baseball (MLB), the oldest rookie ever. In 1971, he was the first Negro Leaguer player selected for the Baseball Hall of Fame. In 1999, Paige was nineteenth on *Sporting News*' list of the 100 Greatest Baseball Players.

Document 5 is drawn from the report of the Chicago Commission on Race Relations that analyzed the causes of the 1919 Chicago Race Riot that was precipitated by the death of Eugene Williams, a black teenager, killed by drowning after he was hit by a brick tossed by whites at a Lake Michigan beach. The authors produced extensive data about the racism and prejudice that African American youths encountered at public sporting facilities before and after the riot that was precipitated by the death of a black teenager. Document 6 is drawn from the research of Frederic Milton Thrasher (1892–1962), an eminent sociologist and a leading member of the Chicago School of Sociology. His dissertation was published in 1927 as *The Gang: A Study of 1,313 Gangs in Chicago* in which he argued that transitional neighborhoods were breeding grounds for gangs. The selection here is based on an ethnographic study that describes how Douglas Park in Chicago served as a buffer zone between Polish and Jewish neighborhoods. There were frequent brawls at this "no-man's land," but the situation did not get out of hand as long as one group dominated. However, if the rival groups were about equal in size, a pitched battle might occur in which rival street gangs and social and basement clubs joined in.

The final document was written by W. Montague Cobb, MD, the first African American Ph.D. in anthropology. His research focused on how the impact of race harmed communities of color. He was an activist scholar, who sought to correct popular misconceptions that were based on racism and prejudice. "Race and Runners" is a well-known monograph that sought to demonstrate that recent African American achievements in sport were not based merely on genetics by employing extensive measurements and physical tests.

1. Richard Henry Pratt Encourages Indian Sportsmanship, c. 1894

First, that you will never, under any circumstances, slug. That you will play fair straight through, and if the other fellows slug you will in no case return it. Can't you see that if you slug people who are looking on will say, "There, that's the Indian of it. Just see them. They are savages and you can't get it out of them." Our white fellows may do a lot of slugging and it causes little or no remark, but you have to make a record for your race. If the other fellows slug and you do not return it, very soon you will be the most famous football team in the country. If you can set an example of that kind for the white race, you will do a work on the highest interests of your people.

2. The *Outlook*'s Dismay with Indian Sportsman Jim Thorpe and the Forfeiture of His Olympic Medals, 1913

When an American Indian, who had won the championship as the best all-round athlete in America, established his right in the Olympic Games at Stockholm last July to be regarded as the greatest amateur athlete in the world, and was so declared by the King of Sweden, there was widespread gratification in America. Now that that great Indian athlete, James Thorpe, has been stripped of his honors because, by his own confession, he had received money for playing baseball, and therefore was not an amateur but a professional and had no right to enter into competition with amateur athletes, the humiliation is not confined to him; it extends to all who value their country's reputation for fairness in sport as in all other matters.

Every such incident lends aid and comfort to those who are constantly looking for proof of their assertions that Americans are constitutionally devoted to the doctrine that nothing should stand in the way of winning. This incident in particular will afford an opportunity to those unfriendly to this country to declare again their opinion that the ideals of the gentleman are beyond the comprehension of

From Richard Henry Pratt, *Battlefield and Classroom: Four Decades with the American Indian, 1867–1914*, ed., Robert M. Utley (New Haven: Yale University Press, 1964), 317.

From "The Amateur," *Outlook* 103 (February 8, 1913): 293–95.

American athletes, and that American sport is thoroughly commercialized. The fact that these aspersions are unjust and ill founded only makes it the more humiliating for such an incident as this to occur....

James Thorpe is a student at the Carlisle Indian School. He is of the Sac and Fox tribe, and, like many other Indians, has sufficient property to afford him support. The Carlisle School is well known for its athletes and its athletic teams. In particular, the Carlisle football team has established a reputation for a peculiar skill and brilliance. Thorpe has been the best-known football player at the School and one of the greatest football players in the country. He is almost as well known as a player of baseball. "In the summer of 1909 and 1910" (this is his own phrase) he played baseball in North Carolina, and for this received money. In the fall of 1911 he was readmitted to the Carlisle Indian School. He took part not only in the sports of the School but also in the athletic meets of the Amateur Athletic Union. Last summer he went with the rest of the American team to Stockholm and competed in the Olympic Games. His achievements there astonished the whole world of athletes. In particular, he took part in two great series of athletic events. One, known as the Pentathlon, is a series of five athletic events; the other, the Decathlon, is a series of ten athletic events. In the first series, out of a possible five firsts he won four; in the Decathlon he registered 8,412 points as against the 7,724 of his nearest competitor, a Swede....

... American public opinion should cordially support the officials of the Amateur Athletic Union, whose action was so prompt and sure in this matter that the repudiation of Thorpe as an amateur was officially made simultaneously with the news of the discovery of his offenses. There was a chance for the representatives of organized amateur sport in America to make clear to the world that their standards of amateur sport were inexorable; and they used that chance to the best advantage. They might have allowed a very legitimate sympathy for this Indian student, and their recognition that he had done only what others had done with impunity, to cloud their judgment and to obscure their sense of duty toward the cause of pure athletics. This they did not do. Like everybody else who thinks about this, they must from the first have seen that there was a large element of individual injustice to Thorpe himself in the consequences that followed his acts as a boy. For a young man to be humiliated before the whole world simply because he played baseball one summer and thoughtlessly accepted money for his playing, as others were doing and as a great many professional players do without any disgrace whatever, seems to be an extraordinarily disproportionate punishment. It might be said that his punishment came from the fact that he concealed his having received money, but the fact that he played for the fun of it and not for the sake of the money may well have led him to believe thoroughly in his own amateur spirit and standing. He was mistaken; but the consequence to him is a very severe penalty for such a mistake.... Humiliating ... as the experience is in one respect, it is emphatically encouraging in another, for it has afforded evidence to the whole world that organized amateur athletics in this country will not countenance disregard of amateur standards.

... In the course of his letter ... acknowledging that he had received money for baseball-playing, Thorpe writes:

> On the same teams I played with were several college men from the North who were earning money by ball-playing during their vacations and who were regarded as amateurs at home. I did not play for the money there was in it, because my property brings me in enough money to live on, but because I liked to play ball. I was not very wise to the ways of the world and did not realize that this was wrong and it would make me a professional in track sports, although I learned from the other players that it would be better for me not to let any one know that I was playing, and for that reason I never told any one at the School about it until to-day.... I never realized until now what a big mistake I made by keeping it a secret about my ball-playing, and I am sorry I did so. I hope I will be partly excused by the fact that I was simply an Indian school-boy and did not know all about such things. In fact, I did not know that I was doing wrong because I was doing what I knew several other college men had done: except that they did not use their own names....

3. Prejudice Against African-American Ballplayers in the St. Louis *Post-Dispatch,* 1911

There is some doubt if baseball, after all, is the great American game. We play it, to be sure, but the colored people play it so much better that the time is apparently coming when it shall be known as the great African game.

The St. Louis Giants, a black baseball team, have easily beaten everything in town but the Browns and the Cardinals, and neither of these latter will play them. The Chicago Giants, all alligator bait, have done the same thing in that city, and there are no end of people up there willing to wager that they can beat either the White Sox or the Cubs.

Your Negro is not a bad athlete. Peter Jackson only missed being heavyweight champion of the world because the holders of that title through the years of his prime would not fight him, and Jack Johnson, more fortunate, bestrides the earth to-day like a black Colossus. The greatest bicycle racer America ever produced was Major Taylor, a Negro. Forced off on the other side of the track by the white conspiracy against him, he rode yards and hundreds of yards further than anyone else in the race, and still usually won it. Subsequently the best riders of Europe sat up on their machines and watched the sunlight flash on his black heels.

But it is in baseball that the descendant of Ham is at his athletic best. Less removed from the anthropoid ape, he gets down on ground balls better, springs higher for liners, has a much stronger and surer grip, and can get in and out of a

From *New York Age*, September 28, 1911.

base on all fours in a way that makes the higher product of evolution look like a bush leaguer.

It requires some courage to predict that colored baseball, like colored pugilism, is to supersede the white brand, but someone has to think ahead and indicate whither we drift, and we therefore wish to go upon record as having said that it will....

4. I Caught Satchel Paige in the 1930s

FRAZIER "SLOW" ROBINSON

... Satchel was about as fast as anyone I ever caught, but it was his control that carried him as far as he went. He had superb control. The way he'd warm up was to hear the top off a book of matches, put it down, and throw the ball over that.... That made the plate look like a mattress when he was out there. He could throw the ball over any part of the plate.

When I first started catching Satchel, he told me, "I don't need a signal. Just catch what I throw.

I couldn't go for that. It's the catcher's responsibility to call the game...."

"I'm not gonna cross you up because I can get *everybody out* with my fastball.... You look for a fastball all the time. Just give me a target and catch it."

The truth was that he didn't have any kind of a curveball. He just threw the ball hard. One day we finally got together on signals.... I'd call him for a fastball, change-up or his hesitation pitch.

Satch was smart out there by outthinking the hitter. He could change his pitch if he saw a batter shift some kind of way. If you were a good low ball hitter, he would pitch to your weakness so much that when he threw the ball in your power, you'd miss it. He knew how to get you out because when he wasn't pitching, he was studying how to break your stride. He'd figure out what he wanted to do with a particular batter, and then he'd set them up. He was very good at changing speeds....

Satchel's most famous pitch, after his fastball, was probably his hesitation pitch ... that ruined the hitter's timing. He would go through his wind-up and stop. Then he would just put his left foot down and throw right from there....

Satchel Paige, besides being the greatest pitcher in our game, was also our greatest attraction.... J.L. Wilkinson, the Monarchs' owner, bought a little two-seater Piper Cub ... and J.L.'s son would fly him around to his games and appearances....

Satchel loved to play to the crowds.... There was always the feeling ... you might see something you'd never seen before.... One time in Spokane ... he called in all three outfielders and moved them to the infield. Then he set the third baseman down on third base, and the first baseman down on first base.

From Frazier "Slow" Robinson with Paul Bauer, *Catching Dreams: My Life in the Negro Baseball Leagues* (Syracuse: Syracuse University Press, 1999), 31–32, 37–38.

Then he struck out the side. He would do things like that just to excite the fans.... He knew that when these fans talked to their friends over in the next town where we'd be scheduled to play, they'd say, "Do you know what that Satchel Paige did?" And when they heard, they'd buy ticket and tell their friends.... Satchel was really made for barnstorming.

5. The Chicago Commission on Race Relations Examines Racial Contacts in Recreation in the Late 1910s

Representatives of each park commission said that they had no rules or regulations of any kind discriminating against Negroes, and that all races were treated in exactly the same way. The only case in which this rule appeared to be violated was in connection with Negro golf players at Jackson Park. Two Negroes participated in the Amateur Golf Tournament at Jackson Park in the summer of 1918 and made good records. The only requirement for entrance into the tournament at that time was residence in the city for one year. In 1919 the requirements were increased, entries being limited to the lowest sixty-four scores, and membership in a "regularly organized golf club" being required. Since Negroes are not accepted in established golf clubs, the Negro golf players met this qualification by organizing a new club, "The Windy City Golf Association." In 1920 the restriction was added that contestants must belong to a regularly organized golf club affiliated with the Western Golf Association. As it was impossible for Negro clubs to secure such affiliation, it is impossible for Negroes to compete in the tournament.

Unofficial discrimination, however, frequently creeps in. According to the representative of the Municipal Bureau, "the person in charge of the park is largely influenced by the attitude of the people outside the park. We had trouble at Beutner Playground because of the tendency on the part of the director, who was a white man, to be influenced by the attitude of the white people in the neighborhood, and either consciously or unconsciously showed by his actions to the colored people that they were not fully accepted." Beutner Playground later became an example of unofficial discrimination in favor of the Negroes, for the Municipal Bureau decided to "turn over the playground particularly to Negroes" and instructed the director "to give them more use of the facilities than the whites." But this was found to be impossible as long as a white director was employed, because he was influenced by the feeling of the whites in the neighborhood who did not want the playground turned over to the Negroes. The desired result was finally obtained by employing a Negro director. "Then the switch suddenly came," said the park representative, "and the playground was turned over to the Negroes almost exclusively."

A similar method was employed with reference to the Twenty-sixth Street Beach, according to the head of the Municipal Bureau, who said: "As the colored population gradually got heavier and more demand came for the use of that beach it gradually developed into a beach that was used almost exclusively by

From Chicago Commission on Race Relations, *The Negro in Chicago: A Study of Race Relations and a Race Riot* (Chicago: University of Chicago Press, 1922), 277, 288–89, 296–97.

Negroes. And we did as we did in the Beutner case: we employed a Negro director when the preponderance was Negro."...

★ ★ ★

Clashes.—Clashes between Negroes and whites at various places of recreation are reported as far back as 1913. These clashes in the main have been initiated by gangs of white boys. In 1913, for example, the secretary of boys' work at the Wabash Avenue Y.M.C.A. (for Negroes) conducted a party of nineteen Negro boys from the Douglas Center Boys' Club to Armour Square. They had no difficulty in entering the park and carrying out their program of athletics. The party then took shower baths in the field house. The Y.M.C.A. secretary had noticed the increasing crowds of white boys near-by but had no misgivings until the party left the park. Then they were assailed with sandbags, tripped, walked over, and some of them badly bruised. They were obliged to take refuge in neighboring saloons and houses in Thirty-third Street west of Shields Avenue. For fully half an hour their way home was blocked, until a detachment of city police, called by the park police, scattered the white gang.

That same year the Y.M.C.A. secretary had found it impossible to proceed east through Thirty-first Street to the lake with groups of Negro boys. When this was tried they inevitably met gangs of white boys, and fights ensued with any missiles procurable. Attempts to overcome this antagonism by continuing to demonstrate that the Negro boys had a right to use these streets were unavailing for the next two years.

In 1915 similar conflicts occurred. That winter Father Bishop, of St. Thomas Episcopal Church, took a group of the Negro Y.M.C.A. boys to Armour Square to play basket-ball. The party, including Father Bishop, was beaten up by white boys, their sweaters were taken from them, and they were otherwise maltreated. The Y.M.C.A. staff then decided not to attempt to use the park or field house during the evenings....

An altercation between white and Negro boys in Washington Park is on record as early as the summer of 1913. These boys were sixteen or seventeen years of age. During the spring and summer of 1919, numerous outbreaks occurred because of the use of the baseball diamonds in Washington Park by Negro players. White gangs from the neighborhood of Fifty-ninth Street and Wentworth Avenue, not far from the park, also came there to play baseball, among them some of "Ragen's Colts." Gang fights frequently followed the games. Park policemen usually succeeded in scattering the combatants. The same season gangs of white boys from sixteen to twenty years of age frequently annoyed Negro couples on the benches on this park. When the Negroes showed fight, minor clashes often resulted.

In Ogden Park, as far back as 1914, there were similar instances of race antipathy, expressed by hoodlums who were more or less organized. A Negro playground director said that if Negro boys attended band concerts in that park, white gangs would wait for them outside the park, and the Negroes were slugged. The white gangs also tried to keep Negro boys from using the shower baths at the park....

★ ★ ★

Though the Negro areas are as well supplied with ordinary playgrounds as the rest of the city, they are noticeably lacking in more complete recreation centers with indoor facilities for the use of older children and adults. Several of these recreation centers ... border on Negro areas but are not used to any great extent by Negroes because the Negroes feel that the whites object to their presence. Though there are three publicly maintained beaches within the main Negro area the Negroes feel free to use only the Twenty-sixth Street Beach, though many of them live as far south as Sixty-sixth Street. Where Negroes do not use nearby facilities to any great extent they have usually either been given to understand, through unofficial discrimination, that they are not desired, or they have been terrorized by gangs of white boys. Few attempts to encourage Negro attendance have been made....

Voluntary racial groupings and serious clashes are found mainly at the places of recreation patronized by older children and adults—the large parks, beaches, and recreation centers. Trouble is usually started by gangs of white boys, organized and unorganized. The members of so-called athletic clubs, whose rooms usually border on the park, are the worst offenders in this respect. If they do not reflect the community feeling they are at least tolerated by it, as nothing is done to suppress them. Some park authorities that have made sincere efforts to have these hoodlums punished are discouraged because they get no co-operation from the courts, and the policeman who takes the boy to court gets a reprimand, while the boy is dismissed....

The most important remedies suggested to the Commission for the betterment of relations between Negroes and whites at the various places of recreation were: (1) additional facilities in Negro areas, particularly recreation centers which can be used by adults; (2) an awakened public opinion which will refuse longer to tolerate the hoodlum and will insist that the courts properly punish such offenders; (3) selection of directors for parks in neighborhoods where there is a critical situation who will have a sympathetic understanding of the problem and will not tolerate actions by park police officers and other subordinate officials tending to discourage Negro attendance; and (4) efforts by such directors to repress and remove any racial antagonism that may arise in the neighborhood about the park.

6. Ethnic Gangs Fight Over Park Turf in Chicago, 1921

FREDERIC M. THRASHER

Warfare on a Jewish-Polish Frontier

In the summer of 1921 it was rumored that a few Jewish boys had been assaulted when passing through the Polish community to the southeast. Thereupon a gang of young Jews (considered "sluggers" in the neighborhood) assembled and, led by "Nails" [Morton], made for the Polish district to seek apologies. They went

---

From Frederic M. Thrasher, *The Gang: A Study of 1,313 Gangs in Chicago* (Chicago: University of Chicago Press, 1927), 196–97.

to the street corners indicated by the boys who had been attacked and started a free-for-all fight. After a sufficient amount of physical punishment had been administered, they withdrew.

During the period that followed, clashes were frequent. One Saturday a group of Jewish boys, who were playing baseball in Douglas Park, were attacked by a gang of about thirty Polish lads. Everything from rotten tomatoes to house-bricks was used for ammunition in the onslaught. The news of the affray reached the poolroom hang-outs and brought the much needed reinforcement. Men like "Nails" [Morton] and "Nigger" [Joe Lebovitz?] went into the fight for revenge. A good many others, including high-school boys, amateur prize fighters, and hangers-on of the poolrooms were eager for the fun of "helping the Hebes lick the Polocks." Their slogan was "Wallop the Polock!" and they rushed fifty strong to the scene of battle. Finally, policemen dispersed what was left of the Polish gang.

It was dangerous for Jewish boys to travel unprotected through Polish territory or through Douglas Park, which was a sort of "no man's land" on the frontier between the two regions. On one occasion a young Jewish boy was sent on an errand by his mother, and came back with a hole in his head, made by a broken milk bottle hurled by a hidden Polish sharpshooter.

Use of the privileges afforded by Douglas Park, which was a common meeting place of the two groups, has always been a bone of contention. There is a refectory and boathouse in the northern portion of the park, which under normal circumstances is open to members of any race or creed. During this period, however, it was a different story. Some days the Jews dominated, but when a gang of Poles larger in number approached, the former would leave. On one occasion the two gangs were of about the same size and the result was a pitched battle.

Not only did the gangs along Roosevelt Road participate in these encounters, but also the social and "basement" clubs of Lawndale found a good opportunity for sport in the "Polock hunt." A club starting out on such an expedition would almost certainly pick up other gangs and become the nucleus for a mob before it finished. Usually the Jewish boys involved were not personally acquainted with their enemies. It was enough that they were Poles, and vice versa. It was a matter of racial, cultural, and religious solidarity.

7. Is There a Connection Between Race and Speed?

W. MONTAGUE COBB

In the 1932 Olympics two American Negroes, Eddie Tolan and Ralph Metcalfe, carried off top places in both the 100- and 200-meter dashes, Tolan setting new Olympic records in each event; and another Negro, Ed Gordon, won the broad jump. Since the tenth Olympiad, Negroes have continued to dominate the

---

From W. Montague Cobb, "Race and Runners," *Journal of Health and Physical Education* 7 (January 1936): 3–7, 52–53, 54, 56.

national field in the sprints and broad jump in the persons of Metcalfe, Jesse Owens, Eulace Peacock, and Ben Johnson....

Jesse Owens, like Metcalfe a persistent performer, won the national AAU broad-jump championship in 1933 and 1934. He has made and equaled various intermediate sprint records. In one afternoon at Ann Arbor, Michigan, in May, 1935, he performed the greatest track feats ever wrought by a single man, breaking three world's records and equaling a fourth. He leaped 26 feet 8 1/4 inches in the broad jump, ran the 220-yard dash in 20.3 seconds, and won the 220-yard low hurdles in 22.6 seconds for new records, besides equaling the world mark of Frank Wykoff of 9.4 seconds for the 100-yard dash....

Wide attention has thus come to be focused on the fact that in the past champion sprinters and broad jumpers have often been Negroes. The first was Howard P. Drew who became national AAU champion at 100 yards in 1912 and 1913 while at Springfield (Mass.) High School. In 1913 he also won the 220-yard title. In 1914 Drew went to the University of Southern California where he became co-holder with Arthur Duffey of Georgetown of the world's record of 9.6 seconds for the 100-yard dash, a mark which stood for many years. Drew also equaled the world's record for the 220-yard sprint, which at that time was 21.2 seconds. His action photographs are displayed today as models of perfect form....

There is ... no running event and few field events to which Negroes have not contributed some outstanding performer and there is no indication of ineptitude in any event in which no champion has yet appeared. It is to be noted, however, that the sprint and broad jump champions have appeared in a rapid succession, culminating in the present group of contemporaneous performers. For this reason they have been especially conspicuous in the public eye. It is this prominence which has probably stimulated the notion that these stars might owe their success to some physical attributes peculiar to their race.

The Old, Old Story

This sort of suggestion is by no means new. In the days when peerless Paavo Nurmi daily fired every youngster's imagination with new world's records broken in Olympic competition, in the months afterward when more records fell during the memorable duels of Nurmi and his doughty Finnish teammate, Willie Ritola, while the two toured America, there were reams written on why the Finns seemed to have a permanent corner on supremacy in the distance runs. The historians extolled the conquests of the mighty Hans Kolehmainen in 1913. Geographers showed how Finland 's rugged climate bred endurance such that the rest of the world might as well turn in its spikes. Moralizing editors completely effervesced on the subject. But still the ancient records (1904) of England's immortal Al Shrubb for the 6-, 7-, 8-, and 9-mile runs are the world's best. Along have come Kansas' Cunningham, Princeton's Bonthron, and New Zealand's Lovelock to run the mile with "impossible speed." Who can say whence the next athletic "trust busters" will come, or what records they will attack?... But to pursue seriously our original inquiry about the relation of the Negro's anatomy to his feats on cinders and pit, track coach and anthropologist must pool their knowledge.

Coach and Anthropologist

To detect and develop athletic talent is the prime function of our track coaches. The track coach is professionally interested only in those qualities of an athlete which make for excellence in performance. He has no concern with the measure in which those qualities may also be characteristic of men of particular occupations or races. These are the business of the physical anthropologist. Let the track coach set down the factors that make a great sprinter and the anthropologist the distinguishing features of the American Negro. If on comparison the two lists have much in common, race may be important; if little, race is of no significance.

Almost at once, however, we are beset with vagaries. The track coach cannot categorically describe the physique and character of the sprint champion, nor can the anthropologist define with useful accuracy the physique and character of the American Negro.... The personal histories and constitutions of our sprinters have not yet been sufficiently analyzed for the formula for the perfect sprinter or jumper to be given. We are not able to say what measure of natural capacity is due to physical proportions, or to physiological efficiency or to forceful personality. Nor can we weight capacity and training scientifically. This does not mean that strongly biased opinions on the subject are non-existent. For instance, it has been said that superior sprinting and jumping ability must be a matter of nine-tenths capacity and one-tenth jumping because the Negro is not disposed to subject himself to rigorous training.

Despite the fact that adequate data are not available for scientific analysis of sprinting and jumping ability, many useful conclusions may be drawn from a common sense approach to the problem. We know first of all that the physique, style of performance, and character of our champions have been highly variable.... When the track coach arrays before his mind's eye the galaxy of stars who have done the hundred in 9.6 seconds or better, he notes no uniformity of physique, style, or temperament....

For fine distinctions, data of desirable precision are not available but we can say from general inspection that there have been long-legged champions and short-legged ones; some with large calves and some with small. Record-breaking legs have had long Caucasoid calves like those of Paddock and short Negroid ones such as Tolan has.... In the matter of style, there have been fast starters like Hubbard and Simpson and slow ones like Paddock and Metcalfe. We have had "powerhouse" sprinters such as Metcalfe and smooth graceful flashes like Owens whose performances see without effort. In respect to temperament again we find no homogeneity.... There have been champions of great courage who were undaunted by defeat or misfortune and others who reacted very severely to "bad breaks...."

We have seen that the variability of the physical, physiological, and personality traits of great sprinters and jumpers, and inadequate scientific data prevent a satisfactory statement as to just what traits are responsible for their success.... Let us now go to the anthropologist. He has to deal with men categorically designated as American Negroes, but they do not look alike. Genetically we know they are not constituted alike. There is not one single physical feature, including skin color, which all of our Negro champions have in common which would identify them as Negroes....

From his photographs Howard Drew is usually taken for a white man by those not in the know. Gourdin had dark straight hair, no distinctly Negroid features, and a light brown complexion. In a great metropolis he would undoubtedly be often considered a foreigner.... [E]xtending his view, the anthropologist fails to find racial homogeneity even among the white sprinters. We find blond Nordic and swarthy Mediterranean types and various mixtures. In fact if all our Negro and white champions were lined up indiscriminately for inspection, no one except those conditioned to American attitudes would suspect that race had anything whatever to do with the athlete's ability.

ESSAYS

The essays in this section examine two of the most important ways in which race and ethnicity influenced American sport. In the first, Gail Bederman, associate professor of history at the University of Notre Dame, examines one of the most important prizefights of the twentieth century, the heavyweight championship bout of July 4, 1910, between the titleholder African American Jack Johnson and the "Great White Hope," Jim Jeffries, the undefeated former champion, perceived as the defender of the white race and the protector of civilization. The fight represented the efforts of the white race to protect its preeminence over other races by demonstrating superiority inside the ring. White supporters anticipated that Jeffries would help restore the presumed natural order of white dominance over the threat of primitive black hypermasculinity. However, Jeffries was soundly defeated. The shocking loss led to widespread race riots throughout the United States, and efforts to ban the film made of the bout.

The other essay is written by historian Gary Ross Mormino who is the Frank E. Duckwall Professor of History at the University of South Florida. His article examines the role of ethnicity in the Italian American community known as the Hill in St. Louis during the 1920s and 1930s by focusing on ethnic sports organizations. Sport channeled forces that had historically divided the city's Italian immigrants, promoted cultural assimilation, and created voluntary organizations that symbolized Italian identity. Thus sport simultaneously promoted Americanization while accentuating the neighborhood's Italianness.

Remaking Manhood Through Race and "Civilization": The 1910 Jeffries–Johnson Fight and Its Impact

GAIL BEDERMAN

At 2:30 PM on July 4, 1910, in Reno, Nevada, as the band played "All Coons Look Alike to Me," Jack Johnson climbed into the ring to defend his title against Jim Jeffries. Johnson was the first African American world heavyweight boxing

From Gail Bederman, *Manliness and Civilization: A Cultural History of Gender and Race in The United States, 1880–1917* (Chicago: University of Chicago Press, 1996), 1–4, 7–10, 41–42. Reprinted by permission.

champion. Jeffries was a popular white former heavyweight champion who had retired undefeated six years before. Although it promised to be a fine match, more than mere pugilism was at stake. Indeed, the Johnson–Jeffries match was the event of the year. Twenty thousand men from across the nation had traveled to Reno to sit in the broiling desert sun and watch the prizefight. Five hundred journalists had been dispatched to Reno to cover it. Every day during the week before the fight, they had wired between 100,000 and 150,000 words of reportage about it to their home offices. Most had assured their white readership that Jeffries would win. On the day of the fight, American men deserted their families' holiday picnics. All across America, they gathered in ballparks, theaters, and auditoriums to hear the wire services' round-by-round reports of the contest. Over thirty thousand men stood outside the *New York Times* offices straining to hear the results; ten thousand men gathered outside the *Atlanta Constitution*. It was, quite simply, a national sensation.

Ever since 1899, when Jeffries first won the heavyweight championship, he had refused to fight any Negro challengers. Jack Johnson first challenged him as early as 1903. Jeffries replied, "When there are no white men left to fight, I will quit the business.... I am determined not to take a chance of losing the championship to a negro." Jeffries' adherence to the color line was not unique. Ever since 1882, when John L. Sullivan had won the title, no white heavyweight champion had fought a black challenger, even though black and white heavyweights had previously competed freely. Sullivan had announced he would fight all contenders—except black ones. "I will not fight a negro. I never have and never shall." It was in this context that Jack Johnson began his career, and eventually defeated every fighter, black or white, who faced him.

For two years Jeffries refused to fight Johnson, but when Jeffries retired in 1905, the remaining field of white contenders was so poor that the public temporarily lost interest in prizefighting. Finally in 1908, the reigning white champion, Tommy Burns, agreed to fight Johnson. By accepting Johnson's challenge, Burns hoped to raise both interest and prize money. Johnson promptly and decisively thrashed Burns, however, and won the title. Faced with the unthinkable—a black man had been crowned the most powerful man in the world!—interest in pugilism rebounded. The white press clamored for Jeffries to return to the ring. "Jeff must emerge from his alfalfa farm and remove that smile from Johnson's face. Jeff, it's up to you," implored Jack London in the New York Herald. In April 1909, the *Chicago Tribune* printed a drawing of a little blond girl begging the former champion: "Please, Mr. Jeffries, are you going to fight Mr. Johnson?" Across America, white newspapers pleaded with Jeffries to vindicate Anglo-Saxon manhood and save civilization by vanquishing the upstart "Negro."

Eventually the aging, reluctant Jeffries agreed to fight, reportedly explaining, "I am going into this fight for the sole purpose of proving that a white man is better than a negro." From its inception, then, the Johnson–Jeffries fight was framed as a contest to see which race had produced the most powerful, virile man. Jeffries was known as the "Hope of the White Race," while Johnson was dubbed the "Negroes' Deliverer." With few exceptions, predictions of the fight's outcome focused on the relative manliness of the white and the black races.

For example, *Current Literature* predicted Jeffries would win because "the black man … fights emotionally, whereas the white man can use his brain after twenty rounds." White men were confident that Jeffries's intrinsic Anglo-Saxon manhood would allow him to prevail over the (allegedly) flightier, more emotional Negro.

Thus, when Johnson trounced Jeffries—and it was a bloody rout—the defenders of white male supremacy were very publicly hoist by their own petards. They had insisted upon framing the fight as a contest to demonstrate which race could produce the superior specimen of virile manhood. Johnson's victory was so lopsided that the answer was unwelcome but unmistakable. After the fight, the black *Chicago Defender* exulted that Johnson was "the first negro to be admitted the best man in the world."

The ensuing violence showed what a bitter pill that was for many white American men to swallow. Race riots broke out in every Southern state, as well as in Illinois, Missouri, New York, Ohio, Pennsylvania, Colorado, and the District of Columbia. Occasionally, black men attacked white men who were belittling Johnson. In most of the incidents, however, rampaging white men attacked black men who were celebrating Johnson's victory. In Manhattan, the *New York Herald* reported, "One negro was rescued by the police from white men who had a rope around his neck.… In Eighth Avenue, between Thirty-Seventh and Thirty-Ninth Streets, more than three thousand whites gathered, and all the negroes that appeared were kicked and beaten, some of them into insensibility.… Three thousand white men took possession of Eighth Avenue and held against police as they attacked every negro that came into sight." Contemporary reports put the overall national toll at eighteen people dead, hundreds more injured.

Even the United States Congress reacted to the implicit aspersions Johnson's victory cast on white manhood. Before the Johnson–Jeffries fight, Congress had refused even to consider a bill suppressing motion picture films of prizefights. The prospect of the filmic reenactment of the "Negroes' Deliverer" thrashing the "White Hope" in hundreds of movie theaters across the nation was too much for them, however. Within three weeks, a bill suppressing fight films had passed both houses and was soon signed into law.

Soon after Johnson won the championship, an even more scandalous public controversy arose: the "Negroes' Deliverer" was making no secret of his taste for the company of white women. White men worried: Did Johnson's success with white women prove him a superior specimen of manhood? The spectacle of dozens of white women in pursuit of Johnson's favor pleased Johnson and infuriated many whites. These women were mostly prostitutes, but racial etiquette held all white women were too "pure" for liaisons with black men. It seemed bad enough that Johnson's first wife was white, although antimiscegenist doomsayers felt smugly vindicated when she committed suicide in 1912. But when authorities discovered Johnson was having an affair with an eighteen-year-old blond from Minnesota, Lucille Cameron, they charged him with violating the Mann Act—that is, with engaging in white slavery. The white American public, north and south, was outraged. In Johnson's hometown, Chicago, a man threw an inkwell at him when he made an appearance at his bank. Effigies of Johnson were hung from trolley and electric poles around the city. Wherever Johnson went he was greeted with cries of "Lynch him! Lynch the nigger!" It didn't matter that Lucille Cameron insisted she was in love with Johnson and soon married him. It made no difference that she turned out to have been an established prostitute, not a seduced virgin. It didn't even matter that no violations of the Mann Act had occurred, and the original charges had to be dropped. By winning the heavyweight championship and by flaunting his success with white women, Johnson had crossed the line, and the white public demanded punishment.

The national Bureau of Investigation was ordered to conduct a massive search to find *something* to pin on Johnson. After an expensive and exhaustive inquiry, it dredged up some old incidents in which Johnson had crossed state lines with a long time white mistress. Although the government usually invoked the Mann Act only to combat white slavery and commercial prostitution, officials made an exception for Johnson. He was convicted of crossing state lines with his mistress and of giving her money and presents. For most American men, these were perfectly legal activities. Johnson, however, was sentenced to a year in prison and a thousand-dollar fine. Hoping to get rid of him, government employees tacitly encouraged him to jump bail and leave the country, which he did. For the next seven years, all Johnson's efforts to make a bargain and turn himself in were rebuffed. Only in 1920 was Johnson allowed to return to the United States to serve his sentence, an impoverished and greatly humbled former champion. The photograph of him losing his last championship bout to white fighter Jess Willard in Havana in 1915 was a standard feature in white bars and speakeasies for many years thereafter.

By any standard, white Americans' response to Jack Johnson was excessive. Why should a mere prizefight result in riots and death? What was it about Jack Johnson that inspired the federal government to use the Bureau of Investigation to conduct a vendetta against him? That moved Congress to pass federal legislation to mitigate his impact? That impelled prominent leaders like former President Theodore Roosevelt to condemn him in print? That caused so many respected Americans to describe Johnson's activities as "a blot on our 20th century American Civilization?" That caused American men to celebrate his ultimate defeat in their saloons for decades?

The furor over Jack Johnson was excessive, yet it was not unique. During the decades around the turn of the century, Americans were obsessed with the connection between manhood and racial dominance. This obsession was expressed in a profusion of issues, from debates over lynching, to concern about the white man's imperialistic burden overseas, to discussions of child-rearing. The Jack Johnson controversy, then, was only one of a multitude of ways middle-class Americans found to explain male supremacy in terms of white racial dominance and, conversely, to explain white supremacy in terms of male power.

★ ★ ★

... [G]ender–whether manhood or womanhood—is a historical, ideological process. Through that process, individuals are positioned and position themselves as men or as women. Thus, I don't see manhood as either an intrinsic essence or a collection of traits, attributes, or sex roles. Manhood—or "masculinity," as it is commonly termed today—is a continual, dynamic process. Through that process, men claim certain kinds of authority, based upon their particular type of bodies. At any time in history, many contradictory ideas about manhood are available to explain what men are, how they ought to behave, and what sorts of powers and authorities they may claim, as men. Part of the way gender functions is to hide these contradictions and to camouflage the fact that gender is dynamic and always changing. Instead, gender is constructed as a fact of nature, and manhood is assumed to be an unchanging, transhistorical essence, consisting of fixed, naturally occurring traits. To study the history of manhood, I would argue, is to unmask this process and study the historical ways different ideologies about manhood develop, change, are combined, amended, contested—and gain the status of "truth."

To define manhood as an ideological process is not to say that it deals only with intellectuals or ideas. It is, rather, to say that manhood or masculinity is the cultural process whereby concrete individuals are constituted as members of a preexisting social category—as men. The ideological process of gender—whether manhood or womanhood—works through a complex political technology, composed of a variety of institutions, ideas, and daily practices. Combined, these processes produce a set of truths about who an individual is and what he or she can do, based upon his or her body. Individuals are positioned through that process of gender, whether they choose to be or not. Although some individuals may reject certain aspects of their positioning, rare indeed is the person who considers "itself" neither a man nor a woman. And with that positioning as "man" or "woman" inevitably comes a host of other social meanings, expectations, and identities. Individuals have no choice but to act upon these meanings—to accept or reject them, adopt or adapt them—in order to be able to live their lives in human society.

Another way to say this is to define manhood as the process which creates "men" by linking male genital anatomy to a male identity, and linking both anatomy and identity to particular arrangements of authority and power. Logically, this is an entirely arbitrary process. Anatomy, identity, and authority have no intrinsic relationship. Only the process of manhood—of the gender system—allows each to stand for the others.

We can see more concretely how this cultural process works by returning to our discussion of Jack Johnson and considering how Johnson's championship was construed by his culture's historically specific way of linking male anatomy, identity, and authority. Late Victorian culture had identified the powerful, large male body of the heavyweight prizefighter (and not the smaller bodies of the middleweight or welterweight) as the epitome of manhood. The heavyweight's male body was so equated with male identity and power that American whites rigidly prevented all men they deemed unable to wield political and social power from asserting any claim to the heavyweight championship. Logically, there was no reason to see a heavyweight fighter's claim to bodily strength as a claim to public power. Yet the metonymic process of turn-of-the-century manhood constructed bodily strength and social authority as identical. Thus, for twenty-seven years African American men, whom whites saw as less manly than themselves, were forbidden to assert any claim to this pugilistic manhood. When Johnson actually won the heavyweight title, white men clamored for Jeffries to ameliorate the situation and restore manhood to what they believed was its proper functioning.

Yet Johnson was not only positioned by these cultural constructs—he also actively used them to position himself. Embittered by years of vainly seeking a title bout, Johnson consciously played upon white Americans' fears of threatened manhood by laying public claim to all three of the metonymic facets of manhood—body, identity, and authority. During his public sparring matches, Johnson actually wrapped his penis in gauze to enhance its size. Clad only in his boxing shorts, he would stroll the ring, flaunting his genital endowments for all to admire, displaying his superior body to demonstrate his superior manhood. In his private life, Johnson also took great pleasure in assuming a more conventional middle-class manly identity, sometimes taking on the persona of a successful self-made man. In 1912, he publicly claimed the right to move into an exclusive white suburb until the horrified residents took steps to prevent him. He also dressed both his beautiful blond wives in jewels and furs and paraded them in front of the press. Johnson, who grew up in Texas, was well aware that throughout the South black men were regularly tortured and lynched for consorting with white women, and that even Northern whites feared that black men lusted irrepressibly after pure white womanhood. Therefore, he made certain the public could not view his wives as pathetic victims of Negro lust. Instead, he presented his wives as wealthy, respectable women whose husband was successful and manly enough to support them in comfort and luxury.

Johnson was equally insistent upon his masculine right to wield a man's power and authority. He treated minor brushes with the law—his many speeding tickets and automobile violations—contemptuously, as mere inconveniences which he was man enough to ignore. In his autobiography, he claims (falsely, according to his biographer) to have "mingled … with kings and queens; monarchs and rulers of nations have been my associates." On a more sinister note, he physically beat and emotionally maltreated his wives and mistresses, implicitly claiming a man's right to dominate women. In short he recognized that dominant white usage prevented him from being treated as the epitome of manhood, as a white heavyweight champion would be treated. Nevertheless he scornfully refused to accept this racial slight. Defiantly, Johnson positioned himself as a real man by laying ostentatious claim to a male body, male identity, and male power.

As Jack Johnson's example suggests, then, gender ideology, although coercive, does not preclude human agency. Numerous ideological strands of gender, class, and race positioned Johnson in a web which he could not entirely escape. He was inescapably a man, a black man, the son of a freed slave brought up in poverty, and so on. Yet although these discourses inescapably defined him, Johnson was able to take advantage of the contradictions within and between these ideologies in order to assert himself as a man and a pro-active historical agent. Recognizing that "Negroes" were considered less than men, he sometimes asserted his manliness in a race-neutral context, as a champion, a self-made man, and a world-famous hero. In other situations, he played upon his blackness, using his champion's body to present himself as an embodiment of highly sexed Negro masculinity. In all these ways, Johnson reinforced his claim to powerful manhood.

In other words, ideologies of gender are not totalizing. Like all ideologies, they are internally contradictory. Because of these internal contradictions, and because ideologies come into conflict with other ideologies, men and women are able to influence the ongoing ideological processes of gender, even though they cannot escape them. Men and women cannot invent completely new formations of gender, but they can adapt old ones. They can combine and recombine them, exploit the contradictions between them, and work to modify them. They can also alter their own position in relation to those ideologies, as Jack Johnson did. Thus, looking at manhood as an ongoing ideological process—instead of as an inherent essence, or a set of traits or sex roles—allows historians to study the ways people have been historical agents of change.

Conclusion

... [L]et us take a final look at the Jack Johnson controversy, focusing on white journalists' reasons for expecting Jeffries, the "Hope of the White Race," to prevail. Frequently, journalists predicted that Jeffries would beat Johnson because manly white civilization had long been evolving toward millennial perfection. *Collier's* magazine asserted that white men expected Jeffries to win because, unlike the primitive negro, he was of a civilized race: "The white man has thirty centuries of traditions behind him—all the supreme efforts, the inventions and the conquests, and whether he knows it or not, Bunker Hill and Thermopylae' and Hastings and Agincourt." The *San Francisco Examiner* agreed, predicting that the "spirit of Caesar in Jeff ought to whip the Barbarian." Faced with rumors of a Johnson victory, the *Chicago Daily News* wailed, "What would Shakespeare think of this if he could know about it?.... Could even Herbert Spencer extract comfort from so dread a situation?" Anglo-Saxon civilization itself might fall if Jeffries were beaten by the "gifted but non-Caucasian Mr. Johnson." In these reports, a Johnson victory was depicted as an affront to millennial advancement of civilization and the power of white manliness.

Yet in other reports, Jeffries was depicted, not as an exemplar of advanced civilization and high-minded manliness, but as a paragon of violent, primitive masculinity. In this context, Jeffries' eagerly awaited victory would show white men's capacity for masculine violence was as powerful as black men's—that civilization had not undermined whites' primal masculinity. Journalists waxed lyrical about Jeffries' primal physical attributes, his "vast hairy body, those legs like trees, the long projecting jaw, deep-set scowling eyes, and wide thin, cruel mouth." They printed pictures of him training for the fight by sawing through huge tree-trunks—which, in urban, twentieth-century America, had primitive connotations redolent of log cabins and the frontier. Jack London, writing in the *New York Herald,* maintained that his own overwhelming desire to witness the match, like other white men's, was itself an Anglo-Saxon race trait. As he saw it, the love of boxing "belongs unequivocally to the English speaking race and ... has taken centuries for the race to develop.... It is as deep as our consciousness and is woven into the fibres of our being. It grew as our very language grew. It is an instinctive passion of our race." For these men, a Jeffries victory would prove that, despite being civilized, white men had lost none of the masculine power which had made their race dominant in the primeval past.

Because both approaches drew upon the discourse of civilization, few people saw any inconsistency. Under the logic of "civilization," Jeffries could be simultaneously a manly, civilized heir to Shakespeare and a masculine, modern-day savage lifted from the forests of ancient England. The crucial point was that Jeffries' racial inheritance made him the superior man; and his superlative manhood would prove the superiority of his race. Whether manly and civilized or masculine and savage, whites were confident that Jeffries would beat Jack Johnson.

Thus, many white men panicked when the black champion thrashed the white. By annihilating Jeffries so completely, Johnson implicitly challenged the ways hegemonic discourses of civilization built powerful manhood out of race. Johnson's victory suggested that the heirs of Shakespeare were not the manly, powerful beings they had thought—that "primitive" black men were more masculine and powerful than "civilized" white men. Many white men could not bear this challenge to their manhood. The men who rioted, the Congress that passed laws suppressing Johnson's fight films, the Bureau of Investigation authorities who bent the laws to jail him—all detested the way Johnson's victory shredded the ideologies of white male power embedded in "civilization."

In sum, when late nineteenth-century Americans began to synthesize new formulations of gender, hegemonic discourses of civilization explained concisely the precise relation between the male body, male identity, and male authority. White male bodies had evolved through centuries of Darwinistic survival of the fittest. They were the authors and agents of civilized advancement, the chosen people of evolution and the cutting edge of millennial progress. Who better to make decisions for the rest of humankind, whether female or men of the lower races? It was imperative to all civilization that white males assume the power to ensure the continued millennial advancement of white civilization.

Sport in an Italian American Community, St. Louis, 1925–1941

GARY ROSS MORMINO

The following essay ... examines the interrelationships between immigrants and urbanization upon two generations of Italian-Americans between the 1920s and World War Two. The article contends that sport played a galvanic role in the acculturation of Italian-American youth, and that athletic voluntary associations became major factors in the evolution of the neighborhood. Sport channeled

---

From Gary Ross Mormino, "The Playing Fields of St. Louis: Italian Immigrants and Sports, 1925–1941," *Journal of Sport History* 9:2 (Summer, 1982), 5–13. Reprinted with permission.

forces that had historically divided Italian immigrants in St. Louis and harnessed these divisive energies into creative participation. Finally, the emergence of a neighborhood athletic federation provided a powerful symbol of ethnic group identity. Recreational enterprise performed a dual purpose. It accentuated the Italianate character of the colony, helping to retard assimilation. But sport also allowed athletes to become Americanized and acculturated them into a larger urban society through the participation of intra-city teams. Indeed, sport encouraged not only the preservation of an ethnic subculture, but the preservation of the community itself.

Several forces helped solidify the Italian-Americans gathered in St. Louis into a cohesive ethnic community. These factors—geographic isolation, the local economy, the Roman Catholic Church, the neighborhood school, the urban gangs, and the many voluntary associations—also contributed to, and were affected by, the phenomenon of sport.

"Six-hundred Italians, a community saloon, the North of Italy tongue, and a $500 Italian flag," constituted the basics of "Dago Hill," which according to a 1901 journalist was "unique among the communities of St. Louis." Attracted by economic opportunities in the clay mines and brick factories of Fairmount Heights, northern Italians from Lombardy and southern Italians from Sicily began arriving in the 1880s and by the turn-of-the-century, the district in southwest St. Louis was dubbed by immigrants as "la Montagna,"—the Hill. Natives derisively called the colony "'Dago Hill."

Geographically and culturally, the Hill remained an isolated and insulated colony for the several thousand Lombards and Sicilians who had arrived by 1910. The colony's cultural homogeneity reinforced the insularity; well over 90% of its residents hailed from Italy. Typically, immigrant colonies were situated in inner-city districts. Not so for the Hill, which was located miles from the congested St. Louis downtown. Not until the 1920s would bus service provide intra-city transportation for area residents. Most first-generation Italians preferred the seclusion of the self-sufficient community. "When I was growing up in the 1920s," recollected Lou Cerutti, a life-long resident, "the Hill was like a little country town." The bus ride to Sportsman's Park widened the social vistas of second-generation Italian-Americans like Joe Garagiola, but his immigrant parents clung securely to their geographic isolation. "Downtown," Garagiola reminisced, "as far as Hill mothers and fathers were concerned, was the place you went to take your citizenship test. Otherwise, downtown was as far away as the Duomo in Milan [Lombardy]."

By 1920, more than 3,000 first and second generation Italians had settled on the Hill. Given the local industrial character of the area and the lack of urban transportation, it was natural that nearly all the residents worked in the local brickyards, clay mines, and foundries. Pay was low and mobility limited. Hill Italians were drastically over-represented at the bottom of the St. Louis occupational ladder; nearly four times as many workers were classified as "unskilled laborers" as in the city (35% vs. 9%).

No-nonsense Italian immigrants had come to St. Louis to work. No work, no dignity. The demands of work and the challenges of building a community exacted harsh sacrifices from these immigrants.... Lombards and Sicilians viewed leisure as a plaything for the *prominenti* (the elite). "A cane, work, and bread make for beautiful children," counseled a Sicilian proverb. Giovanni Schiavo, a pioneering historian writing about the St. Louis Italian community, observed in 1929: "It is well known that as a whole the Italian immigrant has not brought with him any traditions of national games ... the only pastime for which the immigrant is noted is apparently bocce [an Italian game resembling lawn bowling]. National American games do not appeal to the average Italian." However, Schiavo pointed out that the sons of these immigrants were attracted by the lure of sport.... [A]t the moment Schiavo penned those words (1929), Hill Italian-Americans were poised at a pivotal crossroads, as national and local forces were reshaping the values and institutions of ethnic America.

The 1920s witnessed the transformation of American sport and the rise of the athlete as hero. The proliferation of radio and the urban tabloid penetrated ethnic America—even once isolated colonies such as the Hill. Italian-Americans were swept into the sporting vortex both as spectators and participants. Whereas no Italians were represented in the major leagues between 1901-1906, and where only two Italian rookies broke into the circuit in 1920 (out of 133), by 1941 fully eight percent of big league rosters counted Italians, more than double their share of the white population. Individual exploits of Tony Lazzeri, Ernie Lombardi, and Joe DiMaggio popularized the sport in Italian communities. In the boxing ring, Italian-Americans were even more prominent, to the point that by the 1930s that group boasted more champions than any other ethnic cohort. These idols became important role models for second-generation ethnics, who importantly, now had the leisure time to indulge in recreation.

The first waves of Italian immigrants possessed neither the time nor inclination to play soccer or join an athletic club. By the mid-1920s industrial laborers were receiving one and a half-days' rest per week and some paid holidays. Moreover, the young remained in school longer and began work at a later age than their immigrant fathers.

Youth would be served. Italian parents, unconcerned with birth control, produced large families, thus supporting the swelling ranks of the second-generation....

Significantly, these young men were second-generation Italian-Americans, aggressively "new world" in social outlook. In sociological terms, this group was becoming acculturated, acquiring America's language, aspirations, and ideas. Young boys were rebelling against the patriarchal domination of old world fathers, reported social worker Elmer Wood in 1936....

The neighborhood school, another powerful Americanizing and organizing influence, served both as a laboratory for democracy and a cauldron of socioeconomic conflict. Italian parents looked upon the American school with suspicion and distrust. Unlettered immigrants (in 1930, illiteracy rates for foreign-born adults on the Hill approached 40 percent) saw the institution as a threat to parental influence. Compounded by the growing needs of the family, Hill Italo-Americans made limited educational gains.... [F]ew Hill students finished the eighth grade and even fewer finished high school. "Most of the Italian children have difficulty in school because of their language handicaps and poor home training," wrote Wood. Appallingly, in 1940 only eleven Italian-American males over age twenty-five claimed a high school diploma, making that cohort the least-educated group in metropolitan St. Louis....

... [Italian youth] quickly assimilated the essentials of ethnophysical geography. [According to teacher] Lou Berra (no relation to "Yogi"): "... the creek ... railroad tracks ... that was our boundary!... Up the Hill we had the Blue Ridge Gang—Irish. To the northwest we had the Cheltenham Gang—a mixture of Germans and more or less natives. East of Kings Highway was the Tower Grove Gang, what most of us refer to as Hoosiers, people up from small towns ... then the Dog Town Gang to the west.... You go beyond that and you get your ass kicked around, so you stayed within your limits."

The rude confrontation with a hostile outside world presented a difficult transition.... "In school they taught me all about democracy," remembered Sam Chinnici, a Sicilian immigrant. "Then you would come outside and find these antagonisms and would have to fight for all the things they taught you in school...." To outsiders, there was no mistaking the Hill's ethnic boundaries; to insiders, once Italo-Americans left the colony, "Krauts," "Micks," and "Hoosiers" lurked in the shadows. "If you got caught on the other side of Southwest Avenue," reminisced Lou Cerutti, "you got the heck kicked out of you!"

Like urban teenagers across the country, Hill Italo-Americans clustered into their street comer societies. "Every kid on the Hill belonged to a gang or club," remembered Joe Garagiola.... Called the Hawks, Falcons, Ravens, Little Caesars, and Stags, gangs proliferated throughout the 1920s and 1930s climaxing in 1941 when nearly fifty neighborhood clubs boasted a thousand neighborhood members.

Whereas the spirit of *campanilismo* (old-world localism) governed the selection and membership of the mutual aid societies among the first-generation arrivals, second-generation club members relied on block-territorial imperatives, regardless of the parent's old-world ties. "All the kids around my age who lived on Elizabeth Avenue made up a sports club," recollected "Yogi" Berra.

In urban enclaves across the nation, gang members coalesced around territorial loyalties. "There is a definite geographical basis for the play group, ..." contended Frederick Thrasher in his classic study of the gang: "The gang ... is characterized by the following types of behavior: meeting face-to-face, milling, movement through space as a unit, conflict and planning. The results of this collective behavior is the development of tradition, unreflective internal structure, esprit de corps, morale, group awareness and attachment to local territory."

In his classic study, *Street Corner Society*, the participant-observer William Foote Whyte reported the raucous and colorful lifestyle of Comerville. Like Comerville's gangs, Hill athletic clubs mapped out territories, sponsored club houses, respected intricate internal hierarchies, participated in local politics, and bootlegged moonshine.

The Hill also had its William Foote Whyte, in the character of Elmer Shorb Wood. A social worker and graduate student, Wood became a confidant to the colony.... The young sociology student was particularly fascinated by the gang phenomenon, whose characteristics bore great similarity to other working-class, bachelor subcultures: "Boys and young men between ages 16-25 have ... established gangs, or what they term athletic clubs, where they spend their unoccupied time...."

Wood further reported that at one school teachers complained that "Italian boys are not trustworthy, especially on the playgrounds, and always have to be watched, as they delight in hurting someone." The teacher's lament was a familiar complaint on the Hill....

Clearly, Italian "toughs" threatened the future direction of the community. Organized sport would help channel the raw, undisciplined energies of young Italian-Americans into constructive outlets for societally-approved violence. In sports as in life, there exists a fine edge between a keen and healthy rivalry and rancorous, self-destructive competition. Sport had polarized the clubs in the early 1920s. "We had soccer teams nobody could beat," boasted a proud Roland De Gregorio. "But then," he said, his voice slipping noticeably, "we used to fight among ourselves."

The man who helped transform the Hill's athletic direction arrived in 1925. Joseph Causino, son of Italian immigrants, walked into St. Ambrose Church ..., eager to proselytize the gospel of sport and brotherhood. Causino, a new breed of social worker, had been formally trained as a recreation director and was employed by the St. Louis Southside YMCA.

Joseph Causino, despite the Italianate sound of the name, was a third-generation Bohemian.... Having graduated in Fine Arts from Washington University, Causino was forced to cut short a promising artistic career when his family suffered a severe economic setback. Causino found a career with the St. Louis Young Men's Christian Association.

Nationally, the YMCA had made an extensive effort to counsel America's burgeoning youth population. By 1920 the organization had erected over 1000 buildings, valued at ninety-six million dollars....

Causino discovered an enclave in need of formal direction. The Hill contained no recreational center, not even a playing field. Causino represented the ethos of the YMCA—an appeal for citizenship, the Protestant work/play ethic, the creed of Americanization—and he appealed to the youth on their grounds. "He kept us out of jail," volunteered one ... convert ..., "Because, like I said, we had cousins and big brothers who were gangsters.... We let off steam that way (with sports)...."

... Causino—who learned to speak Italian—fully expected opposition from immigrant parents. "My father never liked my playing ball," remembered Yogi Berra. "He always got sore if I came home dirty and he would smack me for sure if my pants were torn!"

Soon after Causino's arrival, an angry parent cornered the youth worker and demanded that he state his intentions. "I want to bring in an organized recreational program," the undaunted Causino replied—in fluent Italian. "I want to make them better citizens, good Americans." The immigrant smiled, satisfied with the answer. "That's what we want," he said, "we want our boys to be good Americans." Sport became a handmaiden for Americanization: "Countless huddles, rap sessions and confrontations later, plenty of good Americans had graduated from Uncle Joe's school. Grown men forcefully swear to Causino's decisive impact upon their lives and the Hill's future. "The greatest.... "Dynamite!" extolled Phil Verga. "If you needed dough, he gave you money. If you needed a job, he'd help you find a job...."

"It finally got to the point," exclaimed Lou Berra, "where Uncle Joe got us working together. One of the things that welded us together was sports." Causino packaged pride, character, unity, and the strenuous life through the appeal of baseball and soccer. Few denied that Causino's techniques and programs were less than a roaring success. His recreational programs, dovetailed with the extensive St. Ambrose Church youth movement, created an effective hold on the colony's young, leaving little room or inclination for deviation.

Causino was aided in his efforts by the parish church.... In 1926 the colony built at immense collective sacrifice, St. Ambrose Church. Immediately the Church became the most important social complex in the community. "The Church at that time," recalled lifelong resident Fr. Anthony Palumbo, "was the center of not only the spiritual activities of the colony, but the social activities gravitated around the church ... it made for a very closely-known community and closely-knit parish."

The Church, aware of the gang problem, set out in the 1930s on an extensive youth program, part of which was the invitation to Causino to help organize athletics.... In order to appeal to the colony's young men, St. Ambrose recruited four young priests in the 1930s two of whom were the first non-Italians to serve the parish.

Fathers Anthony Palumbo and Peter Barabino were exemplary of the new priests; the former appealed to the young with his airplane, the latter with a soccer ball and baseball glove. "No one did more to start it [soccer] on the Hill than Father Anthony Palumbo," observed long-time sports editor of the St. Louis Globe-Democrat, Robert Burns. Fathers Charles Koester and John Wieberg also worked actively with the youth-sport movement. "We priests were the sparkplugs of the community ... "reminisced Koester, today a bishop. "Sports were very important to the Hill. You must remember, the Hill was very poor then and soccer and baseball provided entertainment for the people. It also built character and provided an outlet for our young men."

Soccer and baseball served as a recreational antidote for the Depression strapped Hill. And beyond the colony, Americans continued to indulge in leisure activities with even greater enthusiasm than before. For St. Louisans, free entertainment was offered each Sunday throughout the 1920s and 1930s as millions of soccer, baseball and softball fans crowded into urban parks. In 1927–28, for example, over a million St. Louisans attended soccer matches at a cost to the city of only $1,985.... Sports received a federal boost in the 1930s as New Deal programs sought to involve urban youth. "I was thirteen years old [in 1939] and just as juvenile as our juvenile delinquents of today," reminisced Joe Garagiola. "That was the reason for this league, a project undertaken by the WPA to keep us juveniles off the streets."

The blistering competitiveness, channeled into a community-wide spirit, proved unbeatable on diamond and turf. The Hill's athletic *risorgimento* upset the balance of power in St. Louis soccer, heretofore dominated by the German Sports Club, the Spanish Society, and the Irish Catholic League. "The Hill had some of the city's most fantastic kickers," contended Bill Kerch, veteran reporter for the *Globe-Democrat*. "They were simply outstanding ... very well disciplined ... the best in the city." Trouncing Germans and Irishmen added a new dimension to ethnic rivalry....

Sports offered an acceptable outlet for the free-spirited Italo-Americans. Soccer matches in particular were impassioned affairs. During the 1929–30 Municipal Soccer League season, 51 players were suspended for roughness and fighting. A typical match in 1934 involving Southside rivals Dog Town and Dago Hill nearly ended in a riot before 3,500 not-so-sedate fans. "The game was tough all the way through," complained Coach Norman of Carlstrom's Dog Town.... But the violence and ill feelings were short-lived. Soccer collisions were a mild form of cathartic release, an acceptable outlet for societally-approved violence. "To individuals too ready to follow some subversive drummer," suggested Eugen Weber, "games offered opportunities for self-assertion and sometimes for indulging in competitive violence."

The spirited play exhibited in the 1930s made St. Louis the capital of American soccer, with the Hill shining as one of its brightest jewels. "The Hill was an important breeding ground for soccer players," wrote sports historian James Robinson.... The 1928–29 season was the first in which Hill athletes competed under one banner. That year, soccer players rallied under the banner of Calcaterra Undertakers, winning the title in the city's Foundry League.

In a remarkably brief period, Hill Italians had successfully perfected the team demands of soccer. In 1924, Louis Jean Gualdoni, a Democratic politician, could find no local Italian youths to play on his Fairmount Soccer Team: "This was before Joe Causino and Father Palumbo. What I wanted was a winner ... eventually we got lots of Italians on the team."

The popularity of soccer on the Hill must be explained in terms of the St. Louis environment. German immigrants had introduced the turnverein and soccer in the nineteenth century, and the popularity of the game has persisted.... Moreover, since the Hill's geographic and ethnic neighbors, the Irish and German, played soccer, it was only natural that the community's youth would embrace the sport. Soccer remained a second- and third-generation phenomenon; Italian immigrants had neither played nor understood calcio in the old country.

After 1930, Hill athletes vied for supremacy in nearly every sport. In the early 1930s the gangs were formally organized into an overarching federation ... , the Royal Knights of Italy (later changed to Fairmount Athletic Union because of anti-fascist publicity). The federation, brainchild of Sam Chinicci, a volunteer, promoted tournaments and intramural competition. "I used to organize parades to motivate the boys," said Chinicci, then a filling station operator. "I organized the federation with the help of the National Youth Administration."

Like everything else, sports after 1930 tended to revolve around St. Ambrose, keeping the parish the unquestionable social center of the community. "On Sunday morning, everybody in our neighborhood went to church," reminisced Yogi Berra: "There was never any question about it if you were going....

If you were too sick to go to Mass in the morning, you can bet your life you were going to be too sick to go out and play ball in the afternoon."

When Yogi quit school after the eighth grade, a concerned Papa Berra asked Joe Causino and Fr. Charles Koester of St. Ambrose to guide the errant young man.

Sports, like politics and the brown derby, flourished in urban Catholic America. Sons of Irishmen, Poles, and Italians took to baseball and basketball, football, and soccer. Frank Deford writes:

> In the palmy days of yore, when order reigned over innocent games, sport was uplifting, and a glorious celebration, like the Mass. Sport and the church both stood for authority.... Heroes were larger than life, canonized as athletic saints, a comforting adjunct to the church's own hagiology. The Roman Church has always been perturbed by sex, and for its male adolescents, joining a team was considered the next best thing to a vow of celibacy.

Deford's portrayal ... fits the well-ordered Hill....

"No problem was so big that Father Palumbo couldn't figure it out," reminisced the inimitable Garagiola. When Garagiola was asked to try out for the St. Louis Cardinals, he began to search for a catcher's mitt. "None of our guys had one," he wrote. "The only one we knew of belonged to Louis Cassani. He wasn't one of the boys, but Father Palumbo said that our Johnny Colombo knew Gino Pariani who knew Louie Cassani. The network began operation and we got our mitt."

The Hill had completed a remarkable athletic transformation.... When in the early 1920s local politicians attempted to organize a soccer team, they could find no qualified Italians with which to man the team and thereby attract Democratic voters. By 1929, the first organized Hill soccer team had won the divisional championship, and by 1940 St. Ambrose climaxed the pre-war successes with the Missouri Ozark Amateur Championship. The fiery center from that team, Joe Numi, would return after the war to lead area soccer teams to new heights. Coach Numi was guaranteed quality players, since his farm team, St. Ambrose, won the Sublette Park Parish School League title eleven consecutive years, 1934 through 1945.

Sports had a catalytic impact upon the Hill, an effect measured far beyond tarnished trophies. Potentially the greatest threat to community stability had been the gang, for if the Hill could not win the affections of its young, the neighborhood was doomed.... The assorted gangs on Dago Hill were harnessed by Joe Causino, the Catholic Church, and immigrant fathers. So great a transformation had occurred by 1934 that Causino's colleague, Harold Keltner, published a YMCA guide ironically entitled *Gangs: An Asset to the City of St. Louis*. Keltner described an encounter on the Hill: "Good sportsmanship is one result of the direction of athletics. The Little Caesars, for instance, last year played several ineligible men on their baseball team ... unwittingly and, when they discovered it, wrote a special letter of apology to all the clubs and voluntarily forfeited all of the games."

Sports became a handmaiden for solidarity, a vehicle which helped transform factional conflict into creative competition. By 1941, the Hill had become, partly through the medium of sports, an ethnic phalanx. Young and old, Lombard and Sicilian, old-world mustachioed Petes and new world Yogis passionately identified themselves with the Hill, with St. Ambrose, with neighborhood teams. "What impressed me the most about the kids from the Hill," insisted Fr. Anthony Palumbo, priest and soccer coach at St. Ambrose (1932–1948), "was that they were willing to make a lot of sacrifices to play on the team ... they were willing to sacrifice for the Hill."

That sport played such a critical role amongst Hill youth can be attributed to the ecological characteristics of the locale. These structural factors also reinforced the ethnic dimension of the sport network. Historically, ethnic identification is likely to become intertwined with territorial commonality whenever ethnic residential patterns converge with a working-class population. The Hill presents a striking case of this. Boston's Italian West End—a much studied neighborhood—also exhibited similar characteristics: a strong identification with territorial space, high investments in inter-personal relationships, and strong personal association rather than achievement orientation.

Sports not only crystallized Italo-American feelings internally within the colony, but also provided a public forum from which St. Louisans, and in a broader sense Americans, judged the neighborhood from a different perspective other than busted stills and ethnic caricatures. A St. Louis columnist rhapsodized in 1949: "All is not spaghetti, macaroni and choice wine on the Hill, that famed neighborhood in Southwest St. Louis. The principal occupation is sports and the main export nationally is known athletes...."

Observed a reporter from the prestigious *Post-Dispatch* in 1941: "The Hill is a neighborhood of some 10,000 first, second and third generation Italians. It boasts its own factories and stores, its schools and churches. But best of all, it boasts of being a neighborhood with the lowest juvenile delinquency rate of the city."

Organized athletics had distinctly altered local perception of the Italian Hill. But what role had sports played in retarding or encouraging the acculturation of Italian-Americans? Had athletes promoted assimilation into a greater urban society?

Sports played a complex, often conflicting role in the formation of urban ethnic values. On the one hand, athletics fostered acculturation to American ways of life by mixing nationalities in team play. Sports was a tremendous thing for us Italians," exclaimed Joe Correnti, a dry cleaner who helped organize local soccer teams. "[W]e were almost a closed community. Sports was an outlet for us." Athletic competition forced Hill players outside the sheltered neighborhood.

Local athletic successes also enabled several dozen soccer and baseball players to attend area colleges on scholarships. According to sociologist Richard Rehberg, participation in sport has the most effect on boys least disposed to attend college by raising their educational expectations to attend college. These successful athletes also served as role models for area youth. In 1940, only one Hill resident had obtained a college degree; following the war, college became more attractive, owing to the successes of the GI Bill and athletes. By 1955, the

Hill had spawned a half-dozen professional baseball players, twice that number of professional soccer players, and several national soccer club championships. "It is doubtful," wrote historian Richard Sorrel in describing Woonsocket, Rhode Island, "if any city of comparable size [50,000] produced as many major leaguers [three, including Napoleon Lajoie], let alone from one ethnic group [French]." One neighborhood, the Hill, comprised of only 5,000 Italian-Americans, easily eclipsed Woonsocket's enviable record.

On the other hand, organized recreation promoted ethno-religious identity through competition and the preservation of parish-colony teams. Ironically, the high water mark of Hill athletic competition occurred during a period in which ... mass media and the automobile, were making important inroads into the colony. But the Ford Coupe and Gateway Trolley, the *Post-Dispatch* and Zenith radio, while widening the social vistas of the community, also served to make Hill Italians more conscious of their uniqueness. Urban journalists, eager for unusual copy made a sport of accentuating the Italian character of the Hill and the Latin flavor of its athletes.

The Hill's enthusiasm for soccer accentuated the ethnic dimension of the neighborhood, especially outside St. Louis. John Pooley argues in "Ethnic Clubs in Milwaukee" that soccer fostered ethnoculturalism: "Since the sport of soccer is alien to the core society; and since soccer is the major game of the countries origin of the ethnic groups; and since members of the ethnic groups in question were involved in the activities of soccer clubs ... it is thereby hypothesized that ethnic soccer clubs in Milwaukee inhibit structural assimilation."

In one of the greatest mass movements in modern history, three million Italians immigrated to the United States in the half-century after 1880. Into the maelstrom of an emerging urban-industrial economy sailed the immigrants, most of whom came poorly prepared for the rigors of modern society. They survived, and ... adapted to and adopted the values and institutions of the host society. Historians have made great strides in studying the sensitive issues of *pane e lavoro*—bread and work—but have reluctantly ventured beyond the traditional topics and chronology of the great wave of immigration, 1880–1924. The complex matrix of relationships between immigrant parents and sons, and between second-generation peer groups—a familiar theme in novels—has been largely ignored by immigration historians. One such issue which affected immigrants and sons was ... recreation. Future ethnic scholars might well address themselves to the unexplored seams of sport history and the immigrant community, for the study of athletic voluntary associations provides a microcosmic portrait of the immigrant group.

FURTHER READING

Ashe, Arthur. *A Hard Road to Glory: A History of the African-American Athlete, 1619–1986*, 3 vols. (1988).

Baker, William J. *Jesse Owens: An American Life* (1986).

Baldassaro, Lawrence, and Richard Johnson. *The American Game: Baseball and Ethnicity* (2002).

Baldassaro, Lawrence. *Beyond DiMaggio: Italian Americans in Baseball* (2011).

Bloom, John, and Michael Nevin Willard, eds. *Sports Matters: Race, Recreation, and Culture* (2002).

Buford, Kate. *Native American Son: The Life and Sporting Legend of Jim Thorpe* (2010).

Burgos, Adrian. *Playing America's Game: Baseball, Latinos, and the Color Line* (2007).

Burgos, Adrian. *Cuban Star: How One Negro-League Owner Changed the Face of Baseball* (2011).

Captain, Gwendolyn. "Enter Ladies and Gentlemen of Color: Gender, Sport, and the Ideal of American Manhood and Womanhood During the Late Nineteenth and Early Twentieth Century," *Journal of Sport History* 18 (1991), 81–102.

Carroll, John M. *Fritz Pollard: Pioneer in Racial Advancement* (1992).

Darby, Paul. "Emigrants at Play: Gaelic Games and the Irish Diaspora in Chicago, 1884–c.1900," *Sport in History* 26 (April 2006): 47–63.

Franks, Joel S. *Crossing Sidelines, Crossing Cultures: Sport and Asian Pacific American Cultural Citizenship*, 2nd ed. (2010).

Gems, Gerald. *Windy City Wars: Labor, Leisure, and Sport in the Making of Chicago* (1997).

Greenberg, Hank, in Ira Berkow, ed. *Hank Greenberg: The Story of My Life* (1988).

Hardy, Stephen. *How Boston Played: Sport, Recreation, and Community, 1865–1915* (1982).

Hofmann, Annette R. *The American Turner Movement: A History From its Beginnings to 2000* (2010).

Iber, Jorge, and Samuel O. Regalado, eds. *Mexican Americans and Sports: A Reader on Athletics and Barrio Life* (2007).

Jaher, Frederic Cople. "Antisemitism in American Athletics," *Shofar: An Interdisciplinary Journal of Jewish Studies* 20 (Fall 2001), 61–73.

Lanctot, Neil. *Fair Dealing and Clean Playing: The Hilldale Club and the Development of Professional Baseball, 1910–1932* (1994).

Levine, Peter. *Ellis Island to Ebbets Field: Sport and the American Jewish Experience* (1992).

Llewellyn, Matthew P. "'Viva l'Italia! Viva l'Italia!' Dorando Pietri and the North American Professional Marathon Craze, 1908–10," *International Journal of the History of Sport* 25 (May 2008), 710–36.

Miller, Patrick, and David Wiggins. *The Unlevel Playing Field: A Documentary History of the African American Experience in Sport* (2003).

Mormino, Gary Ross. "The Playing Fields of St. Louis: Italian Immigrants and Sports, 1925–1941," *Journal of Sport History* 9 (Summer 1982), 5–19.

Nendel, Jim. "New Hawaiian Monarchy: The Media Representations of Duke Kahanamoku, 1911–1912," *Journal of Sport History* 31 (Spring 2004), 32–52.

Park, Roberta J. "German Associational and Sporting Life in the Greater San Francisco Area, 1850–1900," *Journal of the West* 26 (1987), 47–64.

Peterson, Robert. *Only the Ball Was White* (1970).

Rader, Benjamin G. "Quest for Subcommunities and the Rise of American Sport," *American Quarterly* 29 (December 1977), 355–69.

Regalado, Samuel O. *Nikkei Baseball: Japanese American Players from Immigration and Internment to the Major Leagues* (2013).

Ribowsky, Mark. *A Complete History of the Negro Leagues, 1884 to 1955* (1995).

Riess, Steven A., ed. *Sports and the American Jew* (1998).

Ritchie, Andrew. *Major Taylor: The Extraordinary Career of a Champion Bicycle Racer* (1988).

Roberts, Randy. *Papa Jack: Jack Johnson and the Era of White Hopes* (1983).

Rogosin, Donn. *Invisible Men: Life in Baseball's Negro Leagues* (1983).

Ruck, Rob. *Sandlot Seasons: Sport in Black Pittsburgh* (1987).

Runstedtler, Theresa. *Jack Johnson, Rebel Sojourner: Boxing in the Shadow of the Global Color Line* (2012).

Tye, Larry. *Satchel: The Life and Times of an American Legend* (2009).

Wiggins, David K. *Glory Bound; Black Athletes in White America* (1997).

Yamamoto, Eriko. "Cheers for Japanese Athletes: The 1932 Los Angeles Olympics and the Japanese American Community," *Pacific Historical Review* 69 (August 2000), 399–431.

Zang, David. *Moses Fleetwood Walker's Divided Heart: The Life of Baseball's First Black Major Leaguer* (1995).

CHAPTER 11

Sports Heroes and American Culture, 1900–1945

Why was sport such an important source of heroes in the early twentieth century? Although there were a few earlier sports idols like pugilist John L. Sullivan, by the 1920s it seemed that every major sport had its own hero or heroine: baseball had Babe Ruth; boxing had Jack Dempsey; football had Red Grange; swimming had Gertrude Ederle; tennis had Bill Tilden; and golf had Bobby Jones. There were not only heroes for the broader society but also certain idols for ethnic subcommunities like boxer Benny Leonard for Jews and baseball star Tony Lazzeri for Italians.

What made certain athletes heroic? Why was there such a great need for heroes at this time? Sociologist Janet Harris in Athletes and the American Hero Dilemma *(1994) states that heroes "provide active displays of prominent human characteristics and social relationships.... They are thought to help define individual and collective identity, compensate for qualities perceived to be missing in individuals or society, display ideal behaviors that people strive to emulate, and provide avenues for temporary escape from the rigors of daily life." How did sportsmen and women become identified as heroes? A sports hero was recognized for athletic accomplishments that were readily measurable, usually gained over a long period, earned, according to historian David Voigt, through "hard work, clean living, and battling obstacles." A hero was more than a celebrity, who was famous simply for his or her athletic accomplishments. Society expected heroes to be morally and socially responsible and to serve as role models. Heroes were thought to be very important for youngsters to emulate (particularly when American society was undergoing many major changes because of industrialization, urbanization, bureaucratization, and immigration). They exemplified stability and direction, certified that traditional values like rugged individualism, self-reliance, and courage still counted, and occasionally also epitomized the relevance of newer traits like teamwork and cooperation.*

DOCUMENTS

Document 1 in this chapter is a fictional account of the athletic exploits of Frank Merriwell at Yale, part of the Merriwell series written by Burt Standish (real name, Gilbert Patten) that dominated the juvenile sports literature market beginning in 1896 when they first appeared in *Tip Top Weekly*. Standish wrote some 208 short novels in the series in which his handsome muscular Christian always triumphs. This extract is taken from *Frank Merriwell at Yale, or Freshman Against Freshman* (1897). In this tale the start of Frank's freshman year is narrated, coming up to the big game against the Harvard freshmen that Frank naturally wins at the last moment with his pitching and batting skill.

Juvenile sports fiction, according to Michael Oriard, "defines exactly who the representative American hero is." Oriard considers Frank Merriwell the epitome of a sports hero. He was a self-made muscular Christian who had great athletic skill, and exemplified such traditional values as hard work, honesty, bravery, loyalty, modesty, and self-sacrifice. American boys who read the Merriwell stories were encouraged by them to emulate the behavior and character of Frank and his younger brother Dick.

Document 2 is a memorial written to honor Christy Mathewson, the athlete generally considered the closest anyone was in real life to the fictional Merriwell boys. Mathewson was a tall, blond, college-educated pitcher, who won 373 games for the New York Giants—the most ever in National League history with a lifetime 2.13 Earned Run Average. "Matty" was an outstanding moral hero who taught Sunday School, never pitched on the Sabbath, and often spoke to youth organizations on clean living and sportsmanship. He served overseas as an officer during World War I and took some mustard gas in France during a training exercise. His weakened condition left him vulnerable to tuberculosis, from which he died prematurely in 1925.

Document 3 focuses on the Black Sox Scandal in which eight players on the Chicago White Sox were thrown out of baseball because of their presumed involvement in fixing the World Series of 1919. This document consists of excerpts from the confession of star outfielder "Shoeless" Joe Jackson, who did not play to lose, batting .375 in the Series. However, he knew of the fix and received a portion of the payoff. Jackson was uneducated and unsophisticated, and he was inadequately represented by attorney Alfred Austrian when he signed the confession. Austrian had ulterior motives because, as the White Sox's lawyer, his agenda was to protect the interests of team owner Charles Comiskey. When the case went to trial, Jackson's confession and those of pitchers Lefty Williams and Eddie Cicotte were reported lost, and the seven indicted players (Utility man Fred McMullin was never charged) were acquitted. The jurors carried them out on their shoulders, having certified the integrity of their heroes. However, Judge Kenesaw Mountain Landis, the newly appointed commissioner of baseball, expelled them anyhow. When Jackson sued the Sox in 1924 for back pay, the confessions suddenly materialized in Comiskey's office, and Jackson lost his suit.

Document 4 describes the emergence of the greatest sports hero of the Age of Heroes, Babe Ruth, a former record-breaking left hand pitcher, turned home run king, who was just traded from the Boston Red Sox to the New York Yankees in 1920. That season he hit 54 home runs, bettering his own previous record of 29 set the year before. His accomplishments dramatically changed the nature of play in Major League Baseball and helped fans forget the ignominy of the Black Sox scandal. Historians consider Ruth a compensatory hero because he was a natural player who exemplified brawn over brain (the opposite of Ty Cobb), and his culinary and sexual excesses flaunted traditional morality, epitomizing the free spirit of the 1920s.

The fifth document is drawn from noted author Maya Angelou's memoir *I Know Why the Caged Bird Sings* (1969). She recounts listening to a radio broadcast at her uncle's store in rural Arkansas of a Joe Louis championship fight. Angelou reminds us how important a hero Louis was to African Americans in the late 1930s.

1. Frank Merriwell at Yale

Yale took the field, and as the boys in blue trotted out, the familiar Yale yell broke from hundreds of throats. Blue pennants were wildly fluttering, the band was playing a lively air, and for the moment it seemed as if the sympathy of the majority of the spectators was with Yale.

But when Hinkley, Harvard's great single hitter, who always headed the batting list, walked out with his pet "wagon tongue," a different sound swept over the multitude, and the air seemed filled with crimson pennants.

Merriwell went into the box, and the umpire broke open a pasteboard box, brought out a ball that was wrapped in tin foil, removed the covering, and tossed the snowy sphere to the freshman pitcher Yale had so audaciously stacked up against Harvard.

Frank looked the box over, examined the rubber plate, and seemed to make himself familiar with every inch of the ground in his vicinity. Then he faced Hinkley, and a moment later delivered the first ball.

Hinkley smashed it on the nose, and it was past Merriwell in a second, skipping along the ground and passing over second base just beyond the baseman's reach, although he made a good run for it.

The center fielder secured the ball and returned it to second, but Hinkley had made a safe single off the very first ball delivered.

Harvard roared, while the Yale crowd was silent....

"Here is where Merriwell meets his Waterloo," said Sport Harris. "He'll be batted out before the game is fairly begun...."

Derry, also a heavy hitter, was second on Harvard's list....

Frank sent up a coaxer, but Derry refused to be coaxed. The second ball was high, but Derry cracked it for two bags, and Hinkley got around to third.

It began to seem as if Merriwell would be batted out in the first inning, and the Yale crowd looked weary and disgusted at the start.

From Burt L. Standish, *Frank Merriwell at Yale, or Freshman Against Freshman* (New York: Street & Smith, 1897).

The next batter fouled out, however, and the next one sent a red-hot liner directly at Merriwell. There was no time to get out of the way, so Frank caught it, snapped the ball to third, found Hinkley off the bag, and retired the side without a score.

This termination of the first half of the inning was so swift and unexpected that it took some seconds for the spectators to realize what had happened. When they did, however, Yale was wildly cheered....

Yedding, who was in the box for Harvard, could not have been in better condition, and the first three Yale men to face him went out in one-two-three order, making the first inning a whitewash for both sides.

... In trying to deceive the first man up Merriwell gave him three balls in succession. Then he was forced to put them over. He knew the batter would take one or two, and so he sent two straight, swift ones directly over, and two strikes were called.

Then came the critical moment, for the next ball pitched would settle the matter. Frank sent in a rise and the batter struck at it, missed it, and was declared out, the ball having landed with a "plunk" in the hands of the catcher.

The next batter got first on a single, but the third man sent an easy one to Frank, who gathered it in, threw the runner out at second, and the second baseman sent the ball to first in time to retire the side on a double play.

"You are all right, Merriwell, old man," enthusiastically declared Heffiner, as Frank came in to the bench. "They haven't been able to score off you yet, and they won't be able to touch you at all after you get into gear."

... Yedding showed that he was out for blood, for he allowed but one safe hit, and again retired Yale without a score.

... Yedding came to the bat in this inning, and Merriwell struck him out with ease, while not another man got a safe hit, although one got first on the shortstop's error.

The Yale crowd cheered like Indians when Harvard was shut out for the third time, the freshmen seeming to yell louder than all the others....

The fourth opened in breathless suspense, but it was quickly over, neither side getting a man beyond second.... [T]he fifth inning brought the same result, although Yale succeeded in getting a man to third with only one out. An attempt to sacrifice him home failed, and a double play was made, retiring the side.

Harvard opened the sixth by batting a ball straight at Yale's shortstop, who played tag with it, chasing it around his feet long enough to allow the batter to reach first....

This seemed to break the Yale team up somewhat. The runner tried for second on the first ball pitched, and Yale's catcher overthrew, although he had plenty of time to catch the man. The runner kept on to third and got it on a slide.

Now Harvard rejoiced. Although he had not obtained a hit, the man had reached third on two errors, and there was every prospect of scoring.

Merriwell did not seem to lose his temper or his coolness. He took plenty of time to let everybody get quieted down, and then he quickly struck out the next man. The third man, however, managed to hit the ball fairly and knocked a fly into left field. It was gathered in easily, but the man on third held the bag till the fly was caught and made a desperate dash for home.

The left fielder threw well, and the ball struck in the catcher's mitt. It did not stick, however, and the catcher lost the only opportunity to stop the score.

Harvard had scored at last!

The Harvard cheer rent the air, and crimson fluttered on all sides.

... At the end of the eighth inning the score remained one to nothing in Harvard's favor. It looked as if Yale would receive a shut out, and that was something awful to contemplate....

In the first half of the ninth Harvard went at it to make some more runs. One man got a hit, stole second, and went to third on an error that allowed the batter to reach first.

Sport Harris had been disappointed when Merriwell continued to remain in the box, but now he said:

"He's rattled. Here's where they kill him."

But Frank proved that he was not rattled. He tricked the man on third into getting off the bag and then threw him out in a way.... Then he got down to business, and Harvard was whitewashed for the last time.

"Oh, if Yale can score now!" muttered hundreds.

The first man up flied out to center, and the next man was thrown out at first. That seemed to settle it. The spectators were making preparations to leave. The Yale bat-tender, with his face long and doleful, was gathering up the sticks.

What's that? The next man got a safe hit, a single that placed him on first. Then Frank Merriwell was seen carefully selecting a bat.

"Oh, if he were a heavy hitter!" groaned many voices.

Yedding was confident—much too confident. He laughed in Frank's face. He did not think it necessary to watch the man on first closely, and so that man found an opportunity to steal second.

Two strikes and two balls had been called. Then Yedding sent in a swift one to cut the inside corner. Merriwell swung at it.

Crack! Bat and ball met fairly, and away sailed the sphere over the head of the shortstop.

"Run!"

In a moment [Frank] was scudding down to first, while the left fielder was going back for the ball which had passed beyond his reach. Frank kept on for second. There was so much noise he could not hear the coachers, but he saw the fielder had not secured the ball. He made third, and the excited coacher sent him home with a furious gesture.

Every man, woman and child was standing.... It was a moment of such thrilling, nerve-tingling excitement as is seldom experienced....

The fielder had secured the ball, he drove it to the shortstop, and shortstop whirled and sent it whistling home. The catcher was ready to stop Merriwell.

"Slide!"

That word Frank heard above all the commotion. He did slide. Forward he scooted in a cloud of dust. The catcher got the ball and put it onto Frank—an instant too late!

..."Safe home!" rang the voice of the umpire.

Then another roar, louder, wilder, full of unbounded joy! The Yale cheer! … The sight of sturdy lads in blue, delirious with delight, hugging a dust-covered youth, lifting him to their shoulders, and bearing him away in triumph. Merriwell had won his own game, and his record was made. It was a glorious finish!

"Never saw anything better," declared Harry. "Frank, you are a wonder!"

"He is that!" declared several others. "Old Yale can't get along without him."

2. *Commonweal* Memorializes Christy Mathewson, a Real-Life Merriwell, 1925

… During these days we have all injected curves and lusty smashes into our vista of world news, showing thus how firm a nucleus for our thoughts and emotions is afforded by the national game. And yet there came also the sudden, saddening, report that one of the supreme gentlemen of sport had died, leaving to the world a fine memory and at least a momentary heartache. Christy Mathewson was, of course, a wonderful pitcher—no other man probably has ever brought a President of the United States half way across the continent to a seat at a crucial game; and certainly no other pitcher ever loomed so majestically in young minds, quite overshadowing George Washington and his cherry tree or even that transcendent model of boyhood, Frank Merriwell. Yet "Big-Six" was very much more than an illustration of diamond craft.

With straightforward, manly character he entered the lists of sport a gentleman, and came out a deserving hero. There was about him no flash, no scandal, no cheap clamor for notoriety. One had a securely comfortable feeling that Mathewson would not betray the trust of his position and uncover flaws over which the cheap journals could grin and sentimentalize. During the years following his war experience, when it became more and more evident that gas had weakened his constitution beyond recovery, there was no attempt to capitalize upon his record, but merely a simple resignation to the circumstances and a brave battle with death. Such men have a very real value above and beyond the achievements of brawn and sporting skill. They realize and typify, in a fashion, the ideal of sport—clean power in the hands of a clean and vigorous personality, a courage that has been earned in combat, and a sense of honor which metes out justice to opponents and spurns those victories that have not been earned.

3. The Black Sox Scandal and the Fallen Hero: The Confession of Joe Jackson, 1920

Q: Did anybody pay you any money to help throw that series in favor of Cincinnati?

A: They did.

From editorial, *Commonweal* 2 (October 21, 1925): 288.

From Joe Jackson, confession before the Grand Jury of Cook County, September 28, 1920 (copy in author's possession). Jackson's entire confession has been published in several books, including David Gropman, *Say It Ain't So, Joe! The True Story of Shoeless Joe Jackson* (New York: Citadel Press, 1992).

Q: How much did they pay?

A: They promised me $20,000, and paid me five.

Q: Who promised you the twenty thousand?

A: "Chick" Gandil....

Q: Who paid you the $5,000?

A: Lefty Williams brought it in my room and threw it down....

Q: You say that you told Mrs. Jackson that evening?

A: Did, yes.

Q: What did she say about it?

A: She said she thought it was an awful thing to do.

Q: When was it that this money was brought to your room and that you talked to Mrs. Jackson?

A: It was the second trip to Cincinnati. That night we were leaving.

Q: That was after the fourth game?

A: I believe it was, yes....

Q: You say Abe Attell and Bill Burns are the two people that Claude Williams told you gave you the double cross?

A: Chick Gandil told me that.

Q: Then you talked to Chick Gandil and Claude Williams both about this?

A: Talked to Claude Williams about it, yes, and Gandil more so, because he is the man that promised me this stuff.

Q: How much did he promise you?

A: $20,000 if I would take part.

Q: And you said you would?

A: Yes, sir.

Q: When did he promise you the $20,000?

A: It was to be paid after each game.

Q: How much?

A: Split it up some way, I don't know just how much it amounts to, but during the Series it would amount to $20,000. Finally Williams brought me this $5,000, threw it down.

Q: What did you say to Williams when he threw down the $5,000?

A: I asked him what the hell had come off here.

Q: What did he say?

A: He said Gandil said we all got a screw through Abe Attell. Gandil said that we got double crossed through Abe Attell, he got the money and refused to turn it over to him. I don't think Gandil was crossed as much as he crossed us.

Q: You think Gandil may have gotten the money and held it from you, is that right?

A: That's what I think, I think he kept the majority of it....

Q: And you were to be paid $5,000 after each game, is that right?

A: Well, Attell was supposed to give the $100,000. It was to be split up, paid to him, I believe, and $15,000 a day or something like that, after each game.

Q: That is to Gandil?

A: Yes.

Q: At the end of the first game you didn't get any money, did you?

A: No, I did not, no, sir.

Q: What did you do then?

A: I asked Gandil what is the trouble? He says, "Everything is all right" he had it.

Q: Then you went ahead and threw the second game, thinking you would get it then, is that right?

A: We went ahead and threw the second game, we went after him again.... "Everything is all right," he says, "What the hell is the matter?"

Q: After the third game what did you say to him?

A: After the third game I says, "Somebody is getting a nice little jazz, everybody is crossed." He said, "Well, Abe Attell and Bill Burns had crossed him," that is what he said to me.

Q: He said Abe Attell and Bill Burns had crossed him?

A: Yes, sir....

Q: Who do you think was the man they approached?

A: Why, Gandil....

Q: Didn't you think it was the right thing for you to go and tell Comiskey about it?

A: I did tell them once, "I am not going to be in it." I will just get out of that altogether.

Q: Who did you tell that to?

A: Chick Gandil.

Q: What did he say?

A: He said I was into it already and I might as well stay in. I said, "I can go to the boss and have every damn one of you pulled out of the limelight." He said, "It wouldn't be well for me if I did that."...

Q: Do you recall the fourth game that Cicotte pitched?

A: Yes, sir.

Q: Did you see any fake plays made by yourself or anybody on [*sic*] that game, that would help throw the game?

A: Only the wildness of Cicotte.

Q: What was that?

A: Hitting the batter, that is the only thing that told me they were going through with it. (Ed.: *He is referring to Game 1.*)

Q: Did you make any intentional errors yourself that day?

A: No, sir, not during the whole series.

Q: Did you bat to win?

A: Yes.

Q: And run the bases to win?

A: Yes, sir.

Q: And field the balls at the outfield to win?

A: I did....

Q: The fourth game Cicotte pitched again? It was played out here in Chicago and Chicago lost it 2 to nothing? Do you remember that?

A: Yes, sir.

Q: Did you see anything wrong about that game that would lead you to believe there was an intentional fixing?

A: The only thing that I was sore about that game, the throw I made to the plate, Cicotte tried to intercept it....

Q: Did you do anything to throw those games?

A: No, sir.

Q: Any game in the series?

A: Not a one. I didn't have an error or make no misplay....

Q: To keep on with these games, the fifth game, did you see anything wrong with that or any of the games, did you see any plays that you would say might have been made to throw that particular game?

A: Well, I only saw one play in the whole series, I don't remember what game it was in, either, it was in Cincinnati.

Q: Who made it?

A: Charlie Risburg.... It looked like a perfect double play. And he only gets one, gets the ball and runs over to the bag with it in place of throwing it in front of the bag....

Q: When did Eddie Cicotte tell you he got $10,000?

A: The next morning after the meeting we had in his room.

Q: Did you tell him how much you got? ...

A: I told him I got five thousand.

Q: What did he say?

A: He said I was a God damn fool for not getting it in my hands like he did.

Q: What did he mean by that? …

A: Why, he meant he would not trust them, they had to pay him before he did anything.

Q: He meant then that you ought to have got your money before you played, is that it?

A: Yes, that's it.

Q: Did you have a talk with any of the other players about how much they got?

A: I understand McMullin got five and Risburg five thousand, that's the way I understand….

Q: Weren't you in on the inner circle?

A: No, I never was with them, no, sir. It was mentioned to me in Boston. As I told you before, they asked me what would I consider, $10,000? and I said no, then they offered me twenty.

Q: Who mentioned it first to you?

A: Gandil….

Q: What did he say?

A: He asked me would I consider $10,000 to frame up something and I asked him frame what? and he told me and I said no.

Q: What did he say?

A: Just walked away from me, and when I returned here to Chicago he told me that he would give me twenty and I said no again, and on the bridge where you go into the club house he told me I could either take it or let it alone, they were going through.

Q: What did they say?

A: They said," You might as well say yes or say no and play ball or anything you want." I told them I would take their word….

THE FOREMAN:

Q: What makes you think that Gandil was double crossing you, rather than Attell and Burns?

A: What made me think it was Gandil going out on the coast, so I was told, I was surmising what I heard, they came back and told me he had a summer home, big automobile, doesn't do a lick of work; I know I can't do that way.

MR. REPLOGLE:

Q: In other words, if he double crossed you fellows he couldn't come back and face them, and he had plenty of money to stay out there. It wasn't at the time that you thought Gandil was double crossing you, you thought Gandil was telling the truth, is that right?

A: No, I told Williams after the first day it was a crooked deal all the way through, Gandil was not on the square with us….

Q: Do you have any suspicion about the White Sox, any of the players throw any of the games this summer?

A: Well, there have been some funny looking games, runs, I could have just my own belief about it, I wouldn't accuse the men….

4. Babe Ruth, the New American Sports Hero, 1920

Next to the leading candidates for the White House, a one-time waif on the streets of Baltimore is perhaps the most discussed person on the American continent to-day. In fact, the name of the abundantly illustrated and illustrious idol of the great American game of baseball, George H. Ruth, is said to be on the tips of more tongues than any living American. And all because he has at this writing batted forty-six home runs during the present baseball season, with the likelihood of increasing the total to half a hundred or more. This tall, broad-shouldered, keen-eyed young man from Maryland plays right field for the New York Americans, the American League team which metropolitan followers of baseball hope will win the pennant. To the millions of baseball enthusiasts, Mr. Ruth is known as "Babe" and his team as "The Yankees."

Ruth and his celebrity make an interesting study. In the first place, the purchase of this player, last winter, from the Boston Americans for $130,000*—two and a half times as much—as the highest price previously paid for a baseball star—created something of a sensation, even in New York. Ruth "took possession" of the metropolis early in the season when he drove home runs for distances that seemed impossible. There are no indications of the craze subsiding. On the contrary, he is being filmed for the movies and is said to have received $100,000 for posing before the camera, in addition to a salary running well into five figures for his services on the diamond. Truly this athlete, as he is quoted in the *New Success Magazine*, as saying of himself, "hits big" or he "misses big," with the accent on the "hit:" "I swing every time with all the force I have," he confided to the *New Success* biographer, "and strike out just as often as others in the .300 class; but when I hit the ball, I *hit* it."

Scientifically, writes Professor A. L. Hodges, in the *Cleveland News-Leader*, Ruth's phenomenal home-run record is largely due to the fact that, consciously or unconsciously, he has found a way of producing the collision between his bat and the ball at the "center of percussion" more frequently than any other player. The weight of the batter has very little to do with the matter of home runs, but, we read, his arm muscles are a controlling factor. Viewed as a mechanical problem, observes this physicist, the home run requires a bat just as heavy as a player can easily swing, the ball to be impelled at an angle of forty-five degrees.

Home runs, we read, depend primarily on quickness of eye and a speedy response of the body's muscles to the message which the eye flashes to the brain. The ball as it leaves the pitcher is often traveling at the rate of a hundred

*Ed. note: Actual cost was $125,000 and $350,000 loan.

From "A New Hero of the Great American Game at Close Range," *Current Opinion* 49:4 (October, 1920) 477–78.

and fifty feet a second or nearly two miles a minute; and the eye-movement necessary to follow it increases greatly as the ball draws nearer to the plate, its speed actually being ten times greater when it crosses the plate. It is of interest to read that "the ball which Ruth hits for a home run weighs about five ounces. If his bat gives it a velocity of five hundred feet a second, we find, by applying a well-known formula of physics that 1,200 foot-pounds of actual energy or work is done. Now, if it takes Ruth one-twentieth of a second to impart this energy by a swing of his bat, this would be at the rate of 24,000 foot-pounds a second, which is about forty-four horse-power. The king of home-run makers is then working at the rate of forty-four horsepower every time he cracks out one of his long hits, but he maintains this rate for such a brief length of time that not very much actual work is involved."

... Ruth is twenty-six years old and is married. In winter he manages his cigar factory in Boston and is possessed of shrewd business sense as well as a sense of humor.

On the humorous side, we read that early in the present season his muff of a fly bait, Ruth being a right-fielder, cost his team their opening game, played in Philadelphia. Prior to the start of the second game, next day, a delegation of Philadelphians marched to the home plate with a package neatly wrapped up, and asked for Ruth. The umpires held up the game while the players of both teams gathered around the fortunate recipient of the gift. Ruth opened the package and pulled out a brown derby hat of the vintage of 1898—a low-crown affair of the kind usually worn exclusively by German comedians. To the uninitiated it may be explained that, "winning the brown derby" is the last word in baseball ridicule. A situation had been created to make Ruth not only appear ridiculous but to give the "fans" of an opposition city an opportunity to jibe him mercilessly. But Ruth donned the brown derby and grinned, thanked the chairman of the presentation committee, wore the hat to the players' bench, and then posed for as many photographers as wanted to snap him in the ridiculous headgear.

Because Ruth came into professional baseball through a Catholic Protectory, in Baltimore, none, say, the *New Success* reporter, should get the impression that he was an incorrigible or a particularly bad boy. His mother died when he was quite young and his father was engaged in a business that was abolished by the Eighteenth Amendment. Their neighbors thought that Ruth would be better off away from home, so he was sent to the protectory.* He learned to play baseball on the protectory team.

His fame as a pitcher and batsman spread to such an extent that he was offered a place on the Baltimore team, of the International League, by the owner of that team, John Dunn. In order to use Ruth on his team, and get him out of the school, it was necessary for Dunn legally to adopt Ruth. As a result of this adoption the Baltimore writers nicknamed him "Babe." The name has clung to him.

Ruth has never lost his fondness for boys.... The home run that gave him more enjoyment than any other, came in New York on a warm sunshiny afternoon last May. Ruth hit a ball far over the grandstand roof out of the Polo Grounds

*Ed. note: Ruth was 7; his mother died 5 years later.

and it landed in Manhattan Field, adjoining. There a group of urchins were having a game with a tattered string ball, which they were keeping together with much difficulty. "The new ball from Ruth's mighty bat came like a gift from heaven."

5. Joe Louis as African American Hero: The Reminiscences of Maya Angelou, 1938

"I ain't worried 'bout this fight. Joe's gonna whip that cracker like it's open season."

"He gone whip him till that white boy call him Momma."

... "A quick jab to the head.... left to the head and a right and another left." ... "They're in a clench...."

... "The referee is moving in to break them up; Louis pushed the contender away and it's an uppercut to the chin. The contender is hanging on, now he's backing away. Louis catches him with a short left to the jaw."

... As I pushed my way into the Store I wondered if the announcer gave any thought ... that he was addressing as "ladies and gentlemen" all the Negroes around the world ... glued to their "master's voice."

... "He's got Louis against the ropes and now it's a left to the body and a right to the ribs.... The contender keeps raining the blows on Louis. It's another to the body, and it looks like Louis is going down." My race groaned. It was our people falling. It was another lynching, yet another Black man hanging on a tree. One more woman ambushed and raped....

... This might be the end of the world. If Joe lost we were back in slavery and beyond help. It would all be true, the accusations that we were lower types of human beings ... stupid and ugly and lazy and dirty and, unlucky and worst of all, that God Himself hated us and ordained us to be hewers of wood and drawers of water, forever and ever....

"He's off the ropes, ladies and gentlemen.... He's moving towards the center of the ring." ... "And now it looks like Joe is mad. He's caught Carnera* with a left hook to the head and a right to the head. It's a left jab to the body and another left to the head. There's a left cross and a right to the head. The contender's right eye is bleeding ... Louis is penetrating every block.... Louis sends a left to the body and it's the uppercut to the chin and the contender is dropping. He's on the canvas...."

"Here's the referee. He's counting.... seven ... eight, nine, ten." ... The fight is all over.... "The winnah, and still heavyweight champeen of the world ... Joe Louis."

Champion of the world. A Black boy. Some Black mother's son. He was the strongest man in the world....

Those who lived too far ... stay[ed] in town [after the fight]. It wouldn't do for a Black man and his family to be caught on a lonely country road on a night when Joe Louis had proved that we were the strongest people in the world.

---

*Ed. note: Carnera was knocked out by Louis in 1935, when neither was world champion.

From Maya Angelou, *I Know Why the Caged Bird Sings* (New York: Random House, 1969), 110–15.

ESSAYS

The first essay in this section focuses on Red Grange and the prominence of sports heroes in the 1920s, often described as "the Golden Age of Sport." Harold E. "Red" Grange (1903–1991) was a three-time consensus All-American halfback at the University of Illinois (1923–1925). In one game in 1924 against the University of Michigan, Grange ran for five touchdowns the first five times he carried the ball at distances of 95, 67, 56, 44, and 56 yards. In 2007 ESPN rated Grange the greatest player in the history of college football. He and his agent signed an extremely lucrative contract with the Chicago Bears moments after his last college game in 1925, at a time when college stars seldom turned pro because the National Football League (NFL) had little prestige and low salaries. His presence drew out the crowds, especially 73,000 who saw him play the New York Giants at the Polo Grounds just a few weeks after ending his college career. Grange helped open the doors for other college stars. John Carroll, Regents Professor at Lamar University and author of *Red Grange and the Rise of Modern Football* (2004), examines the allure of heroes like Grange. Such athletes were renowned, not because they were celebrities, famous for being famous, but because of concrete and readily visible achievements. These heroes seemed to simultaneously represent both traditional small town American values of a bygone era like courage and rugged individualism, as well as teamwork, a trait that reflected the more modern industrial urban society of their current day.

The second essay by Susan E. Cayleff of San Diego State University, author of the outstanding *Babe: The Life and Legend of Babe Didrikson Zaharias* (1995), examines the athletic accomplishments, personal life, and legend of the all-time greatest American female athlete. Babe was extremely versatile, first starring at basketball, and then single-handedly winning the Amateur Athletic Union championship for her company team and setting four world records. She won two gold medals and a silver at the 1932 Olympics; she was limited to three medals only because no woman was permitted to compete in more than three events. Babe subsequently learned golf, and became an outstanding professional.

In the third essay, historian Dominic J. Capeci, Jr., University Distinguished Professor at Missouri State University, and sociologist Martha Wilkerson of Missouri State University, who collaborated on *Layered Violence The Detroit Rioters of 1943* (2009), have written an essay examining how world heavyweight champion Joe Louis first became a hero in the African American community through his boxing exploits when he fought former champion Primo Carnera of Italy. Louis represented opposition to imperialist Italy who had invaded Abyssinia (Ethiopia) in 1935, and then he became world champion in 1937 dethroning James J. Braddock. Joe went on to become an American hero in 1938 when he defended his title against German Max Schmeling, who was perceived as representing Nazism. Louis continued to be a racial and national hero in the ensuing years when the United States went to war, boxing to raise money for the war effort, and serving his country in the U.S. Army, during which time he occasionally spoke out against racism in the military.

Red Grange and American Sport Heroes of the 1920s

JOHN M. CARROLL

During the 1920s, especially after he retired as a football player in 1935, the sports media routinely referred to Red Grange as a football hero. Historians and scholars who study popular culture now debate whether sports figures of that era or today are legitimate American heroes or simply well-publicized celebrities. Peter Williams and Michael Oriard argue, for example, that popular sports are manifestations of archetypal myths, and a select few of the participants should be regarded as heroes. Other scholars such as Richard Schickel and Richard Crepeau question the idea of sports idols as authentic heroes. Schickel, a film historian, maintains that by the 1920s, at least, "The public ceased to insist that there be an obvious correlation between achievement and fame. It was no longer absolutely necessary for its favorites to perform a real-life heroic act, to invent a boon for mankind, to create a business enterprise." Beginning around World War I, it was possible to become a celebrity by just becoming famous—in Daniel Boorstin's phrase, to be "known for your well-knownness." Despite their disagreement on the distinction between a sports hero and a sports celebrity, most scholars agree that the hero-celebrity in athletics was a phenomenon of the early twentieth century and that the 1920s was a germination period for this new type of sports figure.

Grantland Rice provided [in the late 1940s] an uncomplicated explanation for the rise of the sports idol in the postwar years: … "The answer is a simple one. It is because the postwar period gave the game the greatest collection of stars, involving both skill and color, that sport has ever known since the first cave man tackled the mammoth and the aurochs bull." Two more recent studies of heroes and hero-worship in the 1920s hold that it was not the sports stars but the mass media itself, including Rice, that created sports idols during the decade. In a study of Grantland Rice, Mark Inabinett maintains that "the sportswriters of the Golden Age worked in a time when they had a virtual monopoly on sports news" and "the image of unsurpassed greatness attained by the leading athletes of the Golden Age is more attributable to the influence of sportswriters than to the caliber of the sportsmen." Bruce J. Evensen, in a book on the mass media of the 1920s and the rise of Jack Dempsey, is more cautious: "the cultivation of sports celebrity and mass-mediated hero worship during the 1920s" resulted from "a generation's search for significance during a period in American history when for many the world seemed increasingly insensible." Grange himself acknowledged many times that sportswriters played an important role in building up sports personalities during the 1920s and conceded that maybe "it [sport] was built out of proportion."

Richard Schickel has suggested that the press was only one element in a changing postwar society that helped usher in the age of celebrity. The 1920s brought together the emerging forces of modernization that allowed the public

---

to become intimate with outstanding (and sometimes not so outstanding) individuals. Rapid development or improvements in motion pictures, transportation, photography, advertising, and radio ..., created an environment in which "almost anyone could be wrested out of whatever context had originally nurtured him" and turned into a celebrity. Schickel traces the great transformation in modern society to World War I and views developments in the motion picture industry as a precursor to the rise of the cult of celebrity during the 1920s. Many scholars would agree with much of that analysis but quickly point out that not many of the numerous celebrity-heroes of the 1920s have become enduring symbols of the period. In sports, Ruth, Dempsey, Tilden, Jones, and Grange are familiar figures, yet Gertrude Ederle and Gene Tunney, to name two, were celebrities of the golden decade who are less widely known now.

Benjamin Rader argues that the emergence of numerous athletic heroes in the 1920s "went deeper than the skillful ballyhooing of the promoters and journalistic flights of fancy." They were a creation of the public itself. "The athletes as public heroes served a compensatory function ... as the society became more complicated and systematized as success had to be won increasingly in bureaucracies, the need for heroes who leaped to fame and fortune outside the rules of the system seemed to grow. No longer were the heroes the lone business tycoon or the statesman, but the 'stars'—from the movies and sports." Those in the public domain who were obsessed with their individual powerlessness gained the most satisfaction from "the athletic hero who presented an image of all-conquering power"—Babe Ruth's titanic home runs, Dempsey's crushing knockout blows, and Grange's dramatic acceleration on long touchdown runs. Less admired were those athletes who, like Tunney and Ty Cobb, employed a more "scientific style" to achieve victory.

Beyond their personification of raw power, which also symbolized America's emergence as a world economic and political force, many of the enduring sports idols of the era represented traditional Victorian virtues and the ideal of the self-made man. The public image of Grange as a shy, modest, and clean-cut youth who toted heavy chunks of ice to pay his way through college helps explain his appeal as a sports hero. Although not every enduring sports hero-celebrity of the era embodied all the qualities associated with traditional values (Ruth was anything but modest and clean-cut and Bobby Jones came from a wealthy background), most possessed at least some. Grange's stature was enhanced by the popular perception created by the media that he was a product of the West and represented frontier values that were being threatened in an increasingly industrial and urban nation. Although his hometown of Wheaton was rapidly evolving into a suburb of Chicago, the eastern media typically portrayed it as a rustic village. Like Dempsey, Bronko Nagurski, and above all Charles Lindbergh, Grange came to epitomize those virtues of farm, village, and frontier life that many Americans prized but believed to be endangered by the process of modernization. It is also noteworthy that the press focused an inordinate amount of attention on Grange's passion for fast automobiles and his frequent brushes with the law for driving at excessive speeds. John W. Ward has suggested that the extraordinary public acclaim for Lindbergh as the quintessential hero of the

1920s might be partially explained by the fact that he represented both frontier values and the triumph of the machine during a decade in which those issues were central to the lives of many Americans. To a lesser degree, Grange's public image touched on these fundamental concerns of the 1920s.

During his retirement years, Grange occasionally offered ideas on why the 1920s produced so many sports heroes. Like Grantland Rice, he emphasized that many sports celebrities "had great personalities" and acknowledged that a talented group of sportswriters and promoters had given them enormous publicity. Grange particularly focused on the impact of World War I, which he described as a trying time. Sports seemed to provide a natural outlet for the release of pent-up energy and tension as "everyone seemed to let their hair down after World War I." In terms of his emergence as the nation's premier football hero, Grange perceptively pointed out that few outstanding players had preceded him in that category. "I don't think there were any outstanding names in football in those days.... Starting with Jim Thorpe and a lot of them the names were made after most of these people were out of school and the writers wrote about them, and guys that never saw them play started telling how good they were." Grange was undoubtedly correct. Early stars of the game such as William "Pudge" Heffelfinger, Willie Heston, ... and even Thorpe became more widely known in the 1920s and after than they had been in their collegiate days, when football was more a regional sport. It was not until after World War I that the mass media began to promote truly national football heroes.

Although Bruce Evensen and others have emphasized the mass media's responsibility for the rise of numerous sports heroes during the 1920s, a number of other factors also set the stage for this development in the case of football. America's involvement in World War I helped elevate football from a game that had a sometimes-sordid past to one that became associated with fitness, fortitude, and even patriotism. The war also hastened the development of better highways, which made many rural state universities more accessible to students as well as football fans. Universities responded by constructing large stadiums, many of them war memorials, to accommodate the overflow crowds. An increase in automobile ownership, better roads, and new or expanded stadiums combined to make a dramatic impact in the Midwest, South, and Pacific Coast and to make football a genuinely national game. New technology and the further development of radio and newsreels, along with improvements in photography, helped provide the basis for football enthusiasts to closely follow outstanding teams and star players. These innovations, combined with a more nationally oriented print media and an increase in intersectional games, created more interest in football outside the eastern region of the country.

Although Midwestern football was played conservatively by today's standards, in the 1920s it was considered an open game that featured more passing and scoring than the more established eastern game. In general, the eastern press remained skeptical of highly regarded teams and players from outside the region where the game was developed. Red Grange changed the minds of many eastern reporters when he almost single-handedly defeated a highly rated University of Pennsylvania team in Philadelphia on a rain-soaked field in 1925. It may have been the most significant game he played as a collegian. Grange's central place in football history can be attributed to timing. He began his college career just as football was reaping the benefits of being associated with the war effort and the media was perfecting a formula for focusing national attention on hero-celebrities....

It is not clear whether Grange was the best football player of all time or of the 1920s, but he was a gifted athlete who had enormous natural ability, a willingness to work hard, and a great desire to succeed. He competed at a time when fewer of the nation's best athletes played college football (compared with today) and many did not have sound training at the preparatory level. During Grange's years at Illinois, Bob Zuppke complained, "I wish you kids hadn't played in high school—then I wouldn't have to waste so much time correcting the bad habits you've developed." It is not surprising that Grange, with a natural talent for the game, excelled in college football. What helped make him a household name ... was ... that he played three of his best college games (against Michigan and Chicago in 1924 and Penn in 1925) at pivotal times, when, for various reasons, the media focused great attention on him and his team. Grange's extraordinary individual performances also came at a time when some sportswriters were questioning the prevailing view that college coaches were the most important factor in creating winning teams. Although coaches would continue to be revered by football experts ... (Knute Rockne's exalted stature in the 1920s ...), a number of postwar writers began to emphasize that overpaid coaches were of less importance in producing victories than gifted individual performers. Chicago sportswriter Ralph Cannon made the point in 1923, when he wrote that "a couple of halfbacks like Grange are more to be desired than a genius of even a Haughton," ... the famed Harvard coach of the 1910s. Grange's spectacular feats on the gridiron came at a time when the pendulum was swinging, for the moment at least, toward more emphasis on individual performers rather than field generals who directed the game from the bench.

When he signed a professional contract after his final college game, Grange became, at least temporarily, the most written about man in America. Many former collegians played pro football at the time, and a number of them had begun playing before their college classes graduated. College officials made Grange's decision to turn pro a cause célèbre because they were smarting over perceived past abuses by the pros against college football. They were also concerned about the renewed attack against the alleged corruption in the collegiate game that would eventually culminate in the Carnegie Report of 1929 and, above all, by the fact that Grange had come to symbolize college football. Despite the then widely held view that Grange rescued the struggling pro game from the verge of extinction, college coaches and administrators were more concerned about the relative strength of pro football than its weaknesses. Using a strategy perfected by boxing promoter Tex Rickard, C. C. Pyle orchestrated a public relations campaign centered around a near-suicidal schedule of games that embedded Grange's name into the national consciousness. He and Grange helped popularize pro football, but Pyle's strategy of relying on the star system to fill stadiums, emulated by other pro owners, was not in the long-term interest of the game. His reckless scheduling methods designed to maximize profits, which Grange did not oppose, contributed to Red's career-threatening injury and his fall from public grace.

Grange reached his nadir as a football player and public idol in 1928.... [H]e was ridiculed by some journalists and depicted as a fallen hero. After he had gone through a short period of moodiness and defensiveness with the media, his finer qualities reasserted themselves. He admitted making mistakes, refused to blame Pyle for his misfortune, declined public pity, and carried on as an impaired by effective pro football players. Relying on integrity, modesty, and stick-to-itiveness, Grange persevered, and the public forgave him. When the onset of the depression deflated public interest in spectator sport and the fascination with star performers, Grange was almost instantly portrayed in the pres as a throwback to a bygone era. Faced with declining attendance and gate receipts, college coaches and their allies searched diligently for the next Red Grange who might reverse their economic fortunes. Ironically, as Grange's effectiveness as a player diminished he joined the media guild, which had once gloated over his tarnished image, and emerged as one of football's most trusted spokesmen.

Babe Didrikson Zaharias: The "Texas Tomboy"

SUSAN E. CAYLEFF

In the early 1930s, an unsuspecting New York newspaper reporter approached Mildred Ella "Babe" Didrikson. She was already, at the young age of nineteen, nationally known as a championship basketball player and double gold and silver medalist in track and field at the 1932 Los Angeles Olympics. The reporter said, "I'm told you also swim, shoot, ride, row, box, and play tennis, golf, basketball, football, polo and billiards. Is there anything at all you don't play?" "Yeah," the East Texan replied, "dolls."

A life study of Babe Didrikson (1911–1956) presents the women's and sport historian with numerous challenges and possibilities. She was unarguably the most multi-talented athlete of the twentieth century, male or female. She played semi-professional basketball, softball, enjoyed a short stint as a successful harmonica-playing stage entertainer, and when she turned her will and talent to golf in the thirties, forties, and fifties, she won an unprecedented thirteen consecutive tournaments. Ironically, "Didrikson's versatility probably had its roots in the lack of opportunities for women in sports. Male athletes specialized in one sport with aspirations of turning professional in it." But Babe, proficient in two sports that had no pro ranks for women, "moved from sport to sport as opportunities presented themselves to her" and "plied her trade by taking limited engagements in everything."

In addition to her world records and dominance in the high jump, eighty-meter hurdles, javelin toss and softball throw, she was an atypical American

---

From Susan Cayleff, "The 'Texas Tomboy': The Life and Legend of Babe Didrikson Zaharias," Organization of American Historians, *Magazine of History* 7 (Summer 1992): 28–33, by permission of Oxford University Press.

hero. Her ethnic Norwegian background, working-class ways, poor Southern origins, and gender posturing made her an unlikely character to capture the nation's imagination. Sports were her entree into front page headlines, but her clever manipulation of the press and unceasing hustling of gigs and opportunities made her a consummate self-promoter. She told tales of mythic proportion about herself which included scuttling her birth date to make her Olympic victories occur at age fifteen, not nineteen; the wrestling of a bull in downtown Beaumont, Texas; slugging it out with Baby Stribling, then middleweight boxing champion (in fact this was a staged photo session); scaling the outside walls of a multi-story Olympic dormitory to swipe a souvenir flag; typing 186 words per minute at her secretarial position at Employer's Casualty Insurance Company for whom she played sports in Dallas (her scant correspondence reveals rank typing skills and significant grammatical shortcomings); the false claim that she won seventeen, not thirteen consecutive golf tournaments (this "fact" appeared at her Memorial Museum in Beaumont); and her favorite sleight of hand—literally creating larger-than-life size myths about herself. She was, in fact, average in stature—five feet five inches and one hundred forty pounds—but would unabashedly exaggerate her height, weight, and strength. For Babe, the impact of a story justified any hyperbole. She learned story-telling skills from her seafaring father, and regaled her schoolyard buddies, teachers, athletic peers, and sportswriters with dazzling and barely believable feats.

As a personality she was charismatic and willful to the point of abrasiveness: few felt neutrally towards her. Women on the Ladies' Professional Golf Association tour which she helped co-found in 1948 were horrified—and intimidated—by her locker-room antics. She would enter and bellow, "What'd y'all show up for? See who's gonna finish second?" She knew how to psychologically immobilize her opponents and steal their limelight. Not surprisingly, her habit of monopolizing radio interviews with several athletes by belting out a tune on her harmonica did not endear her to many. Her uncanny ability to boast and make good on her predictions of her own accomplishments further infuriated her competitors. She warned the starting forward of the soon-to-be national champion Golden Cyclones women's basketball team (1930–32) that she would usurp her position within weeks. She did just that. She would predict the route of a golf ball's travel, or a final round's score, and delight the press and depress her opponents when her bravado proved true. All of these tactics gave her a competitive edge. In essence, she proclaimed, "I am the greatest!" decades before Muhammad Ali emerged as the king of self-congratulatory behavior.

That she was female, androgynous to the point of boyish-looking as a youth, coarsely spoken and physically brash made her fame and popularity all the more unique. In the years immediately following the Olympics, there was a double-edged reciprocity between Didrikson and the press. Her "deficient femininity" and "disturbing masculinity" sparked constant fears of lesbianism, or worse yet, the existence of a "third sex" in women's sports. Babe played a fascinating role in all of this. She reveled in the (early) persona of the boyish, brazen, unbeatable renegade, but cringed at the innuendos of abnormality. She was the consummate tomboy—beating boys at their own games. In fact, "boyishness" was tolerable and even engaging: "mannishness," on the other hand, insinuated a confirmed condition out of which she would not grow. The latter charge was the greater of the two insults and confirmed her abnormality. One Associated Press release comforted the reader that "she is not a freakish looking character … (but) a normal, healthy, boyish looking girl." Babe was keenly aware of how these portrayals cast her outside of the female gender. Poisonous stories flowed from journalists' pens, likening her to Amazonian creatures. These renditions were so vitriolic that they evoked mothers' warnings that they would "not let their daughters grow up to be like Babe Didrikson."

Yet throughout the condemnation and ridicule, Babe persevered in her attempt to earn a living at sport in an era when it was virtually impossible for a woman to do so. Thus she participated in one-on-one demonstrations that at times had almost carnival-like aspects. She pitched spring training for the St. Louis Cardinals; put on golf ball driving exhibitions with male golf-great Gene Sarazen; played donkey-softball with an all-male, all-bearded touring softball team, prompting the *New York Evening Post* to crow with the headline, "Famous Woman Athlete Pitches for Whisker Team;" sang and ran on a treadmill in a wildly successful albeit short-lived stint in a one-woman vaudeville-type show and even challenged the winning horse of the Kentucky Derby to a foot race.

For these reasons, and her infinitely quotable one-liners, which shocked as much as they entertained (when asked how she drove the golf ball so hard Babe replied, "I just loosen my girdle and let 'er fly!"), Didrikson was a favorite with the press. As her brother, Bubba Didrikson, said when interviewed about his deceased sister, "They called her a sportswriter's dream because she always had time for them…. She never rejected anyone who wanted to interview her. She was wise. She knew that they could make her or break her … she knew that, and she liked it."

This symbiotic relationship debilitated Babe at times. Labeled a "muscle moll" by *Vanity Fair* in 1932, Babe perpetually battled the image of a creature not-quite-female. As she matured, and cultural tolerance for her tomboyishness waned (as it eventually does for young women who excel in male physical endeavors), she deliberately sought to deconstruct her inappropriate past and construct a non-threatening, normal heterosexual, feminine life script.

In this context, Babe experienced the difficulty of being a woman who defied the acceptable parameters of femininity. Middle-class cultural ideals of her era dictated sacrificial devotion to husband, children and home, attention to physical beautification, and a self-effacing demeanor. She consciously set about perfecting the more tolerable aspects of this ideal feminine role. According to Bertha Bowen, a friend and protector who shepherded Babe through the upper-class waters of Texas golf, they began a campaign to feminize her replete with a clothing overhaul, make-up applications, and other accoutrements of femininity such as hairdos, hosiery, and silk slips. Bowen even chased Babe through the former's Texas home with a girdle admonishing her that no decent woman would step outside without wearing one.

Babe realized that further success depended upon recasting herself to conform to acceptable notions of femininity. Women athletes in particular lived with conflicting ideals. A "youthful appearance became fashionable … and an 'athletic' image … made action itself a sort of fashion." For women athletes this meant facing the contradiction between developing the body in what was seen as an "un feminine" fashion versus being a "real" (culturally-constructed) woman. The public attitude, therefore, was ambivalent toward women athletes, not universally approving as many historians claim. If the woman athlete was shapely but not muscular, sporting but not overly competitive, heterosexual, and participating in a "beautiful" sport (defined by sportswriters as swimming, golf, tennis or ice-skating), then and only then did she fulfill the ideal. Babe, like so many other athletes of her era, either adopted an apologetic attitude offering "proofs" of her femininity or struggled with her identity as the criticism and innuendo mounted. In her as-told-to autobiography *This Life I've Led* (1955), Babe offered numerous examples of dating boys, marriage proposals and successes at housekeeping, and sewing and cooking to prove her normality. Much of this was grossly exaggerated or fictitious.

In 1938, Babe's meeting of and marriage to George Zaharias cemented her transition to appropriate womanhood. Their meeting and courtship represented the stuff reporters dream of for they were both media hounds. Zaharias, wealthy and well-known by his wrestling tag-name, "The Crying Greek from Cripple Creek," was also a sports promoter of renown. The credentials he gained as a world-class wrestler from 1932 to 1938 were impressive enough to have him inducted into the … Hellenic Hall of Fame for Greek Athletes in 1982. Significantly, George abandoned his own lucrative career in the ring in order to manage Babe's career. Thus she was the primary wage-earner, although interviews revealed she controlled none of her own monies. So it was that two of sports' most adept hustlers merged their considerable talents. The media idealized their relationship throughout their life together, some resorting to unabashedly sappy prose. The significance of this increases as their marital harmony decreases. Ample evidence exists that Babe's "Greek God" had, in her own words, become "a God Damned Greek." Yet Babe continued to nurture the image of herself as the happily married lady despite increasing periods of wanderlust on George's part, as well as discord and alienation. Babe's wish to present a happy front was most likely due to her desire to keep the ugly innuendos of years past from reemerging.

Her conscious self-transformation was two-fold: stereotypically defined femininity replaced uncouth roughness and golf became her new passion and career focus. This traditionally elite sport promised ascendancy from her gritty and impoverished working-class roots, although prior to her participation, it hardly guaranteed a financial living. Women's golf was in need of a superstar player and personality in 1943 when Babe finally regained her amateur status after an agonizing series of legal stalemates aimed at barring "her ilk" from the game. And while Babe's style provided ample interest, it was often not the kind that golf's higher-ups sought. Yet despite the sport elites' ambivalence toward her, Babe revolutionized women's golf. In 1947, when Pete Martin of the *Saturday Evening Post* interviewed Babe, he wrote of her, "Not much has been made of the undeniable fact that the Babe has revolutionized the feminine approach to golf." Other sports writers said of her, "Babe Zaharias created big-time women's golf ... her booming power game lowered scores and forced others to imitate her." Pushed by her manager/husband and her own high standards well beyond the comfort level, Babe's practice sessions were deservedly legendary. According to Zaharias in a 1957 *Look* magazine interview, in order to win, Babe drove balls with taped, bloodied and sore hands and complied with his grueling schedules. As Babe herself often said, "I've always been a fighter. Ever since I was a kid, I've scrapped for everything. I want to win every time. If a game is worth playing, it's worth playing to win." Babe devoted herself to perfecting her golf game with the same ferocity that she brought to the Olympic high hurdles and javelin toss. She was equally dominant in her newly chosen arena.

As Babe's powerful golf game and trans-Atlantic victories (in 1947 she became the first American woman to win the British Open) gained coverage in the national press, her outlets for competition grew extremely meager. Few professional tournaments existed for women and so Babe and several other women golfers set about establishing the Ladies' Professional Golf Association (LPGA) to introduce more paying tournaments. Sponsored by monies from sporting goods companies, the fledgling women's tour steadily increased its purses, credibility, and consequently, the number of women able to eke out a living in golf. Babe held office in the LPGA's hierarchy during the first several years of its operation and consistently ranked among the top money winners.

In 1953, her athletic career ground to a halt as she battled colon cancer in what would become a recurring struggle. Didrikson utilized sports metaphors to help her cope with her ailment. She conceptualized the disease as "a hurdle she could leap," "a hole she could birdie," and "the toughest competition of my life." By surrounding herself with familiar and successful life strategies, she coped with her ailment admirably. Unfortunately, her public visibility as a cancer self-help role model—in an era when this was virtually unheard of—was based on misinformation. Her husband and closest female friend Betty Dodd, a promising golf protégée from San Antonio who was twenty years Babe's junior, joined with physicians at the University of Texas Medical Branch at Galveston (where she was repeatedly hospitalized for cancer) in not telling her of the extent of her malignancy. Thus, falsely believing herself cured, Babe played a vital educational function for the American public who cheered her posturing as one who could "beat the beast of cancer." She devoted herself to fund raising for and consciousness raising about the disease while staging a dramatic and successful comeback as a championship golfer mere weeks after her operation. Her phoenix-like rise back to the top of the sports world endeared her to a new audience. She was honored by President Eisenhower at the White House, fêted by the Texas state legislature and the American Cancer Society, and given numerous medical humanitarian awards.

Throughout her illness, which recurred in 1955 and claimed her life prematurely in 1956, Didrikson was inseparable from her "other mate," Betty

Dodd. Intimates interviewed readily acknowledge the friendship and care-taking that transpired between the two women. It clearly replaced the emotional intimacy that had waned so dramatically between Zaharias and Babe. In fact, Dodd lived with the couple for the last six years of Babe's life. They were constant travel companions on the tour, music-making buddies, and a persistent source of infuriation and friction to George who had quite literally been replaced in Babe's affections. While this relationship was never admittedly lesbian, it was undeniably the emotional and physical mainstay of Babe's later life. What is so striking is Didrikson's silence about this bond. She does not mention Dodd until the last pages of her 1955 autobiography. Only accounts from hospital and newspaper records revealed the "devoted friend" who slept on a cot beside Babe's hospital bed. Dodd, interviewed repeatedly throughout the late 1980s, openly professed her love for Babe. Theirs is a classic example of a relationship between women that was life-sustaining, yet culturally minimized due to homophobic fears.

Didrikson's life presents numerous challenges to historians and students alike. Discovering a hero with flaws, who was previously portrayed as unblemished, necessitates a new construction of her life story. Her fierce competitiveness, which served her so well on the playing field, was self-serving and at times damaged personal relationships. Her life has always been told as a series of unimpeded successful quests, much like narratives of conquering male heroes in the epic genre. But when gender, homophobia, cultural beliefs about women athletes, and sex-role expectations for women in the era from 1920 to 1960 are analyzed, a far more conflictual and complex life story emerges. Didrikson furthered opportunities for others in women's sports, although not because she was gender conscious and sought to improve opportunities for others that followed after her. She co-founded the LPGA to increase her own opportunities. But she served as a path-breaking role model by virtue of her accomplishments despite her lack of self-conscious effort to do so. Her work with medical humanitarianism was more deliberately altruistic. Thus she leaves a dual legacy: as an athlete and as a public figure who endured scrutiny to help others.

Her shrine-like gravestone in Beaumont, Texas, which fittingly dominates the family burial plot, misleadingly declares the time-worn cliché: "It's not whether you win or lose, it's how you play the game." Ironically, this epitaph embodies the legend of Didrikson as she chose to mythologize herself. It contrasts sharply with the life and values she actually lived. Hers was a life of struggle, disharmony, cultural conflict and unapproved-of intimacy; this amidst much non-introspective fun-seeking. That she worked so hard in her death-bed autobiography to portray her life as harmonious, non-conflictual and ideally bonded to husband and sports peers, speaks to her savvy desire to construct a culturally acceptable life story. Babe's life as she actually lived it allows the historian and student of history a unique chance to unravel the palpable opportunities open to—and extreme limitations encountered by—women athletes and atypical women in general during this era. Babe Didrikson's life is an invaluable window through which larger issues in women's and sport history can emerge, crystallize, and gain meaning.

Joe Louis, African American Hero and American Hero, 1935–1945

DOMINIC J. CAPECI, JR. AND MARTHA WILKERSON

In an effort to interpret race relations during the 1930s and 1940s, [few] historians have studied heroes, those who cast light on how citizens perceive "the essence of themselves" and on the social milieu in which they live. More than any other hero, heavyweight boxer Joe Louis loomed large from 1934 to 1945, … when Afro-Americans encountered severe hardship challenged racial mores and laid foundations for future advances. Amidst both the hostile racism and reform spirit of the Great Depression, he exemplified black perseverance: God, wrote novelist Ernest Gaines, sent Joe to lift "the colored people's heart." More surprising, he emerged an American hero in the Second World War because of the dramatic impact of Nazism on racial attitudes…. [H]e and his admirers inspired, nurtured and reinforced one another, resulting in his playing several, sometimes contradictory—indeed, multifarious—roles. As a black man in a racist environment, his remarkable transition from race champion to national idol signaled the interplay of the individual, society, and changing times; as much as any[one] his experience provides insights into this watershed period of race relations.

Born May 13, 1914 [to] sharecroppers Lily Reese and Munrow Barrow, Louis grew up near Lafayette, Alabama with his seven brothers and sisters…. [who] migrated to Detroit in 1926…. Introduced to boxing by a friend in 1932, he fell in love with the sport, the environment and, most of all, the thoughts of money and respect that came to those in the ghetto who hit hard and moved quick. He turned professional by his twentieth birthday.

Louis was enormously influenced by a handful of people…. [H]is mother taught him to "trust in God, work hard and hope for the best"; she said "a good name" was "better than money" and encouraged him to be somebody. The aspiring, courageous and decent lives that she and her second husband, Pat Brooks, lived impressed young Louis. Managers John Roxborough and Julien Black echoed this message of black dignity. Aware of the resentment triggered by Jack Johnson, the first black heavyweight champion (who challenged racial mores and fled conviction for violating the Mann Act), they instructed Louis in clean living and sportsmanlike conduct; Jack Blackburn, Louis's trainer and father-like confidant, constantly berated "that fool nigger with his white woman, acting like he owned the world." Marva Trotter, whom Louis married in 1935, also reinforced his drive for excellence….

Between his initiation as a professional boxer in 1934 and his rematch with Max Schmeling in 1938, Louis captured the imagination of blacks everywhere. In the throes of economic crises, when white citizens displayed racial intolerance, … and when white liberals, North and South, ignored society's deep-seated, institutionalized anti-black attitude, Louis appeared messianic; as black leadership

---

Dominic J. Capeci, Jr., and Martha Wilkerson, "Multifarious Hero: Joe Louis, American Society and Race Relations During World Crisis, 1935–1945," *Journal of Sport History* 10:3 (Fall 1983): 5–27. Reprinted with permission.

became more aggressive and black masses more aware, he dramatized their struggle between good and evil. After he defeated Primo Carnera in 1935, for example, Harlem residents poured through the streets "shooting, clapping, laughing, and even crying." Given black opposition to Mussolini's invasion of Ethiopia, they celebrated more than a boxing match. Louis seemed invincible in the ring, recording thirty-five wins, twenty-nine knockouts and one loss to Schmeling in 1936 before becoming champion the following year. Graceful, quick and powerful at 6' 1½", 200 pounds, he annihilated all comers, permitting admirers vicarious victories, "even dreams of vengeance," over white society. As significantly, he seemed both Superman and Little Man, greater than his supporters yet acceptable to them; he challenged stereotypes, instilled hope and provided models for racial advancement. Galahad-like, fighting clean and complimenting opponents, he enhanced black respectability; inarticulate and untutored, having stammered as a youth and never advancing beyond sixth grade, he appealed to those ... who understood action as eloquence and poise as bearing. Whether fighting in the ring or starring in "The Spirit of Youth," a thinly veiled biographic film about himself, he portrayed "black ambition without blundering into fantasy." To Maya Angelou growing up in rural Arkansas, he proved that "we were the strongest people in the world."

... [T]he overwhelming majority of blacks identified with Louis. Below the Mason-Dixon line sharecroppers gathered at general stores or in the yards of white neighbors to hear the broadcast of Louis's fights. They honored him with letters and song, as did Florida stevedores who celebrated his defeat of James Braddock: "Joe Louis hit him so hard he turn roun and roun/He thought he was Alabama bound...." Slum-locked welfare recipients helped fill Comiskey Park for that championship night, while most residents of Chicago's South Side, Detroit's Paradise Valley and New York's Harlem huddled in small groups about their radios before reveling in the streets victoriously. Elites, too, cheered Louis. Lena Home noted that Louis "carried so many of our hopes," while Charles C. Diggs, Michigan State Senator from Detroit, convinced legislative colleagues to officially congratulate the new champion for serving as "an example and inspiration to American youth."

Louis genuinely related to all segments of Black America.... He ate black-eyed peas superstitiously on fight day and he gave money to Alabama 'relatives' who appeared on his mother's doorstep in Detroit. Northern blacks knew that Louis roamed the streets of Detroit's eastside and worked at Ford Motor Company, just as they had done.... Perhaps most endearing, Louis organized jobless pals into the Brown Bomber Softball Team and donated to the community chest. Humble origins aside, Louis hobnobbed with celebrities. He became the darling of entertainers like Bill "Bojangles" Robinson, who introduced him to Hollywood. Louis meshed well with all blacks because they worshipped him for his feats and, as pointedly, for his divine mettle. In the poetry of Langston Hughes: Joe has sense enough to know/He is a god/ So many gods don't know.

Yet Louis enamored few whites before the mid 1930s.... Occasionally, writers ... questioned Louis's intelligence, ridiculed his speech or stereotyped him as "kinky-haired, thicklipped," "shuffling." If many whites "stored up" criticism "for Joe," as an NAACP official suspected, white elites embraced him. Small in number, news-hungry celebrities were drawn by his fame and vote-seeking politicians by his popularity among blacks. Intellectuals and liberals, who challenged white supremacy ... and fought for reform primarily along economic lines ... found in Louis a powerful yet unthreatening symbol of black excellence and interracial unity: "Isn't Joe Louis wonderful?" marveled author Carl Van Vechten. Certainly a handful of the champion's personal friends thought so, including Joe DiMaggio and Ed Sullivan.

Inside the ring, racial attitudes began to shift. Louis's handlers knew that prejudice permeated boxing ... [T]he color line that Jack Dempsey and promoter Tex Richard had drawn from 1919 to 1926 carried into the next decade. By that time, however, boxing had fallen into disrepute, marred by scandal, ignoble champions and undesirable gunmen. Roxborough and Black recognized Louis's talent and the opportunity for personal gain and social change ... provided they could avoid scandal and bury the memory of Johnson. They established rules of public behavior for Louis and, in 1935, contracted with white promoter Mike Jacobs. Shrewdly, he scheduled the Carnera bout in Yankee Stadium, which exposed Louis to a known opponent in all important New York City and challenged the Madison Square Garden impresarios who ignored black fighters.... conduct. For his exemplary behavior and victories over Carnera and thirteen other heavyweights that year, Louis became *Ring Magazine*'s "Boxer of the Year" and the Associated Press's "Athlete of the Year:" Even rank-and-file white boxing fans and southern white journalists considered this "well-behaved" "good nigger" as "the savior of a dying sport."

Publicly Louis embodied the Galahad image promoted by his handlers.... Before the Carnera fight ... blacks envisioned him a savior capable of humiliating the symbol of Mussolini's Ethiopian invasion.... Rather than serve as a race symbol, however, he desired to make money and party "with pretty girls." He ... became cocky and out of shape, losing the first Schmeling fight by a knockout. Crestfallen and disturbed that blacks took his defeat to Hitler's [alleged] henchman personally, Louis returned home to nurse his pride and his wounds.

Only twenty-four when winning the title, he understandably failed to grasp his relationship with black society. Publicly the paragon, privately he played with the Brown Bombers against the approval of his managers who feared possible injury; he engaged in numerous sexual encounters and love affairs, sometimes with white women. He received double messages from Roxborough and Black, who directed him never to be photographed with white ladies, but said nothing about dating them. Outwardly, Louis became the person his mother desired and the image his handlers forged.

Louis's personal growth accompanied the national shift from depression to war. Between 1937 and 1941, particularly as a result of the Schmeling rematch, he and Afro-Americans gained confidence. They both smarted over the first bout, which cast doubt on his title and their manhood. In addition, the rise of Hitler abroad placed discrimination at home in bold relief and stimulated black protest for civil rights. Nazism also revealed racism as "an unmitigated evil," forcing white society to question its own moral integrity.... [B]lack and white citizens alike placed the second Louis–Schmeling fight in an international, racial context: American democracy v. Aryan supremacy.... President Franklin D. Roosevelt sent for Louis, felt his biceps and reminded: "Joe, we're depending on those muscles for America." On June 22, 1938, seventy-thousand partisan fans filled Yankee Stadium to see the fight.... When Louis smashed Schmeling to the canvas four times amidst forty-one blows, delivering the K.O. at 2:04 of round one, celebration occurred everywhere.

The victory greatly affected Louis, who became more sure of himself and ... fully understood, possibly for the first time, his meaning for and commitment to black society. No longer isolated, he saw beyond family, friends and personal pride a broader version of people and things black: "If I ever do anything to disgrace my race," he remarked later, "I hope to die." Louis's triumph also appealed to white society's patriotism and need, outside of the South, to appear racially moral in the face of its Nazi-like values. As an integrative force, he seemed capable of bringing the races together ... against common enemies without challenging basic conditions of black life. In fact, sixty-four percent of all radio owners in the nation listened to the rematch—a figure only exceeded in this internationally tense period by two presidential broadcasts.

Louis's mass appeal spread in 1939 and 1940, bringing him greater recognition.... from *Ring Magazine*—"Boxer of the Year" for the third time in six years—and the Schomburg Collection of the New York Public Library and the Association for the Study of Negro Life and History for improving race relations. Aware of his phenomenal popularity, particularly among blacks and white liberals, political brokers sought his support. In the ... presidential campaign of 1940, Roosevelt's advisers shared NAACP [director] Walter F. White's belief that northern black voters could decide the election....

Doubtless the dangers consisted of John Roxborough and his brother, Charles, a prominent Michigan figure in the Republican Party, who persuaded (more likely instructed) Louis to be "in Willkie's corner." During the crucial, closing days of the campaign, Republicans used him ... to ... stump in Chicago, St. Louis and New York, noting Roosevelt's failure to support an anti-lynch bill or get blacks off the WPA rolls; he predicted Willkie would "win by a knockout" and "help my people." Michigan State Senator Diggs, however, assured Roosevelt that "the overwhelming majority" of black voters realized his record and Louis's political ignorance. [W]orried by Willkie's bid for black support, Roosevelt followed the counsel of civil rights advocates and, among other concessions, promoted Colonel Benjamin O. Davis the first black brigadier general and appointed William H. Hastie civilian aide to the Secretary of War....

... Louis retained his heroic stature, nonetheless. His elevation to truly national status was in the offing....

During 1941 ... as world war intensified abroad, so did black militancy and white soul-searching at home. Black leaders, faced with the dilemma of opposing the Axis while protesting homegrown racism, unveiled the Double V campaign [to channel] black frustrations into positive, patriotic actions. By simultaneously seeking victory on two fronts—over foreign and domestic foes—they hoped to bolster black morale and promote racial equality; by linking the struggles and stimulating black defense of the country, they avoided charges of treason and claimed first-class citizenship. White leaders, meanwhile, understood the meaning of Nazism for white supremacy in the United States and the resistance by the larger society to any suggestion of changes in the status quo. Rather than chance alienating whites and hindering preparedness, they played up democratic rhetoric and, when forced by black pressure, compromised on symbolically important issues involving the armed forces and defense industries without fundamentally altering basic conditions. In this context, Louis's forthcoming boxing feats served both personal and societal purposes. He mirrored the aggressiveness of the black masses and the patriotism of their leaders, bringing respect to the race; he embodied the fighting spirit and the interracial symbolism needed by white citizens and leaders during world crisis.

Between January and June, he defended the championship monthly, … in what some called the bum-a-month campaign, before meeting Billy Conn in an historic bout…. Conn, the 175 pound light heavyweight champion, entered as the underdog…. On June 18, 54,487 people … filled the Polo Grounds. Most … rooted for Conn, the cocky Irishman from Pittsburgh who … fought "a brand of battle" few expected. They supported Conn, local reporters opined, because of his dashing underdog appeal rather than his race: Louis believed otherwise, later referring to Conn as a "white hope." No doubt both factors influenced the crowd, but after twelve spirited rounds by Conn, which left Louis "bewildered, dazed and on his way to a decisive defeat," the champion rallied. In the thirteenth round, Conn … ceased to box and threw a long left hook; Louis seized the opening, stunning his opponent with a devastating right cross followed by a fusillade of "crushing fire" with both hands "savagely, thudding home." Conn crumbled, ending one of the greatest heavyweight battles ever.

Louis re-emerged even more heroic and popular among both races. Blacks in Harlem celebrated his victory…. Whites who saw, heard or read about the match understood the epic dimension of Louis. His loss of speed, which probably reflected the smaller challenger's quickness …, and come-from-behind win signaled human imperfection: but his courage throughout the bout and his awesome power and skill in the final round revealed god-like invincibility.

… Having weathered six title defenses, Conn's near win and marital problems, Louis now fought Lou Nova and re-established his own indisputable supremacy. In predictable ritual, 56,549 persons jammed into the Polo Grounds on September 29 to see the champion drop Nova "like a deflated balloon" in the sixth round. Celebrities abounded, including one-time paramour Sonja Henie….; even Roosevelt rearranged his travel schedule to hear the fight broadcast….

Increased renown continued to bring Louis into contact with black leaders and organizations, but his managers always stood between them. Detroit Urban Leaguer John C. Dancy, whose agency benefitted from Louis's generosity, … observed that Roxborough handled all business matters [and], protected Louis from controversial racial issues. They permitted him more exposure in race relations as times changed, but continued to shield him from militant protest…. Black and Roxborough aligned Louis with the more conservative, gradualistic National Urban League and Federal Council of the Churches of Christ....

As the national emergency bound Louis and society more closely together, White thought Louis could best serve Afro-America in the armed forces. In the fall of 1941, he knew of the champion's I-A classification and of increased violence between black servicemen and white citizens, police and soldiers. Behind the scenes he contacted Black and Roxborough, Eleanor Roosevelt and military authorities, negotiating the possibility of commissioning Louis in the Army's Morale Division. Apparently all endorsed his proposal, particularly Army commanders who had no other plans for controlling interracial conflict and imagined Louis capable of boosting black emotions. White, of course, envisioned the champion as both a morale builder for blacks and an integrator for whites. One of the few blacks known and respected by both races, Louis could serve the Double V strategy by encouraging black participation and exemplifying black patriotism at a time when blacks appeared indifferent to the war and whites seemed vulnerable to civil rights propaganda. He fit the needs of black leaders, white liberals and War Department officials.

... White['s] ... influential assistant, Roy Wilkins, warned that public reaction would be "very unfavorable" if Louis somehow avoided the draft. People might resent his enormous income, widely publicized at $2,000,000 in seven years of professional fighting, and compare him with Jack Dempsey, who evoked near lasting criticism for refusing to serve during the last war. Instead they would be "greatly impressed" if Louis entered the service as "a private just like Joe Doakes earning $18 a week"; by not accepting "some soft berth" made possible "though pull with Army higher-ups," he could follow the examples of Hank Greenberg, Winthrop Rockefeller and other famous, wealthy individuals. White agreed with Wilkins and pressed the twenty-seven year old champion and his managers to squelch the story that talk of military service had been ballyhoo for the Nova bout. And if Louis's age would prevent him from being called, White urged that he volunteer.

Black and Roxborough had other plans, however.... They opted for the draft and delayed Louis's November induction by signing a rematch with Buddy Baer. They arranged for Louis and promoter Jacobs to donate their purses for this twentieth title defense to the Navy Relief Society. Such generosity and patriotism enhanced the champion's image and future, as well as their own and boxing's. It also brought raves from whites and sparked debate among Double V-minded blacks aware of the Navy's discrimination. Perhaps realizing the futility of stopping the bout, White complimented Louis for acting "far bigger than the Navy" and hoped his example might influence its policy of relegating blacks to mess men status....

Louis held firm to his commitment despite some black criticism. Many things were wrong with America, he agreed, "but Hitler won't fix them." When asked by reporters why risk his million dollar championship for nothing, he corrected: "I ain't fighting for nothing, I am fighting for my country." On January 9, ... Louis destroyed Baer in round one, donated $47,000 to the Navy Relief Society and received praise from some blacks for having drawn "loop rings" around "ding-donging and complaining" leaders.

Three days after the Baer match Louis passed the Army physical, ending the civilian period more popular than ever before.... By displaying traits—particularly love of country—admired by the larger society, he conformed increasingly to its criteria for heroes; by enhancing his own and black esteem, while ignoring Double V protest, he avoided having to choose one race and set of ideas over another. Honors came to him from all quarters....

Although set in motion by the war crisis, his transition from sports hero to super patriot lay ahead....

Once Louis entered military service, ... he became a national symbol. His physical on January 12 and assignment to Company C at Camp Upton, Long Island drew praise from reporters. Joining the service and being unable to fit into the uniform of "an ordinary man," enhanced his image and instilled national confidence. United States Senator Prentiss M. Brown of Michigan lauded his enlistment, which bandleader Lucky Millander memorialized in "Joe Louis is a Mighty Man." Few, if any, citizens realized how his managers stalled induction for months or how he awaited formal notice rather than volunteer. Instead they believed that he chose freely to forsake luxury, jeopardize life and defend America; they knew of discriminatory military practices and of his segregated unit, making his action even more impressive....

Even before completing basic training, Louis boosted the war effort by agreeing to speak for the Navy Relief Society. Before 20,000 persons on March 10, he stood erect in uniform and dismissed the idea of doing more than any other "red-blooded American." Everyone would do their part, he predicted, and "we'll win 'cause we are on God's side." ... Louis's simple, touching greatness explained columnist Bill Corum, could make him "a symbol" in troubled times. Louis's influence continued well into the war as song writers Sammy Cahn and Jule Styne highlighted his memorable words in "Keep Your Powder Dry."

Fascination grew for Louis as he defined the crisis evangelically. Such beckoned black participation by challenging the argument that this was "a white man's war"; such soothed white consciences by engendering moral self-worth in a racist society fighting for democracy. Blacks understood what Louis meant by being on God's side, but did whites? ... Whether or not whites took the opportunity offered by war "to get on God's side," Louis again bridged racial lines and continued to appear saintly.

He returned to Madison Square Garden on March 27 for another title defense.... Louis dispatched Abe Simon in six rounds, donating his purse of $64,950 to the Army Emergency Relief Organization. Magnanimous as ever, he treated black G.I.'s to almost $3,000 worth of fight tickets.

.... Military authorities ... realized Louis's worth. Placing the champion in special services, they dampened charges of favoritism by treating him routinely. He completed boot camp, rose to corporal and spoke unplaintively of needing to work harder for sergeant's chevrons. A model soldier, he delighted Army personnel who assigned him several roles.

During and immediately after basic training, Louis stimulated the sale of defense bonds.... Officials and private citizens requested his appearance at bond selling rallies in New York and Memphis, claiming that such would increase sales and boost black morale.... 65,000 patrons at the Tam O'Shanter golf tournament

... purchased $933,000 worth of bonds at Louis's urgings. Representatives of labor, academe and mass organizations also requested Louis's services.... More pointedly for race relations, White solicited Louis for NAACP-sponsored events; he believed the champion would help the association achieve an "affirmative note."...

Military leaders, too, understood the value of Louis as morale builder and, especially during his first year of duty, image-maker. He promoted the service by appearing in the film "This is the Army," speaking on the broadcast "Army Hour" and participating in "I am an American Day." ... Later, in the face of the Los Angeles and Detroit race riots, the War Department moved to bolster blacks and educate whites, using clips of Louis in the widely shown docudrama "The Negro Soldier...."

Army officials also arranged for Louis to tour military camps in the United States beginning August 30, 1943. Over the next four months the champion boxed before thousands of soldiers. He visited the G.I.'s in hospitals, lectured on good health and sparred two or three rounds daily. Shortly thereafter he visited the British Isles, France, Italy and North Africa.... [H]e entertained 2,000,000 troops and fought nearly 200 exhibition bouts overseas. Servicemen flocked to watch him fight, "exchange quips, act in skits or just talk."...

Most black spokesmen and white officials also recognized Louis's potential to incite ... violence. Even as the champion's prestige grew among whites in the early 1940s, interracial conflict sprang from his victories over Conn and Baer in locales as far removed as Detroit and Gurdon, Arkansas. Clearly Louis instilled pride, even assertiveness in some blacks, which many whites perceived as a threat to the racial status quo. "Since Joe Louis became so prominent every Negro goes around strutting his stuff." complained one Michigander. Exactly because of the champion's influence among blacks, leaders of both races sought his assistance to curb discord. Following the spring riots of 1943 in Los Angeles, Detroit and elsewhere, Roosevelt supposedly sent Louis as goodwill emissary to Pittsburgh, "the most sensitive spot for another outbreak...."

Louis himself struck "fair" punches for Afro-America. Besides promoting social control over black soldiers and civilians, he helped integrate society and change racial attitudes. Although organized protest lay behind Roosevelt's ordering the placement of black sailors in all naval branches, black newsmen and white officials agreed that Louis's benefit bout for the Navy Relief Society contributed to moving the race beyond mess men duty. Neither black pressure nor Louis's magnanimity integrated the Navy but, judged one editor. "he slapped Jim Crow in the face." He weakened the segregated structure of civilian and military society elsewhere: expressing dissatisfaction with discrimination at bond rallies: integrating promotional golf tournaments: boxing with soldiers of both races before integrated audiences only. Indeed, while the Army used Louis to promote its image and the war effort, he turned the tables on more than one occasion; he informed 20,000 Detroiters that if given defense jobs and "an even break in the Army," blacks "would show the world how to win this war."

When pressed by circumstances, he protested publicly. He ignored a "White Only" sign in the bus depot of Camp Sibert, Alabama (which resulted in his and

Sugar Ray Robinson's arrest) and questioned Jim Crow theater seats in Salisbury, England. More often he inquired privately as to why blacks of Jackie Robinson's athletic ability and education could neither play for post football teams nor attend Officer's Candidate School (OCS). Later Louis exaggerated his significance in correcting some of these wrongs. Nevertheless Louis assisted in bringing about minor, though far from insignificant alterations. Robinson did play some football for Fort Riley, Kansas, and enter OCS, attributing the latter to Louis's efforts. Certainly the champion's intervention in Robinson's behalf and his exhibitions with soldiers of both races "helped broaden the base of athletic competition of many posts." He also might have been instrumental in Robinson going to OCS, but Robinson's ability and education must have been significant in themselves; in any case, military opposition to training more than token numbers of black officers continued throughout the war. Not as assertively, consistently, dramatically or effectively as many others, Louis interacted with racist institutions and turbulent times to advance the struggle for equality....

In the service Louis found himself alone, making "all kinds of decisions." While he completed basic training, Black faced charges and Roxborough served time for running numbers and, pushing Louis to his emotional depths, Blackburn died.... Stripped of his guardians, Louis seemed more independent and concerned about racial justice, particularly for black soldiers and friends like Robinson. The war atmosphere affected him as well, for everyone from Roosevelt to Double V advocates espoused democratic principles. He became sensitized, fighting relief bouts, selling bonds and bolstering morale while witnessing discrimination in the Army....

During the last months of war, Louis continued the model soldier.... From his return to the United States in October 1944 until his discharge a year later, he visited defense plants to spur production or integrate labor forces.... [H]e mustered out of the Army on October 1 amidst great fanfare. Receiving the Legion of Merit "for exceptionally meritorious conduct in the performance of outstanding services" abroad, he expressed characteristic gratitude....

.... Certainly citizens of both races associated themselves, their courage and commitment in the face of disaster with the champion who represented "the best ideals of Americanism." With victory in hand and reconstruction ahead, they again saw in him what they wanted to see in themselves: excellence.

Louis and society ... interacted throughout the world crisis, helping to define one another. Initially, he made most blacks "unafraid of tomorrow" and some whites receptive to changing times. Such was made possible by his awesome fistic skill and attractive human qualities; by his handlers, who understood ... "interracial relations and human psychology"; by black newsmen hungry for copy and their readers equally hungry for heroes; and by white promoters seeking profits and honest trainers wanting scandal-free bouts. His politically symbolic victories over Carnera and Schmeling brought increasing respect from whites and near universal decent treatment from daily presses. His Olympian demeanor and patriotic action thrust him into more historically significant and internationally prominent roles.

Preparedness and war engendered instability and heightened societal needs for someone of Louis's stature.... His enormous appeal and growth occurred because he identified himself with blacks personally and with all citizens representatively; he reflected both cultures and became their champion in and out of the ring. Most importantly, he threatened neither race and unwittingly nurtured the status quo; … He pleased various segments of both communities who played on his prestige as a means to manipulate public behavior: black editors desiring democratic advances without rebellion, southern newsmen taking aim at Hitler without hitting Jim Crow targets, government officials seeking racial peace without social justice, white liberals wanting moral integrity without societal changes and white citizens striving for respectability without recognizing black grievances. Occasionally, he stepped out of character and challenged discrimination, but only in military life and only very tentatively.

Genuinely the people's choice, Louis possessed that quality—"divine grace"—characteristic of heroic leadership. [H]is historical significance lay in the symbolism he represented for black and white societies, their ideologies, their struggles and their "assurances of success." … Louis functioned in all of these categories, played more than theatric parts in the life-and-death drama of war and educated countrymen in decency and democracy. He also marked the transition from earlier, one-dimensional paragons to contemporary, many-faceted heroes who undertake several functions and reveal themselves "warts and all."

FURTHER READING

Alexander, Charles C. *Ty Cobb* (1984).

Baker, William J. *Jesse Owens: An American Life* (1986).

Buford, Kate. *Native American Son: The Life and Sporting Legend of Jim Thorpe* (2010).

Carroll, John M. *Red Grange and the Rise of Modern Football* (1999).

Cayleff, Susan E. *Babe: The Life and Legend of Babe Didrikson Zaharias* (1995).

Creamer, Robert. *Babe: The Legend Comes to Life* (1974).

Cutler, J. L. *Gilbert Patten and His Frank Merriwell Saga* (1934).

Dyreson, Mark. "The Emergence of Consumer Culture and the Transformation of Physical Culture: American Sports in the 1920s," *Journal of Sport History* 61 (Winter 1989), 261–81.

Englemann, Larry. *The Goddess and the American Girl* (1988).

Evensen, Bruce. *When Dempsey Fought Tunney: Heroes, Hokum, and Storytelling in the Jazz Age* (1996).

Gorn, Elliott J. "The Manassa Mauler and the Fighting Marine: An Interpretation of the Dempsey-Tunney Fights," *Journal of American Studies* 19 (1983), 27–47.

Gropman, Donald. *Say it Ain't So, Joe!: The True Story of Shoeless Joe Jackson* (1992).

Inabinett, Mark. *Grantland Rice and His Heroes: The Sportswriter as Mythmaker in the 1920s* (1994).

Lowe, Stephen R. *Sir Walter and Mr. Jones: Walter Hagen, Bobby Jones, and the Rise of American Golf* (2000).

Messenger, Christian K. *Sport and the Spirit of Play in American Fiction* (1981).

O'Connor, Gerard. "Where Have You Gone, Joe DiMaggio?" in Ray B. Browne et al., eds., *Heroes in Popular Culture* (1972), 87–99.

Oriard, Michael. *Dreaming of Heroes: American Sports Fiction, 1869–1980* (1982).

Rader, Benjamin G. "Compensatory Sport Heroes: Ruth, Grange, and Dempsey," *Journal of Popular Culture* 16 (1983), 11–22.

Riess, Steven A. "Sport and Social Mobility: American Myth or Reality," in Donald G. Kyle and Gary Stark, eds., *Essays on Sport History* (1990), 83–117.

Roberts, Randy. *Jack Dempsey, The Manassa Mauler* (1979).

Roberts, Randy. *Papa Jack: Jack Johnson and the Era of White Hopes* (1985).

Roberts, Randy. *Joe Louis: Hard Times Man* (2010).

Roessner, Lori A. "Hero Crafting in *Sporting Life*, an Early Baseball Journal," *American Journalism* 26 (Spring 2009), 39–65.

Runstedtler, Theresa. *Jack Johnson, Rebel Sojourner: Boxing in the Shadow of the Global Color Line* (2012).

Smelser, Marshall. *The Life That Ruth Built: A Biography* (1975).

Smith, Leverett T. *The American Dream and the American Game* (1975).

Spivey, Donald. *"If You were Only White": The Life of Leroy "Satchel" Paige* (2012).

Thomas, Henry W. *Walter Johnson: Baseball's Big Train* (1995).

Vertinsky, Patricia, and Christiane Job. "Breaking Traditions, and Swimming Out of Place: Gertrude Ederle and the Greatest Sports Story in the World," *Stadion* 31 (2005), 111–33.

Ward, John W. "The Meaning of Lindbergh's Flight," *American Quarterly* 10 (Spring 1958), 3–16.

CHAPTER 12

Impact of Title IX on American Women and Sport

A highly significant development in post–World War II American sport has been the recent great increase in women's involvement in sport. American women at first were still largely limited to participation in acceptable "feminine" sports like tennis, gymnastics, figure skating, and swimming to make team sports and "unfeminine" sports acceptable activities for women. In the post–World War II era, the only women who excelled in track and field, for instance, were students at black colleges, who used sport to gain status and respect. Women's involvement in strenuous sports shot up in the 1970s, and has continued to grow ever since. What accounted for this development? Was it the role of women sports heroes? What was the impact of feminism? Did the federal government promote sports as part of the movement to secure equal rights for women? Was the government concerned about the poor performance of female American track and field athletes in international competition in comparison to Russian women at the height of the Cold War? Most scholars attribute the boom to the women's rights movement and to influential role models, especially Billie Jean King. Scholars also agree that fresh attention to sport was furthered by the passage of Title IX of the Education Act of 1972, which sought equal treatment for women in all aspects of higher education. Prior to Title IX, funding for women had comprised less than one percent of intercollegiate budgets. Though Title IX resulted in more funds, historians and other scholars still argue about the program's effectiveness.

DOCUMENTS

Document 1 is drawn from the autobiography of Wilma Glodean Rudolph (1940–1994), the fastest woman in the world who captured three gold medals in sprinting at the 1960 Rome Olympics and helped make women's track and field a major sport in the United States. In this excerpt, she recounts the competition and the gratifying response to her achievements when she returned to the United States at a time when segregation was a way of life in the South.

Document 2 is drawn from the autobiography of Billie Jean King, who was probably the most important female athlete since Babe Didrikson. King was the finest tennis player of her era during a career highlighted by a sweep of the Wimbledon championships in 1967. King helped popularize women's tennis by her personality and style of play and led the fight for women's professional tennis. She helped to organize the Virginia Slims Tour in 1971 and led the struggle to gain purses comparable to those of men at major championships (women originally got only 10 percent of the amount of men's prizes). King also defeated Bobby Riggs in "the Battle of the Sexes" in 1973, one of the most heavily promoted sporting event involving an American woman.

The next three documents examine Title IX of the Education Amendments of 1972. They include the preamble to the law that established the principle of gender equality in education that was interpreted to include equity in interscholastic and intercollegiate sport, followed by a Department of Education explanation of what constituted compliance for institutions of higher education. This is followed by two documents that deal with the implementation of Title IX. In 1993, Baylor University Athletic Director Grant Teaff, a former football coach and a member of the National Collegiate Athletic Association (NCAA) Task Force on Gender Equality, addressed a congressional committee, arguing that football deserved special consideration in any discussion on gender equity. It is followed by the most important legal case in the enforcement of Title IX, *Amy Cohen, et al., v. Brown University, et al.*, in which the federal courts established high standards for compliance. The case was initiated in 1992 after Brown University, which had an excellent record in upholding Title IX, announced plans to eliminate men's water polo and golf, and women's gymnastics and volleyball to save money. Gymnasts and volleyball players argued that since the number of women's sports had just recently achieved comparability to men's, the cuts were unfair. In 1995, the U.S. District Court in Providence, Rhode Island, ruled for the plaintiffs, a decision later upheld by the U.S. Supreme Court.

1. Wilma Rudolph and the 1960 Summer Olympics

WILMA RUDOLPH

Saturday. This was the day. The final in the women's 100 meters. The top three people, out of six, were Jutta Heine, the tall blond girl from West Germany, Dorothy Hyman, from Great Britain, and myself. I really felt insecure about Jutta Heine all that morning. She had won all of her preliminary heats, just as I had, and she was just as tall as I was. I watched her run a heat and noticed that she had a stride just as long as I had, and, yes, she was a good runner. You knew immediately about those things; you can see it in the way runners carry

---

themselves. But I guess I was the favorite going in; my times in the heats were 11.3 twice, and 11.4.

The tension began for all of us in the tunnel which leads out to the stadium. There was no way to get away from each other; you mingle, and you avoid looking, and you try to get yourself in a proper frame of mind. It's a little bit like a fighter before a big championship bout. Yes, you have to build up a little hatred for your opponents, and you have to psyche yourself up to instill the killer instinct. But I was not afraid or intimidated in that tunnel. I never talked, but I always looked the others straight in the eye. I knew that even if I did say something, they wouldn't be able to understand me anyway; the little English they did know would have been lost in my black southern accent. So I just kept quiet and looked them in the eyes. When we got out on the track, I followed my same routine: one practice start, then slowly walk around, with my hands on my hips, near the starting blocks. No rushing, no jumping, no running around; conserve the energy for when it really matters. I was concentrating deeply.

My start was relatively good. I came out second or third in the field, and my speed started increasing the farther I went. When I reached fifty meters, I saw that I had them all, and I was just beginning to turn it on. By seventy meters, I knew the race was mine; nobody was going to catch me. I won by five to seven yards, and Dorothy Hyman was second, and I knew then and there that Jutta Heine would not beat me. I did 11 flat again, and this time there was another mix up involving one of the officials, and the world's record was discounted. I couldn't believe that. I cried, and my coach was upset, but I was happy that I had won my first gold medal easily.

... The next morning, Sunday morning, I had breakfast with Coach Temple. He said to take it easy for as long as I could and, after the 200 meter race, I'd be free to do whatever I wanted in Rome. He told me to rest the ankle as long as I could because on Tuesday, in the 200-meter final, I'd be running curves for the first time since I had sprained it. Tuesday broke raining. It was miserable out there, but I felt good, no real pressure. The 200 was mine, I loved it more than anything else. A little rain meant nothing to me. In fact, before the start of the race, I was saying to myself, as a way of psyching up, "There's nobody alive who can beat you in the 200. Go get it."

The rain did slow me down a little, but I won the race easily, no problem with the ankle, no problem with the start. I really won that race a lot easier than I thought I would, against Jutta Heine and Dorothy Hyman and pretty much the same field that was in the 100. The time was 24 seconds flat, and that was like walking. I was disappointed, because I had been doing a consistent 22.9 in the 200, and 24 flat was embarrassing. Still, I said to myself that night, "That's two gold medals down and one to go."

On Friday, the 440 relay was scheduled. That was my chance to become the first American woman ever to win three Olympic gold medals. I wasn't about to blow it. The team was: Martha Hudson, running the first leg; Barbara Jones, running the second; Lucinda Williams, running the third, and me, running anchor. The teams everybody was talking about were Russia, West Germany, and Britain. Well, we wiped them all out, and we set a world's record in the process.... It was an easy race for us; everybody ran their best, and we won it going away.

When I broke the tape, I had my three gold medals, and the feeling of accomplishment welled up inside of me. The first American woman to win three Olympic gold medals. I knew that was something nobody could ever take away from me, ever. After the playing of "The Star-Spangled Banner," I came away from the victory stand and I was mobbed. People were jumping all over me, pushing microphones into my face, pounding my back. I couldn't believe it. Finally, the American officials grabbed me and escorted me to safety. One of them said, "Wilma, life will never be the same for you again." He was so right.

For one thing, I noticed that some animosity was developing toward me on the part of some other American women runners. There were whispers and rumors and some nasty things said about me getting all of the publicity and the attention and them not getting their share. That may have been so, but I certainly wasn't seeking out any....

I had come to Rome, accomplished what I had wanted to accomplish. I had three gold medals, and now I wanted to share them with the people I loved most. Coach Temple said the plan was to fly from Rome to New York City, then from New York to Nashville. From there, he said, we could drive the fifty miles to Clarksville. So began a strange and tiring journey and a lot of days in airplanes and airports.

Spoils to the Victor

The Clarksville parade for me actually began two miles outside the city, when the police escort picked us up on the highway and started leading us into town. Along the way, the motorcade was joined by a car that included some very important people—my mother and father, one of my older brothers and his wife, and my baby girl, Yolanda. As we got closer to Clarksville, I saw the crowd up ahead and I figured that all 40,000 people in the city had shown up.

As it turned out, this particular parade had a social significance far beyond the welcoming of Wilma Rudolph back home. Clarksville, at the time, was still a segregated city, and parade actually was the first integrated event in the history of the town. So was the banquet they gave for me that night; it was the first time in Clarksville's history that blacks and whites had gathered under the same roof for the same event. That's why it took so long to organize everything; the traditional all-white organizations were going to be represented in the parade, the American Legion, the VFW, the Elks. So were the traditional black groups, the black high school marching band, the black ministers, the various black fraternal organizations.

This parade broke the color barrier in Clarksville, and who was at the head of it but the white mayor of town. I was in an open convertible, standing and waving to everybody along the parade route.... [A]fter the parade was over, we all went over to Fort Campbell, where the generals were all waiting for us. They gave a parachute demonstration for us, and a little reception afterward. When that ended, I had about an hour left to go home, change clothes, and get over to the big banquet they were throwing in my honor at the Clarksville Armory.

I remember that banquet vividly because the armory was jammed with black people and white, and that had never happened before in Clarksville. I also remember vividly a speech that was made that night by this old white judge, Judge Hudson. He got up there that night, knowing exactly what was happening, and he said, "Ladies and gentlemen, you play a piano. You can play very nice music on a piano by playing only the black keys on it, and you can play very nice music on the same piano by playing only the white keys on it. But, ladies and gentlemen, the absolute best music comes out of that piano when you play both the black keys and the white keys together." Everybody applauded. That was a historic day for the town, and certainly for me. But it was only the beginning.

2. Billie Jean King Remembers Life as an Outsider in the 1950s and 1960s

In many respects, I like being different. I also like being successful. I somehow always knew that I would succeed. I had a great sense of destiny from the time I was very young. I remember one incident so vividly. When I was only about five or six years old, I was standing with my mother in the kitchen at home in Long Beach. I told her flat out that when I grew up I was going to be the best at something. She just smiled and kept peeling potatoes or doing whatever it was she was doing. She said, "Yes, dear; yes, of course, dear," as if I had simply said that I was going to my room or going to eat an apple, or whatever....

Of course, much of the reason why I've always felt that I was out of place was because of sports. First, a girl who wanted to excel in athletics was considered to be strange. In the second place, it was all a hopeless dream, anyhow. I think I began to appreciate this when I was only eight or nine, when my father took me to see the old Los Angeles Angels play the Hollywood Stars in the Triple-A Pacific Coast League at Wrigley Field in L.A....

Right away, I loved it, but it was unfair of me to love it, I understood soon enough, because there was no place for an American girl to go in the *national* pastime. This all came back to me when I saw a commercial on television recently and a whole bunch of kids, boys and girls alike, are all climbing out of a station wagon or getting hamburgers or doing something fun together, and they're all dressed up in baseball uniforms. I'm sure that most people who watch this commercial think how forward it is, how progressive, showing girls on the team, girls in uniform just like the boys. And I have such mixed emotions about that commercial. It's great that they include girls, but at the same time it's cruel because all it can possibly do is make some little girl somewhere wrongly

---

think that she can be a baseball player, too. And of course she can't. There is no life for girls in team sports past Little League.

I got into tennis when I realized this, and because I thought golf would be too slow for me, and I was too scared to swim. What else could a little girl do if she wasn't afraid to sweat? But as good as I was, and as much as I loved tennis right from the start, I found myself out of place there, too, because it was a country-club game then, and I came from a working-class family. My father was a fireman, and we didn't have any money for rackets, much less for proper tennis dresses. The first time I was supposed to be in a group photograph was at the Los Angeles Tennis Club during the Southern California Junior Championships. They wouldn't let me pose because I was only able to wear a blouse and a pair of shorts that my mother had made for me. All the other players were photographed.

I had some physical defects also. I had bad eyes—20/400—in a sport where nobody wore glasses. And, even as quick and as fast as I've been, I've been fat all over at times, with chubby little legs, and there are railroad tracks on both my knees from a number of knee operations.... [P]erhaps what has made it even more difficult for me as an athlete is my breathing problem. I inherited sinus trouble from my mother and chest problems from my father. The worst times of all for me have been in England, where I've played my very best and set all those records. I don't think there was one year at Wimbledon when I was entirely well. I always had a problem breathing there. I guess I am nearly a physical wreck. You see, nothing about me is quite what it seems.

People mischaracterized me even before the affair [with Marilyn Barnett]. I am supposed to be tough, loud, brash, and insensitive. In fact, Larry says I am very shy, and I really dislike being in the company of more than five or six people. I'm really a one-on-one person. So many people thought I was scared and crumbling under the pressure before the Bobby Riggs match. There happened to be a regular women's tournament in Houston that same week, and I was forced to play in it if I played Riggs—can you imagine the best players today getting that treatment?—and so, one day, without warning, I showed up in the locker room, and almost every player there was scrambling to bet against me. Rosie Casals was the only one backing me. That really hurt, that they didn't have any faith in me.

I had warned Margaret Court when she first told me that she had signed to play Riggs (for $10,000—she thought that was big money) that she was going to have to deal with a whole *season*—not just a day's match. So I knew the buildup would be even greater for Bobby's and my match; we were working off the Court–Riggs momentum. We signed on July 11 for the September 20 showdown, and the hype never really stopped. If it started to slow down, Bobby would whip it back up again.

So all along, my main strategy was not to get swept along in the promotion.... As much as possible, and right up to curtain time, I tried to stay out of the hoopla. After all, it wasn't as if I was needed to sell tickets and hustle the television. We drew 30,472 to the Astrodome and 40,000,000 American TV viewers—plus millions more abroad—so it did well enough without my becoming another carnival barker. Bobby was quite good enough at that.

Nothing he did surprised me. The reception was very much what I expected, and it didn't faze me. I'd played arenas before, and the circus atmosphere Bobby created just made it all of a piece. The only fear I did have was when they brought me in on the litter like Cleopatra. I don't like heights and I was afraid that they were going to drop me. But even my gift of the pig to Bobby and his gift of the big Sugar Daddy to me passed immediately out of my mind. I was really concentrating on my strategy.

The thing that I thought was especially important going in was to volley well. Obviously, I wanted to hit every shot well, and I planned in practice to play an all-court game, sometimes at the net, sometimes back. But I knew Bobby felt that women were poor players at the net, and when I had seen the tape of the Court match, it was apparent that she had reinforced this opinion by playing so badly at net—on those rare occasions when she could get up there. So, to me, it would be psychologically telling if Riggs suddenly realized that this woman could volley.

... Five of the first six times he tried to pass me with his backhand, I volleyed away winners. He had me down a service break at 3–2, but by then I knew I could take the net at will, and when I broke right back, that pretty much told the tale. Oh sure, almost right to the end there were all those people who thought Bobby fell behind only to get better odds on his courtside bets, but as far as I was concerned, almost from the first I was amazed at how weak an opponent he really was. All I ever feared was the unknown, and soon enough he was a known quantity for me.

That match was such madness. How often in this world can you suddenly have something which is altogether original and yet wonderfully classic? And what could be more classic than the battle of the sexes? The only problem for me is that I think everybody else in the world—Bobby included—had more fun with that match than I did. Men's tennis would not suffer if Bobby lost, so he had nothing to lose.

Perhaps people would have known how much it all mattered to me if they could have seen an incident a few days before.

I was practicing down in South Carolina, and I came in for a snack. Dick Butera, my friend, the owner of the Philadelphia Freedoms of World Team Tennis and the husband of Julie Anthony, another friend, was lying on the floor, watching a college football game. It was halftime, and the Stanford band was entertaining, and suddenly, as I watched, the band began playing "I Am Woman," and then I realized that they had formed my initials, BJK, on the field, and Dick looked up to share this moment with me, and we both had tears in our eyes. I think that was the happiest the Riggs match ever made me.

But it was never the match itself that upset me. It was all the people clamoring after me. My whole life, I wanted to have mobs of people cheer for tennis, but I really become quite frightened when everybody pushes around me and wants to touch me. I hate it when strangers touch me, even though I understand it is almost always for love, and that they don't mean anything harmful. Still, at the time, when it happens, it scares me.

I have often been asked whether I am a woman or an athlete. The question is absurd. Men are not asked that. I am an athlete. I am a woman. I want all other women to have their rights, because above all else, I'm for individual freedom, but there is very much about the goals and methods of the women's movement that I disagree with. That is the refusal to recognize that both men and women view each other through sexual bias. Oh, I know this is going to get me in trouble, but I'm going to mention it anyway. I've got a male friend in business, and he told me once that he'd really rather have a good-looking, well-built blonde who can barely manage as his secretary than some old lady who is a secretarial whiz. That's his privilege, I think. And if the blonde takes the job knowing that she's going to get leered at and chased around the desk, fair enough.

I'm still not even absolutely convinced that we need the Equal Rights Amendment. If it means the end of discrimination on the basis of gender, than I want it. But I don't believe you can legislate people's minds. I believe that it is persuasion you need, not force. Just because you legislate does not mean that people will change....

Sometimes the women's movement reminds me too much of some organized religion, which I can't stand. I was very "religious" as a kid. Also, I was much less tolerant then. That seems to me to be the trouble with movements, be they Women's Liberation or the Moral Majority or whatever. Then you always have to be against somebody on every issue, and I'm not very good at that. I don't like confrontations. But, of course, I always performed my best when the confrontation was most heightened, in the clutch—the most well-known example being the Riggs match. Nothing ever really fits for me.

I was a virgin when I was supposed to be, and I got married to the right cute boy the way I was supposed to at the time I was supposed to, but then we only had a "normal" marriage for a couple years—or, anyway, what most Americans presume a normal marriage to be, even if that ideal barely exists anymore. I never feel comfortable with a lot of so-called "normal" married people because they seem threatened by the way Larry and I live—and this was the case even long before people knew about my affair with Marilyn and could say "I told you so" instead of just "I'll bet she's queer." So I've never really felt at home in that huge world of married people, but I've also never felt at all comfortable when I've been associated with the gay world. Maybe it's mostly that everybody wants reinforcement of their kind of life, and I don't provide that for anybody.

I guess I'm just very much a loner. Except for one thing: I really can't stand to be alone for long. Sometimes I ask myself, Billie Jean, where do you belong? Do you fit in anywhere? Maybe all my life I've just been trying to change things so there would be someplace right for me....

Any woman born around 1943 has had to endure so many changes—in her educational experience, in her working life, in sex, in her roles, her expectations. But with me, it always seemed that I was also on the cutting edge of that change. Any woman about my age—or, for that matter, any person who has had to deal with women, which is just about everybody—has been a part of a great social transition, and just to survive that intact has been an accomplishment for me. I was brought up in a very structured universe—in my family, in school, in tennis, in every part of my world. Then, all of a sudden, the rules all started to change, and it seemed there weren't any rules left. I tried to go with the flow, but always seemed to find myself out in front and on the line.

When I married Larry in 1965, we were going to have babies—lots of them, as far as I was concerned—and I was going to give up tennis, which is the way it was supposed to be. In fact, only two weeks after we were married, I thought I was pregnant. And I was delighted. But even when I found out I wasn't having a baby, I was happy enough just spending so much time with Larry. I'd cook him two meals at home every day and take him his lunch—even when he was on the night shift—to the factory where he worked making ice cream cartons.

As for tennis, it hardly mattered.... It was just fun, and in those days, before professionals were accepted in the main tournaments, there was no money to speak of. We amateurs—"shamateurs" was the accepted term—took what we could in the way of "expenses" under the table, and if it wasn't much, it was still like found money to a young couple, and it helped Larry through law school.

I won Wimbledon three years running, and outside the little tennis community, very few people knew. In 1967 I won all three titles at Wimbledon—singles, doubles, and mixed—and I came back to my country, and there was no one there to meet me, no one at all. And barely six years later, there I was, in the Houston Astrodome, playing prime time to the world in what amounted to the Roman Colosseum [*sic*], with everyone ... chanting my name, hating me or loving me. And everyone wanted—needed—part of me, for tennis or movements or friendship or politics or just for the hell of it.... [P]eople were throwing money at me or grabbing at me or calling me a symbol or a leader or a radical feminist. I didn't know where I was. It was so complicated, and one morning I woke up, and where was I? I was in another woman's bed.

So now I know a lot of people will call me a homosexual, but to me that's just another label.... I'm not concerned for me. I just don't want Larry and my parents and my brother and the other people who love me hurt. And maybe now I can spend some time carving out a place for me in the world around me instead of only in the record books.

3. Title IX of the Education Amendment of 1972, Its Components, and the Three Prong Rule

"No person in the United States shall, on the basis of sex, be excluded from participation in, be denied the benefits of, or be subjected to discrimination under any education program or activity receiving Federal financial assistance."

From U.S. Department of Education, Office for Civil Rights, *Title IX and Sex Discrimination* (Washington, DC, 1998), http://www2.ed.gov/about/offices/list/ocr/docs/interath.html; U.S. Department of Education, Office for Civil Rights *Requirements Under Title IX of the Education Amendments of 1972* (Washington, DC, 1972), http://www2.ed.gov/about/offices/list/ocr/docs/tix_dis.html.

Requirements Under Title IX of the Education Amendments of 1972

The regulation (34 C.F.R. Part 106) implementing Title IX contains specific provisions relating to athletic opportunities. It also permits individual institutions considerable flexibility in achieving compliance with the law.

To clarify the athletic requirements contained in the Title IX regulation, a Policy Interpretation was issued to provide colleges and universities with more guidance on how to comply with the law....

While designed specifically for intercollegiate athletics, the general principles and compliance standards set forth in the Policy Interpretation will often apply to inter-scholastic athletic programs operated by elementary and secondary school systems, and to club and intramural athletic programs.

Student Interests and Abilities

The athletic interests and abilities of male and female students must be equally and effectively accommodated. Compliance with this factor is assessed by examining a school's: (a) determination of the athletic interests and abilities of its students; (b) selection of the sports that are offered; and (c) levels of competition, including opportunity for team competition.

Measuring Athletic Interests Colleges and universities have discretion in selecting the methods for determining the athletic interests and abilities of their students, as long as those methods are nondiscriminatory. The only requirements imposed are that institutions used methods that:

> take into account the nationally increasing level of women's interests and abilities; do not disadvantage the underrepresented sex (i.e., that sex whose participation rate in athletics is substantially below its enrollment rate); take into account team performance records of both male and female teams; and respond to the expressed interests of students capable of intercollegiate competition who belong to the underrepresented sex.

Selection of Sports A college or university is not required to offer particular sports or the same sports for each sex. Also, an institution is not required to offer an equal number of sports for each sex. However, an institution must accommodate to the same degree the athletic interests and abilities of each sex in the selection of sports.

A college or university may sponsor separate teams for men and women where selection is based on competitive skill or when the activity is a contact sport. Contact sports under the Title IX regulation include boxing, wrestling, rugby, ice hockey, football, basketball and other sports in which the purpose or major activity involves bodily contact.

... [A] college or university that sponsors a team for only one sex to do so for members of the other sex under certain circumstances. This applies to contact and non-contact sports. For example, a separate team may be required if there is sufficient interest and ability among members of the excluded sex to sustain a team and a reasonable expectation of competition for that team. Also, where an institution sponsors a team in a particular non-contact sport for members of one sex, it must allow athletes of the other sex to try-out for the team if, historically, there have been limited athletic opportunities for members of the other sex.

Levels of Competition Colleges and universities must provide opportunity for intercollegiate competition as well as team schedules which equally reflect the competitive abilities of male and female athletes. An institution's compliance ... may be assessed in any one of the following ways:

> the numbers of men and women participating in intercollegiate athletics are substantially proportionate to their overall enrollment; or where members of one sex are underrepresented in the athletics program, whether the institution can show a continuing practice of program expansion responsive to the developing interests and abilities of that sex; or the present program accommodates the interests and abilities of the underrepresented sex.

In considering equivalent opportunities for levels of competition, compliance will be assessed by examining whether:

> male and female athletes, in proportion to their participation in athletic programs, are provided equivalently advanced competitive opportunities; or the institution has a history and continuing practice of upgrading the competitive opportunities available to the historically disadvantaged sex as warranted by the developing abilities among the athletes of that sex.

Colleges and universities are not required to develop or upgrade an intercollegiate team if there is no reasonable expectation that competition will be available for that team within the institution's normal competitive region. However, an institution may be required to encourage development of such competition when overall athletic opportunities within that region have been historically limited for the members of one sex....

Athletic Benefits and Opportunities

In determining whether equal opportunities in athletics are available, the Title IX regulation specifies the following factors which must be considered

> accommodation of athletic interests and abilities (which is addressed separately in the section above);
>
> equipment and supplies; scheduling of games and practice time; travel and per diem allowances;
>
> opportunity for coaching and academic tutoring; assignment and compensation of coaches and tutors; locker rooms and other facilities; medical and training services; housing and dining services; and publicity.

The Title IX regulation also permits OCR to consider other factors in determining whether there is equal opportunity. Accordingly, the Policy Interpretation added recruitment of student athletes and provision of support services, since these factors can affect the overall provision of equal opportunity to male and female athletes.

The Policy Interpretation clarifies that institutions must provide equivalent treatment, services, and benefits regarding these factors. The overall equivalence standard allows institutions to achieve their own program goals within the framework of providing equal athletic opportunities. To determine equivalency for men's and women's athletic programs, each of the factors is assessed by comparing the following: availability; quality; kind of benefits; kind of opportunities; and kind of treatment.

Under this equivalency standard, identical benefits, opportunities, or treatment are not required. For example, locker facilities for a women's team do not have to be the same as for a men's team, as long as the effect of any differences in the overall athletic program are negligible.

If a comparison of program components indicates that benefits, opportunities, or treatment are not equivalent in quality, availability, or kind, the institution may still be in compliance with the law if the differences are shown to be the result of nondiscriminatory factors. Generally, these differences will be the result of unique aspects of particular sports or athletic activities, such as the nature/replacement of equipment and maintenance of facilities required for competition. Some disparities may be related to special circumstances of a temporary nature.... Difficulty in compliance will exist only if disparities are of a substantial and unjustified nature in a school's overall athletic program; or if disparities in individual program areas are substantial enough in and of themselves to deny equality of athletic opportunity. This equivalency approach allows institutions great flexibility in conducting their athletic programs and maintaining compliance without compromising the diversity of athletic programs among institutions.

Financial Assistance

To the extent that a college or university provided athletic scholarships, it is required to provide reasonable opportunities for such awards to members of each sex in proportion to the participation rate of each sex in intercollegiate athletics. This does not require the same number of scholarships for men and women or individual scholarships of equal value.

However, the total amount of assistance awarded to men and women must be substantially proportionate to their participation rates in athletic programs. In other words, if 60 percent of an institution's intercollegiate athletes are male, the total amount of aid going to male athletes should be approximately 60 percent of the financial aid dollars the institution awards.

Disparities in awarding financial assistance may be justified by legitimate, nondiscriminatory (sex-neutral) factors. For example, at some institutions the higher costs of tuition for out-of-state residents may cause an uneven distribution between scholarship aid to men's and women's programs. These differences are nondiscriminatory if they are not the result of limitations on the availability of out-of-state scholarships to either men or women. Differences also may be explained by professional decisions college and university officials make about program development. An institution beginning a new program, for example, may spread scholarships over a full generation (four years) of student athletes, thereby, awarding fewer scholarships during the first few years than would be necessary to create proportionality between male and female athletes.

4. Baylor University Athletic Director Grant Teaff Criticizes the Impact of Title IX on Intercollegiate Football, 1993

Madam Chairwoman, ... You first ask whether "full implementation of Title IX" would automatically require severe cuts in football programs. This question is difficult to answer in general terms, because Title IX compliance is fact specific and depends on the situation from campus to campus. If an institution is out of compliance with Title IX, it has latitude to determine how to come into compliance. Whether those steps would include substantial cuts in football would depend on a variety of factors, including the institution's financial condition and its ability to invest additional funds into intercollegiate athletics, the possibility of cutting other men's sports, and the profitability of the football program....

... I understand Title IX to require equality of athletic opportunity and effective accommodation of student interests and abilities, and not necessarily precise equality.

These concerns aside, football by its nature is a resource-intensive sport, requiring more players, more coaches, and more protective equipment than other sports. The disproportionate funding needed to operate a football program makes football the prime target for efforts to identify additional resources for women's athletics or for other funding needs.... [F]ootball, particularly at the Division I level, ... generates revenue and often provides resources for the entire intercollegiate athletics program. Certainly, this is the case at Baylor....

Your second question asks whether I agree with the statement made at the April 1992 gender equity hearing that "spending for football, for which there is no comparable women's sport and in which there is comparatively very large average squad size, contributed greatly to the spending disparities."... Although I cannot state positively that football, in fact, accounts for all spending disparities, I do agree that the resources required to conduct a football program are disproportionate to those required to operate other intercollegiate sports programs, so that football probably is largely, although not exclusively, responsible for the spending disparities.

From Grant Teaff, "Statement," in "Title IX Impact on Women's Participation in Intercollegiate Athletics and Gender Equity," in U.S., Congress, House Committee on Energy and Commerce, *Intercollegiate Sports: Hearings Before the Subcommittee on Commerce, Consumer Protection, and Competitiveness*, (Washington, DC: Government Printing Office, 1993), 16–17.

In some cases, the resources acquired for use in the football program can be used on a broader basis for the benefit of women's sports or the overall athletic program.... For example, ... last year, I centralized access to video equipment, which previously had been used exclusively for the football team, and made it available for use in all sports....

Your last question asks for my reaction to the statement by Ellen Vargyas [prominent attorney at the National Women's Law Center and Title IX advocate] that the university athletic community will not meaningfully address sex discrimination unless it is forced to do so, because special interests want to maintain intercollegiate athletics as "the boys club." I disagree.

First, the statement suggests that the intercollegiate athletic community has not taken steps to eliminate sex discrimination in athletics. Such a suggestion is wrong. The establishment of the NCAA gender equity task force and its work to date represents a true effort of the college community to address gender equity in a serious and practical manner. The statement also fails to recognize the efforts underway at many institutions to improve and strengthen the women's sports program. At Baylor, I have hired a strength coach and conditioning coach who works with all sports, men's and women's. We have two strength and conditioning facilities that are used by all of our student-athletes, male and female. Although my professional life, heretofore, has focused on football, my current goal as director of athletics is to strengthen and improve women's intercollegiate sports at Baylor. I want our women's teams to be competitive and successful ... so that we increase attendance, public interest, and media coverage. I think it is imperative to emphasize promotion and fund raising in women's sports.

Second, while I agree that the college athletic community will not meaningfully address sex discrimination unless it is forced to do so, the statement fails to acknowledge the many external "forces" that are making colleges and universities address Title IX and gender equity. One of the key factors that is "forcing" change at many institutions is simply the public scrutiny and debate over gender equity and opportunities for women. The creation of the NCAA gender equity task force and the emphasis on practical ideas for promoting Title IX compliance are making members of the college community think about the nature of the intercollegiate athletics program on their campus and ways in which opportunities for women can be enhanced, without eliminating existing opportunities for men.

In addition, student interests and demands, congressional oversight, agency enforcement of Title IX, and court orders all operate to "force" colleges and universities to address ways in which to improve the quality and offerings of their women's intercollegiate athletic programs.

Moreover, I think it is overly simplistic to say that colleges and universities will not take action on their own to address Title IX and gender equity because they want to "maintain intercollegiate athletics as a boys' club". On the contrary, I already have commented on the efforts of the intercollegiate athletic community to address gender equity and to expand opportunities for female student-athletes. Whatever it once may have been, college athletics no longer is a "boys' club". Shrinking financial resources and increasing operating costs, not some effort to maintain intercollegiate athletics as an entrenched boys' club, constitute the greatest single obstacle to achieving gender equity.

In summary, we cannot change the nature of football. But that does not mean that we cannot achieve compliance with Title IX and work toward building strong women's intercollegiate athletic programs....

5. Brown University Sued for Violating Title IX, 1996

The plaintiff class comprises all present, future, and potential Brown University women students who participate, seek to participate, and/or are deterred from participating in intercollegiate athletics funded by Brown.... This is a class action lawsuit charging Brown University, its president, and its athletics director ... with discrimination against women in the operation of its intercollegiate athletics program, in violation of Title IX of the Education Amendments of 1972....

This suit was initiated in response to the demotion in May 1991 of Brown's women's gymnastics and volleyball teams from university-funded varsity status to donor-funded varsity status....

As a Division I institution within the National Collegiate Athletic Association ("NCAA") with respect to all sports but football, Brown participates at the highest level of NCAA competition.... Brown operates a two-tiered intercollegiate athletics program with respect to funding: although Brown provides the financial resources required to maintain its university-funded varsity teams, donor-funded varsity athletes must themselves raise the funds necessary to support their teams through private donations ... and that donor-funded teams are unable to obtain varsity-level coaching, recruits, and funds for travel, equipment, and post-season competition.

... Brown saved $62,028 by demoting the women's teams and $15,795 by demoting the men's teams, but ... the demotions "did not appreciably affect the athletic participation gender ratio." Brown's decision to demote the women's volleyball and gymnastics teams and the men's water polo and golf teams from university-funded varsity status was apparently made in response to a university-wide cost-cutting directive.

Thus, plaintiffs contended, what appeared to be the even-handed demotions of two men's and two women's teams, in fact, perpetuated Brown's discriminatory treatment of women in the administration of its intercollegiate athletics program. Plaintiffs alleged that, at the time of the demotions, the men students at Brown already enjoyed the benefits of a disproportionately large share of both the university resources allocated to athletics and the intercollegiate participation opportunities afforded to student athletes.

During the same academic year, Brown's undergraduate enrollment comprised 52.4% (2,951) men and 47.6% [women]. [W]hile nearly all of the men's varsity teams were established before 1927, virtually all of the women's varsity

---

Amy Cohen, et al., Plaintiffs-Appellees, v. Brown University, et al. *65 USLW 2396, 114 Ed. Law Rep. 394, 45 Fed. R. Evid. Serv. 1369.*

teams were created between 1971 and 1977, after Brown's merger with Pembroke College.

At the time of trial, Brown offered 479 university-funded varsity positions for men, as compared to 312 for women.... Of the university-funded teams, 12 were men's teams and 13 were women's teams; of the donor-funded teams, three were women's teams and four were men's teams. The district court found that, in 1993–94, Brown's intercollegiate athletics program consisted of 32 teams, 16 men's teams and 16 women's teams. During the same period, Brown's undergraduate enrollment comprised 5,722 students, of which 48.86% (2,796) were men and 51.14% (2,926) were women. In the course of the trial on the merits, the district court found that, in 1993–94, there were 897 students participating in intercollegiate varsity athletics, of which 61.87% (555) were men and 38.13% (342) were women. Accordingly, the district court found that Brown maintained a 13.01% disparity between female participation in intercollegiate athletics and female student enrollment.... In 1993–94, then, Brown's varsity program—including both university- and donor-funded sports—afforded over 200 more positions for men than for women.

The number of participants in Brown's varsity athletic program accurately reflects the number of participation opportunities Brown offers because the University, through its practices "predetermines" the number of athletic positions available to each gender. The "participation opportunities" offered by an institution are measured by counting the actual participants on intercollegiate teams.

The district court found from extensive testimony that the donor-funded women's gymnastics, women's fencing and women's ski teams, as well as at least one women's club team, the water polo team, had demonstrated the interest and ability to compete at the top varsity level and would benefit from university funding....

The district court did not find that full and effective accommodation of the athletics interests and abilities of Brown's female students would disadvantage Brown's male students.

... [T]he district court found that Brown had not "fully and effectively accommodated the interest and ability of the underrepresented sex 'to the extent necessary to provide equal opportunity in the selection of sports and levels of competition available to members of both sexes.'" The court noted further that, because merely reducing program offerings to the overrepresented gender does not constitute program expansion for the underrepresented gender, the fact that Brown has eliminated or demoted several men's teams does not amount to a continuing practice of program expansion for women. While acknowledging that Brown "has an impressive history of program expansion," the district court found that Brown failed to demonstrate that it has "maintained a continuing practice of intercollegiate program expansion for women, the underrepresented sex."

... The district court concluded that intercollegiate athletics opportunities "means real opportunities, not illusory ones, and therefore should be measured by counting actual participants."

ESSAYS

The first essay is by Susan K. Cahn, a professor of history at the University at Buffalo, State University of New York, and the author of *Coming on Strong: Gender and Sexuality in Twentieth-Century Women's Sport* (1994) and coeditor of *Women and Sports in the United States: A Documentary Reader* (2007). She examines here the rise and fall of the All-American Girls Baseball League (AAGBL) (1943–1954). The AAGBL was largely the idea of Chicago Cubs owner Phillip K. Wrigley, who wanted to sustain interest in the national pastime during World War II when the top major leaguers were in the military. The idea of creating a women's league was a radical notion at a time when competitive team sport, particularly in baseball, was largely a male sphere. The AAGBL was a Midwestern league that recruited talented women ballplayers, who convinced fans that they belonged on the diamond. The AAGBL pointedly tried to promote a feminine image to build up audiences and not to threaten traditional gender roles, requiring players to wear skirts and employ makeup.

The second essay is by Ronald A. Smith, one of the preeminent experts on the history of intercollegiate sport. It is drawn from a chapter in his new book, *Pay for Play: A History of Big-Time College Athletic Reform* (2011). Smith here devotes considerable attention to the rise of Title IX and the federal government's role in reforming women athletics, focusing on the role of the NCAA, which historically prided itself as a leading force (although not always justifiably) in the improvement of all aspects of intercollegiate athletics. The NCAA was aware of the national need to improve elite women's athletic performance that paled during the Cold War by comparison to our adversary, the Soviet Union, and wanted to take a strong leadership role. The NCAA also sought to take a controlling role in amateur women's sport against its rivals for domination, the Amateur Athletic Union that sought to control all amateur sport, and the fledgling Association for Intercollegiate Athletics for Women (AIAW), founded in 1971 to govern intercollegiate women's athletics. The NCAA only became concerned about the impact of Title IX after the bill became a law, since it seemed likely to have a deleterious financial impact upon male intercollegiate sport. The NCAA first tried unsuccessfully to water down implementation of Title IX, and then moved to supplant the AIAW as the governing body for women's intercollegiate sport, which it did in the early 1980s. Smith argues that the NCAA and its constituency played little role in the great reform of gendered American intercollegiate athletics, which he credits to congressional legislation and the federal courts.

The All-American Girls Baseball League, 1943–1954

SUSAN K. CAHN

In 1943 Chicago Cubs owner Philip K. Wrigley launched a bold new baseball enterprise. Fearful that major league baseball might collapse under wartime manpower shortages, he proposed a professional women's baseball league.

From Susan K. Cahn, "No Freaks, No Amazons, No Boyish Bobs," *Chicago History* 18 (March 1989): 26–41.

The All-American Girls Baseball League (AAGBL), as it came to be called, served a dual purpose for Wrigley. He promoted the league as a form of entertainment for a war-weary public in need of wholesome, outdoor recreation. At the same time, he used women's baseball as a temporary replacement for the men's game, keeping stadiums occupied and fan interest alive.

The AAGBL celebrated women's strength and energy, but it also kindled anxieties about traditional gender arrangements in American society. Since the early twentieth century, critics of women sports enthusiasts had cast them in the negative image of "mannish athletes," an image that questioned their femininity and raised the specter of lesbianism. Sport was considered a male activity, the domain of traditional masculine virtues of aggressiveness, competition, physical prowess, and virility. Women athletes were seen as intruders into this male realm.

The AAGBL used the gender issue in sports to its advantage as an ingenious way to market its brand of baseball to the public. By demanding that its players combine "masculine" athletic skill with very feminine appearance, the AAGBL maintained a clear distinction between male and female roles while providing the fans with skillfully played and exciting baseball. The league thus avoided the mannish image that plagued other women's sports.

League managers could assure audiences, amazed at seeing a woman play a "man's game," that the players were feminine and "normal" in every, other respect. Although the AAGBL did not fundamentally challenge existing concepts of masculinity and femininity, it gave a group of gifted women athletes a unique opportunity to compete with the best players in the nation in a game they loved.

The league opened in four Midwestern cities: Kenosha and Racine, Wisconsin; South Bend, Indiana, and Rockford, Illinois. The AAGBL later expanded to include teams in Kalamazoo, Grand Rapids, and Muskegon, Michigan; Fort Wayne, Indiana; and Peoria, Illinois, with short-lived attempts in Chicago, Milwaukee, and Minneapolis; Battle Creek, Michigan; and Springfield, Illinois.... [S]panning the years 1943 to 1954 ... [the AAGBL] ... at its peak operated in ten cities and drew nearly a million fans.

As it became clear that the major league men's game would survive the war, Wrigley lost interest and sold his share of the AAGBL to Arthur Meyerhoff, his close associate and advertising agent. Meyerhoff created the Management Corp. to publicize and coordinate league teams, which typically were owned by businessmen from the sponsoring city. From 1944 through 1950, Meyerhoff's Chicago-based office managed the league with assistance from a board of directors and a league commissioner. In 1951 disgruntled team owners bought out Meyerhoff and decentralized the league's organization during its last four seasons.

... For twelve seasons the league played a four-month schedule of 120 games plus a championship series. Attendance during peak years ranged from 500,000 to one million.... The league recruited women from nearly every state and several Canadian provinces.... [P]layers received $40 to $85 per week in the league's early years and up to $125 per week in later years.... For credibility and name recognition, the AAGBL hired ex-major league baseball managers. Among them were Jimmie Foxx, Marty McManus, and Max Carey.... Though constantly beset by financial problems, high manager turnover, and franchise failure, league teams that survived the initial trial period drew well and commanded tremendous loyalty from hometown fans. For instance, the Racine Belles attracted more spectators than any local male sports team had ever drawn....

No other women's team sport before or since treated such a viable professional organization. Even tennis and golf, the most successful women's professional sports, were still primarily amateur in the 1940s, without professional tours or associations. In order to succeed, a women's professional sports enterprise had to overcome the cultural perception of sport as a masculine activity.... Americans saw sport as a male activity, and they associated athletics with masculine ideals of aggressiveness, competitiveness, physical strength, and virility. Virtues for men, such traits raised the specter of "mannishness" in women. Doctors, scientists, and exercise specialists cautioned that sport posed grave emotional and physical dangers to women, issuing ominous warnings about female hysteria and damaged maternal capacity.... Advocates viewed sport as a step toward emancipation ... denied under restrictive Victorian notions of femininity.

By World War II, women athletes had established a solid institutional base in community recreation programs, industrial leagues, and intramural school programs. Although proponents had by this time settled on a philosophy of "modified athletics" for women, with special rules, uniforms, and chaperone systems in place to differentiate women's athletics from men's, critics continued to evoke the image of the "mannish athlete." Media portrayals frequently referred to successful athletes as "Amazons" with masculine skills and body types. At the organizational level, efforts to curtail women's competitive sports and to eliminate female track and field events from the Olympic Games persisted through the 1950s.

... Meyerhoff especially sought to promote women's baseball by capitalizing on the contrast between "masculine" baseball skill and feminine appearance, describing the league as a "clean spirited, colorful sports show" built upon "the dramatic impact of seeing baseball, traditionally a men's game, played by feminine type girls with masculine skill." Meyerhoff speculated that the novelty ... would attract first-time customers intrigued by the "amazing spectacle of beskirted girls throwing, catching, hitting and running like men...." Unlike barnstorming teams that occasionally featured women players competing against men, the AAGBL needed to sustain interest after the initial effect wore off. Meyerhoff again linked success to the combination of feminine charm and masculine activity....

The management did not consider athletic ability within the boundaries of femininity; they described baseball as a masculine activity and the girls' league as a spectacle. The principal logic behind the league was to find women who played ball "like men," not "like girls," and who looked like "nice girls," not like men. Why did Wrigley, Meyerhoff, and the team owners insist on this distinction? The answer lies in the broader history of sport as a male arena and, specifically, in the tarnished image of women's softball.

Invented in the early 1900s ... softball came into its own as a game in the 1930s. The Amateur Softball Association (ASA) was organized in 1934, and after only one year 950,000 men, women, and children participated in ASA-sanctioned leagues. New Deal programs ... poured money and workers into facility construction projects and community recreation programs...." When the war came, softball's popularity continued to soar so that by the mid-1940s the *New York Times* estimated the sport had grown to include nine million players, 600,000 teams, and 150 million spectators in the United States.... Chicagoans showed a special zeal for the sport. The city hosted several of the first ASA national tournaments and catered to all ages and abilities through park, YMCA, church, business, industrial, and athletic association leagues

Girls and women eagerly joined the throng. Unlike baseball, softball had no masculine stigma at first. If anything, the use of a softer ball, the smaller field dimensions, and early names like "kitten ball" and "mush ball" cast softball in a slightly feminine light as a game appropriate for men, youngsters, and men not rugged enough to excel in baseball.

... Softball thrived in rural areas and urban working-class neighborhoods. In both settings, notions of femininity were expansive and flexible enough to encompass the broad range of women's physically demanding domestic work and wage labor. Unlike middle-class culture, rural and working-class cultures had traditionally defined womanhood more in terms of family and community roles than prescribed feminine attributes and activities. Such flexible definitions allowed for the ... "tomboy" with an avid interest in softball. In addition, by organizing leagues through neighborhood parks, churches, service organizations, and businesses, supporters of softball built upon existing community institutions. During the depression and wartime eras, ... people flocked to their local playing field for an inexpensive evening's entertainment. When women's teams met success, ... they continued to excite loyalty and enthusiasm among hometown fans who were more concerned about players' batting averages than femininity quotients.

However, by the late 1930s, good women's teams began to attract attention as much for their "masculine appearance" as for their superior ability. Within a decade women's skill levels had increased dramatically with the best teams often defeating men's teams in fundraisers and exhibition games. Skilled women players demonstrated speed, power, and competitive zest previously associated only with male athletes. In addition, as women developed physically through training, the size, weight, and musculature of some players evoked negative images of "mannish athletes": During the depression these stereotypes were fueled by cultural anxieties about female intrusion into male realms....

Media accounts of women's softball took a more critical approach by 1940, labeling softball a masculine sport and eyeing skilled women players with suspicion. In their book *Softball! So What*, Lowell Thomas and Ted Shane took an apparently positive view; applauding the women's game.... Yet the authors also observed that women failed to exhibit ladylike manners on the field and resisted "anything effeminate" in the rules.... [T]hey introduced element of ridicule by referring to general prohibitions against women athletes and intimating an association between softball and lesbianism through allusions to Sappho and Amazons....

Wrigley sensed that to make women's baseball attractive to a mass audience beyond the neighborhood appeal of softball, he would have to overcome such negative portrayals and circumvent charges that, as a "male sport," baseball led masculine women.... Insisting that the women play baseball, not softball, Wrigley hoped to sustain interest in baseball as a spectator sport. And by demanding players combine masculine skill with feminine attractiveness, he kept the ideal of feminine womanhood constantly before the public eye. In this way the league would try to establish itself as cut above women's softball, avoiding its mannish image and reputation....

In 1944 the founding of the National Girls Baseball League (NGBL) in Chicago challenged the AAGBL's preeminence and undermined its unique status as the only professional baseball league for women. The NGBL initially consisted of four semipro teams that had dominated women's softball in the Chicago area.... Like the AAGBL, it faded out in the early 1950s.... The NGBL remained closely tied to softball, keeping the underhand pitch and shorter base paths of softball as well as the traditional softball uniforms of shorts or knickers....

The existence of a rival deepened the AAGBL's commitment to its unique brand of feminine baseball. The league had used the underhand pitch in 1943 but quickly legalized a side-arm delivery and eventually switched completely to overhand pitching. Meyerhoff's Management Corp. sought a competitive advantage by continuing to stress femininity and a unique style of ball to contrast with the rough, masculine image of softball. A beauty consultant hired for spring training in 1944 captured the spirit when she substituted the feminine nickname "marygirl" for the more masculine "tomboy" to describe the type of young womanhood desired by the AAGBL.

By associating masculinity with athletic skill and femininity with appearance, the AAGBL maintained a clear sense of appropriate divisions between male and female, even as it gave women an unprecedented opportunity to enter a male sports preserve. The AAGBL adhered to this principle both in the concrete daily operations of the league and in the ideology of women's sport it promoted. The league's dress and conduct codes, its public relations campaigns, and its playing rules all reflect this overarching philosophy.

[T]he AAGBL handbook ... spelled out the logic behind the accentuated contrast of feminine charm with masculine athletic ability. The section called "Femininity with Skill" instructed recruiters to weigh both ability and femininity in prospective players because it was "more dramatic to see a feminine-type girl throw, run and bat than to see a man or boy or masculine-type girl do the same things...." The manual continued: "For the benefit of self and game every player devotes himself to cultivation of both skill and femininity.... It is for the purpose of keeping constantly before the spectator the feminine elements of the show that the All-American girls are uniformed in tennis-type skirts. Conversely, boyish bobs and other imitations of masculine style and habit are taboo."

The carefully crafted impression of femininity included a sexual element. AAGBL officials absolutely forbade bawdiness or sexual antics reminiscent of barnstorming teams, often named "Bloomer Girls," from an earlier era.... [T]he league boasted of All-American Girls' "high moral tone," further safeguarded by the watchful eye of the chaperone. Nevertheless, Meyerhoff understood that the ideal feminine ball player would attract customers with her sex appeal as well as her slugging average. By insisting on short skirts, makeup, and physical attractiveness, he attempted to capitalize on an ideal of wholesome, feminine sexuality....

To ensure that players did in fact embody the desired "feminine mode and attitude," the league's first few spring training sessions featured not only tryouts and preseason conditioning but an evening charm school as well. Led one year by beauticians from the Helena Rubenstein salon … the clinic coached players on makeup, posture, fashion, table manners, and "graceful social deportment at large." Guidelines on personal appearance accompanied the beauty tips. Management ordered players to keep their hair shoulder length or longer, to wear makeup and nail polish, and never to appear in public wearing shorts, slacks, or jeans.

The league dropped the charm school after its value as a public relations stunt ebbed. However, management's stress on feminine dress and manner never wavered.… After buying out Meyerhoff in 1951, team owners adopted a new constitution that further elaborated dress guidelines, stating: "*Always appear in feminine attire….*"

The league introduced several other measures to create the desired effect. The management rejected players it perceived as too masculine. Even after making a team, a player might be fined or released if she violated league rules.…

The AAGBL also had an unwritten policy against hiring minority women, although it did employ several Cuban players. Not until 1951 did the league openly discuss hiring black women, eventually deciding against the idea "unless they would show promise of exceptional ability." This policy reflects the pervasive racism in American society at large and in sport during the 1940s and 1950s. But it can also be understood in relation to the league's special emphasis on femininity, an image rooted in white middle-class beliefs about beauty, body type, and female nature.…

In addition to guidelines on dress and recruiting, the league instituted a player conduct code that forbade most public drinking and smoking, required players to obtain prior approval for social engagements and living arrangements, and imposed an evening curfew. To enforce the rules, each team hired a chaperone.…

… Public relations wizard Meyerhoff developed several promotional schemes. He varied spring training sites annually in order to increase media and audience exposure. In later years, the league established two traveling teams of young players not yet skilled enough for regular league play.…

Other publicity efforts aimed at gaining national media attention and at establishing good community relations in league cities.… Movietone News followed the league to its 1947 spring training in Havana, Cuba, to shoot a preseason game before a crowd of 25,000. Later released as a newsreel called "Diamond Gals," it exposed millions of moviegoers … to the spectacle of All-American Girls Baseball. Articles in national magazines like *Collier's, Saturday Evening Post*, and *Holiday* reported on the league's novel brand of baseball and growing popularity. Meyerhoff's office carefully orchestrated contacts with the media, providing glossy photos of the league's most beautiful players, issuing copies of the league's dress and conduct codes, and emphasizing the difference between baseball and softball. To stress the femininity of the league and quickly silence any suggestions of masculinity or lesbianism, AAGBL officials stressed to the media that league rules allowed "no freaks or Amazons." As proof, it proudly drew attention to the married players and mothers in the league, though due to the young age of most players this group never comprised more than a tiny fraction of the AAGBL players.

While national feature stories highlighted the sex appeal and sensational quality of the league, local promotions stressed the team's contributions to community life and the players' "girl next door" image.... [I]ndividual teams incorporated as nonprofit organizations and returned a portion of their proceeds to the community by supporting local recreation programs and facility maintenance. Ownership by local businesses provided one source of civic backing, while teams gained additional support from local chapters of the Elks, the woman's club, and similar service organizations. Players made personal contact with community members by rooming with local families, giving clinics, ... and making public appearances....

AAGBL teams fared best in medium-sized cities like Rockford and Fort Wayne, where such personal contacts could be cultivated. Unlike the larger cities of Chicago, Milwaukee, and Minneapolis where franchises failed, these small industrial centers combined a keen interest in baseball with the absence of other professional sports ventures to compete for the limited market. Daily newspapers in league towns provided excellent regular coverage, and local radio stations broadcast games in some league cities....

It is not clear whether the femininity concept advocated by the league was instrumental in a team's success or failure.... Many factors contributed ..., including financial backing, competition for the entertainment dollar, team strength, and management ability. While spectators may have responded positively to the feminine style and wholesome values projected by the league, skilled play, intense competition, and intercity rivalries also won the enthusiastic support of baseball fans. The continued popularity of semipro and amateur softball teams suggests at least that alternative approaches, less concerned with expressions of femininity, could succeed [as well]....

... While promotional efforts and dress and conduct codes guaranteed the feminine side of the equation, the impression of "masculine skill" rested on maintaining the distinction between baseball and softball. Management constantly adjusted the rules to more closely conform to the rules of men's baseball. Over the years the league increased the length between bases from 65 to 85 feet, shrunk the ball size, and introduced overhand pitching.

This strategy came back to haunt the AAGBL. The league wanted to highlight the fact that the women could play a man's game—baseball—at the same time denying any resemblance between the All-American Girl and the "pants-wearing, tough-talking female softballer." Eventually this distinction caused the AAGBL to lose contact with its greatest source of talent, semipro and amateur softball players. After the early years the league fought a constant battle to find quality pitching and young talent.... Ironically, the very popularity of organized sport, with youth softball and baseball programs springing up everywhere, may have created unforeseen problems. Organized leagues, especially Little League baseball, tended toward strict gender segregation. By the 1950s fewer girls grew up playing neighborhood baseball on sandlot and playground teams....

... The talent shortage may explain the heightened concern over dress and feminine image expressed in league communications during its last years. The league began signing very young players of fifteen and sixteen as well as courting softball veterans like the Savona sisters, noted in the media for both their "mannish" appearance meant, management may have stepped up efforts to control player behavior and monitor appearance, hoping to reassure the parents of young recruits and to preserve the league's carefully cultivated feminine image.

... The young women shared a common childhood passion for sports and a particular excellence at softball or baseball. Interviews with former AAGBL members suggest that issues of femininity rarely concerned players, who overwhelmingly viewed the league as a fantastic opportunity to do something they really loved—play baseball. Yet looking back, opinion varies about the value of dress codes, rules of conduct, and the AAGBL's overarching femininity principle.

Some players found the league's concern with femininity ridiculous, while others believed it helped the league and improved the image of women athletes. Pragmatic rather than ideological considerations shaped players' views on the pastel skirted uniforms. In a 1985 *Sports Illustrated* interview, Shirley Jameson, ... not[ed], "They were very feminine, and you could do the job—most of the time." But they offered little leg protection when sliding: thus Jameson recalls, "I spent most of the season with strawberries on both legs." Some players believed that if the uniforms created a good public impression, contributing to the league's survival, they benefited the players regardless of personal taste. Still others, like Kalamazoo player Nancy Mudge Cato, loved the sharp look of the uniform and spoke of it with pride. "I loved that uniform.... I thought they were just charming."

Players displayed a similar range of opinion about dress and conduct codes....

Others chafed under the regulations but conformed out of a calculated estimation of the risks. Pepper Paire explained to *Sports Illustrated* reporter Jay Feldman, "You have to understand that we'd rather play ball than eat, and where else could we go and get paid $100 a week to play ball? ... And Faye Dancer, one of the league's more flamboyant players, regaled Sheldon Sunness of *Z Magazine* with her own approach to the rules. "I always respected the rules. I broke them all, but I respected them."

... Players like [Irene] Hickson had grown up in communities where baseball, basketball, and even fist fighting and football were unorthodox but still acceptable activities for girls. Physical strength, competitiveness, and personal toughness were qualities admired in women and men alike. Moreover, in many working-class and rural areas, women's clothing styles were not as restrictive as dominant modes of fashion. To AAGBL players from such backgrounds, the league's dress code and concept of femininity may have appeared strange, irrelevant, or even offensive. Nevertheless, the practical tips on etiquette and social presentation could provide helpful instruction for players unfamiliar with formal dining or public speaking....

Despite this range of opinion, former players seem not to have experienced sport as a masculine endeavor or to have personally felt a tension between sport and female identity. They regarded competitiveness, a love of sport, and the constant quest for improvement as integral aspects of their personalities, neither feminine nor masculine. Players did not express any sense of themselves as less womanly than nonathletes, even though they were aware that to some, baseball was a masculine game requiring masculine qualities. Their love of sport pushed questions of femininity into the background. Sport's masculine connotation presented problems only when it provoked negative responses from others or posed barriers to playing opportunities....

While the All-American Girls played tirelessly and enthusiastically *over* the long summer months, the management waged a constant battle against financial woes and franchise collapse. By the early 1950s ... mainstays like Racine and South Bend withdrew from the league, which shrunk to teams in 1954.... The board of directors cancelled the 1955 season, promising to reorganize the league in the future.

Many factors contributed to the AAGBL's decline. As urbanites joined the postwar suburban exodus and television took the entertainment world by storm, home recreation became the order of the day. Major spectator sports like football and baseball continued to draw large audiences, but attendance suffered at all other levels. Both local and national media expanded their coverage of major sports, nurturing a national sports culture that gradually supplanted small-town boosterism and local loyalties. Softball remained a popular sport, especially in the city and industrial leagues. However, as returning veterans replaced women in the work force. industrial sports as well as jobs once again became the province of men. Girls' and women's leagues continued to operate but as very minor programs. And while topnotch amateur and semipro women's softball teams never ceased providing skilled athletes a place to develop and compete, in most communities Little League baseball, industrial softball, and minor league men's baseball commanded an overwhelming share of funds, facilities, and civic backing.

Finally, the novel combination of "feminine attraction" and "masculine athletics" clashed with the conservative culture of the 1950s [that] witnessed a swift turnabout that propelled women back into domesticity. The emphasis on home, family, and marriage was rooted in return to older, restrictive definitions of femininity. Virulent homophobia ... accompanied the change in gender roles.... With baseball firmly re-established as the national (men's) pastime and femininity once again defined in terms of domestic life, the league's innovative effort to combine sport and femininity and its affirmation of female athletic ability were at odds with the dominant culture. Moreover, in an era of political, legal, and media attacks on homosexuals, the association of women's sport with Amazons or lesbianism jeopardized any attempt to market women's baseball as mass entertainment.

The legacy of the AAGBL lies less in its success or failure than in its fascinating approach to women's sports. The AAGBL management chose to promote the league by accentuating the tension between masculine sport and feminine charm. By continuing to see athletic ability as masculine skill rather than incorporating athleticism within the range of feminine qualities, the league's ideology posed no challenge to the fundamental precepts of gender in American society. In its concern with preserving the distinction between softball and baseball, the

AAGBL disparaged women's softball as unfeminine. Yet it ultimately preserved baseball as a male realm by promoting "feminine baseball" as a spectacle.

Attempting to present an image of femininity consistent with popular and marketable ideals, the AAGBL nevertheless played a part in undermining those ideals. The league's philosophy highlighted the contrast between masculine sport and feminine appearance. But the actual experience of playing and viewing AAGBL baseball challenged the idea that athletic skill belonged in the province of men. The league provided women a once-in-a-lifetime opportunity to develop their skills and to pursue their passion for sport aided by financial backing, quality coaching, and appreciative fans. The players returned the favor. They offered eager crowds the chance to view highly skilled competitive baseball played by women. Whether "tomboys" or "marygirls," the All-American Girls' aggressive, superior play challenged social conventions, defied athletic tradition, and offered the public an exciting and expanded sense of women's capabilities.

Title IX and Government Reform in Women's Athletics

RONALD A. SMITH

Historically, reform generally originated within the National Collegiate Athletic Association (NCAA), conferences, or individual institutions, but possibly the greatest reform in college athletics arose from federal legislation: Title IX of the Educational Amendments Act of 1972. With civil disorder resulting from the Vietnam War, civil rights turmoil, and the women's movement, the U.S. Congress passed legislation that would have a major influence on gender equity, especially as it related to girls' and women's participation in sport. The push for gender equity, found in Title IX, arose not in athletics but in the hiring practice at the University of Maryland, where in 1969 a woman, Bernice Sandler, asked a department member why she was not even considered for the full-time faculty position, a faculty on which she had been teaching part-time. A faculty member told Sandler, "You come on too strong for a woman." Sex discrimination soon dominated Sandler's thoughts, and that one incident led directly to the passage three years later of Title IX.

Shocked into looking at the history of discrimination, Sandler noted that Title VII of the Civil Rights Act of 1964 prohibited discrimination in employment based on race, color, religion, national origin, and sex but said nothing about discrimination in education. Title VI of the same act prohibited discrimination in any program receiving federal financial assistance "on the grounds of race, color, or national origin," but it left out sex. Sandler found out that the Fourteenth Amendment to the U.S. Constitution assured individuals of "equal protection of the laws" by states, yet no Supreme Court case of discrimination against women in education had ever been decided favorably toward women. Furthermore, she discovered that the executive order prohibiting federal

---

contractors from discriminating in employment based on "race, color, religion, and national origin" had been expanded by President Lyndon Johnson to include discrimination based on sex. Eureka! Sandler made the connection between universities, federal contracts, and sex discrimination. Since most universities, including the University of Maryland, received federal contracts, she could help eliminate future sex discrimination at Maryland and elsewhere. With the help of the Women's Equity Action League, she began a national campaign to end discrimination in education, culminating in the passage of Title IX.

When Title IX was under consideration by Congress, there was, at first, little said about gender equity in sport; rather, it was gender equity in education. The American Council on Education, the college president-led group that since World War II had been attempting to reform intercollegiate athletics, was basically silent on the merits of Title IX. At the first congressional hearing on education and employment of women, headed by Representative Edith Green of Oregon, an American Council on Education (ACE) representative told the subcommittee that "there is no sex discrimination in higher education, and even if it did exist, it wasn't a problem." The ACE was silent on Title IX and its stance on gender equity in education and silent on gender equity in sport. The predominantly male college and university presidents were seemingly as uninvolved in the passage of Title IX as was the nation. Little was reported in the press upon its passage, and it generally remained out of sight until questions arose about the negative impact equity for women in sport might have upon men's athletic budgets.

Until the 1960s, few universities offered women's intercollegiate athletics, for most women physical educators for well over a half century had opposed competitive sports for women similar to those conducted for men. When Vassar College had started the first Field Day in 1895, a kind of intramural track meet, there was little thought of competing against other women's colleges in the area, though male-only Harvard and Yale had been rivals for a number of years. Yet, even then, the women of Vassar compared their times and heights to those of the men at Yale: 16 seconds in the 100-yard dash as opposed to 10 seconds for the Yale men and 3 feet 10 inches in the high jump relative to 5 feet 10 inches for the men. Eight decades later, the comparison to men's athletics is what brought women greater equality once Title IX had been passed. By then, women's competitive intercollegiate sport had been established, and not only were most of the sports the same as the men's, but by the force of federal legislation and the courts, the move to equity in the important areas of sport was demanded and enforced.

For about the first century of college women's sport, there was little need to control unethical, commercial, or professional aspects of the sport involvement. Nearly all the activity was controlled by women physical educators, who considered sport to be an integral part of education, not public exhibitions. This was unlike the men's athletics in which students organized the first generation or more of intercollegiate athletics with little or no thought to educational goals. The women physical educators insisted that sport be part of an educational model, strictly under women's control. The male model was a commercial one from the very first intercollegiate contest, a commercially sponsored crew meet between Harvard and Yale on Lake Winnipesaukee in New Hampshire. Women physical educators, nearly all members of the faculty, unlike most male coaches, were emphatic in their desire to keep women's sport under their control and away from the men's commercial-professional model. From the 1870s, when sport was first introduced to college women, to the 1970s, women wielded power and control in college women's sport. Or as sport historian Joan Hult has noted, "[W]ithin the sacred walls of the school gymnasium the women physical educators reigned supreme." The supremacy, until the women's movement in the 1960s, was highly anticompetitive, with no intercollegiate athletics for most colleges.

The century-long tradition of control cannot be overemphasized. It may be the most important point in attempting to understand how women's athletics developed in the twentieth century and how women physical educators remained in power and control until Title IX was implemented in the 1970s. Even in the late 1950s, as Mary Yost of Ohio State University noted, most women's physical education had a number of "dirty words" relative to athletic competition. Three of them were intercollegiate (extramural or sports days were acceptable), coach (teacher was much preferred), and varsity (outgrowth of intramurals was allowed). In the early 1960s, when competition was growing slowly for women, Phoebe Scott, a leader who favored increased competition stated, "Whether we like it or not, we have educated a whole generation of women to believe that somehow there was something slightly evil or immoral in competition for the highly skilled girl." Until the 1970s, there were few concerns by women leaders about athletic scholarships, high school grade point averages, eligibility of freshmen, transfer students, or graduation rates, for the model was educational until the passage of Title IX. The irony, of course, is that with Title IX the women's model of athletics with women physical educators in control quickly vanished, while skilled women athletes, who had been restrained for a century by those same women physical educators, were given opportunities that had not generally existed before. A nearly 180-degree change had occurred in the cliché, "the good of those who play." In the 1920s "the good of those who play" excluded skilled women athletes for two generations, but since the 1960s the statement has emphasized skilled women athletes.

Two major forces changed the direction of women's sport in the 1960s: the women's movement and America's Cold War with the Soviet Union. In the midst of the Cold War, there was a palpable national need to defeat the Soviets in many areas of life, including sports. A special NCAA report in 1962, only months after the Communists began erecting a wall between the Communist countries in Eastern Europe and those of democratic Western Europe, concluded: "Competitive sports have become a vital factor in international relationships and the 'cold war propaganda.'" It was clear that America had lost leadership in Olympic sports, having lost decisively to the Soviets in both the 1956 and 1960 Olympics, with the Soviet women winning twenty-eight medals to the American women's twelve in 1960. Improving women's performance in international competition, especially the Olympics, was not as dramatic but may have been as crucial to America's Cold War image as was the success of President John F. Kennedy in forcing the Soviet Union to dismantle its missiles being constructed in Cuba and aimed at the United States in 1962.

The NCAA saw the need to get involved in raising the level of college women's athletics well before the Association for Intercollegiate Athletics for Women became operational in 1972 at the time of Title IX. A decade before Title IX, the NCAA helped sponsor the educational Institute for Women's and Girls' Sports in cooperation with the U.S. Olympic Development Committee and the Division of Girls' and Women's Sport (DGWS), part of the American Association for Health, Physical Education, and Recreation. In the early 1960s, only a few years after the Soviets appeared to be leading America in scientific developments, such as orbiting the first artificial space satellite and then sending the first astronaut, Yuri Gagarin, into outer space, the United States needed to produce more Olympic winners, and the colleges (except for some Negro colleges) were contributing almost no women Olympians who could compete at the highest levels. At the same time, nearly all male Olympians were participants in intercollegiate athletics. The NCAA also had a self-serving reason to be involved with women's sport development because it was in a generations-old power struggle with the leading amateur athletic organization, the Amateur Athletic Union (AAU), over the control of amateur athletics. If the NCAA was to retain a power position in its longtime fight with the AAU, it was natural to want to be involved on the women's side of athletics.

As competition in women's athletics was rising in the late 1950s and early 1960s, along with the women's movement, college women physical educators organized the Commission on Intercollegiate Athletics for Women (CIAW) in 1966 to govern national championships. The CIAW was organized, in part, as a foil to any NCAA attempt to bring women into the NCAA. The year before the formation of the CIAW, the NCAA's Long Range Planning Committee was discussing the "need for encouraging opportunity for young women to compete in intercollegiate athletics." Thus both women physical educators and the NCAA were discussing women's intercollegiate athletics, but from entirely different perspectives. The women physical educators were responding to the women's movement's desire for greater physical expression and equality of opportunity while fighting to retain women's control of women's sport. The men were far more interested in controlling amateur sport, trying to wrest control of amateur sport from the AAU, and college women's athletics were part of the equation. The die was cast for a fight over control of highly competitive women's college sport before either the Association for Intercollegiate Athletics for Women (AIAW) came into existence or Title IX was passed in 1972. But the legality of Title IX forced action on the issue of equity between men's and women's programs rather quickly.

Title IX of the Education Amendments of 1972 was only thirty-seven words long, but its impact for the reform of women's athletics was eventually profound: "No person in the United States shall, on the basis of sex, be excluded from participation in, be denied the benefits of, or be subjected to discrimination under any educational program or activities receiving federal financial assistance."

There was no discussion that this act would fundamentally reform college sport and women's place in it. In fact, few paid much attention when Title IX was passed, and the all-male NCAA became alarmed only when the law was applied directly to intercollegiate sport and threatened the financial viability of men's sport during the inflationary 1970s. The president of the NCAA, John Fuzak, cried foul, but only after the Department of Health, Education, and Welfare (DHEW) regulations threatened men's sports. The DHEW, Fuzak said, was using an "illegal quota system for determining equality of opportunity." His memorandum to all NCAA members said that "the increasing intrusion of the Federal government into the educational process is repugnant to basic concepts of an institution's freedom to pursue its own education goals." Opposition to Title IX, however, came at the exact time the NCAA was campaigning hard for federal government intrusion to prohibit professional football from televising its games on Friday nights and all day on Saturday, in an effort to preserve its recruiting and financial base. When Title IX was passed, only about 1 percent of the average university athletic budget was expended on women's sports, and the average women's athletic expenditure of institutions of higher learning was about $1 per student. Soon, financing of women's sport rose rapidly when compared to men's sport.

The impact of Title IX on equity for women, ironically, was that the male norm was used as the measure against which to judge equality. The result was that the women's educational model was lost to the male commercial-professional model. That change occurred rapidly in financial aid to women athletes, when in 1972 a tennis player for Florida's Mary Mount College, Kathy Kemper, was denied entry into a collegiate tennis tournament because she had an athletic scholarship. She, her coach, Fern "Peachy" Kellmeyer, and others challenged the antischolarship policy of the AIAW, because denying athletic scholarships to women in an institution of higher education in which men were receiving scholarships violated the equal protection clause of the Fourteenth Amendment. In short, the AIAW was discriminating against its own athletes by denying scholarships. Only months after the challenge to scholarships, the AIAW abandoned its philosophical stance in a pragmatic attempt to save control over women's sport by voting to allow athletic scholarships. Not all women sport advocates favored caving in to athletic scholarships. As two leaders wrote, by voting to allow "talent" scholarships, they were "stooping to do the expedient thing." June Galloway of the University of North Carolina was another. "I believe that not only scholarships are at stake here," she wrote a member of the AIAW Executive Council, "but the entire programs for women in sports." A male supporter of the AIAW, Harold Falls, agreed: "If grants-in-aid are allowed, the educational aspects of the program will no longer exist." He was on target. The Kellmeyer court case and a federal law brought about radical reform in women's athletics, leading directly to far greater participation for women, though at the same time it was destroying the women's educational model.

The Kellmeyer court case broke the bedrock policy of the AIAW and began the movement for equality based upon the male model, a commercially constructed one. Once the AIAW was forced to give athletic scholarships on an equal basis as men, other planks in the education model eroded, including a move toward the male model of recruiting, transfer regulations, negotiations for commercial broadcasts rather than public broadcasting of events, commercial subsidies for AIAW championships, commercial sponsors for all-American teams and all-star contests and alcohol advertising for events. It also eventually led to the end of the sex-separatist policy in women's athletics and the loss of women physical educators' position of influence in college sport. The women's educational model had been sacrificed by the women leaders in an unsuccessful attempt to prevent their loss of power over the control of women's sport. Eventually, the women leaders of the AIAW lost their leadership in women's athletics as its member institutions left to join the NCAA and its far-better-funded national championships, but that took a decade of strife.

Once Title IX regulations were put in place by the mid-1970s and the Kellmeyer court case moved the AIAW model toward the male model, there was an almost unavoidable clash between the NCAA and the AIAW over the control of women's athletics. To be equal under Title IX, the male model was used as a reference. If women did not receive equal scholarships, coaching, practice and game facilities, equipment, and funding relative to men, lawsuits were almost inevitably based upon not only Title IX but also the Fourteenth Amendment to the U.S. Constitution equal protection clause and equal rights amendments of state constitutions. Title IX, however, not the equal protection clause of the Fourteenth Amendment kept women's sport in the public eye and constantly present in the minds of members of the NCAA. As soon as the proposed Title IX regulations were sent out for comment, the NCAA opposed the Department of Health, Education, and Welfare interpretations of the law and began a frontal attack in the legislative and executive branches of the federal government. The NCAA backed Senator John Towers unsuccessful amendment to Title IX, which if enacted would have exempted revenue-producing sports, such as football and basketball, from the regulations, thus limiting perceived damage to men's athletics.

As the efforts to water down the Title IX regulations were failing, the NCAA moved to see if it, rather than the AIAW, should control college women's sports. The NCAA began a concerted effort to portray itself as the only organization that was strong enough to provide equal opportunities for women athletes. As early as the fall of 1974, the NCAA Council began an examination of possibilities of providing national championships for women. When, the following year, the NCAA Council proposed a resolution for possibly conducting "pilot programs for women's national championships," the ire of women in the AIAW was raised higher than it had before. Yet the NCAA Council and legal counsel warned that if the NCAA did not provide championships and athletic scholarships, it would be in violation of the equal protection clause of the Fourteenth Amendment to the U.S. Constitution. A massive telephone campaign by members of the AIAW to NCAA convention delegates put a damper on the Council's resolution for pilot programs. For a short time, the AIAW was able to keep its identity: conducting championships and allowing women to remain in power positions in women's sport.

For the remainder of the 1970s, the AIAW and NCAA made feigned attempts to resolve governance issues so that there might be one organization, but it was clear that the NCAA believed it was the one organization qualified to conduct college athletics. A legal opinion from its counsel in 1975 stated that the NCAA "would be ill-advised to rely upon a 'separate but equal' approach to the administration or operation of programs designed to benefit both males and females." However, as the NCAA was jousting with the AIAW over such issues as combining into one organization or creating common eligibility rules, the National Association of Intercollegiate Athletics, an organization of lesser influential men's college athletics, decided in 1978 to provide championships for women. Compounding defections from the AIAW was the worst inflation in America since the 1920s. Double-digit inflation and compliance to the demands of Title IX placed intercollegiate athletics at all division levels in jeopardy. Obviously, one solution to expanding costs was for individual institutions to form one administrative unit for athletics rather than for each sex. Sex-separate athletic departments and the sex-separate AIAW could not withstand the force of Title IX and equal protection of the Fourteenth Amendment. When the NCAA in 1980 decided to offer championships in Division II and III, the AIAW was doomed, unless the NCAA could be convinced to not implement its championships or a court ruling could save the women's organization. Not only did the NCAA not rescind its Division II and III championships for women in 1981, but it also voted, in a close vote, to begin championships in the big-time Division I.

Moving from what had once been an educational model of the AIAW to the commercial model of the NCAA could be considered reactionary, not reform. However, for women athletes, there is little question that they would be better served athletically with the financial backing of the NCAA. For instance, the AIAW was continuously in financial straights, and from 1974 until its demise it had spent far more each year for its legal counsel, Margot Polivy, than it had for the conduct of national championships. By 1981, the women's model had been effectively lost as the AIAW had gone the commercial route in an effort to survive. As Judith Sweet, women's athletic director at the University of California, San Diego, said, "[S]tudent-athletes may best be served" by creating NCAA championships for women. The disputed vote for women's championships was a reform for athletes but a major defeat for those women who felt betrayed by the loss of what they believed was an educational model for sport in higher education. Title IX, which had been hailed by many for requiring equity in girls' and women's sport, had been cruel to those who clung to an educational model of sport. All that remained was an antitrust lawsuit by the AIAW against the NCAA, one that did not convince the U.S. district judge and a circuit court that the NCAA had used its monopoly to destroy the AIAW. The lawsuit had devoured all the AIAW assets, and the organization lay prostrate with a number of unpaid debts. The educational model and a sex-separatist philosophy were buried with the financial debts.

The reform organization, which was the AIAW, could have had its educational model adopted generally in higher education, but there was no powerful group, other than women in physical education and sport, that supported it. Division III of the NCAA might have gone along with many of the AIAW policies, as, for instance, both opposed athletic scholarships. The power, however, lay with the major athletic powers found in Division I. Within those institutions, there were likely no governing boards, no athletic departments, no alumni groups, no student organizations, and few presidents who would allow an educational model to come into existence, since that model was lifeless among most of the leading institutions of higher education for the entire twentieth century. Only groups of faculty would have been sympathetic toward an educational model, and they had long before been effectively eliminated from the power equation in athletics. The sex-separatist, educational model of intercollegiate athletics had a short shelf life and became a footnote in athletic reform.

While the AIAW died a painful death for many who favored an educational model for athletics run by women, the dynamics of federal Title IX legislation continued its reformation of women's athletics in educational institutions nationally. Title IX did not produce what President W. Robert Parks of Iowa State University believed it would, "the law of equality of millstones," which presumably meant that everyone would drown equally. Rather, it was the driving force reforming college athletics and causing the greatest growth in the number of competitive athletes in American history. Federal legislation had created an athletic reform that would likely have taken decades to achieve had it not passed. It was not easy to get athletic departments, run by males for generations, to treat emerging women's athletics with anything approaching equity. The logic of their argument was, of course, that it had taken decades for men's athletics to reach the stage of general prosperity, and it was unfair for women's athletics to immediately demand an equal division of scholarships, facilities, travel accommodations, equipment, and coaching salaries. The administration of President Ronald Reagan and the U.S. Supreme Court agreed in the 1980s. The same year that the AIAW lost its court case with the NCAA, the U.S. Supreme Court reversed the interpretation of Title IX so that only those programs receiving direct federal aid needed to be mindful of the law. Thus, if the athletic department of the University of Virginia or Stanford received no federal funding, they could legally discriminate against women athletes. Four years later, however, the Civil Rights Restoration Act of 1988 was passed by Congress over the veto of President Reagan, and it specifically applied Title IX to athletic programs.

From that point on, the Title IX reform could progress as rapidly as individual institutions complied with the law and the courts could make decisions, generally in favor of upholding equity rights provided by law. Following a 1979 compliance interpretation of the Office for Civil Rights, an institution could meet the requirements of Title IX in one of three ways: (1) by providing athletic opportunities proportionate to student enrollment, (2) by demonstrating continual expansion of athletic opportunities to the underrepresented sex, and (3) by full accommodation of the interests and abilities of the underrepresented sex. There were numerous court cases testing whether one of the three prongs of compliance was met. Possibly the most important was the 1992 Brown case, in which it was found that Brown University discriminated against women by not supporting female athletes at a level at which male athletes were sustained.

Cohen v. Brown University resulted after the Brown University Athletic Department, for financial reasons, dropped two men's teams, golf and water polo, and two women's teams, volleyball and gymnastics. Outsider lawyers came in to force a court case, claiming that while women made up 51 percent of the Brown student body they represented only 39 percent of Brown's athletes, thus the sports lacked proportionality. Even though Brown University had fifteen women's sports, far more than most universities, it had not added any new women's team since 1982 and thus lacked continuous expansion of women's opportunities. Because it dropped two women's sports, it failed the test of providing for interest and ability of women students. Though *Brown* showed clearly that there was far greater interest among men than women in participation, the judge ruled that the lack of interest was a result of women's place in society, historically, socially, and politically. The Court of Appeals agreed, and the U.S. Supreme Court allowed the decision to stand. The impact of the *Brown* case has been that since 1991, no NCAA Division I school has dropped a women's team, though many men's sports have been eliminated or relegated to intramural-club status. The benefit to women's sports in colleges had been positive, for the *Brown* case has been used, as the U.S. Court of Appeals for the Ninth Circuit has stated, "to encourage women to participate in sports." In this case, passing social legislation through the courts was successful.

In a short period of time, the greatest reform in American intercollegiate athletics had taken place, essentially without major positive action by the NCAA, its faculty representatives, conferences, or individual institutions. Rather, it was the force of federal government legislation and litigation in the court system that brought about reform. Once the action of the federal government had been taken, eventually the male-dominated NCAA and presidents of universities brought about the integration of women's athletics into the cultural mainstream. This was done with increased financing by institutions in providing greater equity in such areas as scholarships, coaching, facilities, and equipment. At no other time was there a period in American history that experienced such rapid growth in intercollegiate competition. The reform that impacted women's athletics was in some ways similar to the reform in integrating African Americans into intercollegiate athletics. In both cases, the federal government and the courts, not individual institutions, conferences, or the NCAA, precipitated the reform. As the reform for women came with the events of the women's movement and Title IX, greater opportunities for African Americans followed on the heels of the *Brown v. Board of Education* decision in 1954 and the Civil Rights Act of 1964.

FURTHER READING

Blue, Adrienne. *Faster, Higher, Further: Women's Triumphs and Disasters at the Olympics* (1988).

Browne, Lois. *Girls of Summer* (1992).

Burton, Mariah Nelson. *Are We Winning Yet? How Women Are Changing Sports and Sports Are Changing Women* (1991).

Cahn, Susan K. *Coming on Strong: Gender and Sexuality in Twentieth-Century Women's Sport* (1994).

Carpenter, Linda Jean. *Title IX* (2005).

Cayleff, Susan. *Babe: The Life and Legend of Babe Didrikson Zaharias* (1995).

Festle, Mary Jo. *Playing Nice: Politics and Apologies in Women's Sports* (1996).

Fields, Sarah. *Female Gladiators: Gender, Law, and Contact Sport in America* (2008).

Fidler, Merrie A. *The Origins and History of the All-American Girls Professional Baseball League* (2006).

Gregorich, Barbara. *Women at Play* (1993).

Guttmann, Allen. *Women's Sport: A History* (1991).

Heiskanen, Benita. *The Urban Geography of Boxing: Race, Class, and Gender in the Ring* (2012).

Howell, Reet, ed. *Her Story in Sport* (1982).

Hult, Joan. "The Philosophical Differences in Men's and Women's Collegiate Athletics," *Quest* 32 (1980), 77–94.

Hult, Joan. "Women's Struggle for Governance in U.S. Amateur Sports," *International Review for Sociology of Sport* 24 (1989), 249–63.

Hult, Joan S., and Marianna Trekell, eds. *A Century of Women's Basketball: From Frailty to Final Four* (1991).

Jay, Kathryn. *More Than Just a Game: Sports in American Life Since 1945* (2006).

Johnson, Susan E. *When Women Played Hardball* (1994).

King, Billie Jean. *Pressure Is a Privilege: Lessons I've Learned from Life and the Battle of the Sexes* (2008).

LeCompte, Mary Lou. *Cowgirls of the Rodeo: Pioneer Professional Athletes* (1993).

Ring, Jennifer. *Stolen Bases: Why American Girls Don't Play Baseball* (2009).

Suggs, Welch. *A Place on the Team: The Triumph and Tragedy of Title IX* (2005).

Verbrugge, Martha H. *Active Bodies: A History of Women's Physical Education in Twentieth-Century America* (2012).

Ware, Susan. *Game, Set, Match: Billie Jean King and the Revolution in Women's Sports* (2011).

Wushanley, Ying. *Playing Nice and Losing: The Struggle for Control of Women's Intercollegiate Athletics, 1960–2000* (2004).

CHAPTER 13

Sport and Race in America Since 1945

Race was an important factor in American sport prior to World War II, and, if anything, it has become an even more prominent variable since then. Before the war Americans had begun to recognize the abilities of African American athletes, most notably Jesse Owens and Joe Louis. Then during the war, when African American soldiers were dying for their country, there were growing demands by civil rights leaders and liberal politicians for racial equality, which included integration of the playing fields.

Jackie Robinson broke color lines in 1946 when he played with the Montreal Royals, the top farm club of the Brooklyn Dodgers, and the professional football leagues followed suit when they hired their first African American players in twelve years. One year later Robinson integrated Major League Baseball when he joined the Brooklyn Dodgers. Historians consider his becoming a Dodger a pivotal event in modern American history.

The full integration of the major professional sports leagues took place at a slow pace—it was twelve years before the last major league team, the Boston Red Sox, became integrated. Furthermore, blacks in baseball and football were "stacked" into the less central positions like outfielder or cornerback rather than catcher or quarterback, and informal quotas limited the number of African Americans that a team might keep on its roster or play at the same time. On the collegiate level, major southern schools would not play football or basketball teams having African Americans as late as the early 1960s, and some southern schools fielded white-only teams until the late 1960s. At this time the Black Athletic Revolt emerged to fight racism, mainly on college campuses, but wherever it existed, most notably the apartheid in South Africa. The movement raised the consciousness of college athletes and their supporters; between 1967 and 1971 there were protests against racism at thirty-seven schools.

What emboldened African American student-athletes to fight prejudice in sports? Historians point to factors such as the civil rights movement, the Black Power movement, and role models—most notably heavyweight champion Muhammad Ali. Ali defied conventional norms by his outspokenness, his conversion to the Islam religion, and his refusal, on religious grounds, to serve in the military. He paid for that decision by having his title taken from him. By the 1980s, when 80 percent of the National Basketball Association (NBA) was black, and most National Football League (NFL) players were black, the most glaring elements of racism had been eliminated, particularly in salaries and stacking. However, African American athletes were still limited when they sought to gain substantial long-term benefits from sport. They disproportionately failed out of college, and these young people remained very underrepresented in athletic leadership positions, both on and off the field. Management opportunities in sports were largely nonexistent. There was no black coach in major professional sports in this era until Bill Russell was hired to coach the Boston Celtics of the NBA in 1966. The first black manager was Frank Robinson of the Cleveland Indians in 1975. There was a black NFL coach in the early 1920s, Fritz Pollard, but the second, Art Shell of the Oakland Raiders, was not hired until 1989.

DOCUMENTS

Document 1 is a private report to the American League by Yankees president Larry McPhail in 1946 on the issue of integrated baseball. It had been strongly pushed by Bill Veeck, a minor league owner who had tried to buy the Philadelphia Phillies in 1943 and stock them with Negro League stars. However, Baseball Commissioner Kenesaw Mountain Landis had blocked Veeck's bid. McPhail, like most of the leaders in organized baseball, opposed integration, and in this presentation he argued that integration would be bad for African Americans. However, the integration of baseball went on despite his criticisms, and Dodgers president Branch Rickey signed Jackie Robinson to a minor league contract.

Robinson was not a star in the Negro Leagues, but he had been an all-around superstar athlete at UCLA and an All-American in football. He had grown up in an integrated world in Los Angeles, was a former army officer, and was married to a sophisticated African American woman. Document 2 examines his first spring training in 1946. What problems did he encounter in his initial experience with white baseball?

Document 3 consists of various statements made by Muhammad Ali during the late 1960s when he was barred from fighting for refusing induction into the Army.

In Document 4, sociologist Harry Edwards of the University of California, Berkeley, reviews the origins of the Black Athletic Revolt he began in 1967 by organizing students at San Jose State to fight racism both at the college and in its athletic program.

Document 5 is an obituary written shortly after the untimely death of Puerto Rican star Roberto Clemente, who played right field for the Pittsburgh Pirates from 1955 to 1972. Clemente was the most outstanding Latino baseball player in Major League Baseball history. He was an excellent batter who had 3,000 hits, led the National League in batting four times, with a lifetime batting average of .317, and he was one of the greatest fielders of all-time (12 Golden Gloves), a winner of two World Series, and a participant in 15 All-Star games.

In this document, sportswriter Bruce Keidan of the *Philadelphia Inquirer* discusses Clemente's great career as well as his character, for Clemente was a great philanthropist who died in an aviation accident while delivering medical aid to Nicaraguan earthquake victims.

1. Yankees President Larry McPhail's Plan to Discourage Integration of Baseball, 1946

The appeal of baseball is not limited to any racial group. The Negro takes great interest in baseball and is, and always has been, among the most loyal supporters of professional baseball....

The American people are primarily concerned with the excellence and performance in sport rather than the color, race, or creed of the performer....

Baseball will jeopardize its leadership in professional sport if it fails to give full appreciation to the fact that the Negro fan and the Negro player are part and parcel of the game. Certain groups in this country, including political and social-minded drum-beaters, are conducting pressure campaigns in an attempt to force major league clubs to sign Negro players. Members of these groups are not primarily interested in professional baseball. They are not campaigning to provide better opportunity for thousands of Negro boys who want to play baseball. They are not even particularly interested in improving the lot of Negro players who are already employed. They know little about baseball—and nothing about the business end of its operation. They single out professional baseball for attack because it offers a good publicity medium.

... Professional baseball is a private business enterprise.... It is a business in which Negroes, as well as whites, have substantial investments in parks, franchises, and player contracts. Professional baseball, both Negro and white, has grown and prospered over a period of many years on the basis of separate leagues. The employment of a Negro on one AAA League club in 1946 resulted in a tremendous increase in Negro attendance at all games in which the player appeared. The percentage of Negro attendance at some games at Newark and Baltimore was in excess of 50 percent. The situation might be presented, if Negroes participate in major-league games, in which the preponderance of Negro attendance in parks such as the Yankee Stadium, the Polo Grounds, and Comiskey Park could conceivably threaten the value of the major league franchises owned by these clubs.

The thousands of Negro boys of ability who aspire to careers in professional baseball should have a better opportunity.... Signing a few Negro players for the major leagues would be a gesture—but it would contribute little or nothing toward a solution of the real problem....

(1) A Major League Baseball player must have something besides great natural ability. He must possess the technique, the coordination, the competitive

---

From Larry McPhail, "Plan to American League on Discouraging Integration of Baseball," in U.S. Congress, Committee on the Judiciary, *Organized Baseball* (Washington, DC: Government Printing Office, 1952), 483–85.

attitude, and the discipline which is usually acquired only after years of training in the minor leagues. The minor-league experience of players on the major-league rosters, for instance, averages 7 years. The young Negro player never has had a good chance in baseball. Comparatively few good young Negro players are being developed. This is the reason that there are not more players who meet major-league standards in the big Negro leagues. Sam Lacey, sports editor of the Afro-American newspapers, says, "I am reluctant to say that we haven't a single man in the ranks of colored baseball who could step into the major league uniform and disport himself after the fashion of a big leaguer.... Mr. Lacey's opinions are shared by almost everyone, Negro or white, competent to appraise the qualifications of Negro players.

(2) About 400 Negro professionals are under contract to the 24 clubs in four Negro leagues. Negro leagues have made substantial progress in recent years. Negro baseball is now a $2,000,000 business. One club, the Kansas City Monarchs, drew over 300,000 people to its home and road games in 1944 and 1945. Over 50,000 people paid $72,000 to witness the east-west game at the White Sox Stadium in Chicago. A Negro-league game established the all-time attendance record for Griffith Stadium in Washington. The average attendance at Negro games in the Yankee Stadium is over 10,000 per game.

These Negro leagues cannot exist without good players.... If the major leagues and the big minors of professional baseball raid these leagues and take their best players—the Negro leagues will eventually fold up ... a lot of professional Negro players will lose their jobs....

(3) The Negro leagues rent their parks in many cities from clubs in organized baseball. Many major and minor league clubs derive substantial revenue from these rentals. (The Yankee(s) ... nets nearly $100,000 a year from rentals and concessions.) ... Club owners in the major leagues are reluctant to give up revenues amounting to hundreds of thousands of dollars every year. They naturally want the Negro leagues to continue. They do not sign, and cannot properly sign, players under contract to Negro clubs. This is not racial discrimination. It's simply respecting the contractual relationship between the Negro leagues and their players....

2. Jackie Robinson on the Struggles of His First Spring Training, 1946

We had a tough time getting to Daytona Beach. At one point we had to give up our seats because the Army still had priority on planes. So we took a train to Jacksonville, and when we got there we found we'd have to go the rest of the way by bus. We didn't like the bus, and we particularly didn't like the back seat when there were empty seats near the center. Florida law designates where Negroes are to ride in public conveyances. The law says: "Back seat." We rode there.

From Jack R. Robinson and Wendell Smith, *Jackie Robinson: My Own Story* (New York: Greenberg, 1948), 65–68, 70–75, 79–80.

When we arrived in Daytona Beach we were met at the bus station by Wendell Smith, sports editor of *The Pittsburgh Courier,* and Billy Rowe, a photographer for the same paper. They had been there about four days and had arranged housing accommodations and other necessities. With them was Johnny Wright, a good friend of mine and a pitcher for the Homestead Grays of the Negro National League. Mr. Rickey had signed Johnny to a Montreal contract not long after he had signed me....

They took us to the home of a prominent Negro family. The rest of the team usually stayed at a big hotel on the ocean front, but this particular time they were quartered at Sanford, Florida, where the Dodger organization was looking over at least two hundred players.

As a result of our transportation difficulties, I was two days late. I learned from Smith and Rowe that Mr. Rickey was a bit upset about my late arrival; so we decided to get up early next morning and drive to Sanford, which is some twenty miles south of Daytona Beach.

We arrived in Sanford the next morning about ten o'clock, but instead of going to the ball park, we decided to go to the home of Mr. Brock, a well-to-do Negro citizen of the town and call Mr. Rickey.... We didn't want to cause a commotion or upset anything by walking into the park and surprising everyone. It was no secret that Johnny and I were going to be there, but we felt it best to remain as inconspicuous as possible.

Smith called Mr. Rickey at his hotel and he told us we should get over to the park as soon as possible. We took our shoes and gloves and hurried over. Clyde Sukeforth met us. We shook hands. "Go right into the dressing room and get your uniforms," he said....

I glanced at the players on the field. They had come from every section of the country—two hundred men out there, all hoping some day to become members of the Brooklyn Dodgers.... Suddenly I felt uncomfortably conspicuous standing there. Every single man on the field seemed to be staring at Johnny Wright and me....

We ducked into the clubhouse. It was empty save for one man, a big, fat fellow. I felt a bit tense and I'm sure Johnny did, too. We were ill at ease and didn't know exactly what to do next. The man saw us then and came right over and introduced himself. "Hiya, fellows," he said with a big, broad smile on his face. "I'm Babe Hamburger...."

"Well, fellows," he said, "I'm not exactly what you'd call a part of this great experiment, but I'm gonna give you some advice anyway. Just go out there and do your best. Don't get tense. Just be yourselves."

Be ourselves? Here in the heart of the race-conscious South? ... Johnny and I both realized that this was hostile territory—that anything could happen any time to a Negro who thought he could play ball with white men on an equal basis. It was going to be difficult to relax and behave naturally. But we assured Babe we'd try....

We finally got dressed and headed for the field. Waiting for us was a group of reporters from New York, Pittsburgh, Baltimore, Montreal, and Brooklyn. They surrounded us and started firing questions:

"What are you going to do if the pitchers start throwing at you?" one of them asked.

"The same thing everyone else does," I answered, smiling. "Duck!"

The next morning we were up bright and early. We went out to the park in a taxi and this time dressed with the rest of the players. Practice that day was a bit long, but not at all strenuous.

When we got back to Brock's, Johnny and I found Wendell Smith and Billy Rowe, our newspaper friends from Pittsburgh, waiting for us. Usually, they joked and kidded with us a lot; but that night they were both exceptionally quiet and sober. We all ate together. The conversation dragged until I began to feel uncomfortable....

Rowe got up from the table suddenly and said to Smith, "I'm going to fill up with gas...." Smith said. "We're all going to Daytona."...

"What about practice in the morning?" I asked. "After all, we came here to make the Montreal Club."

I was angry. What was this all about, anyway? No one had told us to move on to Daytona.... After all, things had been going beautifully. The first two days of practice had passed without a single incident. Surely we weren't being rejected after only a two-day trial! We were just beginning to loosen up a bit....

We piled into the car and started for Daytona. Rowe was driving and Smith was sitting beside him. Johnny was in the back with me. None of us said a word. We stopped at the main intersection of the town for a traffic light. A group of men were standing on the street corner in their shirt sleeves. It looked like a typical small-town bull session.

I suddenly decided that Sanford wasn't a bad town at all. The people had been friendly to us. Apparently they liked ball players. The men on the corner turned to look at us. Easy-going guys, curious over where we were going—certainly not hostile, I thought. I smiled at them. I actually felt like waving.

Rowe broke the silence for the first time as the light changed and we picked up speed. "How can people like that call themselves Americans!" he said bitterly....

"Now just a minute," I said "They haven't done anything to us. They're nice people as far as I'm concerned."...

"Yeah," Smith said, swinging around and looking us in the face. His eyes were blazing with anger. "Sure, they liked you. They were in love with you.... That's why we're leaving."

"What do you mean?" I asked....

"Look," Smith said, "we didn't want to tell you guys because we didn't want to upset you. We want you to make this ball club. But ... we're leaving this town because we've been told to get out. They won't stand for Negro ball players on the same field with whites!"...

The expulsion from Sanford was a humiliating experience. I found myself wishing I had never gotten mixed up in the whole business. When the club moved into Daytona, our permanent training base, what hope was there that I would not be kicked out of town just as I had been in Sanford? I was sure that as soon as I walked out on the field, an objection would be raised. I didn't want to go through that all over again. What could I do? Quit? … I wanted to, but I just didn't have the nerve to walk out on all the people who were counting on me—my family and close friends, Mr. Rickey, the fourteen million Negroes from coast to coast, the legion of understanding white people. Dejected as I was, I just had to stick it out.

The rest of the team was quartered in a big hotel overlooking the Atlantic Ocean. I stayed in the home of a private family in the Negro section of the town. When we finished practice, I'd go home and play cards with Smith, Rowe, and my wife. Once in a while we'd go to a movie. There was only one Negro movie in town and the picture ran for three days.… Often there was absolutely nothing to do. Our life was so restricted and monotonous that sometimes we would go to see the same movie twice.

Now and then some of the local Negroes would invite us to dinner or for a game of cards. There was also a USO Club near-by and some evenings I'd go there to play table tennis or pinochle. But no matter how I tried I couldn't find a sufficient diversion to preoccupy me. I found myself stewing over the problems which I knew were bound to confront me sooner or later.…

We were scheduled to play an exhibition game with the Jersey City Giants in Jacksonville. We made the trip by bus, and when we arrived at the park there was a big crowd waiting outside. We climbed out and went over to the players' gate leading onto the field. It was locked.…

"What's wrong here?" [Montreal manager] Hopper asked a man standing near-by.

"The game's been called off," the man said. "The Bureau of Recreation won't let the game be played because you've got colored guys on your club."

Mel Jones got hold of Charley Stoneham, the Jersey City business manager, and found that the man's report was correct. George Robinson, executive secretary of the Bureau of Recreation, had informed the Jersey City club that he would not allow the game to be played. There was nothing for us to do but drive back to Daytona.…

3. The Thoughts of Muhammad Ali in Exile, c. 1967

"I never thought of myself as great when I refused to go into the Army. All I did was stand up for what I believed. There were people who thought the war in Vietnam was right. And those people, if they went to war, acted just as brave as I did.… People say I made a sacrifice, risking jail and my whole career.… When people got drafted and sent to Vietnam … and came home with one leg and couldn't get jobs, that was a sacrifice.…"

"Some people thought I was a hero. Some people said that what I did was wrong. But everything I did was according to my conscience.… The government had a system where the rich man's son went to college, and the poor man's

From Thomas Hauser, *Muhammad Ali: His Life and Times* (New York: Simon and Schuster, 1991), 171–72, 187–89.

son went to war.... Freedom means being able to follow your religion, but it also means carrying the responsibility to choose between right and wrong.... I wanted America to be America." ...

On the war in Vietnam: "I'm expected to go overseas to help free people in South Vietnam, and at the same time my people here are being brutalized and mistreated.... So I'm going to fight it legally, and if I lose, I'm just going to jail. Whatever the punishment, ... is for standing up for my beliefs, ... I'll face it...."

On being stripped of his title and denied the right to fight: "The power structure seems to want to starve me out. The punishment, five years in jail, ten-thousand-dollar fine, ain't enough. They want to stop me from working...."

On ... financial hardship: ... "What do I need money for? I don't spend no money. Don't drink, don't smoke, ... don't go running with women...."

On lack of black pride: "We've been brainwashed. Everything good is supposed to be white. We look at Jesus, and we see a white with blond hair and blue eyes. We look at all the angels; we see white with blond hair and blue eyes.... We look at Miss America, we see white.... Even Tarzan, the king of the jungle in black Africa, he's white.... All the good cowboys ride the white horses and wear white hats.... When are we going to wake up as a people and end the lie that white is better than black?"

On hate: "I don't hate nobody and I ain't lynched nobody. We Muslims don't hate the white man. It's like we don't hate a tiger; but we know that a tiger's nature is not compatible with people's nature since tigers love to eat people. So we don't want to live with tigers.... So we don't want to live with the white man...."

4. Harry Edwards Reviews the Making of the Black Athletic Revolt, 1967

After the 1964 [Olympic] games, black athletes got together and talked about the possibility of a black boycott of the 1968 Olympics to be held in Mexico....

Then in the fall of 1967, ... First, Tommie Smith, in Tokyo for the University Games, casually commented that some black athletes would perhaps boycott the 1968 Olympics ... to protest racial injustice....

The second event was a revolt of black students and athletes at San Jose State College ... the institution at which ... Smith and ... other "world-class" athletes were matriculating. The significance ... was that sixty of the seventy-two Afro-American students on campus ... banded together and for the first time ... utilized collegiate athletics as a lever [for] social, academic, and political changes at an educational institution ... racism in the fraternities and sororities, racism in housing, racism and out-and-out mistreatment in athletics, and a general lack of understanding of the problems of Afro-Americans by the college administration.

From Harry Edwards, *The Revolt of the Black Athlete* (New York: Free Press, 1969), 40–47.

... We outlined a list of demands and stated publicly what our strategy would be if our demands were not met. We ... declared that we would prevent the opening football game....

Our strategy was ... simple.... [W]e felt that we had to utilize a power lever that would bring the community, student body [and] administration ... into the pressure situation.... We therefore decided to use something more central to the concerns of the entire local community structure—athletics. What activity is of more relevance to a student body than the first football game of the season? ...

The rally was a success and immediately afterward an organization was formed, the United Black Students for Action. It was composed chiefly of Afro-American students.... Our demands were as follows:

We, the affiliates of United Black Students for Action, hereby put forth the following *DEMANDS:*

... Publicly announced pledges from the ... Administration that housing— ... not open to ALL SJS students will not be open to *any* student....

That the Dept. of Intercollegiate Athletics organizes and put into operation *immediately* an effective program that provides the same treatment and handling for all athletes....

That the college administration either work to expand the 2% rule to bring underprivileged minority group members to SJS as students at least in proportion to their representation in the general population of California....

The end result of the confrontation was that the college administration moved to meet our demands, but not before tension had reached such a pitch that the game had to be called off....

... [W]e had learned the use of power—the power to be gained from exploiting the white man's economic and almost religious involvement in athletics.

5. "Roberto Clemente: Baseball's 'Magnificent Militant'"

BRUCE KEIDAN

He was the nicest militant I ever met.

Not that he was much for harsh words or expressions of righteous indignation. Roberto Walker Clemente was far too professional for that sort of thing. But he was a militant nonetheless. A crusader. For the Latin American baseball player. And for the children....

Roberto Clemente has given his last radio interview now. He has, almost unbelievably, struck his last base bit, won his last game for the Pittsburgh Pirates, made his last incredible throw from right field. A plane crash at San Juan, P. R., claimed the 38-year-old superstar late Sunday night. Baseball, Latin America and the children have lost an ambassador.

From Bruce Keidan, "Roberto Clemente: Baseball's 'Magnificent Militant,'" *Philadelphia Inquirer*, January 2, 1973, quoted in *The Congressional Record* (93rd Congress) (Washington, DC: GPO, 1973), 349–50.

"He studied everything and he remembered everything," Phillies manager Danny Ozark [recounted].... "He knew every pitcher and every hitter—whether the hitter had power, where the outfielders should play him, whether or not the guy would try to take the extra base."

He remembered something else, too. Roberto Clemente never forgot his own dirt-poor beginnings on the sandlots and the vacant lots of Carolina, Puerto Rico. He never forgot his obligation to millions of other Spanish-speaking children, growing up poor.

He was on the third of three scheduled relief flights to Managua, Nicaragua, when his plane went down.... Roberto Clemente could have helped the earthquake-stricken city in other ways. He could have written a check.... He could merely have called on the thousands of Influential friends he had made in his 18 major-league seasons to help. But if you knew Roberto Clemente, you knew he would go himself. To save the children.

I remember an interview with Clemente after a game in Philadelphia late last season, when he was closing in on his 3,000th big-league base hit. We were talking about night baseball and the advantage it gave the pitchers.

The handsome, Belafonte-like face shifted into a wry smile. "When I was a boy, we would play baseball all day and much of the night," he said. "There were no lights, but we would keep on playing after it got dark. You didn't have to go home for supper because there was no supper to go home for."

He was a star in a tough Puerto Rican semipro league by the time he was 16. At 19, he was a baseball player in a class by himself on a tropic island crammed full of hungry, agile kids with a dream of escaping from poverty by playing in the major leagues.

The Dodgers signed him for peanuts. In those days, that was what you gave a Latin player to sign him. A Latin kid was supposed to be eternally grateful just for the chance to play in the major leagues, even at a *minimal* salary and without bonus. Long after black Americans were making respectable money in the major leagues, Latins remained second-class baseball citizens.

Clemente fought that bias in his own militant way. He did not sulk or throw tantrums. He was a one-man fifth column. He did it with ability, with hustle, with integrity. He did it by comporting himself like a member of the diplomatic corps. He did it by talking up Latin America and the Latin American ballplayer to anyone who would listen.

"When you talked to Roberto Clemente," said Danny Ozark, "you were talking to Puerto Rico. You had the feeling that he wasn't just FOR his people. He WAS his people."

People said of Roberto Clemente that he was a hypochondriac. They refused to believe that the hundred nagging ailments and injuries of which he complained could be real. Never mind that the doctors agreed with him. Never mind that he played in more than 2,400 games in 18 big-league seasons. A guy who played baseball that well MUST be in the peak of health.

ESSAYS

The first essay by the late Jules Tygiel of San Francisco State University examines the demanding rookie year of Jackie Robinson, the first African American to join the major leagues since the long-forgotten Moses Fleetwood Walker who played for Toledo (American Association) in 1884. Robinson spent the 1946 season in the minors at the Dodgers top farm team in Montreal, winning the Most Valuable Player (MVP), and he was promoted to the Dodgers in 1947. The essay is drawn from Tygiel's seminal monograph *Baseball's Great Experiment: Jackie Robinson and His Legacy*, which is not so much a biography of Robinson, but an examination of the entire process of integration, beginning with the rise of the Negro Leagues through the integration of the Major and Minor Leagues. What kinds of problems did Robinson encounter on and off the field as a trailblazer as he broke the color line? How did he win over his teammates, his opponents, and the fans?

The second essay is a critical analysis of the public image of Muhammad Ali, who *Sports Illustrated* ranked as the "Sportsman of the Century," by David Zang, professor of kinesiology at Towson State University and author of *Sports Wars: Athletes in the Age of Aquarius* (2001), a collection of essays on recent American sport. Zang points out that Ali is widely remembered as a great athlete with enormous courage who stood up for his race, his religion, and his values, even if it meant the loss of his championship and a potential jail sentence for evading the draft. This is the Ali who lit the Olympic Flame at the 1996 Atlanta Olympics, and is a hero to people around the world. Yet Zang also explains that there was another Ali, a man who cruelly taunted opponents, even decent men like Floyd Patterson and Joe Frazier, on their blackness (though the latter's skin tone was much darker than Ali's) and bullied and punished lesser opponents in the ring for his personal gratification. Ali challenged traditional ideas of sport and character and personified the strain between old values and new ones.

A Lone Negro in the Game: Jackie Robinson's Rookie Season

JULES TYGIEL

… [T]he rookie first baseman eked out one bunt single [in his first two games]. "He seemed frantic with eagerness, restless as a can of worms," observed a Boston correspondent. On April 18 the Dodgers crossed the East River to play the New York Giants. Over 37,000 people flocked to the Polo Grounds to witness Robinson's first appearance outside of Brooklyn. Robinson responded with his first major league home run. The following day the largest Saturday afternoon crowd in National League history, more than 52,000 spectators, jammed into the Giants' ball park. Robinson stroked three hits in four at-bats in a losing

---

Baseball's Great Experiment: Jackie Robinson and His Legacy by Tygiel (1983) 3426w from pp.182–85, 188–91, 193, 196, 205–06, 208

cause. Rain postponed a two-game set in Boston, and on April 22 Robinson and the Dodgers returned to Brooklyn, where a swirl of events abruptly shattered the brief honeymoon. The next three weeks thrust Robinson, his family, his teammates, and baseball into a period of unrelenting crises and tension.

The Dodgers' first opponents on the homestand were the Philadelphia Phillies, managed by Alabaman Ben Chapman. While playing for the Yankees in the 1930s Chapman had gained a measure of notoriety for his anti-Semitic shouting jousts with spectators. Now he ordered his players to challenge Robinson with a stream of verbal racial taunts "to see if he can take it." From the moment the two clubs took the field for their first contest, the Phillies, led by Chapman, unleashed a torrent of insults at the black athlete. "At no time in my life have I heard racial venom and dugout abuse to match the abuse that Ben sprayed on Robinson that night," writes Harold Parrott. "Chapman mentioned everything from thick lips to the supposedly extra-thick Negro skull ... [and] the repulsive sores and diseases he said Robinson's teammates would become infected with if they touched the towels or the combs he used." The onslaught continued throughout the series....

The Phillies' verbal assault on Robinson in 1947 exceeded even baseball's broadly defined sense of propriety. Fans seated near the Phillies dugout wrote letters of protest to Commissioner Chandler, and newsman Walter Winchell attacked Chapman on his national Sunday night radio broadcast. Chandler notified Philadelphia owner Robert Carpenter that the harassment must cease or he would be forced to invoke punitive measures.

Chapman, while accepting Chandler's edict, defended his actions. "We will treat Robinson the same as we do Hank Greenberg of the Pirates, Clint Hartung of the Giants, Joe Garagiola of the Cardinals, Connie Ryan of the Braves, or any other man who is likely to step to the plate and beat us," said Chapman, listing some regular targets of ethnic insults. "There is not a man who has come to the big leagues since baseball has been played who has not been ridden."...

The general consensus, however, judged the Phillies' behavior unacceptable. Robinson's Dodger teammates led the protest. By the second day of the series they lashed back at Chapman demanding that he cease baiting Robinson. Chapman's fellow Alabamans marched in the forefront of Robinson's defenders. Eddie Stanky called him a "coward" and challenged him to "pick on somebody who can fight back." Even Dixie Walker reprimanded Chapman, a close personal friend. Rickey later claimed that this incident, more than any other, cemented Dodger support for Robinson. "When [Chapman] poured out that string of unconscionable abuse he solidified and unified thirty men, not one of whom was willing to sit by and see someone kick around a man who had his hands tied behind his back," asserted Rickey.

Robinson publicly downplayed the incident. In his "Jackie Robinson Says" column which appeared in the Pittsburgh *Courier,* the Dodger first baseman wrote, "Some of the Phillies' bench jockeys tried to get me upset last week, but it didn't really bother me."... In later years he revealed his true emotions as he withstood the barrage of insults. "I have to admit that this day of all the unpleasant days of my life brought me nearer to cracking up than I have ever been," he wrote in 1972. "For one wild and rage crazed minute I thought, 'To hell with Mr. Rickey's "noble experiment."' The ordeal tempted Robinson to "stride over to that Phillies dugout, grab one of those white sons of bitches and smash his teeth with my despised black fist."

The daily flood of mail included not only congratulatory messages, but threats of violence. In early May, the Dodgers turned several of these notes over to the police. The letters, according to Robinson, advised "that 'somebody' was going to get hurt if I didn't get out of baseball," and "promised to kill any n——s who interfered with me." In the aftermath of the threats and in light of the burden that answering the mail placed on the Robinsons, Rickey requested that they allow the Dodgers to open and answer all correspondence. In addition, Robinson agreed to refuse all invitations to speak or be honored as well as opportunities for commercial endorsements.

The Dodgers released details of the threatening letters to the press on May 9. On that same day Robinson faced other unpublicized challenges in Philadelphia, the initial stop on the club's first extended road trip. Rickey had been forewarned that Robinson would not get a warm reception in Philadelphia. Herb Pennock, the former major league pitcher who served as the Phillies general manager, had called Rickey demanding that Robinson remain in Brooklyn. "[You] just can't bring that nigger here with the rest of your team, Branch. We're just not ready for that sort of thing yet," exhorted Pennock, according to Parrott who listened on the line. Pennock threatened that the Phillies would boycott the game....

When the Dodgers arrived in Philadelphia on May 9, the Benjamin Franklin Hotel, where the club had lodged for several years, refused to accept Robinson. Team officials had anticipated problems in St. Louis and Cincinnati, but not in the City of Brotherly Love.... Rather than force a confrontation, Robinson arranged for alternative quarters. On subsequent trips, the Dodgers transferred their Philadelphia headquarters to the more expensive Warwick hotel....

At Shibe Park, Robinson endured another distasteful chore. The negative publicity inspired by the Phillies' treatment of him in Brooklyn had led both team owners to request a conciliatory photograph of Robinson and Chapman shaking hands. Chapman, pressured by the Phillies' ownership, went so far as to say that he would "be glad to have a colored player" on his team, though he continued to maintain he had treated Robinson fairly. For Robinson the journey to the Philadelphia dugout to pose with Chapman entailed a painful necessity. "I can think of no occasion where I had more difficult in swallowing my pride and doing what seemed best for baseball and the cause of the Negro in baseball than in agreeing to pose for a photograph with a man for whom I had only the very lowest regard," he later confessed.

Chapman's public moderation notwithstanding the Phillies resumed their earlier harassment. Although Commissioner Chandler had limited their racial repertoire, Phillies bench jockeys replaced it with an act inspired by the recent death threats. "Some of these grown men sat in the dugout and pointed bastes at me and made machine gun-like noise," Robinson later recounted.

A third, more ominous development, which also surfaced on May 9, overshadowed these incidents. New York *Herald Tribune* sports editor Stanley Woodward unveiled an alleged plot by National League players, led by the St. Louis Cardinals, to strike against Robinson.

... Woodward's allegations, exaggerated or not, marked a significant turning point. The account of Frick's steadfast renunciation of all efforts to displace the black athlete, following so closely after Chandler's warning to Chapman, placed the baseball hierarchy openly in support of Robinson. In addition, the uproar created by the Woodward story dashed any lingering hopes among dissident players that public opinion, at least as reflected in the press, endorsed their opinions....

May 9, 1947, marked perhaps the worst day of Jackie Robinson's baseball career. Threats on his life, torment from opposing players, discrimination at the team hotel, and rumors of a player strike simultaneously engulfed the black athlete. The following day, Jimmy Cannon, describing Robinson's relations with his teammates, reported, "He is the loneliest man I have ever seen in sports." And, if as the *Sporting News* argued, "It remains only to judge Robinson on his ability as a player; he appeared to many jurors to present a weak case. Although he had curtailed his 0 for 20 slump, his batting average still languished near the .250 mark. After one month of regular season play, the fate of the great experiment still seemed uncertain.

Amidst the swirl of controversy that followed the Dodgers on their first major road trip, the national interest in Jackie Robinson grew apparent. On Sunday, May 11, the Dodgers faced the Phillies in a doubleheader before the largest crowd in Philadelphia baseball history. Scalpers sold $2 tickets for $6, "just like the World Series." Two days later in Cincinnati 27,164 fans turned out despite an all-day rain "to size up Jackie Robinson." Bad weather diminished the crowds for two games in Pittsburgh, but when the skies cleared, 34,814 fans appeared at Forbes Field for the May 18 series finale. The following day the Dodgers met the Cubs in Chicago. Two hours before game time Wrigley Field had almost filled. A total of 46,572 fans crammed into the ball park, the largest attendance in stadium history. The tour concluded in St. Louis where the Dodgers and Cardinals played before the biggest weekday crowd of the National League season.

"Jackie's nimble/Jackie's quick/Jackie's making the turnstiles click," crowed Wendell Smith. Jimmy Cannon hailed him as "the most lucrative draw since Babe Ruth." By May 23 when the Dodgers returned to Brooklyn, Robinson had emerged as a national phenomenon....

Robinson had also erased all doubts about his playing abilities...

... By June, Robinson had convinced even the most hardened opponents of integration of his exceptional talents.... Starting on June 14, Robinson hit safely in twenty-one consecutive games. At the end of June, he was batting .315, leading the league in stolen bases, and ranked second in runs scored....

Robinson's impressive statistics revealed only a portion of the tale. "Never have records meant so little in discussing a player's value as they do in the case of Jackie Robinson," wrote Tom Meany. "His presence alone was enough to light a fire under his own team and unsettle his opponents." Sportswriter John Crosby asserts, "He was the greatest opportunist on any kind of playing field, seeing openings before they opened, pulling off plays lesser players can't even imagine." Robinson's intense competitiveness provided the crucial ingredient. A seasoned athlete, even in his rookie year, Robinson seemed to thrive on challenges and flourished before large audiences.... Robinson's drive not only inspired his own dramatic performances but intimidated and demoralized enemy players....

At the plate and in the field, Robinson radiated dynamic intensity, but his true genius materialized on the base paths. Sportswriters struggled to capture the striking image of Robinson in motion. They called him "the black meteor" or an "Ebony Ty Cobb," and "The Bojangles of the Basepaths." ...

"He brought a new dimension into baseball," says Al Campanis. "He brought stealing back to the days of the twenties whereas up until that time baseball had become a long-ball hitting game." But the phenomenon went beyond base stealing. Robinson's twenty-nine steals in 1947 were actually less than the league leader of the preceding year. The style of play and the design of his base running antics better measure the magnitude of Robinson's achievement. He revolutionized Major League Baseball by injecting an element of "tricky baseball," so common in the Negro Leagues. In an age in which managers bemoaned the lost art of bunting, Robinson, in forty-six bunt attempts, registered fourteen hits and twenty-eight sacrifices, a phenomenal .913 success rate. His tactics often went against the time-worn conventional wisdom of baseball....

Nor did Robinson's effectiveness require the stolen base. "He dances and prances off base keeping the enemy infield upset and off balance, and worrying the pitcher," reported *Time*.... "Robinson had broken my concentration," recalls [Vic] Raschi of a game in the 1949 World Series. "I was pitching more to Robinson [on first base] than I was to [Gil] Hodges and as a result I threw one up into Gil's power and he got the base hit that beat me."...

Robinson's exemplary demeanor won over his teammates.... When Robinson had joined the Dodgers reporters had described the locker room scene as one of "cool aloofness" amidst a tense atmosphere. In dealing with his teammates Robinson continued the policy that had pursued at Montréal. "Jackie would not sit with any white player that first year unless he was asked to," Recalls Bobby Bragan. In part, this was a face of Robinson's personality. "I sort of kept to myself by habit," he explained.... But this behavior also reflected a decision to avoid forcing himself on those who objected to his presence.

Among northern teammates, playing alongside Robinson posed few problems. For Southerners, on the other hand, it often required a significant adjustment. Several players feared repercussions at home for their involuntary role in baseball integration. "I didn't know if they would spit on me or not," recalled Dixie Walker of his Alabama neighbors. "It was no secret that I was worried about my business. I had a hardware and sporting goods store back home." Pee Wee Reese later said that in family discussions, "The subject always gets around to the fact that I'm a little southern boy playing shortstop next to a Negro second baseman and in danger of being contaminated." Both [Dixie] Walker and Kirby Higbe before the Dodgers traded him, received insulting letters "I got more than a thousand letters from people down South calling me 'nigger-lover,'" writes Higbe, 'Telling me I ought to quit playing baseball and come home rather than play with a nigger."

[JR's play, self-control, and dignity won him fan support.] Only Joe Louis, among black celebrities, had aroused the public imagination as Robinson did in the summer of 1947. Robinson's charismatic personality inspired not merely sympathy and acceptance, but sincere adulation from both whites and blacks alike.

To black America, Jackie Robinson appeared as a savior, a Moses leading his people out of the wilderness.... Thousands of blacks thronged to the ball parks wherever he appeared. At games in the National League's southernmost cities blacks swelled attendance. Many traveled hundreds of miles to see their hero in action. The Philadelphia *Afro-American* reported that orders by blacks for tickets for the first Dodger-Phillies series had "poured in" from Baltimore, Washington, and other cities along the eastern seaboard. For games in Cincinnati, a "Jackie Robinson special" train ran from Norfolk, Virginia, stopping en route to pick up black fans....

As a boy, white columnist Mike Royko attended Robinson's first game at Wrigley Field in Chicago. Twenty-five years later he described the event: "In 1947, few blacks were seen in downtown Chicago, much less up on the white North side at a Cub game. That day they came by the thousands, pouring off the north-bound ELs and out of their cars.... The whites tried to look as if nothing unusual was happening, while the blacks tried to look casual and dignified. So everybody looked ill at ease. For the most part it was probably the first time they had been so close to each other in such large numbers....

⋆ ⋆ ⋆

On the road, hotel accommodations remained problematical. Throughout the Jim Crow era the issue of housing black players had loomed as a major objection to integration. Even in many northern cities, the better hotels did not allow blacks. In border cities like St. Louis and Cincinnati segregation remained the rule. Rickey and his advisers had determined that the Dodgers would not challenge local customs....

In Boston, Pittsburgh, and Chicago, Robinson had no problems. In Philadelphia and St. Louis, officials barred him and he stayed at Negro hotels. The Dodgers anticipated that Robinson would not be allowed to stay with the team in Cincinnati, but the Netherlands-Plaza Hotel accepted him under the provision that he eat his meals in his room so as not to offend other guests.

The Dodgers dared not tamper with one taboo—the prohibition on interracial roommates.... In 1947 Robinson usually roomed with Wendell Smith, who traveled with the team as both a reporter and a Dodger employee....

Throughout most of the season Robinson maintained his batting average over .300, but a late season slump after the Dodgers had clinched the pennant dropped him to .297. He finished second in the league in runs scored and first in stolen bases. Robinson also led the Dodgers in home runs with 12. Despite his reputation for being injury prone, Robinson appeared in 151 of the 154 contests, more games than anyone else on the club.

Robinson's performance also benefited other National League teams. Throughout the season fans continued to watch him in record numbers.... By the season's end Robinson had established new attendance marks in every city except Cincinnati. Thanks to Robinson, National League attendance in 1947 increased by more than three quarters of a million people above the all-time record set in 1946. Five teams set new season records, including the Dodgers, who attracted over 1.8 million fans for the first, and last, time in the club's Brooklyn history.

In October the Dodgers met the New York Yankees in the World Series. The 1947 series ranks as one of the most thrilling in baseball history. Fans remember it for Bill Beven's near no-hitter in the fourth game, Al Gionfriddo's spectacular catch of Joe DiMaggio's line drive in the sixth contest, and the tightly drawn struggles in five of the seven meetings. The Dodgers challenged the Yankees into the last game before succumbing to the effective relief pitching of Joe Page. For Robinson personally, the World Series marked an anticlimax. His presence in the Fall Classic seemed natural, rather than extraordinary. On the field he performed solidly, but not spectacularly. Robinson batted well, hitting .259 despite being robbed of three hits and he drove in three runs. His base running bedeviled Yankee pitchers and catchers and his fielding was flawless....

★ ★ ★

The saga of Robinson's first season has become a part of American mythology—sacrosanct in its memory, magnificent in its retelling. It remains a drama which thrills and fascinates, combining the central themes of the illusive Great American Novel: the undertones of Horatio Alger, the inter-racial comradery [*sic*] of nineteenth-century fiction, the sage advisor and his youthful apprentice, and the rugged and righteous individual confronting the angry mob. It is a tale of courage, heroics, and triumph. Epic in its proportions, the Robinson legend has persevered—and will continue to do so—because the myth, which rarely deviates from reality, fits our national perceptions of fair play and social progress. The emotional impact of Robinson's challenge requires no elaboration or enhancement. Few works of fiction could impart its power.

Indeed, so total was Robinson's triumph, so dominant his personality, that few people have questioned the strategies and values that underpinned Branch Rickey's "noble experiment." Rickey based his blueprint for integration both on his assessment of the racial realities of postwar America and his flair for the dramatic. He believed that the United States was ready for integrated baseball, but the balance remained so precarious that the breakthrough had to be carefully planned and cautiously advanced. Americans—both black and white, players and fans—needed time to accommodate themselves to the idea of blacks in baseball. The slightest false step, Rickey concluded, would delay the entry of nonwhites into the national pastime indefinitely. Rickey felt that the primary burden of this undertaking had to rest on the shoulders of a lone standard-bearer, upon whose success or failure the fate of the entire venture would be determined. The fact that this gradual process accrued publicity and added to the drama was never central to Rickey's thinking, but rather a natural component of his personality, Rickey conceived of schemes on the grand scale and enacted them accordingly....

Understanding Muhammad Ali

DAVID ZANG

... Was [Muhammad Ali's] draft resistance cowardice or conviction? Did America want a heavyweight champ who delivered a heavier wallop with his mouth or his fists?

Overarching all of the answers—indeed, framing the questions themselves—was the issue of race. This is understandable because from the ... late nineteenth century forward the idea of sport as a character builder was intended to elevate and prepare white men as leaders of society. Blacks and women, to the minds of white males, were not going to lead American society in the twentieth century; whatever these lesser beings made of sport—exercise, escape, entertainment—would be for their own lesser reasons.

The color lines that existed in sport into the 1950s had grown from an impeachable but nonetheless widely believed foundation of "scientific" race theory that had, for a century, pinched data on bodies and brains into a shape supporting white assertions of intellectual and moral weakness in blacks. Many whites believed character to be an elusive and unreliable quality among blacks, contending that African heritage imparted even to the economically and socially advantaged a genetic predisposition to bad behavior that might reveal itself at an unfortunate moment. Thus, despite Jesse Owens's rebuke of Hitler, Joe Louis's service in the army, Jackie Robinson's willingness to turn the other cheek, or Wilma Rudolph's defeat of childhood polio, white attitudes toward black athletic success remained reserved.

Young Cassius Clay had overcome some of those reservations, endearing himself to Americans as he returned triumphant and irrepressible from the Rome Olympics of 1960.... [I]n 1964 Clay "shook up the world" by beating Sonny Liston, the prohibitive favorite, to become the world's heavyweight champion. He shook it harder the next day when he forsook ... his "slave name," ... to become Muhammad Ali. To many whites, claimed onetime Black Panther Eldridge Cleaver, Ali's decision to join the Nation of Islam was a "betrayal...." Malcolm X explained the fear underlining the betrayal: "They [whites] knew that if people began to identify with Cassius and the type of image he was creating, they were going to have trouble out of these Negroes because they'd have Negroes walking around the street saying, 'I'm the greatest,' and also Negroes who were proud of being black." Black author Wallace Terry later made clear ... however, that the change was disturbing to some blacks as well....

Ali's transformation from Christian to Muslim seemed to some whites much like going from Stepin Fetchit to Nat Turner. The change broke a compact that Americans had forged with their black athletes—"be good Negroes and enjoy the fruits of athletic success"—and assured that race would be an explicit issue in all that Ali would touch in the next decade.

Nothing was more explicit—or explosive—than the issue of manliness. Tied … to matters of prowess and courage, it was at the dark heart of racial divisions. By the late nineteenth century many white middle-class men believed that a shift from labor of the body to labor of the mind had left Victorian culture "effeminate…." Sigmund Freud tied dominance, aggression, and bonding directly to man's primitive sexual drives and suppression of them, and thereby made the relationship between sexuality and behavior apparent.

Rising attention to the rapidly organizing and expanding structure of sports served two ends. Sports provided an antidote to effeminacy allowing an outlet for dominance and aggression while at the same time promising to dissipate sexual urgency and turn it toward constructive ends. Still, as whites remade manhood…, they were required to give attention to both gender and race, two things that, according to historian Gail Bederman, "linked bodies, identities, and power." As Bederman has written, civilization at the turn of the century had become, in the minds of white men, an "explicitly racial concept."

It was a conceit that reinforced ideas of white superiority but simultaneously made the physical prowess of blacks a constant threat. It could be turned on white men and summon the ghosts of Nat Turner, or it could be turned on white women and summon the myth of black sexuality. In the case of black athletes, trouble could come in both ways. So it was that first black heavyweight champion Jack Johnson, as conqueror of white men in the ring and white women in the bedroom, touched off race riots in the wake of his many affronts to white society in the early 1900s.

Owens, Louis, Robinson, and other black athletes at midcentury appeared safer, following the unspoken but central rules of being a "good Negro," which entailed a repression of sexual appetite and public deference to whites. Still, the myth of black sexuality in America was an old … problem for white males. The image of blacks as promiscuous animals of wanton sexual appetites has been a part of American consciousness for centuries.…

As steps were taken … to desegregate American society, fear of black sexuality presented itself in several ways. In the South, there was militant resistance to the repeal of Jim Crow laws.… One of the stumbling blocks to integrating Baltimore's golf courses and swimming pools in the 1940s was the fear of some parks' board members that those settings would allow black men near to white-women.…

Even in the loftiest of social settings palpable distrust and sexual suspicions were present. Penn's black Rhodes Scholar and basketball star John Wideman told *Look* magazine in 1963: "At college, I've found that there's no cleavage (between the races) beyond the physical fact, although in a way—socially, I suppose—I've often wondered if things would have gone along the same way if I'd had a white girl friend on campus.…"

As the specter of black militancy loomed in the late '60s, it highlighted the second of white fears—that of black revolt. During a 1968 Columbia University fight about where to build a new gymnasium, Harlem blacks instilled fear among whites by threatening to make the situation a violent one. In June of 1966 *Life* magazine investigated the real possibility of black violence in an article titled "Plotting a War on 'Whitey.'" In San Francisco's hippie haven, Haight-Ashbury, an oft-heard belief among whites was "Spades are programmed for hate."

The possibility that the hate would erupt into confrontation was what made the menacing Sonny Liston ... America's worst nightmare. Ali's embrace of his blackness blended both threats: the sexual and the vengeful....

It might have been easier to know what to think had Ali been more like Liston. Instead, he presented a complex puzzle. He boasted constantly of being "pretty," an assertion counter to traditional manliness, yet one that some blacks saw as the anchor for their claim that "black is beautiful." He often laughed with white reporters, yet he was fully aware of white fear. Before his mid-'70s bout with George Foreman he told the press: "What you white reporters got to remember is, black folks ain't afraid of black folks that way white folks are afraid of black folks." As for sex, those who followed Ali closely in the '60s report that he had a healthy libido that was often gratified. If any of his dalliances included white women, they never came to public light.

Of all the factors that constituted manliness, none were more instrumental in defining Ali and confusing white America as his position as a conscientious objector against the draft. For many young men doubts about the value of military service in Vietnam blossomed in two ways: in a preoccupation with the draft that indicated reluctance to serve in Vietnam and in the consequential guilt over not having served. Males either went to Vietnam and fought or they stayed behind with the knowledge that others less fortunate were fighting.

For most draft-age men the most pressing reason for their dilemma was President Lyndon Johnson's commitment to the war.... In February 1965 only 3,000 men were called to service. In the next six months the total was 87,300....

In claiming exemption on religious grounds in early 1966 Ali absolved himself of the guilt. Conscientious objection was a stand that insinuated reflection, not cowardice. When ... stripped of his title shortly after refusing induction in May of 1967, thereby forfeiting what would become three years of income, Ali's refusal to serve appeared, to be one of indisputable moral conviction. For the millions of Americans who supported the Vietnam War, however, Ali's stance looked more like hustle than moral fortitude. But for all those who perceived the war to be unjust, Ali ... became a shining example, though not one without problems.

For one, not fighting in Vietnam seemed to be turning off the very path [of] Joe Louis and Jackie Robinson.... Both had served in the military and, despite Robinson's court-martial, it served their images well. Though a number of black athletes—including Jim Brown, Kareem Abdul-Jabbar, and Bill Russell—supported Ali's decision ..., Louis and Robinson did not.... Wallace Terry, author of *Bloods: An Oral History of the Vietnam War by Black Veterans,* ... met many ...

black soldiers.... "They were absolutely stunned ..., upset ..., angry, frustrated ..., bitter. They hated him for it." Ali's refusal also reinforced the bitter feelings that many Americans felt for athletes who managed to evade combat. The indifferent stance of elite and professional athletes toward military service was certainly not unique, but it was, to many Americans, galling.

A greater puzzle was the irony, apparently unnoticed, that Ali's resistance carried for blacks generally. His membership in the Nation of Islam marked him as a figure ... indivisible from his color, and his use of his Islamic ministry as the basis for avoiding war marked him as someone who could not fight on grounds of pacifism. How strange, then, in 1966 when, in a fit of pique at yammering reporters, Ali declared, "Man, I ain't got no quarrel with them Vietcong." As [Robert] Lipsyte ... has written, the famed comment came from exasperation and may not have accurately (certainly not fully) reflected Ali's draft stance. Nonetheless, antiwar Americans seized upon it as an expression of common sense—rather than religious opposition. This meant that Ali essentially agreed with those whites who claimed generally that the nation had no legitimate quarrel with North Vietnam. It was also precisely what any black draftee, those fighting the war in disproportionate numbers, could have claimed as well. Oddly enough, many blacks who opposed the war did not lean on this practical argument but stood instead on moral grounds, claiming the draft to be institutional genocide. Even then, however, they did not adopt the same antimilitary attitudes that characterized white student opposition, and they did not, by and large, follow Ali's example.

Ali's draft position was further confounded by this question: why did Ali have no remorse about quarreling with unknowns in the ring—the killing game? ... Ali himself openly declared, "There's one hell of a lot of difference in fighting in the ring and going to the War in Vietnam," but the anger in his voice, not any philosophical thinking, lent the claim its sound of conviction.

... In his 1969 work on male bonding, Lionel Tiger proclaimed that "the amalgamation of size, power, dramaturgical savoir faire and dominance" were central to sport's appeal to males. The heavyweight champion was the supreme symbol of dominance. How significant was it, then that the physical aura of Muhammad Ali was one that stung like a bee and floated like a butterfly, particularly when contrasted to the brutish and violent style of the man he dethroned, Liston?

... The deaths of fighters Benny Paret (in the ring in March 1962) and Davey Moore (in March 1963 ..., after sustaining injuries in the ring) drew criticism that depicted boxing as an archaic contest in a civilized world. Bob Dylan's scathing indictment, "Who Killed Davey Moore?" badgered the public conscience with an accusatory chorus, "Why, and what's the reason for?" There were, then, public relations payoffs to be reaped from a heavyweight champ for whom boxing seemed a softer exercise. The portrayal of Ali as a dancer ... masked the brutality that is the essence of the fight game and, once in place, obscured the side of Ali that was cruelty. But cruelty and brutality were integral parts of Ali's ring persona, and obscuring them only contributed to his paradoxical nature.

In the ring he was both Brer Rabbit and John Henry. The aspect of his fighting that was sledgehammer showed intermittently, but when it did Ali was revealed as a warrior willing to club and be clubbed. When he fought Joe Frazier for the third time, in 1975, both men stood toe to toe, drawing on power and resources that tested more than their will to win. It also tested their willingness to punish another man, their will to live, and, thus, their willingness to kill. Ali's cousin Coretta Bavers recalled, "He told me the next morning that he was closer to death than he'd ever been."...

If that contest ... smack[ed] of valor and nobility, the flip side of the champ's brutality was evident in two earlier fights. In the '60s, at the top of the boxing world, Ali had a range of tools at his disposal. Norman Mailer noted that, at times, Ali "played with punches ..., laid them on as delicately as you put a postage stamp on an envelope...." But ..., Ali's attack also included, "a cruel jab like a baseball bat held head on into your mouth." In his November 1965 bout with former champion Floyd Patterson, and then a year and a half later against Ernie Terrell, Ali used mostly the latter, his game turning pitiless and sadistic. Angered because both opponents had dismissed his religious conversion (Terrell insisting on calling him "Clay"), Ali laid on punches and words with venom. Against Patterson, a proud black man well past his prime, Ali was relentless.... [Lypsyte wrote:] "Floyd ... could barely defend himself, and Ali was taunting him and hitting him...." *Life* magazine agreed, calling the fight "a sickening spectacle."

The fight with Terrell was similar, Ali hitting him at will while demanding that Terrell call him by his Muslim name. Ali biographer Thomas Hauser told film documentarians, "Ali went out there to make this a horribly vicious, humiliating experience for Ernie Terrell, and he carried it on long past the time when Terrell was competitive in any way.... It's fifteen rounds of 'What's my name?'"

Perhaps it was just coincidence, but, with the exception of the third Frazier fight, Ali's dark side was most apparent when he was on top.... Ali was never more lovable or popular than when he was the underdog, a phenomenon that brought out his Brer Rabbit cunning, and again connected him to powerful currents of the Vietnam era. He had risen to prominence after slaying Sonny Liston.... Clay ... outfoxed Liston ... with his loudmouthed bravado, appearing manic nearly to the point of insanity. The mythic significance of the win was not lost on Clay or his admirers....

Strangely enough, though the United States was at an impasse against North Vietnam, antiwar protestors and Ali, through his rhetoric ("I ain't got no quarrel with them Vietcong"), both portrayed America's enemy as an underdog, a tiny force trying to hold on against an overwhelming power. It is ironic, then, that as Ali became ensconced as champion, fought as the favorite with power, and a lack of mercy, he increasingly annoyed the establishment but appealed to the counterculture. After he lost his title for refusing induction, his martyrdom appealed to those who opposed the war, but he regained his more widespread popularity only after a loss in the ring reduced him once more to underdog....

In 1974, when he upset George Foreman to regain the crown, the victory seemed moral vindication and proof positive to his many sympathizers in the draft case that the Vietnam War had been immoral. The war, by then, was more widely held to have been wrongful.... [I]t is no surprise that Americans generally applauded Ali's reemergence. Strangely, what was most praised was his cunning—the very type of deceit employed by the Vietcong. During the war, American spokesmen went to great pains to point out that the North Vietnamese's guerilla fighting was an immoral way of fighting—comparable to terrorism—and one at odds with American tactics, in which there was "a vested interest in abstaining from such acts." ... In adopting his strategy for facing Foreman, Ali decided on an indirect attack....

The triumph over George Foreman not only saw many Americans cheering for the reluctant draftee to defeat a man who had proudly waved the American flag in the Olympic ring at Mexico City in 1968, it also delivered a jolt to the concept of worthy opposition. Falling back on an old tendency to demean opponents, Ali had decided on a new tactic for his fight with the huge slugger. Threatening Foreman with a "ghetto whopper" ..., Ali decided instead that the way to beat Foreman was to slump against the ropes and let Foreman hit him until exhausted. The tactic was brilliant, but smacked of the duplicity that many whites believed characterized both blacks and the Vietnamese. It was clearly reminiscent of Brer Rabbit's Tar Baby tactic, and Ali's label for it, "Rope-a-Dope," and his nickname for Foreman, "The Mummy," were best appreciated by a culture now fixated on victory and fast losing touch with the idea of worthy opposition.

Maybe the least noted but most significant aspect of the Foreman fight was that Ali made, victory appear easy. Unlike his fatiguing earlier bouts with Frazier, the "rope-a-dope" seemed to deny the tenet of character-building that demanded hard work. The tactic was ... intelligent and clever.... However, it was also akin to playing possum and ..., thus tied to the trickster of black folklore and white suspicions of blacks as naturally gifted—but not hard, working—athletes. The idea that whites were hard workers while blacks were shirkers was one that had been necessarily absent from much of the discourse on sport during the decades prior to integration.... By the early '60s blacks already constituted percentages of professional teams in numbers disproportionate to their representation in the larger population....

The new prominence of black athletes—and their refusal to acknowledge sport as a confirmation of "good" American values—dramatically undercut the idea of character-building by calling into question the depth and genuineness of American goodness. Besides Ali, important athletes like Henry Aaron, Arthur Ashe, Jim Brown... Oscar Robertson, Bill Russell, and Tommie Smith pointed out the disparities between sport's claim to being a meritocracy and their own experiences as second-class citizens....

The sudden rise of the black athlete—refutation of a century of the myth of white superiority—demanded explanation.... As blacks became increasingly visible on Vietnam era playing fields, the nineteenth-century notion of a primitive, physically superior race was recycled and picked up new adherents, even among blacks....

If blacks were scientifically certified as natural athletic talents, it was one more reason for some whites to deem them unfit for the character-building club. Character meant hard work, and who could be sure of effort in the face of such God-given talent? The notion that blacks had developed a racially distinct style of play, especially in basketball, that touted individual flamboyance at the expense of teamwork, heightened the portrayal of whites as hard workers—and intelligent—while demeaning blacks as something less....

Ali was supremely gifted with physical skill.... "Rope-a-Dope," though widely applauded as shrewd and masterly for an old fighter, nonetheless served to distance Ali from the tenets of character-building. It not only raised entertainment above fair play but also implied an otherworldly sense of self that tapped into another aspect of Vietnam era lore.

It was as poet—in making predictions and then carrying them out—that Ali was at his most perplexing and pleasing. Only Ali the verse maker seemed to know ahead of time what disaster ... might befall his opponents. His poetry in and out of the ring put him at odds with sport's alliance with science. Scientifically grounded theories of athletic achievement, begun in the nineteenth century, produced a performance principle that encouraged people to see athletes as mere representations of their conditioning regimens, nutritional supplements, and illicit drugs—that is, athletes as scientifically created performers. Though the performance principle was necessarily at odds with character-building from the outset—character being a subjective, unscientific measure of a person—one of the reasons that character-building had become so firmly entrenched in public consciousness was that it was effectively disguised as a scientific quest—a submission of the will in step with the demands of a progressive, modern, scientific, and secular world.

The Vietnam era neither quickened nor slowed interest in the scientific quest for enhanced performance.... The sixties were, however, the time that brought science and character into noticeable collision. Ironically, the counterculture, which strove for a more human, less technocratic society, ridiculed what appeared to be human strengths—effort, ethics, discipline—when critiquing sport....

★ ★ ★

... Ali seemed to be, like the Beatles, the rollicking incarnation of another baby boom icon, Peter Pan.... A boxer—subject to so many manly ravages—was unlikely to serve as an Eternal Child, but Clay/Ali fit the bill. He was undeniably playful ... unfettered by material—or adult—concerns. In his early years his skin was smooth and pretty, his verses elementary and comical. Even after his body had begun to go slack, his demeanor remained boyishly mercurial. As trickster supreme he ... wore... the masks that various historians have identified as those that blacks donned to survive slavery: the deferential "Jack," the submissive "Sambo," the ferocious and threatening "Nat." In scheduling his fights from Manila in the Philippines to the African jungles of Zaire, his restless globetrotting made the world his home.

The myth of the Eternal Child also holds that the trickster in that child represents a "powerfully anarchic, anti-authoritarian impulse, a drive to revolt, to disrupt or overturn the existing order." In an age that featured a rejection of old authority and a search for new, Ali was most vivid as a figure who recognized little authority other than his own....

Outside the ring Ali's self-reliance was the archetype of an entire generation's affair with individualism and independence. When Hollywood filmed his biography, *The Greatest*, in 1977, the song that became the film's centerpiece explained that Ali had rejected heroes early in life, settling on self-dependence and self-love as "The Greatest Love of All." In defending his draft resistance he eschewed complexity.... "All I did," he said, "was stand up for what I believed...."

Ali had no qualms about whom he upset.... In spurning the army he thumbed his nose at America's most important civil institutions—the government, the military, and the capitalist economy that supported them both. In converting to Islam, he rejected the Christian God....

When boxing's officials stripped Ali of his crown in 1967 they made him that rarest of treasures—the living martyr—and prepared the way for his resurrection and ascension three years later. Ali reveled in his martyrdom. In April of 1968 he posed for the cover of *Esquire*, his beautiful body riddled with arrows.

All of the ways by which Ali became a symbol—unconsciously or not—were instrumental in his largest rejection, that of the entrenched racial hierarchy. His early fight promoters, draft officials, money men, even Christianity's most important figures were white. Ali chafed at this. His public declamations on politics, wars, and religion were evidence that his actions were undertaken deliberately in the spotlight. His separatist yearnings for a black homeland ..., black pride..., and black sovereignty ... may have derived from his dealings with the Muslim leaders Malcolm X and Elijah Muhammad, but his fame made his stances on civil rights crucial to all of America, particularly to black athletes.

But it was as black athlete that Ali became embroiled in some of his strangest contradictions.... [W]hen sociologist Harry Edwards proposed a black boycott of the 1968 Olympics, one of the unconditional demands for shelving the boycott was the restoration of Ali's title. Edwards often repeated his dictum that whites universally exploited black athletes as modern-day gladiators. How strange, then, that Edwards never hesitated to bring all of his influence to bear on restoring Ali to the top of that gladiatorial world. No doubt Edwards saw Ali as a figure who could help transform the arena into something less exploitative, but historically who has created more capital for entrenched sporting interests than the heavyweight champion of the world?

Even stranger was Ali's own paradoxical contribution to the meaning of race and color: that he, light-skinned and pretty, suspicion of white blood tainting his claims to racial exclusivity, had come to embody the hopes, anger, and venom of so many blacks—had risen to become king of the world not only by beating other blacks but also by humiliating them publicly in the demeaning language used for centuries by whites by addressing them as "nigger" in the most casual of utterances, by pronouncing them dumb and unworthy, and by pointing out their similarity to apes. If Joe Frazier was, as Ali constantly maintained, a "gorilla" in contrast to his own *cafe au lait* look—it was a stern refutation of more than Frazier's countenance. If black was truly beautiful, then how could Frazier be an "ugly gorilla"?

In noting the "intense chords of ambiguity" that Ali struck as a black public figure, writer Gerald Early recently asked if Ali was "a star boxer, or through his genius, the utter undermining of boxing? Was he a militant or the complex unmasking of militancy?" … How could the nation countenance such ambiguity in … heroes or … villains? How could someone so instrumental in undermining traditional notions of character end up idolized decades later as a man of unassailable character? … [I]t was the ambiguity itself that made Ali such an enduring and fitting symbol of the Vietnam era.…

We were never quite sure what to do with Ali … alternately clowning, stinging, mocking, laughing, scorning, and humiliating. As Ali once pointed out: "All kinds of people came to see me. Women came because I was saying, 'I'm so pretty, …' Some white people … came to see someone give the nigger a whuppin'. Longhaired hippies came to my fights because I wouldn't go to Vietnam. And black people …, they were saying, 'Right on, brother; show them honkies.'"

By the time Atlanta hosted the 1996 Olympic Games, we were sure what to do with him. His reputation now softened by time, his many controversial stances left largely unchallenged, his swagger undone by Parkinson's syndrome, we handed him the torch that lit the stadium flame. It was a mighty moment of symbolic reconciliation—of black and white, old and young, amateur and pro. Ali had indeed become the seeming essence of an America more whole than it had been a quarter century earlier.…

… Of the countless athletes who came through the era, none were more representative of the issues related to sport's character-building capacities.

It is probably no coincidence that character-building as the paradigm for sport was eclipsed at the same time that blacks took over the highest levels of play. The idea that blacks and whites were distinct races owed much to Ali. In selecting an identity as "black" rather than "Negro," by adopting separatist leanings after converting to Islam, and by making color matter on his very large stage, Ali reinforced the polarity of the times. What could be further apart, after all, than black and white?…

Much of American sport at the turn of the century owes at least something to Ali's legacy. His collaboration with Howard Cosell embodied the transition from black-and-white to color television. His insistence on being seen prepared the public for the image-wary likes of Andre Agassi, Dennis Rodman, and Hollywood's Rudy. The poetry and the monologues delivered to Terrell and Patterson legitimized and accelerated trash talking. And, against all odds, his most enduring legacy—that of conviction—means that we still take seriously the idea of sports and character.

FURTHER READING

Ashe, Arthur. *A Hard Road to Glory: A History of the African-American Athlete, 1619–1986*, 3 vols. (1988).

Brooks, Dana, and Ronald Althouse eds. *Racism in College Athletics: The African-American Athlete's Experience* (1993).

Cashmore, Ellis. *Tyson: Nurture of the Beast* (2005).

Demas, Lane. *Integrating the Gridiron: Black Civil Rights and American College Football* (2010).

Dyson, Michael Eric. "Be Like Mike? Michael Jordan and the Pedagogy of Desire," in *Reflecting Black: African-American Cultural Criticism* (1993), 64–74.

Early, Gerald. *The Culture of Bruising: Essays on Prizefighting, Literature, and Modern American Culture* (1994).

Garrison, J. Gregory, and Randy Roberts. *Heavy Justice: The State of Indiana v. Michael G. Tyson* (1994).

Gems, Gerald R. "Blocked Shot: The Development of Basketball in the African-American Community of Chicago," *Journal of Sport History* 22 (Summer 1995), 135–48.

George, Nelson. *Elevating the Game* (1992).

Gorn, Elliott J., ed., *Muhammad Ali: The People's Champion* (1996).

Goudsouzian, Aram. *King of the Court: Bill Russell and the Basketball Revolution* (2010).

Gutman, Marta. "Race, Place, and Play," *Journal of the Society of Architectural Historians* 67 (2008), 532–61.

Heiskanen, Benita. *The Urban Geography of Boxing: Race, Class, and Gender in the Ring* (2012).

Hoberman, John. *Darwin's Athletes: How Sport Has Damaged Black America and Preserved the Myth of Race* (1997).

Iber, Jorge, et al. *Latinos in U.S. Sport: A History of Isolation, Cultural Identity, and Acceptance* (2011).

Marcello, Ronald E. "The Integration of Intercollegiate Athletics in Texas: North Texas State College as a Test Case, 1956," *Journal of Sport History* 14 (Winter 1987), 286–316.

Maraniss, David. *Clemente: The Passion and Grace of Baseball's Last Hero* (2006).

Martin, Charles H. *Benching Jim Crow: The Rise and Fall of the Color Line in Southern College Sports, 1890–1980* (2010).

Miller, Patrick B. "The Anatomy of Scientific Racism: Racialist Responses to Black Athletic Achievement," *Journal of Sport History* 25 (Spring1998), 119–51.

Miller, Patrick B., and David Wiggins. *The Unlevel Playing Field: A Documentary History of the African American Experience in Sport* (2003).

Moore, Joseph T. *Pride Against Prejudice—The Biography of Larry Doby* (1988).

Pennington, Richard. *Breaking the Ice: The Racial Integration of Southwest Conference Football* (1987).

Regalado, Samuel O. *Viva Baseball! Latin Major Leaguers and Their Special Hunger*, 3rd ed. (2008).

Regalado, Samuel O. *Nikkei Baseball: Japanese American Players from Immigration and Internment to the Major Leagues* (2013).

Ruck, Rob. *Raceball: How the Major Leagues Colonized the Black and Latin Game* (2010).

Sammons, Jeffrey. *Beyond the Ring: The Role of Boxing in American Society* (1988).

Smith, John M. "'It's Not Really My Country': Lew Alcindor and the Revolt of the Black Athlete," *Journal of Sport History* 36 (Summer 2009), 223–44.

Smith, Maureen M. *Wilma Rudolph: A Biography* (2006).

Smith, Thomas G. *Showdown: JFK and the Integration of the Washington Redskins* (2011).

Snyder, Brad. *A Well-Paid Slave: Curt Flood's Fight for Free Agency in Professional Sports* (2006).

Tygiel, Jules. *Baseball's Great Experiment: Jackie Robinson and His Legacy* (1983).

Wiggins, David K. *Sport, Race, and American Culture: African-American Athletes in a White World* (1997).

CHAPTER 14

The Business of Sport, 1945–2012

The business of sport has changed dramatically since World War II, when the only truly national spectator sports were boxing, thoroughbred racing, and professional baseball (although there was no major league team west of the Mississippi). Today it is now truly national and a "big business." The American population rose from 140 million in 1940 to 249 million in 1990, and 313 million in 2012, with most of this growth occurring in suburbs and the Sun Belt—some at the expense of declining industrial cities in the East and Midwest. How did these demographic shifts enhance opportunities for sports entrepreneurs? They took advantage of the emerging new markets by shifting established franchises in declining Rust Belt metropolises to unexploited growing cities, by expanding established leagues and creating new teams, and by organizing new leagues. These sportsmen were typically super-rich men who utilized their wealth to invest in sporting enterprises to become celebrities and make money by selling tickets and merchandise, and securing lucrative media contracts, with the financial support from local municipalities that built them stadiums and from the federal government through income tax loopholes.

The rise of television profoundly affected professional sports. Boxing was the first big TV sport (discounting wrestling "exhibitions"). It was perfect for the video camera because of its restricted space. Boxing quickly became a mainstay of TV, and in the early 1950s there were bouts on primetime six days a week. However, by the late 1950s interest in boxing was curtailed by its oversaturation on TV, domination by organized crime, the monopolistic promotions like the International Boxing Club, the absence of top white American fighters, and the dearth of charismatic champions. Horse racing benefited less from TV, but enjoyed great success in this era, drawing the largest crowds, eager to gamble at the track, of any sport from the early 1950s until 1984, when it was supplanted by baseball as a spectator sport. Major League Baseball's popularity after World War II was abetted by local TV coverage. However, declining profits in smaller media markets led to the first major league franchise shifts in 50 years, beginning in 1953, when the Boston Braves moved to Milwaukee. Soon teams in major cities were on the move, like the Giants and the highly profitable Dodgers, who moved to the West Coast in 1958.

Professional football lagged far behind baseball in popularity, yet it moved to the West Coast in 1946, a decade ahead of Major League Baseball, made feasible by air travel. The National Football League (NFL) gained significant fan support in the late 1950s, and boomed in the 1960s due to the excitement of the sport, outstanding players and teams, and the game's compatibility with television. The NFL benefited greatly from a national TV contract that was equally divided up among its members. By the 1970s, NFL crowds averaged 90 percent capacity, and it appeared that football had surpassed baseball as the national pastime.

How did players benefit from the boom in professional sports? Players received relatively little of the profits at first because reserve clauses in their contracts limited their negotiating power until the 1960s. Then events started moving in their favor because of court decisions that made all sports, except baseball, liable to antitrust law as well as the growing militancy of players' unions. Salaries began to edge up, especially following player strikes and the achievement of arbitration. Baseball wages rose nearly 250 percent from 1967 to 1975, and basketball by 500 percent. MLB and NBA players averaged over $100,000 a year. Following the introduction of free agency, Major League Baseball and NBA salaries shot up even more, and both surpassed one million dollars on average in 1993. As of 2011, the average salary was $3.31 million in MLB; $5.15 million in the NBA; and $1.9 million the NFL. Nonetheless, sports franchises became increasingly valuable because of multimillion-dollar TV contracts, lucrative licensing agreements, and increased attendance. By 1993, the New York Yankees and Dallas Cowboys were each worth around $200 million, and over $2 billion in 2012, making sports a truly big business.

DOCUMENTS

Document 1 consists of former Los Angeles mayor Norris Poulson's reminiscences about his dealings in the 1950s with Brooklyn Dodgers owner Walter O'Malley and his efforts to bring the team to Los Angeles. The Dodgers then were one of the most profitable franchises in baseball, but O'Malley felt that Brooklyn was in decline, and he had his eyes on potentially huge profits on the West Coast and in pay-TV. Document 2 is Supreme Court Justice Thurgood Marshall's dissent in the case of *Flood v. Kuhn*. St. Louis Cardinals star center fielder Curt Flood, a twelve-year major-league veteran, had sought free-agent status in 1970 after he was traded to the Philadelphia Phillies. When his request was denied, he sued organized baseball, claiming its reserve clause violated the antitrust laws.

In Document 3, Peter Seitz, impartial chairman of the arbitration panel, established under the basic agreement between the 24 major league clubs and the Players Association (that included Marvin J. Miller, executive director of the Players Association, and John J. Gaherin, advisor to the Clubs' Player Relations Committee), explains why he and Miller ruled for Andy Messersmith and Dave McNally in their complaint against the renewal clause in their contracts. Seitz ruled that since the two players completed the 1975 season under renewals of their 1974 contracts, they were hereafter free agents. This supported Miller's prior contention that the Uniform Player's Contract gave owners a right to renew an unsigned player *for one year, and one year only*, contradicting management's claim that the contracts could be renewed yearly every season. The Seitz decision marked a major step forward in the creation of free agency in major professional team sports.

The next documents deal with two major crises that recently bedeviled Organized Baseball. One is the alleged gambling by Pete Rose on baseball. Rose was the manager of the Cincinnati Reds, who had been a great baseball player (1963–1986), hitting .303 for his career, with 4,256 hits, the most ever. When reports emerged that Rose might have bet on baseball, Commissioner A. Bartlett Giamatti assigned John M. Dowd, a lawyer serving as his Special Counsel, to investigate the allegations. Document 4 consists of an extract from *The Dowd Report* (1989) that produced substantial evidence that Rose had bet on baseball during the 1980s, including his tenure as manager, although there was no proof he had bet on the Reds to lose. The outcome was that Rose was banned for life from baseball in 1989, and in 1991 the Baseball Hall of Fame made him "permanently ineligible" for possible induction.

The other big crisis was the use of drugs by ballplayers, which in the 1970s through the 1980s had largely been for recreational purposes. However, at the end of the century, a few players, notably Mark McGuire (70) and Sammy Sosa (66) in 1998, and then Barry Bonds (73) in 2001, were hitting a remarkable number of home runs, obliterating the old record of 61 set by Roger Maris in 1961 and other less distinguished players were hitting far more four baggers than ever before. The public's suspicion led to press investigations, congressional hearings, and an investigation of the Bay Area Laboratory Co-Operative (BALCO), accused of selling tetrahydrogestrinone, a performance-enhancing steroid and human growth hormone. In 2007, Baseball Commissioner Bud Selig invited former U.S. Senator George J. Mitchell (D-Maine), thereafter an envoy in Northern Ireland and Israel, to lead an inquiry into the use of performance-enhancing drugs by baseball players. This document is drawn from the 409-page Mitchell Report that named 89 current and former players who had used performance-enhancing drugs.

Document 6 comes from a 2007 statement made by Congressman Dennis Kucinich (D-Ohio), and former mayor of Cleveland, before the House Domestic Policy Subcommittee investigating publicly funded stadium. He told his colleagues that the Indians had threatened to move without a new field and that developers of a local stadium for the Indians and an arena for the Cavaliers, had promised 28,000 new jobs. The citizens passed an initiative in support of the new facilities. Hence the city spent around $215 million out of a total cost of $305 million for a ballpark and basketball arena in 1994; and $283 million more in 1999 for the Cleveland Browns. He argues all this expenditure did little to promote the city's economy, typical of municipalities that financed local sports buildings.

The final document is a graph that depicts the values of MLB, NFL, NBA, and NHL franchises in the period 2000–2011. The graph clearly indicates the enormous growth in the average value of National Football League teams, especially in comparison to the far more modest appreciation of its rivals.

1. Norris Poulson Reveals How Los Angeles Got the Brooklyn Dodgers in 1958

... When in February, 1957, O'Malley bought the Los Angeles Angels of the Pacific Coast League and the local ball park, Wrigley Field, he sent word confidentially through a friend that he would like to see me. He was then at the Dodger spring-training camp in Vero Beach, Florida. I flew there with a group of our city and county officials.

The meeting was primarily a sparring match. One of our officials promised O'Malley the moon, and Walter asked for more. You couldn't blame him. He had a valuable package in the Dodgers and he knew it. I assured him we wanted desperately to get the team, but made it clear we would have to come up with a plan that wouldn't get all of us run out of the city....

O'Malley gave us no promises at Vero Beach, but did say that if he were to consider our city at all, he would expect us to build a ball park. Land didn't interest him in the least....

O'Malley managed subtly in his conversations with us to point out what other cities would do for him.... He indicated that the "Milwaukee Formula" might be acceptable to him. For the use of County Stadium, Milwaukee, the Braves at the time were giving the city five percent of receipts and fifteen percent of concessions....

... I appointed a citizens committee to study ways and means of developing Chavez Ravine.

When I took office in 1953, some 183 acres of Chavez Ravine belonged to the Los Angeles Housing Authority, which had acquired the land from the Federal Government for public housing. However, estimates for grading the jagged terrain were so high that the idea of building there was growing less feasible.

Secretly, we got Howard Hughes to advance $5000 for a cursory survey.... The survey showed that the cost of building a baseball stadium and parking lot in the hills of Chavez would be exorbitant ... no less than $10,000,000....

In late May, I went to Brooklyn to see O'Malley. I explained that we couldn't raise the money to build a ball park, but suggested that we would try to get him the land at Chavez Ravine for a nominal cost, and he could build his own stadium. He hit the ceiling. "I already have one ball park there!" he exclaimed. "What am I going to do with two?"

He hastened to add that no one had built a ball park with private capital in more than thirty years, and, besides, he would have to lay out cash for indemnification to the Pacific Coast League.

Since O'Malley needed us much less than we needed him, he obviously held the trump cards. In the course of our discussion, he asked if maybe he could sell Wrigley Field to the city. I knew in my heart that the only plausible solution was a trade of Wrigley Field for Chavez Ravine, but I also knew that in

From Norris Poulson interview, "The Dodgers and Chavez Ravine," UCLA Oral History Collection, 1966. UCLA Library Center for Oral History Research.

dealing loosely with city property, I was getting in over my head and playing with political dynamite....

When I returned to Los Angeles, I huddled privately with a small group of our leading citizens [Frank Payne, publisher of the Los Angeles *Examiner,* and Norman Chandler, publisher of the *Times*]....

... They suggested that I get as my representative some top-notch negotiator who understood real estate values and who could hold his own in a bargaining match with the wily O'Malley.

I followed their advice and enlisted the services of Harold C. McClellan, a highly successful business leader who had just returned from a tour of duty as Assistant Secretary of Commerce. McClellan met with City Attorney Roger Arnebergh and Chief City Administrator Samuel Leask to work out some sort of deal to offer the Dodgers. Casually, I suggested the possibility of a trade of Wrigley Field for Chavez Ravine, and the boys took it from there.

These men aren't fools. They realized that baseball would be expensive. But they also knew that the investment was sound. Local business would benefit enormously. The youth of the county would benefit. Hundreds of thousands of sports fans would derive pleasure from major league ball, and the prestige that would come to the city from having a quality team like the Dodgers would be invaluable.

The negotiations were a delicate and complicated matter....

We would give the Dodgers our 185 acres in Chavez Ravine, would buy them an additional 115 acres at a price not to exceed $7,000 an acre, and would contribute $2,000,000 toward grading. With money it received from the State Gasoline Tax Fund, the Country would make available about $2,700,000 for building access roads.

In turn, the Dodgers would hand over Wrigley Field, valued at $2,275,000 for city recreational purposes in a much-needed area. The Dodgers also would set aside forty acres in Chavez Ravine for a recreational area on which they would spend $500,000 for development. For a minimum of twenty years, they would spend $60,000 a year to maintain the area. And they would pay taxes on their property, probably amounting to $350,000 annually.

O'Malley finally agreed to the contract, but not without misgivings. He still would have preferred the City's building the stadium.

I discovered early in my dealings with Walter that he does not run a philanthropic society. He is cool and clever and has the patience required of a good horse-trader. But the man, in truth, was maligned unjustly by many. He didn't make a land grab at Chavez Ravine. The property was more or less thrust upon him by circumstances.... [T]he acreage today is worth a fortune ... it wouldn't have been if he hadn't risked the money to develop it.

Now that he had decided to move to Los Angeles, O'Malley felt that it would be advantageous ... if a franchise could be established in San Francisco. He was reasonably certain that Horace Stoneham was ready to shift the Giants from New York—very likely to Minneapolis–St. Paul where a ball park already had been built. O'Malley asked me if I knew George Christopher, the mayor of San Francisco. Told that I did, he asked if I would set up a private meeting among the three of us. I did—at the Beverly-Hilton Hotel in Beverly Hills. O'Malley invited a fourth party, Matty Fox, president of a pay-TV firm called Skistron.... O'Malley placed a long distance call for Stoneham. He told the Giants president that his team would do much better in California than in Minnesota and assured him that Fox would help finance the San Francisco project in return for subscription television privileges at a future date.

... A few days later, Christopher flew to New York and locked up the Giants for San Francisco. As agreed, Fox began making payments to the club in 1958, but when pay TV never came into focus, Stoneham released him from the contract.

... All that seemed to remain to consummate the deal between the City and O'Malley was the blessing of the City Council.... Political enemies of mine, O'Malley haters, baseball haters, crackpots, intelligent people feeling the city was being slickered, and groups with selfish motives seemed to emerge from the alcoves all at once.

They were backed by two media which seized upon the issue to further or protect their own interests. One was a large segment of community newspapers in Los Angeles and Orange counties. The other was television. The metropolitan dailies in Los Angeles favored baseball. To discredit these publications and make a grab for circulation and advertising, the community papers used Chavez Ravine as the stick with which to beat the drum. They screamed that the mayor, encouraged by the LA dailies, was giving away the people's land.

They were joined by local television, which took an immediate dislike to O'Malley. He was an outspoken advocate of pay TV....

Well, the intrigue now began. To ratify the Chavez Ravine contract, we needed ten of the fifteen votes in the City Council. I was sure of eight. Four were against, one was out of town, and two were on the fence. The issue was debated at great length in the Council Chamber and the vote was delayed repeatedly, making O'Malley understandably nervous. National League President Warren Giles then got into the picture. He warned Los Angeles that unless it ratified the contract before the start of the National League meeting on October 1, the league would look unfavorably upon our city as a place to move a franchise.

I was up against it. On September 30, the Council was still arguing over the contract and not yet ready to vote. My leaders in the Council were Roz Wyman and John Gibson, who carried the discussion late into the night. All the while, I was ... in my office in ... City Hall, listening to the arguments over the intercom. Uneasily, I kept looking at my watch....

... Short two votes, I decided to get help from outside forces. Quietly, I visited some labor unions and asked them to use persuasive charm with one of the fence-sitting councilmen. To put the pressure on the other, I called on downtown businessmen....

On October 7, ... our team turned up with ten votes. We cheered loudly. The battle, at last, was won—or so we thought....

The resourceful enemy circulated a referendary petition for which 53,000 valid signatures were obtained, enough to bring the Chavez Ravine issue to the ballot.... A poll showed that seventy percent of the citizens favored the Chavez Ravine contract....

To counter this competition, I suggested a scare campaign that would strike home with the low-income people who didn't belong to country clubs and social groups and who wanted big league baseball for entertainment. The referendum, we led them to believe, was unalterably a yes-or-no vote for baseball. By this time, the Dodgers had started playing in the Coliseum, and the fans loved them. The prospect of losing them wasn't appealing.

On June 3, 1958, the citizens went to the polls. The battle was touch and go, but we beat the referendum by some 23,000 votes, not too many considering the population of Los Angeles....

2. Justice Thurgood Marshall Dissents in the Curt Flood Case, 1972

Petitioner was a major league baseball player from 1956, when he signed a contract with the Cincinnati Reds, until 1969, when his 12-year career with the St. Louis Cardinals, which had obtained him from the Reds, ended and he was traded to the Philadelphia Phillies. He had no notice that the Cardinals were contemplating a trade, no opportunity to indicate the teams with which he would prefer playing, and no desire to go to Philadelphia. After receiving formal notification of the trade, petitioner wrote to the Commissioner of Baseball protesting that he was not "a piece of property to be bought and sold irrespective of my wishes," and urging that he had the right to consider offers from other teams than the Phillies. He requested that the Commissioner inform all of the major league teams that he was available for the 1970 season. His request was denied, and petitioner was informed that he had no choice but to play for Philadelphia or not to play at all.

To non-athletes it might appear that petitioner was virtually enslaved by the owners of major league baseball clubs who bartered among themselves for his services. But, athletes know that it was not servitude that bound petitioner to the club owners; it was the reserve system. The essence of that system is that a player is bound to the club with which he first signs a contract for the rest of his playing days. He cannot escape from the club except by retiring, and he cannot prevent the club from assigning his contract to any other club.

Petitioner ... alleged, among other things, that the reserve system was an unreasonable restraint of trade....

Americans love baseball as they love all sports. Perhaps we become so enamored of athletics that we assume that they are foremost in the minds of legislators as well as fans. We must not forget, however, that there are only some 600 major league baseball players. Whatever muscle they might have been able to muster by combining forces with other athletes has been greatly impaired by the manner in which this Court has isolated them. It is this Court that has made them impotent, and this Court should correct its error.

From *Flood* v. *Kuhn* 407 U.S. 258 (1972).

We do not lightly overrule our prior constructions of federal statutes, but when our errors deny substantial federal rights, like the right to compete freely and effectively to the best of one's ability as guaranteed by the antitrust laws, we must admit our error and correct it. We have done so before and we should do so again here....

To the extent that there is concern over any reliance interests that club owners may assert, they can be satisfied by making our decision prospective only. Baseball should be covered by the antitrust laws beginning with this case and henceforth, unless Congress decides otherwise.

Accordingly, I would overrule *Federal Baseball Club* and *Toolson* and reverse the decision of the Court of Appeals.

This is a difficult case because we are torn between the principle of *stare decisis* and the knowledge that the decisions in *Federal Baseball Club* v. *National League,* 259 U.S. 200 (1922), and *Toolson* v. *New York Yankees, Inc.,* 346 U.S. 356 (1953), are totally at odds with more recent and better reasoned cases....

In his answer to petitioner's complaint, the Commissioner of Baseball "admits that under present concepts of interstate commerce defendants are engaged therein."... There can be no doubt that the admission is warranted by today's reality. Since baseball is interstate commerce, if we re-examine baseball's antitrust exemption, the Court's decisions in ... *United States* v. *International Boxing Club,* 348 U.S. 236 (1955), and *Radovich* v. *National Football League,* 352 U.S. 445 (1957), require that we bring baseball within the coverage of the antitrust laws....

3. The Arbitrator's Ruling in the Case of John A. Messersmith and David A. McNally and the Coming of Free Agency in 1975

The Association claims that the terms of the Uniform Player Contracts of Messersmith and McNally, respectively, having expired, the two players are at liberty to negotiate contract relationships with any of the other clubs in the leagues and that they are not to be regarded as having been "reserved" by the Los Angeles or the Montreal clubs, respectively, in such a manner as to inhibit other clubs from dealing with them.

The leagues and the clubs assert that the terms of the contracts of these players have not expired; that they are still under contract; and that, in any event, the grievants have been duly "reserved" by their respective clubs; and, accordingly, they are not free to deal with other clubs for the performance of services for the 1976 season; nor are such other clubs free to deal with them for that season excepting under circumstances and conditions not here obtaining....

From "In the Matter of the Arbitration Between the Twelve Clubs Comprising the National League of Professional Baseball Clubs and the Twelve Clubs Comprising the American League of Professional Baseball Clubs." In Marvin and Teresa Miller Papers, Tamiment Library, Robert F. Wagner Labor Archives, Bobst Library, New York University.

The Merits

... Messersmith signed a one-year contract with the Los Angeles Dodgers in 1974. This contract was duly renewed by the Club for what is commonly called the "renewal year" of 1975. The renewal was effected under Section 10(a) of the Uniform Players Contract which provides:

> "10(a) On or before December 20 *** in the year of the last playing season covered by this contract, the Club may tender to the Player a contract for the term of that year ***. If prior to the March 1 next ... the Player and the Club have not agreed upon the terms of such contract, then on or before 10 days after said March 1, *the Club shall have the right by written notice to the Player *** to renew this contract for the period of one year on the same terms*, except that the amount payable to the Player shall be such as the Club shall fix in said notice; provided, however, that said amount *** shall be an amount not less than 80% of the rate stipulated for the next preceding year and at a rate not less than 70% of the rate stipulated for the year immediately prior to the next preceding year." (Emphasis supplied.)

The Players Association claims that Messersmith, having served out and completed his renewal year on September 29, 1975, he was no longer under contract with the Los Angeles Club and, accordingly, was a free agent to negotiate for the rendition of his services with any of the other clubs in the leagues; but that the clubs "have conspired to deny Mr. Messersmith that right and have maintained the position that the Los Angeles Club is still exclusively entitled to his services."

As an affirmative defense, it is the position of the leagues that, by virtue of having sent its reserve list on November 17, 1975 to the appropriate officials and the subsequent promulgation of that list by them, the Los Angeles Club has reserved Messersmith's services for its own use, exclusively, for the ensuing season. This position is based on Major League Rule 4-A(a) which provides:

> "(a) FILING. On or before November 20 in each year; each Major League Club shall transmit to the Commissioner and to its League President *a list of not exceeding forty (40) active and eligible players, whom the club desires to, reserve for the ensuing season* ***.... *[T]hereafter no player on any list shall be eligible to play for or negotiate with any other club until his contract has been assigned or he has been released* *** (Emphasis supplied.)

This Major League Rule is supported and supplemented by Major League Rule 3(g) which reads as follows:

> "(g) TAMPERING. To preserve discipline and competition and to prevent the enticement of players ***, there shall be no negotiations or dealings respecting employment, either present or prospective between any player *** and any club other than the club with which he is under contract or acceptance of terms, or by which he is reserved ***...." (Emphasis supplied.)

Thus, it is the Los Angeles Club's position that Messersmith, having been duly placed on its reserve list in November, 1975, it has an exclusive right to his services in that ensuing season.

The Players Association does not contest that Messersmith was placed on the Club's Reserved List; but it disputes the effect of doing so.... [T]he dispute is whether the fact that the renewal year, which terminated in September, 1975 (as claimed by the Players Association) affected or destroyed the Club's right to reserve Messersmith for the ensuing year of 1976 and to place him on the Club's November 17, 1975 reserve list with the consequences spelled out in Major League Rules 4-A(a) and 3(g). This calls for a decision as to whether Messersmith is still under contract with the Club; and then, if not under contract, whether the provisions of Rule 4-A(a) and 3(g) of the Reserve System prohibit him and any other club from dealing with each other for the 1976 championship season.

... I have reached the conclusion that, as a matter of contract construction, the position of the Players Association in the dispute has merit and deserves to be sustained.

★ ★ ★

No one challenges the right of a Club to renew a Player's contract with or without his consent, under Section 10(a), "for the period of one [renewal] year." I read the record, however, as containing a contention by the leagues that when a Club renews a Player's contract for the renewal year, the contract in force during that year contains the "right of renewal" clause as one of its terms, entitling the Club to renew the contract in successive years, to perpetuity, perhaps, so long as the Player is alive and the Club has duly discharged all conditions required of it. This is challenged by the Players Association whose position it is that the contractual relationship between the Club and the Player terminates at the end of the first renewal year. Thus, it claims that there was no longer any contractual bond between Messersmith and the Los Angeles Club on September 29, 1975.

The league's argument is based on the language in Section 10(a) of the Player's Contract that the Club "may renew this contract for the period of one year on *the same terms*" (Emphasis supplied); and that among those "terms" is the right to further contract renewal....

★ ★ ★

There is nothing in Section 10(a) which, explicitly, expresses agreement that the Player's Contract can be renewed for any period beyond the first renewal year. The point the leagues present must be based upon the implication or assumption, that if the renewed contract is "on the same terms" as the contract for the preceding year (with the exception of the amount of compensation) the right to additional renewals must have been an integral part of the renewed contract. I find great difficulties, in so implying or assuming, in respect of a contract providing for the rendition of personal services in which one would expect a more explicit expression of intention. There are numerous provisions and terms in the Uniform Player's Contract that are renewed in the renewal year when a Club exercises its renewal rights under Section 10(a). Provision of the right to make subsequent and successive renewals is in an entirely different category, however, than the numerous terms in the Player's Contract which deal with working conditions and duties which the Club and the Player owe to each other. That right, critically, concerns and involves the continued existence of the *contract itself* as expressing the mutual undertakings of the parties and the bargain which they struck. All the other "terms" of the Player–Club relationship stand or fall according to whether the contract, as such, is renewed.

★ ★ ★

… I find, on the whole, that the reservation rights of a club, under the rules constituting the Reserve System, contemplate the existence of a player–club contractual relationship. The Basic Agreement incorporated the Uniform Player's Contract therein and provides that during the term of the Agreement no other form of Player's contract will be utilized (Art. III). It goes on to provide that should the provisions of any player–club contract be inconsistent with the terms of the Basic Agreement, the latter shall govern. The Uniform Player's Contract (a part of the Basic Agreement) in Section 10(a), provides that it may be renewed "for the period of one year"; and I have stated that the manner in which the renewal clause has been written does not warrant interpreting the section as providing for contract renewal beyond the contract year. When that year comes to an end the Player no longer has contractual duties that bind him to the Club. Provision for those duties must be found within the rules, which, excepting, possibly, for Rule 3(g) provide for a contractual foundation for the reservation of player's services. To the extent that Rule 3(g) prohibits dealing with a club by a player other than the club by which "he is reserved," it is inconsistent with the provisions of the Basic Agreement and the Uniform Player's Contract which subsume a contractual relationship between the clubs and the players affected.

[I]t is evident that traditionally, the leagues have regarded the existence of a contract as a basis for the reservation of players [since] … the Cincinnati Peace Compact of the National and American Leagues, signed January 10, 1903—probably the most important step in the evolution and development of the present Reserve System. In that document it is provided: "… A *reserve rule* shall be recognized, by which each and every club may reserve *players under contract*, and that a uniform contract for the use of each league shall be adopted." (Emphasis supplied.)

This emphasis on the existence of a contract for reservation of a player to be effective was perpetuated in the Major League Rules.… However, … one may reasonably reach the conclusion: —*no contract, no reservation*. The provision says there shall be no dealings between a player and a club other than the one "with which he is under *contract*, or acceptance of terms, *or by which he is reserved*." (Emphasis supplied.) In other words, *a contract must provide for his reservation*.…

Thus, I reach the conclusion that, absent a contractual connection between Messersmith and the Los Angeles Club after September 28, 1975, the Club's action in reserving his services for the ensuing year by placing him on its reserve list was unavailing and ineffectual in prohibiting him from dealing with other clubs in the league and to prohibit such clubs from dealing with him.

In the case of McNally whom the Montreal Club had placed on its disqualified list, a similar conclusion has been reached.

★ ★ ★

Award

1. *Jurisdiction:*
   It is found and decided that the Messersmith and McNally grievances, ... are within the scope of the provisions of Article X of the Basic Agreement; and, accordingly, are within the duty and the power of the Arbitration Panel to arbitrate....
2. *The Merits*:
   The grievances of Messersmith and McNally are sustained. There is no contractual bond between these players and the Los Angeles and the Montreal clubs, respectively. Absent such a contract, their clubs had no right or power, under the Basic Agreement, the Uniform Player's Contract or the Major League Rules to reserve their services for their exclusive use for any period beyond the "renewal year" in the contracts which these players had heretofore signed with their clubs.
3. *Relief:*
   The leagues ... shall take such steps as may be necessary to inform and instruct their member clubs that the provisions of Major League Rules 4-A(a) and 3(g) do not inhibit, prohibit or prevent such clubs from negotiating or dealing with respect to employment with the grievants in this case; also, that Messersmith shall be removed from the reserve list of the Los Angeles Club and McNally from the reserve or disqualified lists of the Montreal Club....

4. The 1989 Dowd Report on Pete Rose and Gambling on Baseball

... Pete Rose has denied under oath ever betting on Major League Baseball or associating with anyone who bet on Major League Baseball.... The testimony and the documentary evidence gathered in the course of the investigation demonstrated that Pete Rose bet on baseball, and in particular, on games of the Cincinnati Reds Baseball Club during the 1985, 1986, and 1987 seasons.

[W]ith few exceptions, Rose did not deal directly with bookmakers but rather placed his bets through others. [D]uring the 1985 and 1986 seasons, Rose placed bets on baseball with Ron Peters, a bookmaker in Franklin, Ohio ... including Cincinnati Reds games ..., corroborated by the testimony of others and by Rose's own financial records as well. Rose admitted placing bets ... on football and basketball games, but denied placing any bets on baseball games....

Rose placed bets through another friend, Michael Bertolini [who] placed bets on Rose's behalf with an unidentified bookmaker in New York City. One source of this information is a 1988 tape recorded conversation between Bertolini and another of Rose's associates, Paul Janszen. During that conversation, Bertolini mentioned, among other things, that Rose had incurred substantial debts to Bertolini and the New York bookmaker and that Rose had given Bertolini personal checks which Bertolini had had cashed and the proceeds sent to the New York bookmaker. Rose's financial records reveal checks in the amounts described by Bertolini, made out by Rose to fictitious payees. Rose denied placing bets with Bertolini and denied owing anyone money. Rose acknowledged sending eleven $8,000 checks to Bertolini made out to fictitious payees but said that these check were loans to Bertolini to be used as payments to athletes for baseball card shows.

During the 1987 baseball season, Rose utilized Paul Janszen to place his baseball bets after Rose and [Tommy] Gioiosa had a falling out in the spring of 1987. Janszen relayed Rose's baseball bets to an acquaintance of Rose, Steve Chevashore, who in turn placed Rose's bets with a bookmaker in Staten Island, New York, identified only as "Val." Rose's betting on professional baseball, including Reds games, was testified to by Janszen and his girlfriend, Danita Marcum, and was discussed during a taped telephone conversation between Janszen and Chevashore. Rose's betting on baseball is further corroborated by betting records from Rose's home which have been identified by an expert as being in Rose's handwriting. Rose has denied ever placing any bets with Janszen at any time.

In May 1987, "Val" refused to accept bets on behalf of Rose due to Rose's failure to pay his gambling debts. Thereafter, Rose's baseball bets were again placed with Ron Peters. However, instead of being placed by Gioiosa, Rose's bets were placed with Peters by Janszen. Between May and July 1987, Rose bet with Peters $2,000 per game on baseball, including Reds games....

[T]he documentary evidence, including Pete Rose's betting sheets, the betting notebook maintained by Paul Janszen, and the betting records of Ron Peters ... have been analyzed by an expert in gambling investigations who has verified that they reflect actual games played and actual betting lines.

[T]he 1987 betting activity, incorporating information from the betting sheets and telephone traffic between Rose, Janszen, Chevashore, "Val," and Peters between April 8, 1987 and July 5, 1987 [indicates] ... short but frequent telephone calls to and from bettors, and to bookmakers, ... indicative of professional betting activity.

Thus, in sum, the accumulated testimony of witnesses, together with the documentary evidence and telephone records reveal extensive betting activity by Pete Rose in connection with professional baseball and, in particular, Cincinnati Reds games, during the 1985, 1986, and 1987 baseball seasons.

5. The Report on Enhancement Performing Drugs in Major League Baseball, 2007

GEORGE J. MITCHELL

For more than a decade there has been widespread illegal use of anabolic steroids and other performance enhancing substances by players in Major League Baseball, in violation of federal law and baseball policy.... Those who have illegally used these substances range from players whose major league careers were brief to potential members of the Baseball Hall of Fame. They include both pitchers and position players, and their backgrounds are as diverse as those of all major league players. The response by baseball was slow to develop and was initially ineffective, but it gained momentum after the adoption of a mandatory random drug testing program in 2002. That program has been effective in that detectable steroid use appears to have declined. But the use of human growth hormone has risen because, unlike steroids, it is not detectable through urine testing.

This report, the product of an intensive investigation, describes how and why this problem emerged ... from hundreds of interviews and thousands of documents. [T]he evidence we uncovered indicates that this has not been an isolated problem involving just a few players or a few clubs. It has involved many players on many clubs. In fact, each of the thirty clubs has had players who have been involved with performance enhancing substances at some time in their careers.

... There have been many estimates of use. In 2002, former National League Most Valuable Player Ken Caminiti estimated that "at least half" of major league players were using anabolic steroids. Dave McKay, a longtime coach for the St. Louis Cardinals and the Oakland Athletics, estimated that at one time 30% of players were using them.... [B]etween 5 and 7 percent of the major league players who participated in anonymous survey testing in 2003 tested positive for performance enhancing substances. Those figures almost certainly understated the actual level of use since players knew they would be tested ..., the use of human growth hormone was not detectable in the tests that were conducted, and, ... a negative test does not necessarily mean that a player has not been using performance enhancing substances.

Mandatory random testing, formally started in 2004 after the survey testing results, appears to have reduced the use of detectable steroids, but players

---

From George Mitchell, *Report to the Commissioner of Baseball of an Independent Investigation into the Illegal Use of Steroids and Other Performance Enhancing Substances by Player in Major League Baseball* (2007), 1–2, 6–7, 11–16, 18–22.

switched to human growth hormone precisely because it is not detectable. Players who use human growth hormone apparently believe that it assists their ability to recover from injuries and fatigue; … this also is a major reason why players used steroids. Human growth hormone was the substance most frequently sold to players by Kirk Radomski, a former New York Mets clubhouse employee who was a significant source of illegal performance enhancing substances until late 2005.

★ ★ ★

… [W]e interviewed more than 700 witnesses … over 550 … current or former club officials, managers, coaches, team physicians, athletic trainers, or resident security agents. We also interviewed 16 persons from the Commissioner's Office, including Commissioner Selig.…

… We attempted to reach almost 500 former players. Many … declined …, but 68 did agree.… In addition, interviews of 3 former players were arranged.… The Players Association was largely uncooperative. It rejected totally my requests for relevant documents.… It refused my request to interview the director of the Montreal laboratory that analyzes drug tests under baseball's drug program.… The Players Association sent out a companion memorandum that effectively discouraged players from cooperating. Not one player contacted me in response to my memorandum. I received allegations of the illegal possession or use of performance enhancing substances by a number of current players.… Almost without exception they declined to meet or talk with me.

The Problem Is Serious

The illegal use of performance enhancing substances poses a serious threat to the integrity of the game. Widespread use by players of such substances unfairly disadvantages the honest athletes who refuse to use them and raises questions about the validity of baseball records. In addition, because they are breaking the law, users … are vulnerable to drug dealers who might seek to exploit their knowledge through threats intended to affect the outcome of baseball games or otherwise.

The illegal use of these substances to improve athletic performance also carries potentially serious negative side effects on the human body. Steroid users place themselves at risk for psychiatric problems, cardiovascular and liver damage, drastic changes to their reproductive systems, musculoskeletal injury, and other problems. Users of human growth hormone risk cancer, harm to their reproductive health, cardiac and thyroid problems, and overgrowth of bone and connective tissue. Apart from the dangers posed to the major league player himself, however, his use of performance enhancing substances encourages young athletes to use those substances.

… Finally, the illegal use in baseball of steroids and other performance enhancing substances victimizes the majority of players who do not use those substances.… We heard from many former players who believed it was grossly unfair that some players were using performance enhancing substances to gain an advantage.

Governing Laws and Major League Baseball Policies

Anabolic steroids are listed as controlled substances under the federal Controlled Substances Act. Since 2004, the dietary supplement androstenedione and other steroid precursors have been as well.... [I]t is illegal to use or possess steroids or steroid precursors without a valid physician's prescription.... Human growth hormone is a prescription medication....

Many have asserted that steroids and other performance enhancing substances were not banned in Major League Baseball before the 2002 Basic Agreement. This is not accurate.... Major League Baseball's drug policy has prohibited the use of any prescription medication without a valid prescription.... Steroids have been listed as a prohibited substance under the Major League Baseball drug policy since [1991] ... although no player was disciplined for steroid use before the prohibition was added to the collective bargaining agreement in 2002.

Many players were suspended for drug offenses before 2002, even though none of those suspensions related to the use of steroids or other performance enhancing substances....

For many years before 2002, the Players Association opposed any drug program.... The early disagreements ... centered around testing for cocaine and other "recreational" drugs, ... but the effect of the Players Association's opposition was to delay the adoption of mandatory random drug testing in Major League Baseball for nearly 20 years.

... In 2001, the Commissioner ... unilaterally implemented drug testing throughout baseball's affiliated minor leagues. He used that program as the basis for his ... proposal for a major league program ... as part of the 2002 Basic Agreement. For the first time, ... it provided for the possibility of mandatory random drug testing of all major league players if more than 5% of players tested positive for steroids during anonymous survey testing in 2003. After that ..., mandatory random drug testing began in Major League Baseball in 2004. That year, there were 12 undisputed positive tests for steroids. No player was suspended because the program did not provide for suspensions of first-time offenders at that time.

The Major League Baseball Joint Drug Prevention and Treatment Program has been modified twice since ... 2002. In January 2005, human growth hormone (along with seventeen other compounds) was added to the list of prohibited substances. In addition, the Players Association agreed to more stringent penalties for a positive test for steroids (or similar substances) including, for the first time, a suspension of ten days for a player's first positive test. In 2005, 12 players tested positive for steroids and were suspended for ten days.

Later, ... a 50-game suspension for a first positive test; a 100-game suspension for a second positive test; and a permanent suspension for a third positive test.... The penalties for positive drug tests under the major league program are the strongest in major U.S. professional sports leagues. In 2006, two players tested positive for steroids and were suspended for 50 games. In 2007, three players were suspended for 50 games each for positive steroids tests.

In addition, in June 2006 Arizona Diamondbacks pitcher Jason Grimsley was suspended for 50 games based on "non-analytic" evidence that he had violated the policy, specifically his reported admissions to federal agents that he had used steroids and human growth hormone....

The Rise of the "Steroids Era"

Reports of steroid use in Major League Baseball began soon after the widely publicized discipline of Canadian sprinter Ben Johnson at the [1988] ... Olympic Games.... Jose Canseco of the Oakland Athletics was the subject of the first media speculation....

News reports about alleged steroid use in baseball grew more frequent throughout the 1990s. In 1996, ... Ken Caminiti of the San Diego Padres was voted the National League's Most Valuable Player. In a 2002 *Sports Illustrated* article, he admitted ... using steroids ... and credited them for his increased power. In August 1998, coverage of the issue reached what seemed at the time to be a peak, when an article reported that Mark McGwire was using the then legal steroid precursor androstenedione while chasing the single-season home run record.... Then, beginning in the summer of 2000, a number of incidents involving steroids or drug paraphernalia came to the attention of club and Commissioner's Office officials, and the Players Association. They included: In June 2000, state police ... discovered steroids and hypodermic needles in the glove compartment of a vehicle belonging to a Boston Red Sox infielder.... Commissioner Selig asked me to conduct this investigation after the publication of *Game of Shadows*, ... that contained allegations about the illegal use of performance enhancing substances by major league players that were supplied by BALCO and the personal trainer Greg Anderson.

Evidence Obtained of Other Players' Possession or Use

Through the efforts of the United States Attorney's Office for the Northern District of California and federal law enforcement agencies, we obtained the cooperation of former New York Mets clubhouse employee Kirk Radomski.... Radomski identified a large number of current or former major league players to whom he said he illegally sold steroids, human growth hormone, or other substances. Radomski also provided.... (a) the admission by eleven players that Radomski had supplied them with performance enhancing substances.... (b) checks or money orders written to Radomski by some players.... (c) mailing receipts for shipments of performance enhancing substances by Radomski to some players; (d) statements by other witnesses supporting the allegations of use by some players; (e) the names, addresses, and/or telephone numbers of many players were found in Radomski's seized address book; (f) telephone records showing calls between Radomski and some players; and (g) a positive drug test. Six players are named based on information obtained from persons other than Radomski or former major league strength and conditioning coach Brian McNamee … [who] said that he was a direct eyewitness and participant in alleged illegal use by three players who he served as a personal trainer.

6. Congressman Dennis Kucinich on the Failure of Stadiums and Arenas to Positively Impact Their City's Economy, 2007

Today, we are taking a look at the use of tax-exempt financed debt for the construction of sports stadiums, convention centers and hotels. My own city of Cleveland has had experience in this regard. In 1990, the Central Market Gateway Project was formed to develop new stadiums for the Cleveland Indians and the Cleveland Cavaliers. Developers mounted a ballot initiative known as Issue 2 and made claims in their paid advertising that will sound familiar to our witnesses: "Who wins with Issue 2? We all do; 28,000 jobs for the jobless, neighborhood housing for the homeless, $15 million a year for schools for our children, revenues for city and county clinics and hospitals for the sick, energy assistance for the elderly."

The public relations campaign was coupled with hardball threats from Major League Baseball to relocate the Cleveland Indians. The initiative passed by a narrow margin and by 1996, the total cost was up to $462 million, two-thirds of which came from the public, and by 1997, that cost was still rising.…

Cleveland had a municipal football stadium and an intensely loyal fan base, affectionately known as the "Dawg Pound." But that wasn't enough and the Cleveland Browns left Cleveland for a new stadium built with taxpayer subsidies in Baltimore. NFL officials insisted that a new stadium and not renovations would be necessary to get a replacement-football team. Cleveland replaced its stadium with a football only structure paid for primarily with tax money.

After spending hundreds of millions of taxpayer dollars to subsidize stadiums for professional baseball, basketball and football, Cleveland's economy does not show the appropriate progress. We have among the highest poverty rates in the Nation and one of the highest foreclosure rates. This month marks the 132nd month or exactly 11 years in which Ohio's job growth is below the national average.

Whereas Ohio is growing slower than the rest of the country, Cleveland is growing slower than the rest of Ohio. During the 2000 recession, Cuyahoga County lost 75,733 jobs or 9.3 percent of all of its jobs.

From Congressman Dennis Kucinich's Testimony, U.S. Congress, House, Domestic Policy Subcommittee, *Hearing on Taxpayer Financed Stadiums, Convention Centers, and Hotels*, Before the Subcommittee on Domestic Policy of the Committee on Oversight and Government Reform, 110th Congress, First session, March 29, 2007 (Washington, D.C.: Government Printing Office, 2007), 1–3.

The Gateway Project, which promised to generate tens of thousands of new jobs, ushered in a period of net jobs lost since its construction. The Gateway Project neighborhood is particularly striking because the neighborhood is even more vacant and has even fewer jobs after the construction of the Gateway Project than before. Nationally, sports stadium construction is not effective at boosting the local economy and revitalizing urban neighborhoods. Academic research shows that on all counts, sports stadiums add no benefit, no substantial economic benefit to the cities in which they are built, no new jobs, new additional revenue for schools, no new business, no additional value.

In a review of the academic literature, economist Andrew Zimbalist concluded, "Few fields of empirical economic research offer virtual unanimity of findings. Yet, independent work on the economic impact of stadiums and arenas has uniformly found there is no statistically positive correlation between sports facility construction and economic development."

While taxpayer-financed stadiums do not seem to add to the wealth of the public who pay for them, they do add to the wealth of team owners. Consider the Detroit Tigers and the Detroit Lions.... The value of the Detroit Tigers rose from $83 million in 1995 to $290 million in 2001, the year after the team moved into their new stadium. The Lions' increase in value is even more dramatic, rising from $150 million in 1996 to $839 million in 2006. Economic benefit to the team owners was certainly the case for George Bush, who in 1989 spent about $600,000 to buy a small stake in the Texas Rangers baseball team. During his ownership, Mr. Bush and his co-investors were able to get voters to approve a sales tax increase to pay more than two-thirds of the cost of a new $191 million stadium for the Rangers as well as surrounding development. Mr. Bush and his partners also received a loan from the public authority charged with financing the stadium to cover their private share of the construction costs.

By 1994, the Rangers, in their new publicly financed stadium, were sold for $250 million, a threefold increase in value in merely 5 years and one that was largely attributable to a new taxpayer subsidized stadium. Mr. Bush personally came away with a profit of $14.9 million.... [T]he tax-exempt financing indisputably benefited the owners of the Texas Rangers.

Public financing of sports benefits the team owners but not, according to academic consensus, the public. So is tax-exempt financing of stadium construction an appropriate use of taxpayer funds?... [T]he 1986 act removed sports stadiums from the list of eligible private activities that could be financed with tax-exempt private activity bonds. That was the state of affairs until last year when the IRS issued three rulings.

Two of them were private letter rulings favorable to the Yankees and the Mets, allowing them to use previously prohibited private payments for debt service on tax-exempt bonds. Thus, the new Yankees and Mets stadiums can be built at taxpayer expense. The third was a proposed rulemaking that generalized the Yankees and Mets rulings. The effect of these three rulings would seem to subvert the intent of the 1986 Tax Reform Act as regards to public financing of sports stadium construction.

7. The Value of Major League Sports Franchises, 2000–2012

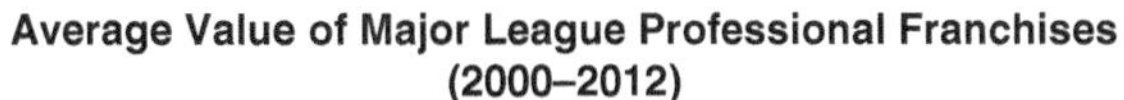

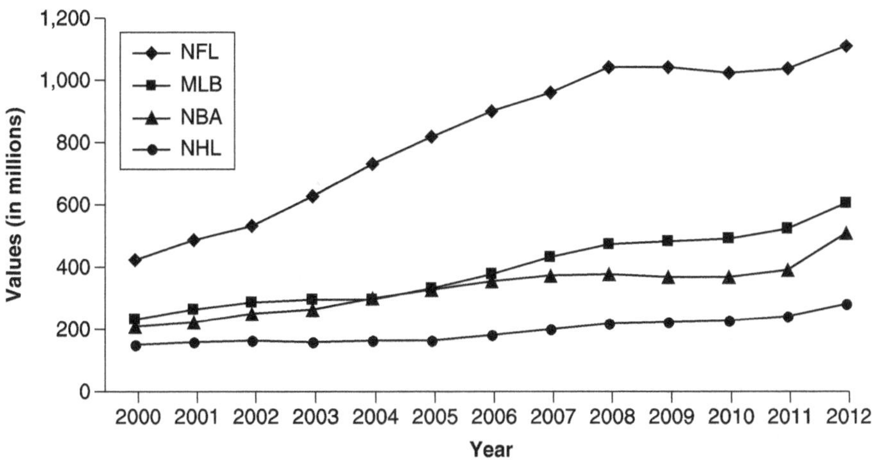

ESSAYS

The first essays on the subject of sport and business are by Michael Oriard, Distinguished Professor of American Literature and Culture at Oregon State University, who himself played in the National Football League (NFL) in the early 1970s. He is the nation's leading expert on the history of intercollegiate and professional football. Oriard's first article discusses the key financial aspects of major college football since the 1960s, with particular attention to the influence of the National Collegiate Athletic Association (NCAA) monopoly over intercollegiate sports. Oriard examines in depth the relationship between the NCAA and network broadcasts of football, which could not keep pace with the growing power of major conferences and even individual schools that created their own networks in the 1980s, especially successful in the era of cable TV. Oriard considers the role of the Bowl Championship Series (BCS), which began in 1998, as an arrangement for guaranteeing lucrative post-season contracts for the big-time football powers, provides extensive data on the profits—and losses—of big time sports programs, and discusses the enormous incomes of top coaches, evidence of student-athlete exploitation, and their sense of entitlement.

In the following paper, Oriard examines the economic world of professional football, the new national pastime. During the 1950s, the NFL was still a relatively modest operation, but thereafter evolved into what is now a

---

multi-billion dollar enterprise with a golden brand, operated by independent and wealthy owners whose franchises currently earn millions of dollars annually. He reports that the past two decades were boom times for the NFL, with the average franchise worth about $100 million 1989, and nearly $900 million in 2006. The big increase is largely due to lucrative national TV contracts and sweet deals with local governments that built new stadia replete with luxury seats that are gold mines for the home team, and, for the most part cooperative relations with the NFL Players Association, whose players often earn seven-figure contracts.

In the third essay, Steven Riess examines the relationship between municipalities and major league franchises over the past 60 years. After half a century of stability, major league teams beginning in 1953 began to relocate to the south and the west, often attracted by publicly financed and operated stadia. Before 1953 there was only one municipal stadium in Major League Baseball, but by the mid-1960s, the majority were publicly owned. In large American cities, municipal support of professional baseball became a common public policy as towns without a big league team competed with other cities to attract. The goal was to promote the city's public image and prime the pump of economic development and urban renewal. Cities without a major league franchise built ballparks to attract tenants. Mayors in cities with franchises that threatened to leave felt compelled to build them expensive ballparks to keep them in town. All the while, economists argued that these projects would not make money for their hosts, but until recently their pleas were ignored. Virtually all new ballparks continue to be heavily subsidized by local governments. However, in the past two decades, teams are increasingly being required to pay part of the costs if they expect public financing.

The NCAA Monopoly: Revenue, Reform, and Exploitation

MICHAEL ORIARD

A Made for TV Football World

... Like academic scandals, $3 million coaches' salaries and $50 million athletic budgets do not result from inexorable external forces but from institutional actions. Over the 1960s and 1970s, the major football powers were continually frustrated over the smaller schools' equal power within the NCAA. The separation into two, then three, divisions, and the further separation of Division I-A from I-AA (now the Football Bowl Subdivision and the Football Championship Subdivision, in the marketing language recently adopted by the NCAA), were attempts by the NCAA to placate its most powerful members. Nothing the NCAA could or would do was enough, however, and in December 1976 the

---

major football-playing conferences, with the exceptions of the Big Ten and Pacific-8 (the Pac-10 in 1978), along with the major independents (chiefly Notre Dame, Penn State, Pittsburgh, Florida State, and Miami), created the College Football Association (CFA) for the purpose of controlling their own football world. The absence of the Big Ten and Pac-10 eventually contributed to the demise of the CFA, but not before it had remade college football. The CFA included the Southeastern, Southwest, and Big Eight Conferences, along with the Atlantic Coast Conference and the Western Athletic Conference.... [T]he big-time football schools continued to receive most of the TV dollars, but as long as the NCAA negotiated television contracts for the entire organization, the football powers would feel vulnerable. When the CFA ... in 1981, attempt[ed] to sign its own contract with NBC, the NCAA ... block [ed] that effort in court. In response, the CFA backed an antitrust lawsuit in the names of the universities of Georgia and Oklahoma, which the Supreme Court ultimately decided in the CFA's favor on June 27, 1984. More than any other single date, this one marks the beginning of the college football world we have today.

Initially, after winning its case, the CFA looked woefully shortsighted. The NCAA had indeed enjoyed a monopoly, and its contracts with ABC, CBS, and ESPN would have paid member schools $73.6 million for the 1984 season. The NCAA had controlled the product, and the networks had paid premium rates for exclusive rights. Now, the CFA had to negotiate its own deal separately from the Big Ten and Pac-10, in a more cluttered, non-exclusive, and regional rather than national TV football marketplace. The CFA signed with ABC and ESPN for a total of $22 million, while the Big Ten and Pac-10 agreed to a joint deal with CBS for $10 million. Individual conferences made additional arrangements with cable networks and local stations for leftover games....

Once the dust settled, three times as many football games were televised in 1984 as in 1983, but for $25 million less in total revenue.... A televised game was now worth about $300,000 to each team, rather than $700,000....

... With its own TV contract in 1990, ... [s]portswriters in much of the country vilified the new Notre Dame arrogant, self-serving, and greedy—for destroying the competitive balance in college football. (With its own TV contract, the Irish would presumably have a recruiting advantage over every other school.)

... Notre Dame's break from the CFA in 1990 triggered a "structural upheaval unprecedented in the history of college athletics." Only Notre Dame could command its own television contract; for everyone else, conferences were the key....

In 1990 Murray Sperber wrote that "intercollegiate athletics has become College Sports Inc., a huge commercial entertainment conglomerate, with operating methods and objectives totally separate from, and mainly opposed to, the educational aims of the schools that house its franchises."...

The first real payoff from deregulation, and the fatal stroke to the CFA, came in 1994, when CBS reacted to losing its NFL rights to Fox by offering the SEC [Southeastern Conference] $85 million over five years, more than double the conference's take under the expiring CFA contracts. Once the SEC went its own way, the Big 12 ($57.5 million from ABC), ACC [Atlantic Coast Conference] ($54 million from ABC), and Big East ($56 million from CBS) followed.... In the summer of 1997, having unleashed the market forces that now ruled college football but doomed itself, the CFA disbanded.

The BCS and College Football for the New Century

Its legacy remains in the Bowl Championship Series (BCS), the latest arrangement for guaranteeing that the big-time football powers receive all that they are due.... [T]he BCS simply consolidated the realignment that began with the CFA and was continued by the Bowl Coalition in 1992, which included the SEC, ACC, Big Eight, Southwest Conference, and Big East but not the WAC (Western Athletic Conference). In 1995 the Bowl Coalition was replaced by the Bowl Alliance, without the Southwest Conference ...; then in 1998 the BCS for the first time reunited the Big Ten and Pac-10 with the original CFA renegades. In one sense, all three bowl arrangements merely recognized the preexisting inequality within college football, except in the case of the Big East, whose inclusion demonstrated absolutely that television ran the show.... The power of the BCS to transform the world of college football then became even clearer in 2003, when the defection of Miami, Virginia Tech, and Boston College from the Big East to the ACC made the ACC for the first time the equal of any football conference in the country and worthy of a $258 million, seven-year TV contract. Within three years, the ACC's overall revenue increased 44.5 percent, while the Big East, deprived of its most legitimate football programs, saw revenues increase only 4.8 percent. Nonetheless, the power of the market itself enabled Louisville, West Virginia, Rutgers, and even South Florida to boast top-20 programs by 2007, able to compete for the best high school players by promising the TV and bowl exposure that recruits with NFL dreams expect....

The BCS instantly became powerful both as a symbol of the division between the upper and lower regions of Division I-A and as a new instrument for maintaining that boundary. Though purporting to be a system for naming a national champion in the absence of a playoff tournament, the BCS more importantly provided a mechanism for divvying up hugely inflated bowl revenues in this new college football world.... With the BCS in 1998, television took greater control of college football. [ABC's] offer of $500 million for the four BCS bowls over seven years, with average payouts initially of about $12 million per team, elevated the four major bowls above the lesser bowls more dramatically than ever before and made the pursuit of a BCS bowl bid an obsession throughout Division I-A.

... [O]ver the first six years of the BCS (1998–2003), the six major conferences took in 93 percent of total BCS revenue and 89 percent of all bowl revenue, while the five mid-majors (Conference USA, Mountain West, Western Athletic, Mid-American, and Big West-Sun Belt) claimed just 4 percent from the BCS....

... [T]otal net bowl revenue ... for the six BCS conferences in 2007–2008 was $126 million, or $21 million per conference....

The disparate impact of the BCS is huge.... Within the SEC, a $1 million guaranteed BCS payout was 1.7 percent of Georgia's $59.5 million in football revenue in 2006–2007 but 8.3 percent of Mississippi State's $12.1 million.... Year to year, the top teams earning BCS bowl berths come predominantly from a fairly small set of perennial superpowers that earn their rewards by having the strongest football teams.... The distorting impact of the BCS lies elsewhere—not just in the separation of non-BCS from BCS schools but also in the guaranteed BCS payout to the fifty-seven or fifty-eight schools from BCS conferences that do not go to a BCS bowl in any given year.... The stakes, along with the distorting consequences, were raised in November 2008, when ESPN outbid Fox to televise the BCS bowls beginning in 2011....

Big-Time College Football in the Twenty-First Century

Because of the controversies generated over its method for selecting bowl participants and its success or failure in determining an unambiguous national champion, the BCS is just the most visible part of the intensified commercializing of big-time college football since the 1990s, which also includes the proliferation of televised contests, corporate branding of stadiums and bowl games, institutional contracts with soft drink and shoe companies, huge expansion in the marketing of team logo merchandise, lavish facilities to lure recruits to campus, and stadiums with luxury suites and seat licenses for the privilege of buying season tickets. Surprisingly, despite these ubiquitous signs of increasing commercialization, the overall economic growth of college athletics and college football actually slowed from the 1980s to the early 2000s.... From 1969 through 1981, the average football revenue (for all teams in whatever was equivalent to Division I-A at the time) increased at an average annual rate of 7.1 percent. From 1981 through 1993, the rate was 12.3 percent; from 1993 through 2003, it was 8.0 percent.

The NCAA's most recent report, for 2004–2006, used median rather than average revenues to eliminate the skewing by one-time large gifts from alumni and boosters—Oklahoma State's single gift of $240 million in 2006, for example—and to help university administrators see more clearly their institution's relative position.... The growth of the *median* revenue ... from 2004 to 2005 was 8.7 percent (from $9.2 million to $10 million); and from 2005 to 2006 ($11.6 million), it was 16 percent. The NCAA also refined the reporting methods by distinguishing revenues "generated" by the athletic department from those "allocated" by the state or the institution (in student fees, direct subsidy, or indirect support for maintenance and salaries). The median *generated* football revenue in 2006 was $10.6 million, up from $9.8 million in 2005 and $8.3 million in 2004.

However growth is measured, the unevenness among institutions is what's most significant.... In 2006 half of the 119 teams in the FBS generated less than

$10.6 million in revenue each. The other half generated revenues ranging from $10.6 million to $63.7 million.... In 2006, 30 percent of FBS football programs generated less than $3.7 million in revenues. The ... top 20 percent, between $23.2 million and $63.7 million.

... Sixty-one of sixty-six BCS teams claimed a profit on football, along with eighteen non-BCS teams. Forty-six BCS and twenty-three non-BCS schools claimed to make money on athletics overall.... [W]ithout institutional subsidies, somewhere between two and four dozen athletic departments actually break even or make a profit in any given year. (Sixteen athletic departments operated in the black in all three years....) The other 100 programs had overall athletics deficits in 2006 averaging $8.9 million, and athletic expenses have increased at a higher rate than revenues. In short, no non-BCS school breaks even on athletics; most lose money on football as well. Most BCS schools make money on football, but less than a third of them make enough to cover the overall athletics budget.

Within the BCS, after Texas and Notre Dame at the top, the next nine BCS schools with the largest football profits are from either the SEC(six) or the Big Ten (three), while seven of the nine at the bottom are from the Big East (four) or the ACC (three).... The wider spreads within the wealthiest conferences created more distinct classes. Big Ten football was led in 2006 by Michigan, with a profit of $36.2 million, followed by Penn State ($29.4 million) and Ohio State ($26.6 million) ... [with] Indiana ($6.9 million) and Northwestern ($4.4 million) on the BCS equivalent of food stamps.

... [T]he gaps between major conferences are widening for reasons unrelated to the BCS. In 2007 the Big Ten launched its own TV network (for broadcasting all sports, not just football), which began with payments of about $6 million a year to each school on top of the $9.3 million from CBS and ESPN. The SEC ... decided in August 2008, to renew its contracts with current TV partners CBS and ESPN. First CBS agreed to increase its payments from $30 million a year to an average of $55 million over fifteen years.... Then ESPN, currently paying about $21 million, took the SEC's remaining games ... for all sports ... for a jaw-dropping $2.25 billion over fifteen years, an average of $150 million a year.... Each SEC school is now guaranteed an average of $17 million a year, beginning in 2011.

... [B]ig-time college football does not depend on television nearly to the extent that the National Football League does (where TV provides $3.7 billion out of roughly $7 billion in total revenue).... [T]icket sales account for 28 percent of generated revenues in athletics overall, while 30 percent comes from alumni and booster contributions. NCAA and conference distributions (which include television and BCS payouts) amount to 17 percent....

Ultimately, the size of the stadium and the demand for tickets determine a football program's financial prospects.... [F]or the 1997 season (pre-BCS), ticket sales amounted to $18.1 million out of $44.2 million of total revenues at Michigan (41 percent), with television and bowl games together contributing less than $10 million.... $15.7 million of Penn State's $25.4 million in football revenue in 1999 (62 percent) came from ticket sales. With donations from boosters for the right to buy tickets bringing in an additional $80.8 million, $24.5 million out of $33.2 million (nearly 77 percent) in football-related revenue was attributable to stadium seating ... when Beaver Stadium held a mere 94,000. With its expansion to more than 100,000, Penn State joined Michigan, Ohio State, and Tennessee in college football's most exclusive neighborhood....

Filling it is the key. It's not just the ... seats ... but also the dollars per seat ... premium pricing for some and the seat licenses or mandatory booster contributions for others. A required donation of $1,000 to buy a $200 season ticket increases gate receipts by a factor of five. Skyboxes or luxury suites—the most anomalous feature of all the strange aspects of education-based college football—add even more.... [A] survey of fund-raising for athletics in 2007–2008 ... found Texas at the top with $16.9 million in gifts for luxury suites (along with $17.6 million for priority seating).... What makes it strange are college football's nonprofit status and claim to a primarily educational purpose.

The Big Ten Network and the SEC's new TV contracts have made the schools at or near the bottom of those conferences less dependent on ticket and seating revenues than the low-revenue programs elsewhere in the BCS. For schools outside the BCS, BCS bowls continue to be the mythical El Dorado, fabled sources of gold that turn out to be fantasies.... So ... the more a program needs bowl and TV revenue today, the less likely it is to get it....

Opportunity, Entitlement, and Exploitation

A New Contract for Coaches

... In the new order that emerged in the 1970s, ... football coaches became free agents in a competitive market. The higher-ed community uttered a collective gasp in 1982 when Texas A&M made Jackie Sherrill the highest-paid university employee in the country by stealing him from Pittsburgh for more than $1.7 million over six years—more than any president, chancellor, or medical-school dean and more than twice the reported $125,000 salary of Michigan's Bo Schembechler, the highest-paid coach in the Big Ten....

A ripple effect was inevitable. When universities and conferences won the right to negotiate their own television contracts in 1984, and the competition for market share intensified, coaches were in position to cash in. By 1986, ... $150,000 had become the norm at the big football schools, while top coaches were now matching Sherrill's $300,000....

By 2001, $1 million was entry level for the upper echelon of college football coaches. [much of which came from media and clothing deals],with twenty-two millionaires [including] ... five each from the SEC and the Big 12.... Spurrier, Bowden, and Oklahoma's Bob Stoops all topped $2 million.... In 2006 ... nine coaches made over $2 million, led by Stoops at $3,450,000 ... and the average salary in Division I-A was $950,000.... [In the] 2008 season ... USC's Pete Carroll [was] ahead of everyone at $4.4 million....

A football coach *always* acts in the name of the university. A coach has no marketable identity except as the head of the university's football team. The … outside income … properly belongs to the university.… The huge sums from Nike and other apparel companies are particularly bizarre in this regard. Why should the coach, not the university, be paid for having the players wear a certain brand of shoes and uniforms?

A New Contract for Athletes, Too

The ripple effect of rising coaches' salaries has not contaminated the purity of the "student-athlete." Under the new contractual model implicitly established in 1973, coaches were to promote the university's image through winning teams. Their players' implied [one-year] contract stipulated an education in return for their athletic endeavors. As football then became a full-time, year-round occupation for the players, with the same low chance of a career in the NFL but with less opportunity to be fully engaged students, the logic of the contractual relationship between athletes and universities became increasingly distorted by assumptions persisting from a vanished era.… [A] scholarship still pays for tuition, fees, board and room, and a little extra for incidentals. In a realignment of the ancient contradiction, as college football became increasingly a commercial enterprise for coaches, it remained an extracurricular activity for players.

In 1973, along with instituting the one-year grants, the NCAA limited the total number of football scholarships to 105. That number was dropped to 95 in 1978 and to 85 in 1994, … as a cost cutting measure.…

Out of the upheavals of the late 1960s, coaches became managers of football teams, not father figures or professors of football and its lessons for life, while players became athletes with annual, renewable contracts who are promised an education in exchange for their athletic services but with major constraints on attaining it.… Economist Richard Sheehan calculated the "implicit compensation" of football players in Division I in the mid-1990s as an hourly wage … for an average of $8.99.… Here in cold numbers we see the bizarre asymmetry of college coaches making CEO salaries while their players earn less than groundskeepers and secretaries in the front office.

The new contractual model treated the players as professionals but without professionals' compensation or rights. It gave the coach complete power to set the terms of the contract, leaving the players only with a choice of whether to accept or reject it.…

… A high school athlete could sign with any college in the country, and he could "play out his option"—transfer to another school—though only by sitting out for a season.… College athletes, … with no bargaining unit or organization to plead their case, have remained wholly subject to the control of their athletic departments and the NCAA.

Entitled or Exploited?

Dishonest football programs are another old story. What was new in the 1980s was the open cynicism of many athletes, eviden[t] … in the aftermath of the conviction of sports agents Norby Walters and Lloyd Bloom in 1989 for fraud and racketeering. Between 1981 and 1987, Walters and Bloom signed agreements with fifty football players whose eligibility had not expired, from almost three dozen schools, including many of the top programs in the country.... Walters and Bloom were convicted of defrauding the universities because, as paid professionals, the players they signed were no longer entitled to the scholarship payments they continued to receive ..., Walters and Bloom conducted a sleazy operation, but a sound argument could be made that, as long as universities insisted on treating students as athletes, the athletes had the right to protect their athletic interests by signing with agents. Many of the young men playing college football themselves figured this out. A few months after the verdict, in a survey of 1,182 current or former NFL players conducted by Allen Sack, a third of the players admitted receiving illicit payments while in college, ranging from "money handshakes" (alumni slipping them a few bucks after a game) to $80,000 over a college career. More telling, 53 percent of the respondents—72 percent of the African Americans—"saw nothing wrong with the practice...."

Entitlement and Thuggery

The idea that star athletes in big-time football programs are exploited might seem laughable to fellow students who resent their lavish facilities and special treatment.... When the NCAA at its "reform convention" in 1991 abolished athletic dorms, it eliminated the most conspicuous symbol of athletic extravagance on many campuses, particularly in the South ... such as the so-called Bryant Hilton (Paul W. Bryant Hall) at Alabama and Bud House (Bud Wilkinson House) at Oklahoma.... The rash of felonies at Bud House in the late 1980s notwithstanding, the defenders of jock dorms claimed that players bonded and coaches could monitor their behavior and academic progress more effectively when athletes were housed together. Critics argued that isolating football players from the rest of the student body was bad for the athletes.

The NCAA had tried to limit the luxury of athletic dorms several years earlier, but by the time it abolished the dorms altogether ... in 1996, new "recruiting showpieces" had already emerged ... as "mammoth training complexes, combination indoor practice facilities and weight rooms situated a few steps from the dorms, allowing football players to exist in a sort of hermetic theme park." Georgia's Dawg Mahal (Butts-Mehre Heritage Hall) and Tennessee's Neyland-Thompson Sports Center set the standard in the late 1980s, soon to be rivaled by other football programs competing for the best high school players.... No country club or Caribbean resort could have been more lavish....

... What's relatively new is the bizarre disparity between such extravagance for the care and feeding of football players and their under compensation relative to the revenues they generate.

What's provided for athletes is, in some ways, what's used to entice all students to the modern university—trendy food courts, country-club quality fitness facilities, recreation centers—only more exclusive and on a grander scale. Football players at the elite level today experience a sort of lavish servitude, and their status as privileged peons—or is it indentured celebrities?—can have some unsavory consequences. Again the story is not altogether new ... but conditions have grown more extreme. An element of conscious privilege, of athletes believing themselves not bound by the rules that govern the rest of society, seems to lie behind much of the boorish and even criminal behavior that has become a distressingly frequent feature of the college sports news.... [E]ither the national media simply began to pay more attention or the degree and scale of misbehavior rose sharply in the late 1980s.

Miami was the first to win notoriety as a football team out of control. with several misdemeanor arrests, a riot in the football dorm, and forty-seven players making $8,346 worth of phone calls through a stolen access number. Miami players reveled in their outlaw image.... *Sports Illustrated* exposed Miami's chief rivals for college football's All-Criminal title. In 1989, under the headline "Oklahoma: A Sordid Story: How Barry Switzer's Sooners Terrorized Their Campus," the cover featured quarterback Charles Thompson in handcuffs after his arrest for selling cocaine. Three of Thompson's teammates had recently been arraigned for gang-raping a woman in the football dorm; another had shot a teammate after an argument. Oklahoma's problems, according to *Sports Illustrated,* began with head coach Barry Switzer, who ran his program like a "loose ship."

A companion story described a Colorado football team from which two dozen players over the past three years had been "arrested, for everything from trespassing to serial rape." Eighteen members from the 1987 squad alone had been arrested and sixty-five "contacted" by police....

... [S]ports sections began including brief wire-service reports under headings on the order of "The Police Blotter."...

... The *New York Times* reported in 1990 ... that athletes were disproportionately involved in rapes and other sexual assaults, and that they were being shielded by authorities—the incidents were often not reported or were excused (as group sex, for example, rather than gang rape), with the intoxicated female victims receiving the blame. The *Boston Globe*'s "College Sports: Out of Bounds" series reported essentially the same state of affairs: athletes receiving more lenient treatment than nonathletes charged with similar offenses (as well as athletic directors not even reporting athletes' failed drug tests to their university presidents).... In the American heartland, at a Nebraska football program run by a famously straight-arrow coach (Tom Osborne), [Lawrence] Phillips and [Christian] Peter went nearly unpunished, despite their convictions for sexual assault, while the athletic department rescinded the scholarship of one of Phillips's victims, a member of the women's basketball team....

... Over the 1990s, a general sense of college football players' criminality settled into public consciousness. The harshest critics contended that so-called student-athletes were acculturated in thuggery and that big-time football programs fostered "rape cultures."

Something was clearly askew in big-time college football....

The NFL as Big Business

MICHAEL ORIARD

The New NFL

In 1989, when Paul Tagliabue replaced Pete Rozelle, the league took in $975 million in revenue and the average franchise was worth about $100 million. The most recent figures ... in 2006 are $6.2 billion and $898 million.... [T]he increase in franchise value since 1998 was 11 times the growth of the S&P 500 over that same period. The "new NFL" that emerged in the 1990s had three cornerstones: labor peace, television contracts, and stadium revenue. Labor peace arrived in 1993 after more than five years of litigation following the collapse of the 1987 strike. Ever-richer television contracts arrived with seeming inevitability, as the NFL always managed to have fewer TV packages than networks to bid for them. And the bounty to be extracted from stadium leases and local marketing was a gift to the NFL from its two "rogue" owners. Al Davis won for every owner the right to move his franchise for a better deal or extort generous stadium financing from the local community to keep him at home. Jerry Jones then showed everyone how to make a stadium pay.

Shrewdness, luck, and unintended consequences have all played a part in the new NFL's prosperity. Davis's fellow owners fought him in court until they lost completely, then they capitalized on the franchise free agency that he won for them all. Tagliabue understood the entertainment business and stadium economics far better than Rozelle, as well as the necessity of labor peace. Tagliabue also managed to hold together an increasingly contentious group of owners.... And television revenues soared, even as ratings slid.... The appearance first of cable and ESPN, then of the new Fox Network, guaranteed competitive bidding for NFL rights, but Tagliabue and the NFL helped themselves maintain their leverage by forming their own network as well.

... In the new NFL, ... football became less completely a "sport" and more a "brand" and entertainment "product" to be moved by marketing men (and women, too).... This chapter will consider the economic foundation of the new NFL.

Labor Peace at Last

In January 1989, as the NFLPA's [NFL Players Association] suit worked its way through the judicial system, and realizing that free agency based on first refusal and compensation was not working, the owners unilaterally imposed so-called Plan B free agency. Each club could now "protect" (that is, restrict) 37 players each season, allowing the rest to become free agents.... Restricted players did see their salaries rise, as free agent signings altered the basic salary structure, but not nearly to the level that they could have negotiated if they were free. Under four years of Plan B, just three "protected" players received offers from other teams. But Plan B backfired on the owners. It proved to the players that free agency could work for stars and journeymen alike, if only it were not restricted.

[I]n November 1989, the NFLPA by decertifying itself as a union gave up its right to sue the NFL on its own behalf, but it now could support individual players' anti-trust suits. In April 1990, the NFLPA backed a new lawsuit ... in the name of New York Jets running back Freeman McNeil and seven others.... This was the beginning of the end of NFL owners' absolute control over professional football.

... The ... McNeil case ... ended with a jury deciding ... that Plan B violated antitrust law. This ... forced the restructuring of the NFL. The players' victory was not quite complete, however. The jury ruled Plan B too restrictive but did not rule out restrictions altogether, if collectively bargained....

... The two groups returned to the bargaining table in November 1992 and worked out a system of free agency.... [T]he NFLPA became certified again as a collective bargaining unit and negotiated a labor agreement over the spring of 1993. The National Basketball Association provided the model: free agency and a guaranteed percentage of gross revenue, but with the NFL's owner-friendly variations—a supposedly "hard" salary cap ... and nonguaranteed contracts.... Under the terms of the agreement, all players became unrestricted free agents after five years. Restricted free agency was possible after three or four years, with the clubs holding the right of first refusal....

Winners and Winners

On the day in 1993 that the NFLPA and the Management Council agreed on the free-agency plan, [NFLPA executive director] Gene Upshaw exulted, "For the first time, we're the partners of the owners." Tagliabue began conferring regularly with Upshaw as a partner in all matters affecting the players.

Free agency also meant millions of dollars ..., whether or not players changed teams or re-signed with their own. Players who had been collectively paid about 30 percent of league revenues in 1998 were now guaranteed twice as much of a much larger pot. In the first round of signings, the average salary of unrestricted free agents more than doubled, from $517,000 to $1.044 million. Restricted free agents did even better, seeing their average salary leap from $293,000 to $780,000. ... A defensive end, Reggie White, came out on top of the initial free-agent signing frenzy with a four-year, $17 million contract.... With a guaranteed percentage of most revenues, players' salaries were now driven by the size of the television contracts.... [I]ncremental average increases followed, ... then a 35 percent leap in 2008 with the signing of new TV contracts...

... The owners had been convinced in 1974 that freedom for the players would mean anarchy for the league.... Instead, labor peace stabilized costs for player salaries and benefits.... [T]he value of an NFL franchise could increase from $140 million in 1993 (for the expansion Carolina Panthers and Jacksonville Jaguars) to $700 million in 1999 (for the Houston Texans). According to the

Minnesota Vikings' owner, Red McCombs, the labor agreement meant as much as the television contract to the value of his franchise.

... A fixed percentage of most of these revenues certainly made the players collectively richer ... but in no way at the expense of the owners. Figures made public during one of A1 Davis's many lawsuits against the NFL revealed that the clubs in 1999 averaged $11.6 million in profit. [Plus] hidden tax benefits.... Alfred Lerner wrote off half the $530 million purchase price for the Browns on his personal income taxes.

The absence of the guaranteed contracts enjoyed by NBA and Major League Baseball players seems to make NFL players relatively less fortunate. [B]etween 1995 and 2002, only about 40 players each season had some guaranteed base salary; ... overwhelmingly ... only signing bonuses were guaranteed.... Because football is less affected by individuals, few NFL players have the clout to command a guaranteed salary....

For both the NFL and the NFLPA as institutions, free agency plus salary cap has been an unalloyed blessing.... Players and owners alike benefit from the public perception of harmonious relations between players and owners, instead of the unseemly spectacle of millionaires fighting billionaires for yet more money. For the NFLPA, the agreement has meant a full partnership in running the business of professional football. For the NFL, the new structure has created long-term stability as well as something close to true parity. With rosters changing each season through free-agent signings, no team (except for the New England Patriots in recent years) can remain dominant for long. Twenty different teams, nearly two-thirds of the NFL, played in the Super Bowl over the 14 seasons following the 1993 agreement....While shared revenues and the salary cap have guaranteed profits for any competently managed franchise, the cap and free agency have also made it extremely difficult to sustain excellence on the field. ... The parity loved by the league has been hard on traditionally well-run clubs.... Once players achieve success, they are easily lost to free agency or become too costly to retain....

For the players, now ... every player now has a shot at free agency after four years, but half of the players in the NFL last fewer than three seasons. In certain fundamental ways, both free agency and the resulting economic disparity among players have altered the meaning of "team...."

The collective benefits enjoyed by all players rose sharply with the 1993 agreement and its guaranteed percentage of revenues. At the same time, free agency separated football players into more distinct economic classes. Roughly 20 percent of the players' guaranteed revenue goes to shared benefits, the remaining 80 percent to individually negotiated contracts.... In 2001 ..., there were 493 millionaires in the NFL ..., earning an average of $2.86 million.... [T]he remaining 1,236 players ... averaged a little over $400,000. In 2005, when the average salary was just under $1.4 million, the median salary was $569,000—a lot of money for everyone, but a whole lot more for some....

... While free agency seems to mostly benefit stars, those designated "franchise" or "transition" players—not allowed to change teams, but compensated at the level of their highest-paid peers—can be particularly frustrated by their inability to capitalize on free-market bidding. The highest-salaried players sometimes become the most vulnerable to being released in order to create room under the salary cap for new free-agent signings.... No club is forced to release any highly paid player whom it wants to keep; players can renegotiate lower salaries; many of those released have gone on to sign with other teams for less money. The hard, cold logic of the market rules. Running backs have become particularly vulnerable in the market-driven football world.... In 2005 running backs ... earned less than offensive tackles, cornerbacks, and defensive ends ... (Left tackles' becoming the highest paid players next to quarterbacks....)

Under the 1993 agreement, the Players Association became, in effect, an adversarial partner in running the NFL: collaborating when possible, pushing for players' rights and financial interests when necessary, though not to the detriment of the league's overall financial stability and not on behalf of the self-interest of every individual player. Some critics have charged that Upshaw has been "much closer to the NFL commissioner than a union boss ought to be."

... [W]hether by necessity or conviction, Upshaw collaborated with Tagliabue in assuring a stable and prosperous NFL into the foreseeable future, to the benefit of future as well as current players, and of owners and fans, too.

... The 2002 collective bargaining agreement, set to expire after the 2007 season, had built-in incentives to settle: for the owners, the salary cap would disappear in the last year of the agreement; for the players, the years required for unrestricted free agency would be extended from four to six. But extending the collective bargaining agreement became entangled with a demand from the less-prosperous clubs for greater revenue sharing among the owners. As negotiations dragged on into 2006, ... Upshaw threatened to decertify the union again.... [T]he two sides seemed locked in ... "a high-stakes game of chicken." Finally, on March 8 ..., the owners agreed to shift about $150 million a year from the 15 wealthiest franchises to the less profitable ones and to share [eventually] 60 percent of all revenues with the players over the six years of the agreement.... Upshaw and the NFLPA were clear winners.... Labor peace now extended through 2011....

Stadium Games

The increasing disparity in club revenue and the shrinking of the players' share came from factors unforeseen in 1993 [when] the NFL still derived most of its income from television and ticket sales, the revenues shared among owners and, as stipulated in the new labor agreement, with players. The tremendous growth after 1993 of unshared local revenues—from luxury boxes, club seats, seat licenses, naming rights, sponsorships, and local advertising—created a pool of funds outside the labor agreement. Much of it went into huge signing bonuses that circumvented the salary cap, creating an advantage for wealthier clubs and widening the gap between stars and ordinary players. It also threatened to undermine the "capitalistic socialism" on which the NFL had thrived since the first national television contract in 1962.

Television made every NFL owner rich in the 1990s.... The free agency that Davis won for owners—the right to move their franchises and thus to extort sweetheart stadium deals from cities eager for "major league" status—had momentous financial consequences for the league unforeseen in 1982. Jones … then showed his fellow owners the enormous profits to be made from their own stadiums.…

Cowboy Capitalism

When Jones acquired the Dallas Cowboys along with Texas Stadium in February 1989 for a reported $140 million, the Cowboys had just completed … the worst record in the NFL.… Jones had the Cowboys back in the Super Bowl by 1993, and twice more in 1994 and 1996, but his financial impact on the rest of the league had greater consequences. As a former oil wildcatter who leveraged his energy company to buy the Cowboys, Jones would not settle for just his share of the common revenue.…

The football-only … stadiums built by the Cowboys and Kansas City Chiefs in the early 1970s had been the jewels of the league and, with their luxury suites, the envy of other owners. [B]ut no one understood their financial potential until Jones … turned Texas Stadium into a playground for wealthy Texans, doubling the price of tickets, replacing 2,500 ordinary seats with 100 more luxury suites (on top of the present 289), and instituting seat licenses of up to $15,000.… Jones's revenue from Texas Stadium went from $700,000 in 1992 to $30 million in 1993, when the Cowboys' gross revenue of $92.9 million exceeded the nearest NFL rival's by more than $18 million. Suddenly, every owner wanted a new stadium with all the trimmings.…

Let's Make a Deal

… 1993 was a pivotal year in the NFL's transformation.… The collective bargaining agreement in the spring ended a quarter-century of labor strife and guaranteed several years of stable player costs. In the fall, the league announced expansion franchises for Charlotte and Jacksonville at a cost of $140 million each—up … from the $16 million paid by Seattle and Tampa in 1976. The inflated franchise price reflected the successively richer TV contracts, the latest of which, in 1990, bumped average annual revenues from $17 million to $32 million per club. It also reflected a new economic reality in the NFL, the enormous profits possible from new stadiums, now that owners had the leverage to exploit them. Existing franchises that sold for well under $100 million in the 1980s were now worth twice as much or more, attracting … the "new breed of debt-laden, swashbuckling owner" in the mold of Jerry Jones.… The NFL's most structurally tumultuous year followed in 1995.… St. Louis lured the Los Angeles Rams with a package of stunning financial inducements, the Raiders returned to Oakland after 13 frustrating years in Los Angeles, … Art Modell (a pillar of the NFL establishment) announced he was uprooting the Browns from Cleveland, and Bud Adams declared that the Houston Oilers would relocate to Nashville. Modell['s] … abandonment of Cleveland made him the most vilified sports owner since Walter O'Malley.…

The professional sports league famous for its stability, and for its cooperative sportsmen-owners, was suddenly in chaos, and chaos had never been so profitable. Several of the league's worst-managed franchises instantly solved their financial problems by moving to new cities for better stadium deals. Los Angeles, the nation's number-two television market, went in one year from having two NFL teams to having none. With outrage in Cleveland so great, Tagliabue promptly promised the city an expansion franchise, which it awarded to Al Lerner in 1998.... This created a 31-team league in need of a thirty-second team.... [T]he NFL in 1999 awarded a franchise for the Houston Texans to Robert McNair for $700 million.... Owners in Cincinnati, Tampa Bay, Arizona, and Seattle all threatened to move, but stayed put after extracting an agreement on a new stadium.

Stadiums were the heart of the new NFL. Television remained the single most important source of revenue, but even as rights fees soared ... from an average of $900 million per year from 1990 through 1993 ..., to $2.2 billion from 1998 through 2005—nontelevision revenue increased even more. In 2003, when the television contracts provided $2.6 billion out of gross revenues of $5.3 billion, TV slipped under 50 percent for the first time since 1977. (The most recent television contracts, beginning in 2006, tipped the balance back to TV revenue.) Television continued to be the largest single pot of money ..., but stadiums became the new economic engine driving the NFL into the financial stratosphere.

Relocation enabled the worst-managed franchises (the Baltimore Colts, St. Louis Cardinals, and Los Angeles Rams) to become highly profitable. Threat of relocation, credible because the NFL was nearly powerless to prevent it, enabled prosperous franchises to become tremendously more profitable. Between 1992 and 2006, 18 teams moved into new stadiums ... [which] meant immediate increases in revenue ranging ... with most clubs seeing gains between 30 and 40 percent.... An additional eight stadiums underwent major renovations, some with comparable impact. (Green Bay's remodeled stadium meant a 36 percent increase in revenue within two years). In 2006, when the Arizona Cardinals moved into their $455.7 million air-conditioned stadium ($310 million paid by the community and state)—with 88 suites going for $75,000 to $125,000 ... (over 90 percent sold), 7,501 club seats at $100—$25 each (100 percent sold), and naming rights purchased by an online university (!) for $154.5 million over 20 years—they immediately began looking on paper like one of the NFL's well-run clubs....

... The club took the profits while the community paid the bills.... Invesco Field cost Denver owner Pat Bowlen $100 million and taxpayers $301 million. The Cincinnati Bengals made out even better: the entire $452 million price tag for Paul Brown Stadium was paid for through an increased sales tax.... *Sports Business Journal* ... reported that for nine new NFL stadiums built between 2000 and 2006, the public contributed $2.27 billion out of $4.24 billion....

Cities cut such deals with NFL owners despite evidence from economists ... that sports stadium were poor economic investments. Communities courted or clung to NFL franchises through lavish public giveaways for the sake of "intangibles," the pride, recognition and "big league" feel that comes from having a team, or for what sociologists Kevin Delaney and Rick Eckstein have called "community self-esteem" and "community collective conscience" (shared values, beliefs, and experiences)....

This calculus has not worked for the NFL in New York and Los Angeles, where civic pride does not depend on a football team, local politicians have more pressing priorities for public investment, and citizens have alternatives for spending their leisure time and money.... Los Angeles simply did not need the NFL as much as the NFL needed Los Angeles, the second-largest TV market....

The threat of losing big-city teams and their television markets ... to the lure of stadium wealth in smaller markets (like Hartford, CT) led to the NFL's G-3 program in 1999, under which clubs annually contributed $1 million each to a common fund for loans to build or renovate stadiums.... A $150 million subsidy through the G-3 program saved the Patriots for Boston, and Boston for the NFL....

[A]s the state surpluses of the 1990s gave way to tight budgets and reduced spending on ... public needs, battles over subsidies of sports franchises intensified.... Yet Arlington, Texas, after defeating referendums for public transit and an urban development project, voted in 2004 to pay half the cost of a new $ 650 million home for the Dallas Cowboys. After a $76.5 million "loan" through the G-3 program and a naming-rights agreement, the fans, not Jerry Jones, would pay the rest through a ticket surcharge and personal seat licenses assessed to season ticket holders.... [T]he price tag for the 80,000-seat stadium was $1 billion and included 200 field-level and upper-level suites, each of them leasing for more than $350,000 annually—the most expensive in the NFL....

Games in publicly financed stadiums ..., are unaffordable for much of the public. [A] family of four in 2005 had to spend from $229.49 (in Buffalo) to $477.47 (in Foxboro) to attend a game.... Tickets alone for premium seats ... ran as high as $566.67 ... for the Patriots.... The NFL still needs ordinary fans from all economic classes to maintain network TV ratings, ... and buy sponsors' NFL-themed merchandise, but new stadiums increasingly resemble all-inclusive resorts where the rich and well connected can party by themselves....

An NFL for Billionaires

In 2003 the Washington Redskins became the NFL's first billion-dollar franchise. The average franchise was worth $733 million, more than three-and-a-half times the $205 million average in 1996 and almost six times the $125 million average in 1991.... Television made every franchise hugely profitable. Even the Arizona Cardinals made a profit in 2003, despite averaging barely 36,000 fans at home (... 17,500 below the next-lowest team). But local revenues created the widening disparity from top to bottom. League wide stadium revenue increased from less than $50 million 1986 to $576 million by 2002, but it was distributed very unevenly. Through the mid-1990s all but a handful of teams made close to the league's average revenue.... The number of luxury suites in NFL stadiums in 2003 averaged 143 but ranged from 68 (Arizona) to 381 (Dallas). The number of club seats averaged a little over 7,000 ..., generating revenue of up to $33 million (Washington). Seventeen teams received annual fees for stadium naming rights ranging from $620,000 (Jacksonville) to $10 million (Houston). The lack of club seats did not prevent Dallas from holding its position as the NFL's second-richest franchise (slipping to third, behind New England, in 2006), but it undoubtedly contributed to Jerry Jones's belief that he needed a new stadium to keep up with the potentially richer Joneses.

The billion-dollar Redskins provided the model for making money in the new NFL. When Daniel Snyder purchased the team for $800 million in 1999, he also acquired a stadium (and its debt). The Redskins were already the NFL's second most valuable franchise (behind Dallas) when Snyder bought it, with revenue in 1998 of $141.1 million, $39 million of that derived from his stadium (compared to the $93.5 million from TV rights, NFL Properties, and the shared portion of gate receipts that every team received). Snyder increased his revenue to $176 million in his first season by selling stadium naming rights to Federal Express for $207 million over 27 years; quintupling his marketing revenue through sponsorships with US Airways, Bell Atlantic, Amtrak, and Mobil; selling 3,000 additional club seats, leasing another dozen luxury suites, and adding 4,000 seats.... By 2004 Snyder had raised his revenue to $287 million, $100 million or more above 19 teams.

... As the 2006 season opened, Forbes pegged the Redskins' value at more than $1.4 billion. *Forbes* attributed just 39 percent of that value to the revenues shared among all NFL clubs, with the Redskins' market, stadium, and brand management accounting for the other 61 percent. The average for the league was almost exactly the reverse: 60 percent form shared revenues, and 40 percent from market and marketing. At the very bottom of the NFL, the Arizona Cardinals, [who] derived a full 80 percent of their franchise value from shared revenues, [were] worth almost $800 million....

To compete in the new NFL, a sweet stadium deal was essential ... to pay down debt and to sign free agents. The 16 new owners who joined the NFL since 1993 [were] already rich and ready to take on huge debts for the chance to become greatly richer.... [I]n 2006, the NFL had 11 billionaire owners.

... Successive television contracts were chiefly responsible for the hugely appreciated values of NFL franchises, but finding additional sources of revenue from sponsorships, premium seating, stadium advertising, and naming rights had become not an option but a necessity....

After debt service, what remained could be spent in the free-agent market. Because the rules of the salary cap allowed signing bonuses to be paid up front, but amortized over the life of the contract fore cap purposes, levels of cash flow created competitive advantages and disadvantages in the NFL for the first time.... Sportswriters and NFL rivals complained that Jones "bought the Super Bowl" that season by spending $61.9 million in salaries and bonuses when the salary cap was $37.1 million....

TV and "Intangibles"

Richer or poorer, all NFL clubs made money because of television. The TV contracts that ran from 1998 through 2005 totaled nearly $18 billion, roughly half of the league's total revenue. [H]owever, ... ABC, CBS, and Fox lost as much as $2 billion on NFL football over that period.... The state of televised football at the turn of the twenty-first century was epitomized by the average of $550 million per year paid by ABC for Monday Night Football. [Back] in 1981, when the rights cost $46 million, Monday Night Football ranked twelfth among all shows in prime time.... Over the next 16 seasons, as rights fees climbed to $230 million, ... *Monday Night Football*'s prime-time rank climbed as high as number 4 among all network programs.... Monday Night Football ... remained in the top 10 for ... [sixteen] consecutive year[s].

... Ratings declined for NFL games on all of the networks. After peaking in 1981 at roughly 17 for three networks combined ... ratings fell ... to 10.2 by 2005. Yet sports in general and NFL football in particular still offered the best opportunity for advertisers to reach a general audience (in 2005, all of the top ten network sportscasts were NFL games, and 22 of the top 25)....

Major League Franchises, Ballparks, and Public Policy, 1953–2012

STEVEN A. RIESS

Today the relationship between urban politics and sports is different than in the early twentieth century when politicians and their close friends often owned baseball teams. Beginning in the 1950s, politicians, especially in cities without professional sports teams, made special efforts to attract or keep major league franchises that included subsidizing ball fields and indoor arenas. Politicians went after a sports franchise just like they would industry and businesses that would improve the community's tax base and quality of life. Keeping a franchise or bringing in a new team enhanced a mayor's personal image, demonstrated his community spirit, and made points for him with urban boosters, contractors, the construction trades, and the tourist industry. On the other hand, a politician who opposed expensive new parks and arenas ran the risk of being labeled an unprogressive killjoy who let a beloved team leave town or failed to bring in a much desired sports franchise. These politicians were invariably backed by powerful local economic elites who comprised a "political regime" who were vigorous advocates of such big-ticket items as stadiums and convention centers that benefit banks, real estate development and tourism. Mayors and other local officials were also under a lot of pressure from clout heavy franchise owners, either fabulously wealthy individuals like Atlanta's Ted Turner, or corporations like the *Chicago Tribune,* Anheuser-Busch, and Disney.

Political scientist Charles Euchner argues that "building stadiums and courting sport franchises have become major parts of city agenda as the emphasis of urban leaders has shifted from redistribution to development." Euchner points

From Steven A. Riess, "Historical Perspectives on Sports and Public Policy." In Wilbur C. Rich, ed. *The Economics and Politics of Sports Facilities* (Westport, CT: Quorum Books, 2000), 13–52.

out that once cities began to stress sports franchises as vehicles for economic development, "cutthroat competition among cities for teams was inevitable" since there were few teams and lots of cities to go around.

Local regimes hoped that by drawing a major league team to their town, they would be adding a valuable new asset that was an economic stimulant that enhanced the city's future development and prestige. Boosters believed that the presence of sports teams could help build feelings of community, promote economic development, development, raise revenue, entertain local residents, encourage tourism, and even support law and order. In the late 1960s, journalists frequently claimed that exciting pennant races in St. Louis in 1967 and Detroit in 1968 curbed summer riots, and attributed Mayor John Lindsay's reelection in 1969 to the Miracle Mets. Boosters promoted fanciful predictions of fabulous returns from publicly built stadiums like the forecast that a new ballpark in St. Petersburg, Florida, in the 1980s would be worth $750 million.

Public Subsidies and the Migration of Franchises

In 1953 the Boston Braves, the "second" team in BeanTown moved to Milwaukee, the first major league franchise shift in fifty years. Milwaukee's quest to become a "big league" city was led by local boosters, especially brewer Fredrick Miller, and the *Milwaukee Journal*. Political leaders made available the minor league County Stadium, which the local government expanded for a major league team. Politicians saw a team as means to gain national prestige for Milwaukee and promote economic development. The Braves were a big success at the box office, and were for a few years the most profitable team in baseball. Furthermore, in their first season, the Braves reportedly attracted $5 million in new business to the city, bringing "an electric vitality" that seemed to effect all local business, and bolster the city's second-rate self-image. The Braves won pennants in 1957 and 1958 and the World's Series in 1957, but thereafter attendance declined, particularly after 1961, once the team slipped out of the first division and popular players were traded. In 1962, Chicago businessmen bought the Braves, and although Milwaukee had the second best major league attendance between 1953 and 1965, decided to move to Atlanta for better media opportunities (a radio-TV package of $2.5 million compared to $400,000 in Milwaukee), and where the city offered an attractive stadium lease. This move foreshadowed a growing problem for franchises whose owners, often faceless corporations, had little if any connections to the hometown.

Atlanta's point man was Mayor Ivan Allen Jr., an unabashed booster, who got the city to build the $42.4 million ($303.34 million in 2011 dollars) Atlanta-Fulton County stadium in 1964 in anticipation of getting a team. Local political leaders welcomed the team with open arms, perceiving it as a way to go "big league" and promote the city's reputation. The extremely favorable terms included the city picking up the legal costs of an antitrust case brought by Wisconsin's attorney general. The new ballpark lost nearly $20 million in its first twenty-five years.

The Braves were eventually replaced by the Brewers in 1970. Twenty-four years later, when the Brewers threatened to exit, voters rejected a referendum to create a special sports lottery to pay for a new field. Nonetheless, the state decided to keep the Brewers in town by paying 77.5 percent of the cost of $400 million Miller Park, funded by a regional sales tax. As historian Glen Gender points out, while municipal leaders might have been indifferent to the problems of jobs leaving town, they go ballistic to protect a major league franchise.

One year after the Boston Braves moved to Milwaukee, the St. Louis Browns, long overshadowed by the Cardinals, migrated to Baltimore where they became the Orioles. The Browns were one of the worst teams in MLB history, with just one appearance in the World Series (1944). They had the worst attendance in the American League for all but two years from 1926 through 1953. Baltimore in 1947 started construction on Memorial Stadium to attract big league sports teams. It was an immediate financial success, earning the city $329,659 through rent and concessions by 1950. Three years later, the Colts moved in, followed by the Orioles in 1954.

The next team to move was the Philadelphia Athletics, a powerhouse team in 1929–1931, but subsequently a frequent cellar dweller. In the early 1950s the A's was surpassed in popularity by the NL's Phillies who won the NL pennant in 1950. Fans stayed away in droves, unhappy with the poor quality of play, the ambiance at old Shibe Park built in 1909 (renamed Mack Stadium in 1953), the price of concessions, and the undesirability of its location in an increasingly dangerous neighborhood. Mayor Joseph Clark and other Philadelphia politicians then paid little attention to the local baseball scene, focusing on urban renewal to revitalize the Central Business District and the industrial base. Consequently, after the Mack family sold the A's in 1955 to businessman Arnold Johnson, he moved the franchise to Kansas City, where he previously had owned the Kansas City Blues of the American Association. Kansas City spent $3 million ($24.85 million in 2011 dollars) to refurbish Municipal Stadium to fit major league requirements.

The most important migration of the 1950s was that of the Brooklyn Dodgers and the New York Giants to the West Coast, dramatically altering the geography of major league baseball. This shift transcended bottom line issues, for as Neil Sullivan wrote, "the Dodgers were more than a business. They represented a cultural totem, a tangible symbol of the community and its values." Most scholars blame Walter O'Malley for deserting Brooklyn, who had just won their first World Series in 1955, and were the second most profitable team in the National League, for greener pastures, thereby grievously harming the borough. The Giants, on the other hand, once an extremely profitable franchise, and world champions in 1954, were struggling, with declining attendance due to its mediocre play, location in a declining neighborhood, and deteriorating ballpark. Owner Horace Stoneham was looking to relocate, probably to Minneapolis, site of the Giants principal minor league affiliate.

Sullivan argues that Dodgers owner Walter O'Malley originally intended to stay in Brooklyn, buy land, and build his own multipurpose stadium to replace undersized (albeit highly profitable) Ebbets Field whose neighborhood was becoming unsafe and less accessible to automobile commuters. O'Malley was concerned about the team's future because after World War II Brooklyn underwent significant demographic changes tied to middle-class white flight to suburban Long Island, and a growing lower class population of people of color, conditions that would eventually hurt attendance. His preferred site was in downtown Brooklyn, but Mayor Robert Wagner, regional planners, and other local and state officials felt that that site was too valuable for baseball and should be saved for greater potential developments. Master builder Robert Moses recommended Flushing Meadows (site of the 1964 World's Fair) in Queens. The power brokers were certain that the Dodgers were not moving, given the team's local ties and the historic stability of major leagues baseball franchises.

In the meanwhile, Los Angeles's regime had been seeking a major league franchise since the early 1940s to promote the city, and even tried to get the Pacific Coast League elevated to major league status. In 1946 the NFL and its rival, the All American Football Conference placed teams there, made viable by air travel. A few years later, Mayor Norris Poulson and other Angeleno leaders sought to bring the Dodgers to Los Angeles to certify their home town's first class status. O'Malley was intrigued by the possibilities of moving to the untapped major league market on the West Coast and the potential for pay-TV. His eyes were on 300-acre Chavez Ravine, the last vacant sector near downtown Los Angeles, previously reserved for public housing. O'Malley offered to trade Wrigley Field, the local minor league ballpark that he had just acquired from Philip K. Wrigley, owner of the Chicago Cubs, for Chavez Ravine, but encountered opposition from various local officials, the courts, and neighborhood activists prior to final approval of the transaction that required a two-thirds majority of the city council. A referendum to fund the project was in doubt until the very last moment when a telethon featuring Hollywood stars helped secure passage by 24,293 votes out of 666,577. The county traded O'Malley 300 acres worth about $6 million and granted him such concessions as a 99-year lease on parking and $4.7 million in new roads and other concessions. O'Malley failed to get the city to build him a ballpark, but still made a great deal. The city got a major league team, and a tax generating property. However, Brooklyn lost their fabled "Bums."

The move west by the Dodgers into Los Angeles and the Giants to San Francisco involved the issues that dominated stadium politics for years, including public vs. private development, eminent domain, competing economic development strategies, neighborhood resistance, and fragmented local political processes. Owners of franchises would keep raising their demands for financial support by playing one city off another in long, drawn-out negotiations.

The attitudes of government officials regarding the subsidizing of their old baseball franchises changed in the 1960s with the rapid deterioration of rustbelt cities as urban planners looked to baseball as a panacea. City leaders became ready to go to any length to keep a franchise. As economist Andrew Zimbalist noted, while "a city reaps unquantifiable benefits from having a team, cities that have teams and lose them are likely to encounter an image problem." Between 1966 and 1970, St. Louis (Busch Stadium), Philadelphia (Veteran's), Pittsburgh (Three Rivers), and Cincinnati (Riverfront) built new modern ballparks in their downtown. These rust-belt cities were losing population and had declining economies which built downtown municipal stadiums to keep their sports franchises and to promote urban development. This was a big change from the historic locations of major league ballparks on the suburban fringes in middle-class residential areas or undeveloped sites, although sports arenas had long been constructed in entertainment zones in or near the CBD. Privately owned ballparks previously avoided downtown sites because of exorbitant property costs, but municipal subsidization of the land (often obtained through eminent domain), and lower construction costs changed that. Planners advocated downtown sites near major highway interchanges and ample parking to facilitate suburban fans that would promote civic development, save the Central Business District, build confidence in the future, and if domed, to serve as convention centers.

Stadium costs escalated rapidly. In 1964, Atlanta's multi purpose Fulton County Stadium, admittedly in a region of cheaper construction costs cost $314 a seat or $19 million, while parks in St. Louis, Anaheim, and San Diego in 1966 and 1967 averaged $25 million. Thereafter costs escalated rapidly. By 1970, ballparks cost from $750 to $850 a seat, or around $45 million, like Riverfront in Cincinnati and $50 million for Pittsburgh's Three Rivers Stadium and Philadelphia's Veterans Stadium. Projects planned at relatively reasonable rates (which had helped convince the public to support them), like the renovation of Yankee Stadium, often ended up with huge overruns. In 1971, when New York City took over the ballpark, it announced that refurbishment would cost $24 million. However, the final bill was $106 million.

O'Malley's $23 million ($178.3 million in 2013 dollars) Dodgers' Stadium, completed in 1962, was the last privately built baseball park for thirty-eight years until $357 million AT&T opened in San Francisco in 2000. By 1970–1971, 69.7 percent of all facilities used by major league sports teams were publicly owned, 23.7 percent were privately owned, and 6.6 percent were university affiliated. Among major professional sports, only hockey still mainly used private facilities (66.7 percent), typically in older multipurpose arenas, compared to the NFL (22.6 percent), and the NBA (16.3 percent). By 1988 the proportion of privately controlled baseball parks had declined to 20.8 percent and 7.1 percent for football.

Public subsidization of private franchises was not limited to construction of ballparks and arenas, but extended to more modest assistance, such as the under pricing of rents and various fees. Direct subsidies included purchasing broadcast rights, and indirect subsidies included constructing highways and exit ramps and giving up future revenues because the edifice was tax exempt. Benjamin Okner estimated that in the late 1960s sports facilities received an average direct government subsidy of $400,000, and $8.8 million in indirect assistance, enough to cover operating costs, but not also cover amortization and interest charges. In 1970, the Seattle Pilots moved to Milwaukee, drawn by low county taxes of $1 for the first million tickets sold, and then just 5 percent thereafter. Seven years later, when the Brewers drew 1.1 million spectators, the county got just $21,149 in taxes. The New York Yankees were also heavily subsidized. In 1973, when George Steinbrenner bought the franchise from CBS, the city rewrote his lease, enabling him to deduct maintenance costs from rent. Thus in 1976, when the Yankees grossed $11.9 million, the city ended up owing the Yankees $10,000, not the $854,504 it would have made under the old contract.

Domed stadiums, modeled after the $41 million Houston Astrodome built in 1965 were particularly expensive. Overly optimistic urban planners built domed facilities as civic monuments that were expected to become centers for public entertainment and an attraction for conventions and other businesses—expectations that were rarely achieved. Historian George Lipsitz found that the Astrodome provided few public benefits, while offering private investors a great opportunity to make a lot of money with little public control. The Astrodome was built by former Houston mayor and Astros owner Judge Roy Hofheinz, whose partner, oilman Bob Smith owned the prospective site. Houston provided its residents minimal public services, yet came up with $3.7 million towards the facility, plus $31.6 million in revenue bonds approved by a referendum. Hofheinz and Smith raised their $6 million for the park by selling luxury boxes. Houston's reward was major league baseball and a famous building that never paid its cost.

The most irresponsible project was the New Orleans Superdome, planned as a $35 million, self-supporting edifice to help redevelop downtown. State legislators gave the Louisiana Stadium and Exposition District a virtual blank check, and ended up with a $163 million 97,000-seat enclosed field that opened in 1975. Yet the true cost was actually far greater because of the high cost bonds purchased to finance the structure. New Orleans never did get a major league baseball team, the project was a huge financial drain and it did not turn around downtown.

The Big Payoff?

New York City politicians in the late 1960s argued for a takeover and rehabilitation of Yankee Stadium to attract tourists, fill up hotels and restaurants, and revitalize its surrounding neighborhood. Bronx borough president Robert Abrams claimed that a new stadium would generate the kind of excitement and energy that New York needed, "not only in real dollars, but in spirit." Abrams argued that fixing up the ballpark would be interpreted as a message to the business community that the city was on the way back from its fiscal crisis.

However, the rebuilt Yankee Stadium created no tangible benefits for the Bronx's residents and merchants. Journalist Robert Lipsyte was told by a local storekeeper, "That's an isolated place over there. People just drive in and out." Lipsyte concluded that the project did not reinvigorate the Bronx, restore public confidence or halt white flight. Nor is there much evidence that expensive, publicly financed sports facilities improved downtowns. None of the promised improvements surrounding Pittsburgh's Three Rivers Stadium ever occurred.

Busch Stadium, built in 1966 at a cost of $55 million ($395.68 million in 2013 dollars), seems to have had a positive benefit in St. Louis's old Skid Row section. The field was intended to be the center of the city's downtown urban renewal to modernize an old decaying industrial city. Cardinals owner August A.

Busch, Jr., and his pals used the downtown park as an entering "wedge to secure tax breaks for adjacent businesses," while the lost revenue was made up by local homeowners and by curtailing city services. The construction led to the removal of "ramshackle tenements and marginal business establishments" for parking, restaurants and new stores. However, it was just one part of the city's major effort at rejuvenating the downtown, symbolized by the Gateway Arch. In the meanwhile, the old Sportsman's Park rusted away along with its industrial neighborhood.

The economic impact of such subsidies fell well short of misguided estimates by paid consultants who overestimated the patronage of out-of-town fans with their "new" money, underestimated the alternate use of discretionary money by local residents, and abused the concept of the multiplier effect (an estimate of how money spent for baseball led to increased local spending). Any consultant producing an unfavorable report would probably be fired and forego future contracts. Tom Ferguson, former president of the Beacon Council that promoted economic development in Dade County, Florida explained, "It's all to sell the local community on making an expenditure." Direct economic benefits include rent, concession shares, parking revenues, jobs, and taxes, but they were less than needed to payoff construction costs and loans, leaving cities with inflated bills, financial losses, underused facilities, and few if any long-term improvements.

Since the seminal 1974 Brookings Institute report on the economics of sports, academic economists have consistently, if not unanimously, took to task the projections made by supporters of municipally financed sports structures. Experts agree that teams are small to medium enterprises that "are not economic engines; they have too few employees and involve too few direct dollars to be a driving force in any city or county's economy." In no city does sports produce even 1 percent of the private sector jobs. In Cook County, Illinois, for instance, sport accounted for merely 0.24 percent of personal income in 1982. Economist Robert Baade of Lake Forest College examined forty-eight cities for the period 1959–1987, including all thirty-five cities that had a major league team in baseball, basketball, football, or hockey. He found that no stadium had a positive effect on real income, and in 63 percent of the cases, the stadium had a negative impact, resulting in economic growth below national urban trends. Economists have also taken to task the false expectations generated by spectacular one-shot events like the Major League All-Star Game, the Superbowl, or college basketball's "Final Four."

Indianapolis, Indiana, which has no major league team, has been the best model for sport supported economic development. Mark S. Rosentraub examined the impact of sport on Indianapolis where the city explicitly tried to use sport to promote itself. Its regime sought to establish a progressive national image with sports as the foundation "on which to build an amenity infrastructure" and thereby promote the quality of life, thereby securing positive national attention, the promotion of investment, and the creation of new jobs.

In 1984, the 60,300-seat inflated roof Hoosier Dome opened with the Colts as its main resident, and the site will have hosted the NCAA Final Four six times by 2015. Indianapolis paid for slightly more than half of the building's $78 million cost, with the rest from philanthropic sources. The city also established a tennis stadium (the SportsCenter), a velodrome, and attracted several national athletic organizations to the city, notably the NCAA in 1999. $2.76 billion was invested in capital development in the downtown area; over one-half from the private sector, 15.8 percent by the city, and most of the rest from the state government. Rosentraub found that "the city was very successful in leveraging funds for its sports strategy," which generated excitement and enhanced its image, but had little direct role in economic development. The sports facilities creates jobs, but they amounted to merely 0.29 percent of the city's workforce.

Economists recognize that team owners benefit from government subsidies (that go beyond construction and land costs), comprising net operating income less depreciation, capital return and property taxes foregone. In other words, "the amount by which revenues fall short of covering all the costs that would have been incurred if the facility were operated by a private owner." This makes it nearly impossible for governments to make up their subsidies. Dean Baim argues that the subsidies are extremely regressive, mainly benefiting rich franchise owners and newly wealthy athletes, and (I would add) the upper middle-class fans who can afford the high price of tickets. In 2011, according to the Fan Cost Index the average cost for a family of four to see a major league game was $197.35. This included four average adult tickets, four small sodas, two small draft beers, four hot dogs, parking, two hats, and two scorecards.

The Baltimore Model: Orioles Park at Camden Yards

Sports teams manipulated Baltimore, a city which in the 1980s was ranked fifth among fifty-eight cities for urban distress. The city's baseball and football teams played at Memorial Stadium into the mid-1980s despite its poor accessibility, distance from the interstate, and limited parking, that made it a losing financial proposition for the city, and beginning in the 1960s, owners Jerry Hoffberger of the Orioles, and Carroll Rosenbloom of the Colts warned the city that they might leave town without a new stadium. In 1972 Rosenbloom traded his team for Robert Irsay's Los Angeles Rams. The local power elite felt that the Colts had an extremely favorable lease, and opposed a new ballpark because of high prevailing interest rates, the need for state and federal funding, and a *Baltimore Sun* report that reported that the Orioles directly generated only about $2 million for the city's income. The town was shocked on May 29, 1984 when the Colts moved in the middle of the night to Indianapolis.

Mayor William Schaefer wanted to avoid building a new stadium, especially since the city had more pressing problems, and focused on revitalizing residential neighborhoods and the oceanfront at Inner Harbor, a blighted area of abandoned warehouses, redeveloped in the late 1970s into an accessible upscale zone of offices, hotels, restaurants, and tourist attractions. However, the departure of the Colts and rumblings from the Orioles convinced Schaefer, who did not want to lose another franchise on his watch, to support a new municipal stadium to help revitalize his city by restoring the city's public image, offering large construction contracts, and promoting economic development. Schaefer won the Democratic nomination for governor in 1986 in which the ballpark was a big issue. As governor he got the quasi-public Maryland Professional Sports Authority (MPSA) to draw up a plan to build a $110 million downtown Orioles Stadium at Camden Yards. Four years later the MPSA built the $220 Ravens Stadium right next door.

Can Cities Attract Teams with a New Ballpark?

Teams play off one city against another to get a sweeter deal. However, since the Washington Senators moved to Arlington, Texas in 1972, the only other franchise to move was the Montreal Expos in 2005, shifted to the national capital to replace the old Senators. The Montreal franchise was at death's door, with the lowest attendance in the National League from 1998 through 2004. In 2002, Major League Baseball bought the franchise with the strong likelihood of folding the team, or moving it, which it did.

This is not to say that teams were not sought by cities. In the Bay Area, several cities actively coveted the San Francisco Giants before the team decided to move from Candlestick Park and built its own ballpark, near downtown, at the China Basin. One city that ardently sought a major league franchise was St. Petersburg, population 238,647, 58th largest in the U.S., and best known as a retirement community, the city had a long history of competition with its more aggressive neighbor of Tampa, home of Busch Gardens, the University of South Florida, and the regional airport. In 1982, the city council granted the Pinellas (County) Sports Authority (PSA) a $1 a year, forty-year lease on the 66-acre downtown Gas Plant redevelopment area, and $7 million to prepare the site for construction of a ballpark. The endeavor was led by "the Vault," city leaders who included the city manager, the assistant city manager, a county commissioner, two councilmen, and the *Petersburg Times* publisher. There was considerable opposition to the proposed new stadium, especially since taxpayers opposed building before any team committed itself to the city.

In 1986, the county and city committed to a new $83 million domed stadium, even though baseball commissioner Peter Ueberroth warned them that there was no guarantee the city would get a major league franchise. Nearly half of the anticipated costs were going to be paid by taxes on the tourist industry. The city's prime target was the White Sox, whose managing partner, Jerry Reinsdorf, was promised an annual $10 million media deal, plus free land for his real estate business to sweeten the pot. The planners produced a 31-page report "Baseball and Florida" that projected the Sox annually bringing in $54.5 million in new business, and $101 million in sales taxes over thirty years.

Reinsdorf's syndicate had purchased the Sox in 1981 from long-time baseball entrepreneur Bill Veeck. Comiskey Park, oldest in the majors, was located in a declining white ethnic neighborhood, separated from the city's largest black ghetto by the massive Dan Ryan Expressway. The Sox, Chicago's second favorite team to the Cubs, were looking to make a splash by moving to the suburbs where there was a large potential fan base who could afford to attend ball games. However, a referendum in 1986 blocked a potential move to the town of Addison. Afterwards, the Chicago and Springfield power brokers established the Illinois

Sports Facilities Authority (ISHA) to build a ballpark in Chicago across the street from the old field. However, squabbling between Mayor Harold Washington and Governor Jim Thompson over control of the ISHA and Sox complaints over proposed terms seriously periled the project. As the legislative session came to a close, it appeared that the Sox were minutes from leaving for St. Petersburg. Then as midnight approached, Governor Thompson turned off the clock, and kept negotiations open until an agreement was reached.

Despite the Sox's decision, St. Petersburg went ahead with its plans to build a domed stadium, turning their eyes to the San Francisco Giants who were up for sale. A local group of investors offered team owner Bob Lurie about $115 million for the franchise, but he sold it to another syndicate that promised to keep the Giants in San Francisco for $95 million. The PSA opened the Florida Suncoast Dome (today Tropicana Field) in 1990 at a cost of $138 million. However, it was not until 1998 that the expansion Tampa Bay Devil Rays moved in.

Cities without franchises could still use the promise of a publicly built ballpark as a means to get an expansion team. Five of the six expansion teams since 1977 played in public facilities, while the Florida Marlins, which began play in 1993 at six-year-old privately built Pro-Player Stadium (formerly Joe Robbie Stadium), home of the Miami Dolphins (today Sun-Life Stadium). The Marlins moved in 2012 to Miami-Dade County's $515 Marlin Stadium. More importantly, cities with franchises continue to use the promise of a publicly built stadium to keep their teams. These new stadiums, beginning in 1994 with Orioles Park at Camden Yards, are often retro designs, including PNC in Pittsburgh, AT&T in San Francisco, and Target in Minneapolis. They typically seat around 40,000, providing for a more intimate experience, quite different from the multi-use parks of the 1960s that had around 60,000 seats. The average park built since 1994 cost $323.9 million, led by $1.3 billion Yankee Stadium.

Since the 1980s, there has been increased taxpayer resistance to subsidization of rich, arrogant franchise owners, who are reaping huge profits and running roughshod over communities, frequently moving to a new field before the old building costs have been amortized. The result was growing scrutiny of public capital budgeting decisions, and public became increasingly successful in getting teams pay a share of costs. Baade and Dye urged that stadiums be employed together with other potential economic anchors and that governments demand that teams use their own money to build stadiums because that makes them more committed to staying. They found that from 1970 to 1985 only two shifting franchises out of twenty-two had left privately built stadia. Since 1995, nineteen new ballparks have been constructed, including Turner Field, erected by Atlanta's Committee for the Olympic Games, which became municipal property after the 1996 Games. Fourteen were joint public-private ventures, three were public, and one (San Francisco) privately owned.

Conclusion

Urban politicians and associated regimes have had a long relationship with professional sports, dating back well over one hundred years, as owners who utilized their clout to help support and protect their sporting investments and promote the reputation of their communities. By the Golden Age of Sports in the 1920s, cities often constructed large outdoor arenas to encourage amateur sport and boost their cities, with the hopes of thereby promoting the local economy. Since the 1950s, cities, especially in the South and West, and since the 1970s, suburbs as well, heavily subsidized new sports franchises by building them ballparks to promote economic development and attest to their metropolitan status. Older, established cities responded by building public stadiums to keep their teams in place, justified as measures to promote economic development. However, the subsidies have not been good financial investments, generating few jobs or long-term economic expansion. municipalities still subsidize sports franchises, either to keep them in town or else to attract them to their towns. The regimes continue to publicize on unsubstantiated forecasts by well paid consultants to support sports as an economic development tool. However, in the past few years, political leaders have put less stress on economic growth, and more on stressing the cultural and psychic returns of having a major league presence in town. Residents seem to accept that justification, especially if the costs do not come directly from their own pocket.

FURTHER READING

Andelman, Bud. *Stadium for Rent: Tampa Bay's Quest for Major League Baseball* (1993).

Beekman, Scott. *NASCAR Nation: A History of Stock Car Racing in the United States* (2010).

Boddy, Kasia. *Boxing: A Cultural History* (2008).

Burk, Robert F. *Much More Than a Game: Players, Owners, and American Baseball Since 1921* (2001).

Chandler, Joan. *Television and National Sport: The United States and Britain* (1988).

Clotfelter, Charles T. *Big-Time Sports in American Universities* (2011).

Danielson, Michael N. *Home Team: Professional Sports and the American Metropolis* (1997).

Fetter, Henry D. *Taking on the Yankees: Winning and Losing in the Business of Baseball, 1903–2003* (2004).

Figone, Albert J. *Cheating the Spread: Gamblers, Point Shavers, and Game Fixers in College Football and Basketball* (2012).

Harris, David. *The League: The Rise and Fall of the NFL* (1986).

Hine, Thomas S. "Housing, Baseball and Creeping Socialism: The Battle of Chavez Ravine, Los Angeles, 1949–1959," *Journal of Urban History* 8 (February 1982), 123–43.

Jay, Kathryn. *More Than Just a Game: Sports in American Life Since 1945* (2006).

Jennings, Kenneth. *Balls and Strikes: The Money Game in Professional Baseball* (1990).

Kahn, Lawrence M. "Cartel Behavior and Amateurism in College Sports," *Journal of Economic Perspectives* 21 (Winter 2007), 209–26.

Miller, James E. *The Baseball Business: Pursuing Pennants and Profits in Baltimore* (1990).

Nagler, Barney. *James Norris and the Decline of Boxing* (1964).

Neal-Lunsford, Jeff. "Sport in the Land of Television: The Use of Sport in Network Prime-Time Schedules, 1946–50," *Journal of Sport History* 19 (1992), 52–76.

O'Brien, Michael. *Vince: A Personal Biography of Vince Lombardi* (1987).

Oriard, Michael. *King Football: Sport and Spectacle in the Golden Age of Radio and Newsreels, Movies and Magazines, the Weekly & the Daily Press* (2001).

Oriard, Michael. *Brand NFL: Making and Selling America's Favorite Sport* (2007).

Oriard, Michael. *Bowled Over: Big-Time College Football from the Sixties to the BCS Era* (2009).

Pierce, Daniel S. *Real NASCAR: White Lightning, Red Clay, and Big Bill France* (2010).

Quirk, James, and Rodney D. Fort. *Pay Dirt: The Business of Professional Team Sports* (1992).

Rader, Benjamin G. *In Its Own Image: How Television Has Transformed Sports* (1984).

Rader, Benjamin G. *Baseball*, 3rd ed. (2008).

Richmond, Peter. *Ballpark: Camden Yards and the Building of an American Dream* (1993).

Riess, Steven A. "Only the Ring Was Square: Frankie Carbo and the Underworld Control of American Boxing," *International Journal of the History of Sport* 5 (May 1988), 29–52.

Roberts, Randy, and James Olson. *Winning Is the Only Thing: Sports in American Society Since 1945* (1989).

Ruck, Rob, Maggie Patterson, and Michael P. Weber. *Rooney: A Sporting Life* (2009).

Sammons, Jeffrey. *Beyond the Ring: The Role of Boxing in American Society* (1988).

Scully, Gerald. *The Business of Baseball* (1989).

Smith, Ronald A. *Play-by-Play: Radio, Television, and Big-Time College Sports* (2001).

Smith, Ronald A. *Pay for Play: A History of Big-Time College Athletic Reform* (2011).

Staudohar, Paul, and James A. Mangan, eds., *The Business of Professional Sports* (1991).

Sullivan, Neil J. *The Dodgers Move West* (1987).

Surdam, David George. *The Rise of the National Basketball Association* (2012).

Trumpbour, Robert C. *The New Cathedrals: Politics and Media in the History of Stadium Construction* (2007).

Voigt, David Q. *American Baseball, Vol. 3, From the Post-War Expansion to the Electronic Age* (1983).

Walker, James R., and Robert V. Bellamy, Jr. *Center Field Shot: A History of Baseball on Television* (2008).

Zimbalist, Andrew. *Baseball and Billions: A Probing Look Inside the Big Business of Our National Pastime* (1992).

Zimbalist, Andrew. *Unpaid Professionals: Commercialism and Conflict in Big-Time College Sports* (1999).

Zimbalist, Andrew. *Circling the Bases: Essays on the Challenges and Prospects of the Sports Industry* (2011).

CHAPTER 15

The Globalization of American Sport

The United States was originally an importer of sporting cultures from England, Scotland, Ireland, and various German states, but after the Civil War, the country became an exporter of sports, particularly baseball, basketball, and volleyball, to promote national prestige, support our growing colonial and neocolonial empire by co-opting local elites, improve living conditions in the underdeveloped world, and make money selling sporting goods. Americans also became much more active in international competition, particularly starting in 1896, the Olympic Games. We believed that success in these contests proved the superiority of our culture and values.

The diffusion of baseball was first promoted by entrepreneurs, missionaries, and educators interested in bringing the finest American attributes to distant lands like the Kingdom of Hawaii in the 1840s, and Japan in the 1870s. Organized Baseball itself initiated world tours in 1874 and 1888–1889 to promote the game overseas and to create a new market for our sporting goods. However, in Cuba, the game was actually imported by Cuban students living in the United States after the American Civil War, who enjoyed playing the game and admired the values it seemed to represent.

Following the Spanish-American War of 1898, the military became an active booster of American sports overseas, particularly in Cuba and the Philippines. The Army used games like baseball to promote political order and social control, substitute for such undesirable amusement like cockfighting, and carry the "white man's burden" by civilizing the local people, improving their health, morals, and character. Playing baseball or basketball would teach such American values as respect for authority, discipline, hard work, and community pride.

American participation in the Olympics first became a diplomatic issue at the London Games in 1908. On the opening day, the Olympic Stadium displayed the flags of all competing nations, except Sweden and the United States. In response, the American flag bearer did not dip his pole while passing King Edward VII in the reviewing standard as was the accepted protocol. National pride was further piqued by questionable decisions by English referees, particularly in the 400 meter finals when an American was disqualified for interference. Officials called for a re-running of the race that the remaining Americans boycotted.

The 1936 Olympics, hosted by the Nazi regime, was a hot issue for Americans because of the German government's racism and its persecution of Jews and other minorities. There was a call in the United States for a boycott of the games. The proposition had the support of prominent journalists, athletic leaders, Catholics, Jews, and Democratic politicians, but was defeated in the end. The American participation was highlighted by the achievements of African American sprinter Jesse Owens, whose four gold medals was a setback for the racist Nazi propaganda machine.

After World War II, sport became an important element of the Cold War. The United States tried to demonstrate the superiority of its economic, political, and social system over the USSR by sending athletes, coaches, and teams (often African American) overseas to win the hearts and minds of the Third World. Furthermore, the United States tried to use its Olympic teams to defeat the Russian teams and those of her allies to "bolster national self-confidence, enhance the respect of allies and nonaligned nations, and demoralize the opposition." However, the United States won more medals than the USSR only twice in the Summer Olympics between 1952, when the Soviet Union made its first Olympic appearance, and 1988, just before the end of the Cold War. The use of the Olympics as a Cold War surrogate was particularly heated in 1980 when the United States shocked the USSR hockey team in the Winter Olympics in possibly the biggest upset in sport history. Later that year, the United States boycotted the Summer Games in Moscow. The Russians retaliated by sitting out the 1984 Games in Los Angeles.

Since the end of the Cold War, the American role in global sport has focused on business. Cable TV made American sports readily viewable around the globe and made heroes of stars like Michael Jordan, who endorsed American made equipment, uniforms, and sneakers that helped to make Nike an $11 billion corporation. The globalization of American sport also led to the international recruitment of athletes by American colleges, the NBA (18 percent of the NBA in 2011), and Major League Baseball (28.4 percent) in 2012.

DOCUMENTS

Document 1 is a secret report filed in 1928 by Zack Farmer, the manager and secretary of the X Olympiad, scheduled for Los Angeles in 1932. He was sent to Amsterdam, the Netherlands, site of the 1928 Summer Games to evaluate the staging of the event. His report was so negative about the Games and its potential for success in Los Angeles that he convinced the California Tenth Olympiad Association in a secret meeting to cancel the proposed spectacle. However, one day later, local city boosters on the committee reevaluated their decision, and the Games were back on. This unpublished critical analysis was a rare case of the seemingly inevitable forward march of American sporting events and sporting institutions not moving ahead. Had the 1932 Los Angeles Summer Olympics not taken place, think how history would have been changed!

Document 2 concerns the effort made by certain European and North American nations to boycott the 1936 Olympics in Berlin, Germany, because of racist Nazi social policies, particularly the government's breaking of Olympic rules forbidding discrimination of athletes based on race and religion. The document is a report by American Counsel George S. Messersmith in late 1935 that delineated in detail evidence of Nazi prejudice against German Jews, and called for the government to support a boycott. However, his report was unheeded by the heavily anti-Semitic State Department. A few weeks later, Amateur Athletic Union voted 58.25 to 55.75 to not boycott. Boycott proponents included Judge Jeremiah Mahoney, president of the Amateur Athletic Union, New York mayor Fiorello La Guardia, former governor Al Smith of New York, Governor James Curley of Massachusetts, and former Assistant Secretary of the Navy Ernst Lee Jahncke, who was expelled from the International Olympic Committee as a result of his opposition.

Document 3 consists of several statements on athletics by President John F. Kennedy who came into office in 1961 with an image of youth and fitness unseen since the presidency of Theodore Roosevelt. President Kennedy was determined to promote physical fitness, writing an article entitled "The Soft American," in *Sports Illustrated* (December 26, 1960), and delivering several lectures as president decrying the state of national fitness and the problems that created over national security. He pointed out that early in the Korean War, the military reported a decline in young men's physical strength and that Selective Service was rejecting nearly half of the draftees because they were mentally, morally, or physically unfit. In addition, 35.7 percent of American children failed one or more strength tests compared to 1.1 percent in Europe. This put the United States at a disadvantage in the Cold War era against our enemy, the USSR. Kennedy would go on to reinvigorate the President's Council on Youth Fitness, established in 1956. Bud Wilkinson, the renowned football coach at the University of Oklahoma, became the president's Physical Fitness Consultant and developed a model physical fitness curriculum.

Document 4 refers to the early efforts by Major League Baseball to send a team to play in Cuba as a goodwill gesture in 1975 during the presidency of Gerald Ford. The government had broken off relations with Cuba in 1961, which had become a Communist dictatorship under Fidel Castro. Proponents of a baseball tour thought that such an action might replicate the "ping pong" diplomacy that helped open Communist China to the United States during the Nixon administration. However, the proposal was rejected by Secretary of State Henry Kissinger. It was not until 1999 that a Cuban team played in the United States against the Baltimore Orioles at Camden Yard.

During the Cold War, sport became increasingly a tool of American foreign policy. This peaked after the 1979 Soviet invasion of Afghanistan, when President Jimmy Carter announced that the United States would suspend arms negotiations with the Russians, condemn the action in the United Nations, and boycott the upcoming Summer Olympics in Moscow unless the Russians withdrew. Carter's naive and moralistic actions were widely opposed by American Olympic athletes who had worked for years to prepare for this one event. In Document 5, Carter explains his reasons for the boycott. The boycott tarnished the image of the Moscow Olympics, which 65 countries did not attend; however, it had no impact on Russian foreign policy.

1. Manager Zack Farmer of the Xth Olympiad Recommends that the United States Olympic Committee Cancel the 1932 Olympics in Los Angeles

August 13, 1928

Confidential report to the Boards of Directors of
The Community Development Association and
California Tenth Olympiad Association only.

Gentlemen:

Conditions affecting Olympism have changed greatly since our invitations were first extended in 1923, particularly since the award of the Games to Los Angeles in 1923, and pronounced changes developed at the recent session in Amsterdam.

I have felt the responsibilities of noting ... for good or for bad, the results that may obtain from holding the Tenth Olympiad in Los Angeles.

... [T]he California Tenth Olympiad Association carries the actual responsibility and liability, economically and otherwise, but is, generally speaking, divested of authority, the latter being in the hands of innumerable and largely intangible and inconstant groups throughout the world, who, in toto, represent the dictating force of the Olympiad.

... [W]e should consider the present status of Olympism as an intended constructive force, on the one hand, and on the other hand whether or not our staging of the Olympiad in Los Angeles will be for the best interests of the city as well as for the institution of Olympism:

... I believe the facts indicate that Olympism has for a long time been and is now, failing to achieve the purposes and results originally expected of it, viz., "Better understanding and the increase of friendly relationships among nations on the fields of sports."

... I seriously question whether the staging of the Games in Los Angeles will strengthen the structure of Olympism, and I am certain, in view of present conditions, which I doubt will improve, that there is a good chance for Los Angeles to be harmed somewhat, as well as benefited, in staging the next Olympiad.

The psychology of the situation is upside down; that is, there is not an even balance of the value between the city upon which the responsibilities rest and the institution of Olympism or world sports.

By the perpetuation of misunderstanding on the part of cities which have clamored for the benefits of being awarded the Olympic Games and the increased blind bidding for such privilege, we have the silly situation of cities begging to the sports world through the International Olympic Committee for something that precedent indicates has been heretofore, of little tangible constructive value to the cities, which have achieved it and which has many positive disadvantages....

From *William May Garland to Avery Brundage*, February 7, 1935 in the Avery Brundage Collection, University of Illinois Archives, Box 56.

These adversities have increased with each successive Olympiad, due largely to the rapidly disintegrating forces within Olympism....

Whereas I believe the sports world should properly be placed in the position of seeking a city willing to undertake the almost thankless task of financing and staging the Olympiad and lending to such city the unified and harmonious enthusiasm and help of all branches of world sports, we find the situation reversed, Amsterdam being a case at hand, and what has heretofore been true with other cities will be particularly accentuated in respect to Los Angeles.

... [T]here is a decided opposition in many important quarters abroad to the staging of the next Olympiad so far away from Europe where it has heretofore had its setting and has become almost a European possession....

[A]side from the question of our ability to adequately finance and competently manage the staging of the Olympic Games, ... there is the bigger question of our being able to produce the games in the face of the adverse conditions existing.

[W]e should be able to look to the International Olympic Committee, which awarded us the Games, as the controlling source of Olympism and to guarantee the existence and exercise of a dominant authority upon the innumerable units of the sports world which would be insurance to us that if we do our part of providing the stage and settings, etc., the show will be delivered to us. This is not so.

There is no central authority that we can look to and depend upon for such service. Nor can we be assured to accomplishing this ourselves, as we have no authority over sports organizations....

This places Los Angeles entirely at the mercy of the many national and international sports federations and athletic organizations, some forty nations being actively involved. These sports federations are themselves, in many instances, at loggerheads with each other and beset with bitter politics and dissension.... There are bitter international feelings evidenced, rivalries and uncontrollable politics. There ... is not, in my opinion, a unified friendly attitude toward staging the games in Los Angeles.

In substance, the International Olympic Committee, the sports federations and other integral groups composing the production side of the Olympiad, are comparable to a ship drifting without a rudder, a mutinous crew aboard and the officers in a state of indisposition.

... [W]e will have on the one hand a definite responsibility of financing and erecting the proper setting, facilities, organization, management, etc., without ever being certain in the preceding four years that the cast and show will be what it should be, as definite commitments from nations entering probably will not be obtainable very far in advance of the actual staging of the Olympiad.

It has been the growing tendency of the International Olympic Committee to decrease rather than to increase the departments of events comprising the Olympiad and to concentrate the staging of the events in the shortest fixed period of the year possible....

Dismissing the winter sports program for a moment, the balance of the Olympiad can be and, accordingly to the present attitude of the Committee, will be concentrated in a few weeks in the summer. Under conditions formerly existing the winter sports, if held in the state, would dominate for several weeks in the winter, … [and] track and field (stadium events) would be the highlight in the summer program.… If the winter sports are not held in California and, … and further considering the aforementioned attitude of the Committee to retrench and concentrate the events, one readily grasps the decided change affecting the scope, duration and the theoretical spread of economic benefits that would accrue to the state.…

Generally speaking, we have considered the two principal benefits to the state and city being the attraction of visitors and the publicity and advertising accruing.… [T]here is danger … that if the show is what it should be our local, statewide and neighboring patronage would purchase the bulk of the show.… If, on the other hand, we fostered a heavy movement of visitor-patrons and disappointed statewide and local fans and tax-payers interested in the financing (if the million dollar bond issue vote is successful November 6th) we would have a serious reaction there.

As to the publicity value: We undoubtedly could guide publicity to our advantage better than … heretofore.… [T]here is as good chance for unfavorable publicity regardless of how well we might perform our task. For example, the world has been told little … about the praiseworthy work of the Dutch in preparing for the Games against unseemly obstacles …, but the world has been told … all about the unfortunate incidents occurring to mar the Ninth Olympiad.… The American Committee's own decision to house its team on a ship led people to believe that the Dutch failed to provide proper housing. The hotheaded action of the French in withdrawing from the ceremonies the first day and threatening to quit entirely because a Dutch gate keeper refused admission to the grounds the night before the opening cast a somber cloud over the Games and created unfavorable publicity.… If an athlete had his pocket picked the story went out that Amsterdam was full of pickpockets and the government had failed to protect the athletes.

Amateur athletics, particularly in the United States, have become so accentuated, over-organized and commercialized, with paid coaches living a life of alibi to sustain their reputations, pampered and tempermental [*sic*] athletes, jealousies and politics dominating the official and directing circle of athletics.…

By some peculiar psychology, applying to athletics particularly, this sort of publicity seems always to take precedence over the more substantial side of the story of an Olympiad.

It is rather natural that the serious propaganda has developed that Los Angeles will not get the foreign athletes without heavy financial assistance.… [T]he foreign countries are worried about the expense and the time lost by their working-men athletes. If our Federal government will provide a ship or two and the railroads special train rates from New York for these countries and we would house and feed the athletes as our guests, the average country's financing would be little different from the past, leaving it to the individual national body to arrange reimbursement to the employer of the athlete for the time lost.…

… [W]hat the million dollars will be spent for … is impossible except in a general way. The Dutch … were unable to answer it because aside from definite costs of facilities, the big bulk of expenses developed as the loose ends of the picture are gradually brought together … [just] a few months before the games.…

We are fortunately situated in that we have our stadium completed and no other Olympic city has been in that position; and we have auditoriums and field facilities to take care of some of the other events. We will have to build a bicycle track and a swimming pool (very expensive structures).… Gate receipts on many of these vents are questionable, especially as compared to the costs.…

The elaborate picture we presented … in connection with the bond issue campaign, respecting the scope, magnitude, importance and benefits of and accruing from the Tenth Olympiad, "was warranted by the conditions existing at the time the picture was painted." The comparatively recent drastic changes heretofore mentioned that have entered the situation require, … I believe, a careful but frank statement to the people of the state before election.…

… [I]f the bond issue is voted, I would recommend against spending any of the bond money to transport athletes or contribute to lost time compensation, using it for the other purposes stated herein, structures, facilities, organization, management, housing, etc. If the money is not voted and we determine to go ahead I would suggest decision so to do be based generally on the following conditions:

That the winter sports be released by Los Angeles;

That we yield to the general tendency to simplify and concentrate the Games;

That the only assurance we give to foreign countries of assistance be an effort to secure oceanic transportation by the Federal government, special train rates to be paid by the countries, and the housing and feeding of the athletes, as differentiated from the sportsmen, be provided by us;

… That the International Olympic Committee be asked to rule permitting the staging of boxing, wrestling, fencing, weight lifting and bicycling and some of the other events off of the stadium grounds.…

Without state or Federal financial aid, it would be safer to have a substantial fund provided by the local governments or by private subscription, to guarantee the Association against loss, although I believe that under the suggested restricted conditions there would be a fair chance for us to pull through without the aid of such a fund; that we could carry on all of the preliminary preparations … out of our own Coliseum reserve funds … and that in 1931 we would begin to have a sufficiently clear picture of the number and quality of the entries to indicate the type of show we would have in 1932.…

2. Counsel George S. Messersmith Advises U.S. to Boycott 1936 Olympics in Berlin

The question of American participation in the Olympic Games arose already several years ago when I was still Consul General in Berlin. It felt at that time that the circumstances were such that American athletic organizations could not

---

From "Report by George S. Messersmith, November 15, 1935," 862.4063 Olympic Games/57. National Archives, Washington, DC.

properly participate in the Olympic Games in Berlin in 1936, and I believe that it is desirable that I should say that nothing that has happened in these two years has changed this view, but, on the other hand, everything that has happened has been in the direction of showing that American participation is undesirable.

When the present Government in Germany came into power and began its program of discrimination, not only on the basis of race and religion, but directed against all persons who were not in accord with National Socialist political, social, and economic doctrine, there was a very definite feeling in sporting and athletic circles in the United States, as well as in other countries, that under the conditions prevailing in Germany and which were likely to continue to exist there, it would be undesirable for the Olympic Games to be held in Berlin. There was a very general conviction that the principles and action of National Socialism were to contrary to the principles of sports and so opposed to the Olympic idea that it would be an anachronism to hold the Olympic Games in Germany under these conditions....

... [T]he same action which has been taken in other aspects of Germany life has been applied to the field of sport. Sport as an activity, particularly of youth, was one of the major aspects of German life which must be coordinated into and definitely controlled by the Party. All German sport is today directly controlled by the Government and is professedly an instrument of the Party for the shaping of youth into National Socialist ideology. There is no tolerance and no freedom in sport, but absolute and definite control by the state.... Sport has ... become a political matter, and sport organizations and activities must be recognized as a political activity of the German State. The authority of the leader of German sports Hans von Tschammer Von Osten, is complete.

... [I]t was recognized at the outset what an instrument the Olympic Games could become in consolidating the position of the Party among the youth of Germany. When the discriminatory measures against the Jews and the Church in particular aroused such widespread resentment and comment outside of Germany and when Jews were excluded from participation in German sports, it was realized that this might bring about reaction in various countries, particularly in the United States and England and in Scandinavia, leading to non-participation in the 1936 Games. It was recognized at the outset also that the decision of the American Olympic Committee would play a predominant part in determining to what degree there would be foreign participation in the Games.

Every endeavor was therefore made to convince the American Olympic Committee that there was no discrimination in Germany, particularly that there was no discrimination against Jews. In order to put the best face on the German situation, Dr. von Lewald, who is partly Jewish, was permitted to remain as the nominal head of the German Olympic Committee.... He was ... retained by the German Government as a façade, but actually had all real power in German sports taken from him. When the American Olympic Committee met in Washington, now almost several years ago, to discuss the question of the attitude it should take towards representation in Berlin in 1936 ... a telegram was addressed by the committee to Dr. von Lewald requesting confirmation or denial of the reports of discrimination which had reached the American Committee.

Dr. Von Lewald replied ... that he could assure the American Committee that Jews were permitted to compete freely in Germany and there was no discrimination. Largely on the basis of this telegram, the American Committee voted favorably on participation in Berlin.

... I may say that I have known Dr. von Lewald well and held him in very high regard. When I asked him what reply he had made to the American Committee, he told me, with tears in his eyes, that he had replied that there was no discrimination. When, as a friend, I reproached him for in this way misusing the confidence which his American friends put in him, he replied that I must know what the consequences would be to him if he had made any other reply....

... To the Party and the youth of Germany, the holding of the Olympic Games in Berlin in 1936 has become the symbol of the conquest of the world by National Socialist doctrine. Should the games not be held in Berlin, it would be one of the most serious blows which National Socialist prestige could suffer within an awakening Germany and one of the most effective ways which the world outside has of showing to the youth of Germany the opinion of National Socialist doctrine.

... As the Jews under the Nuremberg Laws are not first class German citizens, there is no longer any doubt that all persons with any strain of Jewish blood, no matter how attenuated, will not be permitted to compete for Germany. The question, however, is really a much broader and much wider one, for under the strictly state controlled sports which are the rule in Germany today, all the principles of fair-play which sport stands for are disregarded and replaced by those of National Socialist doctrine and discipline.

... The German Government places special value on American participation, for our contingent has always been since the War the most numerous....

... I am informed reliably that there is a wide hope in other national committees that the American Committee may take a more realistic position with respect to the situation in Germany and change its present attitude, which is so strongly for participation. The probabilities are that if the American Committee frankly recognizes the situation which prevails in Germany, American athletic organizations will not participate and that this lead will be followed immediately in many countries.

... I have noticed recently in our press declaration by prominent members of the American Committee that the Olympic Games are not a political matter and that American athletes cannot be brought into a political problem, and that, therefore, our participation should be as numerous as usual in Berlin. It is true that the Olympic Games are not political, and should remain non-political, but it is exactly this situation which seems to be ignored by the American Committee.... German sport is controlled by the State and ... is considered a political instrument. [T]he German Government ... hopes to use them, not only as a political instrument within Germany, but also as a propaganda instrument throughout the world....

... I believe that our dignity and prestige and our adherence to the ideals of fair-pay and the non-political character of sport make it necessary and imperative that the American Olympic Committee revise its attitude and make it clear that the real position is in Germany, leaving it to individual athletic organizations in the United States to take the action which they may see fit with regards to participation.

Unless the American Committee can definitely satisfy itself by first-hand knowledge an observation that this discrimination no longer takes place, I do not believe that it would remain a representative of American sport tradition if American athletes participate in the Olympic Games in 1936.

3. Physical Fitness and National Security, 1960

PRESIDENT JOHN F. KENNEDY

[P]hysical fitness is as vital to the activities of peace as to those of war, especially when our success in those activities may well determine the future of freedom.... We face in the Soviet Union a powerful and implacable adversary determined to show ... that only the Communist system possesses the vigor and determination necessary ... for progress.... Only if our citizens are physically fit will they be fully capable of such an effort.

★ ★ ★

The strength of our democracy and our country is really no greater in the final analysis than the well-being of our citizens. The vigor of our country, its physical vigor and energy, is going to be no more advanced, no more substantial, than the vitality and will of our countrymen. I think in recent years we have seen many evidences in the most advanced tests, comparative tests, that have been made that many of the boys and girls who live in other countries have moved ahead of younger people in this country in their ability to endure long physical hardship, in their physical fitness and in their strength.

This country is going to move through difficult days, difficult years. The responsibilities upon us are heavy, as the leader of the free world. We carry worldwide commitments. People look to us with hope, and if we fail they look to those who are our adversaries.

I think during this period we should make every effort to see that the intellectual talents of every boy and girl are developed to the maximum. And that also their physical fitness, their willingness to participate in physical exercise, their willingness to participate in physical contests, in athletic contests—all these, I think, will do a good deal to strengthen this country, and also to contribute to a greater enjoyment of life in the years to come.

★ ★ ★

From John F. Kennedy, "The Soft American," *Sports Illustrated* (December 26, 1960), 14; John F. Kennedy. "Remarks on the Youth Fitness Program.," July 19, 1961. Online by Gerhard Peters and John T. Woolley, The American Presidency Project. http://www.presidency.ucsb.edu/ws/?pid=8248; John F. Kennedy: "Statement by the President on the Physical Fitness of Young Americans," September 5, 1961. Online by Gerhard Peters and John T. Woolley, The American Presidency Project. http://www.presidency.ucsb.edu/ws/?pid=8309.

I have, on many occasions, expressed my concern over the physical fitness of our youth and I want to stress again the importance of a strong and vital nation—of a physically fit young America.

I am informed by General Hershey, Director of the Selective Service System, that since October 1948 of some 6 million young men examined for military duty, more than a million have been rejected for physical reasons alone. General Hershey likewise has told me that a very substantial number of these physically-unacceptable men were in the preventable category.

The number of these men in the preventable category—men who would not have been rejected had they participated in adequate physical developmental programs—represents more soldiers than we now have stationed in Berlin and West Germany ready to defend freedom.

The situation grows steadily worse. In the last year, more than a thousand men per month—an all-time high—were in the preventable category among those rejected for physical reasons.

I again urge school administrations to implement the basic physical fitness program developed by my Council on Youth Fitness, or a similar one, this fall.

Young Americans must be made fit—to serve our nation in its hour of need—fit to face the future with confidence and strength.

4. Should the United States Send a Major League Baseball Team to Cuba in 1975?

February 19, 1975

Culver Gleysteen of the Office of Cuban Affairs and
William Rogers, Assistant Secretary for Inter-American
Affairs to Secretary of State Henry Kissinger
Department of State, Secret/NODIS Memorandum
SECRET/NODIS*

Additional Talking Points on sending a baseball Team to Cuba

1. *US Public Reaction.*
   The public and the press are skeptical about our Cuba Policy because there is a steady stream of news reporting from the island portraying the regime as stable and self-confident, the life as dreary but providing better social services than most other Latin American countries, and Castro himself as prepared to normalize relations with the US. Cuba watchers among the pres speculate that the lifting of the OAS sanctions will be engineered at the April General Assembly. They think it is just a matter of time before relations are normalized and assume that we are already in the stage of receiving and sending signals. Thus there are over reactions to such measures as the Litton Industries' exception and the travel restriction on Cuban UN diplomats. A public

*NODIS stands for "No Distribution."

From "Beisbol Diplomacy: Declassified Documents from 1975 Reveal Secret U.S.-Cuban Negotiations for Exhibition Games. http://www.gwu.edu/~nsarchiv/NSAEBB/NSAEBB12/nsaebb12.htm.

relations move would correct some of the distortions in the public mind about our Cuban policy—shifting the emphasis to a non-political and non-controversial area.

The Chinese ping-pong players were accepted by the US public as a good way to break the ice between countries separated by decades of hostility.

Baseball with Cuba would serve a similar purpose in bridging the gap between the Bay of Pigs and a new relationship with Castro.

- The President would have a sturdy platform for making an inescapable comment on Cuban policy in Miami next week.
- Picking a game we are likely to win would go well with Americans who are depressed by the regimented victories of the Communists in Olympic games.
- The match would be seen as a shrewd Yankee political move.

2. *The Effect on Castro and Cubans.*
Pre-Castro Cuba was considered the most "Americanized" of any Latin American country in terms of baseball, hot-dogs, and coca-cola. Much of this , and particularly baseball, persists. It still is the most popular spectator and corner lot sport.

Castro wants our technology and spare parts, but we understand he is worried about the effect of American influences on his population in the event of normalization.

- A baseball match would undercut the demonology in Cuban propaganda about the US.
- It would be difficult for Cuban exiles in the US to take issue with despite their general uneasiness about any change in US-Cuban relations.
- Under our existing travel restrictions, athletes have gone to Cuba for competitions. But our allowing a prominent baseball team to go there would be read as a political gesture by Castro.

5. Why the United States Should Boycott the 1980 Olympic Games in Moscow

PRESIDENT JIMMY CARTER

To Robert Kane
President, United States Olympic Committee,
Teagle Hall, Cornell University,
Ithaca, New York 14850

As President of this nation and as Honorary President of the United States Olympic Committee, I write to advise you of my views concerning the Games of the XXII Olympiad scheduled to be held in Moscow this Summer.

From Jimmy Carter, "1980 Summer Olympics Letter to the President of the U.S. Olympic Committee on the Games To Be Held in Moscow." January 20, 1980. Online by Gerhard Peters and John T. Woolley, The American Presidency Project. http://www.presidency.ucsb.edu/ws/?pid=33059.

I regard the Soviet invasion and the attempted suppression of Afghanistan as a serious violation of international law and an extremely serious threat to world peace. This invasion also endangers neighboring independent countries and access to a major part of the world's oil supplies. It therefore threatens our own national security, as well as the security of the region and the entire world.

We must make clear to the Soviet Union that it cannot trample upon an independent nation and at the same time do business as usual with the rest of the world. We must make clear that it will pay a heavy economic and political cost for such aggressions. That is why I have taken the severe economic measures announced on January 4, and why other free nations are supporting these measures. That is why the United Nations General Assembly, by an overwhelming vote of 104 to 18, condemned the invasion and urged the prompt withdrawal of Soviet troops.

I want to reaffirm my own personal commitment to the principles and purposes of the Olympic movement. I believe in the desirability of keeping Government policy out of the Olympics, but deeper issues are at stake.

In the Soviet Union international sports competition is itself an aspect of Soviet government policy, as is the decision to invade Afghanistan. The head of the Moscow Olympic Organizing Committee is a high Soviet Government official.

The Soviet Government attaches enormous political importance to the holding of the 1980 Olympic Games in Moscow, and if the Olympics are not held in Moscow because of Soviet military aggression in Afghanistan, this powerful signal of world outrage cannot be hidden from the Soviet people, and will reverberate around the globe. Perhaps it will deter future aggression.

I therefore urge the USOC, in cooperation with other National Olympic Committees, to advise the International Olympic Committee that if Soviet troops do not fully withdraw from Afghanistan within the next month, Moscow will become an unsuitable site for a festival meant to celebrate peace and good will. Should the Soviet Union fail to withdraw its troops within the time prescribed above, I urge the USOC to propose that the Games either be transferred to another site such as Montreal or to multiple sites, or be cancelled for this year. If the International Olympic Committee rejects such a USOC proposal, I urge the USOC and the Olympic Committees of other like-minded nations not to participate in the Moscow Games. In this event, if suitable arrangements can be made, I urge that such nations conduct alternative games of their own this summer at some other appropriate site or sites. The United States Government is prepared to lend its full support to any and all such efforts.

I know from your letter to me and your meeting with Secretary Vance and Lloyd Cutler of your deep concern for the men and women throughout the world who have trained tirelessly in the hopes of participating in the 1980 Olympic Games. I share your concern. I would support the participation of athletes from the entire world at Summer Olympic Games or other games this summer outside the Soviet Union, just as I welcome athletes from the entire world to Lake Placid, for the Winter Olympic Games.

I have the deepest admiration and respect for Olympic athletes and their pursuit of excellence. No one understands better than they the meaning of sacrifice to achieve worthy goals. There is no goal of greater importance than the goal at stake here—the security of our nation and the peace of the world.

I also urge that the IOC take a further step to eliminate future political competition among nations to serve as hosts for the Olympic Games. I call upon all nations to join in supporting a permanent site for the Summer Olympics in Greece, and to seek an appropriate permanent site for the Winter Olympics.

The course I am urging is necessary to help secure the peace of the world at this critical time. The most important task of world leaders, public and private, is to deter aggression and prevent war. Aggression destroys the international amity and goodwill that the Olympic movement attempts to foster. If our response to aggression is to continue with international sports as usual in the capital of the aggressor, our other steps to deter aggression are undermined.

The spirit and the very future of the Games depends upon courageous and resolute action at this time. I call for your support and your help in rallying the support of the other Olympic Committees throughout the world.

Sincerely,
JIMMY CARTER

ESSAYS

The first essay is written by Louis A. Pérez, Jr., the J. Carlyle Sitterson Professor of History at the University of North Carolina. In this essay, Pérez analyzes the rise of baseball in Cuba. In the late 1860s, young Cubans came to the United States for jobs, education, or to escape political turmoil that peaked in 1868 with the start of the Ten Years War against imperial Spain. They learned about baseball, and brought the game with them upon returning home at a time when Cubans were developing a sense of their national identity. While a sport imported into a country is often used to promote empire and social control, the recipient society can place their own values and norms upon that cultural artifact. Baseball in Cuba became a means of promoting nationalism and liberation. Baseball quickly became perceived as a sport that represented freedom, liberalism, and democracy in an oppressed colony as opposed to the Spanish sport of bull fighting that symbolized oppression and tyranny.

The second essay is by Donald E. Abelson of the Department of Political Science, director of The Canada-U.S. Institute and also the Centre for American Studies at the University of Western Ontario, and author of *A Capitol Idea: Think Tanks and U.S. Foreign Policy* (2002). His study examines one of the most exciting sporting events in American sport history, the semifinal men's ice hockey match between Russia and the United States at the 1980 Winter Olympics. The Russians had won the last four Olympic gold medals, and were universally considered the greatest national team in the world, while the U.S. squad was composed of wet-behind-the-ears college boys. The hockey game took on even greater meaning than a confrontation between Goliath and David because of its symbolic importance as part of the Cold War. The shocking American victory in the "Miracle on Ice" gave the United States an unlikely opportunity to demonstrate the superiority of its cultural, political, and economic system at a time when we were struggling internationally over our hostages in Iran and the Russian invasion of Afghanistan.

The National Pastime Comes to Cuba

LOUIS A. PÉREZ, JR.

Cubans migrated north ... [to study,] as economic émigrés, victims of unemployment and economic depression.... Tens of thousands ... arrived as political refugees.... Between 1868 and 1898, this migration swelled into a diaspora, distributed principally in New Orleans, Key West, Tampa, Philadelphia, and New York.

The Cuban presence in the north was ... a transforming experience, for it occurred as Cubans sought new and alternative means of being "Cuban" as compared with being "Spanish." Cubans in the United States constituted a heterogeneous population, mostly white, almost all of whom had been born on the island. They included young men and women, representatives of both the planter bourgeoisie ... and the powerful ranchers.... They emerged, too, from the rapidly expanding ranks of the *criollo* [people born in the island] middle class.... [T]hey all shared ... discontent with Spanish rule....

In this context experience in the north was decisive in shaping Cuban national identity. Cubans, by the hundreds of thousands, came to know the United States intimately and were themselves shaped by this familiarity....

As the pursuit of *Cuba Libre* stretched across decades and over generations, Cuban susceptibility to North American ways increased....

The process intensified Cuban discontent with the world of their home. Cubans who arrived in the United States were not slow to note the differences and disparities between the colony and the north.... The United States was not only a standard and source of modernity but also an experienced alternative that helped Cubans envision the dismantling of colonial structures and the establishment of a nation, ... deficiencies of the colonial condition and suggested possibilities for transforming their homeland into a nation.

The rising popularity of baseball in the United States coincided with the years when Cuban immigration was the greatest and it centered in many of the cities where the Cuban community was large. Cuban émigrés could not but take note of the sport where it had captured the imagination of the North American public. Jose Marti, the principal organizer of Cuban independence abroad, was living in New York in the mid-1880s, and he viewed the growing popularity of baseball with a mixture of curiosity and wonder....

Cubans in the United States were early susceptible to the appeal of baseball, no doubt for many of the same reasons that North Americans were.... Cubans received baseball as a medium of North American culture, able to reproduce

From Louis A. Perez, "Between Baseball and Bullfighting: The Quest for Nationality in Cuba, 1868–1898," Journal of American History 81 (1994): 493–517, by permission of Oxford University Press.

social relationships and reveal normative boundaries of North American society—a way to mediate the Cuban encounter with the north, to grow familiar with North American ways and participate in those ways.

Cubans played baseball on college and university teams, in their neighborhoods, and at the workplace. Esteban Bellan played on the baseball team at Fordham University near New York City in 1870 and 1871. Cubans in Key West, Florida, formed four baseball teams (Cuba, Fe, Habana, and Esperanza), around which a Sunday municipal league was organized on a ball field provided by the Cuban cigar manufacturer Eduardo Hidalgo Gato.... The first Cuban team in Ybor City (later annexed to Tampa), the Niagara Baseball Club, was organized in 1887, only a year after the founding of the town.... Cubans were also among the first professional ballplayers in the United States. Esteban Bellan—known professionally as Steve Bellan—left Fordham to play third base for the Troy Haymakers (1871–1872) and shortstop for the New York Mutuals (1873) of the National Association.

Cubans returned to the island with a new knowledge of themselves and of the north, conscious of new meanings and mindful of new possibilities. And they returned with a knowledge of baseball ... as a paradigm of progress. They returned bearing modernity, having already started to reinvent themselves self-consciously as agents of change.

Baseball arrived in the island in the 1860s, as Cuban students returned from North American colleges and universities. Almost all the Cubans associated with the early development of baseball on the island had studied or lived in the United States. Emilio Sabourin, manager-player for the Habana Baseball Club, one of the team's founders, attended a business college in Washington, D.C. Other members of the original Habana Baseball Club who studied in the United States included Ernesto Guillo and Francisco Saavedra.... Almost all of the original members of the Matanzas Baseball Club, ... studied in the United States.... The first games were played in Havana, arranged by Cuban players who organized local teams, recruited other Cubans to play, and purchased uniforms and equipment. The first professional team, the Habana Baseball Club, was founded in 1872; a year later, the Matanzas Baseball Club was established. In 1874, Bellan returned to Cuba to play for Habana and organized the first professional game in Cuba. In 1878, a third professional team, the Almendares Baseball Club, was organized. In the same year, the Habana, Matanzas, and Almendares clubs formally agreed to organize themselves professionally into the *Liga General de Base Ball de la Isla de Cuba.*

[I]n 1878, ... peace returned to Cuba, and so too did thousands of Cubans who had emigrated to the United States during the war. Many returned changed by the experience in the north; not least among the changes was a new enthusiasm for baseball. Indeed, the popularity of baseball ... was nothing less than extraordinary.... Havana neighborhood teams (*clubes de barri'o*) multiplied.... Several Afro-Cuban societies organized baseball teams during the 1880s, including the Universo Baseball Club, the Comercio Baseball Club, and the Varo'n Baseball Club in Havana and the Fraternidad Baseball Club in Guanabacoa....

By the 1880s, the Sunday afternoon baseball game had become a fixed feature of social life in Havana.... [O]ne well-known North American travel guide to Cuba recommended Sunday baseball in Havana as an enjoyable afternoon outing and an alternative to the bullfight.

The popularity of baseball also quickly spread across the island and into the provinces. Virtually every town and city of any size organized at least one baseball team.... [M]ore than two hundred baseball teams were organized across the island between the late 1870s and the early 1890s.

Most of the provincial clubs were summer clubs (*clubes de verano*), which were especially popular in the interior towns and cities. The summer months, which followed ... the sugar harvest, were a time of ... seasonal unemployment and idleness.... Baseball quickly developed into a popular summer pastime for fans and players, emerging as one of the principal forms of local recreation.

As baseball grew in popularity and the numbers of teams increased, [and] competition became better organized.... In the late 1880s baseball promoters in Las Villas organized a provincial championship series among teams representing the cities of Santa Clara, Sagua la Grande, and Cienfuegos ... facilitated by the railroads.... [T]elegraph service allowed hometown fans to follow the progress of their local teams on the road.

Cuban baseball teams soon developed sufficiently to compete with North American teams. Increasing numbers of clubs from the United States incorporated Cuba into their barnstorming circuits during the winter and spring months. The first team from the United States to play in Cuba, the Bitter Hops Baseball Club, arrived in 1881 to play Almendares. The Philadelphia Athletics played a series of exhibition games against Cuban professional teams in 1886. In 1890, the New York Giants played winter ball in Havana. A year later an all-star minor league team, on which a young John McGraw played, traveled to Cuba to play a series of exhibition games with a Cuban all-star team. In 1893 a United States women's professional ball club traveled to Havana to play Almendares.

Baseball soon drew a mass audience, in the capital and in the provinces, all year long. In 1886 the final championship game between Habana and Almendares attracted 6,000 fans.... A series of games in [January] 1892 between the visiting Cincinnati Kellys (American Association) and the Fe Baseball Club in Havana drew 5,000 fans weekly.

As game attendance increased, so did the number of ball parks ... comparable to the best professional ball parks in the United States. In 1890, the Habana Baseball Club constructed a home park with a seating capacity of nearly ten thousand.

The expanding economic ties between Cuba and the United States, expressed principally in expanding trade and growing North American investments on the island also promoted the popularity of baseball in Cuba. Crews aboard United States merchant vessels, often idle at Cuban ports for weeks at a time, organized themselves into baseball teams to play local Cuban clubs. In the large provincial ports filled with United States ships during the sugar harvest, especially Matanzas and Cardenas on the north coast and Cienfuegoes and Santiago de Cuba on the South, U.S.–Cuban rivalry became an important aspect of local baseball. North Americans who arrived in Cuba under contract, principally as construction workers, technicians, steamship and railroad crews, and mechanics, also passed some of their leisure time playing baseball against local teams....

Improved maritime transportation between Cuba and the United States also permitted Cubans to travel north, as individual players and as complete teams. During the 1880s and 1890s, Havana teams, including Fe and Esperanza, traveled to Key West to play against the local municipal-league teams. Habana Baseball Club pitcher Adolfo Lujan played for several teams in New York and Key West before returning to Havana. The popularity of baseball was also reflected in the proliferation of weekly baseball newspapers and magazines, in Havana and in the provinces, whose number expanded almost as quickly as the number of baseball teams. Among the most popular Havana weeklies were *El Sport*, *El Base-Ball* ..., and *El Pelotero*. The Habana and Almendares baseball clubs had their own publications (*El Habanista* and *El Almendarista*)....

Baseball in nineteenth-century Cuba offers a measure of colonial society in transition—it was an expression of change and an agent of change. The northern origin of baseball enabled its practitioners in Cuba to participate in modernity.... Cubans celebrated the modernity and progress implied in baseball, associated with the United States, and denounced the in-humanity and backwardness suggested by bullfighting, associated with Spain. Baseball became a means by which Cubans ... give one more expression to their discontent. Cubans subsumed notions of civilization into baseball and of barbarism into bullfighting and drew a Manichaean moral: the contrast between the Old World and the New, Spain and the United States, the past and the future.... Jose Marti was unequivocal about bullfighting: "a futile bloody spectacle ... and against Cuban sentiment as being intimately linked with our colonial past."

This was a view many *criollos* shared. "Public festivals ... observed the Cuban philosopher-poet Enrique Jose Varona in 1887, "... offer one of the clearest indicators of the level of civilization at which each is found.... [M]en and entire classes found at various low levels in this evolution ... come together to witness a spectacle in which the spilling of blood is the inducement" ... Baseball, on the other hand, wrote Varona, "introduces into our customs a valuable element of physical regeneration and moral progress." Journalist Rafael M. Merchan described the bullfight as the "most ferocious and cruel of amusements," while writer, baseball player, and baseball promoter Wenceslao Galvez y Delmonte drew the distinction bluntly: "Baseball is an enlightened spectacle and the bullfight is a barbaric spectacle." ... Novelist Carlos Loveira gave further definition to this dichotomy in his partly autobiographical 1920 novel *Generales y doctores*. The protagonist, Ignacio Garcia, recalled a Sunday afternoon in Havana:

> That afternoon, in addition to a baseball game—enlightened, moral, virile, and wholesome—there was a bullfight, a savage sport that did not appeal to the noble and enlightened Cuban disposition. In the rows of seats and boxes of the baseball stadium, swarmed the Cuban multitude of both sexes.... At the barbaric affair, crammed the foreign multitude ... among whom, naturally, was not to be found a single Cuban....

Certainly baseball sharpened the distinctions between Cubans and Spaniards when those distinctions were increasingly assuming political implications.... Baseball offered the possibility of national integration of all Cubans, of all classes, black and white, young and old, men and women....

From the outset baseball in Cuba involved women as spectators and fans at hometown games and as participants in banquets after the games. The presence of women ... was undoubtedly influenced by Cubans' observation of women at baseball parks in the United States; women spectators thereby became a fixed aspect of the game for Cubans....

Attendance at a baseball game provided women an opportunity to move into the public sphere and to participate in an important facet of creole social life that was loaded with messages and metaphors of nation. Baseball offered a new attraction, a new source of membership, an opportunity to be publicly partisan in an activity that was perceived as distinctly Cuban.

The presence of women, moreover, further ennobled baseball in the eyes of Cubans, who interpreted the *aficion* of women for the game as yet one more confirmation of the gentility and refinement of baseball, in sharp contrast to the brutish and bloody bullfight. Galvez extolled "the delightful company of ladies ... who contribute to the sustenance of baseball by their presence at the games...."

In nineteenth-century Cuba, baseball offered the possibility of social mobility and the blurring of class lines. Cubans constructed out of baseball a usable paradigm of modernity ... in which service to the community gave individuals a chance for mobility and in which membership derived solely from ability....

Baseball promised the possibility of civilization: harmony among competing classes, orderly competition between conflicting interests, a way to reconcile opportunity for individual achievement with group status, and a social progress in which individual skills and personal ambitions bent to community needs.... The code implied a moral framework. Perhaps without fully realizing the nature of the process, Cubans began to connect their experiences in the north with their lives in Cuba.

Cubans detected something else in baseball.... Having suffered defeat ... in 1878, Cuban separatists discerned in baseball a usable moral. The formulation of baseball as *lucha,* as a process in which defeat was temporary and victory a function of preparation (practice) and unity (teamwork), assumed powerful metaphoric resonance....

Baseball offered access to modernity, a status to which all Cubans could aspire, and none more than those disaffected from Spanish rule. Baseball was both symbol and surrogate for opposition at a time when alternative symbols were scarce. In the final years of Spanish colonialism, social and political passions, denied normal outlets, expressed themselves freely in baseball. The ball field was a stage on which select individuals played representative roles that were charged with social and political significance. Simply by not being Spanish, baseball embodied a critique of the colonial regime.

In the capital and in the provinces, in the clubs frequented by creole elites and in working-class neighborhoods, among Afro-Cubans in Guanabacoa and cigar workers in Key West, Cubans played baseball and thus played out a complex drama of a society in transition, of a people contemplating nationhood and searching for means to give form to nationality....

The undoing of colonialism was a gradual process during which normative structures were discredited and cultural forms passed into disrepute and desuetude, during which Cubans turned to alternative forms to repudiate Spanish ways and to express an emerging national identity....

Baseball promoted both local attachments and national allegiance. Nationality obtained new forms of expression when Cubans played North Americans, as team loyalty expanded into a source of national identity. Provincial and municipal rivalries brought Cubans together as townspeople supporting local teams, to compete but also to develop a sense of social integration, and of shared idiom and shared identity. Baseball also incorporated women into the discourse on nation. Women involved with baseball were engaged in the transformation that baseball signified, the affirmation of something Cuban and the pursuit of forms expressive of a separate nationality.

Baseball provided shared images that could bear and disseminate common values. Teams bore names of the[ir] neighborhoods and towns ... and as voluntary associations they offered a degree of popular democracy not readily available.... Cubans discerned that baseball could create a national community out of racially mixed and socially diverse fans, thereby suggesting the possibility of consensus around which to pursue nationhood.... In the end, baseball was a metaphor for the people Cubans wished to become.

Cubans consciously used baseball to embody the moral order from which their vision of nation was derived: to represent a means of nationality no less than an ideal of nationhood. Carlos Ayala had organized the Fe Baseball Club in a Havana neighborhood in the early 1880s, he later wrote, to promote "physical exercise and develop habits of respect and mutual consideration that are developed in the playing of baseball." Aurelio Miranda, one of the founders of the Habana Baseball Club in 1872, consciously subsumed a vision of nation into baseball.... Baseball could teach discipline and patience, virtues necessary to successful nationhood....

The proposition that baseball was a school to promote national identity and patriotic virtues and, more, a training ground to prepare Cubans for the redemptive mission of national liberation early captured the Cuban imagination. Ayala ascribed to the Fe Baseball Club a national mission, a patriotic purpose he believed baseball uniquely capable of fulfilling.... Spanish colonial authorities were not oblivious to the implications of the North American sport. The challenge to colonial rule, Spanish officials understood, came from many different directions.... [O]fficials were unable to restrict or otherwise reverse the growing popularity of baseball in Cuba. That they tried no doubt enhanced the appeal of baseball to many Cubans.... That a sport unfamiliar to Spaniards had so taken hold among Cubans unsettled local authorities.... [T]hey recognized almost from the outset the subversive power of baseball....

That the popularity of baseball increased so quickly, among so many Cubans, caused concern among Spanish residents and led periodically to demands that teams be disbanded and games banned. Indeed, as early as 1873, ..., government authorities banned baseball as an "anti-Spanish activity." The ban was revoked a year later, but Spanish suspicions never abated. In the mid-1880s the conservative newspaper *Diario de Cardenas* commented on the popularity of baseball in Cardenas with concern and suspicion and warned gravely about the "threat" that baseball posed to "the integrity of the country." In 1876, colonial authorities refused to sanction the name Yara for a new baseball team in Havana because of its association with the proclamation of rebellion that precipitated the Ten Years' War, the "Grito de Yara" of 1868.... In 1881 local Spanish authorities ordered the dissolution of the Cardenas Baseball Club after observing an intramural game and concluding that Cuban players were developing new battle tactics to use against Spanish troops.

Disapproval of the bullfight need not have assumed any concrete form.... To support baseball, however, had other implications, for in so doing Cubans constructed an alternative moral order, ... of a superior morality and a higher level of civilization. Baseball was not simply an alternative to the bullfight; it was opposition; it challenged it and the moral universe that it represented. Baseball carried a political subtext that served both to form, and to give form to, Cuban discontent. That increasing numbers of Cubans were turning away from the national pastime of the bullfight to take up baseball offended Spanish sensibilities and aroused Spanish suspicions. Not a few Spaniards suspected—correctly—that the Cuban rejection of the bullfight was simply a thinly disguised repudiation of Spain....

During the early 1890s, as Cuban discontent with colonial rule deepened, even as Cubans prepared for a new war of national liberation, Cubans were playing baseball: in virtually every large city and provincial town, at home and abroad.... The Spanish poet Manuel Curros Enriquez arrived in Cuba ... in 1894. There, he later recalled, he found a people wholly absorbed in baseball.... [When the war for independence began in 1895, the authorities banned baseball as subversive. Many prominent baseball supporters joined the revolution.]

During the 1890s political conditions again forced Cubans to emigrate. Cubans by the thousands dispersed throughout the Caribbean, taking with them their passion for baseball. Indeed, Cubans served as the principal transmitters of baseball in much of the Caribbean region during the late nineteenth century. As early as the 1870s, Cuban émigrés arrived in the Dominican Republic to organize sugar production.... Shortly thereafter, the brothers Ignacio and Ubaldo Alomai arrived in the Dominican capital, Santo Domingo, from Cienfuegos, and within months they had organized two baseball teams. In the early 1890s, the Havana cigar manufacturer Emilio Cramer arrived in Caracas to establish *La Cubana* cigarette factory. Together with other Cuban émigrés and Venezuelans, Cramer organized a Caracas city league of five teams. At about the same time, the Cuban émigré community in the Yucatan introduced baseball in the Mexican cities of Merida and Progreso, with the local municipal teams bearing names suggesting the origins of the organizers: Cuba Baseball Club, Habana Baseball Club, and Matanzas Baseball Club.

Cubans abroad played baseball all through the war, in support of the war, and baseball thereby acquired one more role. In Key West and Tampa, baseball games became patriotic functions designed to raise funds, to obtain public support for local revolutionary juntas, and to make propaganda in behalf of Cuban independence.... Gate receipts from games were donated to the local chapter of the Cuban Revolutionary Party (PRC).... Cramer served as treasurer of the PRC chapter in Caracas and used funds raised by baseball to support the Cuban war effort.

That *aficionados* of baseball—promoters, players, and fans alike—were susceptible to the separatist summons was perhaps predictable.... Cubans associated with baseball perceived themselves already in transition to modernity—a process, they understood, blocked by the continued presence of Spain. Baseball was thus early associated with independence and nation, further heightening the prestige of what Cubans in growing numbers were already calling their "national pastime." Baseball had become identified with the cause of *Cuba Libre*, fully integrated into the mystique and metaphysics of national liberation. For many baseball had proven its value to the nation simply by having promoted the physical stamina of youths who subsequently, as *insurrecto*s, endured the rigors of field operations against the Spanish army....

Baseball resumed in Cuba after the end of the war. The old professional teams resumed play; new neighborhood teams were organized. Many new team names testified to the nationalist tone of the national pastime: *Libertad, Patria, Demajagua, Patriota, Independencia,* and *'98*. Visiting Havana during the final months of Spanish administration in late 1898, Robert P. Porter observed that bullfights were "patronised by the Spanish element exclusively" and that "baseball continues to hold public favour." The United States military occupation, from 1899 to 1902, gave further impetus to baseball in Cuba. Army units across the island organized into local soldiers' leagues, playing intraservice games in which Cubans participated. At the same time, in Havana and in towns and cities across the island, North American army posts organized games between soldiers and local Cuban clubs. The Cuban press carried almost daily stories and line scores of games.... It can only be imagined what values and meanings were assigned to the outcome of games ... against the occupiers.

During the military occupation, the number of United States teams traveling to Cuba increased. In 1899 an "All American" team from New Orleans arrived in Havana to play a series of exhibition games against Cuban teams. Cuban teams also traveled north. An "All Cuban" team played a series of exhibition games in New York in October 1900. Major league teams also traveled to Cuba. In November 1900, the Brooklyn Dodgers, ... the National League champions ..., played the New York Giants in ... Havana. The Brooklyn club also played exhibition games in Havana against the *Cubanos*, an all-star team organized for the occasion, and against the Matanzas Baseball Club....

The popularity of baseball increased during the occupation. The number of organized teams expanded across the island, and game attendance increased. Sunday games in Havana routinely attracted four to five thousand fans....

After 1898 the triumph of baseball over bullfighting was definitive.... [T]he United States military government officially banned bullfighting....

Gradually, too, the possibilities of baseball began to insinuate themselves into North American policy calculations. After 1898, United States officials came to see baseball as a potential instrument of political order and social control. The United States minister to Santo Domingo James Sullivan gave vivid expression to these musings within a decade of Cuban independence: "The American national game of baseball is being played and supported here with great enthusiasm.... It satisfies a craving in the nature of the people for exciting conflict and is a real substitute for the contest on the hillsides with the rifles, if it could be fostered and made important by a league of teams in the various towns in the country...."

Only a year after Sullivan wrote his memorandum, Cubans were assigning different meanings to baseball and evolving a new and complex relationship with the game and with North Americans. "What Cuban who has attended a baseball game between Almendares and one of the great North American major league teams that has visited us in recent years," Jose Sixto de Sola asked rhetorically in 1914, "has not felt linked to our players and the rest of the fans by a powerful bond? ... What is it that produces such intense enthusiasm ...? Ah! It is the national sentiment. All are Cubans and they feel Cuban."

Cubans demonstrated early that they could derive from baseball what they needed and discard the rest, that the meanings, values, and symbols ascribed to baseball could be radically different in a Cuban context than in a North American one, and that they could serve Cuban needs as defined by Cubans. In the course of the twentieth century, baseball emerged as one of the principal expressions of Cuban nationalist sentiment, a way to incorporate Cubans into the nation, a means to project the nation abroad and to promote social integration at home.

Politics on Ice: The United States, the Soviet Union, and a Hockey Game in Lake Placid, 1980

DONALD E. ABELSON

It is known as the "Miracle on Ice" and is widely regarded as the greatest sports moment of the twentieth century. During a snowy afternoon in Lake Placid, New York, on 22 February 1980, the US Men's Hockey Team, coached by the legendary Herb Brooks, defeated the heavily favored Soviet Union 4–3, setting the stage for the US gold medal victory against Finland. Considered a long shot for a medal before the XIIIth Winter Games began, the US Hockey Team captured the imagination and harnessed the spirit of an entire nation.

... It is a story about a coach with a vision, a team of patriotic kids from mostly working-class families who were prepared to make sacrifices for the unknown, and a nation that was desperately searching for someone or something to restore its faith and confidence. But it is also a story of how and why sporting

---

Donald E. Abelson, "Politics on Ice: The United States, the Soviet Union, and a Hockey Game in Lake Placid," *Canadian Review of American Studies* 40 (2010): 63–65, 67–68, 74–83, 85, 87–90. Reprinted with permission from University of Toronto Press (www.utpjournals.com).

events can easily be transformed from athletic contests to political confrontations where athletes, like brave and courageous soldiers, are expected to wage battle with their adversaries. More importantly, it is a story about how a group of athletes were able to remain focused on their goal at a time of considerable political upheaval and nationalistic fervor.

In light of heightened Cold War tensions … is not surprising that what took place in the hockey arena between the Americans and Soviets was catapulted into the political arena. After all, during the Cold War, any major event that involved a matchup between the Soviets and Americans … was bound to be viewed as not only a confrontation between the world's two superpowers, but as a competition between two very different political systems and sets of ideological beliefs. What is interesting is not that the showdown between the US Hockey Team and the Soviets, … it is that despite the political importance the media and policy-makers assigned to this contest, Coach Brooks and his players did not allow themselves to be swept up in what was quickly becoming a political tidal wave.…

For a group of patriotic American college students raised during the height of the Cold War, it would have been tempting to treat the Soviets as their mortal enemy. After all, in the eyes of the media, policy-makers, and the public, the twenty Soviet players proudly displaying CCCP across their chests were more than competitors—they represented a country that had invaded Afghanistan, supplied nuclear weapons to Cuba, and tried to spread communism throughout Europe, Latin America, Asia, and Africa. As President Reagan remarked in the early days of his administration, the Soviets constituted the "Evil Empire" and stood for everything the United States opposed. However, despite widespread fear and animosity in the United States toward the Soviet Union, the US Hockey Team paid little attention to the political dimensions of the US-Soviet rivalry. As Dave Silk, a forward on the 1980 US Hockey Team observed, "For us it was a hockey game. To the rest of the world, it was a political statement.…" The unwillingness of the US hockey players to be drawn into international politics stood in stark contrast to the animosity expressed by several Team Canada players toward their Russian opponents during the historic 1972 Summit, which, in the words of Team Canada's Phil Esposito, was nothing short of a war. Still, by the time the pairings for the medal games were announced, the US players began to realize that they were no longer preparing for just another hockey game.… [T]he US players understood that far more was at stake than a medal. Indeed, despite Coach Brooks's efforts to keep his players out of Cold War politics, the US Hockey Team had been propelled into the national and international spotlight.… Jim Craig, Mike Eruzione, Mark Johnson, and their teammates became America's best hope for reasserting the country's strength and prowess.

The purpose of this paper is to explore the intersection of sport and politics by examining how and to what extent the media, policymakers, and the public drew upon the success of the 1980 US Hockey Team for political purposes. While the spectacular victory over the Soviets—a victory that was cast as nothing short of David versus Goliath—lifted the spirits of a nation at a time of considerable unrest, it also afforded politicians, journalists, and the American public an opportunity to claim supremacy in the political arena. In short, the US Hockey Team's exceptional performance ... did more than convince Americans to proudly display the Stars and Stripes.... After years of frustration over worsening economic conditions at home and a growing sense of powerlessness on the world stage, the American victory gave the United States, not to mention the increasingly disillusioned and despondent Carter Administration, a reason to celebrate. As Mike Eruzione, captain of the US Hockey Team proclaimed, "Winning the gold medal didn't solve the Iranian crisis, it didn't pull the Soviets out of Afghanistan. But people felt better. People were proud. People felt good about being Americans ..."

... It was the perception of millions of spectators that this phenomenal story could happen only in America, the world's greatest democracy—where if you work hard enough, you can accomplish anything—that helped fuel the politicization of the US-Soviet showdown.

... [T]he response of the United States to the success of its hockey team not only gave rise to nationalistic pride. It laid the foundation for ... blatant forms of political opportunism. As American voters were preparing to decide President Carter's fate in the November 1980 election, the president and some of his challengers tried to align themselves with the US Gold Medal Team. On several occasions, President Carter and other leading political figures drew upon the success of the US Hockey Team to mobilize support for their campaigns. In fact, some of the players, including Mike Eruzione and Jim Craig, were asked to join presidential candidates on the campaign trail.

... The US-Soviet game may have provided a perfect platform for politicians and other opinion makers to make claims about the superiority of their country, its political institutions, and its strength of its character, but along the way they overlooked what the hockey team accomplished. [T]hat the United States, a country not known for its love of hockey, produced highly skilled players who could compete successfully with the best Eastern European teams was of secondary importance.... In an ideal world, spectators would simply relish what athletes ... accomplish.... But ... sport is about politics as it is about athletic prowess....

Let the Games Begin

The Olympic torch had not even been lit when the puck was dropped at the Olympic Field House on 12 February 1980, to begin the first game between the United States and Sweden, an event that drew little media interest and even less fanfare.... The United States had been assigned to the Blue Division along with Sweden, Czechoslovakia, Romania, Norway, and West Germany.... Brooks knew that his team would have to at least tie Sweden, a team the United States had not beaten since 1960, to have a fighting chance of making it to the medal round.

... The United States went into the third period with a 1–1 tie, only to watch the Swedes take the lead ... at 4:55. For the next fourteen minutes, Brooks paced the bench calling out instructions as his players tried desperately to even the score. Finally, with thirty-seven seconds remaining, defenseman Bill Baker, … from the right point launched a low slapshot that found its way through Lindbergh's pads. The US bench exploded as Baker raised his stick in the air. Final score, Sweden 2, United States 2.

With Sweden behind them, the United States could now focus its sights on Czechoslovakia, a team that had won the world championship in 1972 and in 1976, a team that was seeded second behind the Soviet Union and a team that had just demolished Norway 11–0. Although few would have predicted that the United States could even skate with the Czechs, they stunned the hockey world by defeating them 7–3.… [I]n the process of defeating a team whose country was firmly under the political control of the Soviet Union, had ignited a flame under the nation.…

… Despite his efforts to keep his team insulated from the press, Brooks could not prevent the media frenzy surrounding future games. By the time his players squared off against Norway on 16 February, media and fan interest in the US team was in full swing.

The win against the Norwegians (5–1) was followed by victories over Romania (7–2) and West Germany (4–2). Having made their way through the initial round undefeated, the United States entered the medal round. Its first opponent—the Soviet Union.…

The Red Scare: Not Quite

… As Brooks stated, his team did not practice for six months to prove to the world the superiority of the American way of life. He said, "If we think we have to win a hockey game or win a medal to prove that our system is the right system, or the way we live is the right way to live, then we are in big trouble.…" But ironically neither Brooks nor his players had much control over how this contest would be viewed.

The national mood was malaise; the citizenry was gloomy, frustrated, angry, helpless. Suddenly, twenty unknown kids, playing a game maybe 20% of the populace knew much about, were finding themselves billed as America's Team.… They were one day away from facing the Russians now, and found themselves carrying the load for the President, the Pentagon, the hostages, General Motors, Dow Jones, the *Saturday Evening Post* and the Four Freedoms.…

… By the time the US-Soviet contest was announced, the players began to understand that they were not simply preparing for another hockey game. Like it or not, they were carrying the weight of the country on their shoulder pads. As Dave Silk remarked, "Heading into the game against the Russians, the only thing that gave us a feel for what was going on outside were all the telegrams.… One telegram read, 'Kill those Commie bastards.' At that point, we began to understand what this game meant to people." In the context of increased Cold War tensions that resulted in, among other things, President Carter's decision to boycott the Moscow Summer Games, this game was viewed by millions of Americans as a superpower confrontation that pitted good against evil, freedom against totalitarianism, and right against wrong.

In the late afternoon on 22 February 1980, the Americans walked briskly from their locker room and stepped onto the ice. But unlike at their first game in the Olympic Field House against Sweden, there were no empty seats. Over 8,500 people had jammed into the arena to cheer on their new-found heroes.... Even before the puck was dropped, thousands of fans began chanting, "USA! USA!" The United States was about to face the Soviet Union, a team that had sailed through the preliminary round outscoring their opponents 51–11. At stake was more than national pride, ... a chance to play for the gold medal, which the United States had not done since 1960.

... Providing color commentary for ABC was Al Michaels and Ken Dryden, the Hall of Fame goaltender of the Montreal Canadians. Michaels was well aware of how the game was being viewed—as a political confrontation between East and West, a battle between David and Goliath—but tried to remind viewers that what was about to take place was "manifestly a hockey game being played on a sheet of ice in Lake Placid." As a result of scheduling conflicts, the game was tape-delayed viewers in the United States....

The United States team were dressed in white, the Soviets in red.... In net for the Americans was Jim Craig, the Boston University All-American whose performance between the pipes was nothing short of exceptional.... At the other end of the ice was Vladislav Tretiak, widely regarded as the greatest goalie in the world.

... [T]he red light behind Craig's net did not flash until midway through the first period when Vladimir Krutov found a hole in his defense. But less than five minutes later, Buzz Schneider broke in on Tretiak and with a hard slapshot beat the goaltender. The Field House erupted ... but it would not take long to break the tie. Sergei Makharov scored at 17:34 and once again the Soviets took the lead. Although their team trailed the Soviets, most American fans were relieved that the United States would head to the locker room only one goal behind. However, with three seconds remaining on the clock, Mark Johnson, [of] the University of Wisconsin ... split the Soviet defense and with one second remaining picked up a Tretiak rebound and shot it past the startled goalie. Once again, the crowd broke into celebration as Johnson evened the score. After one period of play, United States 2, Soviet Union 2.

The second period would result in only one goal—Maltsev from Krutov at 2:18. For the remainder of the period, both teams would have their chances, but neither would be able to capitalize. With one period of play remaining, the Soviets led 3–2. The United States had found themselves in a similar position several times during the tournament when they were forced to come from behind to win....

At 8:39 of the third period, Mark Johnson proved again that he could perform magic by taking a pass from Dave Silk and beating Vladimir Myshkin, who had replaced Tretiak in goal at the beginning of the second period.... [T]he fans were ecstatic.... With ten minutes left, Mike Eruzione, the captain of the US squad ... moved into the slot and blew a twenty-foot wrist-shot past Myshkin.... With the Field House roof about to come off, the Americans had taken the lead for the first time in the game and now had to fend off the Soviets during the second half of the period. The Soviets were relentless. Shot after shot they looked for a way to beat Craig, but to no avail.... [W]ith three seconds remaining on the clock, Al Michaels, anxiously anticipating a US victory, excitedly asked his famous question, "Do you believe in miracles?"... The buzzer sounded. It was pandemonium....

... The US Hockey Team had accomplished what few thought they could. An emotional Jim McKay of ABC compared the US win to a Canadian university football team defeating the Pittsburgh Steelers. Other comparisons would follow. The United States had been outshot 39–16, but they had not been outplayed. They had brought the great Russian bear to its knees.... [T]he United States had defeated what many believed was the greatest hockey team ever to take the ice.... Ironically, the results of the game had not been conveyed to viewers across the United States who ... would be watching the event later that night. Amid the chaos, Herb Brooks found a quiet spot to take a phone call from President Carter congratulating him and his team on their win. Perhaps the president did not realize that the US players had to win one more game before they could be assured a medal. Or perhaps defeating the Soviets at something so important to their national identity was sufficient justification for the White House to call....

[T]he US victory would be front page news for days. Even before the United States defeated Finland 4–2 for the gold medal, it became clear that, for many Americans, beating the Soviet Union was the top story. After years of domestic and foreign policy turmoil that, in President Carter's words, had resulted in "a crisis in confidence." Americans were looking for a reason to feel good about their country again. And what better way to raise the spirits of a nation than to defeat its Cold War adversary at a game that had become such a critical part of its national identity. The United States might have been unable to prevent the Soviet Union from meddling in international affairs, but it had stopped it from claiming hockey supremacy on American soil....

[Jack O'Callahan said], "Looking back, I do believe that our victory was a catalyst for a reawakening of the national spirit that was at a low ebb due to economic, political and social issues. We were the catalyst, but the country was ripe for an awakening. It was all set up and we stepped into the void. We supplied that first big emotional tipping point that got everything else going...."

While the US win over the Soviets might indeed have re-energized the American spirit, to what extent was this important victory responsible for ushering in a new phase in American politics? Did the US win reawaken nationalism in the United States that had lain dormant for years ..., or was it simply seized upon by political leaders, the media, and the public to advance a wide range of political goals? ...

Cold Warriors? From the Hockey Arena to the Political Arena

Like his players ..., Brooks was keenly aware of what was taking place in the international community, but ... made a concerted effort to keep the White House at bay. He was there to coach, not to become immersed in Cold War politics and global diplomacy, although he realized that "politics and athletics are inseparable and anyone who thinks otherwise is kidding himself." Even if he was willing to assume the role of ambassador, there was nothing he or his team could do to free the hostages in Iran, force the Soviets from Afghanistan, or resolve the energy crisis....

However, no sooner had his team returned to the locker room following their gold medal win over Finland, did Brooks ... become involved in the politics surrounding the US victory. Shortly after President Carter placed his second call in two days to congratulate Brooks and his players.... Carter ... told Brooks, "We were working on Iran and economics, but nobody could do business because we were watching TV...."

During the welcoming ceremony for the athletes who participated in the 1980 Winter Games, President Carter said in part, "For me, as President of the United States of America, this is one of the proudest moments that I've ever experienced.... The U.S. hockey team—their victory was one of the most breathtaking upsets not only in Olympic history but in the entire history of sport...." Carter ... was preoccupied with the success of the US Hockey Team and how he could translate their victory ... to his advantage in the political arena ... as he began his uphill battle to hold onto the presidency.

Carter's willingness to draw on the success of the 1980 Hockey Team came as no surprise to Washington insiders. As Haynes Johnson of the *Washington Post* observed, "Jimmy Carter certainly was a political beneficiary of that victory.... What president would have done less?" After three years of overseeing a dismal economy and a mismanaged foreign policy that left the United States feeling victimized by the international community, the US victory in Lake Placid had provided Carter with a glimmer of hope.... The US Hockey Team had galvanized the nation. It was a picture-perfect moment that the often-dejected president could not afford to pass up.... [T]he team had done more to lift the spirits of their country in two weeks than the Carter White House had done since coming to office.

In the days and weeks following their victory, the president, policymakers on Capitol Hill, and the media went to great lengths to claim that what happened ... in Lake Placid exemplified all that was good about America and all that was wrong with the godless communists. In countless speeches on the campaign trail, Carter drew comparisons between the hope that his presidency offered to the hope the US Hockey Team had given the nation.... The storyline ... was clear. The United States had rebounded from years of misery with its integrity and power intact. American hostages were still being held by Iranian militants, but the United States refused to be held hostage. If anything, the victory of the young hockey team has demonstrated that the United States would forever remain a guiding light to all who value freedom and honor....

... [S]ome Americans who had observed how the win in Lake Placid was being politicized were less forgiving. In a letter to the sports editor of the *Hartford Courant*, Frank Francisconi of New London, Connecticut, wrote, "Since the U.S. victory over the Soviets, I have heard more jingoistic claptrap than I care to admit. I also think it is disgraceful that President Carter used the hockey team for political purposes.... Be real! This is a hockey game! ... It is foolish for anyone (including the print medium) to try to turn a game into a symbol of the struggle and/or victory of one economic and social system over another.... Let's rejoice in the U.S. hockey victory. But let's keep it in perspective, too."

Perhaps President Carter read and took to heart Francisconi's advice.... [W]hen the defeated president sat down to write his memoirs, he made only passing reference to the 1980 team.

Conclusion: Nationalism, Political Opportunism, and the Legacy of Lake Placid

Years after the United States Hockey Team struck gold at Lake Placid, people in the sporting world and beyond continue to reflect on what that victory meant to the country.... [T]he success of the US team came at a critical juncture. In the wake of the Vietnam war, the Watergate scandal, and several trying years under President Carter that indeed contributed to a crisis in confidence, the United States found a group of young men who, despite tremendous odds, captured the imagination of the people and the respect of sports enthusiasts around the world.

The extent to which the gold medal victory was politicized by federal and state policy-makers, the media, and the American public was not surprising.... [A]ny major contest that took place between the Americans and Soviets during the Cold War was bound to play out in the political arena. However, while policy-makers and journalists became preoccupied with equating the US victory on ice with American political supremacy, Coach Brooks and the team he assembled to represent the United States refused to allow themselves to become pawns in a global political game. As Brooks and several of his players stated, they came to Lake Placid to play hockey, not to engage in politics.

The United States had every right to feel proud of what the US Hockey Team accomplished and had good reason to celebrate. Moreover, if, as Mike Eruzione, Jack O'Callahan, and their teammates observed, their victory served as a catalyst to reignite confidence in what the United States could achieve at home and abroad, all the better. The importance of boosting national morale, or what others have broadly referred to as feelings of nationalism, should not be overlooked. From time immemorial, political leaders have relied on different tactics to shore up public support for launching major undertakings, including committing the nation to war. As Eruzione stated, the 4–3 win over the Soviets and the 4–2 victory over Finland did not result in the American hostages being freed any earlier. Tough negotiations with the Iranian leadership, which included freezing their considerable assets held in the United States, ultimately led to their release. Nor did the US victory in Lake Placid lead to the eventual collapse of the Soviet Union. Years of poor leadership that resulted in a mismanaged economy and an overly aggressive foreign policy were among many factors that led to the dismantling of the Soviet Empire. By most accounts, the United States hardly had to win a hockey game to demonstrate that the American political system was superior to the one implemented in the former Soviet Union.... Had the United States lost to the Soviets in Lake Placid, could anyone legitimately make the argument that the US political system was inferior?

The temptation to equate success in sport with superiority in politics remains strong but in many respects is completely without foundation. Unfortunately, so long as political leaders believe that they and their country can benefit from making such claims, the relationship between sport and politics will continue to be exploited.

The legacy of Lake Placid should not only be that the US Hockey Team mounted a stunning victory. It should be that the US Hockey Team sent a clear message to policy-makers, journalists, and other opinion-makers that hockey should be about hockey, sport should be about sport, and politics should be about politics.

FURTHER READING

Abelson, Donald. "Politics on Ice: The United States, the Soviet Union, and a Hockey Game in Lake Placid," *Canadian Review of American Studies/Revue canadienne d'études américaines* 40:1 (2010), 63–94.

Ardolino, Frank. "Missionaries, Cartwright, and Spalding: The Development of Baseball in Nineteenth-Century Hawaii," *NINE: A Journal of Baseball History and Culture* 10 (2002), 27–45.

Barney, Robert K. "Born from Dilemma: America Awakens to the Modern Olympic Games, 1901–1903," *Olympika: The International Journal of Olympic Studies* 1 (1992): 92–135.

Bass, Amy. *Not the Triumph But the Struggle: The 1968 Olympics and the Making of the Black Athlete* (2002).

Beezley, William H. *Judas at the Jockey Club* (1987).

Beran, Janice A. "American Sports in the Philippines: Imperialism or Progress through Sports?" *International Journal of the History of Sport* 6 (1989): 62–87.

Bowers, Matthew T., and Thomas M. Hunt. "The President's Council on Physical Fitness and the Systematization of Children's Play in America," *International Journal of the History of Sport* 28 (August 2011), 1496–511.

Brownell, Susan. ed. *The 1904 Anthropology Days and Olympic Games: Sport, Race, and American Imperialism* (2008)

Crawford, Russ. *The Use of Sports to Promote the American Way of Life During the Cold War: Cultural Propaganda, 1945–1963.* (2008)

Dyreson, Mark. *Making the American Team: Sport, Culture, and the Olympic Experience* (1998)

Dyreson, Mark. *Crafting Patriotism for Global Dominance; America at the Olympics* (2009)

Eisen, George. "The Voices of Sanity: American Diplomatic Reports from the 1936 Berlin Olympiad," *Journal of Sport History* 11:3 (1984), 56–79.

Elfers, James E. *The Tour to End All Tours: The Story of Major League Baseball's 1913–1914 World Tour* (2003).

Elias, Robert. *The Empire Strikes Out: How Baseball Sold US Foreign Policy and Promoted the American Way Abroad* (2010).

Fitts, Robert K. *Banzai Babe Ruth: Baseball, Espionage, and Assassination During the 1934 Tour of Japan* (2012).

Gems, Gerald R. *The Athletic Crusade: Sport and American Cultural Imperialism* (2006).

Gripentrop, John. "The Transnational Pastime: Baseball and American Perceptions of Japan in the 1930s," *Diplomatic History* 34:2 (2010), 247–73.

Graham, Gael. "Exercising Control: Sports and Physical Education in American Protestant Mission Schools in China," *Signs: Journal of Women in Culture & Society* 20 (1994), 26–48.

Guthrie-Shimizu, Sayuri. *Transpacific Field of Dreams: How Baseball Linked the United States and Japan in Peace and War* (2012).

Guttmann, Allen. *The Games Must Go On: Avery Brundage and the Olympic Movement* (1984).

Guttmann, Allen. *The Olympics: A History of the Modern Games*, 2nd ed (1992).

Guttmann, Allen. *Games and Empire: Modern Sports and Cultural Imperialism* (1994).

Hill, Christopher R. *Olympic Politics: Athens to Atlanta, 1896–1996*, 2nd ed (1996).

Hulme, Derick L. *The Political Olympics: Moscow, Afghanistan, and the 1980 US Boycott* (1990).

Howell, Colin. "Baseball and Borders: The Diffusion of Baseball into Mexican and Canadian-American Borderland Regions, 1885–1911," *NINE: A Journal of Baseball History & Culture* 11 (2003), 16–26.

Hunt, Thomas M. "American Sport Policy and the Cultural Cold War: The Lyndon B. Johnson Presidential Years," *Journal of Sport History* 33 (Fall 2006), 273–97.

Hunt, Thomas M. "Countering the Soviet Threat in the Olympic Medals Race: The Amateur Sports Act of 1978 and American Athletics Policy Reform," *International Journal of the History of Sport* 24 (June 2007), 796–818.

Klein, Alan M. *Sugarball: The American Game, the Dominican Dream* (1991).

Kruger, Arnd. "'Fair Play for American Athletes:' A Study in Anti-Semitism," *Canadian Journal of History of Sport and Physical Education* 9 (May 1978), 43–57.

Lamster, Mark. *Spalding's World Tour: The Epic Adventure That Took Baseball Around the Globe—and Made It America's Game* (New York, 2006).

Lucas, John A. "American Involvement in the Athens Olympic Games of 1906—A Bridge Between Failure and Success," *Stadion* 6 (1980), 217–28.

Lucas, John A. "American Preparations for the First Post World War Olympic Games, 1919–1920," *Journal of Sport History* 10 (1983), 30–44.

Mathews, George R. *America's First Olympics: The St Louis Games of 1904* (2005).

Perez, Louis A. "Between Baseball and Bullfighting: The Quest for Nationality in Cuba, 1868–1898," *Journal of American History* 81 (1994): 493–517.

Pope, S. W. *Patriotic Games: Sporting Traditions in the American Imagination, 1876–1926* (1997).

Pope, Steven W. "Rethinking Sport, Empire, and American Exceptionalism," *Sport History Review* 38 (2007), 92–120.

Roden, Donald. "Baseball and the Quest for National Dignity in Meiji Japan," *American Historical Review* 85 (1980), 511–34.

Ruck, Rob. *Raceball: How the Major Leagues Colonized the Black and Latin Game* (2011).

Sarantakes, Nicholas Evan. *Dropping the Torch: Jimmy Carter, the Olympic Boycott, and the Cold War* (2011).

Terret, Thierry. "The Military 'Olympics' of 1919: Sport, Diplomacy and Sport Politics in the Aftermath of World War One," *Journal of Olympic History* 14:2 (2006), 22–31.

Thomas, Damion. *Globetrotting: African American Athletes and Cold War Politics* (2012).

Turner, Justin W. R. "1970s Baseball Diplomacy between Cuba and the United States," *NINE: A Journal of Baseball History and Culture* 19 (Fall 2010), 67–84.

Zeiler, Thomas W. *Ambassadors in Pinstripes: The Spalding World Baseball Tour and the Birth of the American Empire* (2006).

MAJOR PROBLEMS IN AMERICAN HISTORY SERIES TITLES CURRENTLY AVAILABLE

Allitt, *Major Problems in American Religious History*, 2nd ed., 2013 (ISBN 978-0-495-91243-9)

Blaszczyk/Scranton, *Major Problems in American Business History*, 2006 (ISBN 978-0-618-04426-9)

Block/Alexander/Norton, *Major Problems in American Women's History*, 5th ed., 2014 (ISBN 978-1-133-95599-3)

Boris/Lichtenstein, *Major Problems in the History of American Workers*, 2nd ed., 2003 (ISBN 978-0-618-04254-8)

Brown/Carp, *Major Problems in the Era of the American Revolution, 1760–1791*, 3rd ed., 2014 (ISBN 978-0-495-91332-0)

Chambers/Piehler, *Major Problems in American Military History*, 1999 (ISBN 978-0-669-33538-5)

Chan/Olin, *Major Problems in California History*, 1997 (ISBN 978-0-669-27588-9)

Chudacoff/Baldwin, *Major Problems in American Urban and Suburban History*, 2nd ed., 2005 (ISBN 978-0-618-43276-9)

Cobbs Hoffman/Blum/Gjerde, *Major Problems in American History*, 3rd ed., 2012
- Volume I: *To 1877* (ISBN 978-0-495-91513-3)
- Volume II: *Since 1865* (ISBN 978-1-111-34316-3)

Fink, *Major Problems in the Gilded Age and the Progressive Era*, 3rd ed., 2015 (ISBN 978-1-285-43342-4)

Franz/Smulyan, *Major Problems in American Popular Culture*, 2012 (ISBN 978-0-618-47481-3)

Games/Rothman, *Major Problems in Atlantic History*, 2008 (ISBN 978-0-618-61114-0)

Gordon, *Major Problems in American History, 1920–1945*, 2nd ed., 2011 (ISBN 978-0-547-14905-9)

Hall/Huebner, *Major Problems in American Constitutional History*, 2nd ed., 2010 (ISBN 978-0-618-54333-5)

Hämäläinen/Johnson, *Major Problems in the History of North American Borderlands*, 2012 (ISBN 978-0-495-91692-5)

Haynes/Wintz, *Major Problems in Texas History*, 2nd ed., 2015 (ISBN 978-1-133-31008-2)

Holt/Barkley Brown, *Major Problems in African American History*, 2000
- Volume I: *From Slavery to Freedom, 1619–1877* (ISBN 978-0-669-24991-0)
- Volume II: *From Freedom to "Freedom Now," 1865–1990s* (ISBN 978-0-669-46293-7)

Hurtado/Iverson/Bauer/Amerman, *Major Problems in American Indian History*, 3rd ed., 2015 (ISBN 978-0-618-06854-8)

Jabour, *Major Problems in the History of American Families and Children*, 2005 (ISBN 978-0-618-21475-4)

Kupperman, *Major Problems in American Colonial History*, 3rd ed., 2013 (ISBN 978-0-495-91299-6)

Kurashige/Yang Murray, *Major Problems in Asian American History*, 2003 (ISBN 978-0-618-07734-2)

McMahon, *Major Problems in the History of the Vietnam War*, 4th ed., 2008 (ISBN 978-0-618-74937-9)

McMillen/Turner/Escott/Goldfield, *Major Problems in the History of the American South*, 3rd ed., 2012
Volume I: *The Old South* (ISBN 978-0-547-22831-0)
Volume II: *The New South* (ISBN 978-0-547-22833-4)

Merchant, *Major Problems in American Environmental History*, 3rd ed., 2012 (ISBN 978-0-495-91242-2)

Merrill/Paterson, *Major Problems in American Foreign Relations*, 7th ed., 2010
Volume I: *To 1920* (ISBN 978-0-547-21824-3)
Volume II: *Since 1914* (ISBN 978-0-547-21823-6)

Merrill/Paterson, *Major Problems in American Foreign Relations,* Concise Edition, 2006 (ISBN: 978-0-618-37639-1)

Milner/Butler/Lewis, *Major Problems in the History of the American West*, 2nd ed., 1997 (ISBN 978-0-669-41580-3)

Ngai/Gjerde, *Major Problems in American Immigration History*, 2nd ed., 2012 (ISBN 978-0-547-14907-3)

Peiss, *Major Problems in the History of American Sexuality*, 2002 (ISBN 978-0-395-90384-1)

Perman/Taylor, *Major Problems in the Civil War and Reconstruction*, 3rd ed., 2011 (ISBN 978-0-618-87520-7)

Riess, *Major Problems in American Sport History*, 2nd ed., 2015 (ISBN 978-1-133-31108-9)

Smith/Clancey, *Major Problems in the History of American Technology*, 1998 (ISBN 978-0-669-35472-0)

Stoler/Gustafson, *Major Problems in the History of World War II*, 2003 (ISBN 978-0-618-06132-7)

Vargas, *Major Problems in Mexican American History*, 1999 (ISBN 978-0-395-84555-4)

Valerio-Jiménez/Whalen, *Major Problems in Latina/o History*, 2014 (ISBN 978-1-111-35377-3)

Warner/Tighe, *Major Problems in the History of American Medicine and Public Health*, 2001 (ISBN 978-0-395-95435-5)

Wilentz/Earle, *Major Problems in the Early Republic, 1787–1848*, 2nd ed., 2008 (ISBN 978-0-618-52258-3)

Zaretsky/Lawrence/Griffith/Baker, *Major Problems in American History since 1945,* 4th ed., 2014 (ISBN 978-1-133-94414-0)